San Diego Trolley System

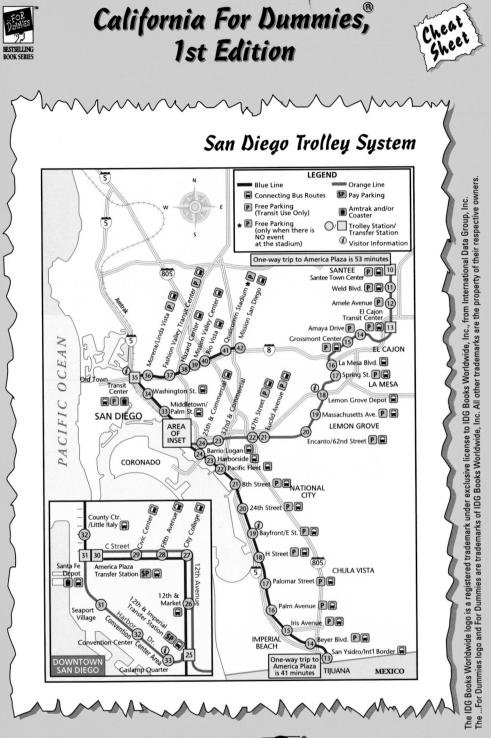

LEGEND

- Blue Line
- Connecting Bus Routes
- P Free Parking (Transit Use Only)
- * P Free Parking (only when there is NO event at the stadium)
- Orange Line
- SP Pay Parking
- Amtrak and/or Coaster
- Trolley Station/Transfer Station
- i Visitor Information

One-way trip to America Plaza is 53 minutes

One-way trip to America Plaza is 41 minutes

DOWNTOWN SAN DIEGO

Copyright © 2000 IDG Books Worldwide, Inc.
All rights reserved.

Cheat Sheet $2.95 value. Item 6158-8.

For more information about IDG Books, call 1-800-762-2974.

IDG BOOKS WORLDWIDE

For Dummies™: Bestselling Book Series for Beginners

California

FOR

DUMMIES®

1ST EDITION

California

FOR

DUMMIES®

1ST EDITION

by Cheryl Farr Leas

IDG Books Worldwide, Inc.
An International Data Group Company

Foster City, CA ✦ Chicago, IL ✦ Indianapolis, IN ✦ New York, NY

California For Dummies®, 1st Edition

Published by
IDG Books Worldwide, Inc.
An International Data Group Company
919 E. Hillsdale Blvd.
Suite 400
Foster City, CA 94404
www.idgbooks.com (IDG Books Worldwide Web Site)
www.dummies.com (Dummies Press Web Site)

Library of Congress Control Number: 00-103382

ISBN: 0-7645-6158-8

ISSN: 1528-2139

Printed in the United States of America

10 9 8 7 6 5 4 3 2 1

1B/RV/QZ/QQ/IN

Distributed in the United States by IDG Books Worldwide, Inc.

Distributed by CDG Books Canada Inc. for Canada; by Transworld Publishers Limited in the United Kingdom; by IDG Norge Books for Norway; by IDG Sweden Books for Sweden; by IDG Books Australia Publishing Corporation Pty. Ltd. for Australia and New Zealand; by TransQuest Publishers Pte Ltd. for Singapore, Malaysia, Thailand, Indonesia, and Hong Kong; by Gotop Information Inc. for Taiwan; by ICG Muse, Inc. for Japan; by Intersoft for South Africa; by Eyrolles for France; by International Thomson Publishing for Germany, Austria and Switzerland; by Distribuidora Cuspide for Argentina; by LR International for Brazil; by Galileo Libros for Chile; by Ediciones ZETA S.C.R. Ltda. for Peru; by WS Computer Publishing Corporation, Inc., for the Philippines; by Contemporanea de Ediciones for Venezuela; by Express Computer Distributors for the Caribbean and West Indies; by Micronesia Media Distributor, Inc. for Micronesia; by Chips Computadoras S.A. de C.V. for Mexico; by Editorial Norma de Panama S.A. for Panama; by American Bookshops for Finland.

For general information on IDG Books Worldwide's books in the U.S., please call our Consumer Customer Service department at 800-762-2974. For reseller information, including discounts and premium sales, please call our Reseller Customer Service department at 800-434-3422.

For information on where to purchase IDG Books Worldwide's books outside the U.S., please contact our International Sales department at 317-572-3993 or fax 317-572-4002.

For consumer information on foreign language translations, please contact our Customer Service department at 800-434-3422, fax 317-572-4002, or e-mail rights@idgbooks.com.

For information on licensing foreign or domestic rights, please phone 650-653-7098.

For sales inquiries and special prices for bulk quantities, please contact our Order Services department at 800-434-4322 or write to the address above.

For information on using IDG Books Worldwide's books in the classroom or for ordering examination copies, please contact our Educational Sales department at 800-434-2086 or fax 317-572-4005.

For press review copies, author interviews, or other publicity information, please contact our Public Relations department at 650-653-7000 or fax 650-653-7500.

For authorization to photocopy items for corporate, personal, or educational use, please contact Copyright Clearance Center, 222 Rosewood Drive, Danvers, MA 01923, or fax 978-750-4470.

About the Author

Cheryl Farr Leas began exploring California more than 15 years ago as a resident of Los Angeles, where she married the man of her dreams in a sushi bar with a view (see Yamashiro in Chapter 21). When she's not traveling the Golden State to visit friends and family — or just to bask in some high-quality California sunshine — she calls Brooklyn, New York, home. She also writes the *Frommer's New York City* travel guides, is author of *Hawaii For Dummies* (new in late 2000), and contributes to such publications as Continental Airlines' in-flight magazine, *Daily Variety,* and *Frommer's USA.*

ABOUT IDG BOOKS WORLDWIDE

Welcome to the world of IDG Books Worldwide.

IDG Books Worldwide, Inc., is a subsidiary of International Data Group, the world's largest publisher of computer-related information and the leading global provider of information services on information technology. IDG was founded more than 30 years ago by Patrick J. McGovern and now employs more than 9,000 people worldwide. IDG publishes more than 290 computer publications in over 75 countries. More than 90 million people read one or more IDG publications each month.

Launched in 1990, IDG Books Worldwide is today the #1 publisher of best-selling computer books in the United States. We are proud to have received eight awards from the Computer Press Association in recognition of editorial excellence and three from Computer Currents' First Annual Readers' Choice Awards. Our best-selling ...For Dummies® series has more than 50 million copies in print with translations in 31 languages. IDG Books Worldwide, through a joint venture with IDG's Hi-Tech Beijing, became the first U.S. publisher to publish a computer book in the People's Republic of China. In record time, IDG Books Worldwide has become the first choice for millions of readers around the world who want to learn how to better manage their businesses.

Our mission is simple: Every one of our books is designed to bring extra value and skill-building instructions to the reader. Our books are written by experts who understand and care about our readers. The knowledge base of our editorial staff comes from years of experience in publishing, education, and journalism — experience we use to produce books to carry us into the new millennium. In short, we care about books, so we attract the best people. We devote special attention to details such as audience, interior design, use of icons, and illustrations. And because we use an efficient process of authoring, editing, and desktop publishing our books electronically, we can spend more time ensuring superior content and less time on the technicalities of making books.

You can count on our commitment to deliver high-quality books at competitive prices on topics you want to read about. At IDG Books Worldwide, we continue in the IDG tradition of delivering quality for more than 30 years. You'll find no better book on a subject than one from IDG Books Worldwide.

John J. Kilcullen

John Kilcullen
Chairman and CEO
IDG Books Worldwide, Inc.

Eighth Annual
Computer Press
Awards ≥1992

Ninth Annual
Computer Press
Awards ≥1993

Tenth Annual
Computer Press
Awards ≥1994

Eleventh Annual
Computer Press
Awards ≥1995

IDG is the world's leading IT media, research and exposition company. Founded in 1964, IDG had 1997 revenues of $2.05 billion and has more than 9,000 employees worldwide. IDG offers the widest range of media options that reach IT buyers in 75 countries representing 95% of worldwide IT spending. IDG's diverse product and services portfolio spans six key areas including print publishing, online publishing, expositions and conferences, market research, education and training, and global marketing services. More than 90 million people read one or more of IDG's 290 magazines and newspapers, including IDG's leading global brands — Computerworld, PC World, Network World, Macworld and the Channel World family of publications. IDG Books Worldwide is one of the fastest-growing computer book publishers in the world, with more than 700 titles in 36 languages. The "...For Dummies®" series alone has more than 50 million copies in print. IDG offers online users the largest network of technology-specific Web sites around the world through IDG.net (http://www.idg.net), which comprises more than 225 targeted Web sites in 55 countries worldwide. International Data Corporation (IDC) is the world's largest provider of information technology data, analysis and consulting, with research centers in over 41 countries and more than 400 research analysts worldwide. IDG World Expo is a leading producer of more than 168 globally branded conferences and expositions in 35 countries including E3 (Electronic Entertainment Expo), Macworld Expo, ComNet, Windows World Expo, ICE (Internet Commerce Expo), Agenda, DEMO, and Spotlight. IDG's training subsidiary, ExecuTrain, is the world's largest computer training company, with more than 230 locations worldwide and 785 training courses. IDG Marketing Services helps industry-leading IT companies build international brand recognition by developing global integrated marketing programs via IDG's print, online and exposition products worldwide. Further information about the company can be found at www.idg.com.   1/26/00

Dedication

In loving memory of Monty (1991–2000), whose first and only airplane trip blessed me with the best three weeks I'll ever have in California.

Author's Acknowledgments

Much love and many heartfelt thanks to Paula Tevis and Stephanie Avnet Yates for their regional expertise and first-rate contributions to this book; Nathaniel R. Leas, Brian Farr, and Elise Soliday for their invaluable research assistance; John Rosenthal for his rockin' map work; and Lisa Renaud for her unflagging support.

Thanks also to editor Alexis Lipsitz and cartographer Roberta Stockwell in New York and editors Kathy Cox and Corey Dalton in Indianapolis for their work in helping to make this book a reality.

Publisher's Acknowledgments

We're proud of this book; please register your comments through our IDG Books Worldwide Online Registration Form located at http://my2cents.dummies.com.

Some of the people who helped bring this book to market include the following:

Editorial

Editors: Kathleen M. Cox and Alexis Lipsitz

Copy Editor: Corey Dalton

Cartographer: Roberta Stockwell

Editorial Manager: Jennifer Ehrlich

Editorial Assistant: Jennifer Young

Production

Project Coordinator: Cindy Phipps

Layout and Graphics: Amy Adrian, Gabriele McCann, Tracy K. Oliver, Kristin Pickett, Jill Piscitelli, Kathie Schutte, Julia Trippetti, Erin Zeltner

Proofreaders: Laura Albert, Corey Bowen, Carl Pierce, Christine Sabooni

Indexer: Liz Cunningham

Special Help
Michelle Conrad, Michelle Hacker, Steve Arany

General and Administrative

IDG Books Worldwide, Inc.: John Kilcullen, CEO; Bill Barry, President and COO

IDG Books Consumer Reference Group

Business: Kathleen A. Welton, Vice President and Publisher; Kevin Thornton, Acquisitions Manager

Cooking/Gardening: Jennifer Feldman, Associate Vice President and Publisher

Education/Reference: Diane Graves Steele, Vice President and Publisher; Greg Tubach, Publishing Director

Lifestyles: Kathleen Nebenhaus, Vice President and Publisher; Tracy Boggier, Managing Editor

Pets: Dominique De Vito, Associate Vice President and Publisher; Tracy Boggier, Managing Editor

Travel: Michael Spring, Vice President and Publisher; Suzanne Jannetta, Editorial Director; Brice Gosnell, Managing Editor

IDG Books Consumer Editorial Services: Kathleen Nebenhaus, Vice President and Publisher; Kristin A. Cocks, Editorial Director; Cindy Kitchel, Editorial Director

IDG Books Consumer Production: Debbie Stailey, Production Director

IDG Books Packaging: Marc J. Mikulich, Vice President, Brand Strategy and Research

♦

The publisher would like to give special thanks to Patrick J. McGovern, without whom this book would not have been possible.

♦

Contents at a Glance

Cartoons at a Glance

By Rich Tennant

Fax: 978-546-7747
E-mail: richtennant@the5thwave.com
World Wide Web: www.the5thwave.com

Maps at a Glance

Table of Contents

Introduction

*I*f you reached for *California For Dummies,* 1st Edition, because it stood out from the overwhelming pack of California guidebooks, or because it just seemed different, pat yourself on the back — you have good instincts.

I assume that this is your first California vacation — or maybe you haven't been in ages, or you haven't visited a particular region. Or maybe you don't want to dedicate your life to trip planning, wasting a whole vacation's worth of time wading through hundreds of dense pages. Maybe you don't like the way that so many conventional guidebooks require you to figure out what hotels, destinations, restaurants, and so forth that the authors actually like and what they're including because they think quantity outweighs quality.

Rather than just throwing out reams of information for you to sift through until you're too tired to tell Bakersfield from Big Sur, *California For Dummies,* 1st Edition, cuts the wheat from the chaff. I've done the legwork for you, and I want you to benefit from my expertise. I know that you work hard to set aside a few precious weeks of vacation time and that money doesn't grow on trees. No matter how much money you have, you don't want to waste it. Consequently, I'm not afraid to take a stand so that you can know what to include in your California vacation — and, even more important, what to pass on. After all, you want to figure this stuff out now, in the planning stage — not after you get there, when it's too late.

I walk you through the whole process of putting together your perfect trip, from the ins-and-outs of laying out a manageable itinerary to choosing the right places to stay to how much time to allot for which attractions and activities. Not that one right answer exists for anybody, of course. This book gives you the tools you need — just what you need, not too much — to really help you discover what works for you and what doesn't. I know your time is valuable, so I strive to get right to the point, to give you the clearest picture of what you need to know, what choices you have to make, and what your options are so that you can make informed decisions easily and efficiently.

Think of building your vacation less as a step-by-step process and more as a jigsaw puzzle. This book helps you choose the right puzzle pieces and assemble them so that a) they interlock smoothly, and b) the finished product reflects the picture *you* want, not someone else's image of what your vacation should be.

What's in This Book and Why — And What's Not Here

Honestly, some parts of California deserve your valuable time and hard-earned money, and others do not. For this reason, I've focused not on covering California comprehensively, but covering the *best* that California offers. This book is a reference tool that answers all of your questions about the state's most terrific destinations — places like Big Sur and Disneyland.

The resulting guidebook directs you to all the worthiest destinations and doesn't bother you with the secondary stuff. You don't have to wade through a big chapter on Sacramento, say, to find the Yosemite National Park recommendations you really want. Capital, schmapital — suggesting Sacramento as a vacation destination is the equivalent of recommending that you cut a New York City vacation short so that you can spend a few days hanging out in Albany. Both Albany and Sacramento are perfectly nice cities, but c'mon — this is about *your* time and money, and California offers many more worthy destinations.

Conventions Used in This Book

I recently tried to extract some information from a guidebook and found so many symbols that I needed training in hieroglyphics to interpret them all. I'm happy to report that the user-friendly *California For Dummies,* 1st Edition, travel guide isn't like that. The use of symbols and abbreviations is kept to a minimum, as follows:

- ✔ The credit card abbreviations are AE (American Express), DC (Diners Club), MC (MasterCard), and V (Visa).

- ✔ I list the hotels, restaurants, and top attractions in A-to-Z order, for the most part, so that moving among the maps, worksheets, and descriptions is easier.

I include some general pricing information to help you as you decide where to unpack your bags or dine on the local cuisine. I've used a system of dollar signs to show a range of costs for one night in a hotel or a meal at a restaurant. Check out the following table to decipher the dollar signs:

Cost	Hotel	Restaurant
$	$75 and under	$15 or under
$$	$75 to $150	$15 to $25
$$$	$150 to $225	$25 to $40
$$$$	$225 to $300	$40 to $70
$$$$$	$300 and up	$70 and up

How This Book Is Organized

California For Dummies, 1st Edition, is divided into six parts. The chapters within each part cover specific travel topics or regions in detail. You can read each chapter or part without reading the one that came before it — no need to read about San Francisco if you're heading to Southern California, after all — but I may refer you to other chapters of the book for more information on certain subjects.

Part I: Getting Started

This first part introduces you to the best of California and touches on everything you'll want to consider before actually getting down to the nitty-gritty of trip planning, including:

- ✔ When to go (and when you may want to stay home).
- ✔ Tips on planning your itinerary, plus actual time-tested itineraries that you can use as a proven blueprint for your own vacation.
- ✔ How much you can expect your trip to cost, with tips on how to save if money is a concern.
- ✔ Special considerations for families, seniors, travelers with disabilities, and gay and lesbian travelers.

Part II: Ironing Out the Details

This is where I get down to the nuts and bolts of travel planning, including:

- ✔ Planes, trains, and automobiles: how to get to California and how to get around California after you're there.
- ✔ The pros and cons of working with a travel agent vs. planning on your own.
- ✔ The advantages of all-inclusive travel packages.
- ✔ Getting ready to go, from the pluses and minuses of buying travel insurance to making advance dinner reservations to what to pack.

Parts III–V: The Destinations

If you think of this book as a meal, these parts constitute the main course. These parts form the bulk of the book and cover the destinations you'll visit. Each chapter offers all of the specific details and recommendations you need for a given destination, including:

> ✔ When to go.
>
> ✔ How much time you'll need.
>
> ✔ How to get there.
>
> ✔ Where to stay.
>
> ✔ Where to eat.
>
> ✔ What to do after you arrive.

Part III covers Northern California: the San Francisco Bay Area; the wild North Coast and tall-tree Redwood Country; and the Sierra Nevada mountains, where you'll find spectacular Lake Tahoe and Yosemite National Park.

Part IV covers California's Central Coast, which includes Santa Cruz and such marvelous destinations as the Monterey Peninsula, Big Sur, Hearst Castle, and that jewel of the coast, Santa Barbara.

Part V focuses on Southern California, namely Los Angeles, San Diego, and Disneyland. And, for those of you who never think the weather is too hot or too dry, I talk about the Desert, including Palm Springs, Joshua Tree National Park, and Death Valley National Park.

For a more thorough destination overview, flip a couple of pages ahead to Chapter 1.

Part VI: The Part of Tens

Every . . . *For Dummies* book contains a part of tens. If Parts III through V are the main course of your meal, think of these fun chapters, each their own top-ten list, as dessert. If you feel like doing homework to get you in the proper California mood, check out Chapter 26. Or maybe you want to catch a whiff of genuine Left Coast zaniness while you're on the road? Read Chapter 27 to learn where you can get down and wacky like real Californians do.

Appendix and Worksheets

The Appendix lists the details for easy reference, putting the facts about California at your fingertips, from locating local AmEx offices to finding the most accurate online weather forecasts, and everything in between. I've also included a bunch of *worksheets* to make your travel planning easier — among other things, you can determine your budget, create specific itineraries, and keep a log of your favorite restaurants so you can hit them again next time you're in town. You can find these worksheets easily because they're printed on yellow paper.

Icons Used in This Book

You'll notice the following icons sprinkled throughout the text. Think of them as signposts; I use them to highlight special tips, draw your attention to things you won't want to miss, and give you the heads-up on a variety of topics.

This icon points out useful advice on things to do, ways to schedule your time, and any other tips I'm sure you won't want to miss.

This icon helps you spot tourist traps, ripoffs, time-wasters, and other things to beware.

These attractions, hotels, restaurants, or activities are especially family-friendly.

Check out this icon for money-saving tips or particularly great values.

This icon points out bits of well-guarded insider advice that give you an edge over those who don't know better.

This icon alerts you to any advance plans that you should schedule before you leave home.

Where to Go from Here

As you read through this book and start to formulate your California vacation, remember this: Planning really is half the fun. Don't think of choosing your destinations and solidifying the details as a chore. Make the homebound part of the process a voyage of discovery, and you'll end up with an entire vacation experience that is much more rewarding and enriching — really. Have a blast with it. Happy planning!

Part I
Getting Started

The 5th Wave   By Rich Tennant

"I think we should arrange to be there for Garlic-Anchovy-Chili Bean Week, and then shoot over to the Breathmint-Antacid Festival."

In this part . . .

This first part introduces you to the best of California and touches on everything you want to consider before you travel so that your California vacation is as spectacular as the state. This part helps you decide the best time to go, plan your itinerary, and budget for your trip. And I include extra tips for people with children, seniors, people with disabilities, and the lesbian and gay community.

Chapter 1

Discovering the Best of California

- -

In This Chapter

▶ Introducing the Golden State's highlights

▶ Exploring San Francisco and the natural wonders of Northern California

▶ Journeying along the gorgeous Central Coast

▶ Reveling in the fun and sun of Southern California

▶ Discovering the unique beauty of California's desert

- -

California isn't just any state in the Union. In fact, it's hardly like a state at all. Way back when I was an intern in Washington, D.C., I learned that national politicians tend to refer to the 31st state as "the nation of California" — a sovereign country all its own, an immense and diverse dominion to be conquered above and beyond the other 49 states.

Their outsize view isn't far from the truth. With nearly 159,000 square miles of land and a 1,264-mile coastline, California is the third largest state in the United States. Sure, both Alaska and Texas are bigger — but California's uniqueness stems from much more than size. California is like the high school homecoming queen whose natural beauty and innate poise make the rest of the student body sneer at her while wanting to bask in her glow at the very same time. They don't call this the Golden State for nothing, after all.

California is really an awesome place, in the truest sense (not the surfer dude sense) of the word. Its jaw-dropping diversity is the real kick in the pants, more than anything else. With two of the nation's largest megalopolises — the San Francisco Bay Area, which has grown beyond speculators' wildest dreams with the rise of Silicon Valley, and metropolitan Los Angeles, whose urban sprawl has a glamorous heart called Hollywood — California has the largest, wealthiest, and most urbanized population of any state in the nation. Yet it's also an agricultural wonderland whose bounty runs the gamut from artichokes, raisins, garlic, and asparagus to some of the finest wine-making grapes in the world. And it still manages to be home to some of the country's most striking and varied wilderness — from purple mountains' majesty to arid, marvelously barren desert.

Within the natural landscape alone, the contrast is unparalleled. Take Mount Whitney and Death Valley as a case in point: At 14,494 feet above and 282 feet below sea level, respectively, they are the highest and lowest points in the continental United States — and just 85 miles separates them. Wow.

Unless you have a couple of months to spare for vacation (lucky you!), though, you're not going to see everything this marvelous, multifaceted state has to offer. You know what? Don't even waste time trying. Frankly, some parts of California are much worthier of your valuable time and hard-earned dollars than others.

These destinations comprise the best of California. You discover more about them as you read on through Parts III through V of this book and begin to plan your trip.

The North Coast

The wild and woolly coastal region north of the San Francisco Bay Area (see Part III) offers some of California's most breathtaking scenery. It's quiet, remote, and ruggedly handsome, with spectacular nature broken only by the occasional picturesque village. Of those villages, none is more lovely than romantic **Mendocino** (see Chapter 11), a postage stamp of a town situated on a majestic headland. Rife with elegant B&Bs, upscale restaurants, and pricey boutiques and galleries, it's definitely built for two — but families with kids will find plenty of outdoor activities to occupy them in the surrounding area. Beware the weather, though, which can be cold and misty at any time of the year — all part of the dreamy Mendocino vibe, aficionados say.

Mendocino also serves as a good jumping-off point for exploring the regal **Redwood Country** (see Chapter 12), which starts just inland and north of Mendocino. The towering coast redwoods — the tallest trees on the planet — extend all the way to the Oregon border, but you won't need to travel that far to get your fill of their majesty. You can follow the scenic 32-mile Avenue of the Giants to the midpoint as a day trip from Mendocino or dedicate a couple of days to the drive, depending on your sightseeing goals.

The Sierra Nevada

Travel inland from the Bay Area or North Coast and you'll soon reach the Sierra Nevada, the magnificently rugged, granite-peaked mountain range that defines northeast and east-central California. This high-altitude region is so uniquely stunning that such geniuses as Mark Twain and Ansel Adams considered it one of their greatest inspirations. The Sierra Nevada stirred John Muir to do no less than found the U.S. National Park system.

Possibly the greatest of the national parks is spectacular **Yosemite National Park** (see Chapter 14), whose natural wonders include such record-setters as Yosemite Falls (North America's tallest waterfall) and El Capitan (the world's largest granite monolith). Beware, though, because Yosemite is the superstar of California's natural attractions, drawing theme-park-worthy crowds in summer — but I tell you how to do your best to skirt them, of course.

Also in the High Sierra rests the United States' biggest and most beautiful alpine lake, sparkling **Lake Tahoe** (see Chapter 13) — California's finest outdoor playground. Come in the winter to ski, in the summer to hike, bike, kayak, sail . . . you name it. If you're a history buff, consider taking a day to visit the **Gold Country** (see Chapter 12), the epicenter of California's 19th-century gold rush hysteria, on your way to or from Tahoe.

The San Francisco Bay Area

The San Francisco Bay metropolitan area has grown by leaps and bounds with the Silicon Valley revolution — all those dot-commies have to live somewhere! The prime draw, however, is still the loveliest and most beguiling city in America, **San Francisco** (see Chapter 9). "The city" (as locals call it — *never* "Frisco") is smaller than you may expect, loaded with personality in all corners, and pleasant to visit year-round. It's also the one destination in the Driving State where you can easily get around without a car.

If San Francisco is the ultimate urban destination, then the gorgeous **Napa Valley** (see Chapter 10) — America's premier wine-growing region — is the embodiment of pastoral escape. This super-fertile valley brims with world-class wine-tasting rooms and some of the country's finest restaurants and inns. Some people consider it hip to prefer the neighboring Sonoma Valley, but not me. If this is your first trip to California's wine country, I advocate starting with the Napa Valley — the biggest, brightest, and best. Grown-ups will find more to interest them here than kids will, needless to say.

The Central Coast

If you ask me (and I guess you did), the central coast — that stretch between San Francisco and Los Angeles — represents California at its very best (see Part IV). The drive along Highway 1 — the world-famous Pacific Coast Highway — is one of the most scenic in the world. Keep in mind, however, that the drive is slow going and quite curvy — real Dramamine territory, so stock up.

Where the San Francisco Bay Area meets the Monterey Peninsula sits **Santa Cruz** (see Chapter 15), California's quintessential, and kinda wacky, surf town. Kids (and kids at heart) will love Santa Cruz — especially the genuine old-fashioned boardwalk, the West Coast's only beachfront amusement park. Santa Cruz is at its best in summer and early fall, when the beach party is going strong.

Pristine nature meets unbridled commercialism on the **Monterey Peninsula** (see Chapter 16) — and fortunately, nature wins out. This stunning knob of land jutting out to sea cradles Monterey Bay, one of the richest and most diverse marine habitats on earth. On land you'll find the **Monterey Bay Aquarium,** one of California's all-time top attractions, plus a collection of delightful communities, from family-friendly Monterey itself to golf mecca Pebble Beach to ultraromantic Carmel-by-the-Sea. The marriage of natural beauty and man-made diversions doesn't get any better than this.

In **Big Sur** (see Chapter 17), on the other hand, the spectacular wilderness and breathtaking views are unhindered by all but the most minimal development. Dedicate a full day to the natural splendor of Big Sur even if you don't want to stay in one of the region's funky hotels; trust me, you won't regret it.

Hearst Castle (see Chapter 18), one of the most outrageous private homes ever built and a real hoot to tour, lies on the other end of the man-versus-nature continuum. Even if this monument to excess isn't your style, you'll enjoy the surrounding countryside — neither Northern California nor Southern, it has a distinct, golden-hued beauty all its own — and the amiable village of **Cambria,** a great place to soak up some small-town charm.

Driving farther down the coast puts you squarely in Southern California. If you have little ones in tow or a strong affinity for good pastry, head inland to Danish **Solvang** (see Chapter 19), a storybook town straight out of Scandinavia. Or visit **Santa Barbara** (see Chapter 20), a seaside jewel that embodies the Southern California dream — perfect for clocking in some top-quality relaxation time.

The Southern California Cities

Southern California is where things get crazy, in a good way. I'll be the first to admit that **Los Angeles (L.A.)** (see Chapter 21) — the poster child for urban sprawl, the city we all love to hate — isn't for everybody. But think twice before you reject it out of hand, culture vultures. In addition to being celeb-rich and gloriously silly, it also happens to be the state's finest museum town. Really.

I'll make no such claims for **Disneyland** (see Chapter 22), just south of L.A. (behind the Orange Curtain, as Angelenos are fond of saying) in Anaheim (Orange County). The Happiest Place on Earth is the original theme park, and it's an unadulterated blast for kids of all ages (even grown-up ones with jobs and mortgages). Consider visiting again even if you've been before, because you'll find plenty of new things to see and do — including a brand-new Disney park, California Adventure, set to open in mid-2001.

Disneyland sets the stage for **San Diego** (see Chapter 23), a significantly more easygoing city than L.A. — or even San Francisco, for that matter. This town's a real beaut, with a wonderfully mellow vibe, golden beaches galore, and plenty of memory-making diversions, most notably three terrific animal parks: the **San Diego Zoo, SeaWorld,** and the **Wild Animal Park**. If that's not enough to keep you and the kids happy and busy, also consider the multifaceted joys of **Balboa Park** (the second-largest city park in the country, after the Big Apple's Central Park) and the metro area's newest theme-park addition, groovy **LEGOLAND**.

The Desert

Unlike the other destinations in this book — which are generally most popular in summer and largely pleasant to visit year-round — California's desert is most fun to visit in any season *but* summer, when the scorching heat can be a bit much to bear. Still, some people (like me) enjoy summer in the desert, when prices are low and crowds are minimal (just pack your sunscreen — number 30 or higher, preferably).

The **Palm Springs** area (see Chapter 24) is the place to go for desert cool. This is the manicured side of the desert, where streets bear names like Frank Sinatra Drive, and golf greens, swimming pools, spa treatments, and martinis rule the day. What's more, easy access to unspoiled nature makes Palm Springs appealing even to those who couldn't care less about the prefabricated glamour or retro-groovy stuff.

You can easily visit unspoiled **Joshua Tree National Park** (see Chapter 25) on a day trip from Palm Springs, and I highly recommend doing so. The stark, scruffy high-desert landscape upends traditional notions of natural beauty, forgoing leafy greenery for mindbending shapes, majestic scale, and otherworldly hues. Both shockingly barren and stunningly beautiful, **Death Valley National Park** (see Chapter 25) pumps up the otherworldliness to new heights. Still, it's awfully remote; unless you have a lot of vacation time, you may be better off saving Death Valley for a future trip.

Chapter 2

Deciding When to Go

● ●

In This Chapter

▶ Getting to know California's weather

▶ Visiting from season to season — and advice for avoiding the crowds

▶ Exploring a year of celebrations, California style

● ●

W.C. Fields once said, "California is the only state in the union where you can fall asleep under a rosebush in full bloom and freeze to death." Surely a gross exaggeration, right? Actually, *no.*

Needless to say, you should uncover a few facts about California's weather patterns before you plan your trip. In addition, you'll want to know the times when everybody else visits California so that you can a) join the party, or b) avoid it like the plague.

Understanding California's Climate

First off, don't be fooled by what you think you know about California's weather. *Really,* you say, *I've seen* Baywatch, *I've set the VCR for* 90210, *I watch* VIP. *What's there to understand? California is all buffed bikini-clad bods and perpetual sun.* Well, yes and no. Sometimes the reality lives up to the myth, and sometimes it doesn't. Frankly, the weather is not all that predictable.

Microclimates are small areas of uniform climate that generally differ from the surrounding climate — and California has lots of them. A perfectly plausible scenario sees you skiing in Tahoe in the morning, cruising around the Napa Valley in shorts and T-shirts in the afternoon, and bundling up against the damp, cold ocean breezes in Mendocino by evening.

The most important weather predictor is your location: coast or inland, north or south.

As a general rule, the weather will likely be cool and windy along the coastline — even in July and August — and warmer and perpetually sunnier as you move inland. The climate will always be warmer and sunnier in inland Sacramento than in famously foggy San Francisco. (The temperature drops again as you climb into the mountains to high-elevation places like Lake Tahoe.) Believe it or not, the rule even holds true in the same city: Downtown Los Angeles is more often than not 10 to 15°F warmer than L.A.'s oceanside beach community, Santa Monica, which benefits from cooling ocean breezes. Latitude matters, too, of course; in general, the southern coast — Santa Barbara and points south — sees better beach weather than its northern counterparts.

The one thing you can say for sure about California weather is how darn changeable it is. The temperature may drop at night more than you're used to, no matter where you're located. In many places, both along the coast and inland, daytime temperatures of 80°F and above may routinely drop down into the low 40s in the evening. Cool fog will cover much of the coastline in the mornings, but if the sun breaks through, temperatures will soar by noon or so. The bottom line: Be prepared for dramatic daily changes, even in summer. Layering your clothes is always a good idea.

Knowing the Secret of the Seasons

California is seasonless to a certain degree — anytime is a good time to visit. The state benefits from glorious conditions year-round, with the weather being generally warmer than most other mainland U.S. spots in winter, and cooler and drier than most in summer.

One of the most surprising ticks in California's weather pattern is that summer generally starts late. As the temperature charts in Table 2-1 show, both San Francisco and Los Angeles (and virtually all points in between) don't really start warming up until July. Even blessedly sunny L.A. is notorious for "June Gloom": Morning gray rolls in and stays until afternoon. (The biggest exception is the desert, where high temperatures and bright sun move in early and unpack to stay awhile.)

Table 2-1   Average Temperatures from Sample Cities and Regions (°F)

Lake Tahoe

	Jan	Feb	Mar	Apr	May	June	July	Aug	Sept	Oct	Nov	Dec
High	40	42	44	51	60	69	77	77	69	59	47	41
Low	20	21	23	27	33	39	45	45	39	32	26	21

San Francisco

	Jan	Feb	Mar	Apr	May	June	July	Aug	Sept	Oct	Nov	Dec
High	58	60	60	61	62	63	64	65	67	67	63	58
Low	43	46	46	47	49	51	53	54	54	52	48	44

Napa Valley

	Jan	Feb	Mar	Apr	May	June	July	Aug	Sept	Oct	Nov	Dec
High	57	62	65	69	75	80	82	82	81	77	65	57
Low	37	41	42	43	48	52	54	54	52	48	42	38

Monterey

	Jan	Feb	Mar	Apr	May	June	July	Aug	Sept	Oct	Nov	Dec
High	60	62	62	63	64	67	68	69	72	70	65	60
Low	43	45	45	46	48	50	52	53	53	51	47	43

Santa Barbara

	Jan	Feb	Mar	Apr	May	June	July	Aug	Sept	Oct	Nov	Dec
High	65	66	66	69	69	72	75	77	76	74	69	66
Low	43	45	47	49	52	55	58	59	58	54	49	44

Los Angeles (downtown)

	Jan	Feb	Mar	Apr	May	June	July	Aug	Sept	Oct	Nov	Dec
High	68	69	70	72	73	78	84	85	83	79	72	68
Low	49	50	52	54	58	61	65	66	65	60	54	49

Palm Springs

	Jan	Feb	Mar	Apr	May	June	July	Aug	Sept	Oct	Nov	Dec
High	70	76	80	87	95	104	109	107	101	92	79	70
Low	43	46	49	54	61	68	75	75	69	60	49	42

On the up side, when the warm weather comes, it almost always stays through September and usually well into October. Indian summer is common, and fall is universally the best season weatherwise. In September and October the fog even lifts from perpetually misty spots along the coast like Monterey and Mendocino. In places where the weather starts to crisp in the fall, like Tahoe, clear air and beautiful colors make for gorgeous conditions.

If you're coming to California to hit the beach in your bikini in January, don't count on it — this ain't Hawaii. Still, the weather will likely be milder here than where you're from (especially if you're from the Northeast or the Midwest). No wonder so many people love visiting in winter — 50° in San Francisco is *way* better than Chicago's, or even New York's, parka weather. Tahoe is prime for skiing, and snow-blanketed Yosemite is crowd-free and gorgeous. And I've often found the coastal destinations — particularly Monterey, Big Sur, and the like — to be more pleasant, with clearer skies, in December or January than they are in June or July. If you get lucky, you may even end up with a beach day in L.A. or San Diego in those months, when the occasional 80° day takes a bow.

Choosing Less Crowded Times

Just about any destination is not necessarily busiest when it's at its best; it's busiest when people have time to come. The busiest months of the year in California are the summer months, from June through September, with July and August being the height of the season. The only exceptions are Tahoe, which gets more winter skiers than summer vacationers, and the desert, where you really *can* fry an egg on the sidewalk from June through September. Always expect high-season prices, the fewest available deals, and the biggest crowds during these peak months — especially on weekends.

Count on paying higher rates on weekends year-round, because you'll not only have to compete with your fellow out-of-staters but also with weekending Californians. Here are a few weekend booking tips:

✔ If you're planning a weekend trip to such hot destinations as Mendocino, the Napa Valley, anywhere at all along the Central Coast, or Palm Springs, book as far in advance as possible, no matter what time of year you visit.

✔ If you're planning a one- or two-week driving vacation throughout the state, try to land in areas like the Wine Country, Carmel, the Hearst Castle area, Solvang, and Santa Barbara midweek rather than on the weekend, when those otherwise restful spots become human zoos.

✔ Schedule your city visits on weekends — any excess of vacationers in San Francisco, L.A., or San Diego is often nicely counterbalanced by the business travelers who've headed home for the weekend, and hotel rates are often lower.

You'll get more for your money and more quiet time (a big plus in a state dominated by natural attractions) by traveling to California outside the summer season. And, in the off-season — from late September through May — you may end up with better weather to boot. Remember, fall is dreamy. You'll find the best deals (and the fewest crowds) in winter.

Using a California Calendar of Events

Here's a brief rundown of the Golden State's top annual events:

✔ **December–March:** This is *whale-watching season* all along the California coast, from Mendocino down to Mexico. Mammoth gray whales migrate from the cold Alaskan waters to warmer climes for their birthing season and then transport their new pups back home. Just look carefully out to sea for a *blow,* the puff of steam that can rise 12 feet from the whale's blowhole.

My favorite place to watch for whales is **Monterey,** which celebrates the annual migration with a two-week party in January called Whalefest. For information, call ☎ **831-649-1770** or point your Web browser to www.monterey.com and search for "Whalefest" for a calendar of this year's events.

Mendocino holds its own celebration, the Mendocino Whale Festival, usually in early March (☎ **707-961-6300;** www.mendocinocoast.com).

✔ **January 1:** New Year's Day sees the **Tournament of Roses Parade,** the mother of all college bowl parades, descend upon Pasadena (near Los Angeles) almost at the crack of dawn. Outrageous floats constructed entirely of fresh roses and other flora compete for the spotlight with high-volume marching bands and high-wattage celebs making appearances. Although the festivities happen on New Year's Day, expect to arrive the night before if you want to get a spot that lets you see anything. Call ☎ **626-449-4100** or visit www.tournamentofroses.com for grandstand tickets, official tour packages, and other information.

✔ **January–February:** The **Chinese New Year Parade and Celebration** in San Francisco, the largest Chinese New Year celebration in the United States, encompasses two weeks of events, the highlight of which is a magnificent parade featuring the legendary Golden Dragon. 2001 is the Year of the Snake, and events ranging from the Miss Chinatown USA pageant to street and flower fairs run from January 20 through February 4, with the parade taking place on February 5. Call ☎ **415-982-3000** for exact details and/or 2002 dates, or go to www.sfvisitor.org.

✔ **Late January–March:** The **Napa Valley Mustard Festival,** a celebration of the petite yellow-petaled mustard flowers that bloom in late winter (and everyone's favorite gourmet condiment), has grown into the Wine Country's biggest event. Two full months of high-end partying runs the gamut from wine auctions to gallery shows to gourmet food competitions. The festival runs January 26 through March 31 in 2001. Call ☎ **707-226-7459** or check www.mustardfestival.org for the full calendar and/or 2002 dates.

✔ **Late February–early March:** **Snowfest** in Tahoe City, a weeklong celebration of the ski season, is the largest of its kind on the world. Features include snow and ice sculpture contests, a polar bear swim in Lake Tahoe, the Incredible Dog Snow Challenge (in which man's best friend competes in freestyle frisbee, search-and-rescue, and sledding competitions), and more. It's the most fun you'll ever have in Polartec. Call ☎ **775-832-7625** or visit the Web site at www.snowfest.org.

✔ **Early May:** Celebrate **Cinco de Mayo,** Mexico's favorite holiday, in San Diego's historic Old Town, the original Spanish birthplace of California, or in the Mexican heart of Los Angeles, El Pueblo de Los Angeles State Historic Monument. Expect festive mariachi music, folk dancing, and lots of yummy eats. Events usually take place over the weekend closest to May 5. Call ☎ **213-625-5045** for L.A. information, ☎ **619-296-3161** or 619-220-5422 for San Diego information.

✔ **Mid-May:** The *San Francisco Examiner* **Bay to Breakers,** the world's largest and zaniest footrace, is actually more fun than run. More than 70,000 runners race across the park in their costumed best For information call ☎ **415-808-5000,** ext. 2222, or point your Web browser to www.sfvisitor.org.

✔ **Memorial Day Weekend:** My personal favorite of Memorial Day weekend events is the **Great Monterey Squid Festival,** a scientific and culinary ode to calamari. Lots of yummy, squid-friendly fun! Dial ☎ **831-649-6544** for details.

✔ **Late June:** San Francisco hosts the **Lesbian, Gay, Bisexual, & Transgender Pride Parade,** the world's largest gay pride parade, bar none. For information call ☎ **415-864-3733.**

✔ **Fourth of July:** Virtually all of California's communities hold their own style of Independence Day celebrations, from San Francisco's fireworks to Monterey's Living History Festival to the Redwood Country's old-fashioned parade and picnic in Victorian-era Ferndale. Contact local visitor bureaus to find out what's on in the town you plan to visit (see "Gathering More Information" sections in the following chapters).

✔ **Early or mid-September:** The **San Diego Street Scene** is a three-day festival of food, music, and fun. Call ☎ **619-557-8490** or visit the Web site at www.gaslamp.org.

✔ **Mid-September:** Solvang's Scandinavian glory reaches its tacky-genuine zenith with **Danish Days,** a historic three-day extravaganza celebrating Solvang's heritage. For details call ☎ **800- 468-6765** or 805-688-6144.

✔ **Mid-September:** The **Monterey Jazz Festival,** the world's longest-running jazz festival (43 years and counting), hosts the biggest names in traditional and contemporary jazz. If you want more information, call ☎ **831-373-3366** or point your Web browser to www.montereyjazzfestival.com.

✔ **Early October: Gold Rush Days** in Marshall Gold Discovery State Historic Park, Coloma, tells the gold rush story in living color through demonstrations, story-telling, and entertainment. Call ☎ **530-622-3470** or 530-622-0390 for information.

✔ **October 31: Halloween in San Francisco** is a wild and wacky fete, complete with over-the-edge costumes, entertainment, and behavior. Call ☎ **415-826-1401.**

✔ **Late November:** The stars brighten Hollywood Boulevard the Sunday after Thanksgiving in the **Hollywood Christmas Parade** in Los Angeles, a classic celebrity-studded parade that launches the holiday season in glittering Tinseltown style. For details call ☎ **323-469-8311** or visit www.hollywoodcofc.org.

Considering all that goes on every year in California, this brief list is merely a microdrop in the bucket. For a complete rundown of events, call the **California Division of Tourism** (☎ **800-862-2543**) and request a copy of *California Celebrations* or point your Web browser to www.gocalif.com and click on "Special Events."

Chapter 3

Great Itineraries

. . . .

In This Chapter

▶ Planning an itinerary

▶ Exploring Northern California in 10 days

▶ Seeing Southern California in 10 days

▶ Taking a romantic trip for two

▶ Bringing the kids along

▶ Discovering the natural side of California

. . . .

*U*nderstand this right now: You will not see all of California. I know retirees who've lived in the Golden State all of their lives who continue to stumble on new discoveries as they putter around.

Still, it's easy to see quite a bit of the Golden State, even if your vacation time is short. Think of your trip as a jigsaw puzzle, and the individual destinations (and the corresponding chapters of this book) as the puzzle pieces. This chapter serves as a primer for putting those interlocking pieces together.

Time-Tested Itinerary Planning Tips

The itineraries I suggest in this chapter should give you an idea of what you can see and do comfortably in the time you have. But remember — no one ideal vacation plan exists. Use the itineraries that appear later in this chapter as you see fit — either as proven, hard-and-fast plans, or simply as starting blueprints that you can then customize by moving the puzzle pieces around, removing one and inserting another as you see fit.

Following are some tips that will help you when determining your own itineraries:

✔ **Embrace the hugeness of California — don't deny it.** You'll do a lot of driving as you move from one destination to another, so factor that in when determining your itinerary. If you're the road-trip type and moving around sounds exciting to you, planning an ambitious itinerary is fine. But if getting to really know a place is important to you, you'll want to make plans to settle in for a few days. Or, if spending too much time in the car with the kids is going to feel more like a chore than a vacation, recognize this fact now so you can plan accordingly.

✔ **Know your travel goals.** If golf is on your agenda, shorten your visit to L.A. for extra time in Palm Springs. If you're more the city type than the nature lover, forgo stops on your drive between San Francisco and L.A. so that you have more time for urban dwelling. If you're planning a family vacation, Disneyland may be a better choice than Napa. You get the idea.

✔ **If you only have one week, limit yourself to two destinations, three max.** If you don't limit yourself, you're going to suffer from the "If it's Tuesday, it must be Big Sur" syndrome. If, for example, you're touring Southern California, start with three days in San Diego, then a day or two in Disneyland, and wrap it up with two or three days in L.A. or Palm Springs. San Francisco and Yosemite National Park alone can tie up a week. The most ambitious among you can add Tahoe to the mix and fly out of Reno, Nevada, but you'll end up with lots of behind-the-wheel time and not really more than two days per destination.

✔ **Seriously consider flying in to one California airport and leaving from another.** The time saved by flying into San Diego and leaving from San Francisco, say, or flying into San Jose and departing from Palm Springs, may be worth the extra airline charges and/or rental-car drop-off charges. What's more, depending on your points of arrival and departure, you may not even incur extra fees. Your best bet is to consider a couple of options and price them out with the airlines and car companies (or put your travel agent to work) before you decide.

✔ **Consider your drive part of the adventure.** The choice is yours: You can either drive straight through without stopping or take a leisurely meander off the beaten path — it all depends on how adventurous you are and how much unassigned time you have. California is a gorgeous state, with lots to admire along just about any route you take. I like to make time for unplanned stops and serendipitous side trips.

✔ **Don't be overly ambitious and try to cram too many activities into a day that you'll be making a long drive.** Driving long distances can really sap your energy. Keep in mind that estimated drive times in this book do not include rest stops, unforeseen traffic or detours, and so on. If you do have time and energy to do more than simply drive and check in to your new hotel on big drive days, consider it a gimme; use the time to relax. (After all, this is a *vacation,* remember.)

✔ **Avoid ending up at a super-popular weekend destination on the weekends.** Restful destinations like the Napa Valley, Mendocino, Carmel, Hearst Castle, Solvang, and Santa Barbara become human zoos when urban dwellers escape the city for the weekend. Many also require two-night minimums over the weekend, which can throw a monkey wrench in your plans. See if you can schedule your city visits over the weekends instead.

You gain no particular advantage by starting at one end of the state over the other, so don't worry about it. Just head north or south based on what's most convenient, appealing, and/or cost-efficient for you.

Northern California in 10 Days

On **Day 1,** fly in to **San Francisco.** Spend **Day 2,** and **Day 3** enjoying the City by the Bay (see "Suggested 1-, 2-, and 3-Day Itineraries" in Chapter 9 for a detailed sightseeing plan for San Francisco).

Itinerary #1

After spending **Day 4** in San Francisco, head to the **Napa Valley** (see Chapter 10) early on **Day 5** and spend **Day 5** and **Day 6** getting to know the Wine Country. For the ideal introduction, plan on a late-morning or early-afternoon winery tour, perhaps one of the reservation-only tours at Schramsberg or Niebaum Coppola, or one of the terrific first-come, first-served tours offered by Robert Mondavi or St. Supéry. See two more wineries after lunch, and mix it up with a little sightseeing or shopping before resting up for a gourmet feast at one of the valley's stellar restaurants. Book ahead if you want to eat at **French Laundry,** often named the best restaurant in the United States. On the morning of **Day 6,** stop at one of the valley's gourmet markets to assemble a lunchtime picnic. Plan some additional activities to mix in with your winery-going, such as a hot-air balloon ride, a bit of bicycling, and/or a mud bath and massage.

On **Day 7,** head north from the Napa Valley in the afternoon for **Redwood Country** (see Chapter 12). Follow Highway 128 north to U.S. 101, and spend the night along the Redwood Highway, perhaps in the charming, Victorian **Ferndale.** On **Day 8,** meander down the Redwood Highway, reaching Mendocino in time for dinner. Spend **Day 9** exploring **Mendocino** (see Chapter 11), hiking the headlands, shopping, or just enjoying the wild beauty of the misty North Coast.

On **Day 10,** drive back to **San Francisco** for your flight home.

You can easily trim this itinerary to eight days by cutting a day off your time in San Francisco and limiting your Redwood Country exploring to a day trip.

Itinerary #2

Depart San Francisco on **Day 4** for **Monterey,** probably my favorite destination on the California coast. Leave in the morning and spend the day playing on the boardwalk and the beach in **Santa Cruz,** arriving in Monterey in time for dinner. If there's just the two of you and you're looking for romance, consider **Carmel** as a base. If your budget is generous, go all out and spend your nights on some of the most spectacular real estate in the nation, **Pebble Beach** (the California destination for golfers).

The Monterey Peninsula (see Chapter 16) deserves a good chunk of time, so spend the evening of **Day 4** and the following two nights here. Start **Day 5** at the **Monterey Aquarium.** (Don't forget to buy your aquarium tickets in advance to save aggravating time in line.) In the afternoon, rent bikes and follow Monterey's gorgeous bayfront bike path (suitable for all riders) for some spectacular views.

Spend **Day 6** exploring the rest of the peninsula by car, including the justifiably famous **17-Mile Drive** (explorable on that rented bike if you have the energy). Spend the afternoon strolling through charming Carmel; even if the weather is chilly, bundle up for a walk along cypress-lined Carmel Beach, one of the world's most beautiful stretches of sand.

On **Day 7,** drive through gorgeous **Big Sur** (see Chapter 17) to San Simeon and **Hearst Castle,** which I discuss in Chapter 18. Resist the urge to stop much along the way (you'll have time for that later). Arrive at your base in **San Simeon** or nearby Cambria in time to see the elephant seals basking in the sun just north of **San Simeon,** and do a little exploring in cute **Cambria** before a leisurely dinner.

Dedicate **Day 8** to **Hearst Castle.** Book yourself a morning tour and an afternoon tour, with time for an IMAX flick at the castle visitor center in between (this makes for good resting-your-tootsies time).

Day 9 is for exploring awesome **Big Sur.** In fact, spend the night along the Big Sur Coast so that you'll have plenty of hiking and/or contemplation time.

Fly home on **Day 10.** Consider flying out of **San Jose** to avoid the drive back to SFO.

Itinerary #3

Depart San Francisco on **Day 4** for **Yosemite National Park** (see Chapter 14). Spend this night and the following two at (or just outside) the park to allow two full days for exploring. Spend **Day 5** poking around Yosemite Valley. Start with the two-hour **Valley Floor Tour** for a good orientation, then set out on one of the many excellent hikes after lunch; you can find one for just about every ability level. Dedicate **Day 6** to seeing other areas of the park, including **Mariposa Grove** (where the giant sequoias grow) and the pristine **High Country** (only accessible in warm weather).

Unless you're setting out on another big day hike, consider spending the afternoon taking advantage of one of the many activities offered in the park, such as horseback riding or river-rafting, or cross-country skiing if it's winter.

On **Day 7,** exit the park on the east side via the **Tioga Pass** and head north on U.S. 395 to Lake Tahoe (see Chapter 13). You can only do this drive between mid- or late June and the first snowfall, usually in November. Call ahead at ☎ **209-372-0200** to check road conditions if you're traveling near the fringes of this time frame. If you're driving in winter, you'll need to reserve most of the day for traveling out the west entrance of the park and following Highway 49 north to U.S. 50 and South Lake Tahoe. Be sure to check the weather along this route, too.

Spend **Day 8** and **Day 9** enjoying **Lake Tahoe,** California's favorite out-door playground. Let the season dictate your activities: summer and fall are great for hiking, jet-skiing, horseback riding, and the like, while winter is ski season. Lady Luck works the casinos year-round, of course.

Day 10 is the day to fly home. Consider flying out of Reno to avoid the four-hour drive back to the Bay Area airports. (**Sacramento,** halfway between Tahoe and San Francisco, is another good bet for saving on drive time.)

Southern California in 10 Days

On **Day 1,** fly into Los Angeles. Spend **Day 2** and **Day 3** enjoying Tinseltown. Check out "Suggested 1-, 2-, and 3-Day Itineraries" in Chapter 21 for a detailed sightseeing plan for Los Angeles.

Itinerary #1

On **Day 4,** go to **Disneyland** (see Chapter 22). In fact, consider making the hour's drive south on the evening of **Day 3** so that you can be first in the park in the morning. (You may even be able to get a jump-start on the masses with an early entrance, a perk enjoyed by Disneyland Hotel guests.) Spend the evening of **Day 4** in Anaheim so that you'll have an entire day in the park. In fact, you may want to consider spend-ing the better part of **Day 5** at Disneyland as well, especially after the new California Adventure park opens in 2001. You may also want to split up your park time, especially if you have little kids who'll tire out easily, if your own theme-park stamina is low, or if you're visiting at a peak time with long lines and wait times for rides. If you've had your fill of Disneyland by **Day 5,** spend that day relaxing by the pool, soaking up some of those California rays.

In any case, head south to **San Diego** (see Chapter 23) in time for dinner on **Day 5,** so that you can start your animal park adventures early on **Day 6.** Whether you have the kids with you or not, don't miss the **San Diego Zoo,** one of the finest zoos in the world and well worth a day of any vacation. On **Day 7,** choose between spending the day at **Sea World,** taking your littlest ones on an excursion to **LEGOLAND,** or treating your older kids to the **Wild Animal Park.** Or, if you've had enough theme-park fun for one trip, split your day between San Diego's culture-rich **Balboa Park** and the beach.

After all this running around, you deserve some rest and relaxation time. So, on **Day 8,** head to **Palm Springs** and spend **Day 9** relaxing under the desert sun. This is the place to get in some quality time on the fairway, or some pampering at the spa (or some of both, if you're so inclined).

If you'd rather avoid a lot of running around, simply stay put in **San Diego** on **Day 8** and **Day 9** — it's another terrific place to kick back — and fly out from there on **Day 10.** Either way, you'll be relaxed and contented enough to head home on **Day 10,** whether you leave from Palm Springs International or San Diego's airport if you've stayed put, or take the easy two-hour drive back to Los Angeles.

Itinerary #2

If theme parks aren't your style at all, head to **Palm Springs** (see Chapter 24) in the late afternoon of **Day 4,** arriving in time for an alfresco dinner. On **Day 5,** take a desert excursion with Desert Adventures Jeep Eco-Tours — or, even better, spend the day exploring **Joshua Tree National Park** (see Chapter 25), an extraordinary place to experience two entirely different, totally pristine desert ecosystems. Spend **Day 6** golfing, spa-ing, or just sitting by the pool sipping fruity drinks garnished with umbrellas.

On **Day 7,** head west again, skirting L.A. as you head northwest to lovely **Santa Barbara** (see Chapter 20), arriving in time for dinner.

If you're driving on a weekday, be sure to pass through L.A. before 3 p.m. to avoid getting stuck in rush-hour traffic.

Spend **Day 8** and **Day 9** hanging out in **Santa Barbara,** Southern California's loveliest beach town. If you're not the beach type (or if the weather's just not beachy), and you feel as if you've seen and done it all by midday on **Day 9,** explore Santa Barbara's wine country or take a ride over to **Solvang** (see Chapter 19) for a slice of Scandinavia, Southern California style.

The drive is an easy 100 miles back to L.A. on **Day 10,** your day to fly home.

Itinerary #3

If **Hearst Castle** appeals to you more than Palm Springs does, arrive in **Santa Barbara** on **Day 4,** and spend **Day 5** and **Day 6** following the plan for **Day 8** and **Day 9** in the preceding "Itinerary #2."

On **Day 7,** head north to **San Simeon** or **Cambria** so you can tour the castle on **Day 8.** You'll have a five-hour drive back to L.A. for your outbound flight, so you may want to meander back down the coast on **Day 9** and spend the night back in the **Santa Barbara** area or, if you have an early-morning flight home on **Day 10,** in an L.A. airport hotel.

Itinerary #4

If theme parks are your purpose, here's an alternate loop: Fly in to **San Diego** on **Day 1.** Spend **Day 2** and **Day 3** enjoying the charms (and parks) of this laid-back town (see "Suggested 1-, 2-, and 3-Day Itineraries" in Chapter 23 for a time-tested sightseeing plan).

On **Day 4,** drive to **Palm Springs.** (The **San Diego Wild Animal Park** makes an easy stop along the way.) Spend **Day 5** and **Day 6** as described in Itinerary #1 or #2, with one day dedicated to discovering the desert's natural beauty and the other committed to enjoying its man-made sybaritic pleasures.

Head to **Los Angeles** on the evening of **Day 6** so you can be at **Universal Studios** bright and early on **Day 7.** Head to Orange County on **Day 8** for a full Disney day on **Day 9** (you can easily work in two **Disneyland** days if you leave L.A. early on **Day 8**). Fly home from San Diego on **Day 10.**

California in Two Weeks — For Romance-Seeking Couples

Fly in to **San Francisco** on **Day 1.** Spend **Day 2** and **Day 3** enjoying the most romantic city in the United States (see "Suggested 1-, 2-, and 3-Day Itineraries" in Chapter 9 for a recommended sightseeing plan of San Francisco).

Itinerary #1

Head north on **Day 4.** If you don't mind a long drive, consider the coastal route on your way up, which winds through lovely, artsy seaside towns. Stop at misty **Mendocino** (see Chapter 11), where picnicking, bike riding, strolling the charming seaside village, and snuggling up in front of a roaring fire in the evening are the primary orders of business. Frankly, towns don't get any more romantic — so spend **Day 5** here, too.

On the afternoon of **Day 6,** pick up curvaceous Highway 128 just south of Mendocino and follow it into the north end of **Napa Valley** (see Chapter 10). Set up camp at one of the valley's ultra-romantic B&Bs (the Cottage Grove Inn is a great choice) and wine and dine each other on **Day 7** and **Day 8.**

On **Day 9,** cut south, back toward the coast, and make magical **Carmel-by-the-Sea** your love nest from which to explore the **Monterey Peninsula** over **Day 10** and **Day 11.** If the weather's good, work in an afternoon kayaking among the elephant seals and sea otters on **Monterey Bay** (see Chapter 16). And don't forget to take a romantic stroll along jaw-droppingly beautiful **Carmel Beach.**

Leave the Monterey area early on **Day 12** to give you the entire day to meander through **Big Sur** (see Chapter 17) on your way to **Hearst Castle** (see Chapter 18). Make **Cambria** your area base, and dedicate **Day 13** to touring Xanadu.

On **Day 14,** drive back to San Francisco (or the **San Jose** or the **Monterey** airport, both a tad closer) to catch a late-day flight home.

Itinerary #2

Spend **Day 4** in San Francisco, and on **Day 5** head directly to the **Napa Valley,** and dedicate **Day 5** and **Day 6** to touring the romantic, adult-oriented Wine Country (see Chapter 10).

On **Day 7,** drive to **Carmel** (or to the brand-new **Casa Palermo** in **Pebble Beach,** if you've got the bucks) and settle in for **Monterey Peninsula** sightseeing on **Day 8** and **Day 9** (see Chapter 16).

On **Day 10,** meander through **Big Sur** country (see "Just the Highlights: Northern California in 10 Days," earlier in the chapter), arriving in **Cambria** (see Chapter 18) in time for a candlelit dinner (the **Sow's Ear** makes a good choice). Make **Day 11** your castle day — and because you're in the romantic mood, ask your guide for tales of Clark Gable and Carole Lombard's visits to "the ranch."

Take **Day 12** to drive south along the Central Coast to **Santa Barbara** (see Chapter 20), a marvelous place to spend **Day 13** at the beach.

On **Day 14,** drive the easy two hours south to the Los Angeles airport (LAX) to catch a flight home.

Itinerary #3

On **Day 4,** head directly to the **Napa Valley,** and dedicate **Day 4** and **Day 5** to touring the Wine Country.

On **Day 6,** drive to **Carmel** (or to the brand-new Casa Palermo in **Pebble Beach,** if you've got the bucks) and settle in for **Monterey Peninsula** sightseeing on **Day 7, Day 8,** and **Day 9.**

Leave early enough on **Day 10** so that you can drive through **Big Sur** country at an enjoyable pace yet still have time to reach **Santa Barbara** in time for a lovely dinner. (Expect the drive to take the full day.) Spend **Day 11** relaxing in perpetually sunny Santa Barbara, resting up for your two days in star-studded, neon-bright La La Land.

On **Day 12,** take the easy drive south into **Los Angeles** for sightseeing today and on **Day 13;** see "Suggested 1-, 2-, and 3-Day Itineraries" in Chapter 21 for suggestions. (Hint, hint, gentlemen: L.A. is a great spot to splurge on an extra-special romantic dinner — **Patina** and **Valentino** are both marvelous choices.) Schedule a late-day flight on **Day 14** to squeeze in some last-day sightseeing.

California in Two Weeks — With Kids

Kids love California as much as adults do — it's sort of like a giant playground with all the latest toys. Anyone traveling with kids won't have a problem finding things to do; the trick is how to fit it all in.

Itinerary #1

On **Day 1,** fly the brood into **San Diego.** Spend **Day 2** and **Day 3** enjoying the local animal parks. (See "Suggested 1-, 2-, and 3-Day Itineraries" in Chapter 23 for suggestions on organizing your time.)

Check out of your San Diego hotel on the morning of **Day 4** and head north to a) **LEGOLAND** in nearby Carlsbad with the little ones, or b) to the **San Diego Wild Animal Park,** in Escondido, with the older kids. Both parks make easy stops along the way to **Anaheim,** where you should check in to your hotel, have an early dinner, and rest up for your big day tomorrow at **Disneyland.** Spread your park time over two days, **Day 5** and **Day 6,** to avoid burnout — your own and the kids'.

On the morning of **Day 7,** head north to **L.A.** Base yourself at the beach for maximum fun. Visit **Universal Studios** on **Day 8.**

On **Day 9,** make the short (two-hour) drive north to cutesy, Danish-themed **Solvang,** which your younger kids are bound to enjoy.

On **Day 10,** head north to **Monterey,** stopping in **San Luis Obispo** for a pleasant lunch break (it's just about exactly at the midpoint of the four-hour drive). The peninsula features plenty to entertain you and the kids on **Day 11** and **Day 12;** the **aquarium,** of course, is a must.

Spend **Day 13** on the beach and boardwalk at **Santa Cruz,** California's historic seaside amusement park (see Chapter 15). It's a real joy, and a must-do for families. You can see the boardwalk in a few ways: You can make it a day trip from your base in Monterey or enjoy it on your way to **San Francisco** (where you're presumably flying out on **Day 14**). However, I recommend spending the night at Santa Cruz so that you can enjoy the neon-lit rides and lively arcades after dark, especially fun in summer.

Only a half-hour or so from Santa Cruz, **San Jose** makes the perfect departure point for your homebound flight on **Day 14.**

Itinerary #2

Fly into **San Francisco** on **Day 1.** The City by the Bay has plenty of kid appeal — in fact, more than enough to occupy **Day 2** and **Day 3.** "Suggested 1-, 2-, and 3-Day Itineraries" in Chapter 9 can help you formulate a sightseeing plan.

On **Day 4,** drive to **Yosemite National Park.** It's an ideal place for kids to learn about and enjoy the natural world on **Day 5** and **Day 6.** (If the weather's warm, consider staying in the tent cabins, which offer both creature comforts and a kid-friendly resemblance to camping.)

On **Day 7,** head back to the coast, basing yourself in **Monterey** or **Santa Cruz** on **Day 8** and **Day 9** for area exploring.

Drive south on **Day 10,** spending the night in **Solvang.** If you choose to spend the day at **L.A.'s Universal Studios,** leave this mini-Denmark early on **Day 11.** (If you must skip one theme park because of time, money, and/or energy concerns, I suggest passing over Universal Studios. Your pre-adolescents and teens may heartily disagree, however, and you may end up on **Day 11** at Universal.)

The distance from Monterey all the way to L.A. is one heckuva drive, so if you'd like to wake up in L.A. on the morning of **Day 11,** I recommend departing **Monterey** or **Santa Cruz** on the afternoon of **Day 9** and basing yourself in the **Hearst Castle** area before heading south on **Day 10.** In fact, you'll even have time to catch a castle tour in the morning before you set out, if you wish.

Head to **Anaheim** on the evening of **Day 11** to spend **Day 12** at **Disneyland** (see Chapter 22).

Depart Anaheim early in the day on **Day 13** to make the hour's drive south to **San Diego** with plenty of time to enjoy **LEGOLAND,** the **San Diego Zoo,** the **Wild Animal Park,** or **Sea World** — pick one for your pleasure. Schedule a late flight out on **Day 14** to finish up at another park — and the kids will sleep on the way home like the angels they are.

If you'd like to spend more time in San Diego without adding another day to your trip, consider cutting back a day in San Francisco; leave the city on the afternoon of **Day 3,** arriving at **Yosemite** in time for dinner. Or skip Universal Studios.

California in Two Weeks — For Nature Lovers

The first two nature-loving itineraries start from Los Angeles. The third uses San Francisco as its take-off point.

Itinerary #1

Fly into **Los Angeles** on **Day 1** — and leave immediately. Drive two hours east to discover the desert beauty of **Palm Springs** (see Chapter 24). (Or avoid the couple hours' drive by flying directly into Palm Springs.) Spend **Day 2** exploring wild, fascinating, untrammeled **Joshua Tree National Park** (see Chapter 25), an excursion that should take the entire day.

Spend the morning of **Day 3** lazing by the pool. After lunch, head out of Palm Springs, skirting L.A. again as you head northwest to **Santa Barbara** (see Chapter 20).

If you're traveling on a weekday, make sure you pass through L.A. before 3 p.m. to avoid getting stuck in rush-hour traffic.

Spend **Day 4** relaxing in the lovely beach town of Santa Barbara, then head to **Big Sur** (see Chapter 17) on **Day 5.** I highly recommend spending at least one night here among the trees, so that you can enjoy this spectacular coast on **Day 6,** too.

On **Day 7,** head to the **Monterey Peninsula** (see Chapter 16), where you should park yourself in **Pacific Grove** for the best outdoors experience today and on **Day 8.**

On **Day 9,** make the drive to **Yosemite National Park** (see Chapter 14), and spend **Day 10** and **Day 11** exploring the park; head for the High Country if you want to avoid crowds, but be sure to dedicate a half day to seeing the icons of Yosemite Valley first.

On **Day 12,** head north to **Lake Tahoe** (see Chapter 13). Spend **Day 13** playing at this magnificent lake. Schedule a late-day flight out of **Reno** so that you have most of **Day 14** to play, too. (Because you're coming to Tahoe to enjoy its natural beauty, the north shore is probably the better base for you.)

Itinerary #2

Fly in to **Los Angeles** on **Day 1** and get a good night's rest for the mammoth 300-mile drive to **Death Valley National Park** (see Chapter 25) on **Day 2.** Expect it to be a *looooong* driving day.

Spend **Day 3** and **Day 4** exploring the vast expanses of the park. (Consider renting a four-wheel-drive if you want to explore some of the primitive park's backcountry roads.)

On **Day 5,** drive out of Death Valley on the western side and take the I-395 route north to the east (Tioga Pass) entrance of **Yosemite National Park** (see Chapter 14). Again, plan on another very full day of driving. Spend **Day 6** and **Day 7** exploring the park.

You can only enter Yosemite through the Tioga Pass entrance between mid- or late June and the first snowfall, which usually occurs in November. Call ahead at ☎ **209-372-0200** to check road conditions if you're traveling near the fringes of this time frame.

On **Day 8,** drive out of the park's south entrance and head to the **Monterey Peninsula** (see Chapter 16). Make forested **Pacific Grove** your base here on **Day 8** and **Day 9** for the best outdoors experience.

On **Day 10,** head to **Big Sur** (see Chapter 17), staying to enjoy this wonderful wilderness on **Day 11** as well.

On **Day 12,** meander south along the view-endowed Pacific Coast Highway to **Santa Barbara** (see Chapter 20), one of the most naturally blessed towns in America; it's a good place to rest up on **Day 13** for the flight home from Los Angeles's LAX on **Day 14.**

Itinerary #3

Fly into **San Francisco** on **Day 1,** and spend **Day 2** appreciating the natural advantages of this glorious city.

On the afternoon of **Day 3,** head up U.S. 101 to the top of the **Redwood Highway**(see Chapter 12). Spend the night here — perhaps in **Eureka's** old town or in Victorian **Ferndale** — and take all of **Day 1** to meander down this most scenic of routes. Arrive in **Mendocino** (see Chapter 11) for dinner, and spend **Day 5** here.

On **Day 6,** make the journey to **Lake Tahoe** (see Chapter 13). Expect the drive to take most of the day (about six hours). Base yourself on the north shore for **Day 7** and **Day 8** for a peak outdoors experience.

On **Day 9,** head to **Yosemite National Park** (see Chapter 14), where you should spend **Day 10** and **Day 11.**

On **Day 12,** drive to the **Monterey Peninsula** (see Chapter 16), setting up camp in **Pacific Grove** for **Day 12** and **Day 13.** (Note that **Big Sur** [see Chapter 17] is within easy reach as a day trip, or add on an extra day for further exploring.)

On **Day 14,** return to **San Francisco** for the flight home — or, better yet, schedule your return flight from **San Jose,** which is an hour closer to Monterey.

Chapter 4

Planning Your Budget

. . . .

In This Chapter

▶ Adding up the elements: transportation, lodging, dining, and sightseeing

▶ Using AAA and American Express membership to your advantage

▶ Cost-cutting tips for wallet-watchers

. . . .

"So — how much is this trip going to cost me, anyway?"

The question is a reasonable one, no matter where you fall on the income ladder. A vacation is a considerable endeavor, with costs that can add up before you know it — especially if you're traveling with kids, when expensive admission tickets and pricier-than-you-thought meals can multiply the damage in the blink of an eye. Therefore, knowing what to expect before you go makes sense.

Adding Up the Elements

The good news is that structuring a California trip to suit any budget is relatively easy. Sure, you can rub elbows with high-profile celebs or dot-com millionaires by choosing to stay at ultra-luxurious resorts and dine at elegant restaurants, but you don't have to; plenty of affordable choices exist in every destination for those of you with less to spend. Sure, you can spend tons of money at many excellent high-ticket attractions, from the **Monterey Bay Aquarium** to **Disneyland** — but pursuing such pleasures as a stroll on the beach or a mountain hike carries no admission price whatsoever. The budget worksheets at the back of this book will help you figure out where your money's going to go and what you can afford to do.

Totaling transportation costs

Most visitors to California fly in and rent a car to get around this mammoth state. The following sections will help you budget enough for comfortable transportation wherever you want to go.

Airfare

Airfare is going to be one of your two big-ticket items (the other being lodging). Predicting airfares is almost impossible, because they can fall to new lows or go through the roof at the drop of a hat. I can tell you, however, that California's main airports — San Francisco, Los Angeles, and San Diego — tend to get so much air traffic (and therefore generate so much competition) that airfares are usually lower than if you're flying into less competitive markets.

Don't quote me on this because prices can always vary, but expect to pay in the neighborhood of $400 to $600 per person for a coast-to-coast flight. You'll pay less if you plan well in advance or get lucky and catch a fare sale; see Chapter 6 for tips on getting the best airfare.

Thanks to Southwest Airlines, prices on air routes within California are usually quite reasonable. At press time, the advance-purchase fare between San Francisco and San Diego was just $71.

What things cost in San Francisco

An average latte in North Beach	$2.50
Shuttle from SFO to any hotel	$10–$12 (plus tip)
Taxi from SFO to city center	$35 (plus tip)
One-way Muni/bus fare to any destination within the city (adult)	$1
Ferry ride and admission to Alcatraz	$12.25
Admission to Exploratorium	$9
A stroll across the Golden Gate Bridge	free!
Luxury room for two at the Huntington	$275–$420
Romantic room for two at Petite Auberge	$120–$265
Budget room for two at the Marina Inn	$65–$135
Dinner for two at Charles-Nob Hill (with wine)	$150
Dinner for two at Grand Cafe (with wine)	$70
Dinner for two at Chow	$36
A 12 oz. microbrew at Thirsty Bear	$3
A tall martini at Top of the Mark	$9.50
Theater ticket for Beach Blanket Babylon	$18–$45

Car rentals

Rental cars are relatively cheap in the Driving State. You can often get a compact for between $100 to $200 a week, depending on your dates and where you pick up your car (Southern California rentals are usually cheaper). If you want something family-size, expect to pay more like $200 to $300 a week — frankly, still quite reasonable.

Do yourself a favor and book a rental car with unlimited mileage. You'll be doing a lot of driving as you travel within California, and you do not want to end up paying for your rental on a per-mile basis. Trust me — you will end up on the short end of this stick. Luckily, most of the major car-rental companies rent on an unlimited-miles basis, but you should confirm this policy when you book.

And because you'll probably cover a good deal of ground, don't forget to factor in gas, which at press time was hovering around $2 a gallon (in some places, it actually topped the $2.50 mark!). Parking is another cost factor, especially in the cities; play it safe and budget $10 a day, more if you're spending lots of time in the cities. Also remember to account for any additional insurance costs.

For further details on renting a car in California, see Chapter 7.

Paying for lodging

California has a wealth of luxury hotels and resorts, but it also offers plenty of affordable choices. The cities specialize in business- and tourist-oriented hotels, while the smaller destinations feature standard hotels, bed-and-breakfast inns, and motels, plus destination resorts in some locales. I've taken care to recommend a range of choices in each of the destinations covered in this book so that everyone has suitable options, no matter what your needs or budget.

In the chapters that follow, you'll see that a number of dollar signs, ranging from one ($) to five ($$$$$), follows each hotel name. These dollar signs represent the median price for a double room per night, as follows:

$ Super-cheap — less than $75 per night

$$ Still affordable — $75 to $150

$$$ Moderate — $150 to $225

$$$$ Expensive but not ridiculous — $225 to $300

$$$$$ Ultra-luxurious — more than $300 per night

In general, you'll find that if you budget between $100 and $175 to spend per night, you'll be able to balance your costs. Make economical choices in the more affordable locations so that you can comfortably handle any pricier destinations down the road, like Carmel. Staying cheap when possible will make digging a little deeper into your pockets later on easier to bear.

So that you don't encounter any unwanted surprises at payment time, be sure to account for the taxes that will be added to your final bill. The base hotel tax is 10 percent, but some municipalities add an additional surcharge, bringing taxes as high as 17 percent in some cities. I've noted the taxes you can expect to pay in the hotel section of each chapter.

Dining with dollars

California prides itself on its culinary prowess — but prepare yourself, because dining out tends to be rather expensive, especially in tourist-targeted destinations like the Wine Country. Main courses tend to run $11 to $18 on the average dinner menu. I've taken care, however, to recommend a range of choices in every destination so that everybody has options, no matter what your needs or budget.

In the chapters that follow, a number of dollar signs, ranging from one ($) to five ($$$$$), follows each restaurant name. The dollar signs are meant to give you an idea of what a complete dinner for one person — including appetizer, main course, one drink, tax, and tip — will likely set you back. The price categories go like this:

$	Cheap eats — less than $15 per person
$$	Still inexpensive — $15 to $25
$$$	Moderate — $25 to $40
$$$$	Pricey — $40 to $70
$$$$$	Ultra-expensive — more than $70 per person

Of course, just about any menu has a range of prices, and the final tally depends on how you order. The wine or bar tab is more likely to jack up the bill quicker than anything else will; desserts will also add to the total.

Saving on sightseeing and activities

Sightseeing admission charges and other activity fees can really add up quickly, especially if you're traveling with the kids. Of course, how much you spend all depends on what you want to do. If you're coming to California largely to discover its scenic towns and natural wonders, you won't have to budget much for sightseeing. Admission to national and state parks is minimal, and activities like hiking, picnicking, and beachcombing are absolutely free (except for the cost of refreshments, natch). Even bike and kayak rentals are inexpensive.

But if you're planning to visit the big-name sightseeing attractions — especially the theme parks — know what your budget can handle. These destinations can be *very* expensive: Expect to pay about $41 a head just to get in the door at **Disneyland,** the same at **Universal Studios,** $39 at **Sea World,** $18 at the **San Diego Zoo,** and $16 at the **Monterey Bay Aquarium.** (Needless to say, the Southern California theme park loop will not be cheap.) Admission is slightly cheaper for kids — but don't worry, they'll find plenty of ways to spend the difference and then some.

Beware, golfers — tee times at California's top courses don't come cheap, either.

In the destination chapters that follow, I tell you how much you can expect to pay for admission fees and activities so that you can budget your sightseeing money realistically.

What things cost in Santa Barbara

An average cup of coffee	$1.25
A ride aboard the Downtown-Waterfront Shuttle	25¢
Surrey for two, two-hour rental	$15
Guided Tour aboard Old Town Trolley	$10
Admission to Santa Barbara Museum of Art	$5
A day at the beach	free!
Strolling State Street	free! (plus shopping budget, of course)
Luxury room for two at the Four Seasons	$280–$550
Romantic room for two at the Bath Street Inn	$110–$170
Budget room for two at first-ever Motel 6	$61–$91
Dinner for two at the Wine Cask (with wine)	$125
Dinner for two at Brophy Bros. (with beer)	$50
Dinner for two at La Super-Rica (with tacos)	$12–$15
Ticket for summer-stock theater production in nearby Solvang	$18–$20

Allotting for shopping and entertainment

Shopping is a huge temptation in California. Many of the Golden State's finest small towns are rich in unique boutiques and other shopping opportunities. I dare you to escape the Napa Valley (see Chapter 10) without spending money on wine or other goodies. But places like Mendocino (see Chapter 11) and Carmel (see Chapter 16) are so pleasant just to stroll through that, if your budget's tight, you won't suffer if you limit yourself to window-shopping while you're there.

Don't blow a wad at the theme park souvenir stands. Anything you buy at **Disneyland** is available at your local mall's Disney Store. And your teenager does *not* need another **Hard Rock Cafe** T-shirt. Save your dough for something special — a one-of-a-kind souvenir that will recall vivid memories of happy vacation times. Or a really good pair of shoes, at least.

The cities are loaded with nightlife and entertainment options. You can spend a hundred bucks on a pair of theater tickets or nurse a couple of $3 beers in a friendly bar all night — the choice is entirely up to you and your wallet. Outside of the cities, California tends to be quiet after dark, with college towns like Santa Barbara and resort destinations like Palm Springs being the exceptions.

Keeping a Lid on Expenses

I don't care how much money you have — nobody wants to spend more than they have to. In this section, I help you rein in your expenses before they get out of control.

Getting the best airfare

This is such a huge topic that I've dedicated the better part of a chapter to it. Before you even start scanning for fares, see Chapter 6, "Getting to California" (also see "Winging Your Way Around" in Chapter 7 if you're interested in traveling within California by plane).

Booking accommodations — and avoiding the rack rate scam

The *rack rate* is the equivalent of the "suggested retail price" for your hotel room. The best way to avoid paying the full rack rate when booking your hotels is stunningly simple: *Just ask for a cheaper or discounted rate.* You may be pleasantly surprised — I've been, many times. But you have to take the initiative and ask, because no one is going to volunteer to save you money.

Here are some other potentially money-saving tips:

- ✔ **Always mention membership in AAA, AARP, or frequent flyer/traveler programs.** You may also qualify for corporate, student, military, or senior discounts.

- ✔ **Call the hotel direct as well as the central reservations 800 number.** I've found that it's worth the extra pennies to make both calls and see which one gives you the better deal. Sometimes the local reservationist knows about special deals or packages, but the hotel may neglect to tell the central booking line.

- ✔ **Consult a reliable travel agent.** Even if you've already booked your own airfare, you may find that a travel agent can negotiate a better price with certain hotels than you can get on your own. For more advice on the pros and cons of using an agent, see Chapter 6.

- ✔ **Bed-and-breakfast inns are generally nonnegotiable on price.** However, always ask if a price break is available during midweek or the off-season; in fact, you'll find that many B&Bs publish discounted midweek and off-season rates.

- ✔ **Travel midweek to popular weekending destinations.** Rates to destinations like the Wine Country, Carmel, the Hearst Castle area, Solvang, and Santa Barbara are at their highest on the weekends. Schedule your visits to the cities on weekends, when business travelers abandon San Francisco, L.A., and San Diego hotels, leaving them open to bargain-hunting vacationers.

- ✔ **Check the hotel listings in this book.** I've taken care to note the types of discounts that each hotel, inn, or motel tends to offer in chapters that follow. I can't guarantee what discounts may apply when you reserve, of course, but these tips should give you a heads-up on the kinds of special deals or discounted rates to ask for when you book.

Taking the AAA advantage

If you aren't already a member, consider taking a few minutes to join the **American Automobile Association (AAA)** before you launch your California vacation. Unfamiliar roads, unpredictable drivers, unforeseen circumstances (a flat that needs fixing, a battery that needs jump-starting), and unexplainable moments of stupidity (hello, lockout!) are just a few of the reasons for hooking into the club's roadside assistance network before you leave home.

But AAA membership offers much more than the occasional roadside rescue. Membership can save you money on hotel rates and admission to attractions throughout California (and other locations). Also included in the annual dues are a mind-boggling array of travel-related and general lifestyle services:

✔ The *AAA Travel Agency* will help you book air, hotel, and car arrangements as well as all-inclusive tour packages — and the staff will always let you know when a AAA member discount is available. American Express traveler's checks are available to members at no charge (see Chapter 8 for more information on traveler's checks).

✔ AAA maps are comprehensive, indispensable, and absolutely free to members. Stop in to your local office or go online to order maps for the destinations that interest you. If you're planning a road trip, ask for a customized *TripTik,* AAA's individual travel planner, with detailed driving directions and maps for your itinerary, plus visitor information for cities and towns along the route — a real boon for California trip planning.

✔ Through AAA's Show Your Card and Save program, members receive discounts and benefits at 3,000 attractions and restaurants and 44,000 retail locations nationwide. You can save a bundle on admissions to attractions throughout California (including Universal Studios Hollywood and SeaWorld), where AAA has a massive presence. Many hotels offer a 10 percent discount on rates (Hilton and Hyatt are two chains that offer even better agreed-upon rates for members). Car-rental companies also offer member discounts. You can really save a lot here — enough over the span of a two-week vacation to justify your AAA dues for a decade, much less a year.

✔ Membership includes a subscription to AAA's bimonthly members-only magazine, which is customized for your region and generally first-rate.

✔ You'll enjoy reciprocal benefits (including emergency roadside assistance) not only throughout the United States but at affiliated auto clubs worldwide.

✔ The *Financial Services* department features CDs, loans, vehicle financing, and other banking products; *Automotive Services* offers new car purchasing at prenegotiated prices; and *Insurance Services* provides a complete line of insurance (car, life, home, renters, small business). They're FDIC insured and offer better rates than most banks, insurance companies, or credit unions.

I hate to sound like a shill, but you really can't go wrong with AAA. Whether you get a 10 percent discount at a Best Western or a stress-relieving flat-tire fix, membership pays itself back before you know it. Annual fees vary slightly from region to region, but you can expect to spend around $55 per individual (primary member) and $25 to $30 for each additional family member. If you're joining solely for your California trip, only one person needs to sign up; back at home, you may want to cover all drivers in case of a roadside emergency.

To find the AAA office nearest you, log onto www.aaa.com, where you'll be linked to your regional club's home page after you enter your home zip code. You can even get instant membership by calling the national 24-hour emergency roadside service number (☎ **800-AAA-HELP**), which can connect you to any regional membership department during expanded business hours (only roadside assistance operates 24 hours a day). If you live in Canada, the **Canadian Automobile Association** (www.caa.com) offers similar services (plus reciprocal benefits with AAA).

Cutting costs in other ways

Here are a few more useful tips:

- Remember that summer, from June through mid-September, is the busy season. If you haven't decided on a travel time yet, *consider the off-seasons,* which are not only cheaper and less crowded but often more pleasant, weather-wise. See Chapter 2 for lots of helpful guidance.

- Consider booking a package deal, which includes airfare and hotel, and sometimes car and attraction costs, in a single price. Check out Chapter 6.

- Keep your eyes posted for the Bargain Alert icon as you read this book. This icon highlights money-saving opportunities and especially good values throughout the Golden State.

- If you live in a nearby state, consider driving to California in your own car. That way, you won't need to spring for a rental.

Bargains from American Express

American Express offers its cardholders a surprisingly good array of discounts at local and national vendors via its "Online Zone" program (previously "Online Extras"). By registering your AmEx card with this free program, you can receive discounts — often 20 percent — from airlines, hotel chains, rental car companies, restaurants, and shops throughout California and the country (even in your hometown), as well as with a good number of online merchants.

Participants change constantly, but the list is usually extensive. American Express is good about keeping these offers current, but be sure to check the expiration dates as well as the terms and conditions carefully. Note that some offers require you to register your American Express card with the Offer Zone program to qualify. Sign up at www.americanexpress.com; click on "Offer Zone" on the home page.

Chapter 5

Planning Ahead for Special Travel Needs

. . . .

In This Chapter

▶ Taking the kids along

▶ Going to the Golden State in your golden years

▶ Dealing with disabilities

▶ Traveling tips for gays and lesbians

▶ Finding help when you're traveling from abroad

. . . .

*G*enerally speaking, California is a forward-thinking state, and plenty accommodating to those of us with special requirements. But you may want to know, more specifically: How welcoming will California be to me and . . . (pick one or more) a) my kids? b) my senior status? c) my disability? d) my same-sex partner? If you need answers, you've come to the right chapter.

Advice for Travelers with Kids

With its wealth of parks — both the theme kind, à la Disneyland, and the natural kind, à la Yosemite — California is the ultimate family-vacation state. Knowing on which side its bread is buttered, the Golden State offers a wealth of family-friendly hotels — from luxury resorts to budget motels — restaurants, and other activities. I note the best kid-friendly spots throughout this book.

Some destinations suit families better than do others. Skip romance-ready Carmel, for example, and head for kid-friendly Monterey. Your kids will probably prefer San Diego over Palm Springs, if you have to choose. Still, families are as individual as snowflakes, and no single blueprint exists for the ultimate family vacation.

Your vacation will go well if you remember to tailor your trip around the things you and your kids like to do. Check out the itineraries in Chapter 3, a number of which take family travel into consideration.

Following are a few tips to help you with your family travel plans:

- ✓ **Don't be too ambitious.** I can't say this too strongly: Too much time spent in the car moving from one place to another will result in a trip from hell — for both you and the kids.

- ✓ **Take it slow at the start.** Give the entire family time to adjust to a new time zone, or just being on the road. The best way to do this is to budget a couple/few days in your initial destination that don't require strict itineraries or lots of moving around.

- ✓ **Look for the Kid Friendly icon as you flip through this book.** I use it to highlight hotels, restaurants, and attractions that families will find particularly welcoming. Zeroing in on these listings will help you plan your trip more efficiently.

- ✓ **Bring plenty of road-trip supplies.** Bring healthy snacks, car-friendly books and games, and a pillow and blanket for naptime. Books on tape are great for entertaining the entire family.

- ✓ **Book some private time for mom and dad.** Most hotels can hook you up with a reliable babysitter who will entertain the kids while you enjoy a romantic dinner or another adults-only activity. Ask about babysitting services when you make your reservations.

The following are excellent resources for advice on family travel:

- ✓ **BabyCenter** (www.babycenter.com/travel) has good advice for planning baby's first trip, and even on traveling while pregnant.

- ✓ **Family.com** (www.family.com) features a travel page with both general and destination-specific advice (albeit with a Disney slant, as Family.com is part of the ABC/Disney Go network).

- ✓ **Family Travel Files** (www.familytravelfiles.com) is a comprehensive Web site dedicated to the subject of family travel featuring both general and destination-specific advice.

- ✓ **Family Travel Times** is an excellent bimonthly newsletter covering all aspects of family travel. Subscriptions are $39 a year, and you can subscribe by calling ☎ **888-822-4388** or 212-477-5524. You can also peruse back issues and subscribe online at www.familytraveltimes.com.

Advice for Seniors

One of the benefits of age is that travel often costs less. Many hotels and airlines give discounted rates to senior travelers, although the minimum age requirement can vary between 55 and 65. Ditto for Amtrak, many public transit systems, museums, attractions, and even theater performances. Always bring an ID card, especially if you've kept your youthful glow, and don't be shy about asking.

If you're not a member of **AARP (American Association of Retired Persons),** 601 E St. NW, Washington, DC 20049 (☎ **800-424-3410,** 800-303-4222, or 202-434-AARP; www.aarp.org), do yourself a favor and join. Members qualify for discounts of up to 25 percent on airfares, hotels, car rentals, and vacation packages. Membership also includes *Modern Maturity* magazine, a monthly newsletter, and special rates on insurance, prescriptions, and more. For just $8 a year, with all the associated benefits, you can't afford *not* to sign up.

Mature Outlook, P.O. Box 9390, Des Moines, IA 50322 (☎ **800-336-6330**), is an organization similar to AARP. It offers discounts on car rentals and hotel stays at many Holiday Inns, Howard Johnsons, and Best Westerns. The $19.95 annual membership fee also gets you $200 in Sears coupons and a magazine.

The Book of Deals is a collection of more than 1,000 senior discounts on airlines, lodging, tours, and attractions around the country; it's available for $9.95 by calling ☎ **800-460-6676.**

Another helpful publication is *101 Tips for the Mature Traveler,* available from **Grand Circle Travel,** 347 Congress St., Suite 3A, Boston, MA 02210 (☎ **800-221-2610;** www.gct.com). Grand Circle Travel is one of the hundreds of travel agencies that specialize in vacations for seniors. But beware: Many of these outfits are of the tour-bus variety, with free trips thrown in for those who organize groups of 20 or more. Seniors seeking more independent travel should probably consult a regular travel agent.

Advice for Travelers with Disabilities

These days, a disability shouldn't stop anyone from traveling. The Americans with Disabilities Act requires that all public buildings be wheelchair accessible and have accessible rest rooms. Most hotels and sightseeing attractions (except those grandfathered by landmark status) are outfitted with wheelchair ramps and extra-wide doorways and halls. Many city sidewalk corners have dropped curbs, and some public transit systems are equipped with lifts. Your best bet is to contact local visitor bureaus, as they can provide you with all the specifics on accessibility in their locale; see "Gathering More Information" at the end of each city and regional chapter.

Because so many of California's hotels are on the newer side, a good number feature rooms dedicated to the needs of disabled travelers, outfitted with everything from extra-large bathrooms with low-set fixtures to fire-alarm systems adapted for deaf travelers. Still, before you book a hotel room, ask lots of questions based on your needs. After you arrive, always call restaurants, attractions, and theaters before you go to make sure they are fully accessible.

These resources provide excellent information on accessible travel:

✔ Both **Moss Rehab ResourceNet** (www.mossresourcenet.org) and **Access-Able Travel Source** (☎ 303-232-2979; www.access-able.com) are comprehensive resources for disabled travelers. Both sites feature links to travel agents who specialize in planning accessible trips. Access-Able's user-friendly site also features relay and voice numbers for hotels, airlines, and car-rental companies, plus links to accessible accommodations, attractions, transportation, tours, and local medical resources and equipment repairers throughout California (and other locations).

✔ You can join the **Society for the Advancement of Travelers with Handicaps (SATH),** 347 Fifth Ave. Suite 610, New York, NY 10016 (☎ 212-447-7284; www.sath.org), to gain access to their vast network of travel connections. Their quarterly magazine, *Open World*, is full of good information and resources.

✔ **Accessible San Diego** (☎ 858-279-0704; www.accessandiego.com), the nation's first nonprofit info center for travelers with disabilities, offers complete information on accessibility issues in San Diego, as well as an *Access in San Diego* travel guide that you can order for $5.

If you'd like to drive yourself around, consider the following:

✔ Many of the big car-rental companies — including **Avis** (☎ 800-230-4898; www.avis.com), **Hertz** (☎ 800-654-3131; www.hertz.com), and **National** (☎ 800-227-7368; www.nationalcar.com) — rent *hand-controlled cars* for disabled drivers at major airport locations throughout California.

✔ **Wheelchair Getaways** (☎ 800-536-5518; www.wheelchairgetaways.com) rents vans and minivans with wheelchair lifts, ramps, hand controls, and/or other features for disabled travelers. Vehicles are available at locations throughout California, including the San Francisco Bay Area, San Jose, L.A., Orange County, Palm Springs, and San Diego; call ☎ **800-638-1912,** or 877-388-4883 (for San Diego and Palm Springs).

Travelers with disabilities may also want to consider joining a tour that caters specifically to them. One of the best operators is **Flying Wheels Travel,** P.O. Box 382, Owatonna, MN 55060 (☎ **800-535-6790;** Fax: 507-451-1685).

Vision-impaired travelers should contact the **American Foundation for the Blind,** 11 Penn Plaza, Suite 300, New York, NY 10001 (☎ **800-232-5463**), for info on traveling with seeing-eye dogs.

Advice for Gay and Lesbian Travelers

In the Golden State, homosexuality is squarely in the mainstream, especially in the cities. San Francisco is mecca for gays, with Los Angeles running neck-and-neck with New York for a close second as gay-friendliest city in the United States. Even relatively conservative San Diego has a huge gay contingent (the Hillcrest neighborhood is their base). Palm Springs is hugely popular with gay travelers, but, by and large, the entire state is welcoming to gays and lesbians.

If you want help planning your trip, **IGLTA,** the **International Gay & Lesbian Travel Association** (☎ **800-448-8550** or 954-776-2626; www.iglta.org), is your best source. IGLTA can link you up with the appropriate gay-friendly service organization or agent. Members are kept informed of gay and gay-friendly hoteliers, tour operators, and airline representatives. The IGLTA site will link you to other useful sites that can also help you plan your California vacation.

Out and About (☎ **800-929-2268** or 212-645-6922; www.outandabout. com) offers a monthly newsletter packed with good information on the global gay and lesbian scene. You can find *Out and About* guidebooks at most major bookstores, but the Web site alone is a first-rate resource.

Advice for Foreign Visitors

The U.S. State Department has a **Visa Waiver Pilot Program** allowing citizens of about 30 countries — including Australia, New Zealand, and the United Kingdom — to enter the United States without a visa for stays of up to 90 days. Citizens of these countries need only a valid passport and a round-trip air ticket upon arrival.

If you're a citizen of a country not included in the Waiver Program, you must have both a *valid passport* that expires at least six months later than the scheduled end of your visit to the United States and a *tourist visa,* which you can get without charge from any U.S. consulate.

For a quick and easy update on current passport and visa issues, plug in to the U.S. State Department's Internet site at www.state.gov. You can get more information from any U.S. embassy or consulate. *Always check for the latest before you leave home.*

You are not allowed to bring foodstuffs and plants into the United States. You may bring in or take out up to $10,000 in U.S. or foreign currency with no formalities; larger sums must be declared to U.S. Customs on entering or leaving. For more information regarding U.S. Customs, call your nearest U.S. embassy or consulate, or contact the U.S. Customs at ☎ **202-927-1770** or www.customs.ustreas.gov.

The United States recognizes most foreign driver's licenses, but you may want to get an international driver's license if your home license is not written in English.

Part II
Ironing Out the Details

In this part . . .

When it comes to California, getting there may not be half the fun, but this part will ease some of your worry. Here, I talk about your travel options: choosing a method of transportation, working with and without a travel agent, using an all-inclusive travel package, and finalizing those last-minute details like making advance reservations, packing, and weighing your insurance options. No glamour — but all necessary.

Chapter 6

Getting to California

In This Chapter

▶ Making your own travel plans versus using a travel agent

▶ Taking advantage of a package deal — or going on a guided tour

▶ Arriving in California by plane, train, or automobile

*G*etting there may not *really* be half the fun, but it's a necessary step — and a big part of the planning process. Should you use a travel agent, or go the independent route? Should you book a package deal, or book the elements of your vacation separately?

In this chapter, I give you the information you need to make the decision that's right for you.

Travel Agent: Friend or Foe?

The best way to find a good travel agent is the same way you locate a good plumber or mechanic or doctor — through word of mouth.

Any travel agent can help you find a bargain airfare, hotel, or rental car. A good travel agent will stop you from ruining your vacation by trying to save a few dollars. The best travel agents can tell you how much time you should budget for a destination, find you a cheap flight that doesn't require changing planes in Atlanta and Chicago, get you a better hotel room than you can find on your own for about the same price, arrange for a competitively priced rental car, and even give recommendations on restaurants.

To get the most out of your travel agent, first do a little homework:

✔ Read up on your destination (you've already made a sound decision by buying this book) and pick out some accommodations and attractions you think you like.

✔ If you want even more recommendations, check out *Frommer's California,* also published by IDG Books Worldwide, Inc., a comprehensive guidebook that goes beyond the the best sites to include just about every place you can think of to go.

> ✔ If you have access to the Internet, check prices on the Web in advance (see "Tips for Getting the Best Airfare" later in this chapter, for ideas) to get a ballpark sense of costs.

Then take your guidebook and Web information to a travel agent and ask him or her to make the arrangements for you. Because they can access more resources than even the most complete Web travel site, travel agents should be able to get you a better price than you can get yourself. They can also issue your tickets and vouchers right on the spot. If they can't get you into the hotel of your choice, they can recommend an alternative, and you can look for an objective review in your guidebook.

Travel agents usually work on commission. The good news is that *you* don't pay the commission; the airlines, accommodations, and tour companies do. The bad news is that unscrupulous travel agents will try to persuade you to book the vacations that reward them the most money in commissions.

Over the past few years, some airlines and resorts have begun limiting or eliminating travel-agent commissions altogether. Consequently, many of these travel agents don't bother booking certain services unless the customer specifically requests them. Some travel agents have even started charging customers for their services — which means that consumers will end up having to pay more or resort to making their own travel plans altogether.

 If you aren't already a member, consider joining the *American Automobile Association (AAA),* which gives you access to the AAA Travel Agency. It's a full-service agency, with experienced travel agents who can book air, hotel, and car arrangements as well as tour packages. And, of course, they'll always tell you when a member discount is available. See "The AAA Advantage" in Chapter 4.

The Ins and Outs of Travel Packages

Package tours differ from escorted tours. Packages are simply a way of buying your airfare and accommodations at the same time.

For popular destinations like California, package tours are the smart way to go. In many cases, a package that includes airfare, hotel, and transportation to and from the airport will cost less than the hotel alone if you booked it yourself. The price is so low because packages are sold in bulk to tour operators, who resell them to the public. The process is kind of like shopping at Sam's Club — except the tour operator is the one who buys the 1,000-count box of garbage bags and resells them at a cost that undercuts the neighborhood supermarket.

Package tours can vary as much as those hypothetical garbage bags. Some offer a better class of hotels than others. Others offer the same hotels for lower prices. Some offer flights on scheduled airlines; others book charters. Some packages may limit your choice of accommodations and travel days. Some let you choose between escorted vacations and independent vacations; others allow you to add on just a few excursions or escorted day trips (also at discounted prices) without booking an entirely escorted tour.

Each destination usually has one or two packagers (tour operators) that are better than the rest because they buy in even bigger bulk. The time you spend shopping around is likely to be well rewarded.

The best places to start looking for a suitable package are your travel agent — who may be able to do the comparison-shopping for you and get you the best overall package rates — and the travel section of your local Sunday newspaper, or the back ads of travel magazines.

Or cut out the middleman and contact a reputable packager directly. Liberty Travel (☎ **888-271-1584**; www.libertytravel.com) is one of the oldest and biggest packagers in the east and runs a full-page ad in many Sunday papers. You won't get much in the way of service, but you will get a good deal. At press time, Liberty was offering good-value packages, with or without air, to the most popular California destinations — including L.A., Disneyland, Palm Springs, San Diego, San Francisco, and Lake Tahoe — and their agents are willing to help you construct a multi-destination trip.

Many airlines also offer travel packages. I always recommend comparison shopping, but you may want to choose the airline that has frequent service to your hometown or the one with which you accumulate frequent-flyer miles; you may even be able to pay for your trip using accumulated miles. The major airlines that offer travel packages to California include these big names:

- ✔ Air Canada Vacations (☎ **800-662-3221**; www.aircanadavacations. com).

- ✔ Alaska Airlines Vacations (☎ **800-468-2248**; www.alaskaair.com).

- ✔ American Airlines Vacations (☎ **800-321-2121**; www.aavacations. com) features one of the more extensive lists of California destinations.

- ✔ Continental Airlines Vacations (☎ **800-634-5555**; www.coolvacations. com).

- ✔ Delta Vacations (☎ **800-872-7786**; www.deltavacations.com) just came out as the price-comparison leader among airline packagers in an informal poll conducted by *Condè Nast Traveler.*

- ✔ Northwest WorldVacations (☎ **800-800-1504**; www.nwaworldvacations. com).

- ✔ Southwest Airlines Vacations (☎ **800-423-5683**; www.swavacations. com) also offers hotel-only reservations — worth noting for those of you whose home airports are not served by the king of the bargain airlines.

- ✔ United Vacations (☎ **800-328-6877**; www.unitedvacations.com).

- ✔ US Airways Vacations (☎ **800-472-2577**; www.usairwaysvacations. com).

If you're considering either arriving in California by train or traveling around the state by train — or both — check into the all-inclusive travel packages offered by Amtrak Vacations (☎ **800-654-5748;** www. amtrakvacations.com).

If you're an AmEx customer, consider going through **American Express Travel** (☎ **800-AXP-6898** [297-6898] or 800-346-3607; www.americanexpress. com/travel), which can book packages through various vendors, including Continental and Delta.

Once again, I'm beating the AAA drum — if you're a member, AAA's travel agency can book excellent-value package deals.

If you're heading to Disneyland, you may want to contact the official Disney travel agency, **Walt Disney Travel Co.** (☎ **800-225-2024** or 714-520-5050; www.disneyland.com). The company offers Disney-focused packages that can also include a wide range of Southern California extras, depending on your wants and needs. For more on this, see "The Art of the (Package) Deal" in Chapter 22.

Universal Studios Vacations offers similar all-inclusive L.A. vacation deals; call ☎ **800-711-0080** or go online to www.universalstudios. com, then click on "Theme Parks" then "Plan a Trip."

The well-conceived escorted tours of California offered by **Tauck Tours** (☎ **800-788-7885;** www.tauck.com) are more luxurious and less structured than your average escorted tour. They're pricey but worth the cost if you'd rather let someone else do the driving.

The information junkies among you may want to search www. vacationpackager.com, an excruciatingly extensive Web-search engine that can link you up with an exhausting list of package-tour operators that offer California vacations. You'll have to wade through a lot of excess at this site, but doing so is the most thorough way to discover *all* of your options.

Be advised that most travel packagers do not offer comprehensive California vacations. They tend to focus on the large-volume destinations — San Francisco, Los Angeles, San Diego, Disneyland, and sometimes Lake Tahoe and Palm Springs. If you want to hit other destinations, you'll likely have to (or have your travel agent) book those legs of your trip directly.

Still, don't give up on the package route; with a little planning, you (or again, your travel agent) may manage to link a few smaller packages into the good-value vacation of your dreams.

For the Independent Trip-Planner: Tips for Getting the Best Airfare

Business travelers who need the flexibility to purchase their tickets at the last minute, change their itinerary at a moment's notice, or want to get home before the weekend pay the premium rate, known as the full fare. Passengers who can book their tickets far in advance, who don't mind staying over Saturday night, or who are willing to travel on a Tuesday, Wednesday, or Thursday pay the least, usually a fraction of the full fare. On most flights to California, even the shortest hops, the full fare is more than $1,000, but a 7-day or 14-day advance purchase ticket is often closer to $500, maybe less. Obviously, I can't guarantee what fares will be when you book, but you can almost always save big by planning ahead.

The airlines also periodically hold sales, in which they lower the prices on their most popular routes. These fares carry advance-purchase requirements and date-of-travel restrictions, but you usually can't beat the price: sometimes no more than $400 for a cross-country flight (less on some discount airlines). Keep your eyes open for these sales, which are advertised in the newspapers, on the Internet, and some-times on TV, as you are planning your vacation. The sales tend to take place in seasons of low travel volume. You'll almost never see a sale around the peak summer vacation months of July and August, or around Thanksgiving or Christmas.

All of the following airlines fly to all major California airports:

- ✔ Air Canada: ☎ **888-247-2262;** www.aircanada.ca
- ✔ Alaska Airlines: ☎ **800-252-7522;** www.alaskaair.com
- ✔ America West: ☎ **800-235-9292;** www.americawest.com
- ✔ American: ☎ **800-433-7300;** www.americanair.com
- ✔ Continental: ☎ **800-525-0280;** www.continental.com
- ✔ Delta: ☎ **800-221-1212;** www.delta-air.com
- ✔ Northwest: ☎ **800-225-2525;** www.nwa.com
- ✔ Southwest: ☎ **800-435-9792;** www.iflyswa.com
- ✔ TWA: ☎ **800-221-2000;** www.twa.com
- ✔ US Airways: ☎ **800- 428-4322;** www.usairways.com
- ✔ United: ☎ 800-241-6522; www.ual.com

Consolidators, also known as bucket shops, are a good place to check for the lowest fares. Their prices are much better than the fares you can get yourself, and are often even lower than what your travel agent can get you. You can see their ads in the small boxes at the bottom of the page in your Sunday travel section. Some of the most reliable consolidators include:

- ✔ Cheap Tickets (☎ **800-377-1000;** www.cheaptickets.com)
- ✔ 1-800-FLY-CHEAP (☎ **800-359-2432;** www.flycheap.com)
- ✔ Travac Tours & Charters (☎ **877-872-8221;** www.thetravelsite.com)

Another good choice, Council Travel (☎ **800-226-8624;** www.counciltravel.com), caters to young travelers, but their bargain-basement prices are available to people of all ages.

Booking your ticket online

Another way to find the cheapest fare is to scour the Internet. Too many travel-booking sites exist to mention them all, but a few of the better-respected (and more comprehensive) ones are Travelocity (www.travelocity.com), Microsoft Expedia (www.expedia.com), and Yahoo Travel (http://travel.yahoo.com). Each has its own little quirks, but all provide variations on the same service. Just enter the dates you want to fly and the cities you want to visit, and the computer looks for the lowest fares. Several other features have become standard to these sites: the ability to check flights at different times or dates in hopes of finding a cheaper fare, e-mail alerts when fares drop on a route you have specified, and a database of last-minute deals that advertises super-cheap vacation packages or airfares for those who can get away at a moment's notice.

You can be notified of late-breaking airfare deals for all the major airlines at once by logging on to *Smarter Living* (www.smarterliving.com), or you can go to each individual airline's Web site and sign up. These sites offer schedules, flight booking, and often information on special deals or fare sales.

Landing an airport

The major California airports include:

- ✔ **San Francisco International Airport (SFO),** 14 miles south of downtown San Francisco via U.S. 101 (☎ **650-876-2377;** www.flysfo.com)

- ✔ **Sacramento International Airport,** north of downtown Sacramento on Interstate 5, just past the junction with Highway 99 (☎ **916-874-0700;** airports.co.sacramento.ca.us/smf)

✔ **San Jose International Airport,** gateway to the Silicon Valley, just north of the U.S. 101/I-880/Highway 17 junction, at the intersection of U.S. 101 and Highway 87 (☎ **408-501-7600;** www.sjc.org)

✔ **Los Angeles International Airport (LAX),** at the intersection of the 405 and 105 freeways, 9½ miles south of Santa Monica and 16 miles southwest of Hollywood (☎ **310-646-5252;** www.lawa.org)

✔ **San Diego International Airport**, locally known as Lindbergh Field, on Interstate 5 right in the heart of San Diego (☎ **619-231-7361;** www.portofsandiego.org)

Chances are good that one of five major airports listed above will serve as your gateway. In addition, major carriers also serve good-size or smaller airports in Oakland, just across the bay from San Francisco (see Chapter 9); in the middle of the state in Fresno, close to the southern gateway to Yosemite (see Chapter 14); in Reno, NV, less than an hour's drive from Lake Tahoe (see Chapter 13); on the northern Central Coast in Monterey (see Chapter 16); in Orange County, just a stone's throw from Disneyland (see Chapter 22); and in Palm Springs (see Chapter 24).

Because the Golden State is so darn big and has so many major airports, you'll need to work out a basic itinerary for yourself before you book your airline tickets. The regional chapters in this book will help you do that, as will the itineraries in Chapter 3. For more information on travel distances between airports and destinations, see Parts III through V as well as Chapter 7.

I've already included this piece of advice in Chapter 3 on planning your itinerary, but it bears repeating here: *Seriously consider flying into one California airport and leaving from another.* The time you save by flying into San Diego and leaving from San Francisco, say, or flying into San Jose and departing from Palm Springs, may justify the extra airline charges and/or rental-car drop-off charges. What's more, depending on your points of arrival and departure, you may happily discover that no extra charges apply. Your best bet is to have a couple of options and price them out with the airlines and car companies (or put your travel agent to work) before you make a final decision.

Driving to California

Driving yourself to California can be a smart move, especially if you live relatively close and you'd prefer to tour the state in your own car.

The major interstates that lead into the state are:

✔ **I-5,** which enters California from Oregon at the northern border and runs south through the middle of the state all the way to San Diego.

✔ **I-80,** which arrives from the east via Reno, NV, and runs west through Sacramento to San Francisco.

✔ **I-15,** which connects Las Vegas, NV, with I-10 just east of Los Angeles.

✔ **I-40,** which runs across the northern half of the southern states, cutting through the Texas panhandle, Albuquerque, NM, and Flagstaff, AZ, before entering California in Needles, CA (where Snoopy's cousin Spike is from, for all you *Peanuts* fans) — otherwise known as the middle of nowhere — and heading west until it connects up with I-15 northeast of Los Angeles.

✔ **I-10,** the most popular route into Southern California, which runs from New Orleans, LA, to Los Angeles, passing through Houston, TX, Phoenix, AZ, and Palm Springs along the way.

✔ **I-8,** which links Tucson and Yuma, AZ, with San Diego.

Here are some handy drive times for you road-trippers:

To San Francisco from:

✔ Portland, OR: 636 miles, 10¼ hours

✔ Reno, NV: 220 miles, 3¾ hours

✔ Boise, ID: 641 miles, 11½ hours

✔ Salt Lake City, UT: 737 miles, 11¾ hours

✔ Las Vegas, NV: 574 miles, 9½ hours

To Los Angeles from:

✔ Salt Lake City, UT: 690 miles, 11 hours

✔ Las Vegas, NV: 270 miles, 4½ hours

✔ Albuquerque, NM: 789 miles, 12½ hours

✔ Phoenix, AZ: 373 miles, 6¼ hours

To San Diego from:

✔ Las Vegas, NV: 332 miles, 5½ hours

✔ El Paso, TX: 725 miles, 11½ hours

✔ Tucson, AZ: 407 miles, 6½ hours

Taking the train

Amtrak (☎ **800-USA-RAIL;** www.amtrak.com) serves multiple California cities, including San Francisco, San Jose, Santa Barbara, L.A., and San Diego.

Arriving by train from another state is much slower and not significantly cheaper than traveling by plane. Therefore, I suggest exploring this option only if saving a little money means more to you than speed of travel, you hate flying, or you're drawn to the romanticism of a train journey. You'll still need to rent a car to do any significant sightseeing, unless you'd prefer to travel around California by train, too; for details, see Chapter 6.

Chapter 7

Getting Around California

● ●

In This Chapter

▶ Traveling around California by car (a rental or your own)

▶ Following the rules of the road

▶ Touring the Golden State by plane or train

● ●

*F*orget the Golden State moniker — California is really the Driving State. You'll need a car to get yourself around, no two ways about it. Even if you choose to move from destination to destination using planes and trains, you'll likely need an automobile after you get to your destination. The only California destinations that you can both easily reach and navigate via other means of transportation are San Francisco, San Diego (some attractions, not all), and Santa Barbara.

Getting Around by Car

If you don't bring your own car to California, you'll probably need to rent one. The following companies rent cars at locations throughout California, including at all the major airports and in the cities:

✔ Alamo: ☎ **800-GO-ALAMO** (800-462-5266); www.alamo.com

✔ Avis: ☎ **800-230-4898;** www.avis.com

✔ Budget: ☎ **800-527-0700;** www.budget.com

✔ Dollar: ☎ **800-800-4000;** www.dollar.com

✔ Enterprise: ☎ **800-325-8007;** www.enterprise.com

✔ Hertz: ☎ **800-654-3131;** www.hertz.com

✔ National: ☎ **800-227-7368;** www.nationalcar.com

✔ Thrifty: ☎ **800-THRIFTY** (800-847-4389); www.thrifty.com

Rental cars are relatively cheap in the Driving State. Of course, I can't guarantee what you'll pay when you book, but you can often get a compact car for between $100 to $200 a week, depending on your dates and where you pick up your car (Southern California rentals are usually cheaper). If you want something family-size, expect to pay more like $200 to $300 a week, which is still quite reasonable.

As mentioned earlier in this book (most notably in Chapter 3), I advocate flying into one airport and leaving from another so you can see as much of California as possible. And depending on your pickup and drop-off points, you may find that you won't have to pay extra for your one-way car rental. Again, no promises, but I've found that more often than not you won't pay more than if you had picked up and dropped off at the same location.

Price car rentals at the same time you price airfares to make sure that flying into one city and out of another is cost-effective on both counts. I've had great luck with one-way rentals with National, but check with a few companies before you make a final decision. If you get a rate quote you like and decide that this is the way you want to go, make your reservation (which will lock in your rate) immediately. This will save you from getting taken to the cleaners after the fact — because policies and prices can change at any time.

For tips on renting hand-controlled cars or vans equipped with wheelchair lifts, see Chapter 5.

Getting the best deal on a rental car

Car-rental rates vary even more than airline fares. The price depends on the size of the car, the length of time you keep it, where and when you pick it up and drop it off, where you take it, and a host of other factors. Asking a few key questions can save you hundreds of dollars.

- ✔ Weekend rates may be lower than weekday rates. Ask if the rate is the same for pickup Friday morning as it is Thursday night. If you're keeping the car five or more days, a weekly rate may be cheaper than the daily rate.

- ✔ As I note in the previous section, some companies assess a drop-off charge if you don't return the car to the same renting location; others do not. Ask when you book. Also ask if the rate is cheaper if you pick up the car at the airport or at a location in town.

- ✔ If you see an advertised special, be sure to ask for that specific rate; otherwise you may be charged the standard (higher) rate.

Don't forget to mention membership in AAA, AARP, frequent-flyer programs, and trade unions. These usually entitle you to discounts ranging from 5 percent to 30 percent. Ask your travel agent to check any and all of these rates. And, don't forget: most car rentals are worth at least 500 miles on your frequent-flyer account!

Using the Internet can make comparison shopping much easier. All the major booking sites — Travelocity (www.travelocity.com), Expedia (www.expedia.com), Yahoo! Travel (www.travel.yahoo.com), and Cheap Tickets (www.cheaptickets.com), for example — feature search engines that can book car rentals for you.

On top of the standard rental price, optional charges can apply to car rentals. You may opt to pay for a *collision damage waiver*, which covers damage in the case of an accident. Many credit card companies offer this coverage automatically, so check the terms of your credit card before you shell out money for this hefty charge (as much as $15/day).

The car-rental companies also offer additional liability insurance (if you harm others in an accident), personal accident insurance (if you harm yourself or your passengers), and personal effects insurance (if someone steals your luggage from your car). If you have insurance on your car at home, that insurance probably covers you for most of these scenarios. If your own insurance doesn't cover you for rentals, or if you don't have auto insurance, consider the additional coverage (as much as $20/day combined). Also keep in mind that car-rental companies are liable for certain base amounts, depending on the state.

Some companies also offer refueling packages, in which you pay for an entire tank of gas up front. The price is usually fairly competitive with local gas prices, but you don't get credit for any gas remaining in the tank. If you reject this option, you pay only for the gas you use, but you have to return it with a full tank or else you face charges of $3 to $4 a gallon for any shortfall. If a stop at a gas station on the way to the airport will make you miss your plane, then by all means take advantage of the fuel purchase option. Otherwise, skip it.

Following the rules of the road

Know these rules of the road before you drive around California:

- ✔ **All passengers must wear seatbelts at all times.** No cheating in the back seat. You must harness children under 4 years or 40 pounds into an approved safety seat (some car-rental agencies now rent these seats; ask when you reserve your car). Motorcyclists must wear helmets.

- ✔ **You can turn right on red** as long as a posted sign doesn't say otherwise. Make sure you make a full stop first — no rolling.

- ✔ **The maximum speed limit on most California freeways is 65 mph,** although some freeways carry a posted limit of 70 mph. For two-lane undivided highways, the maximum speed limit is 55 mph, unless otherwise posted. Speed limits vary in populated areas; defaulting to 25 mph is smart if you're not sure. California law states that you must never drive faster than is safe for the present conditions, regardless of the posted speed limit.

- ✔ **You can pass on the right** on the freeway as long as you act safely and use a properly marked lane.

- ✔ **Pedestrians always have the right of way** in both crosswalks and at uncontrolled intersections.

✔ **Those kids you brought with you can come in handy.** Some freeways, especially those in Southern California, have a High Occupancy Vehicle (HOV) — a carpool — lane, which lets you speed past some of the congestion if three people are in the car (sometimes two; read the signs). Don't flout the rules; if you do, expect to shell out close to 300 bucks for the ticket.

✔ **Always read street-parking signs, and keep plenty of quarters on hand for meters.** Popular destinations and smaller towns with parking crunches often have some of the most stringent rules and gung-ho meter readers. Be extra-vigilant in the metropolitan areas.

Save yourself some hassle and just buy a roll of dedicated parking quarters at your bank before you leave home.

✔ **If you drink, don't drive.** Driving with a blood alcohol level of .08 percent or higher is illegal. Do everyone a favor and refrain from indulging if you plan to get behind the wheel.

✔ **Check the Web for a complete rundown of California state driving guidelines.** The complete *California Driver Handbook* is available online; go to www.dmv.ca.gov, then click on "Publications," where you can also find rules of the road for motorcycles, RVs, and trailers.

In addition to following the rules of the road, include the following tips among your driving practices:

✔ **Always have a good statewide map on hand.** AAA's excellent foldout version, free to members, is a particularly good one and will meet all of your road-warrior needs.

✔ **Know more about the direction you're heading than simply "north" or "south."** California's freeway and highway signs indicate direction, more often than not, by naming a town rather than a point on the compass: If you were heading east on I-10 to Palm Springs, say, you'd follow the signs that say "Ontario" as you drove out of L.A., not the ones that say "Santa Monica." Review your map carefully so that you know which way to go before you hit the road.

✔ **Know how far you have to go.** See Table 7-1 for some sample distances between California destinations:

Table 7-1 Sample Mileage Between CA Destinations

From San Francisco to	From Los Angeles to	From San Diego to
Eureka: 261 miles	Mendocino: 527½ miles	San Francisco: 504 miles
Yosemite National Park: 202 miles	San Francisco: 382 miles	Santa Cruz: 466 miles
Lake Tahoe: 189 miles	Yosemite National Park: 344½ miles	Solvang: 250 miles
Napa Valley: 47½ miles	Monterey: 323 miles	Death Valley: 324 miles
Monterey: 119 miles	Hearst Castle: 231 miles	Los Angeles: 122 miles
Hearst Castle: 211 miles	Death Valley: 262 miles	Disneyland: 98 miles
Santa Barbara: 328 miles	Santa Barbara: 97 miles	Palm Springs: 141 miles
Los Angeles: 382 miles	Disneyland: 26½ miles	Tijuana: 16 miles
Disneyland: 408 miles	Palm Springs: 108 miles	
Palm Springs: 488 miles	San Diego: 122 miles	
San Diego: 504 miles		

✔ **Some routes will take much longer than others.** The scenic routes may be more interesting, but they'll be far slower going than the freeways, so choose your roads carefully. What's more important to you — natural beauty, or getting to your destination as quickly as humanly possible?

The drive between San Francisco and Los Angeles, for example, takes about six hours if you stick to the scenic-free but speedy I-5, which cuts vertically through the unimpressive middle of the state. But count on about a nine-hour drive, plus stops, if you decide to follow the coastal route — one of the most curvaceous and stunning drives on the planet — all the way.

✔ **Prepare your vehicle for the weather.** If you're heading to Yosemite or Tahoe in winter, top off on antifreeze and bring snow chains. If renting a car, ask the agency if chains are provided. Also, check road conditions before you set out. Call the California Department of Transportation (CALTRANS) at ☎ **916-445-1534**, which can fill you in on conditions throughout the state at any time of year. You can also check road and traffic conditions online at www.dot.ca.gov.

✔ **If you're not already a member, consider joining AAA.** The American Automobile Association can be a lifesaver if you get a flat, experience a breakdown, or lock your keys in your car while you're on the road. For a complete rundown of benefits, see Chapter 4.

✔ **Take along your cellphone, if you have one.** A cellphone can be an invaluable lifeline as you drive throughout California, especially in remote destinations — such as Big Sur, or enroute to Yosemite — where you won't find telephone call boxes lining the side of the road. If renting a car, you may be able to rent a cellphone along with your car; ask when you call.

For more advice on how to budget your drive time and what to expect while you're on the road, see Chapter 3. Also check out Chapter 5 for recommendations on road-tripping with the kids.

Winging Your Way Around

If time is short and you want to cover great distances without the long drive, consider flying between California locations. After all, an hour-long flight can save you the entire travel day that driving between San Francisco and Los Angeles or San Diego would consume. Even shorter distances — L.A. to Monterey, say — can save you a good chunk of valuable vacation time. Airfares are generally reasonable, too, often between $60 and $100 per leg.

The following airlines are well-versed in shuttling passengers between multiple California destinations:

✔ Alaska Airlines: ☎ **800-252-7522;** www.alaskaair.com

✔ America West: ☎ **800-235-9292;** www.americawest.com

✔ American/American Eagle: ☎ **800-433-7300;** www.americanair.com

✔ Delta/Skywest: ☎ **800-221-1212;** www.delta-air.com

✔ Southwest: ☎ **800-435-9792;** www.iflyswa.com

✔ US Airways: ☎ **800-428-4322;** www.usairways.com

✔ United/United Express/Skywest: ☎ **800-241-6522;** www.ual.com

For a rundown of California airports, see Chapter 6.

I can't promise who'll be offering the best deals when you're booking, but I've found that Southwest Airlines is often the cheapest and most convenient airline for traveling within California. Why? Three reasons: a) Tickets are sold by segments, which makes it cheap and easy to buy one-way fares; b) full fares are comparatively low, so you have the freedom to change your itinerary without paying a ridiculous markup or penalty; and c) Internet specials often make the airlines' already low fares even lower.

Going the Amtrak Way

Amtrak (☎ **800-USA-RAIL**; www.amtrak.com) runs trains throughout California, including up and down the coast, serving destinations like Sacramento, San Francisco, San Jose, Santa Barbara, Los Angeles, and San Diego, and numerous points in between. Using Amtrak won't save you any time over driving, and may not even save you money over flying; still, it's an option for those of you who'd rather not drive yourselves and don't like to fly, or if you're just enamored with the nostalgia of train travel.

Amtrak one-way coach fares run the gamut from $19 for short-haul routes, such as San Diego to Anaheim or Los Angeles to Santa Barbara, to $93 for long trips like San Francisco to San Diego. Check Amtrak's Web site for regular rail sales.

If you'd like to travel the Amtrak way, consider booking one of the inclusive travel packages offered by Amtrak Vacations (☎ **800-654-5748**; www.amtrakvacations.com). See Chapter 6 for more information.

Chapter 8

Tying Up Loose Ends

- -

In This Chapter

▶ Using credit cards, traveler's checks, and ATMs on the road

▶ Dealing with losing your wallet and other money emergencies

▶ Buying insurance and making reservations before you leave home

▶ Packing what you really need

- -

*T*his chapter helps you shore up the final details — from getting traveler's checks and travel insurance to advance reservations for dining and attractions to packing comfortable walking shoes.

Using Traveler's Checks, Credit Cards, ATMs, or Cash

Traveler's checks are something of an anachronism from the days when people wrote personal checks instead of getting money from an ATM. Because you could replace traveler's checks if you lost them or someone stole them, they provided a sound alternative to stuffing your wallet with cash at the beginning of a trip.

These days, most cities have 24-hour ATMs linked to a national network that almost always includes your bank at home. Cirrus (☎ 800-424-7787; www.mastercard.com/atm/) and Plus (☎ 800-843-7587; www.visa.com/atms) are the two most popular networks; check the back of your ATM card to see which network your bank belongs to. The 800 numbers and Web sites will give you specific locations of ATMs where you can withdraw money while on vacation. The easy accessibility of these ATMS means you can withdraw only as much cash as you need every couple of days, which eliminates the insecurity (and the pickpocketing threat) of carrying around a wad of cash.

 One important reminder: Many banks now charge a fee ranging from 50 cents to *three dollars* whenever a non-account-holder uses their ATMs. Your own bank may also assess a fee for using an ATM that's not one of their branch locations. This means that in some cases you'll get charged *twice* just for using your bank card when you're on vacation. An ATM card can be an amazing convenience when you're traveling in another country (put your card in the machine, and out comes foreign currency, at an extremely advantageous exchange rate). However, banks are also likely to slap you with a "foreign currency transaction fee" just for making them do the local currency-to-dollars conversion math. Given these sneaky tactics, reverting to the traveler's check policy may be cheaper (though certainly less convenient).

If you prefer the security of traveler's checks, you can get them at almost any bank. American Express offers checks in denominations of $20, $50, $100, $500, and $1,000. You'll pay a service charge ranging from 1 percent to 4 percent, though AAA members can obtain checks without a fee at most AAA offices. You can also order American Express traveler's checks by calling ☎ **800-221-7282.**

Visa (☎ **800-227-6811**) also offers traveler's checks, available at Citibank locations across the country and at several other banks. The service charge ranges between 1.5 percent and 2 percent; checks come in denominations of $50, $100, $500, and $1,000. MasterCard also offers traveler's checks; call ☎ **800-223-9920** for a location near you.

Credit cards are invaluable when traveling — they provide a safe way to carry money and a convenient record of all your travel expenses. You can get *cash advances* off your credit card at any bank, and you don't even need to go to a teller; you can get a cash advance at the ATM if you know your PIN number. If you've forgotten your PIN number or didn't even know you had one, call the phone number on the back of the credit card and ask the bank to send it to you. You will usually receive it in 5 to 7 business days, although some banks will give it to you over the phone if you tell them your mother's maiden name or some other security clearance.

Be careful when getting a cash advance because interest rates for cash advances are often significantly higher than rates for credit card purchases. More important, you'll start paying interest on the advance *the moment you receive the cash.* On an airline-affiliated credit card, a cash advance does not earn frequent-flyer miles.

Taking Action if Your Credit Card Is Lost or Stolen

Almost every credit card company maintains an emergency 800-number to call if you lose or someone steals your wallet or purse. The company may be able to wire you a cash advance from your credit card immediately. In many places, they can send an emergency credit card to you within a day or two.

You can usually find the issuing bank's 800-number on the back of the credit card, which won't help you much if the card is lost or stolen. Just to be on the safe side, copy the 800-number from the back of your card into a notebook before you leave and keep the notebook in a secure place. Citicorp Visa's U.S. emergency number is ☎ **800- 645-6556.** American Express cardholders and traveler's check holders should call ☎ **800-221-7282** for all money emergencies. MasterCard holders should call ☎ **800-307-7309.**

If you choose to carry traveler's checks, be sure to keep a separate record of their serial numbers so you can handle just such an emergency.

Odds are that if your wallet or purse is gone, you've seen the last of it — the police aren't likely to recover it for you. After you realize it's gone and you cancel your credit cards, however, call to inform the police. You may need the police report number for credit card or insurance purposes later.

Buying Travel and Medical Insurance

You will encounter three primary kinds of travel insurance: trip cancellation insurance, medical insurance, and lost luggage insurance.

Trip cancellation insurance is a good idea if you've paid a large portion of your vacation expenses up front. Trip cancellation insurance costs approximately 6 to 8 percent of the total value of your vacation.

But the other two types — *medical insurance* and *lost luggage insurance* — don't make sense for most travelers. Your existing health insurance should cover you if you get sick while on vacation (although if you belong to an HMO, check to see whether you are fully covered when away from home). Homeowners' insurance should cover stolen luggage in the event of an off-premises theft. Check your existing policies before you buy any additional coverage. The airlines are responsible for $2,500 on domestic flights (and $9.07 per pound, up to $640, on international flights) if they lose your luggage. If you plan to carry any valuables, keep them in your carry-on bag.

Some credit cards (American Express and certain gold and platinum Visa and MasterCards, for example) offer automatic flight insurance against death or dismemberment in case of an airplane crash. If you still feel you need more insurance, try one of the following reputable companies:

- ✔ Access America, 6600 W. Broad St., Richmond, VA 23230 (☎ **800-284-8300;** fax 800-346-9265; www.accessamerica.com)

- ✔ Travelex Insurance Services, 11717 Burt St., Ste. 202, Omaha, NE 68154 (☎ **800-228-9792;** www.travelex-insurance.com)

- ✔ Travel Guard International, 1145 Clark St., Stevens Point, WI 54481 (☎ **800-826-1300;** www.travel-guard.com)

- ✔ Travel Insured International, Inc., P.O. Box 280568, 52-S Oakland Ave., East Hartford, CT 06128-0568 (☎ **800-243-3174;** www.travelinsured.com)

Be careful not to pay for more insurance than you need. For example, if you only need trip cancellation insurance, don't purchase coverage for lost or stolen property.

Making Reservations and Getting Advance Tickets

In addition to buying your airfare, booking your accommodations, and reserving a rental car, you may want to take care of a few other items before you leave home.

Consider making reservations or buying tickets for the following five types of activities before you leave home:

- ✔ Attractions that have long ticket-buying lines for people who didn't plan ahead (such as the **Monterey Bay Aquarium**) or that have restricted daily admission (like the **Getty Center** in L.A.).

- ✔ Activities that require advance reservations, like a guided hike of **Yosemite** or an extra-special Napa Valley winery tour.

- ✔ Special events and high-profile exhibitions at museums like the **Los Angeles County Museum of Art.**

- ✔ Live theater or musical performances, which often sell out well before showtime.

- ✔ Any special-occasion dinners at high-profile restaurants that you don't want to miss out on — especially in San Francisco, Los Angeles, and any other popular weekend destination where you'll want to celebrate on a Friday or Saturday night. (Don't leave home without a dinner reservation at the Napa Valley's French Laundry if you have *any* hope of eating there.)

As you thumb through this book, look for the Plan Ahead icon. It highlights activities and attractions for which you need to make advance arrangements; otherwise, you may miss out.

I also indicate reservations policies in all restaurant reviews. Be sure to peruse the restaurant listings for those destinations where you may be interested in booking a special meal, and look for red-flag phrases such as "reservations highly recommended," "reservations required," and "reservations a must."

How do you find out what special events and live performances will be available when you're in town? That's easy — just check the section called "Gathering More Information" at the end of each destination chapter, where you find a comprehensive list of destination-specific resources. You'll have the greatest access to information via the Web — especially in San Francisco, Los Angeles, and San Diego, all of which boast many useful sites with copious arts-and-entertainment listings.

Remember, however, that you can always call the local visitors bureau if you want to gather information and recommendations from a real live person.

And don't forget to check with the museums, attractions, and performance venues directly. They'll give you the most up-to-date and comprehensive schedule and ticket info. I include their numbers where appropriate in the listings.

Packing the Right Stuff

Start your packing by taking everything you think you'll need and laying it out on the bed. Then get rid of half of it.

Not that the airlines won't let you take it all — they will, with some limits — but you'll soon discover that carting loads of stuff around California is a big fat drag. Believe me, you really can do without that sixth pair of shoes.

Start by packing the essentials, the stuff you want to be sure to bring along, such as:

- ✔ **Sunglasses:** Because the sun can be quite strong in California, you won't be able to do without them if you're driving. And how else are you going to look cool in Hollywood?

- ✔ **A bathing suit:** Bring one even if you don't expect to encounter beach weather. Finding an enticing Jacuzzi at your hotel and not being able to use it is not fun. And even January can bring the surprise beach day to Southern California. Bring two bathing suits if you think you're going to be doing a lot of beachgoing.

- ✔ **Casual clothes that layer well:** California's weather is frustratingly changeable year-round. You can easily encounter a 20-degree rise in temperature just by moving a few miles inland away from the coast, or a 30-degree drop between 3 and 8 p.m. Be sure to bring a light jacket — yes, even in summer. For more weather guidelines, see Chapter 2 — then prepare yourself for everything.

  In general, you do want to keep your clothes casual. Even the fanciest restaurants are relatively informal; only a few require a sports jacket or tie, and men can get by with a nice pair of khakis and a button-down shirt at most. Women will probably do well with a couple of dresses or pants/top combos that are comfy for day wear and dress up well with accessories for evening.

- ✔ **Good, comfortable walking shoes:** Bring hiking boots, or at least sturdy sneakers, if you plan to hike.

- ✔ **Binoculars:** These come in handy during whale-watching season, or to spot dolphins or seals offshore at any time of year.

✔ **Dramamine or nausea-prevention wristbands:** Be sure to include these if you have a tendency towards carsickness.

✔ **A cellphone, if you have one:** A cellphone can be an invaluable lifeline in the event that you get a flat or your rental car breaks down.

✔ **An extra pair of eyeglasses or contact lenses:** Bringing a spare is always a good idea to prevent an inconvenient "Ack — I can't see!" emergency.

✔ **An umbrella:** Including an umbrella will probably prevent it from raining, of course.

✔ **Prescription medication:** Of course you'll want to bring all of your prescription meds, but don't bother hauling a half-dozen bottles of saline solution, a couple cans of bug spray, or 16 rolls of film from home. California has a fine collection of drugstores throughout the state, and because every community you'll be visiting supports a local population, you won't find an excess of tourist-targeted or prohibitive pricing.

Part III
Northern California: Redwoods, Wine, and Wonder

The 5th Wave   By Rich Tennant

SAN FRANCISCO'S AMAZING CABLE CARS

Travelers can ride from Market Street to the Financial District, through the Rocky Mountains and on to Denver all for the price of one Muni Passport.

©RICHTENNANT

In this part . . .

This part covers Northern California: the San Francisco Bay Area; the wild North Coast and tall-tree Redwood Country; and the Sierra Nevada mountains, where you'll find spectacular Lake Tahoe and Yosemite National Park. San Francisco is the ultimate urban destination, while the gorgeous Napa Valley Wine Country makes a wonderfully pastoral getaway. The wild and woolly coastal region north of the San Francisco Bay Area offers some of California's most breathtaking scenery. It's quiet, remote, and ruggedly handsome, with spectacular nature broken only by the occasional picturesque village. Travel inland from the Bay Area or North Coast and you'll soon reach the Sierra Nevada, the magnificently rugged, granite-peaked mountain range that inspired the U.S. National Park system, of which Yosemite National Park is a spectacular example. Also spectacular is sparkling Lake Tahoe, host to California's finest outdoor playground.

Chapter 9

San Francisco

● ●

In This Chapter

▶ Knowing when to go and how to get there

▶ Getting to know the neighborhoods — and how to get around

▶ Choosing the best places to stay and dine

▶ Seeing the sights, shopping, and enjoying the city after dark

● ●

*S*an Francisco has always been one of America's most enticing destinations. This former gold-rush rowdy may not always bask in the
sunny weather of its Southern California sisters, but where else can
you sample a touch of Asia, a bit of Parisian *joie de vivre,* a taste of
Central America, a hint of Italy, and a good dollop of West Coast style
and eccentricity in a single day? San Francisco's secret weapon is its
winning combination of big-city sophistication and small-town accessibility. You can always discover something new in this walking town of
distinct neighborhoods, from restored Victorians to funky shops to
some of the most delicious restaurants in the country.

San Francisco is currently in the throes of a building boom, and formerly
decrepit corners of the city are undergoing a metamorphosis. An impressive brick-and-concrete baseball park recently emerged on what was
once industrial wasteland. Surrounded by new residential buildings,
upscale restaurants, and shiny Municipal Railway tracks (but no parking
lots), the bayside park is a remarkable piece of urban renewal. South of
Market Street, the enormous **Sony Metreon,** lovely **Yerba Buena
Gardens,** cultural venues, and fashionable hotels have erased much of
what used to be skid row. (Still, expect to see scores of street people
holding signs and asking for handouts nearly everywhere you go.)

What never fails to beguile visitors and locals alike are the much-loved
symbols that are synonymous with the city. The **Golden Gate Bridge,**
the **Palace of Fine Arts, Golden Gate Park,** the cable cars, and
Chinatown have changed little over the years, thankfully. Despite
grumbling from the natives regarding the "good old days," the city
of San Francisco has never been more vibrant.

Timing Your Visit

San Francisco is a year-round city, usually draped in mild to cool temperatures and fog-bound mornings, especially during the summer. If weather is important to you — good weather, that is — come in September or early October, when the city traditionally experiences a hot spell. These, naturally, are the busiest months in the hotel trade, right up there with summer. Be sure to book lodgings ahead of time to ensure a decent place to stay. Winter tends to be cold and drizzly, but you can often get great deals on hotel rooms after the holidays.

 It's always a good idea to check dates with the city's Convention and Visitors Bureau to avoid scheduling a vacation during a convention (see "Gathering More Information" at the end of this chapter).

You can get an idea of what San Francisco is about in three or four days. See "Suggested 1-, 2-, & 3-Day Itineraries" later in this chapter.

Getting There

The Bay Area has two airports:

- ✔ **San Francisco International (SFO)** (☎ 650-876-2377; www.flysfo.com), 14 miles south of downtown

- ✔ **Oakland International Airport** (☎ 800-235-9292; www.flyoakland.com), across the Bay Bridge off Interstate 880

More airlines fly into the considerably larger SFO, but navigating the two-terminal Oakland airport is easier. You'll find tourist information desks on the first floor (baggage level) of both airports as well as ATMs located in every terminal on the upper levels.

Super Shuttle (☎ 415-558-8500; www.supershuttle.com) and other shuttle services offer door-to-door service into the city from San Francisco International. The services are located at center islands outside the upper level, and a guide will direct you to the right area. Fares are around $12; advance reservations are not necessary.

Taxis line up at well-marked yellow columns on the center island outside the lower level of the airport. The fare is about $35 to downtown, plus tip.

All of the major car-rental firms have SFO locations. If you're *renting a car,* a courtesy bus will take you to the building where all the major companies have counters and cars. Catch the bus from the upper-level center islands outside the terminals.

The routine is similar from Oakland International, except that all ground transportation is on one level. Bayporter Express shuttles (☎ 415-467-1800 or 510-864-4000) pick up passengers from Terminal 1 at the center island, and from Terminal 2 around the corner from baggage claim. The fare to San Francisco is $26 for one person, $36 for two people in the same party, and $5 for kids under 12. Making reservations for the 45- to 90-minute ride is best.

A 30- to 40-minute *taxi* ride to downtown will run you about $40.

BART (Bay Area Rapid Transit; ☎ **510-464-6000;** www.bart.org) also runs from Oakland into the city. Take the AirBART shuttle (☎ **510-430-9440**) in front of Terminals 1 or 2, which runs every 15 minutes. The fare is $2 for the 15-minute ride to the Oakland Coliseum BART station. From there, transfer to a BART train into San Francisco; the fare is about $2.45. Purchase your ticket from well-marked kiosks inside the airport or at the BART station. If you're staying around Union Square, the city's commercial hub, exit BART on Powell Street.

By car

Two major highways can bring you into San Francisco: Interstate 5 (I-5) cuts through the center of the state. Drivers traveling along this route are deposited onto Interstate 80 (I-80), which leads over the Bay Bridge into the city. The drive to San Francisco from Los Angeles along I-5 takes 6 to 8 hours.

The other major route is U.S. 101, which heads up from Los Angeles through the city to Marin County, Napa and Sonoma valleys, and other points north. A prettier, more scenic coastal route, Highway 1, takes travelers heading north closer to Monterey and Santa Cruz, but the driving time up from L.A. is approximately 8 to 10 hours.

By train

Amtrak (☎ **800-872-7245;** www.amtrak.com) trains arrive in Emeryville, just north of Oakland. Buses then drop passengers at the CalTrain station, at 4th and King streets, or the Ferry Building, at the foot of Market Street on the Embarcadero.

Orienting Yourself and Finding Transportation

The city covers just seven square miles. Streets are laid out in a traditional grid pattern, except for two major diagonal arteries, Market Street and Columbus Avenue. Market cuts a swath through town from the Embarcadero up toward Twin Peaks. Columbus runs at an angle through North Beach, starting at the Transamerica Pyramid in the Financial District and ending near the Hyde Street Pier.

Numbered *streets* are downtown; numbered *avenues* are found in the Richmond and Sunset districts southwest of downtown.

Other important thoroughfares include Van Ness Avenue, which begins in the Mission District as South Van Ness and terminates at Aquatic Park; and Geary Street, which begins at Market and wends through the city to Ocean Beach.

San Francisco's neighborhoods

Along with the lovely natural setting, it's the neighborhoods — each with its own unique personality — that invest San Francisco with so much charm. Because this isn't a big city, size-wise, you'll be no more than 20 minutes or so by cab from all the major sites, shopping areas, and restaurants no matter where you stay.

Union Square

The center of tourist activity, Union Square is tucked inside Sutter, Grant, Market, and Mason streets. Big department stores, expensive boutiques, theaters, many exceptional restaurants, and the greatest concentration of hotels in the city surround the actual square. If you stay here, Chinatown, Nob Hill, the Tenderloin, the Financial District, and SoMa are all within walking distance.

A few blocks west is the Tenderloin, a gritty patch of poverty bounded by Sutter and Mason streets and Van Ness and Golden Gate avenues. The only reason to linger in the 'loin is to visit **Glide Memorial Church,** 330 Ellis St. (☎ **415-771-6300**), for rousing Sunday services. The multicultural choir sings soulful hymns that bring the congregation to their collective feet. Come early to secure a seat.

Chinatown

This densely packed area roughly between Broadway, Taylor, Bush, and Montgomery streets is as colorful and exotic as advertised. The Dragon Gate entrance on Grant Avenue leads to touristy shops, but after you wander up and around Stockton Street, you'll feel as if you're in another country. See "The top attractions" later in this chapter for Chinatown's sightseeing and shopping highlights.

Nob Hill

Tony Nob Hill is a rather rarefied residential district, crowned by **Grace Cathedral,** the magnificent Episcopal Church at the top of California Street. A string of pricey hotels cascades down the hill toward the Financial District, along with the California Street cable car line. If you're ready for the challenge of walking up and down steep grades, Nob Hill is just a short stroll from Union Square.

The Financial District

The Financial District encompasses prime bay real estate roughly between Montgomery Street and the Embarcadero, on either side of Market Street. Major corporations call this area home, and the **Transamerica Pyramid,** at Montgomery and Clay streets, is a skyline landmark. Seek out Belden Place, an alley between Kearny, Bush, and Pine streets, which is full of outdoor dining opportunities.

The Embarcadero

Liberated from the pylons and cement of the Embarcadero Freeway, which was damaged by the 1989 Loma Prieta earthquake and subsequently torn down, this area runs along the bay from the eastern edge of Fisherman's Wharf to the beginning of China Basin. **Embarcadero Center,** a collection of five multi-use buildings connected by bridges and walkways at the end of Market Street from Drumm to Sansome, houses upscale chain stores, restaurants, and movie theaters. Take the F streetcar from Union Square.

SoMa

South of Market Street (or SoMa for short) has exploded in the past 10 years, particularly between Second and Fifth streets, and it's only becoming bigger and better. Attractions include **San Francisco Museum of Modern Art,** the **Ansel Adams Center for Photography, Yerba Buena Gardens,** and the kid magnet **Sony Metreon** (see "The top attractions," later in this chapter).

North Beach

North Beach isn't an actual beach; it's the former Italian enclave that Chinatown is encroaching upon. This is the place to hop from one cafe to another, to browse for books and Italian pottery, and to examine the delectables at the various Italian delis and pastry shops. Columbus Avenue is the main thoroughfare, but family-style restaurants and crowded bars dot the streets from Washington to Grant, while the XXX-rated clubs stick together on Broadway. Use the Powell-Mason cable car to get here from Union Square.

Fisherman's Wharf

Sixteen million tourists per year can't all be wrong, but this most touristy section of town is all a matter of taste. Located on Bay Street between Powell and Polk streets, the former working piers have been stripped of their glory and turned into an embarrassment of commercialism. Step gingerly past Pier 39 and the plethora of schlock shops to the **Hyde Street Pier, Ghirardelli Square,** and the **Cannery** to discover a few legitimate reasons to spend time here. Parking is dreadful, so take the F streetcar from Union Square.

The Marina

Many glorious sites are within walking distance of this high-priced district, including the **Exploratorium.** The Marina's commercial blocks along Chestnut Street, between Franklin and Lyon streets, are full of coffeehouses, restaurants, and shops. Take a walk to the **Golden Gate Bridge** by way of Marina Boulevard. Get to the Marina by the 30-Stockton, 22-Fillmore, 41-Union, or 45-Union/Stockton buses.

The marina is the gateway to the fabulous playground that is the **Presidio,** 1,500 acres on the westernmost point of the city that once belonged to the U.S. Army. They're now part of the **Golden Gate National Recreation Area.** Stop in the visitor center, in the Main Post at Fort Mason on Montgomery Street, for maps and suggestions for hikes. Take the 29-Sunset bus to get here.

Cow Hollow

A residential paradise between Broadway, Lyon, and Lombard streets, and Van Ness Avenue, the district's main claim to fame — among locals and tourists alike — is Union Street, a fashionable haven of shops, restaurants, and those young, urban professionals we all love to hate. To get here, take the 30-Stockton, 22-Fillmore, 41-Union, or 45-Union/Stockton buses.

Civic Center

Bordered by Van Ness and Golden Gate avenues and Franklin, Hyde, and Market streets, Civic Center is home to local politicians, city offices, and cultural centers; the **SF Ballet, SF Symphony,** and **SF Opera** line up along Van Ness Avenue. **City Hall,** on Van Ness Avenue between McAllister and Grove streets, recently underwent a spectacular renovation, and its glittering black-and-gold dome makes a splendid landmark. Note that Civic Center also attracts a large homeless contingent. You can reach this area via the F streetcar.

The Castro

The Castro is famous for its ties to an active, activist gay community. You'll see beautifully restored Victorian homes and shops catering to buff guys. Shopping and people-watching take place mainly on Castro Street between Market and 18th streets. Take the F streetcar from Union Square.

Haight-Ashbury

Commonly known as the Haight, and bounded by **Golden Gate Park,** Divisadero, Fulton, and Waller streets, Haight-Ashbury hasn't fully recovered from what must have been a real bummer to some — the demise of the '60s. Haight Street — where the action is — continues to hold a magical appeal over scruffy groups of youngsters campaigning for handouts.

Should you be curious enough to drop by, you'll stumble upon a multitude of used clothing stores competing for space with all kinds of commercial endeavors, most of which are perfectly legal. The stretch from Masonic to Stanyon is particularly good for vintage wearables. The N-Judah Muni Metro line will take you to Haight (pronounced like "hate") Street.

Japantown

Japantown consists of some downright unattractive indoor shopping centers off Geary Street between Webster and Laguna streets. It's a shame that this area isn't more visually appealing, because the dismal gray buildings attached by a pedestrian walkway house some good, inexpensive noodle restaurants and interesting shops. **Kabuki Hot Springs** is a great place to have a massage and a soak. Across Sutter Street, between Fillmore and Webster streets, look for **Cottage Row,** all that's left of the real Japantown before redevelopment got hold of the neighborhood. Catch the 38-Geary or 22-Fillmore bus to get here.

The Mission District

This is a busy, largely Hispanic community spanning the area from Cesar Chavez (formerly Army) Street to Market Street between Dolores and Potrero streets. The oldest building in the city (1776), **Mission Dolores** (on Dolores and 16th streets) attracts visitors, as do a wealth of inexpensive restaurants and murals that burst out from the landscape. Valencia Street between 16th and 23rd streets has become a serious destination for foodies. Take BART to the 24th Street stop.

Telegraph Hill

This area is a residential neighborhood just to the east of North Beach, behind **Coit Tower** and the **Filbert Steps. Russian Hill** is just to the northwest, where you'll find the wiggly part of **Lombard Street** and Macondry Lane, fictionalized in Armistead Maupin's *Tales of the City.* You can reach Telegraph Hill via the Powell-Mason cable car.

Pacific Heights

Pacific Heights, bordered by Broadway, Pine, Divisadero, and Franklin streets, is where the city's rich and elite live in lavish, beautifully landscaped mansions. The 22-Fillmore, 12-Folsom, 27-Bryant, 47-Van Ness, 49-Van Ness/Mission, and 83-Pacific will all get you to Pacific Heights.

The Richmond District

Largely residential, the Richmond District features **Golden Gate Park** as one edge — *ahh*-inspiring, and a great place to relax — and the Pacific Ocean as the other. The N-Judah Muni Metro line provides the easiest way to get here.

Getting around

San Francisco is relatively compact and offers good public transportation, so don't plan on driving around the city. Traffic is very heavy downtown, and one-way streets confuse drivers unfamiliar with the territory. That, combined with the lack of parking and the heavy-handed meter maids, makes leaving your car outside the city limits (or in a parking garage) the sensible thing to do.

Renting a car downtown is simple, so if you're starting your California trip with a few days in San Francisco and then setting out to explore, arriving carless in the city and arranging to pick up your rental just before you leave town is a good idea.

From Union Square, where most hotels are located, it's an easy walk to Chinatown, North Beach, SoMa, and the Financial District. Buses, Muni streetcars, and cable cars are both convenient and inexpensive ways to reach outlying neighborhoods, and taxis are plentiful.

Here are a couple of transit tips that will make your life much easier:

✔ Get a copy of the official Muni map, which costs $3 and is invaluable for public transportation users. It shows all bus, streetcar, cable car, and BART routes and stations. Maps are available for purchase at the Convention and Visitors Bureau Information Center. You can also phone ☎ 415-673-MUNI for route information.

✔ The one-stop-shopping number to call for local traffic or public transit information is ☎ 415-817-1717. This number connects you to whatever info line you need, be it BART or Muni routes, or the latest on traffic conditions. You can also find public transit schedules on the Web at www.ci.sf.ca.us/muni.

Muni Passports — accepted on buses, streetcars, and even cable cars, but not BART — are a bargain for visitors. A 1-day passport is $6, a 3-day pass is $10, and a 7-day pass is $15. You can purchase them at the Convention and Visitors Bureau Information Center at Hallidie Plaza, at the Union Square TIX Bay Area booth, and at the cable car booth at Sutter and Hyde streets. You can also purchase single-day passes on board the cable cars.

Hoofing it

Walking is the preferred method of travel in San Francisco and the only way to catch the nuances of the neighborhoods. Be careful, however, as a rash of vehicle/pedestrian accidents has occurred lately. Watch for drivers running red lights or turning right on a red, and make sure bus drivers see you entering the crosswalk.

Taking the Muni Metro streetcars

The San Francisco Municipal Railway, known as *Muni* (call ☎ 415-673-6864 for gracious directions on how to get where you want to go; www.ci.sf.ca.us/muni), is much maligned by locals for inefficiency, but tens of thousands of commuters rely daily on its buses and electric streetcars for a lift.

Muni Metro streetcars run underground downtown and aboveground in the outlying neighborhoods. The five streetcar lines, the J, K, L, M, and N, make the same stops as BART (see the next section) along Market Street, including Embarcadero Station, Montgomery and Powell streets (both near Union Square), and the Civic Center. Past the Civic Center, the routes branch off in different directions. The *N-Judah* line services the Haight-Ashbury and parallels Golden Gate Park on its way down Judah Street to the ocean. The *J-Church* line passes near Mission Dolores and the Castro. My personal favorite is the *F-Market,* whose vintage streetcars run from the Castro Street station down Market Street, over to Mission Street, then down the Embarcadero to Fisherman's Wharf. Muni cars marked "Mission Bay" end their journey at the CalTrain Station on King Street just past the spanking new San Francisco Giants baseball park.

The *fare* to ride a bus or streetcar anywhere in the system is $1 for adults and 35¢ for seniors and children, and includes a transfer good for two hours; exact change is required.

Riding the bus

A fleet of buses chugs throughout the city from 6 a.m. to midnight. Street-corner signs and painted yellow bands on utility poles and on curbs mark bus stops, and buses are clearly numbered on the front. Depending on your destination and the time of day, buses arrive every 5 to 20 minutes. They aren't the quickest means of transportation, but with 80 transit lines, they are the most complete. During rush hours (7 to 9 a.m. and 4 to 6 p.m.), buses are often sardine-can crowded.

Going underground with BART

Bay Area Rapid Transit (☎ 650-992-2278; www.bart.org) is different from Muni, although visitors often get the two systems mixed up because they share the same underground stations downtown. Within the city limits, that's not a problem. BART, however, runs all over the Bay Area, and more than one unsuspecting traveler has ended up in Oakland when he intended to exit at the Embarcadero.

Purchase BART tickets from machines at the station. *Fares* to and from any point in the city are $1.10 each way; outside the city, fares vary depending on how far down the line you go.

Hopping aboard the cable cars

No trip to San Francisco would be complete without a ride on a cable car. Three lines traverse the downtown area. The *Powell-Hyde line,* the most scenic and exciting run, begins at Powell Street and ends at the turnaround across from Ghirardelli Square. The *Powell-Mason line* goes through North Beach and ends near Fisherman's Wharf. The *California Street line,* the tamest and least scenic, crests at Nob Hill and then edges its way to Van Ness Avenue. Rides are $2 one way. You may only board a cable car at specific, clearly marked stops. Cable cars operate from 6:30 a.m. to 12:30 a.m.

Catching cabs

Taxis are easy to hail downtown, especially in front of hotels, but you have to call a cab to come get you almost anywhere else. Reaching the taxi companies by phone can take a long time, so keep this in mind. Have these numbers handy: Yellow Cab (☎ 415-626-2345); Veteran's Cab (☎ 415-552-1300); Desoto Cab (☎ 415-673-1414); Luxor Cabs (☎ 415-282-4141); and Pacific (☎ 415-986-7220). Rates are about $2 for the first mile and $1.80 for each additional mile.

Staying in Style

The following listings reflect the city's best choices in various price categories. You also won't find the biggest hotels in town mentioned — we're leaving them for the conventioneers.

The hotel occupancy rate is high almost all year-round, so rates don't fluctuate greatly. For bargains, try the winter months or ask about weekend packages at hotels that cater to business travelers. Be

San Francisco Transit

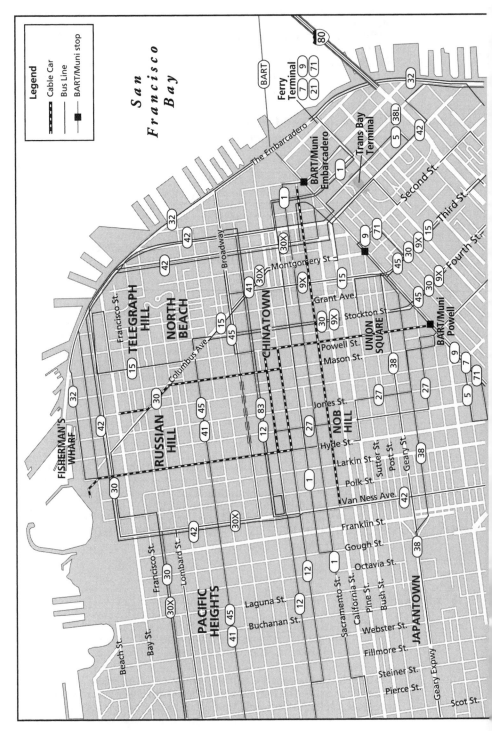

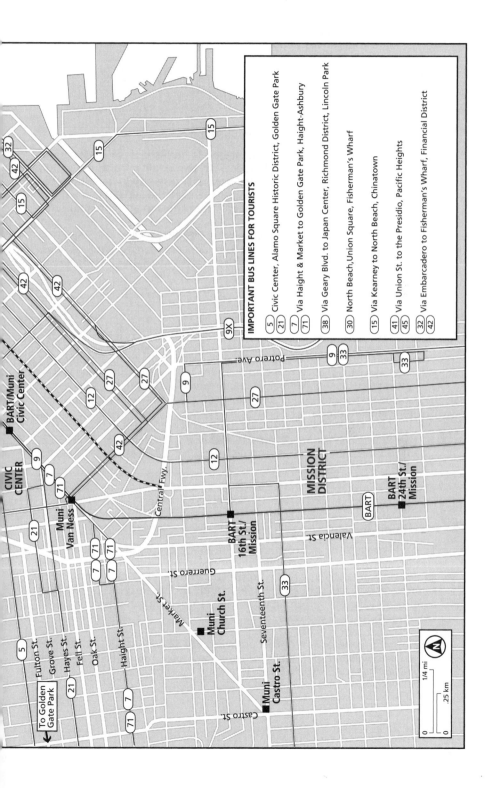

IMPORTANT BUS LINES FOR TOURISTS

5 Civic Center, Alamo Square Historic District, Golden Gate Park
21

7 Via Haight & Market to Golden Gate Park, Haight-Ashbury
71

38 Via Geary Blvd. to Japan Center, Richmond District, Lincoln Park

30 North Beach, Union Square, Fisherman's Wharf

15 Via Kearney to North Beach, Chinatown

41 Via Union St. to the Presidio, Pacific Heights
45

32 Via Embarcadero to Fisherman's Wharf, Financial District
42

advised that lots of hotels in older buildings, especially around Union Square, have surprisingly tiny rooms and baths. If you plan to keep a car, prepare yourself for hefty parking fees.

Count on an extra 14 percent in taxes being tacked on to your hotel bill.

Best Western Tuscan Inn

$$$–$$$$ **North Beach/Fisherman's Wharf**

Compared with the rest of the chain hotels on Fisherman's Wharf, the Tuscan has some soul. It isn't loaded with personality, but the location is appealing to kids, and the rooms are fairly large by local standards. The concierge is friendly and enthusiastic, and all the expected amenities are available. In warm weather, you can dine alfresco at the restaurant.

425 North Point (between Mason and Taylor sts.). ☎ *800-648-4626 or 415-561-1100. Fax: 415-561-1199. Internet:* www.tuscaninn.com. *Valet parking: $20. Rack rates: $175–$245 double. Deals: Packages available; also ask about AAA, corporate, and senior discounts. AE, CB, DC, DISC, MC, V.*

Campton Place

$$$$$ **Union Square**

The harpsichord music piped into the classically decorated lobby tells you right away that this is one genteel hotel. Intimate, clubby, reserved — you'll want to use your company manners even as the valet unpacks your bags, fluffs up the bathrobes, and shows off the many luxury amenities in the just-renovated rooms.

340 Stockton St. (at Post St.). ☎ *800-235-4300 or 415-781-5555. Fax: 415-955-5536. Internet:* www.camptonplace.com. *Valet parking: $28. Rack rates: $315–$435 double. AE, DC, DISC, JCB, MC, V.*

Chancellor Hotel

$$ **Union Square**

This 137-room hotel offers a level of intimacy and value you just won't find in many other comparable inns. It's also right on the Powell Street cable car line, a stone's throw from Saks Fifth Avenue. The little bathrooms are well-stocked, and the bedrooms are brightly decorated and comfortably furnished. For views, request front rooms ending in 00 to 05. Ceiling fans instead of A/C.

433 Powell St. (between Post and Sutter sts.). ☎ *800-428-4748 or 415-362-2004. Fax: 415-362-1403. Internet:* www.chancellorhotel.com. *Valet parking: $24. Rack rates: $155 double. AE, DC, DISC, MC, V.*

Golden Gate Hotel

$$ Union Square

The 23 rooms at this charming small hotel have few amenities, but they're cheerful and light on the wallet. Some share baths. The locale is great for walkers and cable-car lovers, and the free breakfast and afternoon goodies make the bargain even better.

775 Bush St. (between Powell and Mason sts., two blocks from the Chinatown gate). ☎ *800-835-1118 or 415-392-3702. Fax: 415-392-6202. Internet:* www.goldengatehotel.com. *Parking: $12. Rack rates: $78–$85 double with shared bath, $109–$119 double with private bath. Rates include continental breakfast and afternoon tea. DC, MC, V.*

Harbor Court Hotel

$$$$ The Embarcadero

This Embarcadero hotel is especially classy and romantic. Along with concierge services and express check-in, the hotel features a happenin' restaurant/bar with live entertainment. Guests have free access to the state-of-the-art Embarcadero YMCA pool and health club next door. Rooms are spacious and include half-canopy beds and all the amenities.

165 Steuart St. (between Mission and Howard sts.). ☎ *800-346-0555 or 415-882-1300. Fax: 415-882-1313. Valet parking: $24. Rack rates: $235–$250 double. Deals: Check for specials and packages. AE, CB, DC, DISC, MC, V.*

Hotel Bohème

$$–$$$ North Beach

What can be more satisfying than a charming, very intimate hotel in the heart of North Beach? The 15 beautiful rooms with iron beds and vivid wall colors are small; bathrooms are equipped with showers only, but in-room amenities are generous. The accommodating staff will assist with restaurant reservations, tours, and rental cars, but you'll have to schlep your own luggage up a flight of narrow stairs. Rooms do not have A/C.

444 Columbus Ave. (between Vallejo and Green sts.). ☎ *415-433-9111. Fax: 415-362-6292. Internet:* www.hotelboheme.com. *Parking: $23 in a garage a few blocks away. Rack rates: $149–$169 double. AE, CB, DC, DISC, JCB, MC, V.*

Hotel Del Sol

$$ The Marina

Paint, mosaic tiles, and a lively imagination can do a lot to reinvent a motel, and you won't find a better example of how well this works than the Del Sol. You'll think you're in Southern California (after the fog lifts, anyway), but here pedestrians can walk around without getting startled looks from drivers. A hammock suspended between palm trees and the heated pool complete the hallucination. Multicolor guest rooms and suites contain a few amenities like nice soap. Some rooms include kitchenettes.

San Francisco Accommodations

Best Western Tuscan Inn **3**
Campton Place **12**
Chancellor Hotel **10**
Golden Gate Hotel **7**
Harbor Court Hotel **15**
Hotel Bohème **4**
Hotel Del Sol **1**
Hotel Milano **14**
Hotel Monaco **13**
Hotel Rex **8**
The Huntington **5**
Kensington Park Hotel **11**
Marina Inn **2**
Petite Auberge **6**
Sir Francis Drake Hotel **9**

Golden Gate
← Bridge

GOLDEN GATE NATIONAL Fort Mason
RECREATION AREA

THE MARINA

Bay St.
Francisco St.
Chestnut St.
Lombard St. **2**
Greenwich St.

COW HOLLOW   **1**

PACIFIC HEIGHTS

Divisadero St.
Scott St.
Pierce St.
Steiner St.
Fillmore St.
Webster St.
Buchanan St.
Laguna St.
Octavia St.
Gough St.
Franklin St.

Washington St. Pacific   Lafayette
Clay St.   Medical   Park
Sacramento St. Center
California St.
Pine St.
Bush St.
Sutter St.
Post St.   Japan
Geary St.   Center
O'Farrell St.   **JAPANTOWN**
Ellis St.
Eddy St.
Golden Gate   Turk St.
← Bridge
Golden Gate Ave.
McAllister St.
Fulton St.
Grove St. Alamo
Square   Ivy St.   **HAYES VALLEY**
Hayes St.
Fell St.   Fell St.
Oak St.
Page St.
Haight St.
Waller St.
Duboce   Hermann St.
Park   Duboce Ave.
Duboce Ave.
101
McCoppin

Octavia St.
Gough
McCoppin

Castro
Noe St.
Sanchez St.
Church St.
Dolores St.
14th St.
Guerrero St.
Valencia St.
Mission St.

15th St.

THE CASTRO   **MISSION**
16th St.   **DISTRICT**
17th St.

Legend

California Line	————
Powell-Mason Line	- - - - - -
Powell-Hyde Line	————

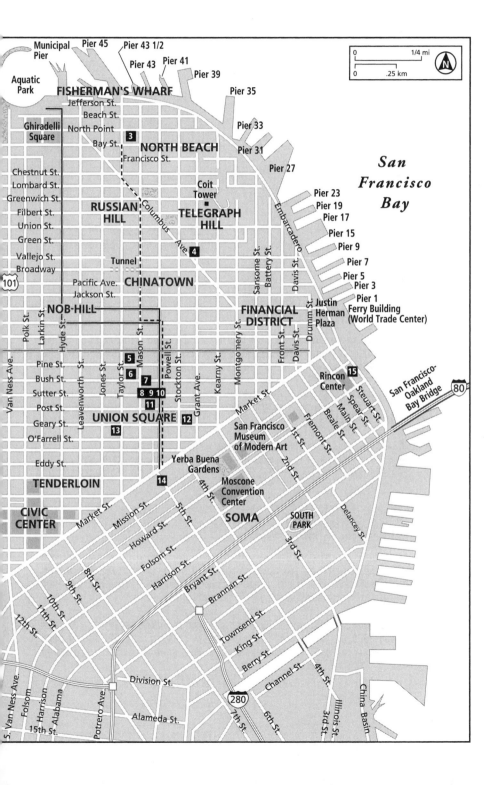

Pier 45
Municipal
Pier
Pier 43 1/2
Pier 43
Pier 41
Pier 39
Aquatic
Park
Pier 35
FISHERMAN'S WHARF
Jefferson St.
Beach St.
Ghiradelli
Square
North Point
Pier 33
Bay St.
3
NORTH BEACH
Pier 31
Chestnut St.
Francisco St.
Pier 27
Lombard St.
Greenwich St.
Coit
Tower
Pier 23
Filbert St.
RUSSIAN
HILL
TELEGRAPH
HILL
Pier 19
Union St.
Pier 17
Green St.
4
Pier 15
Vallejo St.
Pier 9
Broadway
Tunnel
Pier 7
101
Pacific Ave.
CHINATOWN
Pier 5
Jackson St.
Pier 3
NOB HILL
Pier 1
Justin
Herman
Plaza
Ferry Building
(World Trade Center)
FINANCIAL
DISTRICT
Polk St.
Larkin St.
Hyde St.
Pine St.
5
Van Ness Ave.
Bush St.
6
Rincon
Center
15
San Francisco-
Oakland
Bay Bridge
80
Sutter St.
7
Leavenworth
Jones St.
Taylor St.
Mason St.
Powell St.
Stockton St.
Grant Ave.
Kearny St.
Montgomery St.
Front St.
Davis St.
Steuart St.
Spear St.
Main St.
Beale St.
Fremont St.
1st St.
2nd St.
Post St.
8 9 10
Geary St.
11
O'Farrell St.
UNION SQUARE
12
13
Market St.
Eddy St.
San Francisco
Museum
of Modern Art
TENDERLOIN
Yerba Buena
Gardens
14
Moscone
Convention
Center
CIVIC
CENTER
Market St.
Mission St.
5th St.
4th St.
SOMA
SOUTH
PARK
Delancey St.
3rd St.
Howard St.
Folsom St.
8th St.
Harrison St.
9th St.
Bryant St.
Brannan St.
10th St.
11th St.
Townsend St.
12th St.
King St.
Berry St.
Channel St.
4th St.
Illinois St.
3rd St.
China Basin
Division St.
S. Van Ness Ave.
Folsom
Harrison
Alabama
280
Potrero Ave.
7th St.
6th St.
Alameda St.
15th St.

San
Francisco
Bay

Sansome St.
Battery St.
Drumm St.
Davis St.
Embarcadero

Columbus Ave.

0   1/4 mi
0   .25 km

3100 Webster St. (at Filbert St.). ☎ ***877-433-5765*** *or 415-921-5520. Fax: 415-931-4137. Internet:* www.sftrips.com. *Parking: Free! Rack rates: $139–$149 double. AE, DC, DISC, MC, V.*

Hotel Milano

$$$ SoMa

There isn't anything flashy or exciting about this well-designed and maintained modern-Italian-themed boutique hotel, but you won't find a better value in SoMa. It sports one of the more spacious on-site fitness rooms, plus a concierge, restaurant, and all the expected amenities, including minibars. The multi-story San Francisco Shopping Centre is a few feet away and Yerba Buena Gardens is just around the corner, so you won't lack for things to do nearby.

55 Fifth St. (between Market and Mission sts.). ☎ ***800-398-7555*** *or 415-543-8555. Fax: 415-543-5885. Valet parking: $24. Rack rates: $169–$269 double. Deals: Ask about weekend packages. AE, DC, MC, V.*

Hotel Monaco

$$$$ Union Square

Scare up a vintage Vuitton steamer trunk and a foxtail-trimmed scarf, and sashay into this Roaring '20s-themed Monaco. The medium-size rooms are replete with canopied beds, floral prints, and modern furniture. All the amenities — a fitness center, room service, robes, and so forth — are on-board, along with the appropriately named Grand Cafe restaurant. The hotel is a little overwhelming for some visitors, but quite impressive overall. It is also close to theaters.

501 Geary St. (at Taylor St.). ☎ ***800-214-4220*** *or 415-292-0100. Fax: 415-292-0111. Internet:* www.hotelmonaco.com. *Valet parking: $24. Rack rates: $219–$309 double, from $399 suite. Deals: Ask about packages and specials. AE, CB, DC, DISC, MC, V.*

Hotel Rex

$$$–$$$$ Union Square

At this attractive and sophisticated 94-room gem, room sizes vary from smallish doubles on up. All accommodations are colorfully decorated and smartly designed. This is a full-service hotel, including a concierge and thoughtful amenities such as CD players.

562 Sutter St. (between Powell and Mason sts.). ☎ ***800-433-4434*** *or 415-433-4434. Fax: 415-433-3695. Internet:* www.thehotelrex.com. *Parking: $19 to self-park, $25 to valet. Rack rates: $175–$255 double, $575–$675 suite. Rates include evening wine. AE, CB, DC, DISC, MC, V.*

The Huntington

$$$$$ Nob Hill

The Boston Brahmin in you will adore this refined, quiet oasis with its subtle elegance and impeccable service. The 1924 building originally housed apartments, so guest rooms and baths are larger than average. Rooms above the 8th floor have views; the ones below are extra-spacious. Children are welcome, and the staff, concierge included, will anticipate your every need. Manicured Huntington Park, complete with playground, is across the street.

1075 California St. (at Taylor St.). ☎ 800-227-4683 or 415-474-5400. Fax: 415-474-6227. Internet: www.slh.com. *Valet parking: $19.50. Rack rates: $275–$420 double. AE, CB, DC, DISC, JCB, MC, V.*

Kensington Park Hotel

$$$ Union Square

This 86-room gem, with a theater on the second floor and a well-known restaurant next door, is a find among Union Square hotels in any price range. Larger-than-average rooms were renovated in 1998; the bathrooms were already among the handsomest in the area. A long-time employee who's both porter and concierge couldn't be friendlier or more willing to assist guests. Request a room above the 7th floor, Nob Hill side or on a corner, if you like views. The hotel includes workout facilities.

450 Post St. (between Mason and Powell sts.). ☎ 800-553-1900 or 415-788-6400. Fax: 415-399-9484. Internet: www.personalityhotels.com. *Valet parking: $22. Rack rates: $185–$249 double. Rates include continental breakfast and afternoon tea. AE, CB, DC, DISC, JCB, MC, V.*

Marina Inn

$–$$ The Marina

This modest 40-room Victorian inn is furnished with simple wooden beds, armoires, and small tables. Streetside rooms are bright but noisy; inside rooms are quieter and darker, but natural light comes from a light well. The staff will make tour, restaurant, and airport shuttle reservations, but no room service is available.

3110 Octavia St. (at Lombard St.). ☎ 800-274-1420 or 415-928-1000. Fax: 415-928-5909. Internet: www.marinainn.com. *Parking: $9.50 at the nearest public garage. Rack rates: $65–$135 double. Rates include continental breakfast. AE, MC, V.*

Petite Auberge

$$–$$$$ Union Square

Romantics will find happiness here among the florals and French-country effects. The high-end rooms are enormous; the less expensive are cozy and have showers only, but are equally comfortable. Along with a full breakfast served downstairs in the homey dining room, the hotel offers complimentary tea, wine, and hors d'oeuvres in the afternoon. It's well-known and exceedingly popular, so if you want to experience the charms of this Provençal-style inn, book way ahead.

863 Bush St. (between Mason and Taylor sts.). ☎ *800-365-3004 or 415-928-6000. Fax: 415-775-5717. Internet:* www.foursisters.com. *Valet parking: $19. Rack rates: $120–$265 double. Rates include full breakfast and afternoon snacks. AE, DC, MC, V.*

Sir Francis Drake Hotel

$$$ Union Square

Uniformed valets open the doors into the elegant lobby of this historic building. The medium-size, up-to-date rooms won't take your breath away, but if you can secure a corner room above the 10th floor, the view will. A small workout room, cafe, excellent restaurant, and nightclub are on-site. Services, including concierge, are superlative.

450 Powell St. (at Sutter St.). ☎ *800-227-5480 or 415-392-7755. Fax: 415-391-8719. Internet:* www.sirfrancisdrake.com. *Valet parking: $25. Rack rates: $179–$269 double, $350–$650 suite. Deals: Packages available. AE, CB, DC, DISC, MC, V.*

Dining Out

Eating is not beside the point when visiting San Francisco. The number of restaurants in the city (around 3,300) is astonishing, and the quality of the food in many of them is equally so.

So much food and so little time . . . but plenty of competition. Call for reservations before arriving at any but the most casual of restaurants.

Want to eat at the most sought-after tables in town? Try calling the day you'd like to go, right after the reservation line opens. The most popular restaurants often require that guests confirm their reservations by noon, so you may luck out and get in on a cancellation.

Boulevard

$$$$ The Embarcadero   CALIFORNIA

An elegant turn-of-the-century setting and generous plates of seasonal California-French cuisine combine to ensure a rousing good time at this deservedly popular restaurant. Guests without reservations can take a seat at the counter, but you should call three or four weeks in advance to get a prime table.

1 Mission St. (at Steuart St.). ☎ *415-543-6084. Reservations a must. To get there: Muni Metro to the Embarcadero Station; walk one block east to Mission St. Main courses: $18–$28. AE, CB, DC, D, MC, V. Open: Lunch Mon–Fri, bistro menu Mon–Fri 2:30–5:15 p.m., dinner nightly.*

Charles–Nob Hill

$$$$ Nob Hill CALIFORNIA

Two small, elegantly appointed dining rooms tucked inside a swanky apartment building give Charles an extra-intimate feel. Dishes are exquisitely prepared and presented, from the tiny appetizers brought gratis by the mannerly waitstaff to the memorable main courses and desserts. This is the perfect place to celebrate a special occasion. Dinner is also served in the bar if you don't have reservations.

1250 Jones St. (at Clay St.). ☎ 415-771-5400. Reservations are a must. To get there: California line cable car; exit at Jones and walk three blocks north to Clay. Main courses: $25–$33. AE, DC, MC, V. Open: Dinner Tues–Sun.

Chow

$–$$ The Castro AMERICAN

Straightforward pasta dishes, brick-oven roasted chicken, and thin-crusted pizzas make this great price performer perfect for kids and grown-ups alike. The pleasant wood-paneled room is casual and comfortable.

215 Church St. (at Market St.). ☎ 415-552-2469. Reservations not taken. To get there: Take Muni Metro J-Church or F-Market to Church St. Main courses: $6.50–$13. MC, V. Open: Lunch and dinner daily.

Delfina

$$ Mission District TUSCAN ITALIAN

A wonderfully friendly and casual bistro that defines what's incredible about the city's neighborhood restaurants. Dishes such as Chianti-braised beef ravioli, quail with spring onion-chanterelle bread salad, or roasted beets with local goat cheese are full of flavor and are made from only the freshest ingredients, a smattering of herbs, and brilliant preparation.

3621 18th St. (between Dolores and Guerrero sts.). ☎ 415-552-4055. Reservations a must. To get there: Muni J-Church to 18th; walk one block east. Main courses: $10–$15. MC, V. Open: Dinner nightly.

Enrico's Sidewalk Cafe

$$–$$$ North Beach CAL-ITALIAN

Dining on a patio with a view of the bawdy section of Broadway would liven up any evening, but this friendly, cosmopolitan bar and restaurant also offers jazz and a menu of knockout seasonal fish and meat dishes.

504 Broadway (at Kearny St.). ☎ 415-982-6223. Reservations recommended. To get there: 30-Stockton bus to Broadway; walk two blocks east. Main courses: $10–$22. AE, DC, MC, V. Open: Lunch and dinner daily.

San Francisco Dining

Boulevard **8**
Charles–Nob Hill **6**
Chow **22**
Clift **13**
Delfina **21**
Enrico's Sidewalk Cafe **3**
Foreign Cinema **19**
Grand Cafe **15**
Green's **1**
The House **2, 23**
Jardinière **17**
King George **14**
Kokkari **4**
Neiman Marcus **11**
Plouf **7**
R&G Lounge **5**
Scala's Bistro **10**
Sheraton Palace **9**
Slanted Door **20**
Thirsty Bear **16**
Westin St. Francis **12**
Zuni Cafe **18**

Golden Gate
← Bridge

GOLDEN GATE NATIONAL   Fort Mason
RECREATION AREA

THE MARINA

Bay St.
Francisco St.
Chestnut St.
Lombard St.
Greenwich St.

COW HOLLOW

PACIFIC HEIGHTS

Divisadero St.
Scott St.
Pierce St.
Steiner St.
Fillmore St.
Webster St.
Buchanan St.
Laguna St.
Octavia St.
Gough St.
Franklin St.

Washington St.   Pacific
Clay St.   Medical   Lafayette
Sacramento St.   Center   Park
California St.
Pine St.
Bush St.
Sutter St.
Post St.
Geary St.   Japan
Center
O'Farrell St.   JAPANTOWN
Ellis St.

Eddy St.
Golden Gate   Turk St.
← Bridge
Golden Gate Ave.   Golden Gate
McAllister St.   ← Bridge
Fulton St.
Grove St.   Alamo
Square   Ivy St.   HAYES VALLEY
Hayes St.
Fell St.   Fell St.
Oak St.
Page St.
Haight St.
Waller St.

Octavia St.

Duboce   Hermann St.
Park
Duboce Ave.
Duboce Ave.

Gough
McCoppin
101

Castro
Noe St.
Sanchez St.
Church St.
14th St.
Dolores St.
Guerrero St.
Valencia St.
Mission St.

15th St.

THE CASTRO
17th St.   16th St.

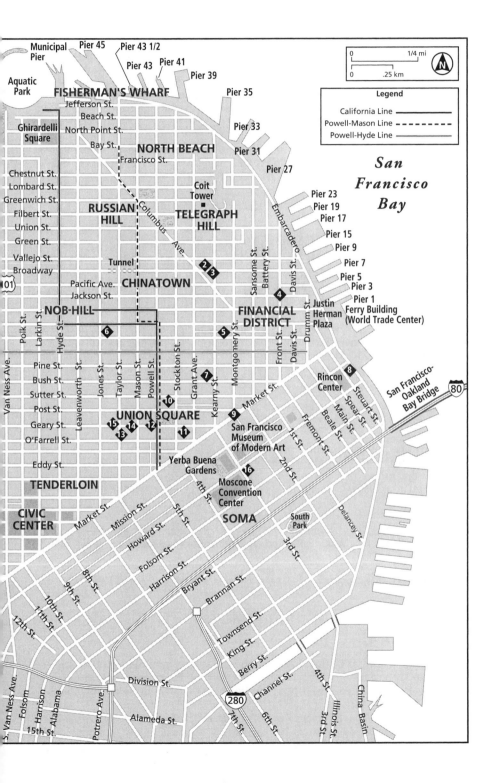

Foreign Cinema

$$$ Mission District   NEW AMERICAN/FRENCH

Mission District regulars nearly lost their *empanadas* when the shiny, chic Foreign Cinema opened in 1999. The expansive dining room — plus outdoor patio where foreign films are screened on a concrete wall — would throw anyone at first, but an elegant plate of escargots or some oysters from the raw bar helps to lower any resistance to the inevitable changes in the neighborhood.

2534 Mission St. (between 21st and 22nd sts.). ☎ *415-648-7600. Reservations highly recommended. To get there: BART to 24th St. Main courses: $11–$19. AE, MC, V. Open: Dinner Tues–Sun; late-night menu until 1 a.m.*

Grand Cafe

$$$ Union Square   CALIFORNIA

Living up to its name in every aspect, this vast, high-ceilinged, muraled bistro is abuzz with activity and energy. People gravitate here pre- and post-theater for brick-oven pizzas, roasts, grilled fish and chicken, and desserts. Kids get crayons and can order from the Petit Cafe menu.

501 Geary St. (at Taylor St.). ☎ *415-292-0101. Reservations accepted. To get there: Muni Metro to Powell St.; walk two blocks to Geary and two blocks south to Taylor. Main courses: $14–$22. AE, CB, DC, DISC, MC, V. Open: Breakfast, lunch, and dinner daily.*

Green's

$$ The Marina/Cow Hollow   VEGETARIAN

If you've never eaten in a gourmet vegetarian restaurant, or if your past encounters with vegetarian dining have been less than inspired, you're in for a marvelous culinary experience. The Saturday evening prix-fixed menu is a deal, especially when you see the gorgeous views that come with the meal.

Fort Mason, Bldg. A (off Marina Blvd. at Buchanan St.). ☎ *415-771-6222. Reservations highly recommended at least two weeks in advance. To get there: Take the 30-Stockton to Laguna and transfer to the 28-19th Ave. into Fort Mason. Main courses: $10–$14; prix-fixe menu (Sat only) $38. DISC, MC, V. Open: Lunch Tues–Sat, dinner Mon–Sat, Sun brunch.*

The House

$$ North Beach   CALIFORNIA/ASIAN

East meets West in the House kitchen, and the resulting relationship is pleasing and harmonious. Another location on Ninth Avenue near Golden Gate Park gives you two opportunities to try this fresh, seasonal cuisine.

1230 Grant St. (near Columbus Ave.). ☎ *415-986-8612. Reservations recommended. To get there: Bus 30-Stockton. Main courses: $11–$17. AE, DC, MC, V. Open: Lunch Mon–Fri, dinner Mon–Sat.*

Jardinière

$$$$ Civic Center   CAL-FRENCH

This is where the upscale crowd sups before the opera, ballet, or symphony. Expect sophisticated surroundings, a lively bar, and highly touted food. The duck confit is heaven-sent. A jazz combo plays upstairs Sunday through Tuesday.

300 Grove St. (at Franklin St.). ☎ *415-861-5555. Reservations a must. To get there: Muni Metro to Civic Center; walk 4 blocks north on Franklin. Main courses: $20–$28. AE, DC, DISC, MC, V. Open: Dinner nightly, bar menu until midnight.*

Kokkari

$$$–$$$$ Financial District   GREEK

Your average Mediterranean shipping tycoon would feel perfectly comfortable seated beneath the beamed ceilings of this richly appointed *taverna*. The California-meets-Greek menu takes familiar dishes to Mount Olympus–style heights. Order the *Yiaourti Graniti* (yogurt sorbet with tangerine ice) for dessert even if you're full.

200 Jackson St. (at Front St.). ☎ *415-981-0983. Reservations a must. To get there: 2, 3, or 4 bus; transfer to 42 Downtown loop exit at Sansome and Jackson sts. and walk two blocks west to Front. Main courses: $14–$27. AE, DC, MC, V. Open: Lunch Mon–Fri, dinner Mon–Sat.*

Plouf

$$$ Financial District   FRENCH

One in a row of terrific restaurants on Belden Place, Plouf has a menu of fresh fish prepared with a French twist and served by waiters who look as if they were extras in the movie *Gigi.* The leek tart also elicits raves. Eat outside on the street and pretend you're in Paris.

40 Belden Place (an alley between Pine, Kearney, and Bush sts.). ☎ *415-986-6491. Reservations advised. To get there: Walk on Stockton St. north from Union Square to Bush St. and turn east for two blocks. Main courses: $14–$23. MC, V. Open: Lunch and dinner Mon–Sat.*

R&G Lounge

$ Chinatown   CHINESE

Downstairs, in a setting reminiscent of an airport lounge, excellent Hong Kong Chinese dishes are served. The small dining room upstairs is more attractive, so talk your way to a table there. Try live spot shrimp from the downstairs tank and fresh crisp vegetables such as Chinese broccoli and *yin choy* (a leafy green vegetable with a red root that's often boiled, then braised with garlic).

631 Kearny St. (between Sacramento and Clay sts.). ☎ *415-982-7877. Reservations accepted. To get there: Bus 15-Third. Main courses: $6.50–$8.50. AE, MC, V. Open: Lunch and dinner daily.*

Scala's Bistro

$$$ Union Square ITALIAN

The seductively masculine dining room, with mahogany paneling and warm lighting, complements the well-rounded menu of Italian favorites, including an excellent Caesar salad and flavorful local bass.

432 Powell St. (between Post and Sutter sts., next to the Sir Francis Drake Hotel). ☎ *415-395-8555. Internet:* www.scalasbistro.com. *Reservations recommended. To get there: Powell-Hyde-line cable car. Main courses: $12–$24. AE, DC, DISC, MC, V. Open: Breakfast, lunch, and dinner daily.*

Slanted Door

$$–$$$ Mission District VIETNAMESE

Savvy travelers and locals of every stripe swoon over the buttery steamed sea bass, caramelized chicken, and plates of "shaking" beef. If dinner reservations seem impossible to come by, show up around 6 p.m. and you may get lucky (they hold a few tables for walk-ins).

584 Valencia St. (at 17th St.). ☎ *415-861-8032. Reservations a must. To get there: BART to 16th and Mission; walk west one block to Valencia. Main courses: $11.50–$19.50. MC, V. Open: Lunch and dinner Tues–Sun. Vietnamese.*

Thirsty Bear

$$$ SoMa SPANISH

The tasty little appetizer-style treats of Spanish cuisine, tapas, are all the rage around these parts, but no one serves small (and large) plates of authentic Catalan food like this cavernous restaurant/brewery. Don't miss the fish cheeks. *Really.*

661 Howard St. (near Third St.). ☎ *415-974-0905. Reservations recommended. To get there: Bus 15-Third, 30-Stockton, or 45-Union/Stockton; exit at 3rd and Howard. Main courses: $14–$18. AE, MC, V. Open: Lunch Mon–Sat, dinner nightly..*

Zuni Cafe

$$$ Civic Center CALIFORNIA

You can always detect a palpable buzz from the smartly dressed crowd hanging around Zuni's copper bar drinking vodka and scarfing up oysters. Everything from the brick oven is great, but the roast chicken and bread salad for two is simply divine. Don't opt for an outside table, as the view on this section of Market Street isn't all that pleasant.

1658 Market St. (between Franklin and Gough sts.). ☎ *415-552-2522. Reservations recommended. To get there: Muni Metro F-Market to Van Ness; walk two blocks southwest. Main courses: $16–$20. AE, MC, V. Open: Lunch and dinner Tues–Sat, brunch and dinner Sun.*

Exploring San Francisco

You can save money on entrance fees to six major attractions by purchasing the *CityPass* for $33.25. It's good for admission to the **Museum of Modern Art, M. H. de Young Memorial Museum, Palace of the Legion of Honor, California Academy of Sciences, the Exploratorium,** and a Blue & Gold Bay cruise. You can get your CityPass at the aforementioned attractions, or order it in advance from Ticketweb at ☎ **510- 601-8933** or online at www.citypass.net.

The top attractions

Alcatraz Island

If not for the movies, Alcatraz Island (a.k.a. "The Rock") would never have morphed from a rundown, deserted maximum-security prison to a must-see tourist attraction. Self-guided 2 ½-hour audio tours and talks facilitated by National Park rangers are full of interesting anecdotes. The walk uphill to the Cell House is steep, so wear comfortable shoes, and don't forget to bring a jacket because the island gets windy. Another path up to the prison is now wheelchair-accessible. In the summer, order tickets far in advance for the ferry ride to the island. Plan on a minimum of three hours for the entire excursion.

Pier 41, near Fisherman's Wharf. ☎ *415-773-1188 for information only.* ☎ *415-705-5555 to purchase tickets over the phone; this service charges a $2.25-per-ticket service fee. Internet:* www.blueandgoldfleet.com *or* www.telesails.com. *To get there: F Market streetcar; Powell-Mason cable car (the line ends a few blocks away); or bus 30-Stockton, which stops one block south. Admission (includes ferry and audio tour): $12.25 adults, $10.50 seniors 62 and older, $7 children 5–11. Open: Winter, daily 9:15 a.m.–2:30 p.m.; summer, daily 9:15 a.m.–4:15 p.m. Ferries run approximately every half-hour from Pier 41. Arrive at least 20 minutes before sailing time.*

The Cable Cars

These cherished wooden cars creak and squeal up and around hills, while unwitting passengers lean out into the wind, running the risk of getting their heads removed by passing buses. San Francisco's three existing lines comprise the world's only surviving system of cable cars. (Brown signs with a white cable car on them indicate stops.) All three routes are worth your time, but the Powell-Mason line conveniently wends its way from the corner of Powell and Market streets through North Beach and ends near Fisherman's Wharf, and the Powell-Hyde line, which starts at the same intersection, ends up near the Maritime Museum and Ghirardelli Square. The less-thrilling California line begins at the foot of Market Street and travels along California Street over Nob Hill to Van Ness Avenue.

Cars run from 6:30 a.m. to 12:30 a.m. The fare is $2 per person one-way, payable on board; Muni passports are accepted. For more information, see "Getting around" earlier in this chapter.

San Francisco's Top Attractions

0 _____ 1 mi
0 _____ 1 km

Legend
Cable Car – – – – – –

PACIFIC

OCEAN

Golden
Gate
Bridge ❶

❷

Golden Gate Promenade

101

GOLDEN GATE
NATIONAL
RECREATION AREA

THE PRESIDIO

Lincoln Blvd.

Arguello Blvd.

Baker Beach

①

China Beach

34

Lake St.

California St.

LINCOLN PARK

Clement St.

Geary Blvd.

Point Lobos
Ave.

Park Presidio Blvd.

10th Ave.

8th Ave.

6th Ave.

Arguello Blvd.

Univ.
of S.F.

Cliff 35
House

43rd Ave.

36th Ave.

34th Ave.

30th Ave.

25th Ave.

RICHMOND
DISTRICT

Fulton St. ①

J. F. Kennedy Dr.

32 31

30

GOLDEN GATE PARK

28

33

29

Lincoln Way

Ocean
Beach

Great Highway

Irving St.

25th Ave.

Irving St.

9th Ave.

7th Ave.

Parnassus
Ave.

Judah St.

Judah St.

Sunset Blvd.

SUNSET DISTRICT

19th Ave.

Adventure Bicycle Company **14**	Chinatown **16**	Golden Gate Bridge **1**
Alcatraz Island Ferries **11**	Chinese Culture Center **19**	Golden Gate Fortune
Ansel Adams Center for Photography **24**	Coit Tower **13**	Cookies Company **17**
California Academy of Sciences **28**	Exploratorium/Palace of Fine Arts **3**	Golden Gate Park **33**
California Palace of the Legion of Honor **34**	Fisherman's Wharf **9**	Holiday Adventures **4**
Cartoon Art Museum **23**	Fort Point **2**	Japanese Tea Garden **31**
Children's Playground **27**	Ghirardelli Square **5**	Kabuki Hot Springs **25**

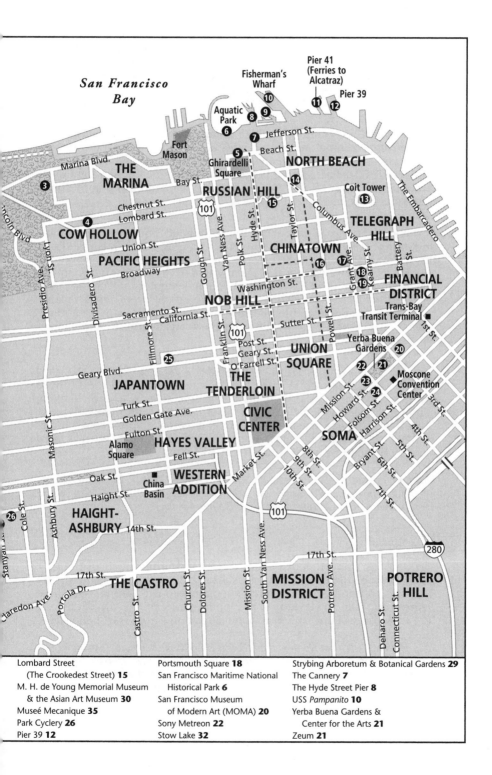

Chinatown

Crowded with pedestrians and crammed with exotic-looking shops and vegetable markets whose wares spill onto the sidewalks, Chinatown is genuinely fascinating. If you want an authentic experience, veer off Grant Avenue and explore the side streets and alleys. On weekends, Chinatown is extra-jammed with shoppers examining fruits and vegetables piled on outdoor tables. Just walking down the street can be an experience.

The **Golden Gate Fortune Cookies Company,** 956 Ross Alley (between Jackson and Washington streets near Grant Avenue), is a working factory where you can purchase inexpensive fresh almonds and delicious fortune cookies (terrific gifts for the folks back home!). It's very tight quarters, but you can stand for a few minutes watching rounds of dough transmogrify. Open daily from 10 a.m. to 7 p.m.

Portsmouth Square, a park above the Portsmouth Square parking garage on Kearny Street (between Washington and Clay streets), is the site of the first California public school, which opened in 1848, and marks the spot where San Francisco was originally settled. A compact but complete playground attracts all the neighborhood preschoolers and, in the morning, elderly Chinese who come to practice tai chi exercises. The landscape includes comfortable benches, attractive lampposts, and young trees. The distinctly S.F. view includes the Transamerica Pyramid looming above the skyline.

The pedestrian bridge over Kearny Street leads directly into the third floor of the Chinatown Holiday Inn, where you can find the **Chinese Culture Center.** A gift shop leads to the sole gallery, where changing exhibits may feature, for example, photographs from pre-earthquake Chinatown, Chinese brush painting, or exquisitely embroidered antique clothing and household items. Admission is free, and the center is open Monday through Saturday from 10 a.m. to 4 p.m.

Location: 750 Kearny St., Portsmouth Square. ☎ *415-986-1822. To get there: Take Muni Bus 1 California, 9AX San Bruno "A" Express, 9BX Xan Bruno "B" Express, 15 Third. Admission: Free. Open: Tues–Sun 10 a.m .–4 p.m.*

Coit Tower

You can see this 210-foot concrete landmark from much of the city, but everyone should see it up close. The walls inside are painted with dramatic, not-to-be-missed murals commissioned during the Great Depression. Take an elevator to the top for panoramic views of city and bay. This visit will probably take about 30 minutes from start to finish.

Atop Telegraph Hill (near North Beach). ☎ *415-362-0808. To get there: Take the 39-Coit bus or walk from Lombard St. where it meets Telegraph Hill Blvd. (two blocks east of Stockton St.). Parking: The drive up and the parking lot are always a mass of cars. Admission: $3.75 adults, $2.50 seniors, $1.50 kids 6–12. Open: Daily 10 a.m.–6 p.m.*

Exploratorium/Palace of Fine Arts

One of the finest hands-on science museums anywhere, this attraction makes an interesting stop for all ages. The changing exhibits explore technology, human perception, and natural phenomena with well-written text. Visiting with kids can be humbling if you're science-impaired, but a staff of alert volunteers is on hand to help with the tough questions. When you need to decompress, stroll the lovely grounds surrounding the Palace of Fine Arts. If the weather's balmy, bring a picnic and stay awhile.

3601 Lyon St. (at Marina Blvd.), the Marina. ☎ **415-561-0360.** *Internet:* www.exploratorium.edu. *To get there: 30-Stockton bus to Marina Stop. Parking: Free and easy. Admission: $9 adults, $7 seniors and students over 18, $5 kids 6–17, $2.50 kids 3–5. Free to all first Wed of the month. Open: Memorial Day–Labor Day, daily 10 a.m.–6 p.m., Wed to 9 p.m.; Labor Day–Memorial Day, Tues–Sun 10 a.m.–5 p.m., Wed to 9 p.m.*

Fisherman's Wharf

Don't be disappointed when you arrive at Fisherman's Wharf and see lots of people wandering around, none of whom seem to be fishing for a living. This was once a working set of piers, but today it's a seemingly endless outdoor shopping mall masquerading as a bona-fide destination. Some people really enjoy examining the refrigerator magnets and cable car bookends stocked in one olde shoppe after another; others, dazed in the presence of so much kitsch, hastily plan their escape. Still, because most folks make their way to the wharf for one reason or another, here's a run-down of what's there.

Even when the weather is cold and gray, tourists pack **Pier 39,** a multi-level Disneyesque shopper's dream (or nightmare, depending on your point of view). Arcade halls lined with deafening video games anchor the pier on each end, with T-shirt shops and fried food filling the void. The only plausible reasons to join the mob are for the golden view of Alcatraz from the end of the pier, and to watch the sea lions loitering on the west side of the pier (follow the barking). If you're arriving by car, park on adjacent streets or on the wharf between Taylor and Jones streets. (Be advised — the parking garage charges $5.50 per hour! Do your best to avoid these price-gougers, or just don't bring a car here.)

The San Francisco Maritime National Historical Park (☎ 415-556-3002) is a small, two-story museum displaying exhibits and photos marking the city's maritime heritage. Examining the museum's schooners, figure-heads, and photographs only takes about 15 minutes, although children may lose interest after the first five minutes. Still, the museum is very sweet, and admission is free. Open daily from 10 a.m. to 5 p.m.

If you've got little kids in tow (or anyone interested in history), you won't want to miss touring the **USS *Pampanito,*** Pier 45 (☎ **415-775-1943**). This submarine saw active duty during WWII and helped save 73 British and Australian prisoners-of-war. The $27 family pass (for 2 adults and up to 4 children) also gets you into the Hyde Street Pier (see the next paragraph). Otherwise, submarine-only admission is $6 for adults, $4 for seniors, students, and children 6 to 12 (kids under 6 are free). Open daily from 9 a.m. to 6 p.m. in winter, and until 8 p.m. in summer.

The Hyde Street Pier, at the foot of Hyde Street (at Beach Street, two blocks east of the Maritime Museum), houses a number of refurbished historic ships, which you can roam around. Of particular note is the 112-year-old *Balclutha,* a square-rigger with a past. You'll probably want to spend at least an hour or so touring the vessels. In summer, admission is $4 adults, $2 for kids 12 to 17, free for kids 11 and under; winter admission is half price. Open daily from 9:30 a.m. to 5 p.m.

Ghirardelli Square, the former chocolate factory across the street from the Maritime Park at 900 North Point (between Polk and Larkin streets; ☎ 415-775-5500), is one of the more pleasant shopping malls in the area. Granted Landmark status in 1982, the series of brick buildings hosts a roster of special events, including an annual chocolate-tasting benefit in September. Street performers entertain regularly in the West Plaza. Open daily from 10 a.m. to 6 p.m., to 9 p.m. in summer.

One block east in what was once peach-canning facilities is **the Cannery,** 2801 Leavenworth St., at Beach Street (☎ 415-771-3112), with yet more shops, jugglers, musicians, and food. Open daily from 10 a.m. to 6 p.m., until 9 p.m. summer.

At the foot of Polk St., on the western edge of the Embarcadero. To get there: Take the Powell-Hyde cable car line to the last stop; the F-Market streetcar; or the 19-Polk, 30-Stockton, 32-Embarcadero, 42-Downtown Loop, or 47-Van Ness bus. Parking: Pricey lots and garages; street parking is difficult.

Golden Gate Bridge

The quintessential San Francisco landmark. A walk across the windy, 1.7-mile-long span, hundreds of feet above the water, underscores the point that San Francisco really is like no other city. Bundle up, then set out from the Roundhouse on the south side of the bridge. The stroll is noisy and chilly, but exhilarating. The only way to return from the other side is on foot, so assess your fatigue in the middle of the span before continuing on toward Marin. After your stroll, take some time to climb below the bridge to see the five-acre garden there.

No phone, but you can check the Web site: www.goldengate.org. *To get there: The 28-19th Ave. or the 29-Sunset bus will deposit you across from the viewing area, right by a parking lot. Open: to pedestrians daily 5 a.m.–9 p.m.*

Lombard Street

The part of Lombard with the moniker "crookedest street in the world" begins at Hyde Street below Russian Hill. The whimsical, flower-lined block attracts thousands of visitors each year. If you intend to drive this redbrick street (it's one-way, downhill, so take the curves slowly), go early in the morning before everyone else revs up their Chevys. Better yet, walk down the stairs to fully admire the flowers, the houses with their long-suffering tenants, and the stellar view.

Lombard St. between Hyde and Leavenworth sts. To get there: Powell-Hyde cable car line.

San Francisco Museum of Modern Art (MOMA)

It was a big deal when the city finally built a handsome, grown-up museum to house its collection of modern paintings, sculptures, and photographs. The interior is especially beautiful and exudes a warmth that makes viewing the exhibits — including works by Henri Matisse, Jackson Pollock, and Ansel Adams — even more enjoyable.

151 Third St. (two blocks south of Market St., near Howard St.). ☎ ***415-357-4000.*** *Internet:* www.sfmoma.org. *To get there: Take any Muni Metro to the Montgomery St. Station and walk one block south to Third St. then two blocks east; or take the 15-Third, 30-Stockton, or 45-Union/Stockton bus. Admission: $8 adults, $5 seniors, and $4 students with ID; half-price Thurs 6–9 p.m.; free for kids under 12. Free to all first Tues of the month. Open: Thurs 11 a.m.–9 p.m., Fri–Tues 11 a.m.–6 p.m.; from 10 a.m. in summer.*

Golden Gate Park & its attractions

The 1,017 rectangular acres of greenery and cultural attractions that comprise **Golden Gate Park** contain something for everyone. Locals use the park for everything from soccer practice to wedding receptions to fly-casting lessons. On Sundays, when John F. Kennedy Drive is closed to street traffic, bicyclists ride with impunity and in-line skaters converge for dance parties.

A grand new *park entrance* on Stanyan Street (off Waller Street) will bring you to the massive **Children's Playground** and a beautifully restored carousel. The imaginative structures and swings will occupy kids for as long as you allow. A remodeling of the entrance cut down on the rather large numbers of street people who hung out there, but you never know if that will change. In any case, don't let that keep you from enjoying the park; the street folks can look a little scary to the uninitiated, but they are generally harmless. *Another entrance* at 9th Avenue on Lincoln Way brings you to the botanical gardens, the **Japanese Tea Garden,** the **Academy of Sciences,** and the **de Young** and **Asian Art** museums.

Joggers and parents pushing baby strollers make regular use of the path around manmade **Stow Lake.** The boathouse (☎ **415-752-0347**) rents paddleboats, bikes, and in-line skates by the hour, half day, and full day. If you aren't driving, walking to the boathouse is a bit of a hike. The boathouse is west of the Japanese Tea Garden on Martin Luther King Drive; open daily from 9 a.m. to 4 p.m.

The *N-Judah* Muni Metro streetcar drops you off on 9th Avenue and Judah Street; walk three blocks to the park from there. Numerous bus lines drive close to or into the park, including the 44-O'Shaughnessy, which you can catch on 9th Ave.; the 21-Hayes; and the 5-Fulton.

Golden Gate Park houses the following museums and attractions:

California Academy of Sciences

Traveling exhibits on everything from dinosaurs to spiders complement permanent natural-history exhibits that put to shame the dusty moose dioramas you may remember from grammar-school field trips. The Earth and Space exhibit includes a popular earthquake simulation — it's as close as you'll want to get to the real thing. Also inside you'll find the **Morrison Planetarium** and the **Steinhart Aquarium;** kids love the hands-on tide pool, where they get to poke (gently) at starfish and sea urchins. Staff members feed the seals and dolphins every two hours, beginning at 10:30 a.m. and the penguins at 11:30 a.m. and 4 p.m. Plan on spending an hour or two here, longer if you attend a planetarium show.

On the Music Concourse. ☎ *415-750-7145, or 415-750-7141 for planetarium show schedules. Internet:* www.calacademy.org. *Admission: $8.50 adults, $5.50 seniors and students 12–17, $2 children 4–11; free for all the first Wed of the month. Planetarium show, $2.50 adults, $1.25 seniors and children under 18. Open: Memorial Day–Labor Day, daily 9 a.m.–6 p.m.; Labor Day–Memorial Day, daily 10 a.m.–5 p.m.*

M. H. de Young Memorial Museum & the Asian Art Museum

These two museums share a building across the Music Concourse from the Academy of Sciences. Steel beams set up to help reinforce the structure (in the event of an earthquake) lend an erector-set ambience to the once-stately surroundings. If you're interested in American art and textiles, or 6,000 years of Asian history, you'll forget about the outside of the building after you're inside. Free docent tours are available. The de Young also operates the excellent Cafe de Young, which serves salads and sandwiches. Touring both museums will take you 1 ½ hours.

75 Teagarden Dr., across from the Music Concourse. **M. H. de Young Memorial Museum:** ☎ *415-863-3330. Internet:* www.deyoungmuseum.org. **Asian Art Museum:** ☎ *415-379-8801. Internet:* www.asianart.org. *Admission to both museums: $7 adults, $5 seniors, $4 children 12–17, free for children under 12; free to all first Wed of the month. Open: Wed–Sun 9:30 a.m.–5 p.m., until 8:45 p.m. first Wed of the month.*

Strybing Arboretum & Botanical Gardens

This splendid oasis contains more than 6,000 species of well-tended plants. It's exceptionally lovely in late winter, when the rhododendrons blossom and wild iris poke up in corners, and no more peaceful a place exists when the skies are drizzling. I recommend the guided tours, offered daily at 1:30 p.m., for anyone who finds identifying any but the most basic of flowers and trees difficult. Plan to spend at least a half-hour just wandering around.

9th Ave. at Lincoln Way (turn left of the tour bus parking lot by the Music Concourse). ☎ *415-661-1316, ext. 314 for guided tour info. Internet:* www.strybing.org. *Admission: Free! Free guided walks daily 1:30 p.m. Open: Mon–Fri 8 a.m.–4:30 p.m., Sat–Sun 10 a.m.–5 p.m.*

Japanese Tea Garden

This tranquil spot includes colorful pagodas, koi ponds, bridges, and a giant bronze Buddha. Young children find this piece of the park particularly memorable, because they can climb over a steeply arched wooden bridge. Passengers spill through the entry gate of this major tour bus destination with alarming regularity. To avoid the onslaught, arrive before 10 a.m. or after 4 p.m. in summer. Japanese tea, accompanied by a few paltry snacks, is served in the teahouse for $2.95 per person. While the garden is worth the small admission fee, the food isn't.

To the left of the de Young Museum. ☎ **_415-752-4227._** _Admission: $3.50 adults, $1.25 seniors and children 6–12. Open: Oct–Feb, 8:30 a.m.–dusk; Mar–Sept, 8:30 a.m.–6:30 p.m._

Yerba Buena Gardens and Center for the Arts

Yerba Buena Center for the Arts

You can find the following attractions in and around the Yerba Buena Gardens and Center for the Arts:

Where once sat nothing but parking lots and derelicts, this 22-acre complex now stands as a micro-destination. A collection of galleries showing a rotating exhibition of contemporary visual and performance art by local artists, gardens, a dance space, and a theater has been joined recently by an ice-skating rink/bowling alley, a children's garden and carousel, and an arts/technology studio for older kids. An entertainment behemoth in a separate building across the street — **Sony's Metreon** — houses restaurants, retail shops, and a multiplex movie screen. If you take in all that Yerba Buena Center has to offer, you can easily spend the day and evening here. Parking is difficult and/or expensive, so use public transportation if at all possible.

Yerba Buena Center for the Arts is at 701 Mission St. (between 3rd and 4th sts.). ☎ **_415-978-2700,_** _or 415-978-ARTS for the box office. Internet:_ www. yerbabuenaarts.org. _To get there: Muni Metro to Powell St. or Montgomery St. and walk two blocks down Third St.; or 14-Mission or 15-Third bus. Admission to the galleries: $5 adults, $3 seniors and students. Open: Galleries, Tues–Sun 11 a.m.–6 p.m._

Zeum

This wonderful art/technology center is probably the only attraction specifically designed for older kids and teens that doesn't rely on video games. The hands-on labs give visitors the opportunity to create animated video shorts with clay figures, learn about graphics, sound, and video production in the studio, and interact with the changing gallery exhibits. Any bored adolescent would find resisting a Zeum offering difficult.

☎ *415-777-2800. Internet:* www.zeum.org. *Admission: Adults $7, seniors and students $6, kids 5–18 $5. Open: Sat–Sun 11 a.m.–5 p.m. during the school year, daily in summer.*

Sony Metreon

Four stories of glass and brushed metal anchoring one block of Yerba Buena Center, the new Sony Metreon is quite the sight. Some people call it the future of entertainment centers, and, for the moment at least, nothing else on the planet is quite like it. Of course, eating and spending money are big themes. The third floor houses 15 — count 'em — 15 movie screens and the city's first IMAX theater. You'll also find what Sony refers to as family-friendly attractions, two of which are cleverly based on popular children's books, *The Way Things Work* and *Where the Wild Things Are.* The third is an interactive game arena, likely to swallow up a generation of video-enhanced teens and young adults. Noisy and lit like a Vegas casino, Metreon is best described as awesome.

Mission St. at 4th St. ☎ *800-METREON. Internet:* www.metreon.com. *Admission: Free! Tickets for all three attractions are $17 adults, $13 seniors and kids 3–12; individual attraction prices $7–$10. Open: Daily 10 a.m.–10 p.m.*

Pursuing the arts & other cool stuff to see & do

The **California Palace of the Legion of Honor,** in Lincoln Park between Clement Street and 34th Avenue in the outer Richmond District (☎ **415-750-3600;** www.famsf.org), exhibits an impressive collection of paintings, drawings, sculpture, and decorative arts. The grounds around the palace are a draw as well. The museum is open Tuesday through Sunday from 9:30 a.m. to 5 p.m., and admission (including the **Asian** and **de Young** art museums in **Golden Gate Park**) is $7 adults, $5 seniors, $4 kids 12 to 17, free for those under 12 (free for all on the second Wednesday of the month). Take the 38-Geary bus to 33rd and Geary, then transfer to the 18-46th Avenue bus for a ride to the museum entrance.

You can also check out the **Ansel Adams Center for Photography,** 250 4th St., between Howard and Folsom streets, in SoMa (☎ **415-495-7000;** www.friendsofphotography.org), which has five galleries, one de- voted entirely to Adams. Open daily from 11 a.m. to 5 p.m.; admission is $5 adults, $3 students, $2 seniors and teens 12 to 17. The **Cartoon Art Museum,** also in SoMa at 814 Mission St. and 4th Street (☎ **415–227-8666;** www.cartoonart.org), produces exhibits on all forms of cartoon art and often showcases local cartoonists, such as Bill Griffith and the late *Peanuts* creator Charles Schultz. Open Wednesday through Friday from 11 a.m. to 5 p.m., Saturday 10 a.m. to 5 p.m., Sunday 1 to 5 p.m.; admission is $5 adults, $3 seniors, $2 children 6 to 12.

Museé Mecanique, below Cliff House at 1090 Point Lobos Rd., at the Great Highway (☎ **415-386-1170**), contains lovingly restored and maintained mechanical marvels that were the forerunners to pinball machines. Open daily from 10 a.m. to 8 p.m. Admission is free. To get there, take the 38-Geary Bus — and bring along a roll of quarters.

Taking a hike

Fort Point (☎ **415-556-1373**), underneath the Golden Gate Bridge at the tip of the peninsula, dates from 1857. The distance is an easy 3 ½-mile stroll to Fort Point from the Hyde Street Pier along the paved **Golden Gate Promenade,** which hugs the coast as it passes through the Marina Green and the Presidio. Alternatively, you can reach Fort Point by taking the 28-19th Avenue or the 29-Sunset bus to the Golden Gate Bridge and climb down from the viewing area to a short trail leading to the fort. Open Wednesday through Sunday from 10 a.m. to 5 p.m.

Riding a bike

If you plan to ride in Golden Gate Park, your best bet is one of the bike stores nearby, such as **Park Cyclery,** 1749 Waller St. (☎ **415-751-7368**). **Holiday Adventures,** 1937 Lombard St. (☎ **415-567-1192**), will pick you up at your hotel and drive you to their store in the Marina, which is convenient for rides around the Presidio or over the Golden Gate Bridge. Both shops charge $5 per hour; per-day rates are $25 and $19 respectively for bike, helmet, and locks.

Walking the beach

Ocean Beach, at the end of Geary Boulevard on the Great Highway, attracts picnicking families and teenagers looking for a place to swill some beer. Great for oceanside strolls if the tide is low, and the waves can be magnificent. Swimming is dangerous and not allowed, though. The 38-Geary bus gets you within walking distance of the beach, or you can take the N-Judah Muni Metro streetcar to the end of the line.

Soaking it up

For some pampering with a Japanese twist, take the 38-Geary bus to **Kabuki Hot Springs,** 1750 Geary Blvd. at Webster Street in Japantown (☎ **415-922-6000**). This is a most respectable communal bathhouse, where you can soak your feet, have a massage, or take a steam bath. Women may use the facilities on Sundays, Wednesdays, and Fridays; men get it the rest of the week. Massages are by appointment.

Seeing San Francisco by Guided Tour

An introductory tour is a good bet for those of you with limited time to explore the city.

The old soft shoe (s)

Friends of the Library sponsors **City Guides** walking tours (☎ 415-557-4266; www.hooked.net/users/jhum). These tours trod 26 different paths each week, all for free — that's right, no charge! All you have to do is decide which tour appeals to you and show up at the proper corner on time. You can explore the haunts of the original 49ers on the "Gold Rush City" tour, admire the Painted Ladies (San Francisco's collection of beautifully resorted Victorian homes) on the "Landmark Victorians of Alamo Square" tour, or get an insider's view of Chinatown. Highly recommended!

Local cookbook writer and luminary Shirley Fong-Torres operates Chinatown food tours that will have you classifying noodles like an expert. **Wok Wiz Chinatown Walking Tours & Cooking Center,** 654 Commercial St., between Kearny and Montgomery streets (☎ 800- 281-9255 or 415-981-8989; www.wokwiz.com), offers daily tours for $37 for adults, $35 for seniors, and $28 for kids under 12. Tours include a seven-course dim sum lunch.

Everyone's favorite neighborhood reaches new heights of giddiness on Saturdays when food writer GraceAnn Walden leads **Mangia! North Beach** (☎ 415-397-8530; www.sfnorthbeach.com/gawtour.html), a 4 ½-hour, $45 walking, eating, shopping, and history tour. GraceAnn and her followers traipse in and out of a deli, an Irish pub, a truffle factory, a bakery, a pottery store, and two lovely churches before ending with a multi-course, family-style lunch at one of her favorite restaurants. This tour offers lots of samples, lots of tidbits about the Italians, and lots of fun. Reservations are a must.

Trevor Hailey can introduce you to gay and lesbian history from the Gold Rush to the present on her four-hour **Cruisin' the Castro** walking tour (☎ 415-550-8110). The $40 tour price includes brunch; reservations are required.

Bay cruises

The **Blue & Gold Fleet** (☎ 415-773-1188; *Internet:* www.blueandgold-fleet. com, or www.telesails.com for online tickets) operates ferry-boats to and from Marin County from Fisherman's Wharf. This is also the only company that serves Alcatraz Island. Blue and Gold's one-hour bay cruise ($17 for adults, $13 for seniors and kids 12 to 18, $9 for kids 5 to 11) travels under the Golden Gate Bridge; past Sausalito, Angel Island, and Alcatraz; then back to Fisherman's Wharf. If you're not interested in landing on these shores, this tour will provide a satisfy-ing, if brief, encounter with the bay.

Suggested 1-, 2-, and 3-day itineraries

On **Day 1,** find **Market Street** and catch one of the historic F-Market streetcars heading toward **Pier 39** and **Fisherman's Wharf.** If you haven't eaten breakfast, try the **Eagle Cafe** on the second floor of the pier, but if it happens to be a Saturday, stop at Green Street on the Embarcadero and breakfast at the **Ferry Plaza Farmers' Market.**

At Pier 39, greet the sea lions (follow the barking) and continue to the end of the pier for a dead-on view of Alcatraz Island. Walk to **Aquatic Park** to complete a tour of Fisherman's Wharf. You'll pass the **Hyde Street Pier** and the **Maritime National Museum** — pop in if you like ships — as well as **Ghirardelli Square.**

On Bay Street, catch a 30-Stockton bus to Chestnut Street. If it's not too soon to shop or eat, **Cafe Marimba** is a great choice for Mexican food. The bus ends up at Beach Street. The walk from the **Palace of Fine Arts** through the **Presidio** to the **Golden Gate Bridge** is lovely. Follow the joggers on the path along the bay. The 29-Sunset bus will also take you there and back.

End the afternoon around Union Square, window-shopping along Stockton and Sutter. Change your clothes, then go to the **Top of the Mark** (see "Bars & lounges" later in this chapter) for an aperitif and a grand view. For dinner, see what's cooking on Belden Place. Afterward, if you still have a bit of steam left, drop by **Biscuits and Blues** for a musical nightcap.

Day 2 starts with another transportation highlight. Fling yourself onto a Powell-Hyde cable car for the brief ride to **Lombard Street.** Walk down via the staircases on either side and, heading north, find the **San Francisco Art Institute** at 800 Chestnut St. Inside the campus, follow the signs to the cafe for breakfast or a snack. This is a funky place with unobstructed views of the bay and a menu of sandwiches, bagels, and vegetarian entrees priced for starving artists.

Follow Filbert Street to **Washington Square Park** in North Beach, a modest pocket of green with plentiful benches on the perimeter and the twin spires of Saints Peter and Paul's Church solidly cutting into sky to the north. Park yourself on a bench, maybe with a latté in hand from **Mario's Bohemian Cigar** on the corner. Then, stroll around North Beach or walk up Grant Avenue past Union Street and follow the signs to **Coit Tower.** From there, return to North Beach for a leisurely lunch at **Moose's,** which is on the east side of the park, or pick up a sandwich at one of the delis and have a picnic in **Portsmouth Square,** a short walk away.

Spend the afternoon exploring **Chinatown.** If you're in the mood for Chinese cuisine for dinner, see "Dining Out" for suggestions. Then head back to North Beach for a performance of Beach Blanket Babylon (see "Nightlife" later in this chapter).

Day 3 is a walk in **Golden Gate Park,** where you can get in some culture at the **de Young** and **Asian** art museums and some fresh air in the **Strybing Arboretum.** Find lunch over on 9th Avenue.

In the afternoon, a trip downtown to the **Museum of Modern Art** finishes the artistic portion of your San Francisco visit. Take a rest stop in **Yerba Buena Gardens** across the street.

Dine around Union Square if you're ambitious enough to see an 8 p.m. show at ACT or another theater. Otherwise, hail a cab and head to a **Mission District** restaurant such as **Delfina,** and pretend you're a local. Night owls can finish the evening catching the second set at the **Boom Boom Room.**

Shopping 'til You Drop

Jump right in; the shopping's fine and dandy in San Francisco.

Union Square

With all big department stores within shouting distance of one another, Union Square gets a body in the mood for retail therapy faster than you can say "Charge it!" Stand in the square and turn around slowly; you'll see **Saks Fifth Avenue** on the corner of Powell and Post streets (☎ 415-986-4300); **Neiman Marcus** at Stockton and Geary streets (☎ 415-362-3900); and **Macy's** (☎ 415-397-3333) everywhere else.

A half-block north of Neiman's on Stockton Street is **Maiden Lane,** which is lined with designer shops. You can also find an entrance here to **Britex Fabrics** (☎ 415-392-2910), probably the most well-stocked notions and fabric store in the country.

Chinatown

Grubby curio shops line Grant Avenue, selling all manner of cheap trinkets and clothing. If you venture off Grant, you'll find many herbal shops with strange remedies and jewelry stores full of jade of varying quality. The merchants in the less touristy stores don't always speak English and they may not seem friendly, but don't let that keep you from looking around.

Chong Imports, in the Empress of China building at 838 Grant Ave., between Clay and Washington streets (☎ 415-982-1432), stocks a little of everything. **Tai Yick Trading Company,** 1400 Powell St., at Broadway (☎ 415-986-0961), sells porcelain and pottery at reasonable prices; locals swear this is the best store of its kind in town, and the owners are helpful and friendly. The **Imperial Tea Court,** 1411 Powell St. near Broadway (☎ 415-788-6080), sells everything you'll need to brew a proper cup of Chinese tea.

North Beach

Completely different from the street of the same name in Chinatown, Grant Avenue from Green to Greenwich streets has a Parisian accent, with many stylish boutiques for clothes and accessories. **Biordi Art Imports,** 412 Columbus Ave., at Vallejo Street (☎ 415-392-8096), stocks the most beautiful hand-painted Majolica dishes and serving pieces — as close as you can get to eating off a work of art. **City Lights Bookstore,** the famous Beat-generation bookstore founded by renowned Beat poet and Ginsberg crony Lawrence Ferlinghetti, sits on Columbus Avenue at Broadway (☎ 415-362-8193), and is still a bastion of left-of-center literature.

Union Street, the Marina

Folks who love wandering in and out of specialty shops will think they've hit pay dirt between Fillmore Street and Van Ness Avenue in the Marina District.

Carol Doda, who shaped a career out of her chest long before implants were considered accessories, runs a lingerie shop, **Carol Doda's Champagne and Lace**, at 1850 Union St. (☎ **415-776-6900**). The store carries bras in regular and hard-to-find sizes, plus lots of other fun things. Sinus help comes in the form of **Gazoontite,** 2157 Union St. (☎ **415-931-2230**), where useful products for your favorite asthmatic or allergy-prone relative are attractively displayed. **Mudpie,** 1694 Union St. (☎ **415-771-9262**), sells expensive children's clothes and gifts; sticker shock is slightly lessened in the downstairs sale room, where everything is half-price.

Enjoying the Nightlife

Still have energy after all that sightseeing? *Great.* So what do you want to do? For up-to-the-minute listings, get a free copy of the *San Francisco Bay Guardian* from sidewalk kiosks or in cafes.

Beach Blanket Babylon, baby

A veritable institution, *Beach Blanket Babylon* is the only-in-San Francisco musical revue famous for outrageous costumes and wildly inventive hats that appear to lead lives of their own. The spectacle is so popular that even after celebrating 25 years of poking fun at stars, politicians, and San Francisco itself, seats for the constantly updated shows are always sold out. Purchase tickets ($18 to $45) through the TIX window on the Stockton Street side of Union Square (☎ **415-433-7827**), by mail, or by fax at the number listed below at least three weeks in advance, especially if you want to attend a weekend performance. Children may only attend Sunday matinees, when liquor isn't sold.

At Club Fugazi, 678 Green St., between Powell St. and Columbus Ave., North Beach. ☎ *415-421-4222. Fax: 415-421-4187. Internet:* www.beachblanketbabylon. com. *To get there: The 15-Third, 30-Stockton, or 45 to Columbus and Union St.; Green St. is one block south of Union.*

Play it loud: Live music

Biscuits and Blues

This all-ages jazz-and-blues venue is in a basement room near the theater district. The Southern food is inexpensive ($9.95 entrees), and the musicians range from local faves to legends.

410 Mason St. (at Geary St.), Union Square. ☎ *415-292-2583. To get there: Take the 38-Geary bus to Mason St.*

Boom Boom Room

John Lee Hooker's Boom Boom Room is open every night for dancing to live music, cocktails, and jiving. Lines often form on the weekends, so arrive on the early side and sip your drink slowly.

1601 Fillmore St. (at Geary St.), Japantown. ☎ *415-673-8000. Internet:* www. boomboomblues. com. *To get there: Take the 38-Geary bus to Fillmore St.*

The Great American Music Hall

This venue presents big-name acts in an ornate, comfortable setting. Call for an events calendar.

859 O'Farrell St. (near Polk St.), the Tenderloin. ☎ *415-885-0750. To get there: Take a cab to avoid the dangers of the Tenderloin at night.*

Jazz at Pearl's

Pearl's features a Monday Big Band Night and local jazz musicians Tuesday through Saturday. A menu of ribs, burgers, pizza, and other snacky items is available. No cover, but expect a two-drink minimum.

256 Columbus Ave. (at Broadway), North Beach. ☎ *415-291-8255. To get there: The 15-Third, 30-Stockton, or 45 bus to Columbus and Union sts.; walk south on Columbus three blocks to Broadway.*

The Plush Room

This intimate showroom books local and national cabaret acts for runs lasting from a weekend to a few weeks. Expect torch and standards singers, musical revues, or duos of some repute. Reservations are strongly suggested.

In the York Hotel, 940 Sutter St. (between Hyde and Leavenworth sts., four blocks west of Union Square). ☎ *415-885-2800. Internet:* www.plushroom.citysearch.com.

The Saloon

This should be your first stop on a walking tour of North Beach blues bars. It's a quintessentially loud, raucous blues bar, and the locals like it. Just follow the crowds.

1232 Grant Ave. (at Fresno St., near Vallejo St.). ☎ *415-989-7666. To get there: 30-Stockton bus or 45 to Columbus and Union Street; Grant is one block east of Columbus.*

Come here often? Bars & lounges

Backflip

Backflip serves good cocktails in an aqua-blue setting designed to give patrons the impression that they are drinking in the deep end. The staff wears vinyl. You get the picture, I'm sure.

At the Phoenix Hotel, 601 Eddy St. (at Larkin St.), the Tenderloin. ☎ **415-771-3547.** *To get there: Take a cab.*

Blondie's Bar and No Grill

Blondie's is on the sizzling Valencia Street corridor in the Mission District. The young and the restless make good use of the free jazz jukebox.

540 Valencia St. (between 16th and 17th sts.), Mission District. ☎ **415-864-2419.** *To get there: Take BART to 16th St. and walk one block west to Valencia.*

The Blue Lamp

This place includes a fireplace, a pool table, and a handful of tables for two along with a well-stocked bar. Music starts after 10 p.m.

561 Geary St. (between Jones and Taylor sts.), a short walk south from Union Square. ☎ **415-885-1464.**

Harry Denton's Starlight Room

This venue is popular for dancing, drinking, and mingling in an upscale way.

In the Sir Francis Drake Hotel, 450 Powell St. (at Sutter St.), Union Sq. (three blocks from the Powell St. Muni Station). ☎ **415-395-8595.**

Top of the Mark

The Top of the Mark has it all — views, music from 9 p.m., dancing, and a convivial crowd of suits. The hotel recently began serving a $39 prix-fixe dinner on Friday and Saturday nights; with 7:30 p.m. reservations, a night on the town is a done deal.

In the Mark Hopkins Intercontinental Hotel, 1 Nob Hill (at Mason and California sts.). ☎ **415-616-6916.** *To get there: For fun, take the California St. cable car and exit at the top of Nob Hill.*

Experiencing the finer side of the arts

Theater

Union Square houses at least 10 professional theaters of varying sizes, and experimental theaters are scattered about the SoMa and Mission districts in converted warehouses and gallery spaces. The preeminent company in town is the **American Conservatory Theater (ACT),** which produces a little of everything during its October to June season. The sets and costumes are universally brilliant, and the acting is first-rate. Productions take place in the lovely Geary Theater, 415 Geary St., at Mason Street (☎ **415-749-2228;** Internet: www.act-sfbay.org).

Opera

The **San Francisco Opera** season opens with a gala in September and ends quietly in early January. Performances are produced in the War Memorial Opera House, 301 Van Ness Ave., at Grove Street (☎ **415-864-3330;** Internet: www.sfopera.com), in the Civic Center.

Classical music

The **San Francisco Symphony** performs in the Louise M. Davies Symphony Hall, 201 Van Ness Ave., at Grove Street (☎ **415-864-6000;** Internet: www.sfsymphony.org), in Civic Center.

Dance

Classical and modern dance groups abound, the most recognized being the **San Francisco Ballet,** whose season runs from February to June. The troupe performs in the War Memorial Opera House, 301 Van Ness Ave., at Grove Street (☎ **415-865-2000;** Internet: www.sfballet.org).

Quick Concierge

AAA:
The office at 150 Van Ness Ave. in the Civic Center provides maps and other information to members. Call ☎ 415-565-2012 for information.

American Express:
City locations include 560 California St., between Montgomery and Kearny streets (☎ 415-536-2686), and 455 Market St., at First Street (☎ 415-536-2600).

Baby-Sitters:
Call **A Bay Area Child Care Agency** (☎ 415-991-7474).

Emergencies:
For police, fire, or other emergencies, phone **911.** From cell phones, call ☎ 415-553-8090.

Hospitals:
Saint Francis Memorial Hospital, 900 Hyde St., between Bush and Pine streets (☎ 415-353-6000), offers 24-hour emergency-care service. The hospital's physician-referral service number is ☎ 415-353-6566.

San Francisco General Hospital, 1001 Potrero Ave. (☎ 415-206-8111), accepts uninsured emergency patients, but the wait can be brutally long and uncomfortable. The patient assistance number is ☎ 415-206-5166.

Internet Centers: Cafe.com is closest to Union Square at 970 Market St., near 5th and 6th streets (☎ 415-922-5322); open Monday through Saturday from 8 a.m. to 10 p.m.

Newspapers & Magazines:
The *San Francisco Chronicle* is the major daily. The Sunday Datebook section lists goings-on about town. The weekly *Bay Guardian,* free at sidewalk kiosks and in bookstores, bars, and coffeehouses, is an excellent source for entertainment listings.

Police:
Dial **911** in an emergency. For non-emergencies, call ☎ 415-553-0123.

Post Office:
The Rincon Center houses a post office at 180 Steuart St., in the Embarcadero. Call ☎ 800-ASK-USPS or log onto www.usps. gov to find the branch nearest you.

Taxes: Sales tax is 8.5%. Hotel tax is 14%.

Taxis:
Yellow Cab
(☎ 415-626-2345);
Veteran's Cab
(☎ 415-552-1300);
Desoto Cab
(☎ 415-673-1414);
Luxor Cabs
(☎ 415-282-4141).

Transit Info:
☎ 415-817-1717.

Weather:
For forecasts, go online to www. wunderground.com/US/CA/ San_Francisco.html.

Gathering More Information

The San Francisco Convention & Visitors Bureau Information Center is on the lower level of Hallidie Plaza, 900 Market St., at Powell Street (☎ **800-220-5747** or 415-391-2000). It's open Monday through Friday from 9 a.m. to 5:30 p.m., Saturday from 9 a.m. to 3 p.m., Sunday from 10 a.m. to 2 p.m.

Closer to Fisherman's Wharf is the Visitors Information Center of the Redwood Empire Association on the second floor of the Cannery, 2801 Leavenworth (☎ **800-200-8334** or 415-543-8334). The center stays open Monday through Saturday from 10 a.m. to 6 p.m.

You'll find the city's official Web site at www.sfvisitor.org. For up-to-date information on the city and surrounding areas, try Citysearch at www.bayarea.citysearch.com; the *San Francisco Chronicle* Web site at www.sfgate.com; or the *San Francisco Bay Guardian* site at www. sfbg.com.

Chapter 9 written by Paula Tevis

Chapter 10

The Napa Valley Wine Country

*J*ust an hour's drive north of San Francisco is the gorgeous Napa Valley, America's most celebrated wine-growing region. Less than 30 miles from end to end, this super-fertile area brims with world-class wine-tasting rooms, excellent restaurants, and marvelous resorts and country inns.

If I had to pick my favorite place in all of California, the Napa Valley would be it. The stresses and strains of regular life just fade away as you cruise gentle Highway 29, the verdant valley's main thoroughfare, stopping in at wineries, pausing between tastings for a gourmet picnic, a hot-air balloon ride, or a bit of boutique shopping. Visiting the Napa Valley is like taking a trip to the south of France, without the jet lag or the language barrier.

You're not a wine connoisseur, you say, and all this sounds just a tad intimidating? (Not to mention a bit expensive.) Don't turn to another chapter just yet. Sure, the valley does hold some pretentious wine-tasting rooms and five-star restaurants geared to know-it-alls with deep pockets. In general, however, Napa Valley is surprisingly visitor-friendly and down-right welcoming to casual wine drinkers. First-time visitors will feel right at home. And, although Napa may not be the bargain destination of your vacation, affordable places to stay, eat, and drink abound.

What's that? You say you've heard that Napa is crowded, commercialized, and that the neighboring Sonoma Valley is a better bet? Plenty of prickly pretentious types will tell you just that — and they're dead wrong. The quieter, less tourist-oriented Sonoma is indeed lovely — and equal to Napa as a wine-growing region — but Napa is *the* Wine Country destination for first-timers. Napa is more beautiful, has more wineries and other attractions, and is easier to explore. Believe me, Napa will more than occupy your time; I've been visiting annually for more than 10 years now, and Napa still contains hundreds of things that I have yet to see and do. Leave Sonoma for a later trip.

Timing Your Visit

Summer and autumn are the most popular seasons for touring the Napa Valley. The valley is especially gorgeous in fall, and September and October bustle during the grape harvest, or *crush,* which fills the air with the sweet fragrance of *must* (the pulp and skins of crushed grapes). If you plan to visit during these seasons, make reservations early.

As long as the weather is dry, Napa's a treat during the winter and spring, when the roads, restaurants, and tasting rooms are relatively unclogged, and you can more easily book hotels. With the vines stripped of their heavy fruit, the valley's not quite so beautiful, however, and touring can be a downright drag in the rain.

Weekends are always more crowded than weekdays, and the traffic heading north on the Golden Gate Bridge from San Francisco on Friday afternoons (and south on Sunday afternoons) can be murder. Do what you can to plan your visit midweek, while the weekenders are at work; not only will you avoid the crowds and enjoy your stay more, but you're bound to save a few bucks on accommodations.

Although you can easily entertain yourself for a week here, three days and two nights can provide an ideal introduction to the Wine Country. That gives you plenty of time to start with a winery tour, spread out your winery visits over the next couple of days, and work in some other local pleasures — a hot-air balloon ride, perhaps, or some leisurely bicycling or a spa treatment.

A single day simply can't do the area justice and will leave you wanting more. But if you can only spare a day out of your San Francisco time, come anyway. Start out from the city early, because virtually all of the wine-tasting rooms shut their doors by 5 p.m. Plan to visit no more than three to four wineries (all anyone can really handle in a day, anyway), followed by an early dinner before you head back to the city. Drive immediately to Calistoga, at the north end, and work your way down the valley along Highway 29 to make your return to San Francisco a bit shorter.

Don't make this day trip on a summer weekend, as the bumper-to-bumper traffic on Highway 29 will ruin it.

Getting There

Really, only one way exists to arrive in the Napa Valley: by car.

Driving yourself

From San Francisco, two roads will take you to Napa Valley:

✔ If you decide to take *the San Francisco-Oakland Bay Bridge,* head east from downtown over the bridge (I-80) and north to the Napa/Highway 29 exit near Vallejo; follow Highway 29 north into the heart of the valley. The trip takes about 70 minutes.

✔ From the *Golden Gate Bridge,* continue on U.S. 101 north to Novato, where you'll pick up Highway 37 east. Take Highway 121 (the Sonoma Highway) north toward Sonoma and then east to Napa, where you'll end up on Highway 29. Make sure to have a map handy. This drive is more scenic but takes about 90 minutes.

If you're coming from the North Coast, take Highway 128 out of Mendocino, and follow the road straight into the north end of the valley, which will take a little more than 2 hours.

From Lake Tahoe, pick up I-80 west and take it to Highway 12, which will lead you in about six miles to Highway 29 north, Napa's main drag. Expect the drive to take about 3 ½ hours, whether you're coming from the north or south shore.

Along for the ride — Guided tours

If you don't want to drive yourself to or around the Wine Country, you can join an organized tour. Taking a tour is a good alternative if you don't feel comfortable driving; otherwise, I strongly suggest the do-it-yourself option. On a tour, you'll cover a lot of ground in way too short a time, you won't have time to linger in places that catch your fancy, you won't have much of a choice as to where you eat, and you'll miss some great wineries that aren't part of the package.

The best tour operator is Great Pacific Tour Company (☎ **415-626-4499**), which will pick you up and deliver you back to your San Francisco hotel after tastings at two Sonoma wineries, a picnic lunch, and a tour of **Domaine Chandon,** a sparkling wine producer in Napa. The cost is $66 adults, $64 seniors, and $56 for kids 5 to 11.

Another option is to ride the **Napa Valley Wine Train** (☎ **800-427-4124** or 707-253-2111; www.winetrain.com), basically a gourmet restaurant on wheels that chugs 36 miles through the valley from end to end. Lunch, brunch, and dinner tours range in price from $29.50 to $99 per person. This is a dining and take-in-the-scenery tour only; only the **Grgich Hills Private Winery Tour and Tasting,** a lunchtime ride ($75 per person), includes a stop. The train sports a wine-tasting car with an attractive bar and knowledgeable host. You can purchase and taste wine without worrying about driving safely back to the station. The three-hour tours depart from 1275 McKinstry St. in downtown Napa, at the south end of the valley. Reservations are essential. If you don't want to drive to Napa to pick up the train, Grayline (☎ **800-826-0202;** www.graylinesanfrancisco.com) will transfer you by bus from San Francisco to the wine train station for the 3-hour lunch excursion; the total cost is $99 per person.

Getting Your Bearings

The Napa Valley is compact and very easy to explore. The town of Napa at the south end is just 28 miles from Calistoga at the north end. Take a look at a map of the valley, and you'll see that it resembles a ladder, with two main roads running (roughly) north-south — Highway 29, the main drag, along the west side and the Silverado Trail along the east side — and east-west cross streets at regular intervals, every half-mile or so. The valley is more commercial and developed at the south end, growing increasingly bucolic and spread out as you move north.

At the south end is the town of Napa, the commercial center of the Wine Country and the gateway to Napa Valley. This is where the real people live — hence the fast-food joints and discount superstores. Stop by the visitor center (see "Gathering More Information" at the end of this chapter) if you want to pick up a winery map, but head north from there; you'll hit the Wine Country vibe you're looking for in a matter of minutes.

Just north of Napa is Yountville. Both St. Helena and Calistoga boast more genuine old-fashioned charm, but Yountville wins in the convenience department. Good restaurants abound, and you can't be more centrally located.

Immediately north of Yountville is Oakville, then Rutherford, two blink-and-you'll-miss-'em towns that really just qualify as map markers. Next is St. Helena, about 18 miles north of Napa, a quiet, attractive little town with upscale shops tucked away in beautifully restored wooden storefronts.

Around St. Helena, the terrain starts to open up and look like the agricultural landscape it is. In another 10 miles, you'll reach Calistoga, California's version of Saratoga Springs, the east coast's favorite spa town (the name "Calistoga" is a cross of the two: *Cali*fornia and *Sara*toga). This well-preserved, super-charming gold-rush town boasts the natural hot springs that make the Wine Country a first-class spa destination, too. I highly recommend basing yourself here, because this is the Napa Valley at its absolute best. The down side is distance; Yountville is a good half-hour drive south, so you'll spend a bit more time in the car if you base yourself here. Because the driving is so gorgeous, it's easily worth it — but you should be aware of the distance, especially if your time is limited.

Be very careful while driving always-busy Highway 29. Even if you're a teetotaler, remember that virtually everybody else has imbibed a bit. This two-lane road serves as the scene of too many accidents, especially at night.

Napa Valley & The Wine Country

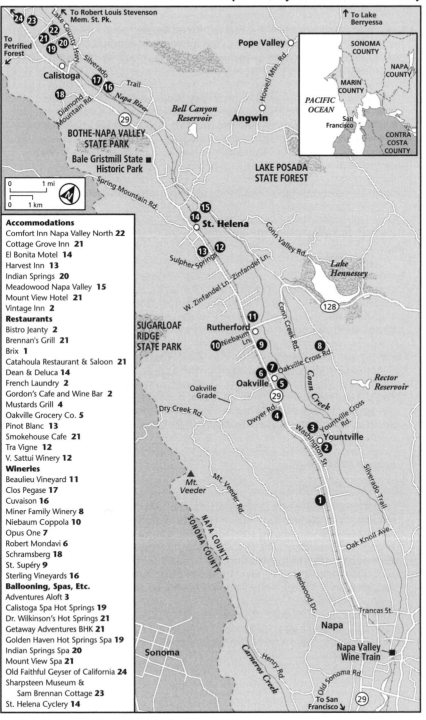

To Robert Louis Stevenson Mem. St. Pk.

To Petrified Forest

Calistoga

To Lake Berryessa

Pope Valley

SONOMA COUNTY

NAPA COUNTY

MARIN COUNTY

PACIFIC OCEAN

San Francisco

CONTRA COSTA COUNTY

Silverado Trail

Napa River

Diamond Mountain Rd.

Bell Canyon Reservoir

Angwin

Howell Mtn. Rd.

BOTHE-NAPA VALLEY STATE PARK

Bale Gristmill State Historic Park

LAKE POSADA STATE FOREST

Spring Mountain Rd.

0   1 mi
0   1 km

St. Helena

Conn Valley Rd.

Lake Hennessey

Sulpher Springs

W. Zinfandel Ln.   Zinfandel Ln.

128

SUGARLOAF RIDGE STATE PARK

Rutherford

Niebaum Ln.

Conn Creek Rd.

Rector Reservoir

Oakville Grade

Oakville Cross Rd.

Oakville

Conn Creek

Dry Creek Rd.

Dwyer Rd.

Yountville Cross Rd.

Washington St.

Yountville

Mt. Veeder

Mt. Veeder Rd.

NAPA COUNTY
SONOMA COUNTY

Silverado Trail

Oak Knoll Ave.

Redwood Dr.

Trancas St.

Napa

Sonoma

Carneros Creek

Henry Rd.

Old Sonoma Rd.

Napa Valley Wine Train

To San Francisco

29

Accommodations
Comfort Inn Napa Valley North **22**
Cottage Grove Inn **21**
El Bonita Motel **14**
Harvest Inn **13**
Indian Springs **20**
Meadowood Napa Valley **15**
Mount View Hotel **21**
Vintage Inn **2**

Restaurants
Bistro Jeanty **2**
Brennan's Grill **21**
Brix **1**
Catahoula Restaurant & Saloon **21**
Dean & Deluca **14**
French Laundry **2**
Gordon's Cafe and Wine Bar **2**
Mustards Grill **4**
Oakville Grocery Co. **5**
Pinot Blanc **13**
Smokehouse Cafe **21**
Tra Vigne **12**
V. Sattui Winery **12**

Wineries
Beaulieu Vineyard **11**
Clos Pegase **17**
Cuvaison **16**
Miner Family Winery **8**
Niebaum Coppola **10**
Opus One **7**
Robert Mondavi **6**
Schramsberg **18**
St. Supéry **9**
Sterling Vineyards **16**

Ballooning, Spas, Etc.
Adventures Aloft **3**
Calistoga Spa Hot Springs **19**
Dr. Wilkinson's Hot Springs **21**
Getaway Adventures BHK **21**
Golden Haven Hot Springs Spa **19**
Indian Springs Spa **20**
Mount View Spa **21**
Old Faithful Geyser of California **24**
Sharpsteen Museum &
   Sam Brennan Cottage **23**
St. Helena Cyclery **14**

Staying in Style

Despite a wealth of choices, high demand keeps room rates on the pricey side, and most lodgings have a two-night minimum on weekends. Make reservations as far in advance as possible, especially for stays between May and October.

If my favorites are full, call Napa Valley Reservations Unlimited (☎ **800-251-NAPA** or 707-252-1985), a free central reservations service. Or contact B&B Style (☎ **800-995-8884** or 707-942-2888; www.bbstyle. com), which places an emphasis on smaller, more intimate choices. You can find other credible Napa Valley reservations bureaus online at www.napavalleyonline.com.

Count on 12 percent in taxes being tacked on to your hotel bill.

Comfort Inn Napa Valley North

$–$$ Calistoga

Situated on neatly manicured grounds just east of Calistoga town, this clean, well-kept motel offers great value in an expensive neighborhood. The chain-standard rooms are boosted up a notch by big new TVs, coffeemakers, and hair dryers, as well as on-property extras including a hot natural mineral pool and whirlpool. Nice!

1865 Lincoln Ave. (west of Silverado Trail), Calistoga. ☎ *707-942-9400. Fax: 707-942-5262. Internet:* www.comfortinn.com *or* www.travelbase. com/destinations/calistoga/comfort-napa. *Parking: Free! Rack rates: $60–$152 double. Rates include continental breakfast. AE, DC, MC, V. Deals: Discounts for seniors and AAA members; also check the Web site for Internet-only discounts. Guests get 10 percent off spa services at a nearby spa.*

Cottage Grove Inn

$$$–$$$$ Calistoga

These two picture-perfect rows of cozy cottages are strictly for couples, preferably the cooing kind. Each is beautifully furnished and features a deep, two-person, Jacuzzi tub, fireplace, vaulted ceilings, a sitting area (perfect for cuddling), VCR, CD player, minifridge, coffeemaker, and a supremely comfy bed. The themes — Audubon, Library, Fly Fishing — add color without being overbearing, and service is friendly without being intrusive. You can easily walk to some terrific restaurants and spas.

1711 Lincoln Ave., Calistoga. ☎ *800-799-2284 or 707-942-8400. Fax: 707-942-2653. Internet:* www.cottagegrove.com. *Parking: Free! Rack rates: $195–$275 double. Rates include continental breakfast, bottle of wine, and afternoon wine and cheese. DC, MC, V.*

El Bonita Motel

$$–$$$ St. Helena

This very cute Depression-era motel sits a bit too close to Highway 29, but the 2 ½ acres of gardens out back — complete with pool, Jacuzzi, and sauna — and low rates make it a very good value, especially for families, who can really make themselves at home in the suites. The smallish rooms are immaculate and well-furnished, with microwaves, minifridges, and coffeemakers. A bargain for everybody — and you can't beat the central location.

195 Main St. (on Hwy. 29, at El Bonita Ave.), St. Helena. ☎ *800-541-3284 or 707-963-3216. Fax: 707-963-8838. Internet:* www.elbonita.com. *Parking: Free! Rack rates: $119–$199 double, $169–$249 1- or 2-bedroom suite. Rates include continental breakfast. AE, DC, DISC, MC, V.*

Harvest Inn

$$$–$$$$ St. Helena

This Tudor-style inn doesn't have quite as much personality as I'd like, and service is a bit too impersonal, but the rooms are attractive, comfortable, and roomy enough for a family. Two pools and two Jacuzzis are set in lovely gardens against a dramatic mountain backdrop. A $2-million renovation in 1999 brought lots of little luxuries into the rooms, including feather beds, CD players, and VCRs. The mid-valley location is central to everything.

1 Main St., St. Helena. ☎ *800-950-8466 or 707-963-9463. Fax: 707-963-4402. Internet:* www.coastalhotel.com. *Parking: Free! Rack rates: $149–$319 double, $399–$649 suite. Rates include continental breakfast. Deals: Check Web site for packages. AE, DC, DISC, MC, V.*

Indian Springs

$$$ Calistoga

Booking these comfortable, old-fashioned bungalows in summer is not easy; you'll have to edge out the families that come here year after year, drawn by the excellent location and great value. (Hint: Call 48 hours ahead and see if you can get in on a cancellation.) Guests can use the Olympic-size mineral pool until late in the evening (day visitors have to leave by 6 p.m.). The spa offers a full range of treatments.

1712 Lincoln Ave., Calistoga. ☎ *707-942-4913. Fax: 707-942-4919. Internet:* www.indianspringscalistoga.com. *Parking: Free! Rack rates: $175–$360 double studio or 1-bedroom, $450–$500 3-bedroom. Deals: Check Web site for room and spa specials. MC, V.*

Meadowood Napa Valley

$$$$$ **St. Helena**

If you really want to splurge, stay at this sprawling Relais & Chateaux resort. Each individual accommodation is nestled among the oaks on the 250 wooded acres, which boast two pools, tennis courts, world-class golf, and more than a few deer. Rooms are supremely luxurious, but in a kick-off-your-shoes way — you'll find no fussiness here. Service is stellar, of course, and the amenities list is as long as your arm. The icing on the cake? The restaurant is one of the finest fine-dining rooms in the valley.

900 Meadowood Lane (off Silverado Trail), St. Helena. ☎ *800-458-8080 or 707-963-3646. Fax: 707-963-3532. Internet:* www.meadowood.com. *Parking: Free! Rack rates: $335–$700 double, $540–$3,030 suite. Deals: Ask about packages and other promotional deals. AE, DISC, DC, MC, V.*

Mount View Hotel

$$$ **Calistoga**

Ideally situated in the heart of Calistoga, this charming and attractively restored historic hotel is a pleasing place to stay. Done in a cozy California-country style, the rooms are comfortable and well-appointed. The secluded cottages, which have private patios with Jacuzzis, are worth the splurge for romance-seeking couples. A pool and Jacuzzi in the cute courtyard, a well-regarded spa, and one of the valley's favorite restaurants, Catahoula, round out the appeal.

1457 Lincoln Ave., Calistoga. ☎ *800-816-6877 or 707-942-6877. Fax: 707-942-6904. Internet:* www.mountviewhotel.com. *Parking: Free! Rack rates: $130–$250 double, suite, or cottage. Rates include continental breakfast (delivered to your room). AE, DISC, MC, V.*

Vintage Inn

$$$–$$$$ **Yountville**

This big, attractive French-country inn is conveniently situated at the southern end of the valley, near some terrific restaurants. Done in a light and airy style and clustered throughout the lovely flowering grounds, the pretty rooms are equipped with fireplaces, fridges, Jacuzzi tubs, coffeemakers, and terry-cloth robes. Tennis courts and a heated pool make this a comfortable mini-resort, good for couples exploring the area.

6541 Washington St., Yountville. ☎ *800-351-1133 or 707-944-1112. Fax: 707-944-1617. Internet:* www.vintageinn.com. *Parking: Free! Rack rates: $150–$350 double. Rates include continental champagne breakfast and afternoon tea. AE, CB, DC, DISC, MC, V.*

Dining Out

With excellent restaurants at every turn, the Napa Valley is a wonderful place to eat well. However, the best dining rooms often book up ahead, so reserve in advance. If you're visiting on a weekend, calling before you even leave home is a good idea.

Bistro Jeanty

$$$ Yountville   FRENCH

This very French bistro is much applauded around the Bay Area for its authenticity, great menu, and vivacious dining room. Eating here satisfies both the appetite and the spirit. The seasonal menu includes rustic dishes like lamb tongue and potato salad or rabbit and sweetbread ragout, plus typical bistro items including coq au vin and steak frites. Both adventuresome and timid eaters will find something to like here.

6510 Washington St., Yountville. ☎ 707-944-0103. Reservations recommended. Main courses: $12.50–$22.50. MC, V. Open: Lunch and dinner daily.

Brennan's Grill

$$$ Calistoga   CALIFORNIA-CONTINENTAL

Brennan's isn't exactly breaking any new culinary ground — and that's precisely why it's so popular. Expect well-prepared grilled hangar steak, seared day-boat scallops, and blue cheese-and-walnut-crusted filet mignon, all served in a lovely, lodge-style dining room with well-spaced tables draped in white linens and stylish arts-and-crafts accents. Brennan's is super-romantic after the sun goes down.

1374 Lincoln Ave., Calistoga. ☎ 707-942-2233. Reservations recommended. Main courses: $7–$18 at lunch, $14–$24 at dinner. AE, MC, V. Open: Lunch and dinner daily.

Brix

$$$$ Yountville/Rutherford   ASIAN FUSION

This airy, contemporary restaurant is one of my Napa Valley favorites, thanks to the bold Asian-inspired, French-accented cooking of Tod Michael Kawachi. His innovative cuisine is very similar to the nouveau island cooking known as Hawaii Regional Cuisine, and no wonder — Kawachi studied under Hawaii's master chef, Roy Yamaguchi. Look for such cross-pollinated successes as macadamia nut-crusted goat cheese on greens with chardonnay vinaigrette, and grilled quail with Thai basil sweet potatoes in a orange-ginger hoisin sauce. The patio seating is gorgeous in warm weather.

7377 St. Helena Hwy. (Hwy. 29), 1½ miles north of Yountville. ☎ 707-944-2749. Internet: www.brix.com. *Reservations recommended. Main courses: $9–$13.50 at lunch, $16–$25 at dinner. AE, DC, DISC, MC, V. Open: Lunch and dinner daily.*

Catahoula Restaurant & Saloon

$$$ Calistoga

You will detect a strong hint of New Orleans in the food and atmosphere of this fun and funky restaurant, both a critical and local favorite. If you didn't make reservations, dine at the bar in front of the wood-fired ovens, where you can watch in awe as busy chefs crank out plate after plate of seasonal Southern-accented dishes, such as an oven-roasted tomato pizza topped with andouille sausage and onion confit; spicy seafood paella with housemade chorizo; and cornmeal-fried catfish with lemon-jalapeño meuniére and Mardi Gras slaw. Excellent!

In the Mount View Hotel, 1457 Lincoln Ave., Calistoga. ☎ *707-942-2275. Internet:* www.catahoularest.com. *Reservations recommended. Main courses: $11–$20. MC, V. Open: Breakfast and lunch Sat–Sun (check for Fri daytime hours in summer), dinner nightly.*

French Laundry

$$$$$ Yountville FRENCH

Regarded as one of the finest chefs in the United States, Thomas Keller prepares superb multicourse meals for a lucky crowd in his intimate, elegant, universally celebrated restaurant. If you're serious about food, book a table well in advance, and arrive hungry — you won't want to miss a beat. The French Laundry experience is sublime on every front.

6640 Washington St. (at Creek St.), Yountville. ☎ *707-944-2380. Internet:* www.sterba.com/yountville/frenchlaundry. *Reservations required. Prix-fixe meals: $70–$80; chef's tasting menu $95. AE, MC, V. Open: Lunch Fri–Sun, dinner nightly.*

Gordon's Cafe and Wine Bar

$–$$ Yountville CREATIVE AMERICAN

Chef-owner Sally Gordon's delicious food is served in a warm atmosphere reminiscent of a general store. Besides comfort-food favorites at breakfast and creative sandwiches at lunch, Gordon's serves a three-course prix-fixe dinner on Friday nights, making the cafe a prime destination for food lovers. The shop is well-known for its meticulous selection of fine wines and gourmet condiments, including more kinds of olive oil than you ever imagined existed.

6770 Washington St., Yountville. ☎ *707-944-8246. Reservations essential at dinner. Main courses: $3.50–$8 at breakfast and lunch; $32 prix-fixe dinner. AE, MC, V. Open: Breakfast and lunch daily; dinner Fridays only.*

Mustards Grill

$$ Yountville CALIFORNIA

The California version of a classic pub, this Napa Valley institution is always filled to overflowing with a festive, food-conscious crowd, drawn in by the lengthy menu of delicious American dishes that are always well-prepared but never too challenging. You won't have room for dessert, but loosen your belt and give it a go anyway — you won't be disappointed.

7399 St. Helena Hwy. (Hwy. 29), Yountville. ☎ *707-944-2424. Reservations recommended. Main courses: $11–$17. CB, DC, DISC, MC, V. Open: Lunch and dinner daily.*

Pinot Blanc

$$$$ St. Helena FRENCH

All butter-yellow walls and rich upholstery fabrics, this gorgeous country-French dining room has to be Napa's loveliest. It's also my favorite of famed L.A. chef Joachim Splichal's mini-chain of Pinot bistros. Look for innovative twists on rustic French classics like perfectly seared foie gras with melted apricots and honeysuckle jus, and steak frites with Pernod butter. If the figs with goat cheese and pancetta-wrapped arugula are on the menu, don't skip it.

641 Main St. (Hwy. 29), St. Helena. ☎ *707-963-6191. Internet:* www.patinagroup. com. *Reservations recommended. Main courses: $9–$22 at lunch, $14.50–$25 at dinner. AE, DC, DISC, JCB, MC, V. Open: Lunch and dinner daily.*

Smokehouse Cafe

$–$$ Calistoga BBQ

Sick and tired of fancy Wine Country food? Hankering for some good, old-fashioned American grub? Then head to this simple, wood-hewn diner, which serves up some of the best barbecue west of the Mississippi and north of the Mason-Dixon line. Expect hearty crawfish cakes, Louisiana hot links, Texas beef brisket, and ribs — hickory-smoked pork or mesquite-smoked baby-backs, your choice. This place serves up giant portions, friendly service, and cornbread to die for, natch.

In the Calistoga Train Depot, 1458 Lincoln Ave., Calistoga. ☎ *707-942-6060. Main courses and full BBQ plates: $5–$8 at breakfast, $6.50–$19.50 at lunch and dinner. MC, V. Open: Breakfast, lunch, and dinner daily.*

Tra Vigne

$$$ St. Helena ITALIAN

This is an elegant, but not stuffy, place for a Northern Italian meal. The homemade mozzarella and house-pressed olive oil alone (recently celebrated in no less than *Gourmet* magazine) make a visit worthwhile. Come for lunch on the courtyard patio, and you'll feel as if you've stepped into

Tuscany. The restaurant also features a delicatessen, the **Cantinetta,** where you can purchase reasonably priced pizza, wine, and prepared foods to eat here or down the road at a winery.

1050 Charter Oak Ave., St. Helena. ☎ 707-963-4444. Reservations recommended. Main courses: $12.50–$19. CB, DC, DISC, MC, V. Open: Lunch and dinner daily.

Touring the Wine Country

The Napa Valley is home to more than 220 wineries, some owned by corporations, and others the domain of individuals so seduced by the grape that they abandoned successful careers to devote themselves to viticulture. While no correlation exists between the size of a winery and the quality of the product — which has more to do with the talents of the vintners and variables such as weather and soil conditions — the bigger wineries offer more to visitors in terms of education and entertainment.

If you don't know anything about wine — or you know what you like but want to learn more about the growing, blending, and bottling processes — the first winery you visit should be one that offers an in-depth tour, so you can familiarize yourself with the winemaking process. **Robert Mondavi** offers an excellent introductory tour, as does **St. Supéry.** Book the superb tour offered by **Schramsbuerg** if you're interested in the production of sparkling wine (a.k.a. champagne; only the French winemakers from the Champagne region fundamentally have the right to call it that).

Don't expect a deal on wine purchased directly from the producers. Wineries sell at full retail so as not to undercut their primary market, wine merchants. Only buy and carry what you think you can't get at home. If you're concerned that you won't be able to locate a particular vintage at home, most wineries will mail order. If you live outside of California, see the sidebar "Bureaucracy in a bottle: Shipping your wine purchases home" later in this chapter.

How to tell a Cabernet from a Pinot Noir

The most prominent varieties of grapes produced in the area include Cabernet Sauvignon, Pinot Noir, and Zinfandel grapes grown for red wines, and Chardonnay and Sauvignon or Fume Blanc grapes grown for white wines.

Of course, the best way to really tell a Cab from a Pinot is to read the label on the bottle. The label identifies the type of grape used if the wine contains at least 75 percent of that particular variety. The appellation of origin indicates where the grapes were grown — either a viticulture area such as the Carneros region of the Napa Valley, a county, or the state itself. The vintage date is important as it explains when at least 95 percent of the grapes were crushed. Because many wines taste better as they get older, and some years produce better grapes than others, you'll want to make a note of the vintage.

You can greatly enhance your knowledge of wine by tasting correctly — and what better classroom than a French-style chateau smack in the middle of a vineyard? Remember that wine appreciation begins by analyzing color, followed by aroma, then taste. You do this with your eyes first, then your nose, then your mouth. Don't be shy about asking questions of the person pouring — he or she will happily answer your questions because the more you learn about his or her product, the more likely you are to become a steady customer. And that makes everybody happy!

Here are a few wine-tasting do's and don'ts:

- ✔ Before the pour, sniff your glass. It should have a clean aroma. If not, ask for a fresh glass.

- ✔ Never pour the wine yourself.

- ✔ Taste wines in the proper order: whites first, reds second, dessert wines last. This reflects the order in which food is generally served — white wines with a first course, reds with a hearty main course, and dessert wines with dessert.

- ✔ Swirl the wine to coat the inside of the glass. This introduces more oxygen and helps open up the wine flavors and aromas.

- ✔ Smell the wine. Think about what the different aromas bring to mind — spice, fruit, flowers, and so forth.

- ✔ Take a sip and coat the back of your tongue with the wine.

- ✔ Along with baseball, wine tasting is one of the few sports where spitting is not only allowed, it's encouraged. Just make sure you hit the target — a bucket or some other container will be available for this purpose. Spitting is a nifty way to sample many wines without becoming fuzzy-headed.

- ✔ Don't mistake a tasting room for your friendly neighborhood bar — this is not the time to swill with drunken abandon. And lose the chewing gum.

If you really want to get into this wine thing, pick up a copy of *Wine For Dummies* by Mary Ewing Mulligan and Ed McCarthy, published by IDG Books Worldwide, Inc.

The best wineries for first-time visitors

The Napa Valley is home to more than 220 wineries, so the handful discussed here represent only the tip of the iceberg. But the valley contains plenty of other worthwhile wineries, so get a winery map (they're easily available throughout the region) and explore those back roads — let your adventurous spirit rule the day.

Wine-tasting rooms charge no admission fees, and the tours are usually (but not always) free. Be aware, however, that most wineries charge a fee for tasting, usually minimal and deducted from any purchases you make. In the listings below, we've noted current wine-tasting fees and touring policies; keep in mind that wineries can — and do — change their minds. In any case, the tasting fee should always be clearly posted at the tasting counter; if you're not sure, ask.

Beaulieu Vineyard

The vintners at this well-regarded establishment, founded in 1900 and Napa's third-oldest winery, aim to set visitors at ease the moment they walk through the door by passing out glasses of Chardonnay. After you relax, take the free half-hour tour through the production facility, given daily from 11 a.m. to 4 p.m. Each tasting thereafter is $5, or $18 for five delicious reserve vintages; be ready to shell out if you want to take home one of these special bottles. Don't be frightened away, however: A number of award-winning regular labels sell for less than $20 a pop.

1960 St. Helena Hwy. (Hwy. 29, just north of Rutherford Cross Rd.), Rutherford. ☎ *707-967-5230. Internet:* www.bv-wine.com. *Open: Daily 10 a.m.–5 p.m.*

Clos Pegase

Attention, architecture buffs: Even if you're not interested in the free 30-minute tour (given daily at 11 a.m. and 2 p.m.; no reservations needed), come to see the house. This stunning Michael Graves-designed winery is a temple to modern winemaking. It's plenty easy to while away a happy hour or more here studying the terrific art collection, walking around the sculpture garden, and picnicking on the vast lawn (you must reserve a picnic table). Wine tasting is $2.50 for current releases, and $5 more to taste three reserve wines. Bottles don't come cheap here, but this is a good place to pick up something special.

1060 Dunaweal Lane (west of Silverado Trail), Calistoga. ☎ *707-942-4981. Internet:* www.clospegase.com. *Open: Daily 10:30 a.m.–5 p.m.*

Cuvaison

Headquartered in a wonderful Mission-style house, this intimate, excellent winery is a great place to taste and learn. Winemaker John Thatcher has crafted world-renowned Chardonnay — refreshing, not over-oaked — as well as superb Merlot, Pinot Noir, and Cab. The tasting room is one of the most hospitable in the valley; tastings are $4, and you even get to keep your logo glass as a souvenir. A free tour will take you into the state-of-the-art wine cave daily at 10:30 a.m. Bring home a bottle of the rich, ruby Eris Pinot Noir if it's in stock — you won't find this memorable vino in your local wine shop. Picnic tables are here for your use.

4550 Silverado Trail (just south of Dunaweal Lane), Calistoga. ☎ *707-942-6266. Internet:* www.cuvaison.com. *Open: 10 a.m.–5 p.m.*

Miner Family Winery

This warm, attractive modern winery is a great bet for those who prefer an easygoing vibe and well-priced wines. Virtually all wines are in the $12 to $20 range, and I walked out with excellent $6 bargain bottles on my last visit. The tasting fee is $5, which is reimbursed if you buy two or more bottles. Expect big, oaky reds, and look out for the excellent smoky Viognier, available only here. A couple of cute umbrella-covered picnic tables are available for your use.

7850 Silverado Trail (just north of Oakville Cross Rd.), Oakville. ☎ **707-944-9500.** *Internet:* www.minerwines.com. *Open: Daily 11 a.m.–5 p.m.*

Niebaum Coppola

I've found the staff here to be a tad pretentious, but this impressive estate is still well worth visiting. Its neo-Medieval grandeur is marvelous — straight out of *Falcon Crest.* A museum traces the history of the winery, the former Inglenook Vineyards, and its world-famous current owner, filmmaker Francis Ford Coppola, while the second floor houses Coppola-related movie memorabilia, including the surfboard used in *Apocalypse Now.* The wines are sophisticated, yet most bottles are surprisingly well-priced. Regular tastings are $7.50, and you can keep the glass.

If you want to take the 1½-hour historical tour (at $20 a pop), which ends with a formal sit-down tasting in one of the wine cellars, make reservations two weeks in advance for either a 10:30 a.m. or 2:30 p.m. slot. Sorry, no picnic facilities (a shame on these fabulous grounds).

1991 St. Helena Hwy. (Hwy. 29, at Rutherford Cross Rd.), Rutherford. ☎ **707-968-1100** *or 707-968-1161. Internet:* www.niebaum-coppola.com. *Open: Daily 10 a.m.–5 p.m.*

Opus One

Don't expect a warm and fuzzy welcome at pretentious Opus One, the brainchild of Robert Mondavi and Baroness Phillipine de Rothschild. This imposing facility — the Caesar's Palace of the Napa Valley — is dedicated to the production of one, and only one, wine: Opus One, a dry-as-a-bone, mostly Cab blend that goes for a whopping $120 a bottle. The $25 tasting fee (for 4 oz.) is well worth it for wine buffs who want to see what all the fuss is about. If the name means little to you or you're in search of real bottles to buy, you can better spend your money elsewhere.

Free one-hour tours are offered daily at 10:30 a.m. by appointment only (book well in advance).

7900 St. Helena Hwy. (Hwy. 29, at Oakville Cross Rd.), Oakville. ☎ **707-944-9442.** *Internet:* www.opusonewinery.com. *Open: Daily 10:30 a.m.–3:30 p.m.*

Robert Mondavi

You'll recognize this grand Mission-style winery from the labels on Mondavi's popular wines. It's a bit corporate, but excellent for novices. The first to conduct public tastings, Mondavi continues its dedication to wine education.

A top-notch 1½-hour winery and vineyard tour — the best in the valley for first-timers — is offered daily throughout the day. The fee is $10, and I highly recommend making advance reservations. More in-depth seminars on wine-growing, wine and food, and other subjects are offered for fees ranging from $10 to $65 (reservations required). Call or visit the Web site for a complete schedule of tours and special events.

7801 St. Helena Hwy. (Hwy. 29, just north of Oakville Cross Rd.), Oakville. ☎ *888-RMONDAVI or 707-226-1395. Internet:* www.robertmondavi.com. *Open: Daily 9:30 a.m.–5 p.m.*

Schramsberg

You can't just stop by this elegant and completely unpretentious 200-acre champagne estate — but advance booking one of the by-appointment-only tours, offered daily from 10 a.m. to 2:30 p.m., is well worth the trouble. Schramsberg is the best sparkling-wine producer in the United States, and the free 1 ½-hour tour (followed by a $7.50 tasting) is the country's best champagne tour. You'll explore caves that were hand-dug a hundred years ago and learn the whole bottling process, which has hardly changed a whit since then. Follow the tour with a walk through the impeccable gardens. Book at least a week in advance on weekends.

1400 Schramsberg Rd. (turn off Hwy. 29 at Peterson Dr.), Calistoga. ☎ *707-942-2414. Internet:* www.schramsberg.com. *Open: Daily 10 a.m.–4 p.m.*

St. Supéry

If you want an excellent introductory tour that's a little more intimate than the one offered by Mondavi, come to this friendly, first-class winery. Everybody makes a big deal about "SmellaVision," which teaches you about aromas common to certain varietals, but the real highlights are in the demonstration vineyard, where you'll learn about growing techniques up close (I even got to taste grapes right off the vine!), and get an excellent lesson in tasting at the end of the one-hour tour. Tours are free, but you'll have to buy a $5 lifetime tasting card. Reserve tastings are in the "Divine Wine" room, where $10 will get you half glasses of the really good stuff (the Meritages are well worth the price).

8440 St. Helena Hwy. (between Oakville and Rutherford Cross rds.), Rutherford. ☎ *800-942-0809 or 707-963-4507. Internet:* www.stsupery.com. *Open: Daily 9:30 a.m.–6 p.m. (to 5 p.m. Nov–Apr).*

Sterling Vineyards

An aerial tram transports you to this whitewashed Mediterranean-style hilltop mega-winery, currently owned by the Seagram Company. After you land, a self-guided tour takes you through the entire operation and into the tasting room, where the helpful staff serves up tastings. A bit too corporate, but the spectacular views alone are worth the $6 ticket price (which includes the tasting). Plan on spending at least an hour here.

1111 Dunaweal Lane (a half-mile east of Hwy. 29), Calistoga. ☎ *707-942-3344. Internet:* www.sterlingvineyards.com. *Open: Daily 10:30 a.m.–4:30 p.m.*

Bureaucracy in a bottle: Shipping your wine purchases home

Having a winery ship a few bottles directly to your home should be no problem, right? Wrong. Due to absurd and constantly fluctuating "reciprocity laws" — designed to prevent you from easily buying direct from the manufacturer in order to protect the middleman (the nation's wine distributors) — varying state regulations in each of the 50 states limit wine shipping across state lines.

What that means is this: Currently, California's wineries can only ship to private individuals within the Golden State and to about 20 other states. Wineries used to look the other way, but now that a few have been punished with severe fines, most will not ignore your state's laws. If you live in a nonreciprocal state, you'll have to figure out another way to get those precious bottles home.

Do your homework before you buy more wine than you can physically carry home. Be skeptical of any winery that tells you it can ship to nonreciprocal states — chances are good that you'll never get your wine. Although boxing your own wine and sending it to a nonreciprocal state is technically illegal, some shippers will do it for you. Not that we're recommending you do

this, of course, but you may want to carry your wine out of the Napa Valley and send it from a post office, UPS, or other shipping company in another area of California where the issue isn't such a hot potato. Feel free to ask for advice at the winery; they're usually very willing to help, because they want you to buy.

If you need to ship your — ahem — socks home from the valley, try Buffalo's Shipping Post, 2471 Solano Ave., Napa (exit at Lincoln off Hwy. 29; ☎ 707-226-7942); Aero Packing, 163 Camino Dorado, (off N. Kelly Rd.), just south of the town of Napa (☎ 707-255-8025); or Wrap-It Transit, in the Riverpark Shopping Center, 1325 W. Imola Ave., Napa (exit at Imola off Hwy. 29; ☎ 707-252-9367). Remember that no guarantees exist; companies have every right to change their policies at any time.

This direct-shipping issue is a super-controversial subject that is evolving all the time. If you want to learn what the current regulations are in your state before you leave home, point your Web browser to www.wineinstitute.org/shipwine and click on "State Control Authority Directory," or visit www.freethegrapes.org.

Picknicking and Other Cool Stuff to See and Do

Sure, the restaurant scene is great — but hardly a better place on the planet exists for picnicking than the Napa Valley. A number of fabulous gourmet grocers can supply the vittles, and many friendly wineries provide pastoral picnic grounds.

My favorite picnic supplier is the **Oakville Grocery Co.,** 7856 St. Helena Hwy. (Hwy. 29), at Oakville Cross Road (☎ **800-736-6602** or 707-944-8802; www.oakvillegrocery.com). Here you can put together your own gourmet picnic from the excellent bread selection, the deli counter (which runs from first-rate cold cuts to top-quality foie gras), and yummy pastry offerings.

A little less country store-ish is **Dean & Deluca,** 607 St. Helena Hwy. (Hwy. 29, north of Zinfandel Lane), St. Helena (☎ **707-967-9980;** www.deandeluca.com), the Big Apple's favorite gourmet grocer. Everything at this first-class mega-mart is beautifully displayed — and very pricey. Still, you'll get your money's worth.

Just across the street from Dean & Deluca is **V. Sattui Winery,** 1111 White Lane (at Hwy. 29), St. Helena (☎ **707-963-7774;** www.vsattui.com), whose mammoth tasting room also serves as a bountiful gourmet shop. If you buy here, you can also dine here on the justifiably popular picnic grounds.

After you put your picnic together, where should you go? In addition to **V. Sattui, Clos Pegase, Cuvaison, Oakville Ranch,** and **St. Supéry** are among the many wineries that offer pleasant picnic spots (remember to reserve a table ahead at Clos Pegase). You can also take your picnic to **Old Faithful,** where you can munch on your lunch while you enjoy the natural show.

Do not bring a bottle of wine from one winery to enjoy at another. If you're going to use a winery's picnic grounds, buy a bottle of wine inside first to enjoy during your alfresco meal.

Getting pampered in Calistoga

People have been taking to Calistoga's rejuvenating mud baths — a blend of ancient volcanic ash, imported peat, and naturally boiling mineral water, which simmers at a comfy 104°F — for more than 150 years. Calistoga's spas are generally friendly, rustic, comfortable places borne out of a therapeutic tradition — nothing like the marble-tiled glamfests that are most resort spas.

Treatments are relatively affordable. Expect to pay between $100 and $125 for a mud bath and 1-hour massage. You can reserve a tub, followed by a mineral shower and a massage or a facial, at:

✔ **Dr. Wilkinson's Hot Springs,** 1507 Lincoln Ave. (☎ 707-942-4102; www.drwilkinson.com), probably the most well-known of Calistoga's spas.

✔ **Mount View Spa,** 1457 Lincoln Ave. (☎ **800-772-8838** or 707-942-5789; www.mountviewspa.com), very nice but a tad pricier than most.

✔ **Golden Haven Hot Springs Spa,** 1713 Lake St. (☎ **707-942-6793;** www.goldenhaven.com), which boasts late hours and private mud-bath rooms for couples.

✔ **Calistoga Spa Hot Springs,** 1006 Washington St. (☎ **707-942-6269;** www.calistogaspa.com), whose mud bath/massage packages are a very good buy.

Check for Internet specials. And if mud just sounds icky to you, these spas all offer alternatives, such as salt baths and aromatherapy wraps.

Hot-air ballooning

Soaring over the vineyards under a colorful balloon, with just a few other souls sharing your basket, is a joy. **Bonaventura Balloon Company** (☎ **800-FLY-NAPA** or 707-944-2822; www.bonaventuraballoons.com) is one of Napa's most trusted hot-air balloon operators, with a range of packages available. Or call **Napa Valley Aloft/ Adventures Aloft** (☎ **800-944-4408** or 707-944-4408; www.nvaloft. com), whose early-morning lift-off includes a preflight snack and a postflight brunch with bubbly. At $175 to $225 per person (depending on the flight and extras you choose), however, you may want to keep those feet on the ground.

Two-wheeling it

If you want to join the many bicyclists you see pedaling down Napa's scenic roads, **St. Helena Cyclery,** 1156 Main St., St. Helena (☎ **707-963-7736**), will set you on the Silverado Trail for $7 per hour or $25 per day. **Getaway Adventures BHK** (Biking, Hiking, and Kayaking), 1117 Lincoln Ave., Calistoga (☎ **800-499-BIKE** or 707-942-0332), runs full-day bike trips with lunch and winery tours.

Seeing Old Faithful blow off steam

The **Old Faithful Geyser of California,** off of Hwy. 29 north of Calistoga at 1299 Tubbs Lane (☎ **707-942-6463;** www.oldfaithfulgeyser.com), is one of only three "old faithful" geysers in the world. The natural geyser has been blowing off steam at regular intervals for just about as long as anyone can remember. The 350°F water spews out to a height of about 60 feet every 30 to 40 minutes or so (depending on barometric pressure, the moon, tides, and tectonic stresses). The performance lasts about a minute, and you can watch the show as many times as you wish. Bring your picnic lunch; a few redwood tables offer a front-and-center view.

The natural geyser is a wonder, but what's really so great about Old Faithful is its old-time roadside attraction vibe. The stop includes a video show, a small geothermal exhibit hall, a snack bar, and a few odd-ball narcoleptic goats that suddenly fall asleep on occasion (see what I mean by roadside attraction?).

Admission is $6 for adults, $5 for seniors, $2 for children 6 to 12. Old Faithful is open daily from 9 a.m. to 6 p.m. (to 5 p.m. in winter).

Stepping back in time

Interested in learning how Calistoga and the rest of the Napa Valley got off the ground? The tale is fascinating, and the **Sharpsteen Museum & Sam Brennan Cottage,** 1311 Washington St. (2 blocks north of Lincoln Avenue), Calistoga (☎ 707-942-5911), tell the story well. The little museum is well-curated and easy to explore in a half-hour or so. The visionary behind the museum, Ben Sharpsteen, was an animator and director for Disney, so an out-of-place but interesting room details his personal and professional history.

Shopping

The valley is a shopper's delight. Outlet-a-holics have two stops to make: the 50-store Napa Premium Outlets, off Hwy. 29 at the First Street exit, Napa (☎ 707-226-9876); and its smaller sister complex, the 10-store St. Helena Premium Outlets, 2 miles north of downtown St. Helena on Hwy. 29 (☎ 707-963-7282). These are high-end outlets, so expect such big-name shops as Donna Karan, Coach, J. Crew, Tommy Hilfiger, Cole Haan, and more.

If you prefer one-of-a-kind boutiquing, you'll find a cute little stretch of shops along St. Helena Highway (Hwy. 29) in St. Helena. The Old West-style storefronts along Calistoga's Lincoln Avenue house a pleasing mix of local services and unusual boutiques.

Gathering More Information

Call the Napa Valley Conference and Visitors Bureau (NVCVB) at ☎ 707-226-7459, or go online to www.napavalley.com. After you arrive, stop by the NVCVB's office at 1310 Napa Town Center in downtown Napa, where you'll find helpful counselors on staff as well as a wealth of information; exit Hwy. 29 at First Street.

Chapter 11

Mendocino

*I*f you want a taste of California's wild and wonderful North Coast, Mendocino is the perfect place to get it. This secluded, artsy, and enchanting town is a West Coast version of a New England seashore village (it actually served as Cabot Cove, Maine, in *Murder, She Wrote*). Mendocino is magically situated atop craggy headlands that jut out into the Pacific, giving the town ruggedly gorgeous coastline on three sides. The spectacular setting — a world apart from the seaside landscape farther south, even near San Francisco — makes it an ideal spot for a bit of nature-inspired relaxation.

Hugely popular as a romantic getaway from the Bay Area, the town is dedicated to the laid-back, weekending life. You won't find a whole lot to do in Mendocino — and that suits weary travelers just fine. Couples come to stroll, shop, bike, hike, and generally take it slow. Families are welcome, though disaffected teens may not be happy campers among the high-falutin' galleries, and wallet-watching parents (or anybody on a tight budget, for that matter) may decry the overall high prices.

Mendocino also offers a good starting point for exploration of California's one-of-a-kind redwood country; see Chapter 10.

Timing Your Visit

Summer or early fall is the best time to come. Mendocino is lovely from May through mid-October. Don't expect warm, though: average highs run between 59 and 66°F, and lows can dip below 50°F even in August. Mornings are misty and generally give way to afternoon sun; fog prevails in July and August and sometimes early September. Dress warm, and in layers. Leave your bathing suit at home, because these waters are never warm enough for swimming. If you travel inland, up the Redwood Highway (see Chapter 10), expect temperatures to increase as much as 15 or 20 degrees.

Visit during the week to avoid the maximum-capacity crowds, highest room rates, and mandated two-night minimum stays.

The weather can be a crapshoot in winter (frankly, this far up the coast, it can be a crapshoot at any time of year). Still, it's not much colder on average — about 10 degrees across the board — and you'll save a bundle on accommodations. You'll also find yourself in prime whale-watching territory if you visit between mid-December and mid-April. Don't be surprised if you run into some rain, though.

How much time do you need? Two nights will do the trick. You may want to stop by just for one night, to sample the vibe on your way up to the Avenue of the Giants (see Chapter 10).

Getting There and Getting Around

Mendocino's seclusion is a big part of its charm — but also makes reaching it a big fat drag. The town is 155 miles from San Francisco, 95 miles from the north end of the Napa Valley. The problem is that no major highway runs to the town; you either have to battle the slow-going mountains, or the even slower-going coast, to get there.

✔ **From San Francisco:** The fastest route is to take U.S. 101 north to Cloverdale, then take Highway 128 west to Highway 1, then go north along the coast; the drive takes about 4 hours.

✔ **From the Napa Valley:** The valley's main highway, 129, meets up with Highway 128 in Calistoga, at the north end. Follow 128 west all the way to the coast, which takes 2 ½ to 3 hours.

Curvaceous Highway 128, which crosses the mountains, is a Dramamine route all the way from U.S. 101 to the coast, which is the bulk of the trip no matter what your starting point. If you have a sensitive tummy and would prefer to keep your nausea in check, take U.S. 101 to Willits, pick up Highway 20 west to the coast, and head south on Highway 1. This alternative route will add 45 minutes or an hour to your trip — and Highway 20 is no joy, either — but it's an appreciably smoother ride.

The most scenic drive from the Bay Area is to take the coastal route, Highway 1, all the way. The drive is stunning, but expect it to take 6 long, nausea-inducing hours.

After you've arrived in Mendocino, park your car and set out on foot. The town is entirely walkable and easy to get a handle on. Main Street runs perpendicular to Highway 1 along the oceanfront. Lansing is the main north-south street in town, meeting Main at the ocean. The rest of the town unfolds along a basic grid from there, no more than six blocks deep or wide.

Staying in Style

Most places require a two-night minimum stay on weekends. Count on 10 percent in taxes being tacked onto your hotel bill at checkout time.

Contact **Mendocino Coast Accommodations** (☎ **707-937-5033;** www.mendocinovacations.com), a free central reservations service, if my favorites are full.

If Mendo's high rates are too much for you, trek 10 miles up Highway 1 to Fort Bragg and the very nice, value-minded **Harbor Lite Lodge,** 120 N. Harbor Dr., Fort Bragg (☎ **800-643-2700** or 707-964-0221; www.harborlitelodge.com.), which boasts rustic appeal, a pleasing maritime vibe, and spacious rooms for $64 to $225 double. Ask for one away from the bridge to avoid traffic noise.

Alegria Oceanfront Inn & Cottages

$$$ Mendocino

This former sea captain's home is the only accommodation in town with direct beach access. Gorgeous ocean views, pretty gardens, and a lovely California contemporary interior set a relaxing coastal tone. Each room has a private entrance, a coffeemaker and fridge, TV, and either a fireplace or a woodburning stove. The copious redwood decks with Adirondack chairs offer views galore. Mendo marvelous!

44781 Main St. (west of Evergreen St.). ☎ 800-780-7905 or 707-937-5150. Internet: www.oceanfrontmagic.com. Parking: Free! Rack rates: $180–$210 double. Rates include full breakfast. Deals: Ask about off-season and midweek rates. DISC, MC, V.

Blackberry Inn

$$ Mendocino

If you can get past the hokey Old West theme, you'll have one of the best values on the coast. The motel is designed as a frontier town — the rooms have names like the Saloon, the Millinery, the Livery Stable, and so forth. Inside they're bright, pretty, spacious, and spotless; even the cheapest has a sitting area, a well-dressed king-size bed, and distant ocean views. Set on a bluff on the opposite side of Highway 1, it's a long walk or a two-minute drive into town. Resident deer contribute to the storybook vibe.

1865 Larkin Rd. (on the inland side of Hwy. 1). ☎ 800-950-7806 or 707-937-5281. Fax: 707-937-5281. Internet: www.innaccess.com/bbi. Parking: Free! Rack rates: $95–$145 double, $175 2-bedroom, 2-bath cottage. MC, V.

Mendocino Hotel & Garden Suites

$$–$$$ Mendocino

This 1878 hotel (a leftover from Mendocino's logging days) makes a pleasing choice in the heart of town, especially if you prefer the anonymity of hotel life over the sometimes stifling intimacy of a B&B. It evokes the gold rush spirit with a mix of antiques and reproductions, yet offers all the modern comforts. Rooms are spread throughout a two-block complex; each is distinct and boasts period appeal, and many have fireplaces or woodstoves. This hotel is not extra-special, but nice.

45080 Main St. (between Kasten and Lansing Sts.). ☎ *800-548-0513 or 707-937-0511. Internet:* www.mendocinohotel.com. *Parking: Free! Rack rates: $85 double with shared bath, $120–$205 double, $250–$275 suite. Rates include morning coffee. Deals: Ask about AAA and off-season discounts, and check Web site for packages. AE, MC, V.*

Reed Manor

$$$–$$$$ Mendocino

Sitting on a bluff just above town, this mansion-like home makes a luxurious romantic escape. A gorgeous, library-like lobby leads to a handful of large, impeccably decorated rooms, each with a fireplace, Jacuzzi tub, VCR, minifridge, coffeemaker, and a deck or patio. The home is somewhat formal in style, but not stiff. Ask for a top-floor room for the best ocean and village views. The town is a short walk away.

Palette Dr., just off Lansing St. ☎ *707-937-5446. Internet:* www.reedmanor.com. *Parking: Free! Rack rates: $175–$300, $450 suite. Rates include in-room continental breakfast. MC, V.*

Stanford Inn by the Sea

$$$$ Mendocino

This rustic-sophisticated lodge sits on extraordinary tiered grounds populated by llamas, horses, and other critters in a woodsy setting near the Big River, a 5-minute drive from town. The wood-paneled rooms are done in a supremely comfy California-country style and boast working fireplaces, fridges, and VCRs; the suites are great for families. The grounds feature a gorgeous greenhouse with a lap pool, sauna, and Jacuzzi; a gym; a good vegetarian restaurant; and canoes and mountain bikes for rent. It's one of the pet-friendliest hotels in California, too.

At Hwy. 1 and Comptche-Ukiah Rd. ☎ *800-331-8884 or 707-937-5615. Fax: 707-937-0305. Internet:* www.stanfordinn.com. *Parking: Free! Rack rates: $215–$275 double, $275–$640 1- or 2-bedroom suite. Rates include full breakfast, afternoon tea, and evening hors d'oeuvres. AE, CB, DC, DISC, MC, V.*

Whitegate Inn

$$$–$$$$ Mendocino

For romance in the heart of town, you can't beat this splendid Victorian B&B, whose caring owners have an impeccable eye for detail. The big, luxurious, antique-filled rooms feature enveloping featherbeds, gorgeous private baths, fireplaces, TV, and bucketloads of classic Victorian style. The inn boasts gracious public spaces and lovely gardens, too. This place is classic, elegant, and utterly marvelous.

499 Howard St. (at Ukiah St.). ☎ 800-531-7282 or 707-937-4892. Fax: 707-937-1131. Internet: www.whitegateinn.com. *Parking: Free driveway and street parking. Rack rates: $139–$279 double. Rates include full breakfast and evening wine and snacks. Deals: Check Web site or ask about winter specials. AE, DC, DISC, MC, V.*

Dining Out

Far be it from me to encourage hotel dining, but also consider the **Victorian Dining Room ($$$$)** at the Mendocino Hotel. My husband and I enjoyed a terrific dinner here. It's a bit more formal than most in town, with exemplary service and a pleasing continental cuisine with California flair; main courses run $13 to $30.

Stanford Inn by the Sea also has a pretty dining room, **The Ravens ($$),** which serves creative vegetarian cuisine prepared with organic home-grown veggies and lots of Asian slants; entrees cost $10 to $16.

Bay View Cafe

$–$$ Mendocino AMERICAN

This casual, second-story restaurant serves up just-fine food and excellent ocean views. Expect sandwiches, burgers, homestyle breakfasts, and liberal use of the fryer, plus Southwestern-style selections at dinner. This restaurant is hugely popular, so expect a wait on weekends.

45040 Main St. (between Kasten and Lansing sts.). ☎ 707-937-4197. Reservations not taken. Main courses: $5–$8 at breakfast, $6.50–$15 at lunch and dinner. No credit cards. Open: Breakfast, lunch, and dinner daily.

Cafe Beaujolais

$$$ Mendocino CAL-FRENCH

Here's Mendocino's best-known restaurant. The room is pretty, dimly lit, almost Victorian, but the attention-getting cuisine — creative Cal-French with a Southwest flair here and there — is thoroughly 21st-century modern. The menu changes regularly, but past successes have included wild sturgeon pan-roasted in truffle emulsion and ahi wrapped in apple-wood-smoked bacon and dressed in a spicy tomatillo salsa. Key notes include organic produce, house-baked breads, and inventive wine pairings. The midweek fixed-price meal is a relative bargain.

961 Ukiah St. (at Evergreen St.). ☎ *707-937-5614. Internet:* www.cafebeaujolais.com. *Reservations recommended. Main courses: $18–$21; Tues–Thurs 3-course prix-fixe $25. DISC, MC, V. Open: Dinner nightly.*

Mendo Burgers

$ Mendocino BURGERS

You want the best burger on the coast? You got it. Six variations are on hand, including fresh ground chuck, turkey, grilled fish (petrale sole), and homemade veggie (falafel, carrots, sweet red peppers). Be sure to ask for a side of generously cut, finger-lickin'-good fries when you place your order in the luncheonette-style kitchen. If it's a nice day, opt for one of the pleasant courtyard picnic tables over the plain dining room. Look for the sidewalk sandwich board; it's down the path, in back (behind the Mendocino Bakery & Cafe).

10483 Lansing St. (between Ukiah St. and Little Lake Rd.; you can also enter from Ukiah St.). ☎ *707-937-1111. Reservations not needed. Burgers: $5–$10. No credit cards. Open: Daily for lunch and early dinner (Mon–Sat to 7 p.m., Sun to 5 p.m.).*

The Moosse Cafe

$$—$$$ Mendocino CALIFORNIA

A bit more casual, and less romantic than its compatriots, this charming restaurant is housed in a simple warren of rooms clad with contemporary art. The short but smart menu features well-prepared crowd pleasers like baby-back ribs with housemade BBQ sauce, a garlicky roasted free-range chicken, pistachio-crusted local halibut, and yummy pastas. The only sour note? The famous Caesar salad is highly overrated — but the fab bittersweet chocolate pudding salved my disappointment.

In the Blue Heron Inn, 390 Kasten St. (at Albion St.). ☎ *707-937-4323. Internet:* www.theblueheron.com. *Reservations recommended. Main courses: $11–$20. MC, V. Open: Lunch and dinner daily.*

The 955 Ukiah Street Restaurant

$$–$$$ Mendocino CAL-FRENCH

Cafe Beaujolais has a higher profile, but many locals consider this cozy, unpretentious restaurant to be the most consistently excellent in town. The extensive, creative, and reasonably priced menu includes a good number of low-priced pastas and veggie dishes for diners on a budget, as well as heartier steaks, lamb shank, duck, and the like. Ask for a table overlooking the gardens for maximum romance and comfort.

955 Ukiah St. (between Howard and Evergreen sts.). ☎ *707-937-1955. Internet:* www.955restaurant.com. *Reservations recommended. Main courses: $8–$22. MC, V. Open: Dinner Wed–Sun.*

Picnicking

Come summertime, picnicking is practically a religion in this neck of the woods. Whether you want to pack a basket for the woods or grab a takeout sandwich to nosh in town, Mendocino's got you covered.

- ✔ **Mendocino Market,** 45051 Ukiah St., between Lansing and Kasten (☎ 707-937-3474), makes great sandwiches and a to-die-for free-range chicken that you can enjoy at garden tables.

- ✔ **Tote Fête,** 10450 Lansing St., at Albion (☎ 707-937-3383 or 707-937-3140), boasts a wide selection of takeout goodies.

For an utterly divine finish, stop by the **Mendocino Cookie Company,** also at 10450 Lansing St. (☎ 707-937-4843; www.mendocinocookies. com), which bakes cookies so yummy you won't even feel guilty.

Exploring Around Mendocino

The primary occupation of most visitors to Mendocino is . . . nothing. Most people come to stroll through town, enjoy the charming seacoast vibe, soak up the views, and separate themselves from some of their disposable income.

Gallery hoppers should head to the visitor center at the Ford House Museum to pick up the *Mendocino Gallery Guide,* which offers a good gallery map. If local lore interests you, visit the **Ford House Museum,** on Main Street at the end of Kasten Road (☎ 707-937-5397), and the **Kelley House Museum,** just a few doors down and across Main (☎ 707-937-5791), both legacies from Mendocino's 19th-century boomtown days as logging capital of the North Coast.

A great place to start gallery-hopping is the **Mendocino Art Center,** 45200 Little Lake Rd., at Williams Street (one block west of Kasten; ☎ 707-937-5818), Mendocino's unofficial cultural headquarters. Multiple gallery exhibits are always on display; you'll find plenty of art to buy and lovely gardens.

Straightforward shopping highlights include **Silver & Stone,** 45005 Ukiah St., near Lansing (☎ 707-937-0257), a wonderful jewelry shop with lots of creative pieces, including many affordable ones. Also stop in at the **Main Street Book Shop/More Used Books,** 990A Main St., across from the Presbyterian Church (☎ 707–937-1537), a pleasing shop that used-book hounds should seek out.

Exploring the Headlands

Basically, all the waterfront territory that surrounds town makes up **Mendocino Headlands State Park**. In spring, wildflowers blanket the spectacular area; winter is a great time to watch for California gray whales, who cruise close to shore between mid-December and mid-April.

Three miles of easy trails wind through the park; stop by the visitor center at the Ford House (described in the previous section) for an access map. Easiest access is behind Mendocino Presbyterian Church, on Main Street, where a trail leads to stairs that take you down to a small but picturesque beach.

Drive out to Heeser Drive (via Little Lake Road) to reach more remote areas of the park. A number of parking lots along the route lead to short trails and magnificent views along the wild coast, which reminds me very much of Scotland. (Aye!)

Big River Beach, the park's finest stretch of sand, is accessible from the highway just south of Comptche-Ukiah Road. The beach is good for picnicking, walking, and sunbathing, but don't even think about going in the water.

Big River Beach meets the mouth of the Big River, which you can explore via top-sitting kayak or canoe. Rent one for $18 per hour ($54 for the full day) from **Catch a Canoe & Bicycles Too,** just below the Stanford Inn at Highway 1 and Comptche-Ukiah Road (☎ 707-937-0273; www.stanfordinn.com). They'll also rent you a top-flight mountain bike for $10 per hour ($30 a day).

Visiting Russian Gulch

Several other state parks dot the rugged coastline around Mendocino. The best of the bunch is **Russian Gulch State Park** (☎ 707-937-5804 or 707-937-4296), located off Highway 1 two miles north of Mendocino. It's more remote and foresty than Mendocino Headlands, and quite spectacular. Picnic Area Drive leads right to the park's main attraction, a churning collapsed sea cave with marvelous swirling tides called the **Devil's Punchbowl** that's well worth checking out. The well-marked, three-mile **Falls Loop Trail** is an easy walk through the redwoods to a lovely waterfall. The day-use fee is $5.

Riding the Skunk Train

Riding the Skunk Train is an easy way to see the redwoods without having to drive yourself. Founded in 1885 as a logging railroad, the **Skunk Trains** (☎ 800-77-SKUNK or 707-964-6371; www.skunktrain.com) are vintage train cars that will take you through gorgeous — and otherwise inaccessible — North Coast redwood territory. (Originally gas powered, the trains emitted a distinctive odor that prompted locals to claim "you can smell 'em before you can see 'em" — hence the name.) The line runs 40 miles between Fort Bragg and Willits to the north. Half-day trips, which take three hours and turn around at the midpoint, Northspur, are $27 for adults and $14 for kids. The full-day loop, which traverses the entire route and takes 8 hours (including a lunch stop in Willits), is $35 for adults, $18 for kids. You should book summer excursions a month in advance.

Taking in the sweet smell of Fort Bragg

Fort Bragg is the commercial hub of North Coast life (car dealerships, fast-food joints — you get the picture). It's also home to the **Mendocino Coast Botanical Gardens,** 18220 N. Hwy. 1 (☎ **707-964-4352;** www.gardenbythesea.org). This lovely public garden blooms year-round and features gentle trails with terrific ocean views — well worth a couple of hours for green thumbs. Admission is $6 for adults, $5 for seniors, $3 for kids 13 to 17, $1 for younger kids. The gardens are open March through October daily from 9 a.m. to 5 p.m., and November through February daily from 9 a.m. to 4 p.m.

You can book winter whale-watching excursions and deep-sea fishing charters for tuna, halibut, and salmon at Fort Bragg's Noyo Harbor. Call **North Coast Fishing Adventures** (☎ **877-546-4263;** www.fortbraggfishing.com).

Enjoying the local theater scene

For some reason that escapes me, community theater is a big deal in these parts. Mendocino does not offer a whole lot to do after dark, so why not see what's on? Of course, you never know what you could end up with, but dear friends of mine caught a terrific production of *My Fair Lady* that was the highlight of their Mendocino trip. (Do scenes from *Streetcar!* pop to mind, *Simpsons* fans?) Check with the **Mendocino Theater Company,** 45200 Little Lake Rd. (☎ **707-937-4477;** www.mcn.org/1/mtc), where the $10 to $15 ticket prices minimize the risk (half-price for kids under 16).

Gathering More Information

Before you arrive, call the Fort Bragg/Mendocino Coast Chamber of Commerce (☎ **800-726-2780** or 707-961-6300), or point your Web browser to www.mendocinocoast.com. You can visit the chamber's walk-in center in Fort Bragg at 332 N. Main St. (Highway 1), between Laurel and Redwood streets, across from the Guest House Museum.

In Mendocino, stop at the **Ford House Museum,** on the ocean side of Main Street near Kasten (☎ **707-937-5397**). Free publications and maps are available at shops and restaurants around town, and your hotel can also supply you with a wealth of information.

For more information on Mendocino's state parks, visit the official California State Parks Web site at www.cal-parks.ca.gov; click on "North Coast," and then "Mendocino County." At the visitor center, ask for a copy of the *Mendocino Coastal Parks Guide,* an informative newspaper that's well worth the 25-cent price tag.

Chapter 12

Redwood Country

● ●

In This Chapter

▶ Deciding on the length of your visit

▶ Separating the trees from the cheese along the Avenue of the Giants

▶ Finding a place to stay among the redwoods

● ●

*Y*ou don't have to drive all the way up to **Redwood National Park,** in the far reaches of Northern California near the Oregon border, to experience the state's giant redwoods. Frankly, by the time you got there, some 300 miles north of San Francisco, you'd have already seen enough of the towering trees to last a lifetime. A day excursion from Mendocino that takes you partway up the famed Avenue of the Giants — or a trip that incorporates one night in Mendocino with a second night farther north along the route — will provide plenty of exposure to the towering, majestic trees.

The **Avenue of the Giants** is a 32-mile scenic byway that follows a portion of the old two-lane Highway 101, and parallels the modern freeway (as well as the Eel River) from Phillipsville at the south end to Pepperwood at the north. The "giants" are the magnificent coast redwoods, the tallest trees on earth, which often exceed 300 feet in height. These trees are the longer, lankier cousins to the stout giant sequoias of the Sierra Nevada. The Avenue is a relatively easy drive, curvaceous but not too challenging, that passes through some of the most spectacular territory offered by California. If you drive as far as **Humboldt Redwoods State Park** (roughly the midpoint of the route), you'll witness the largest stand of virgin redwoods in the world.

Unfortunately, you won't see just pristine nature. Tacky attractions blight the route, turning the gorgeous highway into a schlocky sideshow. From drive-through trees to a statue of Bigfoot, many of the attractions feel like leftovers from the Eisenhower era — like a '50s B-movie that's lost its kitschy kick. The good news is that the sheer majesty of the trees makes stomaching *le grand frommage* easy.

Redwood Country

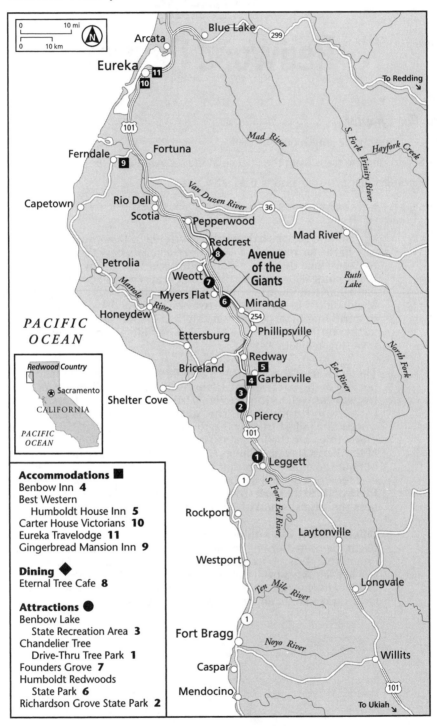

0   10 mi
0   10 km

Blue Lake
Arcata
299
Eureka **11**
10
To Redding

101
Ferndale
Fortuna
9
Mad River
S. Fork Trinity River
Hayfork Creek

Capetown
Rio Dell
Scotia
Van Duzen River
36
Pepperwood
Mad River

Petrolia
Redcrest
8
Avenue of the Giants
Ruth Lake

Weott **7**
Myers Flat
6
Miranda
254

PACIFIC OCEAN
Honeydew
Mattole River
Ettersburg
Phillipsville
North Fork

Briceland
Redway
5
4 Garberville
Eel River

Redwood Country
Sacramento
CALIFORNIA
PACIFIC OCEAN

Shelter Cove
3
2
Piercy
101

1 Leggett
1

Rockport
S. Fork Eel River
Laytonville

Westport
Longvale

Ten Mile River
1

Fort Bragg
Noyo River
Willits

Caspar
Mendocino
101
To Ukiah

Accommodations ■
Benbow Inn **4**
Best Western
   Humboldt House Inn **5**
Carter House Victorians **10**
Eureka Travelodge **11**
Gingerbread Mansion Inn **9**

Dining ◆
Eternal Tree Cafe **8**

Attractions ●
Benbow Lake
   State Recreation Area **3**
Chandelier Tree
   Drive-Thru Tree Park **1**
Founders Grove **7**
Humboldt Redwoods
   State Park **6**
Richardson Grove State Park **2**

Timing Your Visit

Whether you visit the Avenue of the Giants on a day trip or an overnighter, try to set aside plenty of daylight hours to truly appreciate the mammoth redwoods.

Day tripping from Mendocino

You can make the Avenue of the Giants a day trip from Mendocino, leaving in the morning and returning for dinnertime. (This timetable works best in summer, when you have more daylight hours to enjoy.)

You don't have to follow the entire route to get an eyeful of the tall trees. A number of towns exist along the way where you can stop and eat lunch, and connecting back up with U.S. 101 is easy at about a half-dozen points if you tire of the meandering roadway. Those of you with day-trip stamina can travel as far as **Humboldt Redwoods State Park** and back in the course of the day, with time to stop for some communing with nature. The drive is about 98 miles, or 2½ hours in each direction (not counting stops).

If that sounds like too much for you, just go as far as **Richardson Grove State Park,** off Highway 101 before the start of the Avenue, about 68 miles (about 1½ to 2 hours) north of Mendocino. This marvelous park makes a great place to discover the coast redwoods, which serve as the area's main tourist attraction. Also, the first leg of the drive takes you past some spectacular coastline. Beyond the park lies more of the same, with one-horse logging towns and tacky attractions thrown in. However, you will find some marvelous pristine stretches if you venture farther, with pullouts to hiking trails and day-use areas.

Because pickings are slim along the route, putting together a picnic lunch at Mendocino Market or Tote Fête (see Chapter 11) before you leave Mendocino is a very good idea, especially if you'd like more than a grilled-cheese sandwich from a lunch counter. The drive will present you with plenty of picnic spots from which to choose.

Finding options for overnighters

If you want to spend more time among the trees, you can (see "Staying in Style Along the Route" later in this chapter). If you want to take it slow, consider taking a full day to meander north from Mendocino and up the Avenue of the Giants; then stay in a Ferndale or Eureka B&B for a night (it's 134 miles to Ferndale, 145 to Eureka). In the morning, hop on U.S. 101 for a speedy return south.

If your goal is the redwoods and you don't care about the coast — or you don't want to subject yourself to the nausea-inducing ride to the coast — skip Mendocino altogether. The weather is much warmer and sunnier inland, and you'll save time and energy (not to mention a few bucks on accommodations) by sticking to U.S. 101 for northern destinations. Garberville makes a great southern base (especially the very nice **Benbow Inn**) if you follow this strategy. You can also zip your way to the top, stay in Eureka or Ferndale, and meander down the Avenue the next day. Driving the route northbound presents no particular advantage.

Getting There

From Mendocino, follow Highway 1 north along the shoreline to Leggett, where you'll pick up U.S. 101 (the Redwood Highway) north. The distance to Leggett is about 53 miles, with the first 30 or so winding along the coast; the scenery becomes really spectacular after you pass through Fort Bragg. It's slow going, so be prepared. Pick up U.S. 101, and 15 miles later you'll reach **Richardson Grove State Park.** The Garberville exit is another 8½ miles. Six miles beyond Garberville you can pick up the southern end of the Avenue of the Giants, formally known as Highway 254.

If you're bypassing Mendocino and coming from the south, take speedy U.S. 101 all the way north to the Avenue of the Giants exit at Phillipsville (6 miles north of Garberville). This exit is 211 miles from San Francisco straight up the 101, 158 miles from Calistoga (at the north end of Napa Valley) via Highway 128 to U.S. 101.

Driving the Avenue of the Giants

You can see these highlights as you proceed north on the Redwood Highway, U.S. 101, picking up the Avenue of the Giants, Highway 254, at its southernmost gateway. You'll also pass much more of both the sublime and the obscure: pristine woodland stretches with pullouts that lead to wonderful hiking trails and day-use areas in the woods, and more silly attractions than you can shake a stick at. Watch for any number of blink-and-you'll-miss-'em towns along the road where you can stop to buy a casual lunch or a kitschy souvenir.

At the junction of Highway 1 and U.S. 101 sits the **Chandelier Tree Drive-Thru Tree Park** in Leggett (☎ **707-925-6363**), the first of many such attractions on the Redwood Highway. Other corn-pone variations along the route include the "world famous" treehouse and the one-log house. If you're doing the cheeky Roadside Americana version of this tour, don't worry — you can't miss 'em. Each attraction sports a massive sign (usually a whole set) that's more attention-getting than a 10-foot-tall carnival barker.

Lest you think this drive-thru tree business is anything natural, Chandelier will dispel that notion right quick. Way back whenever, somebody cut a car-size hole in the base of a mammoth redwood, and you pay three bucks for the right to drive your car through. This cheesy activity is not really worth the $3, but if you're curious (I was!), this is as good a place as any to get it out of your system. And I defy you to bypass it with a kid in your car. In fact, this stop is better than most, because the picnic area provides a pretty spot for lunch. We spotted deer coming out of the woods for a sip from the pond on our stop. The park also boasts the requisite gift shop.

Here's where things really start to get good. Any itinerary should include a visit to **Richardson Grove State Park,** 15 miles north of Leggett (7 miles south of Garberville) on U.S. 101 (☎ **707-247-3318,** 707-247-3319, or 707-247-3415; Internet: www.cal-parks.ca.gov/DISTRICTS/ncrd/ rgsp.html). The park includes a terrific visitor center with a grocery store and a nice shop, where you can pick up maps and pamphlets covering the entire region. A short (10-minute) interpretive loop offers an excellent introduction to the towering trees, complete with explanatory placards. More extensive trails include an easy 1.6-mile woodland loop; stop in at the staffed center for a map. The day-use fee is $5.

Even if you're not staying at the Benbow Inn, the adjacent **Benbow Lake State Recreation Area** (☎ **707-247-3318;** Internet: www. cal-parks.ca.gov/DISTRICTS/ncrd/blsra.htm) makes an excellent stop for picnicking, sunning, and lake swimming in summer, and includes nice grassy areas and a rocky beach. The lake was closed for dam repairs in 2000, but is scheduled to reopen to the public in the summer of 2001. Still, calling the park (or the hotel) for an update before you get your heart set doesn't hurt. The dining room over at the **Benbow Inn** (see "Staying in Style along the Route" in this chapter) makes a good stop for lunch (served in summer only).

About 14½ miles from Phillipsville, the first access point for the Avenue of the Giants is **Humboldt Redwoods State Park** (☎ **707-946-2409;** Internet: www.humboldtredwoods.org). Much larger than Richardson Grove, this 53,000-acre park is the real heart of the Avenue. Humboldt Redwoods features the Redwood Highway's main visitor center, plus 100 miles of hiking trails. You can pick up a trail map in the visitor center. If you want to spend some serious time here, check out the extensive Web site. The day-use fee is $5.

About two miles north of the visitor center, still in Humboldt Redwoods State Park, is **Founders Grove,** one of the most impressive redwood groves in the region. Its name honors the enlightened folks who founded the Save-the-Redwoods League way back in 1917. A gentle, half-mile interpretive loop meanders through the grove. This walk is an enjoyable introduction to coast redwood ecology, and also takes you past the *Dyerville Giant* — a 370-foot monster of a tree that was designated the "Champion Coast Redwood" before it fell about a decade ago. Here it remains, lying on the forest floor, its rootball alone measuring three stories long.

In the logging town of *Redcrest*, the unassuming **Eternal Tree Cafe** serves freshly made sandwiches and boasts a nice outside dining area.

Staying in Style along the Route

If you want to spend quality time among the redwoods, here are a few good places to stay. *Garberville* is a charm-free bend in the road off

Highway 101 near the southern gateway of the Avenue of the Giants. The town is perfectly serviceable if you'd like to skip the coastline altogether and head straight for the trees.

The tiny but stately burg of *Ferndale* presents a picture-perfect ginger-bread slice of authentic Victoriana just past the north end of the drive. A visit to the town is well worth the five-mile detour off U.S. 101.

Eureka is about 10 miles north of the Avenue's northern gateway. The largest town on the North Coast doesn't look like much at first glance, but if you turn west off U.S. 101 between B and M streets, you'll discover a charming Victorian Old Town along the waterfront.

For more choices, contact the visitors bureau (see "Gathering More Information," later in this chapter), whose Web site offers an excellent rundown of options throughout the area.

Hotel taxes in this neck of the woods vary; count on 7.9% to 10% being tacked onto your bill at checkout time.

Benbow Inn

$$–$$$ Garberville

This wonderful Tudor-style hotel is tucked away in the woods on swimmable Benbow Lake. The appealing Americana-style rooms vary from petite to grand, but all are homey and comfy with pretty, tiled bathrooms; some have VCRs, pullout sofas, terraces, and/or fireplaces. The hotel has lovely lakefront grounds, a nice terrace restaurant, and attentive service. All in all, it's a great value — and an ideal place to base yourself as you play among the redwoods.

445 Lake Benbow Dr. (off Hwy. 101), Garberville. ☎ *800-355-3301 or 707-923-2124. Fax: 707-923-2897. Internet:* www.benbowinn.com. *Parking: Free! Rack rates: $115–$225 double, $305 cottage. Rates include afternoon tea and scones and evening hors d'oeuvres. Closed Jan–Mar. Deals: Ask about off-season deals. AE, DISC, MC, V.*

Best Western Humboldt House Inn

$–$$ Garberville

This good-value chain motel is a perfectly fine choice if you're looking for a bed at the south end of the Avenue. Rooms are pleasant enough, and the facilities include a pool and Jacuzzi.

701 Redwood Dr. (off Hwy. 101), Garberville. ☎ *800-528-1234 or 707-923-2771. Fax: 707-923-4259. Internet:* www.bestwestern.com. *Parking: Free! Rack rates: $67–$96 double, $92–$140 cottage. Rates include continental breakfast. Deals: Ask about off-season deals as well as AAA, senior, corporate, and government discounts. AE, CB, DC, DISC, MC, V.*

Carter House Victorians

$$–$$$ Eureka

This grand collection of Victorians is well-situated in Eureka's Old Town. Let price and taste dictate your booking, which may be in the magnificent Carter House mansion that also houses the highly regarded **301 Restaurant;** the full-service Hotel Carter; or one of two quaint cottages. No matter which you choose, you can count on impeccable accommodations, plush bedding, terry robes — the works. Peruse the full range of options online.

301 L St. (at Third St.), Eureka. ☎ **800-404-1390** or 707-445-1390. Fax: 707-444-8067. Internet: www.carterhouse.com. Parking: Free! Rack rates: $85–$187 double, $125–$297 suite, $497 cottage. Rates include two-course breakfast and evening wine and hors d'oeuvres. AE, DC, DISC, MC, V.

Eureka Travelodge

$ Eureka

A just-fine motel for those in search of a budget-friendly bargain at the northern end of the Redwood Highway. Rooms have coffeemakers, and a heated pool is open in summer.

4 Fourth St. (between A and C sts.), Eureka. ☎ **888-515-6375** or 707-443-6345. Fax: 707-443-1486. Internet: www.travelodge.com. Parking: Free! Rack rates: $40–$70 double. Deals: Ask about AAA, senior, corporate, and government discounts. Check Web site for Internet-only promotions; a printable $5-off coupon was available at press time. AE, DISC, MC, V.

Gingerbread Mansion Inn

$$$ Ferndale

In a town of pristinely preserved Victorian homes, this one stands head and shoulders above the rest. It has been exquisitely restored and furnished in high Victorian style. Each room includes a private bathroom (some with clawfoot tub and/or a fireplace) and luxurious extras like plush bathrobes and turndown service.

400 Berding St., Ferndale (use the Fernbridge/Ferndale exit off U.S. 101 and go 5 miles). ☎ **800-952-4136** or 707-786-4000. Internet: www.gingerbread-mansion.com. Parking: Free! Rack rates: $140–$185 double, $180–$350 suite. Rates include full breakfast and afternoon high tea. Deals: Check Web site or ask about romance packages and other current specials. AE, MC, V.

Gathering More Information

Your best bet is to contact the _Eureka! Humboldt County Convention & Visitors Bureau;_ call ☎ **800-346-3482** or 707-443-5097, or go online to www.redwoodvisitor.org, where you'll find individual city links in addition to information on the area as a whole.

For more information on the region's state parks, including campground info, visit the official California State Parks Web site at www.cal-parks.ca.gov; click on "North Coast" and then "Mendocino County" and/or "Humboldt County."

The main visitor center is midway along the route, at **Humboldt Redwoods State Park** (☎ 707-946-2409), 2 miles south of Weott (near the Burlington Campground) and 20 miles north of Garberville, but you can get all the maps you'll need at **Richardson Grove State Park.**

Chapter 13

Lake Tahoe

● ●

In This Chapter

▶ Deciding when to visit, where to go, and how long to stay

▶ Finding the perfect places to stay and eat

▶ Getting active on shore — and out on the water — in any season

▶ Mixing it up with lady luck at the casinos

▶ Stepping back in time with a side trip to the Gold Country

● ●

*I*f you're looking for the Golden State's biggest and best playground, look no farther — you've found it. When Californians — particularly Northern Californians, who have more than their fair share of beautiful places to visit — want to get outside and ski, snowmobile, boat, hike, mountain bike, ride horseback, fish, kayak, jet ski (the list goes on), they come to Tahoe.

Lake Tahoe is a testament to their ultimate good taste. For it isn't just any ol' lake; it's one of the most spectacular lakes in the world, and definitely the most beautiful lake I've ever seen. Tahoe is the largest alpine lake in North America — 22 miles long and 12 miles wide, with a surface area of nearly 192 square miles, which means it can hold about a half-dozen Manhattans (and I don't mean the cocktail).

Calling it "sparkling" barely does this crystalline lake justice. Science even has an explanation for it: The water is 99.9 percent pure, about the same purity as distilled water. It's so clear that a dinner plate resting 75 feet below the surface would be visible to the naked eye. What's more, Lake Tahoe is the eighth-deepest lake in the world; it holds so much water that, if you tipped it on its side, the contents would flood the entire state of California to a depth of 14 inches.

Evergreens and snowy peaks rising from the shoreline make the lake look that much deeper, broader, and majestic. Don't just take my word for it; listen to Mark Twain, who called Lake Tahoe "the most beautiful picture the whole earth affords." Come and see for yourself — and play to your heart's content.

Timing Your Visit

When's the best time to visit? Simple: Come in winter if you want to ski. If you want to do anything else, come in summer — or autumn. Fall is the secret season in Tahoe. The colors are beautiful, the air crisp, activities abound, and hotel rates are low, low, low. Skip yucky spring altogether. The snowmelt turns the terrain into mud.

Even if you come in summer, prepare yourself for cool weather. In July, average highs don't hit the 80s, and evenings can dip well below 50. And because the upper 12 feet of the lake only warms to about 68°F, don't expect to splash around in your floaties. Chances are, it'll be all you can do to dip your toes in.

Tahoe is a favorite weekend getaway among San Franciscans, so you'll always save money — and, even more important, avoid the crowds — by scheduling your stay for Monday through Thursday.

A three-night stay in Tahoe will give you plenty of time to fully explore the area and play. If you cut your stay back to two, you risk spending too much time in the car (getting there and leaving), and not enough time in Tahoe. Budget four nights if you want to experience both shores. For more on this topic, check out the next section.

Choosing between Two Shores

The 30-mile drive between Lake Tahoe's north and south shores can become a two-hour bumper-to-bumper (or snowstorm-y) nightmare in the high seasons, so choose your shore carefully. Both boast first-rate skiing, good restaurants, lake views, and plenty of on-the-water fun — but that's pretty much where the similarities end.

South Lake Tahoe is more developed and generally cheaper; more hotels mean more competition, so you'll get better accommodations for your money. The Nevada casinos are at hand (in town for all intents and purposes), so this is your shore if you want some gambling action or nightlife. Getting out on the water is easier from the south shore, too, because it boasts more marinas, more outfitters, plus some excellent shoreline state parks not far from town.

The north shore, on the other hand, is prettier. It's more remote and resortlike, with a diverse selection of ski resorts and first-class accommodations. **Squaw Valley,** six miles from the lakeshore, is one of my favorite outdoor playgrounds. Still, although not as commercially spoiled as South Lake Tahoe, **Tahoe City** can be way too crowded for its own good in the high seasons. And because the emphasis is on luxury and inexpensive choices are fewer, you won't get as much value for your dollar if affordability is your priority.

If you have the time to spare, budget a couple of nights on the south shore and a couple of nights on the north shore. Doing so will also grant you the opportunity to enjoy the marvelous drive along Highway 89 at an easy pace.

Getting There

Lake Tahoe straddles the California/Nevada border, a four-hour drive east (slightly northeast, actually) from San Francisco.

✔ **If you're coming from San Francisco:** Take I-80 east to Sacramento, then U.S. 50 to South Lake Tahoe on the south shore, or stay on I-80 east to Highway 89 south to reach Tahoe City on the north shore.

✔ **If you're coming from Yosemite:** Take Highway 120 east out of the park to I-395 north to U.S. 50 east; at the U.S. 50/Highway 28 split, follow U.S. 50 to South Lake Tahoe, Highway 28 to Tahoe City on the north shore.

The 3½-hour drive is doable only between late June and first snowfall (usually early November), as Yosemite's east gate closes in winter. Otherwise, the drive becomes a 5- or 6-hour trek north on winding Highway 49 to I-50, which can be slow going in bad weather.

✔ **If you're coming from points south:** Take I-5 through central California to Sacramento, then pick up I-80 east to the north shore or U.S. 50 east to the south shore.

Whether you're taking I-80 to the north shore or U.S. 50 to the south shore, you can easily work in a side trip to the Gold Country on your way to Tahoe. All you need is a few hours to spare and a yen for those golden days; for details, see "Side-Tripping to the Gold Country" at the end of this chapter.

✔ **If you're heading to Squaw Valley:** Follow Highway 89 (River Road) at the 89/28 split in Tahoe City. Go 5 miles and turn left at Squaw Valley Road.

Reno/Tahoe International Airport is at U.S. 395 just south of I-80 in Reno, NV (☎ **775-328-6400;** www.renoairport.com/reno-tahoe). All of the national car-rental companies have airport locations. The drive takes 50 minutes to Tahoe City on the north shore; take U.S. 395 north to I-80 west to Highway 89 south. For South Lake Tahoe, take U.S. 395 south to U.S. 50 west, a 70-minute drive.

These airlines fly into Reno/Tahoe:

- ✔ Alaska Airlines: ☎ **800-426-0333;** www.alaskaair.com
- ✔ America West: ☎ **800-235-9292;** www.americawest.com
- ✔ American Airlines: ☎ **800-433-7300;** www.aa.com
- ✔ Continental: ☎ **800-525-0280;** www.continental.com
- ✔ Delta/Skywest: ☎ **800-221-1212;** www.delta-air.com
- ✔ Northwest: ☎ **800-225-2525;** www.nwa.com
- ✔ Southwest: ☎ **800-435-9792;** www.southwest.com
- ✔ United: ☎ **800-241-6522;** www.ual.com

Getting Your Bearings

On the south shore, two main highways meet at a prominent "Y" intersection in South Lake Tahoe: U.S. 50, which continues up the east (Nevada) shore of the lake to midpoint and then shoots off east; and Highway 89, which runs up the west (California) side of the lake to Tahoe City, then turns northwest away from the lake. Highway 28 picks up where 89 leaves off, running along the north shore from Tahoe City to midpoint on the Nevada side, where it meets up with U.S. 50, completing the continuous 72-mile circle around the lake.

Lake Tahoe's biggest town is South Lake Tahoe, which runs along the south shore. Its main drag is U.S. 50, which is called Lake Tahoe Boulevard in town. After you cross the California/Nevada border, you're immediately in Stateline, Nevada. The casinos are just on the other side of the line; the sidewalks don't even pause.

Follow Highway 89 about 31 miles north along the west shore, past camp-like resorts and stunning lakefront homes, and you'll reach Tahoe City, the commercial hub of the north shore. Go six miles northwest on Highway 89 to breathtaking Squaw Valley, whose thriving Olympic Village was built for the 1960 Winter Games.

Another prominent community sits on the northeast shore, Nevada's Incline Village, but I've concentrated on the California side because I like it best — and this *is* a book about California, after all.

Lake Tahoe

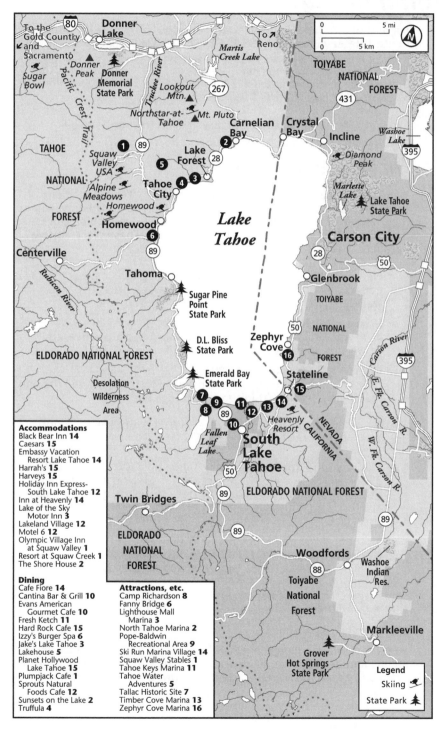

Accommodations
Black Bear Inn **14**
Caesars **15**
Embassy Vacation
    Resort Lake Tahoe **14**
Harrah's **15**
Harveys **15**
Holiday Inn Express-
    South Lake Tahoe **12**
Inn at Heavenly **14**
Lake of the Sky
    Motor Inn **3**
Lakeland Village **12**
Motel 6 **12**
Olympic Village Inn
    at Squaw Valley **1**
Resort at Squaw Creek **1**
The Shore House **2**

Dining
Cafe Fiore **14**
Cantina Bar & Grill **10**
Evans American
    Gourmet Cafe **10**
Fresh Ketch **11**
Hard Rock Cafe **15**
Izzy's Burger Spa **6**
Jake's Lake Tahoe **3**
Lakehouse **5**
Planet Hollywood
    Lake Tahoe **15**
Plumpjack Cafe **1**
Sprouts Natural
    Foods Cafe **12**
Sunsets on the Lake **2**
Truffula **4**

Attractions, etc.
Camp Richardson **8**
Fanny Bridge **6**
Lighthouse Mall
    Marina **3**
North Tahoe Marina **2**
Pope-Baldwin
    Recreational Area **9**
Ski Run Marina Village **14**
Squaw Valley Stables **1**
Tahoe Keys Marina **11**
Tahoe Water
    Adventures **5**
Tallac Historic Site **7**
Timber Cove Marina **13**
Zephyr Cove Marina **16**

Legend
Skiing
State Park

Staying in Style

For additional choices throughout the region, contact **Lake Tahoe Central Reservations** (☎ **888-434-1262**, 800-824-6348, or 530-583-3494; www.tahoefun.org), a free reservations service. You can also try **Tahoe Reservations.com** (www.tahoereservations.com), another free service that specializes in South Tahoe. For ski packages, contact **Ski Tahoe** (☎ **888-982-1088**; www.skitahoe.com).

Expect to see 10 to 12 percent in taxes added to your hotel bill.

On the south shore

Want a little Vegas spice in your Tahoe vacation? Then stay at one of these big-name Stateline, Nevada, casinos. They're fairly equivalent in their middle-of-the-road comforts and $$-$$$$ prices, which can range from $89 to $259 depending on day and season. These places thrive on packages, so always ask.

- ✔ **Harrah's** (☎ **800-427-7247** or 775-588-6611; www.harrahstahoe.com) is a perennial crowd-pleaser — low-key, attractive, and well-done.

- ✔ **Harveys** (☎ **800-427-8397** or 775-588-2411; www.harveystahoe.com) is the rock-and-roll casino. It's sharp and attractive, and draws in a young, sophisticated crowd.

- ✔ **Caesars** (☎ **800-648-3353**, 800-235-8259, or 775-586-7771; www.caesars.com) is the most glamorous of the casinos, and the only real themed casino (think grown-up toga party).

In addition to the more unique choices below, South Lake Tahoe also has some excellent-value motels:

- ✔ **Holiday Inn Express,** 3961 Lake Tahoe Blvd. (☎ **800-544-5288** or 530-544-5900; www.holidayinnexpresstahoe.com), has high-quality rooms tucked among the trees to ensure quiet. Rooms run $69 to $159, family-size suites $139 to $209, including continental breakfast.

- ✔ **Motel 6,** 2375 Lake Tahoe Blvd. (☎ **800-4-MOTEL-6** or 530-542-1400; www.motel6.com), is the best motel value in town for penny-pinching travelers. Rooms run $39 to $70.

Black Bear Inn

$$$ South Lake Tahoe

Wow! This stunning lodgelike B&B looks like it jumped straight out of a Ralph Lauren catalog, complete with gleaming knotty-pine woodwork and a two-story riverstone fireplace in the soaring living room. Extraordinary craftsmanship, impeccable rustic-goes-chic style, beautifully outfitted rooms (gorgeous bathrooms!), lots of lounging space, and super-friendly hosts add up to my favorite place to stay in Tahoe, period. Geared more toward adults than families with kids, though.

1202 Ski Run Blvd., South Lake Tahoe. ☎ *877-BEAR-INN (232-7466) or 530-544-4451. Fax: 530-544-7315. Internet:* www.tahoeblackbear.com. *Parking: Free! Rack rates: $150–$200 double, $350–$425 cabin. Rates include full breakfast. MC, V.*

Embassy Vacation Resort Lake Tahoe

$$$ **South Lake Tahoe**

Skip the bland Embassy Suites business hotel down the street and book in to this terrific lakefront condo resort instead. The sun-filled suites are gorgeously decorated in subdued Southwest colors and high-quality everything. Each suite comes with a cute balcony and a fully equipped kitchenette or kitchen. This hotel offers excellent indoor/outdoor pool, pretty grounds, exercise room, video-game room, coin-op laundry, and far more style and value-for-dollar than you'd expect. A winner!

901 Ski Run Blvd., South Lake Tahoe. ☎ *800-737-9884, 800-362-2779, or 530-541-6122. Fax: 530-541-2028. Internet:* www.embassytahoe.com. *Parking: Free! Rack rates: $109–$469 studios, 1- and 2-bedroom suites (1-bedrooms from $129, 2-bedrooms from $159). Deals: AAA and senior discounts available; ask about packages. AE, CB, DC, DISC, JCB, MC, V.*

Inn at Heavenly

$$–$$$ **South Lake Tahoe**

These upscale motel rooms are not big, but they're done in a dreamy-cute wooden lodge style, each with a one-of-a-kind gas fireplace, VCR, ceiling fan, and kitchenette with microwave, fridge, and coffeemaker. Swings and picnic sets dot the lovely grounds. Amenities include steam room and sauna, warm-hearted innkeepers, and a cozy common room with games and videos. Pet-friendly, so bring Fido.

1261 Ski Run Blvd. (just downhill from Heavenly ski resort), South Lake Tahoe. ☎ *800-MY-CABIN (692-2246) or 530-544-4244. Fax: 530-544-5213. Internet:* www.inn-at-heavenly.com. *Parking: Free! Rack rates: $125–$185 double, $350–$450 cabin (sleeps 8–12). Rates include continental breakfast, snacks. Deals: AAA and senior discounts available. Some kind of discount or package deal almost always exists; off-season rates as low as $69. AE, DISC, MC, V.*

Lakeland Village

$$–$$$ **South Lake Tahoe**

If your lodging ideal is a home away from home, look no farther. At this lakeside residential complex/condo resort, the spacious, contemporary-style units run the gamut from studios to four-bedroom townhouses. All are very comfortably furnished and have fully equipped kitchens, fireplaces, and a balcony or deck. Also on-site: 1,000 feet of private beach, two pools, two spas, a sauna, and tennis courts with pro. Heck — it's better than home!

3535 Lake Tahoe Blvd., South Lake Tahoe. ☎ *800-822-5969 or 530-544-1685. Fax: 530-541-6278. Internet:* www.lakeland-village.com. *Parking: Free! Rack rates: $90–$190 double, $130–$220 suite, $145–$750 town house (sleeps 4–10). Deals: Plenty o' packages — ski, golf, and more. AE, MC, V.*

On the north shore

Lake of the Sky Motor Inn

$$ Tahoe City

This '60s motel is a walk from restaurants, but far enough from the tourist fray to offer some measure of peace. Expect nothing beyond the basics, but rooms have been recently remodeled, beds are firm, housekeeping is neat, and beamed ceilings add a lodgelike touch. The lakeview rooms include fridges. The friendly owners keep the coffeepot on all day. The motel offers a pool and free local calls, too.

955 N. Lake Blvd. (Hwy. 28), Tahoe City. ☎ *530-583-3305. Fax: 530-583-7621. Parking: Free! Rack rates: $79–$129 double. Rates include continental breakfast. Deals: Rates as low as $59 off-season. AE, DC, DISC, MC, V.*

Olympic Village Inn at Squaw Valley

$$–$$$ Squaw Valley

This Swiss chalet–style all-suite hotel is the best value in the gorgeous Olympic Valley, bar none. The suites are attractively done in a country accent and boast fully equipped mini-kitchens, VCRs, and stereos. The lovely grounds are a stone's throw from Squaw Valley USA activities. Time-share owners get first dibs, so call early (midweek is your best bet).

1909 Chamonix Pl. (off Squaw Valley Rd.), Squaw Valley. ☎ *800-845-5243 or 530-581-6000. Fax: 530-583-4165. Internet:* www.sierraweb.com/ovi. *Parking: Free! Rack rates: $95–$335 one-bedroom suite. AE, DISC, MC, V.*

Resort at Squaw Creek

$$$$$ Squaw Valley

This stunning destination resort is built to take prime advantage of the valley and forest views. The rooms themselves aren't overly special. Come, instead, for the unparalleled facilities, which include a wonderful pool complex, a brand-new spa, first-rate dining, golf, tennis, biking, cross-country ski center, and ice-skating in season, private chairlift at Squaw Valley USA, great kids' program, and more.

400 Squaw Creek Rd., Squaw Valley. ☎ *800-403-4434 or 530-583-6300. Fax: 530-581-6632. Internet:* www.squawcreek.com. *Parking: $15 to valet, free self-parking. Rack rates: $250–$350 double, $420–$525 suite, from $750 penthouse. Rates include continental breakfast. Deals: Ask about golf, ski, spa, valley-view upgrades, and other packages. AE, DC, DISC, MC, V.*

The Shore House

$$$–$$$$ Tahoe Vista

This wonderful B&B is a marvelous choice for lakefront amour. The house sits 15 minutes from Tahoe City, in gorgeous, upscale Tahoe Vista. The rustic-romantic rooms are built for two and have private entrances, knotty-pine walls, cuddly Scandia down comforters on the custom-built log beds, gas fireplaces, and CD players (no TV). The B&B offers a sandy beach next door, welcoming and attentive innkeepers, and plenty of lake-facing lounge spaces — including a lakeside hot tub.

7170 North Lake Blvd., Tahoe Vista (eight miles east of Tahoe City). ☎ *800-207-5160 or 530-546-7270. Fax: 530-546-7130. Rack rates: $160–$255 double. Rates include full breakfast. DISC, MC, V.*

Dining Out

Tahoe is at full capacity most weekends, so book Friday and Saturday dinners in advance to avoid disappointment.

On the south shore

You'll find Tahoe's own **Hard Rock Cafe ($$)** at Harveys, Stateline Avenue at U.S. 50 (☎ **775-588-6200**). **Planet Hollywood ($$)** is next door at Caesars (☎ **775-588-7828**).

Cafe Fiore

$$$ South Lake Tahoe   ITALIAN

Lower profile than neighboring Nepheles, Cafe Fiore is definitely the superior restaurant. The dining room is rustic but lovely, with just seven white linen–dressed tables, plus a handful more on the alfresco terrace in summer. The creative Italian fare is prepared with expertise and culinary care; the garlic bread alone is enough to bring me back, begging for more. A regular winner of the *Wine Spectator* Award of Excellence, this restaurant is ultra-romantic and simply divine.

1169 Ski Run Blvd. (between U.S. 50 and Pioneer Trail), South Lake Tahoe. ☎ *530-541-2908. Internet:* www.cafefiore.com. *Reservations highly recommended. Main courses: $13–$22. AE, MC, V. Open: Dinner nightly.*

Cantina Bar & Grill

$$ South Lake Tahoe   CAL-MEXICAN

This Southwestern cantina is consistently named best Mex by locals. It's attractive and lively, with first-rate margaritas and 30 different beers free-flowing during the weekday 3 to 6 p.m. happy hour and beyond. The kitchen gets creative with specialties like rock shrimp quesadillas and calamari rellenos, but you're welcome to stick to tried-and-true faves such as top-notch burritos, taco combos, and the like.

765 Emerald Bay Rd. (at Hwy. 89 and 10th St.), South Lake Tahoe. ☎ **530-544-1233.** *Internet:* www.cantinatahoe.com. *Reservations not taken. Main courses: $8–$15. MC, V. Open: Lunch and dinner daily.*

Evans American Gourmet Cafe

$$$–$$$$ South Lake Tahoe   CONTEMPORARY AMERICAN

Tucked away in a vintage ski cabin in the woods is Tahoe's best restaurant, on any shore. It's intimate and sophisticated, but completely unpretentious. Ingredients are fresh and top-quality. Preparations are somewhat complex, but Chef Aaron Maffit's hand is so practiced and his touch so light that even the foie gras starter doesn't seem too heavy. Desserts are divine, too. This terrific restaurant could stand on its own in New York or San Francisco.

536 Emerald Bay Rd. (on Hwy. 89, a mile north of U.S. 50), South Lake Tahoe. ☎ **530-542-1990.** *Internet:* www.evanstahoe.com. *Reservations highly recommended. Main courses: $18–$23. DISC, MC, V. Open: Dinner nightly. Contemporary American.*

Fresh Ketch

$$–$$$$ South Lake Tahoe   SEAFOOD

The well-worn, casual downstairs bar offers first-rate seafood and good views, while the pretty upstairs dining room maintains a more formal atmosphere. I like the bar for lunch; golden-wood backgammon tables even let you settle in for a game as you nosh on oysters on the halfshell, delicately breaded calamari with a zippy dipping sauce, fish-and-chips, and ahi tacos. I can't be sure, of course, but I believe the New England clam chowder may be the best you'll find west of the Mississippi.

At Tahoe Keys Marina, 2433 Venice Dr. (off U.S. 50 at the end of Tahoe Keys Blvd.), South Lake Tahoe. ☎ **530-541-5683.** *Reservations recommended for dining room. Main courses: $7–$14 at downstairs bar, $16–$24 in upstairs dining room. AE, CB, DC, DISC, MC, V. Open: Lunch and dinner daily (dining room dinner only). AE, DC, DISC, MC, V.*

Sprouts Natural Foods Cafe

$ South Lake Tahoe   HEALTHY EATS

This health-minded deli is an excellent choice for hearty salads, sandwiches, fresh-baked goodies, and fresh-fruit smoothies. Eat in, cozy up to an outdoor table, or have yours packed as a picnic to go.

3123 Harrison Ave. (at U.S. 50 and Alameda Ave.), South Lake Tahoe.
☎ *530-541-6969. Main courses: $4–$7. No credit cards. Open: Breakfast, lunch, and dinner daily.*

On the north shore

Jake's Lake Tahoe

$$$ **Tahoe City AMERICAN**

This big, handsome restaurant serves up great lake views, tropical cocktails, fresh seafood, good steaks, and a party-hearty vibe. Keeping the bill down is easy by noshing on burgers, pastas, sandwiches, and salads in the marina-facing bar.

At the Boatworks Mall, 780 N. Lake Tahoe Blvd. (Hwy. 28), Tahoe City.
☎ *530-583-0188. Internet:* www.hulapie.com. *Reservations highly recommended. Main courses: $7–$13 at lunch, $13–$22 at dinner; bar menu $7–$12. AE, DC, MC, V. Open: Lunch and dinner daily.*

Lakehouse

$–$$ **Tahoe City AMERICAN/PIZZA**

This restaurant features just-fine American eats served in a spectacular lakefront setting. You can hardly find a better seat in town than on the deck in nice weather. You can also catch good views from the casual fire-lit dining room in winter. The food includes hearty breakfasts, well-stuffed sandwiches, ribs, and surprisingly good pizza pies.

120 Grove Court, off N. Lake Blvd. (turn off Hwy. 28 at the sign for Lakehouse Mall), Tahoe City. ☎ *530-583-2222. Reservations not taken. Main courses: $4–$12. AE, MC, V. Open: Breakfast, lunch, and dinner daily.*

PlumpJack Cafe

$$$$ **Squaw Valley CONTEMPORARY AMERICAN**

The best restaurant in Squaw Valley is this first-rate resort version of the San Francisco fave. The Mediterranean-accented modern cuisine revolves around seasonal ingredients. On my visit, the homemade tagliatelle pasta with chanterelle mushrooms, sweet corn, and green tomatoes sang with fresh flavors. The room is 100 percent high-design chic but utterly comfortable nonetheless. Service is impeccable in a not-too-formal way, and the wine list boasts well-chosen, lesser-known labels at reasonable prices. Excellent through and through.

At PlumpJack Squaw Valley Inn, 1920 Squaw Valley Rd., Squaw Valley. ☎ *530-583-1734 or 530-583-1576. Reservations highly recommended for dinner. Main courses: $17–$27. AE, MC, V. Open: Breakfast, lunch, and dinner daily.*

Sunsets on the Lake

$$$–$$$$ Tahoe Vista CAL-ITALIAN

This terrific restaurant in gorgeous Tahoe Vista is well worth the 15-minute drive east from Tahoe City. Spectacular lake views transform the pretty modern dining room into something really special. You'll get your money's worth from the crowd-pleasing entrees, such as garlic chicken spit-roasted to moist perfection, or the stellar braised lamb shank with a shiitake demi-glace. Try the rustic wood-fired pizzas, too. Come early for a sunset cocktail at the heated alfresco Island Bar.

7320 N. Lake Blvd. (Hwy. 28, about eight miles west of Tahoe City), Tahoe Vista. ☎ *530-546-3640. Reservations recommended. Internet:* www.sunsetslaketahoe. com. *Main courses: $8–$12 at lunch, $14–$28 at dinner. AE, DC, DISC, MC, V. Open: Dinner nightly; lunch daily in July and Aug.*

Truffula

$$$$ Tahoe City CONTEMPORARY AMERICAN

Sick and tired of yet another hip "New American" restaurant? Hold fast a little longer, until you try this excellent left-of-center variation, a self-professed purveyor of "wild food from land and sea." You can tread familiar waters with pan-roasted halibut with purple tomatoes and golden tomato vinaigrette, or go wild with blackhorn antelope with prosciutto-flecked polenta and roasted fig sauce. A suitably adventuresome wine list accompanies. This restaurant is a must for audacious eaters.

550 N. Lake Blvd. (Hwy. 28 at Grove Ct., above Village Sports), Tahoe City. ☎ *530-581-3362. Reservations recommended. Main courses: $19–$24. MC, V. Open: Dinner Thurs–Mon.*

Enjoying Lake Tahoe

You have to get out on the water to truly appreciate the grandeur of Lake Tahoe.

The 570-passenger **M.S. Dixie II** (☎ **775-588-3508** or 775-882-0786; www.tahoedixie2.com), an authentic paddle wheeler, offers lake cruises year-round from Zephyr Cove Marina, on U.S. 50, which is four miles east of the CA/NV state line. I like the two-hour Emerald Bay Sightseeing Cruise best. This cruise gives you a general feel for the lake and takes you into the stunning bay where you can see Fanette Island and Vikingsholm up close without the difficult walk (see "Driving along the spectacular shore" later in this chapter). Fares are $20 adults, $5 for kids under 12; reservations are recommended.

If you'd like a more intimate ride, book with **Woodwind Sailing Cruises** (☎ **888-867-6394**; www.sailwoodwind). Trips start at $20 for adults, $18 for seniors, $10 for kids 12 and under. The sunset champagne cruise is ultraromantic.

On the north shore, catch a ride aboard the **Tahoe Gal** (☎ **800-218- 2464** or 530-583-0141; www.tahoegal.com), which offers tours from the Lighthouse Mall Marina, 850 N. Lake Blvd., in Tahoe City from mid-April through October. Prices start at $17 adults, $7 kids.

Boating for do-it-yourselfers

Expect to pay in the neighborhood of $75 to $120 per hour for a power-boat and between $80 and $100 for a jet ski; the fourth hour is often free. Always reserve ahead.

On the south shore, choose between:

- ✔ Zephyr Cove Resort Marina, a very nice marina with a red-sand beach on U.S. 50 four miles east of the CA/NV state line (☎ **775- 588-3833**; www.tahoedixie2.com), rents late-model boats between 16 to 28 feet, plus runabouts, ski boats, pontoons, pedalboats, kayaks, and canoes. If you'd rather rent a jet ski or go parasailing, call ☎ **775-588-3530**.

- ✔ Tahoe Keys Boat Rentals (☎ **530-544-8888**, 530-541-8405, or 530-541-2155) rents powerboats from Tahoe Keys Marina, conve-niently located in South Lake Tahoe off Lake Tahoe Boulevard (U.S. 50) at the end of Tahoe Keys Road.

- ✔ A great place to launch a kayak is Timber Cove Marina, on Lake Tahoe Boulevard at the end of Johnson Boulevard, which has the largest public beach on the south shore. Rentals are available from Kayak Tahoe (☎ **530-544-2011**; www.kayaktahoe.com). Call ahead to arrange for a guided tour.

- ✔ Camp Richardson Marina at Camp Richardson Resort, two miles west of the U.S. 50/Highway 89 junction (☎ **530-542-6570**; www.camprichardson.com), rents a full slate of boating equip-ment similar to that at Zephyr Cove.

On the north shore:

- ✔ North Tahoe Marina, 7360 N. Lake Blvd. (Highway 28, one mile west of Highway 267), in Tahoe Vista (☎ **800-58-MARINA** or 530-546-8248; www.northtahoemarina.com), rents 19- to 24-foot powerboats, plus skis and tow lines.

- ✔ Tahoe Water Adventures is at the Lakehouse Mall, just off North Lake Boulevard at the end of Grove Street, in Tahoe City (☎ **530-583-3225**). They'll rent you powerboats with wakeboards or skis, canoes, kayaks, jet skis, or environmentally friendly inflatable watercraft.

Sportfishing

The most respected charter company around is Tahoe Sportfishing, which operates from two south-shore locations: Ski Run Marina, off U.S. 50 at the end of Ski Run Boulevard, a mile west of the state line (☎ 800-696-7797 or 530-541-5448); and Zephyr Cove, on U.S. 50 four miles east of the state line (☎ 800-696-7797 or 775-586-9338). Four- to seven-hour trips run $65 to $95 per person, including all gear, tackle, and bait. If you're lucky enough to hook a salmon or a big Mackinaw lake trout, the fee includes cleaning and sacking.

Driving along the spectacular west shore

The entire drive along Highway 89 offers spectacular scenery. It's worth dedicating the better part of a day to explore (be sure to make your exploration day a bright, clear weekday to avoid traffic).

Here are your best stops, from south to north:

✔ The best public-access beaches are part of the **Pope-Baldwin Recreational Area,** which begins just west of the Y intersection with U.S. 50. Expect to pay $3 to park at most public beaches, such as pretty **Pope Beach** and at the beach at **Camp Richardson.** Camp Richardson's **Beacon Bar & Grill** is the ideal place to enjoy a sunset Rum Runner (practically the official Tahoe cocktail) because the patio is right on the sand, just a stone's throw — literally — from the water.

✔ Next up is the **Tallac Historic Site,** a landmarked 1920s resort undergoing restoration. Far more interesting is **Visitors Center Beach** (turn right at the USFS Lake Tahoe Visitors Center sign). Follow the **Rainbow Trail,** an easy 10-minute walk along a paved walkway dotted with interpretive placards, to the **Stream Profile Chamber,** which offers an eco-lesson in water clarity and the freshwater food chain through a submerged window onto **Taylor Creek.** The view is like looking into an aquarium, only it's the real thing — very cool. Walk 10 minutes in the opposite direction from the visitor center, following the "Beach access" sign, to a very nice stretch of beach.

Hikers should stop into the visitor center itself to pick up a copy of the invaluable *Lake of the Sky Journal,* which details a number of great hikes throughout the area.

✔ From the **Visitors Center Beach,** the highway begins to climb northward. Soon you'll see the aptly named **Emerald Bay,** a 3-mile-long finger of sparkling green water jutting off the lake. This bay also has the lake's only island — tiny **Fanette Island** — where you'll find the ruins of an old stone teahouse.

Pull into the lot marked "Emerald Bay State Park/Vikingsholm" for my favorite lake photo op, bar none. The walk down to the lakeshore is 1½ miles long, but at the end you'll find **Vikingsholm,** a Danish-style castle built by the same (kinda wacky) lady behind the teahouse on Fanette Island. Back in 1928, the lake so reminded her of a Scandinavian fjord that she decided to drive the theme home. The castle is a sight to see — but remember, you'll have to walk back *up* that steep 1½-mile hill. The mansion is open for tours in summer only (☎ 530-525-7277).

✔ A couple of miles farther up the road sits **D. L. Bliss State Park** (☎ 530-525-7277), a gorgeous park with one of the lake's finest beaches (come early in summer to insure a parking spot). Attention, hikers: Moderate-level **Rubicon Trail** is a worthy 5-mile hike along Emerald Bay.

✔ Another 7 miles on is **Sugar Pine Point State Park** (☎ 530-525-7982). This terrific park offers 1¾ miles of shoreline with sandy beaches, more than 2,000 forested acres laced with hiking trails, the historic Ehrman Mansion (open for guided tours in summer), and a nature center. Parking is $5.

✔ After you reach Tahoe City, take note of **Fanny Bridge,** on Highway 89 just south of the Y intersection with Highway 28 (next to **Izzy's Burger Spa,** a great spot for juicy burgers and thick shakes), so named for the view of derrieres as folks bend over the rail to catch sight of the leaping trout below.

Golfing and other warm-weather fun

Hitting the links is a very big deal in North Tahoe. A half-dozen excellent courses lie within easy reach of Tahoe City, including the award-winning Robert Trent Jones, Jr.–designed links-style course at the **Resort at Squaw Creek** (see "Where to Stay on the North Shore" earlier in this chapter), honored by *Golf* magazine as one of the Top 10 resort courses in America. For tee times here or at another course, contact North Lake Tahoe Central Reservations (☎ 800-824-6348 or 530-583-3494; www.tahoefun.org). These friendly folks can also direct you south-shore vacationers to great courses, too.

Taking a heavenly tram ride

When it's not busy shuttling skiers, the Heavenly Aerial Tram (☎ 775-586-7000; www.skiheavenly.com) will take you on a mile-high ascent for some of the most spectacular views ever, here or anywhere. After you're done gawking at the scene during the five-minute ride, you can follow a two-mile path through a lovely forest, or dine at the Monument Peak Restaurant, which offers standard American eats. The ride costs $12.50 for adults, $9.50 for kids 4 to 12; ask for pricing on dining combo tickets, and make a reservation if you intend to eat. Guided hikes are offered in summer; call for the schedule. Heavenly is off U.S. 50 at the top of Ski Run Boulevard.

River rafting

Truckee River Rafting (☎ **888-584-7238** or 530-583-7238) offers one of my all-time favorite north-shore activities: taking a leisurely float along a five-mile stretch along the Truckee River from Tahoe City to River Ranch Pond. You'll even hit a couple of baby rapids for a few thrills. The kids will just love it. The ride is $25 for adults, $20 for kids, including all equipment and pickup at the end. Reserve ahead, and allow two to four hours for the adventure.

Playing at Squaw Valley's High Camp

Squaw Valley High Camp (☎ **530-583-6955;** www.squaw.com) is a marvelous place to play in summer, and a great way to experience the Olympic Village. After a scenic cable-car ride to 8,200 feet, you can ice-skate at the mountaintop Olympic Ice Pavilion, or swim and spa in the Swimming Lagoon. Hikers can pick up a trail map at the base information desk and follow any one of a half-dozen mountain trails, ranging from easy to difficult. Mountain bikers can rent a front-suspension bike at the Squaw Valley Sport Shop, in the Olympic Village (☎ **530-583- 3356**), take it to the top, and explore the snowless slopes. Expect half-day rentals around $30, and full-day rentals in the neighborhood of $40, helmets included; call to book a bike and avoid disappointment.

Hitting the slopes in ski season

Tahoe is more popular as a ski resort than anything else. It's home to the state's best skiing, and the country's largest concentration of downhill slopes. The ski season usually lasts from November through April, but has been known to extend into the early summer. Most resorts welcome snowboarders, but always check first.

Lift tickets for adults usually cost between $45 and $60 for a full day, $30 to $40 for a half day. Resorts often issue money-saving multiday tickets, and kids and seniors usually qualify for discounts.

Contact the local visitor centers (see "Gathering More Information" later in this chapter) for more information about all of the ski resorts in the area. Also inquire about *ski packages,* which can usually save you a small fortune, especially if you schedule to ski midweek.

The top south shore slopes

Heavenly (☎ **775-586-7000;** www.skiheavenly.com) is off U.S. 50 at the top of Ski Run Boulevard (turn left). It features the region's steepest vertical drop (3,500 feet) and one of its largest ski terrains (4,800 acres), not to mention one of the world's largest snowmaking systems. A third of the trails are set aside for envelope-pushers, but the rest are dedicated to beginners and intermediates. Excellent for families, with everything from kiddie ski schools to daycare.

Kirkwood (☎ **209-258-6000;** www.skikirkwood.com) is a 30- to 45-minute drive outside of South Lake Tahoe on Highway 88 (from U.S. 50, take Highway 89 south to 88 west). This resort ranks among

Ski magazine's Top 10 in North America for snow, terrain, and challenge. A terrific choice for spring skiers thanks to high average snowfall. It's now a destination resort, so inquire if you want to stay.

The top north shore slopes

Midsize **Alpine Meadows** (☎ **800-441-4423** or 530-583-4232; www.skialpine.com), 8 miles west of Tahoe City, has the best spring skiing around. In early May 2000, when everybody else was closed for the season (even Kirkwood), Alpine Meadows was still going strong. A local favorite, it maintains a committed following.

Diamond Peak (☎ **775-831-3211** or 775-832-1177; www.diamondpeak.com) is 17 miles east of Tahoe City in Incline Village, Nevada. Diamond Peak has taken great care to target families, and it's the north shore's best resort for kids. It's also smaller and less expensive than most. Kids as young as 3 can learn to ski, and the resort maintains a terrific snowplay area.

If you want spectacular lake views while you ski, take to the slopes at **Homewood** (☎ **530-525-2992.** www.skihomewood.com), right on the lake's west shore, 6½ miles south of Tahoe City. It's small, intimate, and a local favorite. Ask about Wild Wednesdays, when grown-ups ski two-for-one.

Northstar-at-Tahoe (☎ **800-466-6784** or 530-562-1010; www.skinorthstar.com), 11 miles east of Tahoe City, is a terrific choice for families, with 75 percent of the ski terrain devoted to beginners and intermediates. A well-rounded resort, with lots of good facilities and other activities.

Ever dream of Olympic glory? Live the fantasy at **Squaw Valley USA** (☎ **888-766-9321** or 530-583-6955; www.squaw.com), 9 miles from Tahoe City, site of the 1960 Olympic Winter Games. Spanning six Sierra peaks, gorgeous, excellently outfitted Squaw Valley is Tahoe's most state-of-the-art ski area and boasts its most challenging array of runs. A must for serious skiers.

Cross-country skiing and snowmobiling

The north shore offers the most — and best — cross-country options. **Lakeview Cross Country Ski Area** (☎ **530-583-9353**) has more than 40 miles of groomed trails, a full-service day lodge, state-of-the-art equipment, and a convenient location, just 2 miles east of Tahoe City off Highway 28 at Dollar Hill (turn at Fabian Way).

Northstar-at-Tahoe (☎ **530-562-2475**) has a terrific cross-country, telemark, and snowshoe center with 40 miles of groomed trails. **Diamond Peak** (☎ **775-832-1177**) lets you bring Bowser along as you explore more than 20 miles of groomed trails and more backcountry area on skis or Atlas snowshoes. See "Hitting the Slopes in Ski Season" for details on both resorts. The **Resort at Squaw Creek** (☎ **530-581-6637**) is much smaller, with just 11 miles of trails, but the Squaw Valley setting is unparalleled.

On the south shore, head to the **Cross-Country Ski & Snowshoe Center** at Camp Richardson Resort, on Highway 89 which is 2½ miles north of the U.S. 50/89 "Y" intersection (☎ **530-542-6584**).

The south shore's **Zephyr Cove Snowmobile Center,** on U.S. 50, 4 miles east of the state line (☎ **775-882-0788** or 775-588-3833; www.tahoedixie2.com), is the largest snowmobiling center in the United States. You can rent and set out on your own (kids as young as 5 can accompany you on a double machine), or take a guided tour (recommended if you're a newbie). Reservations recommended.

On the north shore, contact **Snowmobiling Unlimited** (☎ **530-583-5858** or 530-583-7192). Tahoe's oldest snowmobile touring company, this company leads two- and three-hour guided tours.

Trying your luck at the Stateline casinos

One of the great advantages of a south shore vacation is the proximity to the casinos just a walk across the border in Stateline, Nevada. The following 24-hour fun palaces are my favorites, and you can throw a stone and hit each of 'em from the California side. Just go east on Lake Tahoe Boulevard until you reach Stateline Avenue.

- ✔ **Harrah's** (☎ **800-427-7247** or 775-588-6611; www.harrahstahoe.com) is low-key, attractive, and well-done, drawing a generally older crowd. The jam-packed showroom schedule offers a wide array of entertainment, from crowd-pleasing Vegas-style revues starring leggy showgirls to big-name headliners, including many baby-boomer faves (Ringo Starr, Smokey Robinson, the Smothers Brothers, and so forth).

- ✔ **Harveys** (☎ **800-427-8397** or 775-588-2411; www.harveystahoe.com) rocks, with video monitors and speakers blasting radio-friendly sounds throughout the largest and most stylish casino in Tahoe. Terrific racing and sports book. Harveys draws in a young, sophisticated crowd. The showroom focuses on cabaret-style shows and sexy revues, while the **Hard Rock Cafe** hosts live music on Friday and Saturday nights.

- ✔ **Caesars Tahoe** (☎ **800-648-3353** or 775-586-7771; www.caesarstahoe.com), the only real theme casino in Tahoe, is also the most glam. Caesars contains the best of the sports books, although Harveys gives it a run for its money. It offers the best showroom, too, with such heavyweight headliners as Wynonna, David Copperfield, and Tom Jones as well as championship boxing. Attention party animals: Caesars houses **Nero's 2000,** Tahoe's biggest and best dance club.

If you hope to catch a big-name headliner, check the schedule before you leave home and make reservations to avoid disappointment.

The casinos make sure families feel welcome. Harrah's, Harveys, and Caesars all offer sizable video arcades where classics like Pac Man and Donkey Kong buzz and beep alongside the latest virtual-reality games. In addition, the casino showrooms often offer all-ages entertainment, such as magic shows, at earlier family hours.

Gathering More Information

Lake Tahoe offers far more to do beyond what I mention here. Contact one of the local visitor organizations for more information, especially if you're interested in an activity I haven't discussed.

The Lake Tahoe Visitors Authority (☎ **800-AT-TAHOE,** 530-544-5050, or 530-583-3494; www.virtualtahoe.com) can give you all the information you'll need on South Lake Tahoe and environs. After you arrive, stop by the South Lake Tahoe Chamber of Commerce, located at 3066 S. Lake Tahoe Blvd., just east of Altahoe Boulevard (☎ **530-541- 5255;** www.tahoeinfo.com), open Monday through Saturday from 8:30 a.m. to 5 p.m.

For info on the north shore, contact the North Lake Tahoe Resort Association (☎ **800-824-6348**, 888-434-1262, 530-583-3494, or 530-581-8736; www.tahoefun.org). After you arrive, stop by their terrific visitor center at 245 North Lake Blvd. (on the north side of Highway 28; the sign says "Chamber of Commerce") in Tahoe City, open Monday through Friday from 9 a.m. to 5 p.m., Saturday and Sunday from 9 a.m. to 4 p.m.

If you'd like information on the Nevada side of the north shore, contact the Incline Village/Crystal Bay Visitors Bureau (☎ **800-468-2463** or 775-832-1606; www.gotahoe.com).

For Tahoe road conditions, call ☎ **800-427-7623;** for weather, call ☎ **800-752-1177.**

Side-Tripping to the Gold Country

California's gold-rush country is rich in color and history. Dotted with 19th-century-mining-towns-turned-cutesy-B&B-havens, the region is a big weekend destination for northern Californians (especially wooing couples, natch). The area has plenty to see and do, but nothing so major that you should devote the half week you'd need to drive the region's main thoroughfare, Highway 49, from end to end. Leave that drive for a future visit, after you've covered so many of California's highlights that you have the time to dedicate to it.

But (you knew there was a but!) a portion of the Gold Country is so easy to reach on your drive to or from Lake Tahoe that I highly recommend that you dedicate half a day to seeing its main (and most fascinating) attraction, the **Marshall Gold Discovery State Historic Park**, where the gold rush began. You can also stop in a gold-rush town or two just to get a taste of what the Gold Country's like.

Getting there

The section of Highway 49 — the **Gold Chain Highway** — on which I suggest you focus runs roughly north-south between I-80 (the road to North Tahoe) and U.S. 50 (the road to South Tahoe). I-80 connects with Highway 49 at **Auburn,** about 35 miles (or 40 minutes) east of Sacramento, 78 miles (or a gorgeous 1½-hour drive) west of Tahoe City. U.S. 50 connects with the section of Highway 49 you're concerned with on the south end, in **Placerville** (originally dubbed Hangtown for its single-minded justice system), about 43 miles (or 45 minutes) east of Sacramento, 55 miles (or a little more than an hour's drive) west of South Lake Tahoe.

The roughly 23-mile drive between Auburn and Placerville along the Gold Chain Highway takes about an hour thanks to one narrow lane in each direction and more than a few hairpin turns. **Coloma,** the hairsbreadth of a town where you'll find the Marshall Gold Discovery Park, is roughly midway between the two.

Because all roads lead through Sacramento, you can easily work a trip along the Gold Chain Highway into your journey to or from Tahoe.

If you're heading to South Tahoe: Pick up I-80 (which you may already be on if you're coming from the Bay Area) in Sacramento, turn south on Highway 49 to do your exploring, and then head east and on to South Tahoe after you meet up with U.S. 50. If you're leaving **from South Tahoe,** reverse the process by taking U.S. 50 west, Highway 49 north for exploring, then I-80 west on when you're done.

If you're heading to North Tahoe: Take U.S. 50 east from Sacramento, then take Highway 49 north, then I-80 east to Tahoe City. **From North Tahoe?** You got it — I-80 west, Highway 49 south, U.S. 50 west to your destination.

The Gold Country can be brutally hot in summer, so dress accordingly.

Hitting the highlights

The **Marshall Gold Discovery State Historic Park** is nestled in the golden Sierra foothills on Highway 49 between Auburn and Placerville at Coloma (☎ **530-622-3470** or 530-622-0390; parks.ca.gov/districts/goldrush/mgdshp/mgdshp.htm or www.windjammer.net/coloma). Actually, about 70 percent of Coloma *is* the park. This is where James Marshall, a carpenter, discovered two itsy-bitsy gold nuggets on

January 24, 1848, at John Sutter's mill on the dusty banks of the American River. This discovery managed to launch gold-rush mania and redirect California history in the process.

A working re-creation of Sutter's mill, a few intact gold-rush-era buildings, and enlightening exhibits capture the pioneering spirit and excitement of that day and the "'49ers" get-rich-quick craze that followed. This place is very cool, and kids will enjoy it more than you may expect. To take maximum advantage of this historic site, start out at the **Gold Discovery Museum Visitors Center,** just off Highway 49 at Bridge Street. Come early, and ask the rangers about guided discovery tours and sawmill demonstrations (usually Thursday through Sunday 11 a.m. and 1 p.m. in summer). You may even get a chance to pan for gold yourself! The buildings are open daily from 10 a.m. to 5 p.m., and the fee is $5 per car. Bring a picnic lunch or snack.

By the way: James Marshall, poor soul, never saw a dime of the gold in them thar hills.

Old Town Auburn

In Auburn, the area just off the I-80 at Nevada Street (bounded by Court Street, Lincoln Way, Washington Street, and Maple and Commercial streets), is **Old Town Auburn.** This is an ideal example of an Old West gold town transformed into a boutiqued downtown. Nevertheless, it still maintains a strong historic feel with original buildings boasting false storefronts along steep, cobbled streets. Head to the **Bootleggers Old Town Tavern & Grill ($$-$$$),** 210 Washington St. (☎ 530-889-2229), for a lunch stop with an appealing local vibe.

To get some background history on the area, stop at the **Placer County Courthouse,** the notable neoclassical building with a mismatched hat — a Renaissance gold dome — at the top of the hill at 101 Maple St. (at Court Street and Lincoln Way). Inside is the petite **Placer County Museum (☎ 530-889-6500),** which tells the story of Auburn's rise as a mother-lode gold-rush town. This is a great place to pick up information on other attractions in the area.

Seeing more of the Gold Country

If you want to spend more time in Gold Country, the following places are good bets for lodging.

- ✔ Located within the bounds of the Marshall Gold Discovery Park, the **Coloma Country Inn Bed & Breakfast ($$)** (☎ 530-622-6919; www.colomacountryinn.com) captures the spirit of the locale in a lovely and well-appointed 1852 farmhouse.

- ✔ In Auburn, your best bet is the **Holiday Inn of Auburn ($$),** on Highway 49 within walking distance of Old Town (☎ 800-814-8787 or 530-887-8787; www.holiday-inn.com).

For more information on the Auburn area, including local B&B recommendations, check out www.auburnweb.com, or contact the Placer County Visitors Council (☎ **530-887-2211**; www.placer.ca.gov/visit).

If you're going to spend more time in the region, consider heading south to cute-as-a-button Sutter Creek (whose **Chatterbox Cafe** The *New York Times* noted "may be the finest luncheonette in North America"), and nearby Jackson. The Amador County Chamber of Commerce (☎ **209-223-0350**; www.cdepot.net/chamber) can provide more information.

Or head to the far north end of Highway 49 to Nevada City and Grass Valley, which many consider to be the finest tourist towns in the Gold Country. Contact the Grass Valley/Nevada County Chamber of Commerce (☎ **800-655-4667** or 530-273-4667) or the Nevada City Chamber of Commerce (☎ **800-655-6569** or 530-265-2692), or go online to the very useful site www.ncgold.com.

Certain accommodations near **Yosemite National Park** make ideal bases for exploring the region, especially the **Groveland Hotel** and hotels in Oakhurst, such as **Château du Sureau.** See Chapter 14 for details.

Chapter 14

Yosemite National Park

- -

In This Chapter

▶ Planning your trip to America's favorite national park

▶ Deciding where to stay and dine within Yosemite

▶ Weighing your options in the nearby gateway towns

▶ Exploring Yosemite — On and off the beaten path

- -

*P*repare to meet one of the most spectacular places in the world. **Yosemite National Park** encompasses nearly 1,200 square miles and a wildly diverse landscape that soars from 2,000 feet to an awesome 13,000 feet above sea level. It's a blue-ribbon destination all the way: home to the world's most impressive glacier-carved canyon (Yosemite Valley); three of the world's 10 tallest waterfalls, including North America's longest (2,425-foot Yosemite Falls); the world's largest granite monolith (El Capitan); and the world's biggest and oldest trees (the Giant Sequoias). However, those nature-bending records don't even begin to describe Yosemite's majesty — you must come and see this breathtaking place for yourself.

The mile-wide, seven-mile-long **Yosemite Valley** is the attraction-laden heart of the mammoth park, much of which is unreachable wilderness. When you arrive, you see why this valley is called the ultimate example of a glacier-carved canyon: Its flat, open meadows and oak and mixed-conifer woodlands come to an abrupt halt on all sides, where sheer walls suddenly soar to the sky. The towering cliffs, craggy monoliths, rounded domes, and tumbling waterfalls will wow you. And, between Memorial and Labor days, the mammoth crowds may give you a migraine, because 90 percent of the park's visitors congregate there. Think of the valley as the Waikiki of Yosemite.

You shouldn't miss the valley, but schedule some time to poke around the quieter areas of the park, especially if you're craving a more genuine wilderness experience. Head for the serene, (largely) crowd-free **High Country** in the summer. The entire Sierra Nevada doesn't get any more beautiful than this splendid mix of verdant subalpine meadows and forest, crystal-blue glacial lakes, granite spires, and domes. Or make time for **Mariposa Grove,** the sky-scraping stand of giant sequoias at the lovely, woodsy, civilized south end.

The beauty of Yosemite is that it's a foolproof park. To accommodate all those tourists, Yosemite has become very visitor-friendly, offering lots of available guidance, great facilities, and easy hikes and river access, making it an ideal place to vacation with children. The summer madness horning in on your communion with nature just seems like the biggest, best summer camp in the world to a kid.

Remember: Even at the height of the summer chaos you can have a genuine wilderness experience in Yosemite if you want one. You don't have to be a survivalist to venture out of the valley and into one of the more remote areas of the park. Whenever you visit, give yourself the space and time (at least two days; more is ideal) to truly appreciate this humbling, awe-inspiring place.

Timing Your Visit

Overwhelmingly, most people visit Yosemite in June, July, and August — which means that if you don't have to come during those months, you shouldn't. The Yosemite Valley becomes so crowded in the summer that it seems more like a theme park than a natural wonderland. But if your vacation falls during these months, don't feel that you have to stay away.

If you're not staying in the park, enter early (the superintendent has been known, on a few occasions, to close the gates when the park reaches maximum capacity), and plan to spend much of your visit in areas other than the Yosemite Valley, where most visitors congregate. On the up side, summer is the best time to visit **Tuolumne** (pronounced "too-ALL-oh-mee") **Meadows,** glorious subalpine meadows at an altitude of 8,600 feet, and take the drive to the summit of **Glacier Point,** at 7,214 feet, for spectacular views over the valley.

Mid-September through October is a magical season. Visitorship drops but the park remains fully accessible; the roads to Tuolumne Meadows and Glacier Point generally don't close until November.

If you really want the park all to yourself, visit in winter. The valley is marvelously peaceful, the snow provides a nice contrast to all that granite, and cross-country skiing opportunities abound. (The average annual accumulation on the valley floor is about four feet.) You can easily get accommodations and even discounted rates. The **High Country** is under about 20 feet of snow from November through May, however, and pretty much off limits.

When you're deciding how much time to spend touring Yosemite, go with more rather than less. I learned this lesson on my first visit to Yosemite: One day, even a full one, is simply not enough. Give yourself at least two days; three full days comes closer to the ideal.

Accessing the Park

You can enter the park through any one of four main entrances:

✔ The most commonly used entrance (and most traffic-congested in summer) is the *Arch Rock Entrance,* on the west side of the park via Highway 140, through the blink-and-you'll-miss-it town of El Portal. (Note: This entrance closes nightly between 10:30 p.m. and 6:30 a.m.) This gateway offers the most direct access to Yosemite Valley, where your first stop should be the main Valley Visitor Center after you dump your car in a day-use lot (if you're staying outside the park) or at your accommodation. The center is open daily from 8:30 a.m. to 5 p.m.

✔ On the west side, north of Arch Rock, is the *Big Oak Flat Entrance,* on Highway 120, which takes you through Groveland first. It's also valley-convenient, but allows you to pass by the congested valley and head straight for the High Country if you so choose. If you're going to bypass the valley, be sure to stop by the Big Oak Flat Information Station (☎ **209-379-1899**), just inside the park gate, for information and maps; open daily from 9 a.m. to 6 p.m.

✔ You can also arrive via the *South Entrance,* on Highway 41, about 35 miles south of Yosemite Valley. It's the most convenient entrance for those coming from points south, and it boasts some of the most wonderful vistas in the park. You'll also use it if you choose to stay at **Tenaya Lodge** (see the listing of places to stay outside the park later in this chapter) or at one of the accommodations options in Oakhurst. The Wawona Information Station (☎ **209-375-9501**) is open only in summer from 8:30 a.m. to 4:30 p.m. daily. Turn off Highway 41 at Chilnualna Falls Road and take the first right after the stables.

✔ The *Tioga Pass Entrance,* the eastern High Country gateway on Highway 120, is open only in summer. You'll use this entrance if you come from Lake Tahoe (see Chapter 12), or from **Death Valley National Park** (see Chapter 26). The Tuolumne Meadows Visitor Center (☎ **209-372-0263**) is open daily in season from 9 a.m. to 7 p.m.

Getting there by car

From Lake Tahoe, you can take U.S. 50 west out of Tahoe to I-395 south to Highway 120, which will lead you into the park's High Country via the summer-only Tioga Pass Entrance. The 3 ½-hour drive is doable between late June and the first snowfall (usually early November). Otherwise, you'll have a 5- or 6-hour drive down winding Highway 49, which can be extra-slow going in bad weather.

From San Francisco, the drive is about 3½ hours. Take I-580 west to I-205 to Highway 120, then plan the rest of your route along highways 120, 99, or 140, depending on where you're staying.

From the Central Coast, you have a couple of options, depending on your departure point. From the Monterey Peninsula, take U.S. 101 to Highway 152 to Highway 99 north to Highway 140 to the Arch Rock Entrance — roughly a 5-hour drive — or Highway 99 south to 145 to 41 north to the South Entrance. If you're starting farther south on the coast, take U.S. 101 or Highway 1 to Highway 41 (near Morro Bay) and follow it all the way to Yosemite's south gate. Expect to spend about 5½ hours on 41.

From Los Angeles, the drive lasts about 6½ hours. Take I-5 north to Highway 99 to either Highway 41 or Highway 140, depending on where you're staying.

Winging it

Fresno Yosemite International Airport, 5175 E. Clinton Ave., Fresno (☎ 559-498-4095; www.fresno.com/flyfresno), is 90 miles south of Yosemite. From the airport, take Highway 180 to Highway 41 north to the park's South Entrance. These airlines fly in:

- ✔ Alaska Airlines: ☎ 800-426-0333; www.alaskaair.com
- ✔ America West: ☎ 800-235-9292; www.americawest.com
- ✔ American Airlines: ☎ 800-433-7300; www.aa.com
- ✔ Continental: ☎ 800-525-0280; www.continental.com
- ✔ Delta: ☎ 800-221-1212; www.delta-air.com
- ✔ Horizon: ☎ 800-547-9308; www.horizonair.com
- ✔ United/United Express: ☎ 800-241-6522; www.ual.com

The following national car-rental companies have airport locations:

- ✔ Avis: ☎ 800-331-1212; www.avis.com
- ✔ Budget: ☎ 800-527-0700; www.budgetrentacar.com
- ✔ Dollar: ☎ 800-800-4000; www.dollar.com
- ✔ Hertz: ☎ 800-654-3131; www.hertz.com
- ✔ National: ☎ 800-CAR-RENT; www.nationalcar.com

Arriving by train

Another option is to arrive in Merced, 73 miles southwest of the Arch Rock Entrance, via Amtrak (☎ 800-872-7245; www.amtrak.com). You can then book transportation or a park tour with VIA Adventures/Gray Line of Yosemite (☎ 800-842-5463), which also offers packages that include accommodations.

Entering and navigating the park

Admission to the park is $20 per car, $10 per person if you arrive by bus, bike, or on foot. Your ticket is good for 7 days, so keep it handy. At press time, reservations are not required and you are free to drive around the park as you please, but these policies can change; call ☎ **209-372-0200** or visit the official site at www.nps.gov/yose to check the latest before you go.

Do everybody a favor while you're in Yosemite Valley: Park your car once (you'll be directed right to a day-use lot if you're not staying within park bounds) and use the shuttle system, bikes, or your own tootsies to move around the valley floor. Free shuttle buses loop the valley daily year-round, and as frequently as every 10 minutes in high season. Park management is so eager for you to take advantage of this alternative that they make it a breeze to use. If you'd rather two-wheel it, bike rentals are available for the entire family at **Curry Village** (☎ **209-372-8319**) year-round, and from April through November at **Yosemite Lodge** (☎ **209-372-1208**). Use your car only to reach other far-flung areas of the park.

In May 2000, in an effort to alleviate some traffic congestion, the Yosemite Area Regional Transportation System (YARTS) started offering bus service from some of the gateway communities, allowing you to leave your car behind at the motel. This service is particularly useful for those of you staying at **Cedar Lodge** and **Yosemite View Lodge** just outside the Arch Rock Entrance, both of which have on-site pickups. You can also meet the bus if you're staying farther west on Highway 140 in Mariposa. Those of you staying at the **Wawona Hotel** in the southernmost section of the park can use YARTS to reach Yosemite Valley. For exact schedule and fare information, call ☎ **877-989-2787** or 209-372-4487, or visit www.yarts.com.

Preparing for Your Visit

Here are a few tips to help you get your visit off on the right foot:

- ✔ **Wear appropriately sturdy shoes.** Hiking boots are best, but at the least bring sneakers. I cannot tell you how many women I've seen walking around the park in platform slides.

- ✔ **Always bring a jacket.** Even if the valley floor is hot, the air can really cool off after you ascend to the High Country. Rain is most common in the colder months, but thunderstorms can happen at any time.

- ✔ **In summer, bring a swimsuit.** A hot day may tempt you to take a dip in the Merced River. An excellent swimming hole exists at Stoneman Bridge, near Curry Village in the valley.

✔ **In winter, come with the appropriate snow gear.** Bring snow boots, snow coats — the works. Don't leave home without tire chains in the trunk if you're driving your own car, or inquire about them when you book your rental vehicle.

✔ **In the High Country, opt for an easier hiking trail than you might normally choose.** The thinness of the air at these elevations can really tax your system and sap your energy.

✔ **Heed all warnings about the bear problem.** Terribly spoiled by years of human leftovers, black bears have decided that they prefer your Big Macs, Cheetos, and PB&J sandwiches to Mother Nature's eats. As a result, they've become a real menace to personal property (and to themselves — Yosemite's bears are in danger of losing their natural hunting and gathering instincts).

✔ **Do not leave food in your car.** Don't even leave a stray french fry in the trunk. Bears have become experts at ripping open cars as if they were tin cans (most often, they just wiggle their claws into the gap above the door and bend down). Statistics prove that they're particularly fond of white minivans — why, nobody knows. During the month of April 2000 alone, bears broke into 45 cars — and trust me, you do not want to have to explain this to Avis. If you camp or stay in a tent cabin, *diligently use the metal food storage boxes.*

Staying and Dining Inside the Park

If you're not thrilled with your lodging or campground reservation, call back within 30 days of the date of your arrival. Most cancellations occur within that 30-day period, so you may be able to upgrade to your preferred choice.

Yosemite Eats

In addition to the food choices available in the accommodations themselves (noted in the following sections), **Yosemite Village** boasts a number of casual restaurants, including a deli, a pizza-and-pasta joint, and a burger grill in summer. The choices may not be gourmet, but you won't go hungry here.

Yosemite Concession Services manages all in-park accommodations. You can make reservations up to 366 days in advance. Call central reservations at ☎ 559-252-4848 to reserve, ideally 366 days before your intended arrival to avoid disappointment. The phone lines are open Monday through Friday between 7 a.m. to 6 p.m. , Saturday and Sunday 8 a.m. to 5 p.m. (PST), and the service accepts all major credit cards. The park hotels book up further in advance than you may expect in season, so call as early as possible. You can make online reservations through www.yosemitepark.com, but at press time, no provision existed for instant guarantee, so calling may be your best option.

All rates are based on double occupancy. Expect to pay between $3 and $11 for each extra person ($20 at the Ahwahnee). Kids can sometimes stay free, so ask. Call the special offer hotline at ☎ **559-454-0555** for discounted prices on winter stays (mid-November through March).

Ahwahnee Hotel

$$$$ Yosemite Valley

The park's finest place to stay is this baronial, ultra-romantic landmark lodge, gorgeously done in a Native American motif. Despite the elegance, it's right at home in the valley — it has the same grand scale. Afternoon tea is served in the great lounge, and dinner is a reservations- and jacket (or sweater)-required affair in the stunning (and surprisingly good) dining room. Feel free to come for lunch in your shorts and tennies.

Rack rates: $241–$287 double, $515–$860 suite.

Curry Village

$–$$ Yosemite Valley

Sitting in the shadow of Glacier Point is Curry Village, whose accommodations include a few standard motel rooms, rustic wood-frame cabins (some with private bath, some without), and canvas-covered tent cabins that are halfway to camping but still have wood floors, electricity, and maid service; they share a couple of central bathhouses. The whole place has a summer-camp-gone-to-heck vibe about it, but it's convenient and fun if privacy isn't a big concern. The village includes a cafeteria, a burger shack, a coffee and ice cream counter, and a pizza parlor, plus an activities desk with bike rentals (cross-country skis in winter).

If you book a tent cabin at Curry Village, ask when you arrive if any cancellations have cleared the way for an upgrade. If it's available, chances are good they'll give it away for free. It never hurts to ask, especially outside the summer season.

Rack rates: $40–$92 double.

Housekeeping Camp

$ Yosemite Valley

This arrangement is the closest you can get to roughing it without toting your own tent. The camp basically consists of a collection of semi-furnished concrete-and-canvas lean-tos on the banks of the Merced River. The experience is like camping at a KOA, with shared bathhouse, laundry, and a small grocery store.

Rack Rates: $43 double.

Yosemite National Park Accommodations

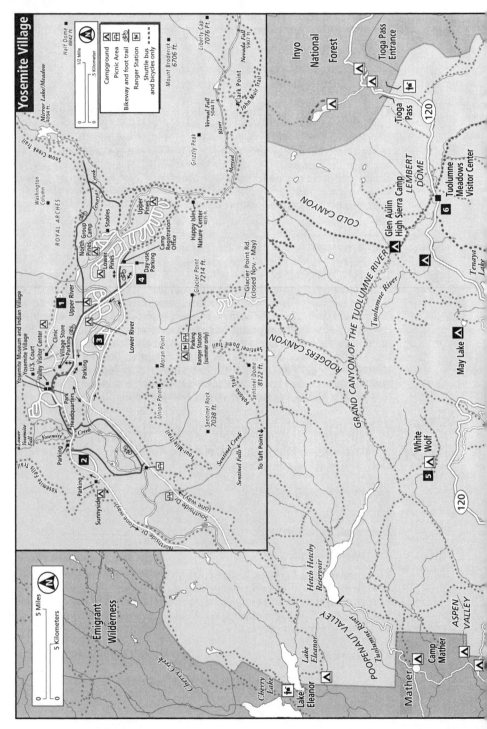

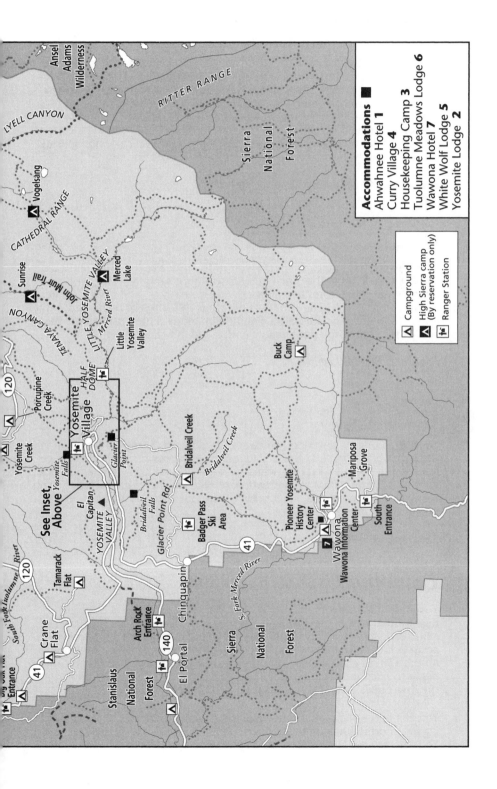

Accommodations ■
Ahwahnee Hotel **1**
Curry Village **4**
Housekeeping Camp **3**
Tuolumne Meadows Lodge **6**
Wawona Hotel **7**
White Wolf Lodge **5**
Yosemite Lodge **2**

△ Campground
▲ High Sierra camp
(By reservation only)
🏠 Ranger Station

Tuolumne Meadows Lodge and White Wolf Lodge

$ High Country (North Yosemite)

Both of these lodges have the same metal-frame canvas tent cabins that Curry Village has, but without the chaotic squatters' vibe. They are clean and neat, and most cabins sleep four and have wood-burning stoves. (White Wolf also has four cute wood cabins with private baths.) White Wolf is a bit more out of the way but has fewer facilities; breakfast and dinner are served in the restaurant/general store. Tuolumne Meadows is larger and has a burger stand, a grocery store, stables, a mountaineering school, a gas station, and a dining tent for breakfast and dinner.

Rack rates: $42–$46 double. Open summer only.

Wawona Hotel

$$ South Yosemite

The Wawona isn't quite as spectacular or luxurious as the Ahwahnee, but this landmark lies in the much quieter southern section of the park (providing great relief from the valley crowds in summer) and boasts oodles of Victorian charm. The rooms contain no TV or telephones, and only about half offer private baths. Facilities include a nice restaurant that serves three meals; a pool; tennis court; and nine holes of golf.

Rack rates: $94–$121 double.

Yosemite Lodge

$$ Yosemite Valley

Yosemite Lodge is a perfectly nice standard motel (sorry, no TV) right in the heart of the valley bustle. The standard rooms are just fine, but go for a lodge room if you can, which will get you a bit more space and a view of Yosemite Falls from a patio or balcony. The lodge includes two midpriced restaurants (one sit-down, one buffet-style) and a cafeteria, plus a snack shack by the pool.

Rack rates: $92–$115 double.

Camping

Yosemite has so many campsites that managing them is its own cottage industry. Still, they book up very quickly, so call as early as possible, especially for stays from May through September. Park services accepts campsite reservations up to five months in advance, starting on the 15th of each month. (In other words, on February 15th you can begin to make reservations for June 15th through July 14th.) Calling on the first day is wise if you want your first choice.

You can find a complete rundown of the camping options online, including fee information and locations, at www.nps.gov/yose/camping.htm. You can also get all the information you need by calling the reservations line at ☎ **800-436-PARK** (436-7275) or 301-722-1257 daily between 7 a.m. and 7 p.m. (PST). You can make online reservations at reservations. nps.gov. If Yosemite campgrounds are full, the reservations agents will gladly refer you to the National Forest campgrounds just outside the park.

Staying and Dining Outside the Park

Each of the hotels in this section is near one of the park's main gates. In addition to the two motels closest to the park, Cedar and Yosemite View lodges (see the listings below), Yosemite Motels (☎ **888-742-4371;** www.yosemite-motels.com) also runs the just-fine **Comfort Inn Oakhurst ($–$$),** 15 miles south of the South Entrance, as well as two motels in Mariposa: the **Best Western Yosemite Way Station ($–$$)** and **Comfort Inn Mariposa ($–$$).** The Mariposa motels are fine choices if everything else is booked, but you're better off trying to stay closer to the park first.

If you stay at **Cedar Lodge** or **Yosemite Lodge** (see the individual listings later in this section), or at any of the Mariposa choices discussed previously, you can leave your car behind and use the YARTS shuttle to reach the park if you choose (see "Entering & Getting Around the Park" earlier in this chapter).

The area can get booked up in the busy season, so if my favorites are full, contact the Yosemite Sierra Visitors Bureau (☎ **559-683-4636;** www.yosemite-sierra.org) for additional options.

Because the region is so rural, expect to eat at your hotel restaurant. Only those who stay at an Oakhurst or Mariposa base will have other restaurants to choose from. Even there, pickings are slim — limited largely to pizza and fast food — so don't let dining dictate your choice of base. The exception: **Erna's Elderberry House** at the sumptuous **Château du Sureau** in Oakhurst (see the listing later in this section).

Best Western Yosemite Gateway Inn

$–$$ Oakhurst

This perfectly nice motel, 15 miles due south of the park, offers pleasant rooms that are big enough for families. All rooms have coffeemakers, many have microwaves and fridges, and some have kitchens. Facilities include an indoor pool area with a spa, sauna, and exercise equipment; an outdoor pool and spa; and coin-op laundry.

40530 Hwy. 41, Oakhurst. ☎ *800-528-1234 or 559-683-2378. Fax: 559-683-3813. Internet:* www.bestwestern.com. *Parking: Free! Rack rates: $44–$110 double, $79–$144 suite. Rates include continental breakfast. Deals: Ask about off-season deals. AE, DISC, MC, V.*

Cedar Lodge

$$ El Portal

Another nice motel, this one is located 8 miles outside of the Arch Rock entrance in hilly setting along the Merced River. Rooms are motel-standard but quite comfortable. On site are two pools (one indoor, one outdoor), a spa, a grocery store, and two restaurants — one a nice dining room and the other a casual pizza parlor.

9966 Hwy. 140, El Portal. ☎ *888-742-4371 or 209-379-2612. Fax: 209-379-2712. Internet:* www.yosemite-motels.com. *Parking: Free! Rack rates: $85–$99 double, $135 suite. AE, MC, V. Deals: Off-season rates as low as $59 double, $99 suite.*

Château du Sureau

$$$$$ Oakhurst

Finding one of America's finest inns in the rinky-dink town of Oakhurst, just a 20-minute drive from Yosemite's South Entrance, is wild. Staying at this gated Relais & Chateaux villa is like being entertained by European royalty, complete with maids to bring you tea and cookies and butlers to press your dinner clothes. The inn is supremely gorgeous and comfy — and the staff won't bat an eye when you stumble in dusty after a day in the park. Even if you're accustomed to luxury travel, you'll never forget this place. One of California's most celebrated restaurants, **Erna's Elderberry House,** is on the premises. The French Provençal–style cuisine is well worth a special-occasion splurge, even if you don't stay here ($72 prix-fixe).

48688 Victoria Lane (just off Hwy. 41, 15 miles south of Yosemite's South Entrance), Oakhurst. ☎ *559-683-6860, or 559-683-6800 for restaurant reservations. Fax: 559-683-0800. Internet:* www.chateaudusureau.com. *Parking: Free! Rack rates: $325–$510 double. Rates include an elegant two-course breakfast. AE, MC, V.*

Groveland Hotel

$$ Groveland

The charm of this sweet historic inn and the Wild West–style one-horse town makes up for the drive (23 miles outside the Big Oak Flat Entrance). The hotel houses the finest restaurant in town, plus a groovy gold-rush-era saloon. Rooms are furnished with antiques and have private baths. A great in-between base for those who'd also like to do a bit of Gold Country exploring along Highway 49.

18767 Main St. (Hwy. 120, east of Hwy. 49), Groveland. ☎ *800-273-3314 or 209-962-4000. Fax: 209-962-6674. Internet:* www.groveland.com. *Rack rates: $125–$145 double, $200 suite. Rates include continental breakfast and evening wine. Deals: Ask about midweek winter getaway specials. AE, DISC, MC, V.*

Tenaya Lodge

$$$–$$$$ Fish Camp

This gorgeous destination lodge draws in parkgoers as well as conference groups with its stone's-throw proximity to the park, terrific facilities, on-site activities, and rustic-glamorous wilderness-lodge-goes-modern ambience. The ultra-comfy rooms are done in area-appropriate style and boast all the latest comforts. The facilities include two pools, three restaurants, game room, gym, spa services, and a terrific kids' program.

1122 Hwy. 41, Fish Camp (2 miles south of the South Entrance). ☎ 888-514-2167 or 559-683-6555. Fax: 559-683-8684. Internet: www.tenayalodge.com. *Rack rates: $169–$259 double, $199–$379 suite. Deals: You'll always save a few bucks by choosing midweek over a weekend stay. Winter rates as low as $89. Check for packages and Internet specials, as low as $139 in season. AE, DC, DISC, JCB, MC, V.*

Yosemite View Lodge

$$ El Portal

Just 2 miles outside the Arch Rock Entrance, this large motel complex is the closest you can get to Yosemite without actually staying within park bounds. Rooms are large and very comfy; all have kitchenettes, and many have Jacuzzi tubs, gas fireplaces, and balconies overlooking the rushing Merced River (I recommend spending a little extra for one of these). On site are three pools (two outdoor, one indoor) and five spas, a just-fine restaurant, a bar, a pizza parlor, and a well-stocked general store.

11136 Hwy. 140, El Portal. ☎ 888-742-4371 or 209-379-2681. Fax: 209-379-2704. Internet: www.yosemite-motels.com. *Parking: Free! Rack rates: $119–$149 double, $179–$199 suite. MC, V. Deals: Off-season rates as low as $79 double.*

Exploring the Park

I highly recommend launching your visit with the two-hour guided *Valley Floor Tour,* conducted aboard an open-air tram in warm weather, a cozy bus in winter. The tour is an absolute must if your visit is limited to one day, as it's the only way you'll see all of the park's major features. You can see the valley highlights by tour in the morning, and then spend your afternoon exploring the High Country or heading south to Wawona. Tours run daily year-round, at regular intervals throughout the day. Tickets are $17.50, and you can buy them at a booth just outside the Valley Store in Yosemite Village, or at any park accommodations tour desk. For more information, call the Yosemite Lodge Tour Desk (☎ 209-372-1240). Also ask about similar seasonal tours of other regions of the park.

If you're driving into Yosemite Valley from the South Entrance along Highway 41, stop at **Tunnel View** for one of the park's most stunning vistas. Pull over along with everybody else after you pass through the Wawona Tunnel on Route 41 for a majestic bird's-eye overview of the valley. You can also catch this view on the drive south from the valley to Glacier Point Road or the Wawona section of the park.

Yosemite Valley Highlights

The mile-wide, seven-mile-long **Yosemite Valley** is the attraction-laden heart of the mammoth park. Most park services are located in **Yosemite Village,** which even has a post office and a sizable store.

Make the Valley Visitor Center your first stop in Yosemite Village. You can pick up all the maps and info you need here, watch a short intro-ductory movie, check the schedule of orientation programs and ranger-led activities, and learn enough about glacial geology and the local flora and fauna to give you a basic understanding of the park.

Next to the visitor center sits the **Yosemite Museum and Cultural Center,** where you can learn about life in the valley before the Europeans showed up, and the **Ansel Adams Gallery,** which is wonderful for both browsing and buying the works of the master photographer as well as contemporary photogs who have a special talent for training their lens on Mother Nature. Shuttle service can take you to all corners of the valley from here (see "Entering & Getting Around the Park" earlier in this chapter).

You won't want to miss these Yosemite Valley highlights:

- ✔ Even before you reach the valley, you'll see beautiful **Bridalveil Fall** on your drive in; just look to the right. It's one of the prettiest falls in the park. You can pull into the parking lot and follow an easy, short trail to the base of the falls.

- ✔ To your left as you drive in, past Bridalveil, is **El Capitan,** the largest piece of solid granite in the world. Pull in to the turnout at El Capitan meadow to scour the immense face of this 3,593-foot-tall monolith for rock climbers. (Climbers are a cinch to spot after dark, when they turn their headlamps on.)

- ✔ From shuttle stop no. 7, just west of the visitor center, take an easy half-mile round-trip walk to the base of lower **Yosemite Fall.** As you stand on the bridge facing the spray, you'll really feel the impressive force of the continent's tallest waterfall.

- ✔ From the valley floor, look to the northeast and you can't miss **Half Dome,** Yosemite's most famous feature — 4,733 extraordi-nary feet of 87-million-year-old brawny rock.

- ✔ The **Nature Center at Happy Isles,** on the easternmost shuttle loop (stop no. 16), has great hands-on nature exhibits for kids, plus wheelchair-accessible paths that run along the banks of the Merced River. Stop here early in your visit for information on the Valley Junior Ranger Program, which gives kids the opportunity to earn awards for completing special park projects.

Glacier Point

In summer, you can drive the 32 miles from the valley floor to 3,200-foot **Glacier Point,** which offers the park's most stunning panoramic views. Not only will you be able to see all of the valley's highlights, but you'll catch views of the High Sierra to the north and west that are beyond breathtaking. From the valley, take Highway 41 to the Chinquapin junction and turn left onto Glacier Point Road (turn right if you're coming up from the South Entrance); allow about an hour each way for the drive. Sunrise from Glacier Point is spectacular.

If you're visiting in winter, bring your cross-country ski gear. You can drive as far as Badger Pass Ski Area (less than halfway), and ski your way to Glacier Point from there. Call ahead to inquire about overnight cross-country-ski excursions to the point.

Wawona/South Yosemite

Mariposa Grove, at the quieter, woodsy southern section of the park (about 35 miles south of the valley via Highway 41), is one of my favorite spots in Yosemite. It's the most impressive of the park's three groves of giant sequoias, the world's largest trees. Giant sequoias are shorter but more massive than their lanky cousins, the coast redwoods (see Chapter 10), with distinctive bell-bottom bases as large as 35 feet in diameter. That is one big tree — and you'll find a whole stand of 'em here! Grizzly Giant, the oldest tree in the grove, is one of the largest sequoias in the world.

An easy interpretive trail leads through the grove from the parking area, with placards offering a self-guided tour. The grove also has a small museum. From the valley, follow Highway 41 south and take the signed turnoff; expect the drive to take about 1¼ hours. You can also hop on a shuttle bus to reach the grove, but the far distance from the valley makes driving more efficient for time-challenged visitors. The grove is open year-round, but heavy snow occasionally closes the access road.

The High Country

At 8,600-feet elevation, stunning **Tuolumne Meadows** bursts with wild-flowers in summer (this high up, where the snow sticks around through June, summer seems more like spring). The 55-mile drive from the valley takes 1½ hours along the gorgeous Tioga Road (Highway 120; open in summer only). The magnificent drive alone is half the fun, so allow more time to stop at the myriad overlooks. You'll pass lush meadows, thickly wooded forest, granite domes, and ice-blue glacial lakes — the most notable being **Tenaya Lake**, a popular spot for wind-surfing, fishing, and canoeing.

Consider buying a copy of *The Yosemite Road Guide* at the visitor center before you set out. This publication contains a good self-guided driving tour of the route. Once you arrive, stop at the Tuolumne Meadows Visitor Center for orientation, trail, and program information.

Walking the walk: Hiking and nature trails

With 860 miles of trails, Yosemite has a hike for you, no matter what your level of stamina and experience. Nature writers dedicate whole volumes to hiking the park, so you're better off referring to a more complete source for the full range of options.

In addition to the walks to **Yosemite Fall** and **Bridalveil Fall** (see "Yosemite Valley Highlights" earlier in this chapter), here are some of the best day hikes. Check the *Yosemite Guide* newspaper for additional day-hiking options. A very useful "Yosemite Valley Day Hikes" single-sheet handout is also generally available. Be smart and remember to check conditions at the visitor center before you set out.

✔ The easy mile-long round-trip walk to **Mirror Lake** will reward you with remarkable views. The trailhead leaves from shuttle stop no. 17 (behind the stables). You can then follow the lovely 5-mile loop around the lake if you choose.

✔ The **John Muir/Mist Trail** is the park's most popular hike, so set out early or save it for later in the day. The trail leaves from **Happy Isles** (shuttle stop no. 16) and climbs alongside the Merced River (whose rushing whitewater naturalist and park godfather John Muir called "the symphony of the Sierras") to **Vernal Fall.** The initial ⁷⁄₁₀-mile portion of the trail is moderately difficult and follows a paved but steep trail that leads to a bridge with terrific views of the falls.

The hardiest of you can continue along the strenuous ³⁄₁₀-mile "Mist" portion, which sharply ascends 600 more feet (for a total elevation gain of 1,000 feet) directly alongside the fall (expect spray) and includes countless granite steps (that StairMaster experience will really come in handy here, folks) before you reach the pool at the top. Allow 2 to 4 hours.

✔ Up at Tuolumne Meadows, try the easy 1½-mile round-trip walk to **Soda Springs**. The trailhead leaves from just east of the visitor center and follows a gurgling river through a peaceful section of meadow to a bubbling carbonated spring.

✔ Hardcore hikers may want to tackle the 17-mile cable-hike ascent to the top of **Half Dome**, a full-day affair that's only for the hardiest. You'll need hiking boots with serious traction and leather gloves. Call the info line ☎ **209-372-0200** for details or consult a ranger before you go.

If you'd like to tour the park with a knowledgeable guide — an excellent idea, especially if you want to venture off the busiest trails — go with Yosemite Guides (☎**877-425-3366;** www.yosemiteguides.com). They'll lead you on natural history walks, birding tours, and even take you fly-fishing. They have a desk at the **Yosemite View Lodge** (see "Where to Stay and Dine Outside the Park"), but I highly recommend booking before you arrive.

Talking the talk: Ranger-led programs

In addition to guided tram and bus tours (see "Exploring the Park" earlier in this chapter), the park rangers offer a phenomenal number of guided walks and interpretive programs throughout the park. The calendar is chockfull from morning until night with morning-light photo walks, birding walks, bear talks, Discover Yosemite family programs, brown-bag lunch lectures, fireside discussions . . . you get the picture. A number of children's programs are offered, and the Junior Ranger program is excellent. Some activities carry a fee, but many are free. Check the *Yosemite Guide* newspaper or inquire at the visitor center for the complete schedule.

The artist in you may want to check the schedule of free, informal, outdoor art classes offered in various media throughout the summer by the **Art Activity Center,** located in Yosemite Village next to the Village Store. You can find the schedule on the Yosemite Valley Activities page at www.nps.gov/yose.

The highly respected **Yosemite Theater** program, which stages dramatic interpretive programs (actorly portrayals of *John Muir in Yosemite,* for example, or *A 49er's Life with the Yosemite Indians*), as well as occasional concerts in the evenings. Tickets are usually under $10 for adults and under $5 for kids. These events are hugely popular, so buy your tickets early in the day to avoid disappointment.

Finding more cool stuff to do

Fun activities abound year-round, from horseback riding, river rafting, and rock-climbing for beginners to ice-skating, snowshoeing, and skiing (both downhill and cross-country) in winter. Whatever you want to do, one thing's for sure: It's administered by Yosemite Concessions Services (☎ **209-372-1000**). Check their easy-to-use Web site at www.yosemitepark.com and click on "Activities & Adventures" for a rundown of available activities with all the details — including prices, access, and reservations information.

Gathering More Information

Call the park's 24-hour information line at ☎ **209-372-0200,** or go online to www.nps.gov/yose. You can also use this number to check road conditions (always a good idea). More information is available from Yosemite Concessions Services at ☎ **209-372-1000** or www.yosemitepark.com. Request a copy of the official *Yosemite Guide* when you call. You can easily find this seasonal newspaper in the park, but it contains lots of invaluable trip-planning information — including the latest on road construction and policy changes to mitigate traffic congestion — that can come in handy before you go.

The Yosemite Association maintains a useful site at www.yosemite. org, complete with an online bookstore where you can order materials to read up on the park before you go. The association has a helpful information line at ☎ **900-454-YOSE** (454-9673) that lets you talk to a real person. Be prepared with your questions and talk fast, because the meter will tick at $1.95 for the first minute, 95 cents per minute thereafter (all proceeds go to benefit the park).

For information on the surrounding area, your best source is the Yosemite Sierra Visitors Bureau, 40637 Hwy. 41, Oakhurst (☎ **559-683-4636;** www.yosemite-sierra.org). In addition to providing general visitor info, they're happy to help with just-outside-the-park lodging reservations. Another good site is www.yosemite.com.

Part IV
The Central Coast

The 5th Wave — By Rich Tennant

"SINCE WE LOST THE DOLPHINS, BUSINESS HASN'T BEEN QUITE THE SAME."

In this part . . .

*P*art IV covers California's Central Coast, which includes such marvelous destinations as the Monterey Peninsula, Big Sur, Hearst Castle, and that jewel of the coast, Santa Barbara.

Where the San Francisco Bay Area meets the Monterey Peninsula sits Santa Cruz, California's kinda wacky surf town. If you ask me (and I guess you did), the Central Coast — that stretch between San Francisco and L.A. — represents California at its very best. The drive along coastal Highway 1 is breathtaking, in more ways than one. The Monterey Peninsula cradles Monterey Bay, one of the richest and most diverse marine habitats on earth, plus a collection of the state's most delightful communities, from family-friendly Monterey itself to world-class golf mecca Pebble Beach to ultra-romantic Carmel-by-the-Sea. Be sure to dedicate a full day to the natural splendor of Big Sur, even if you don't want to stay in one of the region's funky hotels; trust me, you won't regret it. Hearst Castle, Cambria, fairytale Solvang, and dreamy Santa Barbara complete this thoroughly charming part of the state.

Chapter 15

Beach Blanket Babylon: Santa Cruz

. . . .

In This Chapter

▶ Deciding when to visit and where to stay and eat

▶ Enjoying the boardwalk — and other surfside fun

▶ Shopping, strolling, and riding through the redwoods

. . . .

Santa Cruz, the quintessential beach town and surf mecca, sits just a stone's throw from the Bay Area, at the northwestern end of Monterey Bay. Monterey is the prime destination along the coast (see Chapter 16), but Santa Cruz is within easy reach of San Francisco — perfect for northern California vacationers who want a taste of genuine Golden State beach life, or anyone who wants to avoid the tourist throngs that can overwhelm Monterey in summer.

Families with kids in tow will especially enjoy the Santa Cruz Beach Boardwalk, the West Coast's only seaside amusement park. If you hail from the East Coast, push those visions of the gritty Jersey boardwalk from your mind — Santa Cruz's version is everything a seaside boardwalk was meant to be. It's clean, family-friendly, and filled with amusements, from arcade games ("Getcha stuffed Elmo right he-ah! Three plays for a dol-lah!") to cotton-candy and funnel-cake vendors to thrill rides — even an old-fashioned wooden roller coaster that's rickety good fun. And, in summer, the beach scene out front is straight out of the movie *Gidget*.

Inland from the beach lies a charming downtown whose hippie element has been minimized, but not eliminated, by necessary post-earthquake gentrification (Santa Cruz was seriously damaged in the 1989 Loma Prieta earthquake.) As a result, you'll find a nice blend of affordable but high-quality restaurants and boutiques, and a genuine and appealing laid-back California coast vibe.

Timing Your Visit

California's middle coastline enjoys mild weather all the time, with highs in the mid-70s in summer and the mid-50s in winter. Late summer — from mid-July through September, and often into October — is usually best for sunny beachgoing and boardwalk fun. Crowds do not present a huge problem; in fact, I like Santa Cruz best on summer weekends, when it's at its liveliest.

Boardwalk operation is limited to weekends in spring and fall and restricted to holidays in winter, so be sure to check the schedule before you head here with the kids in the off-season.

If you want to stay in Santa Cruz, plan on one or two nights and a couple of days to enjoy it all, with maybe a third full day to book a fishing charter or kayak trip. If you're driving between Monterey and the Bay Area, allot at least a few hours to stop and enjoy the boardwalk and downtown a bit before continuing on your journey.

Getting There

Santa Cruz is 76 miles southeast of San Francisco. You can choose the quick route or the scenic route:

- ✔ **For the quick route:** Take I-280 to Highway 85 to Highway 17, which deposits you onto Ocean Street, leading right to the beach.

- ✔ **If you prefer the scenic route:** Take Highway 1 the entire way, which takes about twice as long. One stretch of Highway 1, called Devil's Slide, isn't for the faint of heart — as you may have guessed from the name — but the rest is pretty easy driving.

If you're heading to Santa Cruz on a weekend morning, skip the "quick route" in favor of Highway 1, because Highway 17 tends to logjam with Bay Area beachgoers.

If you're coming from Monterey, 45 miles away, take Highway 1 north. The drive takes about an hour.

Getting Your Bearings

Santa Cruz is small and easy to navigate. Both Highway 17 and Highway 1 take you straight into the heart of town. Exit Highway 1 from River Street and follow it to Front Street to reach the shopping and dining district in the heart of downtown (Front Street is the main drag).

Proceed down Front to oceanfront Beach Street to reach the beach. Head west along Beach until it becomes West Cliff Drive, whose beachfront path offers gorgeous ocean views and an excellent look at the local surfing action (and probably a few clusters of fuzzy sea lions sunning themselves on the rocks below).

Santa Cruz

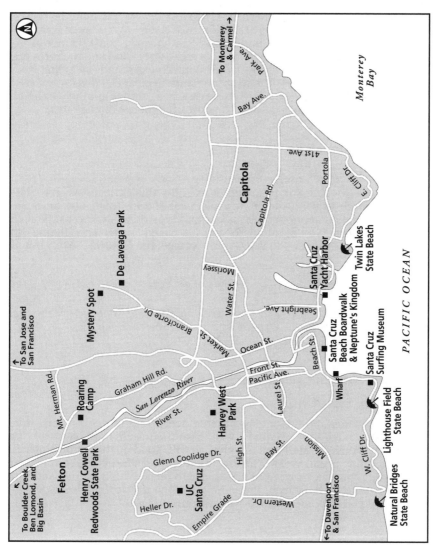

Staying in Santa Cruz

Because Santa Cruz is a beach destination, summer rates are significantly higher than winter rates. You'll also pay more for the privilege of visiting over the weekend — and expect a two-night minimum if you include Saturday in your stay.

If you'd like more options, call the **Santa Cruz County Accommodations Hotline** at ☎ 800-833-3494.

Count on an extra 12 percent in taxes being tacked on to your hotel bill.

If the summer weekend rates at the hotels that follow are too rich for your wallet, try the Sea & Sand Inn's sister property, the **Carousel Motel ($),** near the boardwalk at 110 Riverside Ave. (☎ **800-214-7400** or 831-425-7090; www.beachboardwalk.com/lodging/carousel.html). This motel is much more budget-basic and doesn't boast the ocean views, so don't expect much. But the location is good and the rates are considerably lower — as low as $59 double year-round (including continental breakfast). The **Best Inn Santa Cruz** at 600 Riverside Ave. (☎ **831-458-9660;** www.bestinnssantacruz.com) is another economical choice. Rates go as low as $75; check for special online rates.

Babbling Brook Inn

$$$ Santa Cruz

If you're looking for romance, book into this little oasis. It's just a 2-minute drive (or a 10-minute walk) west of downtown, but, because it sits among an acre of gorgeous gardens, you'd hardly know it. You can choose from 14 charming rooms, all based on an arty theme (the Cezanne, the Monet, the Van Gogh — you get the picture). Lovely but not too cutesy, thank goodness — a real romantic treat.

1025 Laurel St. (at California St.). ☎ 800-866-1131. Fax: 831-427-2457. Internet: www.cacoastalinns.com/babbling-frame.html. Parking: Free! Rack rates: $150–$195 double. Rates include full breakfast and afternoon wine and hors d'oeuvres. Deals: Check Web site for frequent midweek discounts; golf packages may also be available. AE, DC, DISC, MC, V.

Sea & Sand Inn Santa Cruz

$$–$$$ Santa Cruz

This friendly and fabulously situated oceanfront motel is a gem. It lies clifftop above the surf, just a walk from the beach and boardwalk. The motel rooms are standard but nice, all with good-quality furnishings and panoramic ocean views. The lovely garden, with furnished terrace overlooking the water, is a wonderful place to relax. With a kitchen and a private patio with Jacuzzi, the suite is well worth it if you're looking to splurge or have the kids in tow. A terrific choice.

201 W. Cliff Dr. ☎ 831-427-3400. Fax: 831-466-9882. Internet: www.beachboardwalk. com/lodging/sea.html. Parking: Free! Rack rates: $89–$179 double, $129–$249 double with spa, $189–$319 studio or suite. Rates include continental breakfast, plus afternoon refreshments in most seasons. AE, MC, V.

West Coast Santa Cruz Hotel

$$$ Santa Cruz

This very nice hotel is the only lodging in town with direct beach access. The rooms are unremarkable but very comfy; in-room extras like Sony Playstations, minifridges, and coffeemakers mean they're family-friendly, too. The beachfront pool area is well-furnished and leads right to Santa Cruz's prime stretch of sand. This pleasing choice is hard to beat if it suits your budget.

175 W. Cliff Dr. (adjacent to the Santa Cruz Wharf). ☎ *800-426-0670 or 831-426-4330. Fax: 831-427-2025. Internet:* www.westcoasthotels.com/santacruz. *Parking: Free! Rack rates: $159–$249 double, $200–$480 suite. AE, DISC, MC, V.*

Dining Out

Santa Cruz boasts a thriving restaurant scene, so you can expect to eat well here. The following are my local favorites.

Bittersweet Bistro

$$$ Rio Del Mar   CALIFORNIA

A meal at this stylish and hugely popular restaurant is well worth the 20-minute trip south of town. Chef Thomas Vinolus uses the freshest produce and a wood-fired oven to craft hearty, not-too-fussy California cuisine with a Mediterranean accent. The large menu offers something for everyone, from excellent seafood preparations and steaks to creative mini-pizzas for more casual tastes. The restaurant regularly receives the *Wine Spectator* Award of Excellence. The desserts are divine, too, named "Best in County" three years running.

In the Deer Park Shopping Center, 787 Rio Del Mar Blvd. (off Hwy. 1, about 10 miles SE of Santa Cruz), Rio Del Mar. ☎ *831-662-9799. Internet:* www. bittersweetbistro.com. *Reservations recommended. Main courses: $7–$12 at lunch and brunch, $16–$22 at dinner. AE, MC, V. Open: Brunch Sun, dinner nightly.*

Casablanca Restaurant

$$$$ Santa Cruz   CONTINENTAL/SEAFOOD

This wonderful restaurant is one of the most romantic in town. The white linen–covered tables are terraced so that every diner has ocean views, and twinkling white lights add to the ambience. The old-school, seafood-heavy menu more than lives up to the stellar setting. Look for such winning dishes as ruby-red ahi crowned with fresh mango and roasted green chili sauce, and New York steak in a bourbon-peppercorn demi-glace. Excellent service and a great wine list, too.

In the Casa Blanca Inn, 101 Main St. (at Beach St.). ☎ *831-426-9063. Reservations recommended. Main courses: $17–$26. AE, DC, DISC, MC, V. Open: Dinner nightly.*

El Palomar

$$ Santa Cruz   MEXICAN

This airy, cheerful Mexican restaurant in the heart of downtown is a great place to enjoy an affordable meal. It doesn't have the best Mexican grub in California, but the generous plates are well-prepared and quite pleasing. Expect all your favorites, from saucy enchiladas to sizzling fajitas. Seafood lovers shouldn't miss the excellent ceviches, all freshly prepared and perfectly seasoned with lime (the octopus is particularly good). The Santa Cruz Harbor location is cheaper and even more casual.

1336 Pacific Ave., downtown. ☎ 831-425-7575. Reservations recommended for dinner. Main courses and combo plates: $7–$19. AE, DISC, MC, V. Open: Lunch and dinner daily. **Cafe El Palomar ($):** *At the Santa Cruz Harbor, 2222 E. Cliff Dr. ☎ 831-462-4248.*

Gabriella Cafe

$$ Santa Cruz CALIFORNIA

This super-charming restaurant is a terrific bet for those who want a touch of sophistication for not a lot of money. Expect fresh, seasonal veggies; well-poached local sturgeon and pan-seared pork loin; daily-made gnocchi and risotto; and "pan amore" — homemade focaccia with delectable roast garlic, basil pesto, and heirloom tomato spreads. The restaurant also offers alfresco seating in the cute alley garden.

910 Cedar St. (between Locust and Walnut sts., 1 block over from Pacific Ave.), downtown. ☎ 831-457-1677. Reservations recommended. Main courses: $7–$15. AE, DC, DISC, MC, V. Open: Lunch Mon–Fri, brunch Sat–Sun, dinner nightly.

Pearl Alley Bistro

$$$ Santa Cruz CALIFORNIA FRENCH

This attractive, slightly funky bistro is an excellent spot to enjoy an innovative meal. Expect French classics like vichyssoise and bacon-wrapped sweetbreads; but don't be surprised when the chef takes California-style liberties in preparation, offering such dishes as giant sea scallops served on artichoke bottoms and aromatically seasoned with lavender and thyme. An oddity is the do-it-yourself Mongolian barbecue, which you cook at your table on a sizzling rock. The restaurant offers friendly service and a nice wine selection, too.

110 Pearl Alley (between Lincoln and Walnut sts.), downtown. ☎ 831-429-8070. Internet: www.pearlalley.com. *Reservations recommended. Main courses: $13–$24.50. Open: Lunch and dinner daily.*

Hitting the Boardwalk

All of the good-time boardwalk fun detailed in this section faces **Cowell Beach,** a vast stretch of sand that really comes alive in summer. So grab your beach towel and catch some rays alongside the bevy of beachgoers, which range from vacationing Bay Area families to bikini-clad co-eds to volleyball-playing surfer dudes.

The Santa Cruz Beach Boardwalk

This landmark oceanfront boardwalk — the only beach amusement park on the West Coast — is a retro jewel. The well-kept, beautifully maintained wooden boardwalk (here in one form or another since 1907) offers nearly 30 rides, plus dozens of skill games, tacky souvenir shops, and food vendors (hot dogs, cotton candy, funnel cake) — more than enough to entertain kids of all ages well into the evening, when a rainbow of bright lights heightens the appeal. The boardwalk boasts two national landmarks: the wooden **Giant Dipper** roller coaster, a 1924 original and still a marvelous thrill ride; and the 1911 **Looff Carousel,** a work of art with hand-carved wooden horses and a magnificent pipe organ. The boardwalk also includes a good kiddie area with nine rides. You'll pay for rides with tickets you buy at booths strategically placed along the boardwalk; the booths also offer unlimited-ride passes for committed thrill-seekers. The boardwalk is hugely popular, especially in summer, but the crowds are all part of the fun.

Along Beach St., between Pacific and Riverside aves. ☎ *831-426-7433 or 831-423-5590. Internet:* www.beachboardwalk.com. *Admission: Free! Rides $1.50–$3. All-day unlimited ride pass $26.95. Open: Memorial Day–Labor Day, daily from 10 a.m.–late; spring and fall, Sat–Sun noon–5 p.m.; limited holiday operation in winter. Hours change regularly, so call for current schedule.*

Buy your unlimited ride passes online and save $5; also check for online coupons.

Neptune's Kingdom & Casino Fun Center/Supercade

Think the boardwalk is limited to nostalgic entertainment? Think again! These enormous indoor family fun centers feature loads of millennium-worthy fun, including the **MaxFlight CyberCoaster,** the world's only rider-programmable virtual roller coaster; laser tag; a two-story miniature golf course with a pirate theme; and enough classic and cutting-edge arcade games to exhaust the National Mint's supply of quarters.

Adjacent to the boardwalk at 400 Beach St. ☎ *831-426-7433 or 831-423-5590. Internet:* www.beachboardwalk.com. *Admission: Free; charges vary for individual games and attractions. Adventure Package (includes one bowling game with shoe rental, one round of Laser Tag, one miniature golf game, and $5 in arcade tokens) $10. Open: Daily 11 a.m.–11 p.m.; limited hours in winter.*

Santa Cruz Municipal Wharf

This old-time pier isn't as grimy or commercial as Monterey's; it has a nice maritime vibe, but it's still a shade on the tacky side. Locals cast and crab from the wooden pier, which is lined with cheesy shops, sportfishing charters, and a succession of mediocre seafood restaurants, the best of which is **Riva** (☎ **831-429-1223**). **Santa Cruz Boat Rentals** (☎ **831-423-1739**) offers equipment rentals as well as bait and tackle. **Stagnaro's Fishing Trips** (☎ **831-427-2334**) can take you deep-sea fishing as well as on whale– and sea lion–watching cruises. The wharf also offers an excellent photo op of the boardwalk.

You can park here, too, for a minimal charge, but be aware that traffic can really back up; you may be better off putting your wheels in a street lot.

On Beach St. just west of the boardwalk. ☎ *831-420-6025. Admission: Free! Open: Daily 5 a.m.–2 a.m. (most shops open daily 7a.m.–9 p.m.).*

Surfing and Other Cool Stuff to See and Do

Follow Beach Street west from the boardwalk and it quickly turns into West Cliff Drive, a gorgeous clifftop road lined with marvelous old houses on one side and spectacular ocean views on the other.

At Lighthouse Point (within walking distance of the wharf) sits the petite **Santa Cruz Surfing Museum** (☎ 831-420-6289; www.cruzio. com/arts/scva/surf.html), which traces surfing history from both local and broader points of view (with a nice accent on oft-neglected female surfers). You can easily see the collection of surfboards and other memorabilia in an hour or less. It's open daily except Tuesday from noon to 4 p.m. The suggested donation is $1.50.

Lighthouse Point also serves as the perfect vantage for **Steamer Lane,** Santa Cruz's infamous surfing spot. If you're lucky and the surf's up, you'll see some daredevil pros riding the waves.

Kayaking the bay

Monterey Bay is a fabulous place to kayak in summer, even for beginners. You'll glide right by sunbathing sea lions and snacking sea otters as shorebirds swoop through the air around you. **Venture Quest Kayaking** rents kayaks to experienced paddlers at their wharf location (☎ 831-425-8445). You can schedule a guided bay adventure ($24 to $28 per person) by calling the Beach Street location (☎ 831-427-2267; members.cruzio.com/~venture). Venture Quest also offers a guided tour of Elkhorn Slough, a calm-as-can-be, wildlife-rich estuary of Monterey Bay ($52).

Browsing Pacific Avenue

One of the best things about Santa Cruz is its charming downtown, which boasts a quintessential laid-back California coast vibe — not to mention a fair amount of shopping, most of it unique and affordable. The main drag for browsers is Pacific Avenue, which is chock-a-block with boutiques, bookstores, and record shops from Mission to Laurel streets. You'll find some gems on the side streets just off Pacific, too, such as **Annieglass,** at 109 Cooper St. (☎ 831-427-4260), an outlet store for locally made art-glass jewelry and housewares — a real find if you're looking for gifts.

Marveling at the Mystery Spot

Okay, so you won't exactly marvel at the **Mystery Spot,** 465 Mystery Spot Rd. (☎ **831-423-8897**; www.mystery-spot.com), but lovers of kitsch will enjoy this funhouse in the woods. Ads tout it as a natural phenomenon where the accepted rules of gravity, perspective, compass, velocity, and height no longer exist (phooey on you, Newton!). It's a real hoot if you like silly stuff, and it's open daily from 9 a.m. to 5 p.m. The tour only lasts 35 minutes, but expect an hour-long wait in summer. Admission is $5 for adults and $3 for kids.

Finding the Mystery Spot alone can be a mystery: From Pacific Avenue, turn right on Water Street and left on Market Street, which turns into Branciforte Drive; follow the signs.

Taking a ride through the redwoods

Want a glimpse of California's majestic redwoods and pioneering past, but don't have time to visit the North Coast or the Gold Country? Catch a ride on the **Roaring Camp & Big Trees Narrow Gauge Railroad** (☎ **831-335-4484**; www.roaringcamprr.com), which takes riders aboard the nation's last steam-powered passenger railroad through the majestic Santa Cruz Mountains on a 1 ¼-hour round-trip. The journey provides good fun, especially for families and train buffs. Trips leave from Roaring Camp, a half-hour's drive from Santa Cruz, daily year-round (weekends only in December). Rates are $14.50 adults, $9.50 kids 3 to 12. They also offer a beach-to-redwoods round-trip for $16 adults, $11 kids.

At press time, a 10 percent discount was available to those who made their reservations online.

Gathering More Information

Call the Santa Cruz County Conference and Visitors Council (☎ **800-833-3494** or 831-425-1234), or point your Web browser to www.scccvc.org. After you arrive, stop in at the friendly and helpful staffed visitor center at 1211 Ocean St., at Kennan Street, across from McDonald's and next to the Baker's Square restaurant.

Chapter 16

The Monterey Peninsula

*P*repare yourself for some of the most spectacular real estate you've ever seen when you visit this rocky, cypress-dotted stretch of California coast. A mystical, foggy shoreline rich with natural beauty and steeped in maritime history, it's home to the continental United States' largest marine sanctuary as well as some of the state's most charming communities.

The Monterey Peninsula juts out into the ocean at the south end of Monterey Bay. The bay is the deepest part of the ocean just off the North American coast, twice as deep as the Grand Canyon. As a result, it houses one of the most diverse collections of marine animals on the planet. Sea lions, otters, pelicans, gulls, even whales are a major presence and set the tone for life here. (More than one hotel manager has told me that guests in ocean-facing rooms frequently call to complain about the barking dogs that wake them in the predawn hours — to which the manager explains that sea lions don't respond well to requests for quiet.)

The biggest draw on the peninsula is the town of *Monterey,* home to the justifiably world-famous **Monterey Bay Aquarium**, one of the premier attractions in the Golden State, and **Cannery Row**, the sardine-canning center immortalized by John Steinbeck and since transformed into a family-friendly tourist zone. The aquarium actually lies half in Monterey and half in neighboring *Pacific Grove,* which I discuss in conjunction with Monterey because the dividing line is unnecessary for our purposes. From a base in either town, you can easily enjoy the charms and attractions of both.

Monterey Peninsula

Accommodations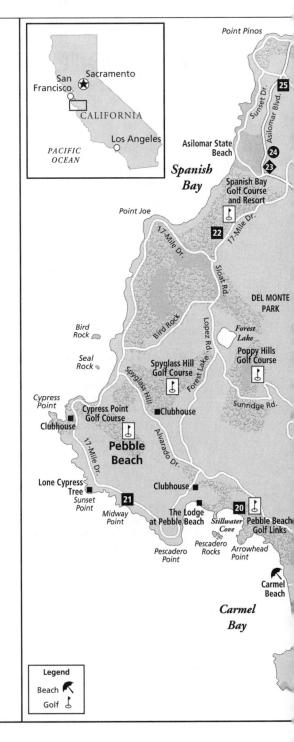
Asilomar Conference Grounds **25**
Best Western Victorian Inn **8**
Casa Palermo **21**
Cobblestone Inn **32**
Cypress Inn **31**
Cypress Tree Inn **17**
Grand View Inn/Seven
   Gables Inn **1**
The Inn at Spanish Bay **22**
The Lodge at Pebble Beach **20**
Mission Ranch **19**
The Monterey Hotel **14**
Monterey Plaza Hotel and Spa **9**
Pacific Gardens Inn **26**
Quail Lodge Resort and
   Golf Club **18**
Rosedale Inn **26**
Village Inn **28**

Dining ◆
Cafe Fina **10**
Cafe Gringo **30**
Caffé Napoli/Little Napoli **31**
Casanova **27**
Flying Fish Grill **29**
The Duck Club **9**
First Awakenings **3**
The Fishwife at Asilomar Beach **23**
Hula's **4**
Jack London's Bar and Grill **26**
Montrio **12**
Sea Harvest Fish Market
   & Restaurant **7**
Stokes Adobe **13**
Turtle Bay Taqueria **15**

Attractions ●
Cannery Row **6**
Carmel Mission **19**
Dennis the Menace
   Playground **16**
Fisherman's Wharf **11**
Garland Regional Park **18**
Maritime Museum of
   Monterey **11**
Monarch Grove Sanctuary **24**
Monterey Bay Aquarium **5**
Monterey State Historic Park **11**
Pacific Grove Museum of
   Natural History **2**

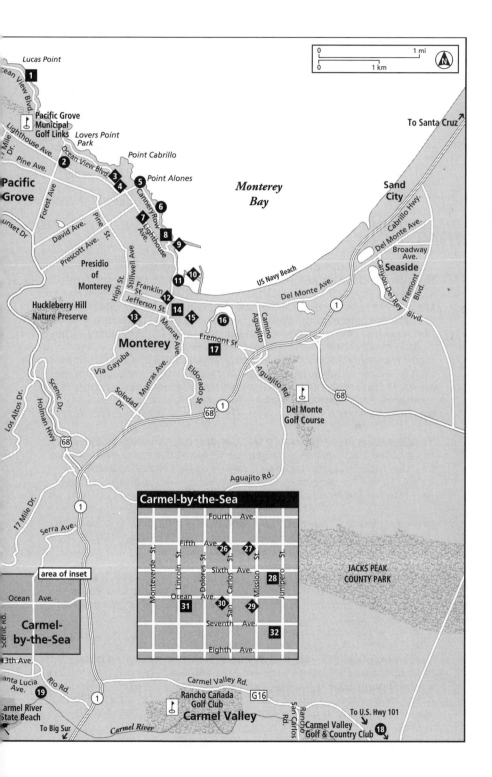

Lucas Point

1

Pacific Grove
Municipal
Golf Links

Lovers Point
Park

Lighthouse Ave.

Ocean View Blvd.

Pine Ave.

2

Point Cabrillo

**Pacific
Grove**

Forest Ave.

David Ave.

Ocean View Blvd.

3

4

5

Point Alones

Cannery Row

*Monterey
Bay*

To Santa Cruz

**Sand
City**

Cabrillo Hwy.

Del Monte Ave.

Broadway
Ave.

Canyon Del Rey

Fremont Blvd.

Seaside

unset Dr

Pine St.

Prescott Ave.

6

7

Lighthouse
Ave.

8

9

**Presidio
of
Monterey**

Stillwell Ave.

High St.

10

11

Franklin
St.

12

US Navy Beach

Del Monte Ave.

1

**Huckleberry Hill
Nature Preserve**

Jefferson St.

14

15

13

Munras Ave.

Fremont St.

16

Camino
Aguajito

Monterey

Via Gayuba

Munras Ave.

Eldorado St.

17

Aguajito Rd.

1

68

Del Monte
Golf Course

68

Los Altos Dr.

Scenic Dr.

Holman Hwy.

Soledad
Dr.

68

Aguajito Rd.

17 Mile Dr.

Serra Ave.

1

area of inset

Ocean   Ave.

**Carmel-
by-the-Sea**

Scenic Rd.

3th Ave.

Carmel-by-the-Sea

Fourth   Ave.

Fifth   Ave.

Monteverde St.

Lincoln   St.

Dolores   St.

San Carlos   St.

Mission   St.

Junipero   St.

26

27

Sixth   Ave.

28

Ocean   Ave.

31

30

29

Seventh   Ave.

32

Eighth   Ave.

**JACKS PEAK
COUNTY PARK**

anta Lucia
Ave.

19

Rio Rd.

Carmel Valley Rd.

Rancho Cañada
Golf Club

G16

San Carlos Rd.

Rancho San Carlos Rd.

To U.S. Hwy 101

Carmel Valley

armel River
State Beach

To Big Sur

Carmel River

Carmel Valley
Golf & Country Club

18

0   1 mi

0   1 km

Sculpted out of the midsection of the peninsula is *Pebble Beach,* home to some of the most beautiful woodlands, priciest residential real estate, and best championship golf resorts in the country. If you're looking for world-class clubbing, this is the place to be — but be sure to pack that platinum card, because it doesn't come cheap. Still, you can tour this spectacular territory at a bargain-basement price — $7.50, to be exact — along the *17-Mile Drive,* a gorgeous private road that traverses hill and dale along a meandering loop.

At the south end of the peninsula is *Carmel-by-the-Sea,* one of the sweetest towns I've ever laid eyes on, and home to one of California's most stunning beaches. This upscale haven is a mecca for gourmet dining and boutique shopping, but don't worry: You can enjoy its charms without blowing a wad in the process.

Timing Your Visit

The weather on the Monterey Peninsula is moderate year-round — the average daily temperature along the coast only varies by about 12 degrees throughout the calendar year, with average highs in the mid 60s and average lows in the low 50s. Fog can be a factor, consistently keeping the summers misty and gray, especially in the morning hours; I've regularly enjoyed more sun in December or January than I've seen in June or July. Don't let fog-bound days keep you away, however — the misty haze only adds to the Monterey mystique. Still, the best time to visit is Indian summer, from August through October, when days are sunniest and warmest. Jazz fans may want to plan their trip around the **Monterey Jazz Festival,** which takes over the town for a three-day weekend every September.

Temperatures are appreciably warmer and days sunnier inland, but most of the area's prime destinations lie along the coast. Still, you only have to drive inland 20 minutes or so — to visit the new **Steinbeck Center** in Salinas, say, or to tour area wineries — for temps to climb well into the 80s or 90s in July or August.

Expect spikes in summer and weekend hotel rates. The good news for off-season travelers: You just may end up with the best weather at the lowest prices.

Even if you're visiting in the height of summer, shorts and T-shirts just won't do. Be sure to take along a jacket, a sweater, and long pants. For the current local forecast for the Monterey Peninsula, call ☎ 831-656- 1725.

The distance is less than 5 miles from Monterey on the north end to Carmel on the south end, but this action-packed peninsula boasts lots of attractions. Exploring the entire area can easily occupy you for 5 or 6 days. If your time is limited, two days is enough to explore Monterey thoroughly, but set aside at least a half-day for the aquarium. Plan to spend a third day in Carmel (you can enjoy a lovely stretch of the 17-Mile Drive on your way there) or on the golf course.

Getting There

The Monterey Peninsula is just off Highway 1, about 46 miles south of Santa Cruz, 122 miles south of San Francisco, and 86 miles north of Hearst Castle. To get there:

- ✔ **From Santa Cruz:** Take Highway 1 south for about an hour; follow the exit signs into Monterey, or proceed another three miles south to the Ocean Avenue exit, which leads you to Carmel. (Watch for the Ocean Avenue exit, because it doesn't explicitly say "Carmel.")

- ✔ **From San Francisco:** Follow the route suggested in Chapter 15 to Santa Cruz and pick up Highway 1 as described above.

- ✔ **If you're heading north from Cambria:** Follow Highway 1 through Big Sur. This spectacular drive is slow going and can easily take a full day with stops; see Chapter 17 for details.

You can fly into Monterey Peninsula Airport, located on Olmsted Road four miles east of Monterey off Highway 68 (☎ **831-648-7000**; www.montereyairport.com). Serving the airport are:

- ✔ America West Express: ☎ **800-235-9292**; www.americawest.com

- ✔ American Airlines/American Eagle: ☎ **800-433-7300**; www.aa.com

- ✔ United Airlines: ☎ **800-241-6522**; www.ual.com

The national car-rental companies that have airport locations include:

- ✔ Avis: ☎ **800-331-1212**; www.avis.com

- ✔ Budget: ☎ **800-527-0700**; www.budgetrentacar.com

- ✔ Enterprise: ☎ **800-RENT-A-CAR**; www.erac.com

- ✔ Hertz: ☎ **800-654-3131**; www.hertz.com

- ✔ National: ☎ **800-CAR-RENT**; www.nationalcar.com

You can also catch a ride with Yellow Cab/Carmel Taxi (☎ **831-624-3885**), which usually has cabs circling the airport; expect the fare into Monterey to cost about $15.

Before you pay for a taxi, check with your hotel to see if they offer a complimentary shuttle service.

Monterey and Pacific Grove

As the capital of California when under Spanish rule, the first capital of the Golden State, and the hub of West Coast nautical life, Monterey is rich with history. The **Monterey State Historic Park** and the nicely preserved downtown boast beautifully restored Spanish adobes. Despite the dissolution of the sardine-canning industry, the town still thrives on its maritime past. Barely a day goes by without someone making a reference to the city's favorite son, novelist John Steinbeck.

Don't come expecting some bastion of historic high-mindedness, however — Monterey is quite comfortable maintaining its mass-market appeal, thank you very much. In fact, some feel that the town fathers have gone too far, succumbing to the worst impulses of tourism — witness campy **Cannery Row** and tacky **Fisherman's Wharf,** they say. It's true — you have to wade through some touristy schlock in these areas. But you can't argue with the appeal of the marvelous aquarium and that one-of-a-kind bay (be sure to get out on it if you can). And even Cannery Row and the wharf are good for a bit of fun, as long as you take them with the grains of salt they deserve. Beyond the prime tourist zones, you'll discover a genuine ocean community with beautifully preserved architecture, stunning panoramic vistas, top-quality restaurants, and more.

Gorgeous *Pacific Grove* makes a great base for those who'd rather revel in the area's natural wonders, and who don't mind the short drive or bike ride it takes to reach the main attractions. If convenience is more important to you, or bustle is more your style, book a room in Monterey proper.

Getting your bearings and getting around

Monterey is divided into two main sightseeing areas:

✔ **Downtown** (centered on Alvarado Street) and adjacent **Fisherman's Wharf,** where you'll also find Monterey State Historic Park.

✔ The **Cannery Row** area (sometimes referred to as "New Monterey"), where the aquarium is also located.

Cannery Row is roughly to the west/northwest of downtown and the wharf; beyond Cannery Row is Pacific Grove, which is easily reachable by bicycle and perfect for exploring on two wheels. The downtown–Fisherman's Wharf area and Cannery Row are both very pedestrian-friendly, but you'll most likely need to drive, bike, or take public transport between the two.

Parking can be somewhat difficult in Monterey's tourist areas, so you may want to park your car at your hotel when you arrive and leave it there for the duration of your stay. (All of the hotels I recommend are centrally located, making it easy to do just that.) If you do drive between sites, your best bet is to park in one of the paid lots. If you choose to rely on metered spots, be sure to have quarters, and pay attention to time.

If you visit between Memorial Day and Labor Day, you can use the *Waterfront Area Visitor Express (WAVE)* shuttle to get around. The WAVE operates buses between all the major tourist sites and hotel areas in Monterey and Pacific Grove daily from 9 a.m. to 7:30 p.m. in season. Rides were absolutely free in 2000 — a bargain at twice the price, considering what you'll save on parking fees and headaches. For the latest information, contact Monterey Salinas Transit (☎ **831-899-2555**), or visit www.mst.org.

For the lowdown on renting bikes — a very popular pastime — see "More Cool Stuff to See and Do" later in this chapter.

Choosing a place to stay

You may want to try booking your room through a free reservations service such as Monterey Peninsula Reservations (☎ **888-655-3424**; www.monterey-reservations.com); Time to Coast Reservations (☎ **800-555-WAVE** or 877-MONTEREY; www.timetocoast.com), serving Monterey only; or Resort II Me (☎ **800-757-5646**; www.resort2me.com). Because they have established relationships with local hotels and inns, they may be able to negotiate a better rate for you than if you call the hotel directly; your best bet is to compare. They can also refer you to other reliable properties in the area if the choices I recommend in the sections that follow are full.

Many hotels require a two-night minimum on weekends. Count on an extra 10 percent in taxes being tacked on to your final hotel bill.

Always inquire about packages — which may include aquarium tickets or other incentives — even at the cheapest motel.

Asilomar Conference Grounds

$$ Pacific Grove

Situated on 105 gorgeous oceanfront acres of pines and dunes, this woodland conference center is now open to individual bookings, and it's a great bargain for families on a budget. Rustic but immaculately kept stone-and-log lodges house basic guest rooms (private baths, but no TVs), plus a great room for lounging. Facilities include a heated pool, ping-pong, and billiards; a boardwalk leads to the beach and tidepools. This is a wonderful outdoorsy, summer camp– like retreat, with Monterey's attractions just minutes away. Cafeteria-style dining halls (pay-one-price lunch $7.75, dinner $12.40) mean you save on meals, too.

800 Asilomar Blvd., Pacific Grove. ☎ 831-642-4242 or 831-372-8016. Fax: 831-372-7227. Internet: www.asilomarcenter.com. Reservations accepted up to 90 days in advance. Parking: Free! Rack rates: $78–$97 double, $130–$190 cottage or suite. Rates include full breakfast. MC, V.

Best Western Victorian Inn

$$$ Monterey

This nice motel is just two blocks from Cannery Row. Don't let the "Victorian" theme fool you; the office is housed in a period home, but guest rooms are in a modern annex. Still, they're pleasant and feature nice extras: marble fireplaces, minibars, coffeemakers, and VCRs. Rack rates are *way* too high, but snagging a good rate through Best Western is pretty easy. Book a concierge-level room if you can, which adds cathedral ceilings, featherbeds, whirlpool tub, CD player, and robes to the mix.

487 Foam St., Monterey. ☎ *800-232-4141 or 831-373-8000. Fax: 831-373-4815. Internet:* www.innsofmonterey.com *or* www.bestwestern.com. *Parking: Free! Rack rates: $169–$449 double. Rates include continental breakfast and afternoon wine and cheese. Deals: Promotional packages as low as $129; rates as low as $89 (from $81 for seniors and AAA members) through* www.bestwestern.com

Cypress Tree Inn

$–$$ Monterey

Fremont Street is not my favorite place to stay in the area — its budget motels don't have the charm of those in woodsy Pacific Grove — but if you want a freeway-convenient location and don't mind a short drive to Monterey's main attractions, stay here. The rooms are spotless and spacious; all have minifridges, and some have private hot tubs, fireplaces, and/or kitchenettes. On-site you'll find a Jacuzzi, sauna, coin-op laundry, a barbecue area, and a bake shop serving free coffee and tea.

2227 N. Fremont St., Monterey. ☎ *800-446-8303 (in CA only) or 831-372-7586. Fax: 831-372-2940. Internet:* www.cypresstreeinn.com. *Parking: Free! Rack Rates: $46–$110 double; $58–$140 double with kitchen, hot tub, and/or fireplace; $125–$160 suite. Deals: Ask about attraction, romance, and other packages. AE, DISC, MC, V.*

Grand View Inn/Seven Gables Inn

$$$–$$$$$ Pacific Grove

These gorgeous sister inns are two of the most spectacular I've ever seen — and they're ideally located to boot, along the stunning coast road and situated so that just about every room has an ocean view. I prefer the subtler Edwardian style of the 1910 Grand View over the Seven Gables' more elaborate 1886 Victorian (which you may remember from old American Express commercials), but it's really a matter of taste. Everything is impeccable, from the marble baths to the faultless service. Romance-seeking couples simply can't do better. Book well ahead.

555–557 Ocean View Blvd., Pacific Grove. ☎ *831-372-4341. Internet:* www.7gables-grandview.com. *Parking: Free! Rack rates: $165–$375 double. Rates include full breakfast and afternoon tea. MC, V.*

The Monterey Hotel

$$$ Monterey

This charming Victorian hotel is beautifully located in the retail heart of downtown Monterey, just a walk from Fisherman's Wharf. It's impeccably restored and cute as a button, with beveled-glass details and mahogany polished to a high sheen. The smallish but lovely period rooms are elegantly furnished and have very nice marble-tiled baths; go for a double-double for the most space. The staff is attentive, too.

406 Alvarado St., downtown Monterey. ☎ *800-727-0960 or 831-375-3184. Fax: 831-375-2899. Internet:* www.montereyhotel.com. *Valet parking: $12. Rack rates: $139–$189 double, $219–$309 suite. Rates include continental breakfast and afternoon and evening refreshments. Deals: Ask about weekday rates and aquarium packages. AE, DC, DISC, MC, V.*

Monterey Plaza Hotel and Spa

$$$–$$$$$ Monterey

Monterey's best waterfront hotel is ideally located, and dramatically situated to maximize the spectacular bay views. Elegant teak-paneled public areas lead to spacious, extremely comfy guest rooms with big marble baths and all the little luxuries. Go ocean-view if you can, but even guests in the cheapest inland-view rooms can relax on the bayfront terrace. Service is excellent, and facilities include a gym, a full-service spa, and a restaurant worthy of attention in its own right (see "Dining Out").

400 Cannery Row, Monterey. ☎ *800-631-1339, 800-368-2468, or 831-646-1700. Fax: 831-646-5937. Internet:* www.woodsidehotels.com. *Valet parking: $13. Rack rates: $185–$420 double, from $460 suite. Deals: Ask about spa, golf, aquarium, breakfast, romance, and Steinbeck Center packages. AE, CB, DC, DISC, MC, V.*

Pacific Gardens Inn

$$ Pacific Grove

This cute, AAA three-diamond choice is a little more motel-like than the Rosedale Inn, but it's pleasing nonetheless. All of the simple but clean country-style rooms contain coffeemakers and popcorn poppers, and most have wood-burning fireplaces; suites offer full kitchens and large living rooms (great for families). Two on-site Jacuzzis and a coin-op laundry round out the appeal of this good value.

701 Asilomar Blvd., Pacific Grove. ☎ *800-262-1566 or 831-646-9414. Fax: 831-647-0555. Internet:* www.pacificgardensinn.com. *Parking: Free! Rack rates: $120–$135 double, $155–$185 suite. Rates include continental breakfast and afternoon wine and cheese. Deals: Ask about off-season rates Nov–Feb. AE, MC, V.*

Rosedale Inn

$$ Pacific Grove

Here's my favorite among Pacific Grove's sweet cottage-style motels. The dreamy lodgelike complex is actually much nicer than a motel. All of the large rooms are beautifully done in a comfy country style and feature cathedral ceilings (with ceiling fans), VCR, fireplace, kitchenette with microwave and minifridge, and whirlpool tub and hair dryer in the very nice bath. About half are two-room suites, which also have a sleeper sofa in the living room — perfect for families. Management is super-friendly, too. This place is a winner.

775 Asilomar Blvd., Pacific Grove. ☎ *800-822-5606 or 831-655-1000. Fax: 831-655-0691. Parking: Free! Rack rates: $125–$135 double, $175–$215 two-room suite. Rates include continental breakfast. AE, DISC, MC, V.*

Dining Out

Cafe Fina

$$$ Fisherman's Wharf, Monterey   ITALIAN/SEAFOOD

This restaurant stands head-and-shoulders above the mostly mediocre eateries on the wharf. After a friendly greeting, a host will lead you into the attractive bilevel dining room, all clean lines and water views, where an Italian-accented seafood menu lets you dine as casually or elaborately as you like. Expect fresh local and flown-in fish, pizzas-for-one from the wood-burning oven, and mesquite-broiled steaks, plus veal marsala and other authentic Italian specialties.

47 Fisherman's Wharf, Monterey. ☎ *800-THE-FINA or 831-372-5200. Internet:* www.cafefina.com. *Reservations recommended. Main courses: $7–$16 at lunch, $9–$22 (most under $17) at dinner. AE, CB, DC, DISC, MC, V. Open: Lunch and dinner daily.*

The Duck Club

$$$$ Monterey   CONTEMPORARY AMERICAN

A marvelous over-the-water setting and a skilled kitchen using top-quality seasonal ingredients make this a winner in the special-occasion category. It's a bit more clubby and formal than most local restaurants, but it's still comfortable. Chef James Waller has created a contemporary menu that's strong on wood-grilled and -roasted fish and meats (including an excellent caramelized duck, natch). The hearty dishes are pleasing across the board, and the knowledgeable staff will help you pair your choices with a bottle from the award-winning wine list.

In the Monterey Plaza Hotel & Spa, 400 Cannery Row, Monterey. ☎ *831-646-1706. Internet:* www.woodsidehotels.com. *Reservations recommended. Main courses: $19–$28 at dinner; 3-course prix-fixe $32. AE, MC, V. Open: Breakfast and dinner daily.*

First Awakenings

$ Pacific Grove   WHOLESOME AMERICAN

This airy, cheery restaurant is the place to satisfy morning and midday cravings. Yummy oatmeal and granola and a whole slate of creative egg dishes are available, and pancakes don't get more divine. The menu expands at lunchtime to include fresh, hearty salads and sandwiches. Go for an umbrella-covered outdoor table on nice days.

In the American Tin Cannery, 125 Ocean View Blvd., Pacific Grove. ☎ *831-372-1125. Main courses: Breakfast $4–$7, lunch $5.50–$7. AE, DISC, MC, V. Open: Breakfast and lunch daily (to 2:30 p.m.).*

The Fishwife at Asilomar Beach

$$ Pacific Grove   SEAFOOD

This hugely (and justifiably) popular fish house serves up affordable, top-quality meals in a pleasing ocean-view room that bustles with a friendly mix of tourists and locals. The always-fresh seafood comes grilled, golden-fried, included in excellent house-made pastas, and as tasty sea-garden salads. The lunch menu features sandwiches, too, as well as steak and non-seafood pastas. Kids get their own color-in menu.

1996½ Sunset Dr. (Hwy. 68), at Asilomar Blvd., Pacific Grove. ☎ *831-375-7107. Internet:* www.fishwife.com. *Reservations recommended. Main courses: $6–$10 at lunch, $8–$15 at dinner. AE, DISC, MC, V. Open: Lunch and dinner daily.*

Hula's

$$ New Monterey   ISLAND-STYLE

This kitschy-cute place is straight out of Waikiki in the '50s. Voted 1999's best new restaurant in the local *Coast Weekly,* Hula's serves up satisfying casual meals with island twists — fish tacos, coconut-crusted mahi mahi, teriyaki steak. I loved the ahi wasabi wrap, a hearty spinach-tortilla burrito stuffed with fresh ruby tuna, beans, rice, cabbage, daikon, and a not-too-spicy wasabi cream. The burgers are yummy, too.

622 Lighthouse Ave., Monterey. ☎ *831-655-HULA. Reservations recommended for dinner. Main courses: $6.50–$11 at lunch, $9.25–$14 at dinner. MC, V. Open: Dinner Tues, lunch and dinner Wed–Sun.*

Montrio

$$$$ Downtown Monterey   CREATIVE AMERICAN

Montrio is the most stylish restaurant in town. The high-design room buzzes with nattily dressed diners as a bevy of chefs bustle around the open kitchen, preparing such award-winning bistro-style dishes as Dungeness crab cakes with spicy rèmoulade, and golden rotisserie chicken (or apple-smoked filet mignon, your choice) on garlicky mashies.

414 Calle Principal (at Franklin St.), downtown Monterey. ☎ 831-648-8880. Internet: www.montrio.com. Reservations recommended. Main courses: $10–$14 at lunch, $11.50–$22 at dinner. AE, DISC, MC, V. Open: Lunch and dinner daily.

Sea Harvest Fish Market & Restaurant

$–$$ Monterey SEAFOOD

This friendly place is a fish market first and a restaurant second — which means that you pick your fillet right out of the case. It's grilled or fried right up, and served along with soup or salad at one of the casual tables. Fish simply doesn't come more off-the-boat fresh. The kitchen prepares delicious homemade Louis dressing and stellar chowder, too. Perfect for those who'd rather avoid the Cannery Row tourist traps in favor of an authentic local meal.

598 Foam St. (2 blocks inland from Cannery Row, at Hoffman St.), Monterey. ☎ 831-646-0547. Full meals: $7–$16. MC, V. Open: Daily lunch and early dinner (to 8 p.m. Sun–Thurs, to 9 p.m. Fri–Sat).

Stokes Adobe

$$$$ Monterey CALIFORNIA-MEDITERRANEAN

If Montrio sounds too high-profile and the Duck Club too formal, head to this historic adobe, which gets major points for its Southwest-style charm and constant raves for its contemporary Cal-Med fare. Chef Brandon Miller makes the most of the local bounty in his innovative but unfussy cuisine, which the *San Francisco Chronicle* calls "possibly the best food on the Monterey Peninsula." The restaurant is simply wonderful on all fronts.

500 Hartnell St. (at Madison St., just east of Pacific St.), Monterey. ☎ 831-373-1110. Internet: www.stokesadobe.com. Reservations recommended. Main courses: $7–$10 at lunch, $13–$21 at dinner. AE, MC, V. Open: Lunch and dinner Mon–Sat, dinner Sun.

Turtle Bay Taqueria

$ Downtown Monterey MEXICAN

The people behind the local fave The Fishwife (see the entry earlier in this section) have brought casual coastal Mexican eats to downtown Monterey. Everything is prepared with fresh regional produce, fish, and meats. Take out or sit down at this cute, colorful joint, where you can nosh on hearty burritos, Caribbean-inspired rice-and-black bean bowls, hearty salads topped with char-broiled fish and meats, and well-prepared Mexican staples. Beer and wine is available.

431 Tyler St. (at Bonifacio St.), downtown Monterey. ☎ 831-333-1500. Internet: www.fishwife.com/turtlebay.htm. Main courses: $4–$6.50. AE, DC, DISC, MC, V. Open: Lunch and dinner Mon–Sat.

Monterey's top attractions

Cannery Row

Immortalized on the page by Monterey's favorite son, John Steinbeck, this former super-smelly row of working sardine canneries is now a temple to the tourist dollar, rife with mass-appeal shopping, dining, and nightlife. The fish that fed the local sardine-canning industry — the largest in the world, processing ¼-million tons in 1945, the year Steinbeck's *Cannery Row* hit bookshelves — disappeared in the late 1940s from overfishing of the bay. Complaining about what replaced the canneries is easy (and believe me, locals do), but even Steinbeck found it to be an improvement over what was. In the '60s he wrote, "The beaches are clean where they once festered with fish guts and flies. The canneries that once put up a sickening stench are gone, their places filled with restaurants, antique shops, and the like."

Stay away if you're averse to this kind of commercialism. But if you're not, you'll find that the T-shirt shops and theme restaurants haven't entirely quashed the row's maritime character. It's a nice renovation, and recent years have brought in a better quality of merchant to supplant some of the cheesier businesses. Highlights include the **Taste of Monterey** Wine Tasting Center (see "More Cool Stuff to See & Do," later in the chapter), and the **Ghirardelli Chocolate Shop and Soda Fountain,** in Steinbeck Plaza, 660 Cannery Row (☎ 831-373-0997), where you can indulge your sweet tooth in true San Francisco style.

Just off the Pacific Grove end of the row, on Ocean View Boulevard, is the **American Tin Cannery Premium Outlets** (☎ 831-372-1442; www. chelseagca.com), which boasts such big names as Reebok and London Fog among its 50 or so stores. Just off the other (Monterey) end is the **Cannery Row Antique Mall,** 471 Wave St. (☎ 831-655-0264), housing two levels of antiques and collectibles dealers.

What's probably the world's finest bike path parallels the row, connecting up with it at a couple of points; for details, see "More Cool Stuff to See & Do" later in this chapter. Also look for a brand-new IMAX theater to pop up along the Row next to the Monterey Plaza Hotel over the next couple of years.

Cannery Row: Bayfront west of downtown Monterey, between David and Reeside aves. (the heart of the action is between David and Drake aves.). ☎ 831-373-1902.

Fisherman's Wharf

Cannery Row not cheesy enough for you? Don't worry — Fisherman's Wharf will be. Larger and more touristy than Santa Cruz's wharf but not quite as touristy as San Francisco's (thankfully), this wooden pier is packed with T-shirt shops, seafood restaurants, and bay-cruise and sportfishing operations out to snare a tourist buck or two. That said, it's still worth a look, primarily because the bay views are to die for, and this is one of Monterey's best perches for watching the frolicking seals and barking sea lions that populate the bay.

If the weather's good, buy yourself a chowder-filled sourdough-bread bowl and park yourself along the pier to watch the offshore action. If it's not, find a bayfront seat at one of the pier's seafood restaurants; the best of the bunch is Italian-accented **Cafe Fina** (see "Dining Out").

If you're the plan-ahead type who'd like to hit the water for some sportfishing or whale-watching, contact these operators:

Monterey Sportfishing and Cruises, 96 Fisherman's Wharf (☎ **800-200-2203** or 831-372-2203), offers daily year-round whale-watching cruises. Be aware, however, that you'll only spot the big'uns — California gray whales — from December through March. This company also offers fishing trips for salmon, halibut, albacore, and cod, which start at $45 per person.

Chris' Fishing Trips, 48 Fisherman's Wharf (☎ **831-375-5951;** www.chrissfishing.com), has four large (51 to 70 feet) boats leaving on daily deep-sea hunts; cod and salmon are main catches. Full-day trips run $30 to $45 per person.

If you'd rather watch the pros haul in their daily catches, head over to **wharf no. 2** (just next door to Chris's), which is today's working commercial pier. If you'd like to wiggle your toes in the chilly surf, head a bit farther east to **Monterey Bay Park,** where the big white-sand beach gradually slopes into sandy shallows that are just warm enough.

Fisherman's Wharf: *Waterfront at the end of Alvarado St., downtown Monterey.* **Wharf no. 2:** *At the end of Figueroa St.* www.montereywharf.com. *Admission: Free!*

Monterey Bay Aquarium

This marvelous aquarium, one of the best, largest, and most enjoyable on the planet, sits on the shore of one of the most spectacular marine habitats in the world. It's terrific for all ages, with gliding bat rays and other sea creatures to touch, instructive shows throughout the day (some featuring friendly, spotlight-savvy sea lions), interactive exhibits, and well-written placards at every display that even younger children can understand and enjoy. Exhibits tie in closely to the immediate surroundings, really bringing home the reality of the marine environment and the message of conservation.

Have I mentioned how jaw-droppingly awesome this aquarium is? It displays more than 300,000 sea plants and animals representing 570 different species. At the heart of the loftlike, indoor/outdoor complex is a three-story tank replicating a kelp forest, which you can walk around up a spiral ramp, viewing the leopard sharks and bay fish from all sides.

Better yet is the **Outer Bay** exhibit, featuring inhabitants of the open ocean in a phenomenal million-gallon tank with the *largest window on earth.* Almost cooler than the giant green sea turtles, schools of sharp-toothed barracuda, and threatening-looking sharks are the jellyfish, which move in slo-mo, translucent unison like a modern art exhibit come to life.

Aquarium time-savers

The ticket lines just to get into the Monterey Bay Aquarium can be a nightmare, especially in summer. Even on a Tuesday I've seen 15- to 30-minute waits throughout the day. Do yourself a favor: Avoid the lines at the gate by arranging for admission tickets in advance.

Many of Monterey's hotels offer packages that include aquarium tickets. Even if you just book a straight daily rate, call ahead and ask the front desk if they sell advance tickets; most do.

If your hotel doesn't sell aquarium tickets, you can order them directly from the aquarium by calling ☎ 800-756-3737; the flat $3-per-order service charge is well worth the time saved. Don't worry about mailing time; the tickets can be left at will-call, where you'll never encounter a wait.

Here are some tips to help you make the most of your aquarium visit:

✔ Allow a minimum of 3 hours to see the aquarium; budget 4 or 5 if you want to see everything.

✔ You're allowed to leave and come back in the same day, as long as you get your hand stamped. I highly suggest leaving for lunch or a rest, which will give you a break from the ever-present crowds and rejuvenate you for more looking.

✔ Review the "Today at the Aquarium" schedule as soon as you arrive, so that you can budget your touring around any live programs you'd like to see (they usually last 15 to 30 minutes).

✔ If time is limited, head straight for the **Outer Bay,** followed by a visit to the two-story **Sea Otter** exhibit, and then a walk along the **Habitats Path** to the **Touch Pool** for maximum satisfaction.

Come before January 2002 if you want to see the mind-blowing 7,000-feet **Mysteries of the Deep** exhibit, the largest deep-sea exhibit ever — many of these otherworldly critters have never been on display before *anywhere*. New in 2000 is **Splash Zone,** a hands-on gallery for kids that combines live-animal exhibits (including tuxedoed penguins) with staff-led learning programs and good old-fashioned play areas.

886 Cannery Row, Monterey. ☎ *800-756-3737 or 831-648-4937 for tickets, 831-648-4888 for 24-hour information.* www.mbayaq.org. *Admission: $15.95 adults, $12.95 students (13–17 or with college ID) and seniors 65 and over, $7.95 disabled visitors and children 3–12. Open: Daily 10 a.m.–6 p.m. (from 9:30 a.m. on holidays and in summer); check for extended hours in summer.*

Monterey State Historic Park

At the gateway to Fisherman's Wharf sit a dozen or so beautifully restored historic adobes that served as California's capitol under Spanish, Mexican, and initial U.S. rule. The state now collectively protects these buildings as Monterey State Historic Park. Even if you're not a big history buff, I suggest checking out this area, simply for the beauty of the buildings and the setting. You can tour this area in a number of ways.

Do-it-yourselfers who just want to explore a bit can stop into the **Visitor Center** at the Maritime Museum and pick up the free Path of History map. The center shows a free 20-minute continuous-loop film on the history of Monterey. The map will lead you through the historic park and adjacent Old Monterey (the beautifully restored downtown area), highlighting buildings of note along the way. You won't be able to enter the buildings, but the exteriors alone are worth a look.

If you'd like a little more background, take the **guided-tour** route. A number of tours are offered daily; you pay one price, and your ticket is good for any tours you wish to take. I recommend starting with the introductory walking tour (offered at 10 a.m., 11 a.m., and 2 p.m.), which provides a general exterior overview. Follow that tour with a house tour or two (or a garden tour, if you're visiting between May and September) of the buildings that caught your fancy in the course of your initial tour. Highlights include the **Cooper-Molera Adobe,** which depicts family life in the mid-1800s with living-history demonstrations throughout the three-acre complex, and the **Larkin House,** generally considered to be the finest still-standing example of Monterey Colonial architecture.

You can also explore the **Maritime Museum of Monterey** (☎ 831-372-2608; www.mntmh.org/maritime.htm), which tells the story of Monterey's seafaring past, from the Spanish conquistadors through the sardine fishers (note the separate admission fee).

Visitor Center: *At the Maritime Museum of Monterey, Stanton Center, 5 Custom House Plaza (at the end of Alvarado St.).* ☎ *831-649-7118.* www.mbay. net/~mshp. *Guided tour fees: $5 adults, $3 teens 13–17, $2 kids 6–12. Maritime Museum admission: $3 adults, $2 seniors and teens 13–18, free for kids 12 and under. Open: Visitor center, museum, and most buildings daily 10 a.m.–5 p.m. Call for tour schedules.*

More cool stuff to see and do

Don't miss the **Monterey Peninsula Recreation Trail,** one of the most scenic walking paths in the country. And the good news is that you don't have to hoof it; bikers and in-line skaters are welcome, too. You can pick up the paved path anywhere along Monterey's coastline and follow it into Pacific Grove all the way to Asilomar Beach.

Past the aquarium, in Pacific Grove, you'll ride along the beach side of Ocean View Boulevard. If you look inland, you can admire the gorgeous ocean-facing homes (including some stunning Victorians); on the bay side, gorgeous purple heather and the occasional gnarled cypress separates you from the frolicking sea lions and colorful kayaks gliding along the water.

Go at least as far as **Lovers Point Park** (where Ocean View meets Pacific Avenue in Pacific Grove), a gorgeous grassy point that juts out to sea. With a sheltered beach and tables for picnickers, it's the perfect place to take a load off and relax. From here, push on around the curve, where the road becomes Sunset Drive, and take it past picturesque **Point Pinos Lighthouse** (the oldest continually operating lighthouse in the West, since 1854) to undeveloped **Asilomar State Beach,** where you can spend a quiet day among the dunes, tidal pools, and barking sea lions. Hardy folks can continue along the **17-Mile Drive;** you'll find a gate on Sunset Drive just past Asilomar Avenue, and bicyclists can enter for free. (For more on the 17-Mile Drive, see the section later in this chapter.)

Rent your bike or skates from **Adventures by the Sea** (www. adventuresbythesea.com), which has a few convenient locations: 299 Cannery Row, across from the Monterey Plaza Hotel (☎ 831-372-1807); 201 Alvarado Mall, next to the Maritime Museum (☎ 831-648-7235 or 831-648-7236); and at Lovers Point Park in Pacific Grove (summer only; no phone). Bikes cost $6 an hour or $24 per day ($30 overnight); locks and helmets are provided. Skates are $12 for two hours or $24 for the day, with all safety equipment included. Service is very friendly, and gear is in good condition. Advance reservations are gladly accepted.

Kayaking the bay

Monterey Bay is a great place to kayak in summer, even for beginners. You'll glide right by sunbathing sea lions and snacking sea otters as shorebirds swoop through the air and schools of jellyfish skirt just below the surface of the water (a kayaking companion of mine once called it "a horror movie in the making," but the gooey creatures are simply mesmerizing).

Again, contact **Adventures by the Sea** (see the preceding section for locations and contact info). Kayaks cost $25 per person for the day, including waterproof gear and instruction to get you started. The bay is glassy enough for fearless novices to set out on their own in summer, but I highly recommend booking a tour if you're the least bit nervous, or if the surf is kicking up. The cost is $45 per person for a two- to three-hour tour, and you should reserve ahead.

Exploring the underwater world

If you're an experienced scuba diver, pack your certification card — this national marine sanctuary is a dive you shouldn't miss. Contact **Monterey Bay Dive Center,** 225 Cannery Row (☎ 800-60-SCUBA or 831-656-0454; www.mbdc.to), a PADI dive center that can arrange guided dives with pro divemasters. Call at least 48 hours in advance to schedule your dive, sooner if possible.

Tasting the local grape

Monterey's wine country has really grown up in recent years, becoming California's third most prominent wine-growing region, behind Napa and Sonoma (even the *New York Times* has called it "The Next Napa"). Go ahead, review the shelves at your local wine store or the next wine

list you're handed. The number of Monterey labels there will surprise
you, as will the number of Monterey County winery names you know:
Morgan, Estancia, Jekel, Talbott, J. Lohr, Smith & Hook, Chalone, and
many others. The local vintners tend to specialize in Chardonnay, Pinot
Noir, and Cabernet Sauvignon — all popular grapes that are suited to
the region's A-1 soil and growing conditions — and they're making
some of the best wines that the California wine country has to offer.

Where to start? That's easy. Stop by **A Taste of Monterey,** the
Monterey County Wine and Produce Visitors Center, upstairs at 700
Cannery Row, next to the Bubba Gump Shrimp Co. (☎ **831-646-5446;**
www.indian.monterey.edu/icn/nonprofit/atom), open daily from
11 a.m. to 6 p.m. This bayfront tasting room is a serious wine-tasting
center and a great place to learn about, taste, and buy local wines —
ideal for one-stop shoppers.

Adventurous types who want to wend their way through Monterey
County's vineyards and visit the wineries' own tasting rooms in person
can easily make a day of it. Stop by **A Taste of Monterey** to pick up the
Monterey Wine Country Wine-Tasting Guide, a free map to the region's
wineries; don't be afraid to also ask the friendly folks for tips on where
to go. The map is also available at local visitor centers (see "Gathering
More Information" at the end of this chapter).

Or you can arrange your wine-country touring in advance by going
online to the very useful Web site run by the Monterey County Vintners
and Growers Association at www.wines.com/monterey. At this site
you can preview the wineries you'd like to visit and order a free copy of
the aforementioned wine-tasting guide (or order an advance copy by
phone at ☎ **831-375-9400**).

Side-tripping to the National Steinbeck Center

The **National Steinbeck Center** is a 20-mile drive northeast from
Monterey, at 1 Main St. in the agri-town of Salinas (☎ **831-775-4720;**
www.steinbeck.org). The state-of-the-art museum is well worth a visit
if you're a fan of the county's favorite son, author John Steinbeck
(*Cannery Row, East of Eden, Of Mice and Men*).

Even if you're not a literary buff but are simply interested in the history
of the region, you'll find the tour engaging, as many of Steinbeck's
works were rooted in the local culture. The tour also appeals to film
fans, because the multimedia approach makes prime use of the many
first-rate, star-studded films that were crafted from Steinbeck's stories.

The museum is deliberately designed to be multi-sensory, and it largely
succeeds. A few of the exhibits fall flat — who wants to scrub rags on a
fake washboard, and does that really help anybody to better understand *The Grapes of Wrath?* — but most are well-thought out and com-
pelling. You can easily make your way through the museum in an hour
or two; the kids will have enough to keep them busy. The center is

open daily from 10 a.m. to 5 p.m. Admission is $7.95 for adults, $6.95 students and seniors, $5.95 kids 13 to 17, $3.95 kids 6 to 12. To get there from Monterey, take Highway 68 east, which will lead you right through Old Town Salinas to the center (the biggest, brightest building in town — you can't miss it).

Strolling and shopping Old Monterey

Monterey's charmingly restored downtown, inland from Fisherman's Wharf and centered on Alvarado Street, is well worth exploring. History and architecture fans should pick up the **Path of History Walking Tour** (see the section on the Monterey State Historic Park earlier in this chapter), while shoppers should just hit the streets.

Vintage-clothing buffs can wander off the main drag to the **Blue Moon Trading Co,** 176 Bonifacio Place, which runs perpendicular to Alvarado (☎ **831-641-0616**).

Wintering with the monarch butterflies in Pacific Grove

Pacific Grove is also known as "Butterfly Town, USA." Why, you ask? Because monarch butterflies, it seems, know a good thing when they see it. Thousands of brilliant black-and-orange monarch butterflies converge on the town annually in October or early November, and stay until February or March. The best place to see them is in the **Monarch Grove Sanctuary,** between Grove Acre Avenue, Ridge Road, and Lighthouse Avenue (☎ **888-PG-MONARCH** or 831-373-7047), where they alight in the eucalyptus trees. Tour guides are usually on hand on the weekends in season to answer questions about the fluttering beauties.

You can also peruse a detailed display on the winged winter visitors at the **Pacific Grove Museum of Natural History,** 165 Forest Ave., at Central Avenue (☎ **831-648-3116**). It's open Tuesday through Sunday from 10 a.m. to 5 p.m., and admission is free.

Leave your nets at home, collectors — the fine for harassing a butterfly in Pacific Grove is $1,000.

Playing with Dennis the Menace

Families with kids should definitely budget a couple of hours to run and jump at the **Dennis the Menace Playground** (☎ 831-646-3866), at Camino El Estero and Fremont Street, just east of downtown Monterey. Designed by Dennis creator (and Pacific Grove homeboy) Hank Ketcham, the way-cool playground boasts an old steam train to climb on, more colorful jungle gyms than I could count, rope-and-plank suspension bridges, a giant swing ride, and lots more low-tech, old-fashioned fun. It's open Tuesday through Sunday and Monday holidays from 10 a.m. to dusk; admission is free.

Pebble Beach: Nirvana for Golfers

Carved out of the middle of the peninsula is a whole different kind of world, Pebble Beach, where platinum cards and nine-irons rule the day. Rolling championship fairways, lush woodlands, and magnificent vistas are broken only by million-dollar homes and a few ultra-luxury resorts that cater to a big-money, high-profile crowd. In golf terms, this is the big time — Pebble Beach is home to some of the most famous golf courses in the world. It hosts the star-studded annual **AT&T Pebble Beach National Pro-Am,** which has paired club-swinging celebs with PGA Tour stars annually (late January or early February) since 1937, and has played host to multiple U.S. Open Championships throughout the years (including 2000's).

If you need to ask how much it costs to stay at Pebble Beach, you can't afford to stay here. Even if you can, but you're the jeans-and-T-shirts type, Pebble Beach may not be for you. But you don't have to stay over — or buy into the big-budget golf life — to enjoy the marvelous scenery. Everybody can — and should — tour this spectacular territory along the *17-Mile Drive* (see "Cruising the 17-Mile Drive" later in this chapter), a gorgeous private loop road.

If you don't want to stay but do want to play a round of unparalleled golf, you can do that, too — with a little effort and luck.

Staying & playing at the resorts

The **Pebble Beach Company** (☎ **800-654-9300;** www.pebblebeach.com) runs all of the Pebble Beach resorts, making price-shopping and comparing amenities easy. Always ask about packages that may include greens fees in the price. And always check with a travel agent, who may be able to get a better package price at these super-luxury resorts than you can get on your own.

Guests at any of the Pebble Beach resorts get preferred service at all of Pebble Beach's facilities; facilities are accessible to nonguests on a more limited basis. (Read: The high-paying resort guests get first dibs.) See "Hitting the Links" later in this chapter for details on the world-class golf courses, with information on greens fees and tee-time availability for resort guests and nonguests. You can play tennis at the **Beach and Tennis Club** and the **Spanish Bay Club** for $10 per 1 ½ hours; call ☎ **800-654-9300** for reservations.

New in January 2000 is the 22,000-foot Mediterranean-style **Spa,** which promises to be world-class on all fronts; call ☎ **888-565-7615** or 831-622-6443 to schedule appointments.

Book your tee times at the same time that you reserve your room.

Casa Palermo

$$$$$ **Pebble Beach**

Pebble Beach's newest resort is very exclusive — just 24 super-luxurious suites housed in a magnificent Mediterranean villa right on the fairway. It feels like a private estate, complete with fireplace-lit living room, cozy library, and clubby billiards room. You'll want for nothing here — and if you do, your personal concierge will be happy to get it for you in a snap. Shockingly priced, but stunning.

17-Mile Drive, Pebble Beach. ☎ *800-654-9300 or 831-625-8557. Fax: 831-644-7960. Internet:* www.pebblebeach.com. *Parking: Free. (At these prices, it should be.) Rack rates: $475–$1,500 cottage or suite, plus $20 gratuity per night. Rates include continental breakfast. AE, CB, DC, DISC, JCB, MC, V.*

The Inn at Spanish Bay

$$$$$ **Pebble Beach**

One of the few resorts to hold Mobil's highly coveted five stars — and named the second-best place to stay in North America in *Travel & Leisure*'s 1999 World's Best poll — Spanish Bay is a marvelous choice if you like big resorts. Rooms are large and done in a super-luxurious contemporary style. I'd choose this one over the Lodge for its winning facilities and its location in the heart of the gorgeous Scottish-style Links at Spanish Bay. Still, it's hard to go wrong at either property.

17-Mile Drive, Pebble Beach. ☎ *800-654-9300 or 831-647-7500. Fax: 831-644-7960. Internet:* www.pebblebeach.com. *Parking: Free. Rack rates: $350–$500 double, from $675 suite, plus $18.50 gratuity per night. AE, CB, DC, DISC, JCB, MC, V.*

The Lodge at Pebble Beach

$$$$$ **Pebble Beach**

The Lodge is somewhat more stately and formal than its sister resort at Spanish Bay, but it's equally elegant, service-oriented, and satisfying. The amenity-laden, utterly luxurious guest rooms are scattered throughout the glorious oceanfront property — most convenient for golfers set on teeing off on the legendary Pebble Beach Golf Links

17-Mile Drive, Pebble Beach. ☎ *800-654-9300 or 831-624-3811. Fax: 831-644-7960. Parking: Free. Rack rates: $395–$525 double, from $675 suite, plus $15 gratuity per night. AE, CB, DC, DISC, JCB, MC, V.*

Cruising the 17-Mile Drive

The only private toll road west of the Mississippi, the stunning 17-Mile Drive is well worth the price of admission: $7.50 per car.

Bicyclists can enter for free; see "More Cool Stuff to See and Do" earlier in the chapter for details on renting bikes. The ride is easy — mainly downhill — toward Carmel, but average folks may find it a real chore to make the uphill climb back. If you're not a long-distance biker, either stick to the Pacific Grove portion of the drive, or arrange for a pick-up at the **Lodge at Pebble Beach** or in Carmel.

The spectacular loop wends through the Monterey Peninsula, linking Pacific Grove to the outskirts of Carmel along the coast, then turning inland, hitching up with the main highway for a moment, and then heading back toward Pacific Grove through the **Del Monte Forest.** It takes you along the breathtaking rocky coastline, past the most beautiful cypress trees on the peninsula, and through unspoiled woodlands. (FYI: The gnarled, windbent cypress trees that lend the peninsula such a distinct beauty are native only to this region; they can live to be 4,000 years old.) You'll see championship golfers and native deer cohabiting on some of the most scenic golf greens in the world, and watch sea lions and harbor seals bark and cavort in the whitecaps just offshore. The only buildings you'll see are massive luxury homes tucked discreetly among the trees, and three world-class resorts, should you wish to seek them out (see the previous section).

You can enter the drive through five different gates, paying your fee in exchange for a handy-dandy full-color map and brochure of the highlights along the route. You're likely to use one of these three:

- ✔ From Monterey or Pacific Grove, the most convenient gate is the *Pacific Grove Gate.* Follow Ocean View Boulevard from Monterey to Sunset Drive; after the road turns inland, you'll soon see 17-Mile Drive on your right.

- ✔ From Carmel, enter at the *Carmel Gate;* from downtown, turn right off Ocean Avenue onto San Antonio Avenue (one block before the beach).

- ✔ If you're just passing by the peninsula and want to take a gander at this remarkable real estate, enter at the *Highway 1 Gate,* just off the main road at the Holman Highway exit.

Leisurely dining along the 17-Mile Drive

If you're not staying in Pebble Beach but you'd like to enjoy an elegant breakfast, lunch, or dinner here (and maybe a glimpse of a luxe resort in the process), book a table at **Roy's Pebble Beach ($$$$)**, at the **Inn at Spanish Bay** (☎ 831-647-7423). Roy's is the best of Hawaii celebrity chef Roy Yamaguchi's mainland restaurants. Expect well-prepared Euro-Asian cuisine with inspired sauces and pleasing California and island twists. Entrees are pricey, averaging in the $20s, but keeping the bill down is easy if you make a meal of Roy's signature wood-fired pizzas or choose from the extensive appetizers list; don't miss those killer short ribs (better than dessert!).

If you'd rather put together a picnic to enjoy along the drive, stop into the **Pebble Beach Market ($$)**, a gourmet deli at the **Lodge at Pebble Beach**, which has a lawn where you can spread out and enjoy your ready-to-eat meats, veggies, cheeses, and other gourmet goodies.

Allot a leisurely afternoon for the drive. If you don't have a few hours to spare, you can see part of the route by using it to travel between Monterey and Carmel (or vice-versa). The disadvantage of this plan is that you'll have to choose between coastal and inland portions; I say go coastal, but it all depends on your aesthetic sensibilities.

The map features about 20 points of interest, and you can use pullouts at scenic points all along the drive. If you'd rather avoid a lot of stop and go, focus on these natural highlights:

✔ **Point Joe,** on the northern end of the coast, which offers a gorgeous vantage for spotting migrating whales between December and March.

✔ About midway down the coast are **Seal Rock** and **Bird Rock,** where you can spot countless gulls, cormorants, and other offshore birds, plus harbor seals and sea lions, gathering just offshore.

✔ **Fanshell Overlook** offers awesome views of Fanshell Beach, where harbor seals gather to birth their pups each spring.

✔ **Cypress Point Lookout** offers the drive's most spectacular coastal view and is ideal for sunset mavens.

✔ A little farther down the coast is the famous **Lone Cypress**, one of the peninsula's most distinctive and mesmerizing images. The magnificently gnarled, windblown tree looks as if it's growing right out of bare rock, but its insistent roots have actually burrowed deep through the rock's crevices. You're not allowed to get up close, but the view from the deck beside the parking area is magnificent.

✔ You can see the best forest-and-ocean panorama from **Huckleberry Hill,** along the inland curve a little bit north of the Highway 1 Gate, which is the highest point along the drive.

Hitting the links

I won't lie to you — getting a tee time on one of the prime Pebble Beach courses without booking a room at one of the resorts can be difficult, even in the off-season (November through March).

Pebble Beach Golf Links, The Links at Spanish Bay, Spyglass Hill Golf Course, all on the 17-Mile Drive, and **Del Monte Golf Course,** in Monterey, are all administered by the Pebble Beach Company (☎ **800-654-9300;** www.pebblebeach.com). If you'd like to book a lesson, call the **Pebble Beach Golf Academy** (☎ **831-622-1310**), home to two of _Golf Magazine_'s Top 100 Teachers in America for 1999–2000, Laird Small and Dan Pasqueriello.

✔ **Pebble Beach Golf Links**, at the Lodge at Pebble Beach, is the Big Kahuna of Pebble Beach golf courses. A links legend since 1919, this par-72, 6,799-yard rolling oceanfront beauty regularly ranks among the top five courses in the world, and many of golf's biggest names have called it the finest course they've ever played. This is a mature course with old-root trees and massive bunkers, at one with the land like few courses on earth.

Unless you're willing to foot the bill for a Pebble Beach hotel room, don't get your heart set on playing here, though — nonguests can book tee times just a day in advance, which means you have to get very lucky and catch a last-minute cancellation (near to impossible). And expect to pay to play, big time: Greens fees are $300 for resort guests, $350 for nonguests.

✔ **Spyglass Hill Golf Course,** at Stevenson Drive and Spyglass Hill Road in Pebble Beach, Robert Trent Jones, Sr.'s par-72, 6,859-yard legend is one of the toughest golf courses in the world. Expect to test your skills — and every club in your bag — if you get to play here. Greens fees are $225 for resort guests, $250 for nonguests. Nonguests can book tee times up to a month in advance for this course — easier to get on than Pebble Beach, but still tough. (Even winter tee times were booked up a month in advance when I last checked.)

Your best bets for garnering available tee times are the **Del Monte Golf Course** and **The Links at Spanish Bay,** where nonguests can book up to two months in advance. I found tee times regularly available within a few weeks of the date I called at Spanish Bay and Del Monte. Still, you should call as early as possible, even marking your calendar to dial at the two-month and one-month mark. If that fails, just call back and try to snag a cancellation.

✔ **Del Monte Golf Course,** at the Hyatt on Sylvan Road and Hwy. 1 in Monterey, is the oldest course west of the Mississippi. This par-72, 6,339-yard inland course has been challenging golfers since 1897, as well as wowing them with its tree-lined charm. And by Pebble Beach terms, greens fees are reasonable: $75 for resort guests, $103 for non-resort guests.

✔ Designed by Robert Trent Jones, Jr., Tom Watson, and Frank Tatum, **The Links at Spanish Bay,** at the Inn at Spanish Bay, is the U.S.'s foremost Scottish linksland-style course; Tom Watson has said "It's so much like Scotland, you can almost hear the bag-pipes." Greens fees are $185 for guests, $235 for nonguests.

It's an even playing field for tee times at the public **Poppy Hills Golf Course,** just off 17-Mile Drive on Lopez Road (☎ 831-625-2035; www.ncga.org/poppy.htm), where everybody has an equal shot. Robert Trent Jones, Jr., designed this par-72, 6,865-yard, which is a favorite among duffers. The course accepts reservations up to 30 days in advance. I advise calling as early as possible within that time frame for your choice of tee times, but you can usually snare a slot a week in advance. Greens fees are lower, too: $115 Monday through Friday, and $130 Saturday, Sunday, and holidays.

Carmel-by-the-Sea

If Monterey sounds too touristy, Pebble Beach too expensive, and Big Sur's accommodations too woodsy or rustic for you, consider Carmel. This high-end haven is the star of the California coast, and one of the loveliest towns in all of America. It's more like an elite artists' colony than a mass-market tourist town, with galleries and boutiques galore, quaint views or sweeping vistas at every turn, and a relaxed vibe that whispers "away from it all" like sweet nothings in your ear.

Like the celebrity it is, Carmel exudes charisma by the bucketload. This charmer displays its assets to their best advantage, with picture-perfect, cypress-dotted streets leading gradually downhill to one of the most spectacular beaches on the California coast.

Not everyone likes Carmel. For one, complaints of commercialism abound from those who knew it when, before Saks Fifth Avenue and all those cute inns moved in. And like its most famous resident, Clint Eastwood (who served a high-profile stint as mayor a few years back), virtually all of the residents are seven-figure types. As a result, prices are high across the board, restaurants are more upscale than casual, and an air of elitism prevails.

Also, Carmel isn't really suited for the young'uns; romance-seeking couples rule the day here. If you have the kids in tow, you'll probably be happier basing yourself in family-friendly Monterey or Pacific Grove instead. You will find, however, that no one's more welcome in Carmel than the family pet; this is West Coast Nirvana for those who like to travel with Fido.

Carmel is rather quiet and not overloaded with sightseeing "attractions" per se. Visiting is more about slowing down a bit — browsing the boutiques, ambling the backstreets to admire the fabulous homes, and strolling that breathtaking beach. If you're looking for relaxation, stay awhile. All you need is a day or so to explore the village itself, but Carmel also makes a good base for exploring the entire peninsula, and even the stupendous Big Sur Coast (see Chapter 17).

Orienting yourself and getting around

Carmel-by-the-Sea is petite and easy to navigate. The town is laid out on a basic grid pattern, with Ocean Avenue running due west from Highway 1 to Carmel Beach and serving as the village's main drag.

Parallel to Ocean Avenue run numbered avenues: Fourth, Fifth, and Sixth avenues to the north, and Seventh and Eighth avenues to the south. (The town extends farther in each direction, but these streets shape downtown.)

Perpendicular to Ocean and the numbered avenues run a number of name streets: Mission Street, San Carlos, Dolores, Lincoln, and so on. You can get an easy-to-follow, cartoony map of downtown labeling most major businesses almost everywhere about town; for a preview, point your Web browser to www.carmelfun.com.

Note that this quaint village has no need for such big-city affectations as street addresses. Thus, all addresses are given in general terms: San Carlos Street at Seventh, Sixth between Lincoln and Monte Verde, and so on.

Everything in town is within walking distance. Most likely, you'll be able to park your car at your inn or motel and leave it there for the duration of your stay. Parking has strict time limits in the downtown area, but moving a few blocks off Ocean Avenue into more residential territory usually yields less restricted space. A free lot sits at Third Avenue and Torres Street, and another at the beach, plus a paid lot at Eighth Avenue and San Carlos Street.

Staying in style

Carmel is just so gosh-darn cute that it's a hugely popular weekend destination. Book well in advance if you're planning a visit over the weekend. And be aware that most places require a two-night minimum stay on weekends.

You may want to try booking your room through a free reservations service such as **Monterey Peninsula Reservations** (☎ **888-655-3424;** www.monterey-reservations.com); **Resort II Me** (☎ **800-757-5646;** www.resort2me.com); or the **Carmel Area Reservation Service** (☎ **888-434-3891** or 831-659-7061; www.carmel-california.com). You can sometimes get a better rate through these services than you can obtain by calling direct, and they'll make alternative suggestions if my suggestions are full.

Count on 10 percent in taxes being tacked on to your final hotel bill.

Cobblestone Inn

$$–$$$ Carmel-by-the-Sea

This charming B&B offers flowery, romantic accommodations at moderate prices. The 24 rooms encircle a lovely courtyard. Each room features a fireplace, TV (not a given in B&Bs), and minifridge. The staff serves afternoon goodies in a warm and lovely living room. On the down side, the cheapest rooms are very small, and only two of the rooms with private baths have tub/shower combos. But the sacrifices are minimal considering the charms. Bikes are available for exploring.

Junipero St. between Seventh and Eighth aves. ☎ *800-833-8836 or 831-625-5222. Fax: 831-625-0478. Internet: www.foursisters.com. Parking: Free! Rack rates: $115–$195 double, $230 suite. Rates include full breakfast and afternoon wine and hors d'oeuvres. AE, DC, MC, V.*

Cypress Inn

$$–$$$ Carmel-by-the-Sea

Carmel's pet-friendliest hotel is also a good bet for pet-free travelers. This Moorish-Mediterranean inn is co-owned by screen legend Doris Day, whose movie posters grace the bar. Some of the standard doubles are small and on the spare side, but they do the trick. You can enjoy breakfast in the lovely courtyard on nice days, and the oh-so-comfy fireplace-lit living room is a guest magnet in the evenings. The service is accommodating, too.

Lincoln St. and Seventh Ave. ☎ *800-443-7443 or 831-624-3871. Fax: 831-624-8216. Internet:* www.cypress-inn.com. *Parking: Free! Rack rates: $125–$225 double, from $275 suite. Rates include a generous continental breakfast spread. AE, DISC, MC, V.*

Mission Ranch

$$–$$$ Carmel-by-the-Sea

With the helping hand of Dirty Harry himself, Clint Eastwood, this 1850s farmhouse and its outlying buildings have been transformed into an elegant country inn. The ranch lies on the outskirts of town, a good walk away from the village, but sheep-filled pastures and ocean views make it almost picture-perfect. Rooms vary depending on price and location, but all have an appealingly cozy ranchland vibe; ask questions when you book to be sure you end up in the one that's right for you. On-site is an excellent restaurant, plus a fitness room and tennis courts.

26270 Dolores St. (near the Carmel Mission). ☎ *800-538-8221 or 831-624-6436. Fax: 831-626-4163. Parking: Free! Rack rates: $85–$225 double, $195–$225 1- or 2-bedroom cottage. Rates include continental breakfast. AE, MC, V.*

Quail Lodge Resort and Golf Club

$$$$–$$$$$ Carmel Valley

Inland from town lies Carmel Valley, a playground for wealthy types who prefer fun in the sun to misty coastal charms. Owned by the Peninsula Group — one of the world's finest hotel chains — this magical destination resort spreads across 850 pastoral acres with gorgeous gardens, sparkling lakes, wildlife-dotted woodlands, and championship fairways. Luxuries abound in the spacious French-country rooms, and the extensive facilities — tennis courts, pools, hiking paths, more — will keep you happy for days on end.

8205 Valley Greens Dr., Carmel Valley (4 miles east of Carmel-by-the-Sea). ☎ *800-538-9516 or 831-624-2888. Fax: 831-624-3726. Internet:* www.peninsula.com. *Parking: Free! Rack rates: Apr–Nov $245–$345 double, $395–$1,350 suite, plus $15 service charge per night. Ask about golf, romance, and holiday packages. AE, CB, DC, JCB, MC, V.*

Village Inn

$$ Carmel-by-the-Sea

This superbly located motel is Carmel's best bet for budget-minded travelers. The cute rooms have a bit more charm than you usually find at such bargain rates, as well as fridges and nice, newish baths. The attractive property is spic-and-span, and management is conscientious and friendly. The double queens are a good bet for families.

Junipero and Ocean aves. ☎ *800-346-3864 or 831-624-3864. Fax: 831-626-6763. Internet:* www.carmelvillageinn.com. *Parking: Free! Rack rates: $69–$185 double, $89–$360 suite. Rates include continental breakfast. AE, MC, V.*

Dining Out

It's really hard to go wrong dining out in Carmel. The locals have loads of discretionary income, so they can afford to demand the best. Of the more than 60 restaurants in this tiny town, most are better than average. This section describes my favorites — but if you pass something else that strikes your fancy, chances are good that it won't disappoint you.

Reservations are a must on weekends.

Cafe Gringo

$$ Carmel-by-the-Sea   MEXICAN

Tucked away in a charming courtyard, Café Gringo offers pleasing nouveau-Mexican fare. Chef Zenda Willemstein takes a creative, health-conscious approach to the Tex-Mex style of cooking, using all-fresh ingredients and shunning lard and deep-frying. The food is zesty and flavorful, but not too spicy for uninitiated palates. Choose between the colorful, unpretentious dining room or the heated brick patio.

In the Paseo San Carlos, San Carlos St. between Ocean and Seventh aves. ☎ *831-626-8226. Reservations accepted. Main courses: $8–$14. AE, MC, V. Open: Lunch and dinner Thurs–Tues.*

Caffé Napoli/Little Napoli

$$ Carmel-by-the-Sea   ITALIAN

These mirror-image sister restaurants bring a true slice of Naples to Carmel. Between the charming decor (think red gingham, garlic braids), the excellent country-style cooking, the extensive all-Italian wine list, and the low prices, it's no wonder that these restaurants inspire such local loyalty. Expect hearty favorites like crispy-crust pizzas, hand-stuffed cannelloni, and Neapolitan-style seafood. Everything's fresh from the field or the bay. This restaurant is terrific — and a grade-A value to boot.

Caffé Napoli on Ocean Ave. near Lincoln St. ☎ *831-625-4033. Little Napoli in the El Paseo Building, Dolores St. between Ocean and Seventh aves.* ☎ *831-626-6335.*

Internet: www.littlenapoli.com. *Reservations highly recommended for dinner. Main courses: $8–$16. MC, V. Open: Lunch and dinner daily (Little Napoli open for lunch Fri–Sun only).*

Casanova

$$$$ Carmel-by-the-Sea FRENCH/ITALIAN

In a town full of dreamy restaurants, this is far and away the most romantic. The Mediterranean-style house (former home of Charlie Chaplin's cook) spills over with candlelit old-world charm. But don't let all this talk of ambience fool you: The French-Italian menu is top-notch, the service is excellent, and the 30,000-bottle wine cellar is an award-winner. Considering that the meals include antipasti and dessert, prices aren't bad, either.

Fifth Ave. between San Carlos and Mission sts. ☎ *831-625-0501. Internet:* www.casanovarestaurant.com. *Reservations recommended. Three-course prix-fixe: $22–$40. MC, V. Open: Lunch Mon–Sat, brunch Sun, dinner nightly.*

Flying Fish Grill

$$$–$$$$ Carmel-by-the-Sea PACIFIC RIM/SEAFOOD

Chef/owner Kenny Fukumoto's dark and intimate pan-Asian seafood house is one of my favorite restaurants on the Monterey Peninsula. Expect creative, beautifully prepared seafood dishes with Japanese accents — almond sea bass and *yosenabe* (clay-pot seafood) are shining stars on the universally pleasing menu — plus specialties like rib-eye *shabu-shabu* for nonseafood eaters. Marvelous!

In Carmel Plaza, Mission St. between Ocean and Seventh aves. ☎ *831-625-1962. Reservations highly recommended. Main courses: $15–$23. AE, DISC, MC, V. Open: Dinner nightly (closed Tues in winter).*

Jack London's Bar and Grill

$$–$$$ Carmel-by-the-Sea AMERICAN

Come here when you tire of Carmel's high prices and snooty airs. This quarter-century-old bar and restaurant is a completely unpretentious hangout that has nevertheless been lauded by the *New York Times* for its local charms. The huge menu ranges from burgers and chicken-breast sandwiches to pizzas, Tex-Mex specialties, and Black Angus steaks. It offers great bathtub-size margaritas, too.

San Carlos St. at Fifth Ave. ☎ *831-624-2336. Main courses: $7.50–$21. AE, DISC, MC, V. Open: Lunch and dinner daily.*

Exploring Carmel-by-the-Sea

At the foot of Ocean Avenue sits **Carmel Beach,** one of the most heavenly beaches in the United States, if not the world. A wide crescent of white sand skirts gorgeous, tidepool-dotted Carmel Bay. A screen of gnarled cypresses separates street from sand, and emerald-green cliffs of Pebble Beach rise in the distance. Swimming is a no-no, as the waves are too rough (and the water's too cold year-round, anyway), but the beach is great for strolling, picnicking, and playing fetch with Fido, who's allowed to run off leash here (you'll see lots of happy dogs cavorting in the sand). Take time to walk along this stretch of beach no matter what time of year you're visiting; walk north for the best views.

The small parking lot at the end of Ocean gets crowded year-round, but you can often find additional spots along Scenic Road, from which wooden staircases lead down to the beach at various points along the road. (Note that the only restrooms are in the parking lot on Ocean Avenue.)

If you want a little sand space to yourself, follow Scenic Road south around the promontory to **Carmel River State Beach**, a more remote, white-sand, dune-dotted stretch that's a paradise for birders.

Shopping and strolling

Shopping is tops among Carmel activities. Pricey apparel and home-furnishing boutiques, jewelry stores, and art galleries line the streets of downtown. Don't expect to find anything too funky; still, you can do lots of one-of-a-kind browsing to do. Gallery hounds should pick up the free *Carmel Gallery Guide,* available throughout town. Be sure to peek into Carmel's various courtyards, which often hide some of the best finds. The alfresco **Carmel Plaza,** at Ocean Avenue and Mission Street (☎ **831-624-0137**), houses about 50 shops, including familiar names like Saks Fifth Avenue and Banana Republic.

Stepping into the past

Mission San Carlos Borromeo del Rio Carmelo, more commonly known as the **Carmel Mission,** 3080 Rio Rd. (☎ **831-624-3600;** www.carmelmission.org), is one of the largest and most beautiful of the 21 Spanish missions established by Father Junípero Serra, Spanish founder of California's mission chain. Built in a baroque style with a towering Moorish bell tower, it has been in continuous operation since 1771. The burnished terra-cotta facade and soaring, romantic curves make it worth strolling by even if you don't go inside. Still, history buffs will want to make the effort.

It's open for self-guided tours daily from 9:30 a.m. to 4:15 p.m. (from 10:30 a.m. on Sunday), with extended hours in summer. Admission is $2, $1 for kids. To reach the mission, take San Carlos Street south from town and follow the signs, or take Rio Road west off Highway 1 and follow it for a half-mile.

TIP

If you'd like to learn more about the local history and color, take a two-hour guided walk with **Carmel Walks** (☎ 831-642-2700; www. carmelwalks.com). The walks take place Tuesday through Friday at 10 a.m., Saturday at 10 a.m. and 2 p.m., for $15 per person. Tours leave from the Pine Inn at Lincoln Street and Ocean Avenue; call ahead to reserve your spot.

Sampling Big Sur's natural beauty

The spectacular beauty of the Big Sur Coast (see Chapter 17) begins just three miles south of Carmel-by-the-Sea at **Point Lobos State Reserve** (☎ 831-624-4909; www.pointlobos.org). A cypress-dotted headland, the Big Sur Coast has been variously called "the greatest meeting of land and water in the world" and "the crown jewel of the state parks system." It's a natural wonderland, all right, with sea lions, otters, harbor seals, and seabirds populating the ocean coves; spectacular coastal vistas (perfect for whale-watching in winter); picnic areas; and miles of hiking trails. The entrance fee is $7 per car, which includes a trail map. Open from 9 a.m. to dusk. Arrive early, especially on weekends; if the lot is full, you'll have to wait for someone to leave before you can enter.

Gathering More Information

For peninsula-wide information before you arrive, point your Web browser to www.monterey.com, or contact the Monterey Peninsula Visitors & Convention Bureau on their 24-hour info hotline (☎ 831-649-1770; www.monterey.com). Another useful source of information is the Monterey County Travel & Tourism Alliance (☎ 888-221-1010; www.gomonterey.org). For Carmel-specific information, you can call ☎ 888-434-3891 to order the "Carmel Sample Packet" ($12.95), or visit www.carmel-california.com.

In Monterey

Stop in at the well-staffed and well-stocked Monterey Visitors Center, near downtown at Camino El Estero and Franklin St. (one block inland from Del Monte Avenue). It is open Monday through Saturday from 9 a.m. to 6 p.m. (to 5 p.m. November through March), Sunday from 9 a.m. to 5 p.m. (to 4 p.m. November through March).

There's also a staffed information desk at the **Maritime Museum** at Monterey State Historic Park, near the entrance to Fisherman's Wharf.

In Carmel

You can pick up information from the Carmel Business Association, upstairs next to the Eastwood Building on San Carlos Street between 5th and 6th avenues in Carmel-by-the-Sea (☎ 831-624-2522). You can also call ahead to have a visitor's guide sent to you. The office is open Monday through Friday from 9 a.m. to 5 p.m. and Saturday from 11 a.m. to 3 p.m. (check for Sunday hours in summer).

You can also stop by the Monterey County Visitors Center at the Crossroads Shopping Center, off Hwy. 1 at the Rio Road exit, Carmel; open Monday through Friday 10 a.m. to 5:30 p.m., Saturday 10 a.m. to 6 p.m., Sunday 11:30 a.m. to 5:30 p.m.

Chapter 17

The Spectacular Big Sur Coast

• •

In This Chapter

▶ Enjoying the state's most spectacular natural scenery

▶ Choosing the best places to stay and dine

▶ Exploring Julia Pfeiffer Burns State Park and other highlights

▶ Watching sea lions, otters, and seals at Point Lobos State Reserve

• •

*F*ew shorelines in the world are as breathtaking as the Big Sur Coast. Skirted by rugged shores and crescent-shaped bays, this pristine wilderness of towering redwoods and rolling hills is tranquil, unspoiled, romantic, dramatic, and overwhelmingly beautiful — and, as you may have guessed by now, perfect for relaxing. If you really want quiet, this is the place to get it.

Although, technically, a Big Sur Village does exist (about 29 miles south of the Monterey Peninsula on Highway 1), blink and you'll miss it. "Big Sur" actually refers to the gorgeous 90-mile stretch of land between Carmel-by-the-Sea and San Simeon. The main thoroughfare and scenic byway is Highway 1, blessed on one side by the 167,000-acre Ventana Wilderness, with the splendid Santa Lucia mountain range rising just beyond, and on the other by the wild, rugged, spectacular coast. The region is at its most woodsy and breathtaking in the northern half, but the entire coastline drive is stunning.

Development is minimal, and you'll find little more to do here than commune with nature — but oh, what spectacular nature it is! Make time to enjoy it. Hike the state parks, walk the beaches, stop regularly along the drive to watch windsurfers pirouette among the waves and sea lions sun on the rocks, or just perch yourself atop the cliffs and take in the sea breeze. You won't believe the effect Big Sur can have on your soul: Modern life fades into the background as you become absorbed in Mother Nature's world.

The Big Sur Coast

To Monterey and
Point Lobos State Reserve

Point Sur
Lighthouse

VENTANA
WILDERNESS

Point Sur
State Historic Park

South Fork

Santa

Little Sur River

Lucia

Point Sur

Gate

ANDREW MOLERA
STATE PARK

△
Adams Hill

Los Padres

*False
Sur*

California
Sea Otter
Game Refuge

Gate

Gate

Camp
Parking

Gate

2

Big Sur

Range

*Molera
Point*

Gate

Big Sur River

National Forest

Gate

Gate

Pfeiffer
Falls Pfeiffer Big Sur
State Park

3

Park
Headquarters

4

△Sawmill
Flat △Weyland

*Cooper
Point*

Accommodations ■

Big Sur Lodge **4**
Deetjen's Big Sur Inn **7**
Glen Oaks **2**
Post Ranch Inn **5**
Ragged Point Inn & Resort **9**
Ventana Inn & Spa **6**

Dining ◆

Big Sur River Inn **3**
Cielo **6**
Deetjen's Big Sur Inn **7**
Glen Oaks Restaurant **2**
Nepenthe/Cafe Kevah **8**
Rocky Point Restaurant
& Lounge **1**

Pfeiffer Beach

Pfeiffer Point

Wreck Beach

5

South Park
Entrance

6

1

To
San Luis
Obispo

7

8

California Sea Otter Game Refuge

9

*PACIFIC
OCEAN*

| 0 | | 1 mi |
| 0 | | 1 km |

Ⓝ

The flip side to all this poetic waxing, however, is that Big Sur requires some effort to enjoy. With just one winding, hairpin-plagued lane in each direction, Highway 1 is slow going and can be tummy-turning. Tourist facilities along the route are limited, so don't expect a gas station every few miles, or any chain motels or fast-food joints at all. The region's remoteness has fostered a special breed of local: quiet types who fiercely protect their privacy, their rustic lifestyle, and the unspoiled nature around them. A hippie vibe still prevails — most residents came here to get away from it all, and they mean to keep it that way. Stay off private property and unmarked driveways, and stick to clearly marked pullouts, public areas, and parks. Take a cue from the locals: Appreciate Big Sur for what it is — glorious and unspoiled. Enjoy it, respect it, and leave no mark. Pack out *everything* you bring in.

Timing Your Visit

Like much of California's central and northern coast, Big Sur is at its clearest, warmest, and sunniest best in Indian summer — September and October. Summer is the busiest season traffic-wise and hotel-wise, so plan ahead and expect to pay top dollar.

What's the tradeoff for cooler weather in winter and spring? Clear skies, little fog, no crowds, lower hotel rates, and fabulous offshore views of the mammoth gray whales that migrate from Alaska to Mexico and back again between November and April. For a month-by-month breakdown of the seasons and events, point your Web browser to www.bigsurcalifornia.org and click on "Calendar."

Leave yourself plenty of time to mosey along the Big Sur Coast. Even though the distance is only about 110 miles from Carmel to San Simeon, you can't really drive the twisty-turny road in less than 3 hours. And trust me — you don't want to.

Allow a whole day for the drive. New and exciting views present themselves at every turn, with plenty of vista points for stopping. An entire day gives you time to go hiking at one of the spectacular parks along the way, along with time for a picnic or a leisurely lunch.

If you want to spend more time among the trees, book a place to stay for a night or two. However, be aware that the accommodations in this funky neck of the woods fall into two categories: big-money luxurious, or comfort-challenged rustic. You won't find any affordable country inns or reliable chain motels in between, and TVs are not a common amenity no matter which budget level you choose. If the choices in "Staying in Big Sur" don't suit you but you still want more than a day to explore Mother Nature's handiwork, base yourself just to the north on the Monterey Peninsula (Carmel is particularly convenient) or near Hearst Castle to the south for easy access.

Getting There

You can access all the main attractions via Highway 1. If you're dedicating a day to the drive, set out early so you can take full advantage of daylight. The slow, curving drive is not only a drag at night, but you can't see any of the spectacular scenery — so why bother? Leaving early is especially important if you're heading north, as the region's finest parks, Pfeiffer-Big Sur and Julia Pfeiffer Burns state parks, are about two-thirds of the way up the coast.

Staying in Big Sur

Expect 10½ percent in taxes to be tacked on to your hotel bill.

Camping is certainly the truest way to experience this unspoiled region. If camping's your thing, visit www.bigsurcalifornia.org for a complete list of campground options.

Big Sur Lodge

$$ Big Sur

Tucked among the redwoods of Pfeiffer-Big Sur State Park are these 61 rustic cabins, many large enough to house families. Well-kept and spacious, all have private baths and patios with lovely views, but no TV or telephone to interrupt as you commune with nature. Spend a bit more for a fireplace and/or kitchenette if you can afford it; nights get cool, and who wants to run out for coffee in the morning? A restaurant, country store, and heated pool, plus all park amenities, are on-site.

In Pfeiffer-Big Sur State Park, Hwy. 1, Big Sur (26 miles south of Carmel). ☎ *800-424-4787 or 831-667-3100. Fax: 831-667-3110. Internet:* www.bigsurlodge.com. *Parking: Free! Rack rates: $89–$189 1-bedroom cottage, $119–$219 2-bedroom cottage. Rates include day-use fees for five Big Sur-area parks. AE, MC, V.*

Deetjen's Big Sur Inn

$$–$$$ Big Sur

Built by a Norwegian homesteader and his missus in the 1930s and now a national historic site, Deetjen's is quintessential Big Sur: Lovely, rustic, and funky to a fault. You'll love the oddball collection of hand-hewn cabins if you don't mind sacrificing creature comforts for rustic-cozy. The cabins do not include phones, TVs, or central heating. Walls are single-board thin, so don't pass on a fire-heated room — even in summer — and don't expect privacy or quiet (families with kids under 12 must book two adjoining rooms). The restaurant is one of the local best. Book well ahead, as the inn fills up two months or more in advance.

Hwy. 1, Big Sur (30 miles south of Carmel). ☎ *831-667-2377. Parking: Free! Rack Rates: $75–$160 double with shared bath, $110–$180 double with private bath. MC, V.*

Glen Oaks

$–$$ Big Sur

This well-run, well-maintained post-adobe-style motel is Big Sur's best standard lodging. The basic rooms are clean and comfortable but, in true Big Sur fashion, have no TVs or phones. Rooms with two queen-size beds can accommodate families. Two cottages feature well-outfitted kitchens and tub/shower combos in lieu of the standard walk-in showers. The dinner-only restaurant is a cozy local favorite, and a cafe next door serves breakfast and lunch.

Hwy. 1, (1 mile north of Pfeiffer-Big Sur State Park, 25 miles south of Carmel).
☎ *831-667-2105. Fax: 831-667-1105. Internet:* www.glenoaksbigsur.com.
Parking: Free! Rack rates: $60–$99 double, $110–$138 cottage. No credit cards.

Post Ranch Inn

$$$$$ **Big Sur**

Wide expanses of glass bring the outside in to 30 gorgeous, amenity-filled oceanfront cottages, spread out over 98 unspoiled acres at this environmentally friendly, ultra-exclusive resort. No TVs, but you'll have CD players and everything else you could want — even your own private slice of spectacular Big Sur to explore. A full menu of spa treatments is available in your room or outdoors — you decide. The restaurant is excellent, too. This place is ridiculously expensive (not to mention a tad pretentious), but worth every penny.

Hwy. 1 (28 miles south of Carmel). ☎ *800-527-2200 or 831-667-2200. Fax: 831-667-2824. Internet:* www.postranchinn.com. *Rack rates: $455–$755 double, $695–$900 house for 2–6. Rates include continental breakfast. AE, MC, V.*

Ragged Point Inn & Resort

$$–$$$ **Ragged Point**

This rustic motel at the southern gateway to Big Sur isn't perfect — expect worn tiled entryways and dated baths — but the spectacular oceanfront setting makes up for any deficiencies. Rooms are clean and feature new furnishings, comfy beds, and furnished patios for enjoying the views. Upstairs rooms are pricier, but you'll have better coastal vistas. The resort includes a gorgeous stone-pillared restaurant with perfectly decent food and a spectacular ocean-facing patio. The grounds are fab, too — stop by for the sightlines even if you don't stay here.

19019 Hwy. 1 (14 miles north of Hearst Castle). ☎ *805-927-4502. Fax: 805-927-8862. Parking: Free! Rack rates: $89–$179 double. AE, DISC, MC, V.*

Ventana Inn & Spa

$$$$$ **Big Sur**

Here's another stunning luxury oasis similar to Post Ranch, this one spread over a whopping 243 meadowy, ocean-facing acres. *Travel & Leisure* named much-lauded Ventana as the second-best small hotel in the world in 1998, so expect to be wowed. The gorgeous rooms are more country cozy than contemporary, and include TVs, VCRs, and CD players among the luxuries. You can't argue with the fabulousness of the grounds, which include a new 2,100-foot spa — with amenities ranging from massages and mud treatments to aromatherapy sessions — and the first-rate **Cielo** for fine dining.

Hwy. 1 (28 miles south of Carmel). ☎ *800-628-6500 or 831-667-2331. Fax: 831-667-2287. Internet:* www.ventanainn.com. *Parking: Free! Rack rates: $340–$850 double or suite. Rates include continental breakfast and afternoon wine and cheese. AE, CB, DC, DISC, MC, V.*

Dining Out

In addition to the options listed below, also consider these excellent choices at Big Sur's top places to stay:

✔ Moderately priced, highly regarded **Glen Oaks Restaurant ($$$),** across the street from the Glen Oaks motel on Highway 1 a mile north of Pfeiffer-Big Sur State Park (☎ **831-667-2264**), is a warm and cozy local favorite particularly well-known for its homemade pastas. The restaurant is open nightly for dinner except Tuesday; main courses run about $10 to $19.

✔ **Cielo ($$$$)** at the Ventana Inn & Spa, two miles south of Pfeiffer-Big Sur (☎ **831-667-2331**), is tops for a sophisticated lunch stop or a special dinner. Grab a midday table on the outdoor patio in nice weather — the views are incredible. The California cuisine doesn't disappoint, either. Main courses run $11 to $17 at lunch, $24 to $30 at dinner, and an afternoon light-bites grill menu is on offer in between the major meals.

✔ Housed in four wood-polished, candlelit rooms, the lovely restaurant at **Deetjen's Big Sur Inn ($$$$),** four miles south of Pfeiffer-Big Sur (☎ **831-667-2377**), is regaled for its hearty cooking and intimate ambience. Breakfast ($7 to $10) includes all of your farmhouse favorites, while dinner ($17.50 to $25) features such sophisticated but unfussy dishes as New York steak with twice-baked potato and herb-crusted New Zealand rack of lamb. A country delight.

Reservations are recommended at all of the above choices. For further details, see "Staying in Big Sur" earlier in this chapter.

Big Sur River Inn

$$ Big Sur   AMERICAN

This popular, unpretentious place is ideal for taking a break at any time of day. Cozy up to the huge stone fireplace in cold weather, or snag a table on the alfresco deck when the sun shines. Expect American classics ranging from hearty breakfasts to burgers and sandwiches to fresh fish, pastas, and ribs. Service is friendly, and the crowd is a nice mix of locals and visitors. The inn provides live entertainment on Saturday evenings and Sunday afternoons, usually of the foot-stomping variety.

Hwy. 1 (2 miles north of Pfeiffer-Big Sur State Park). ☎ *831-667-2700. Internet:* www.bigsurriverinn.com. *Reservations recommended for dinner in season. Main courses: $8–$12 at lunch, $8–$20 at dinner. AE, DC, DISC, MC, V. Open: Breakfast, lunch, and dinner daily.*

Nepenthe

$$$ Big Sur AMERICAN

Nepenthe's prices are way too high if you only consider the strictly average American fare — steaks, broiled fish, burgers, quiche — but the stupendous views alone are worth the price. The redwood-beamed indoor/outdoor restaurant has a wonderful lodgelike atmosphere, and a casual party vibe prevails. The panoramic views are awe-inspiring, and starlit nights are pure magic. Come by for a drink if you don't want to pay for the food. Or, better yet, on nice days, head a level down to the alfresco **Cafe Kevah ($)**. Kevah's amazing patio boasts the same stellar views, and the casual healthy-gourmet daytime fare goes for a fraction of the dough.

Hwy. 1 (2 miles south of Pfeiffer-Big Sur State Park, just south of the Ventana Inn). ☎ *831-667-2345. Internet:* www.nepenthebigsur.com. *Reservations accepted for five or more. Main courses: $11–$26 at Nepenthe, $5.50–$11 at Cafe Kevah. AE, MC, V. Open: Lunch and dinner daily at Nepenthe, breakfast and lunch daily at Cafe Kevah.*

Rocky Point Restaurant & Lounge

$$$$ Big Sur STEAKS/SEAFOOD

This pleasing clifftop chophouse at the northern end of Big Sur is one of the area's most spectacularly situated restaurants, second only to Nepenthe — and you'll get better food for your money. You have an incredible ocean view no matter where you sit, either indoors or out. Sunset views are phenomenal, and floodlights play off the waves after dark. The surf-and-turf menu is traditional and satisfying. Everything is flame-grilled over hardwoods, and all dinners include soup or salad and sides.

Hwy. 1, about 10 miles south of Carmel. ☎ *831-624-2933. Internet:* www. rocky-point.com. *Reservations highly recommended for dinner. Main courses: $10–$15 at lunch, $19–$32 at dinner. AE, DISC, MC, V. Open: Breakfast, lunch, and dinner daily.*

Exploring the Big Sur Coast

The highlights in this section are discussed as you proceed along Highway 1 southbound. This is strictly to match the existing structure of this book. Making the drive southbound brings no particular advantage, scenic or otherwise. In addition to these stops, a number of smaller parks and scenic vistas with pullouts exist along the way.

✔ Just three miles south of Carmel lies **Point Lobos State Reserve** (☎ 831-624-4909; www.pointlobos.org), a cypress-dotted headland that has been variously called "the greatest meeting of land and water in the world" and "the crown jewel of the state parks system." It's a natural wonderland, all right, with sea lions, otters, harbor seals, and seabirds populating the sea coves; superb coastal vistas (perfect for whale-watching in winter); picnic areas; and miles of hiking trails. The entrance fee is $7 per car ($6 if you have a senior citizen on board), which includes a trail map.

Arrive early, especially on weekends. If the lot is full, you'll have to wait for someone to leave before you can enter.

✔ About 13 miles south of Carmel is the **Bixby Bridge,** which you'll probably recognize, even if you've never been to Big Sur. Rising 260 feet over **Bixby Creek Canyon,** the much-photographed bridge is one of the world's highest single-span concrete bridges, and one of Big Sur's most iconic images. Park your car in the lot on the north side so that you walk across the span and take in the magnificent views.

✔ South of Bixby Bridge is **Point Sur Lighthouse Station,** in Point Sur State Historic Park (☎ **831-625-4419** or 831-667-2315; www.cal-parks.ca.gov/DISTRICTS/monterey/psshp.htm). Built 361 feet above the surf and first lit in 1889 — and in continuous operation ever since — Point Sur is the only working 19th-century lighthouse on the California coast that's open to the public. Three-hour tours are scheduled on weekends (Sat 10 a.m. and 2 p.m., Sun 10 a.m. only), with some weekday and moonlight tours added in summer. The fee is $5 for adults, $3 for teens 13 to 18, $2 for kids 5 to 13, free for under 5s.

The tour includes a steep half-mile hike each way, including stairs, so wear sturdy shoes and a (preferably waterproof) windbreaker to guard against the elements. Call for exact schedule and meeting-place details.

✔ About 20 miles south of Carmel is **Andrew Molera State Park** (☎ **831-667-2315;** www.cal-parks.ca.gov/DISTRICTS/ monterey/amsp.htm), the largest park on the Big Sur Coast, and the least crowded. Miles of trails meander through meadows and along bluffs. The 2 ½-mile-long beach is accessible via a lovely mile-long path flanked by wildflowers in spring. At low tide, you can walk the entire length of the beach. Otherwise, stick to the bluff trail. No swimming, of course — the water's way too cold. But you can take a horseback ride along the sand with **Molera Horseback Tours** (☎ **800-942-5486** or 831-625-5486; www. molerahorsebacktours.com). Prices are $36 to $108 for one- to three-hour guided rides.

✔ Across from Molera State Park you can pick up the **Old Coast Road,** the original 1880s thoroughfare, when only wagons traversed these parts. If you're heading south, you can follow it as a rough scenic alternative for about eight miles by turning left before crossing the Bixby Bridge, but if you just backtrack about a mile north from this entrance you get a spectacular view of the Big Sur Valley, Point Sur Lighthouse, and the Pacific beyond.

Don't try the road in wet weather, though; you will get stuck.

✔ Another five miles or so down the road (26 miles south of Carmel) is **Big Sur Station** (☎ **831-667-2315**), a terrific source for maps, ranger advice, and other Big Sur information.

✔ Big Sur Station is just past the entrance to **Pfeiffer-Big Sur State Park,** 800 acres of wildlife-rich parkland that includes excellent hiking opportunities for all levels of ability; pick up the map available at the park entrance.

One excellent moderate walk is the 40- to 60-minute route to towering 60-foot-high **Pfeiffer Falls,** which takes you through one of Big Sur's most impressive redwood groves. If you're feeling energetic, add on another hour to follow the trail to the **Valley View Overlook** (a mile from the main trailhead, a half-mile from the falls) for spectacular panoramic views.

On-site is the **Big Sur Lodge,** plus more than 200 campsites (see "Staying in Big Sur" earlier in this chapter for details). The park has a good day-use picnic area, too, and a country store where you can buy provisions. This is the most active of Big Sur's state parks, with extensive ranger and campfire programs in season; call ☎ **831-667-2315**. The day-use fee is $6 per car.

✔ About a mile south of the Pfeiffer-Big Sur park entrance is Sycamore Canyon Road, which leads to beautiful **Pfeiffer Beach.** An arch-shaped rock formation just offshore makes for a distinctive view.

Although the sunsets are spectacular, locals advise that you come to Pfeiffer Beach in the morning hours to avoid windblown sand (the winds can kick up in the later hours). But first you have to find Sycamore Canyon Road: The unmarked route is the only paved, ungated road west of Highway 1 between the Pfeiffer-Big Sur State Park and the Big Sur Post Office (you should see a "Narrow Road" sign as an additional clue). Take the sharp turn toward the coast and follow the road slowly for about two winding miles to a parking lot; parking is $5. A short path leads to the beach. Skip this trip if you have a trailer or a motor home.

✔ Two miles south of Pfeiffer-Big Sur State Park is **Nepenthe,** one of the best spots on the planet to enjoy a burger and a view. For details on it and its sister alfresco **Cafe Kevah,** see "Dining Out," earlier in this chapter. Also on-site is the **Phoenix** (☎ **831-667-2347;** www.nepenthebigsur.com), a highly browsable book and gift shop.

Other great shopping along this stretch includes the **Hawthorne Gallery,** just south of Nepenthe on Highway 1 (☎ **831-667-3200**). Another five or six miles along sits the **Coast Gallery** (☎ **831-667-2301**), considered the premier local showcase for the works of the many super-talented artists and artisans who consider Big Sur the ultimate muse.

✔ **The Henry Miller Memorial Library** (☎ **831-667-2574;** www.henrymiller.org) is on the mountain side of Highway 1, a quarter-mile south of **Nepenthe.** It is dedicated to the life and work of Miller, who lived in Big Sur from 1844 to 1962 and wrote such classics as *Tropic of Cancer.* First editions of his writings as well as some of his artwork are on display, as is a rotating exhibit of local art. The library makes a pleasant place for a short stop, especially for Miller fans. Admission is free. Open Thursday through Sunday from 11 a.m. to 6 p.m.

✔ Twelve miles south of Pfeiffer-Big Sur is **Julia Pfeiffer Burns State Park**, a gem of a park and my absolute favorite spot for spectacular ocean views.

Everyone can follow the **Overlook Waterfall Trail** — it's even wheelchair-accessible. The flat and easy ⅓-mile (each way) trail leads to a cliff top with spectacular views of **McWay Falls** plunging into a gorgeous cove where seals and sea otters play in the white-crested blue-green water. Cypress trees stepping down the rocky coast in the background give the view an only-in-Big-Sur mystique. In winter, park yourself on one of the benches to look for migrating whales. The view is particularly spectacular at sunset.

Above the parking lot is a small picnic area and trailheads to two more of the park's hiking trails. The ⅓-mile **Canyon Trail** is steeper and ungraded but still not difficult, and the payoff is a lovely forest waterfall and a bench from which to contemplate it (and rest your weary toes). The day-use fee is $6 per car; ask the park attendant to sell you a trail map for an additional buck.

The big attractions end after Julia Pfeiffer Burns State Park, but the drive is still stunning, and scenic turnoffs abound. About 59 miles south of Carmel, just south of the U.S. Forest Service Station in Pacific Valley, is **Sand Dollar Beach**, which features a very nice picnic area. Take the stairs to reach the beach, which may be devoid of sand if you visit in winter (it usually washes back in summer).

Farther south — just north of **San Simeon,** where the landscape opens up to rolling, golden hills — you'll see elephant seals sunning themselves on rocks and maybe a few colorful windsurfers dancing on the waves beyond. That's when you know you've almost reached the outrageous, infamous, legendary **Hearst Castle,** which is just around the bend. I discuss the Hearst Castle in Chapter 18.

Gathering More Information

Your best source for Big Sur information is the Big Sur Chamber of Commerce Web site at www.bigsurcalifornia.org; you can also call the chamber at ☎ **831-677-2100.** Additionally, the Monterey Peninsula Visitors & Convention Bureau (☎ **831-649-1770;** www.monterey.com) and the Monterey County Travel & Tourism Alliance (☎ **888-221-1010;** www.gomonterey.org) can also provide you with information on Big Sur.

If you'd like more information on Big Sur's state parks, call California State Parks' Big Sur Station at ☎ **831-667-2315,** or point your Web browser to www.cal-parks.ca.gov, then click on "Central Coast," and scroll down to "Monterey County." Located 26 miles south of Carmel, a half-mile south of the entrance to **Pfeiffer-Big Sur State Park,** Big Sur Station is your prime information stop for the region after you've arrived.

Chapter 18

Hearst Castle and Cambria

● ●

In This Chapter

▶ Visiting the mind-boggling castle that Hearst built

▶ Deciding on the best places to stay and dine nearby

▶ Strolling the village and bumming around the beach

● ●

*T*he Japanese have a well-known saying about the town where Japan's most pompous shogun built the country's most outrageous, ostentatious temples. It goes like this: "Don't say 'kekko' ('enough!') until you've seen Nikko."

Well, Nikko has a Western soulmate, and its name is Hearst Castle.

Like that 18th-century shogun — and the fictional counterpart he so detested, Charles Foster Kane (of *Citizen Kane*) — publishing baron and man-about-Hollywood William Randolph Hearst was not a man of small visions. In 1922, he set out to build a dream house beyond all imagination. He called his marvelous new estate "La Cuesta Encantada" — the Enchanted Hill — and enchanting it was, for a time. In its heyday, the '30s and '40s — the Golden Age of Hollywood — this real-life Xanadu was the playground for the silver screen's elite, including Carole Lombard, Clark Gable, Charles Lindbergh, Shirley Temple, and many others.

If the place fails to enchant you, it will at least leave you awestruck. The 130-room main house — along with three Italian Renaissance guest "cottages," magical gardens, and two of the most fabulous swimming pools you'll ever lay eyes on — brims with a you-have-to-see-it-to-believe-it collection of priceless antiques and art that's less a statement on one man's taste or artistic vision and more a commentary on excess and the awesome power that money can buy.

Yes, the castle is well worth visiting. It's a sight to behold — sometimes a beautiful one, but always an over-the-top, only-in-California testament to a Gilded Age glory. Come for the marvelous stories of the building process, the fabulous people, and the spectacular parties. Little ones probably won't get much out of a visit, but older kids will enjoy it just as much as the grown-ups.

Hearst's sprawling compound sits high above San Simeon, which isn't really much of a town. But six miles to the south is Cambria (pronounced

CAM-bree-uh, like "camera," with a short "a" rather than a long one), which makes an excellent base of operations. Not quite northern Californian and not quite southern, not quite coastal and not quite inland, this charming village has a distinct and winning personality and offers terrific opportunities for dining and strolling.

Timing Your Visit

Hearst Castle and Cambria are enjoyable in any season. The biggest considerations are money and crowds.

You'll snare the lowest hotel rates in winter, and the castle is quiet enough that you needn't make advance tour reservations. Spring and fall are pleasant — you'll have the opportunity to take the evening tour (only offered in these seasons), and you'll still beat the crowds if you visit midweek.

You'll pay the highest hotel rates and wrestle with the biggest crowds in summer. You should make weekend hotel reservations, in particular, as far in advance as possible, and I highly recommend purchasing advance tickets for castle tours (more on this subject under "Touring the Castle," later in this chapter).

Set aside two days to enjoy the castle and the charms of Cambria. If you're just coming to see the castle, one day will do, but expect it to be a longish one and sandwich it between a two-night stay.

Getting There

Cambria is right off Highway 1, smack dab in the middle of the coast. It is located 223 miles south of San Francisco, 105 miles south of Monterey, 130 miles north of Santa Barbara, and 230 miles north of L.A. San Simeon, home to the Hearst Castle Visitor Center, is on Highway 1, six miles north of Cambria.

Driving from points north: If you're following the scenic route through Big Sur, just keep going — stay on Highway 1 until you see signs for Hearst Castle, and for Cambria a few minutes beyond.

If you're coming directly from San Francisco or Monterey, take U.S. 101 south to Paso Robles, then Highway 46 west to Highway 1, and Highway 1 north to Cambria and the castle.

Driving from points south: Take U.S. 101 north to San Luis Obispo, where you'll pick up Highway 1 north to Cambria and the castle.

Getting Your Bearings

San Simeon is less a town than a stretch of Highway 1 lined with motels and services catering to castle visitors. The entrance to Hearst Castle rests just north of San Simeon on the inland side of the road.

Cambria lies six miles south of the Hearst Castle Visitor Center. The town's Main Street runs roughly parallel to Highway 1 inland, connecting up with the highway at each end of town.

Tiny Cambria actually has three distinct parts. Along Main Street is *"the Village,"* which is divided into two sections: The West Village and the East Village. The *West Village* is the newer, somewhat more touristy end of town where you'll find the visitor information center. The more historic *East Village* is a bit quieter, more locals-oriented, and a tad more sophisticated than the West Village.

The Cambria & San Simeon Area

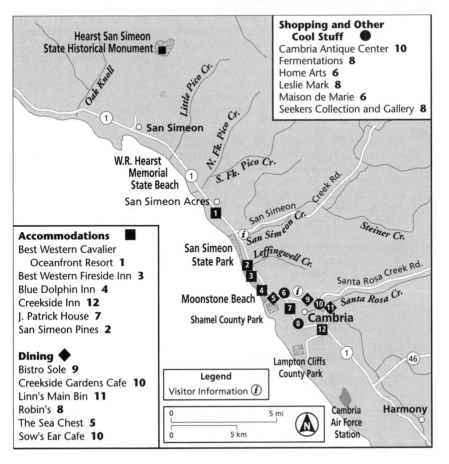

Hearst San Simeon State Historical Monument

Oak Knoll

Little Pico Cr.

1 — San Simeon

W.R. Hearst Memorial State Beach

N. Fk. Pico Cr.

S. Fk. Pico Cr.

San Simeon Acres — **1**

San Simeon Cr. Creek Rd.

San Simeon Cr.

Steiner Cr.

Shopping and Other Cool Stuff ●
Cambria Antique Center **10**
Fermentations **8**
Home Arts **6**
Leslie Mark **8**
Maison de Marie **6**
Seekers Collection and Gallery **8**

Accommodations ■
Best Western Cavalier Oceanfront Resort **1**
Best Western Fireside Inn **3**
Blue Dolphin Inn **4**
Creekside Inn **12**
J. Patrick House **7**
San Simeon Pines **2**

Dining ◆
Bistro Sole **9**
Creekside Gardens Cafe **10**
Linn's Main Bin **11**
Robin's **8**
The Sea Chest **5**
Sow's Ear Cafe **10**

San Simeon State Park — **2** **3**

Leffingwell Cr.

Santa Rosa Creek Rd.

Santa Rosa Cr.

Moonstone Beach — **4** **5** **6** ⓘ **9** **10** **11**

7

Shamel County Park — **8** **Cambria** **12**

1 — 46

Lampton Cliffs County Park

Legend
Visitor Information ⓘ

0 ——— 5 mi
0 ——— 5 km

N

Cambria Air Force Station — **Harmony**

If you cross Highway 1 to the coastal side at the far west end of town (or the north end, if you're considering how the freeway runs), you'll reach Cambria's third part, **Moonstone Beach.** Lined with motels, inns, and a few restaurants on the inland side of the street, ocean-facing Moonstone Beach Drive is my favorite place to stay in Cambria.

Staying Near the Castle

If you're planning to explore both Hearst Castle and the Big Sur Coast from one perch, consider staying at the **Ragged Point Inn & Resort,** just 14 miles north of Hearst Castle near the southern gateway to Big Sur (see "Staying in Big Sur" in Chapter 17).

Expect an extra 9 percent in taxes to be tacked on to your Cambria or San Simeon hotel bill.

If you want a super-cheap choice, try the **Creekside Inn ($)**, 2618 Main St., Cambria (☎ **800-269-5212;** www.moonstonemgmt.com). It's more basic than the motels in the following listing and doesn't boast the same oceanfront perch, but the village location is extremely convenient and the rates are considerably lower — $50 to $85 double, year-round.

Best Western Cavalier Oceanfront Resort

$$ San Simeon

This upscale oceanfront motel is freshly renovated and a real gem. It's well situated along the coast, with lots of ocean-view rooms. Every room is very comfortable (cozy bedding!) and outfitted with a VCR, minibar, and hair dryer. Coastal evenings can be chilly year-round, so book one with a fireplace if you can. On-site extras include two heated pools, a Jacuzzi, an exercise room, two restaurants, and a coin-op laundry, plus video rentals next door. The motel welcomes pets, too.

9415 Hearst Dr. (3 miles south of Hearst Castle on Hwy. 1), San Simeon. ☎ *800-826-8168, 800-780-7234, or 805-927-4688. Fax: 805-927-6472. Internet:* www.bestwestern.com. *Parking: Free! Rack rates: $89–$184 double, $105–$121 family room (2 queens). Deals: Rates as low as $69 in the off-season. Discounts for AAA members, seniors, and government and military employees. AE, CB, DC, DISC, MC, V.*

Best Western Fireside Inn

$$ Cambria

This inn is my favorite of the Moonstone Beach motels. Well done in a charming country style with floral prints and warm woods, the spacious rooms are a few steps above motel standard. Each has a coffeemaker and minifridge, most have gas fireplaces, and some have Jacuzzi tubs; VCRs (and movies) are available for rent. Extras include a nice heated pool and spa, and a friendly staff.

6700 Moonstone Beach Dr., Cambria. ☎ *888-910-7100, 800-780-7234, or 805-927-8661. Fax: 805-927-8584. Internet:* www.bestwesternfiresideinn.com *or* www.bestwestern.com. *Parking: Free! Rack rates: $89–$189 double. Rates include continental breakfast. Deals: Rates as low as $75 in the off-season. Discounts for AAA members, seniors, and government and military employees. AE, CB, DC, DISC, MC, V.*

Blue Dolphin Inn

$$$ Cambria

Part country inn, part upscale motel, the Blue Dolphin is an excellent choice for those who don't mind paying a bit more for high-quality accommodations. The beautifully outfitted rooms have nice amenities — gas fireplaces, big TV with VCR, hair dryer, and minifridge — and cozy, frilly, chintzy English country decor. The best rooms (and most expensive, of course) have private patios with ocean views. The inn is very attractive and professionally run, but has no pool.

6470 Moonstone Beach Dr., Cambria. ☎ *805-927-3300. Fax: 805-927-7311. Internet:* www.cambriahotels.com. *Parking: Free! Rack rates: $75–$220 double. Rates include continental breakfast and afternoon tea. AE, DC, DISC, MC, V.*

J. Patrick House

$$–$$$ Cambria

Tucked away on a woodsy hill just minutes above the East Village is this utterly lovely B&B, Cambria's best. The main house is an elegant log cabin; the nearby carriage house contains seven of the eight impeccable, unfussy rooms. Named for the counties of Ireland and brimming with country warmth, each room boasts beautifully chosen antiques, a wood-burning fireplace, and a private bath. The innkeepers couldn't be more agreeable or attentive. Wonderful!

2990 Burton Dr., Cambria. ☎ *800-341-5258 or 805-927-3812. Fax: 805-927-6759. Internet:* www.jpatrickhouse.com. *Parking: Free! Rack rates: $125–$180 double. Rates include full breakfast, early evening wine and hors d'oeuvres, and bedtime cookies and milk. 2-night minimum. Deals: Check Web site for packages and special deals. AE, DISC, MC, V.*

San Simeon Pines

$$ San Simeon

This camplike resort is nothing fancy, but it's a great alternative to a family motel, and a good choice for anyone looking for a top-notch value. To meet everyone's needs, the resort divides units between family and adult areas. The well-kept grounds feature a solar-heated pool, a playground, and a par-3 golf course. The grounds have no view, but they do feature private beach access. Ask for a room away from the highway for total quiet.

7200 Moonstone Beach Dr. (at the north end of Moonstone Beach, just off Hwy. 1), San Simeon. ☎ *805-927-4648. Internet:* www.sspines.com. *Parking: Free! Rack rates: $74–$130 double, $80–$94 family room (2 queens). AE, MC, V.*

Dining Out

Bistro Sole

$$$ Cambria ECLECTIC/MEDITERRANEAN

This sophisticated but casual indoor/outdoor bistro is one of Cambria's most contemporary restaurants, and one of its most pleasing. The preparations are almost decadent, from saffron risotto with rock shrimp and asparagus to charbroiled rack of lamb in a delectable cabernet sauce. Don't miss the awesome oysters rockefeller, finished with a glazed hollandaise — better than dessert! If the weather's nice, take a seat on the leafy garden patio. Service is attentive, plus there's live music at brunch.

1980 Main St., Cambria. ☎ *805-927-0887. Reservations recommended. Main courses: $6–$10.50 at lunch and brunch, $10–$20 at dinner. MC, V. Open: Lunch and dinner daily, Sun brunch.*

Creekside Gardens Cafe

$ Cambria AMERICAN/MEXICAN

This unpretentious local favorite is *the* place for breakfast. The pancakes are to die for. Adventuresome types shouldn't miss the Danish *ableskiver,* ball-shaped pancakes served with Solvang sausage. Lunchtime brings tasty sandwiches, salads, and Tex-Mex specialties, while dinner is strictly dedicated to the head chef's Jalisco roots. The results are authentic Mexican specialties accompanied by fresh-from-the-oven corn tortillas.

2114 Main St., Cambria. ☎ *805/927-8646. Internet:* www.cambria-online. com/CreeksideGardensCafe. *Reservations not taken. Main courses: $4–$6 at breakfast, $6–$10 at dinner. No credit cards. Open: Breakfast and lunch daily, dinner Mon–Sat.*

Linn's Main Bin

$ Cambria AMERICAN HOME COOKING

This comfortable and charming farmhouse restaurant/bakery/gift shop is a great place to relax over a hearty home-style meal morning, noon, or night — or just enjoy a midday cappuccino and a generous slice of olallieberry pie (a local specialty; the berries taste somewhat like blackberries). Order anything with a crust and you can't go wrong. The homemade pot pies are pure comfort in a pastry dish.

2277 Main St., Cambria. ☎ *805/927-0371. Internet:* www.linnsfruitbin.com. *Reservations not needed. Main courses: $4.50–$7.50 at breakfast, $6–$13 at lunch and dinner. AE, DISC, MC, V. Open: Breakfast, lunch, and dinner daily.*

Robin's

$$ Cambria   INTERNATIONAL

Hugely popular Robin's comes through on all counts: It offers cozy ambience, dedicated service, and satisfying cooking from around the globe. Well-prepared with fresh ingredients and a healthy bent, dishes range from house-specialty pastas and bouillabaisse to Indian-spiced lamb and Asian curries. A bit schizophrenic for my tastes, but I can't argue with success. The menu features lots of good choices for vegetarians, too. Don't miss dessert if you respect your sweet tooth.

4095 Burton Dr., Cambria. ☎ *805-927-5007.* www.robinsrestaurant.com. *Reservations recommended. Main courses: $4.50–$10 at lunch, $9.50–$17 at dinner. DISC, MC, V. Open: Lunch and dinner daily.*

The Sea Chest

$$$ Cambria   SEAFOOD

This place is everything a good seafood house should be: Casual, bustling, and dedicated to serving the freshest seafood in preparations that let the quality of the fish shine through. Start with bluepoints on the half shell, follow with a fresh green salad, follow that with one of the day's catches (usually lightly grilled with just a little lemon and butter), and the world is your oyster. You may have to wait for a table, but the wait will be well worth it. My only complaint? Skip the lackluster chowder.

6216 Moonstone Beach Dr., Cambria. ☎ *805-927-4514. Reservations not accepted. Main courses: $14–$19. No credit cards. Open: Dinner daily except Tues.*

Sow's Ear Cafe

$$$ Cambria   CONTEMPORARY AMERICAN

The kid's menu makes the Sow's Ear good for families, but the relaxing and intimate ambience makes it the place to go for casual romance as well. You'll know that it's special from the moment you're presented with the marvelously addictive signature marbled bread, baked and served in a terra-cotta flowerpot. The beautifully prepared gourmet comfort food includes such reassuring favorites as fried brie, shrimp scampi, barbecued baby backs, and chicken and dumplings. This restaurant is one of my long-standing Cambria favorites.

2248 Main St., Cambria. ☎ *805/927-4865. Internet:* www.thesowsear.com. *Reservations recommended. Main courses: $14–$22; early dinner specials (5–6 p.m.) $11–$14. DISC, MC, V. Open: Dinner nightly.*

Visiting the Castle

The only way to see Hearst Castle (which is now run by the California State Parks system and is officially known as **Hearst San Simeon State Historical Monument**) is via guided tour. The castle is open daily except on Thanksgiving, Christmas, and New Year's Day.

Getting on the bus!

Four different 1¾-hour tours depart regularly throughout the day. Each one includes the outdoor Greco-Roman-style Neptune Pool (which you'll likely recognize from photos) and the indoor Roman Pool, a looker lined with Venetian glass and gold.

Each tour departs from the visitor center and is led by a well-schooled guide. The first tour leaves the visitor center at 8:20 a.m.; the last one leaves at 3:20 p.m. in winter, later at other times of the year.

- ✔ **Tour 1** is the introductory tour. It focuses on the opulent public spaces in *Casa Grande* (as the main house is called), including the movie theater, where you'll see a few minutes of Hearst's home movies (starring more than a few famous faces). You'll also see the art-filled gardens and some of the luxurious guest quarters in the 18-room *Casa del Sol* guest house.

- ✔ **Tour 2** should be called the Kitchens and Baths tour. It's my favorite, as it concentrates on the more casual (I use that term loosely) and private spaces on Casa Grande's upper floors. These rooms include the impressive library (one of the most memorable rooms in the house), Hearst's private suite, the massive kitchen and pantry, and guest rooms with lots of fabulous bathrooms. The stories are great on this one.

- ✔ **Tour 3** focuses on the construction of Hearst Castle, which never really ended. You'll see a portion of the estate that wasn't completed, all of the 10-room *Casa del Monte* guest house, and a wing of guest suites in Casa Grande that were completed in Hearst's final years and show the castle's most modern face. Great for anybody interested in the story behind the design and construction of the house.

- ✔ **Tour 4** runs only between April and October, and it's a good one. At the heart of this tour is a detailed overview of the gardens and grounds, including a "hidden" area that was never completed and only recovered during restoration. You'll also see more of the *Neptune Pool* building; *Casa del Mar,* the largest and most eye-popping of the guest houses; and the wine cellar.

For each tour, a bus takes you on the 15-minute ride up the hill from the visitor center to the castle and back. You cannot linger at the castle on your own or wait for your next tour there. No matter how many tours you take in a day, you must return to the visitor center each time and ride the bus back to the top of the hill with your tour group, so _allow at least 2 hours between tours_ when you buy your tickets. All tours involve a good deal of walking, including climbing between 150 and 400 steps, so be sure to _wear comfortable shoes_.

Specialty tours worth considering

Evening Living History tours are held most Friday and Saturday nights during spring and fall, and usually nightly around Christmas. This 2¼-hour tour is a real gem, and worth the extra money (see "Getting tour tickets" later in the chapter). Led by guides in period costume, the moonlight tour offers all the castle highlights, plus the closest glimpse of what life may have been like in Hearst's heyday. In December, when the house is decked out for Christmas, it's pure magic. Don't miss this one if it's offered.

Family Tours are now available in summer, generally between Memorial Day and Labor Day. These are standard tours reconfigured just a bit so that the young'uns in your group will understand and enjoy what they're seeing. Ask about these tours when you reserve your tickets (see "Getting tour tickets" later in the chapter).

Physically Challenged Accessible Tours are offered at least three times a day. Book them at least 10 days in advance by calling ☎ 805-927-2070.

For information on **Focus Tours** — where such themes as architecture, textiles, or tilework serve as the topic of discussion — call ☎ 805-927- 2020 or check `www.hearstcastle.org`.

Selecting the tour that's right for you

I usually recommend taking two of the four standard 1 ¾-hour tours; this way, you can see a few different views of the estate without being overwhelmed. You can easily suffer from museum overload here, however — all the wow!-inducing, over-the-top excesses can really start looking the same after a while. Taking in two tours and the other castle attractions makes for quite a full day.

You'll need at minimum 2 hours between tours, but that won't allow you any more than a potty break. You may want to set aside more time between tours for a bit of lunch and for perusing the museum, or perhaps taking in a movie at the visitor center's theater (see "Keeping busy between trips to the top" later in the chapter).

Because you'll pay for each tour individually, you may want to spread your castle visit over two half-days, especially if you quickly tire of walking, crowds, or theme park–like bureaucracy. I strongly suggest this approach if you decide to take more than two tours.

The general wisdom says that you should always start with Tour 1. That's a good recommendation, especially if you know little or nothing about the castle and its history, but it's not a must. Pass on Tour 1 if you're going to take the Evening Tour, as it covers much of the same ground. If the private spaces interest you more than the public ones, start with Tour 2. Tour 3 makes a great follow-up after either 1 or 2, but it's too detail-oriented to start out with. Tour 4 is a must-do second tour for horticultural buffs and oenophiles, so try to visit in warm weather if this means you.

Getting tour tickets

Tickets for tours 1 through 4 are $10 for adults, and $5 for kids 6 to 12. The evening tour is $25 for adults, and $13 for kids.

Booking your tour tickets in advance is always a good idea. You can buy tickets right at the visitor center, but you have no guarantee that they'll be available — a day's slate of tours can easily sell out. You pay no fee for advance reservations, and you can make them from 1 hour to 8 weeks in advance. Call the California State Parks Reservations line at ☎ **800-444-4445,** where a knowledgeable operator will assist you. Ask about packages that include big-screen movies at the new National Geographic Theater (see the next section). By the time you read this, you'll be able to order tickets via the Internet at www.hearstcastle. org. If you're ordering tickets from outside the United States, call ☎ **916-414-8400, ext. 4100.** If you need more information, call ☎ **805-927-2020.**

Keeping busy between trips to the top

You'll find plenty to keep you busy at the visitor center before, after, and in between tours. In addition to an observation deck offering a good view of the Enchanted Hill, two gift shops, and food vendors (think ball-park variety and you'll get the picture), the center also includes a surprisingly good small museum. The **Conservation Room** is a glassed-in area where you can watch conservators work on whatever restoration project is in process during your visit.

The center's newest attraction is **Hearst Castle Experience National Geographic Theater** (☎ **805-927-6811;** www.ngtheater.com). In this theater, you can watch larger-than-life films, including the 40-minute *Hearst Castle: Building the Dream* and other films (*Grand Canyon* was also on the schedule at press time), in 5-story-high iWERKS format (just like IMAX) with 7-channel surround sound. Shows begin every 30 minutes past the hour throughout the day. Tickets are $7 for adults, $5 for kids 12 and under, or $12 adults and $8 kids if you take in a double feature.

Hitting the Central Coast Beaches

Just across Highway 1 from the entrance to the Hearst Castle Visitor Center is **W. R. Hearst Memorial State Beach.** This pleasant day-use beach is generally too cold for swimming, but picnic tables, barbecues, and bathrooms make it perfect for in-between- or after-tour picnicking. Look for whales offshore in winter.

Just north of San Simeon is a wonderful unnamed beach where you can watch elephant seals doing their natural thing up close and personal, frolicking and sunning themselves on the rocks year-round. Finding this beach is easy — just stop at the packed parking lot and follow the crowds along the short, sandy walk for a good vantage. Keep your distance from these giant mammals, and don't go beyond the marked areas — not only is it unhealthy for them, but it can be dangerous for you.

In Cambria, **Moonstone Beach** is great for strolling and whale-watching in season. Keep your eye on the sand for the semi-precious jasper stones that give the beach its name.

Exploring Cambria

Strolling the streets of laid-back Cambria is a pleasant change of pace after a day of lines and hectic sightseeing at Hearst Castle. This charming artists' colony doesn't have more than four or five blocks to explore, but they're worth checking out even if you're based up in San Simeon and not here. You'll find the area's best restaurants (see "Dining Out" earlier in this chapter) and shops, less of the tacky touristy variety and more focused on good-quality crafts.

The shopping highlight of the West Village is Home Arts, 727 Main St. (☎ **805-927-ART1;** www.home-arts.com), which boasts an appealingly eclectic mix of country and contemporary home fashions and gifts.

The East Village has lots of worthwhile stops. Tops among them is Seekers Collection and Gallery, 4090 Burton Dr. (☎ **800-841-5250** or 805-927-4352; www.seekersglass.com), a museum-quality art-glass gallery. I also love Fermentations, 4056 Burton Dr. (☎ **800-446-7505;** www.fermentations.com), which serves as a great introduction to the Central Coast wine country through tastings, wine sales, and wine-themed gifts. While you're at it, check out Leslie Mark, upstairs at 4070 Burton Dr. (☎ **800-543-4390** or 805-927-1434; www.lesliemark.com), whose original line of natural-fiber casual womenswear has made this a must-stop for me for years now.

Gathering More Information

For Hearst Castle info, call ☎ **800-444-4445**, or visit the comprehensive Web site at www.hearstcastle.org.

For information on Cambria, contact the Cambria Chamber of Commerce, which operates a visitor center at 767 Main St. (☎ **805-927-3624**), or go online to www.cambriachamber.org. Another terrific source is www.cambria-online.com.

American Express's official travel office in Cambria is Traveltime, 4210 Bridge St. (☎ **805-927-7799**).

Chapter 19

Solvang, California's Own Little Denmark

Come for the cookies.

Sure, this faithful re-creation of a Danish hamlet tucked away in the golden southern California hills has lots to recommend it, including shopping, smorgasbords, windmills, thatch-roof cottages, and other cutesy old-world architecture. Not to mention the whole Hans Christian Andersen angle. The town is like a Brothers Grimm fairy tale retold as a Golden Book come to life.

Still, the cookies are the reason to come. Those rich, golden-brown butter cookies — the kind that come in the wax tubs — are just scrumptious, and nobody bakes 'em better than the old-country bakeries of Solvang.

Of course, to get to the cookies, you have to put up with a good amount of kitsch. My recommendation? Take it with a grain of salt. Stay just long enough to enjoy the scenery — a day, maybe two if you have a high tolerance for cute. Balance your visit with a stop in the neighboring artists' colony, Los Olivos, to cut the saccharine.

And if sugar and spice and everything nice just doesn't work for you? Nobody said you had to stay. Remember — you can always just stop by for the cookies.

 If you're traveling with the young'uns in winter or you're not into beachy pursuits, Solvang may make a better local base for you and your family than nearby Santa Barbara (see Chapter 20), thanks to its kid-friendly storybook vibe and almost-consistently sunny skies.

Getting There and Orienting Yourself

Solvang lies a stone's throw inland from the coast in the Santa Ynez Valley, where the weather is pleasing year-round (though it can get appreciably hotter than the coast in summer).

Solvang is an easy stop if you're traveling along the coast. It's 110 miles southeast of Hearst Castle, 35 miles north of Santa Barbara, and 130 miles northwest of L.A. To reach Solvang from U.S. 101, turn east onto Highway 246 at Buellton; go 3 miles to the heart of town.

Navigating petite Solvang is a breeze. Highway 246 turns into the town's main thoroughfare, Mission Drive. The majority of the sights and attractions are located along, or in the blocks south of, Mission Drive between Fifth Street and Alisal Road (one block east of First Street). The whole town is walkable, even for the laziest among us.

A Don't-Miss Detour: If you're coming from Santa Barbara or other points south, I highly recommend taking the San Marcos Pass instead of 101 to reach Solvang. This route adds only 15 minutes or so to your drive — but oh, what a glorious drive it is. At Goleta (just north of Santa Barbara), exit U.S. 101 at Highway 154. This scenic two-lane highway rises from sea level to about 2,200 feet, passing gorgeous golden ranchlands and breathtaking views of **Los Padres National Forest** and shimmering **Cachuma Lake,** before descending into the Santa Ynez Valley. At Santa Ynez, turn left (west) at Highway 246, and you'll be in Solvang in no time.

Attention, coast travelers: You can enjoy the San Marcos Pass even if you're not stopping in Solvang. Just continue straight on Highway 154 through artsy Los Olivos (see "Exploring Nearby Los Olivos" below); you'll connect up with U.S. 101 again north of Buellton.

Booking a Place to Stay

Solvang is booked up year-round on weekends. If you're visiting over Friday and/or Saturday, call as far in advance as possible. And be prepared — weekends often demand two-night minimum stays.

If Solvang's weekend rates are too high for you, try the **Best Western Pea Soup Andersen's Inn,** three miles west of town on Highway 246 (☎ **800-PEA-SOUP** or 805-688-3216; www.bestwestern.com), where you can have a well-kept room for just $69 to $79. Next door is **Andersen's Pea Soup Family Restaurant,** a local cottage industry that has grown into a regional institution.

Expect 10 percent in taxes to be tacked onto your final hotel bill.

Best Western King Frederik Inn

$–$$ Solvang

This very nice chain motel is right in the heart of town. The rooms have a bit of charm and a few frills, service is very friendly, and you can't beat the location. It has a nice pool, too. Call early — this good bargain sells out fast.

1617 Copenhagen Dr., Solvang. ☎ 800-549-9955 or 805-688-5515. Fax: 805-688-2067. Internet: www.bestwestern.com. Parking: Free! Rack rates: $69–$109 double. Rates include continental breakfast. Deals: Discounts for AAA members and seniors; also ask about breaks for families. AE, DC, DISC, MC, V.

The Inn at Petersen Village

$$$ Solvang

Solvang's only AAA four-diamond award-winner is also its finest, most kitsch-free place to stay. The individually decorated rooms are graceful, tasteful, and well-priced for what you get. They're done in a chintzy European-country style that's old-world evocative (think canopied beds, bold florals, antique reproductions) without sacrificing modern comforts. An elegant wine bar and piano lounge round out the appeal.

1576 Mission Dr., Solvang. ☎ 800-321-8985 or 805-688-3121. Fax: 805-688-5732. Internet: www.peterseninn.com. Parking: Free! Rack rates: $140–$200 double, $235 suite. Rates include full breakfast buffet and evening wine, cheese, and desserts. Deals: Midweek discounts available (usually $20 off); also ask about AAA-member discounts. AE, MC, V.

Solvang Royal Scandinavian Inn

$$ Solvang

This full-service hotel is nicely located in the heart of town but away from the congested main drag. It's nothing special, but perfectly comfortable. On-site is a Danish-American restaurant, a cocktail lounge, and a heated pool and a Jacuzzi.

400 Alisal Rd., Solvang. ☎ 800-624-5572 or 805-688-8000. Fax: 805-688-0761. Internet: www.solvangrsi.com. Parking: Free! Rack rates: $81–$141 double or junior suite. Deals: Mid-week discounts for AAA and AARP members. AE, DC, DISC, MC, V.

Storybook Inn B&B

$$–$$$ Solvang

This irony-free B&B is perfect for romance-seeking couples looking to buy into Solvang's cutesy charm. Each attractive and comfortably outfitted room is done in a fairy-tale theme, with lots of frilly accents and country touches. On-site is **Brothers,** the best restaurant in town.

409 First St., Solvang. ☎ 800-786-7925 or 805-688-1703. Fax: 805-688-0953. Internet: www.solvangstorybook.com. Parking: Free! Rack rates: $120–$205 double. Rates include full breakfast and afternoon wine and cheese. DISC, MC, V.

Dining Out

As the "Danish capital of America," Solvang's cuisine is far from ordinary. In addition to butter cookies, pastries, and *aebleskivers* (those powdered-sugared ball-shaped cookies), you can get traditional Danish fare such as meatballs (*frikadeller*) and red cabbage (*rodkaal*), as well as standard American eats.

Bit o' Denmark

$$ Solvang DANISH

Sure, the restaurant offers a regular menu, but the real reason to come is the all-you-can-eat smorgasbord, widely regarded as the best and freshest smorgasbord in town. Expect Danish specialties galore. Weekend lunchers pay a bit more, but get a bigger spread.

473 Alisal Rd. ☎ *805-688-5426. Main courses: $6.50–$8 at lunch (smorgasbord $8.50 Mon–Fri, $8.95 Sat–Sun), $12–$17 at dinner (smorgasbord $12.95). AE, DISC, MC, V. Open: Breakfast, lunch, and dinner daily.*

Brothers

$$$–$$$$ Solvang CALIFORNIA

This restaurant is the best in town, and one of the best on the Central Coast. Sibling chefs Jeff and Matt Nichols emphasize the season in their small but immensely appealing nightly menu. Expect unfussy, beautifully prepared dishes like rosemary grilled chicken and horseradish-crusted Alaskan halibut. The dining room is warm and intimate, and the service is assured and friendly. Well-chosen local vintages round out the appeal.

In the Storybook Inn, 409 First St. ☎ *805-688-9934. Internet:* www.solvang storybook. com/brothers.htm. *Reservations recommended. Main courses: $15–$27. MC, V. Open: Dinner Wed–Sun.*

Cafe Angelica

$$–$$$ Solvang AMERICAN/ECLECTIC

Come here if you're dying for some fresh greens after all those butter cookies and Danish meatballs. This casual cafe specializes in fresh salads and sandwiches at lunch, pastas and heartier fare — veal parmigiana, filet mignon — at dinner. The breezy patio is very pleasant.

490 First St. (across from Hans Christian Andersen Park). ☎ *805-686-9970. Reservations recommended. Internet:* www.solvangca.com/html/angelica. html. *Main courses: $5–$9 at lunch, $11–$17 at dinner. AE, MC, V. Open: Lunch and dinner daily.*

Paula's Pancake House

$ Solvang   DANISH-AMERICAN

Solvang's favorite place to start the day is this pleasing, unpretentious diner, which specializes in the morning meal. The mammoth menu boasts a whole slate of pancake choices, including crepe-thin Danish pancakes; French toast and waffles; a host of omelettes and egg dishes; and burgers and salads for lunchers who don't like to flaunt tradition. The umbrella-covered patio tables make the perfect perch for watching the world go by.

1531 Mission Dr. ☎ 805-688-2867. Main courses: $3.75–$7.25. Open: Breakfast and lunch daily. AE, DC, DISC, MC, V.

Exploring Solvang and Environs

Solvang's most distinctive feature is its cutesy architecture. Take time to stroll the town to see the windmills and Danish farm-style *bindingsvaerk* buildings, distinguished by their dormers and exposed timber cross beams (similar to English Tudor style). This isn't a serious architecture tour, however. After you get the gist, you're likely to find yourself paying more attention to the shops housed within instead. Don't expect anything wild or funky; the boutiques are largely cute and affordable, with a few famous-name outlet stores sprinkled in the mix. While you're exploring, look up; many roofs are decorated with wooden storks, which bring good luck to everyone.

Seeing the highlights

Remember those yummy butter cookies I mentioned at the start of this chapter? They're Solvang's ultimate enticement, and the best in town can be found at **Birkholm's Bakery,** 1555 Mission Dr. (☎ **805-688-3872;** www.birkholms.com). Their multiple varieties of Danish butter cookies come in 1 ½ lb. wax tubs ($8.95) — easy to carry or send home. (Birkholm's will even ship the tubs for you!) If you ask one of the friendly staff nicely, they may even let you taste a cookie before you buy. The bakery also sells fresh-baked goodies and coffee. Open Monday through Thursday 8 a.m. to 5:30 p.m., Friday 8 a.m. to 6 p.m., 8:30 a.m. to 6 p.m. on weekends.

Discovering Solvang's roots

If you're interested in knowing how a southern California town ended up feeling like a Danish transplant, stop into the **Elverhøj Museum of History and Art,** 1624 Elverhoy Way, at the end of Second Street, 4 blocks south of Copenhagen Drive (☎ **805-686-1211;** www.solvangca.com/museum/elverhoy.htm). This pleasing museum is a bastion of authenticity in the sea of Solvang kitsch — well worth a half-hour visit. Open Wednesday through Sunday from 1 to 4 p.m. No admission fee, but donations are warmly accepted.

Focusing on fairy tales

Upstairs at the Book Loft, at 1680 Mission Drive (between First Street and Alisal Road), is the one-room **Hans Christian Andersen Museum** (☎ 805-688-2052), dedicated to Denmark's favorite fairy-tale spinner. The display is actually quite interesting. Open daily from 10 a.m. to 5 p.m. Admission is my favorite price — free!

Going on a mission

Old Mission Santa Ines, 1760 Mission Dr., just east of Alisal Road (☎ 805-688-4815; www.missionsantaines.org), is one of Solvang's few buildings without a windmill or copper roof. The 19th of California's 21 Spanish missions was founded by Franciscan friars and built by Native American workers in 1804; restoration work is returning the handsome adobe to its 19th-century grandeur. It features a museum, semi-formal gardens, and ornate tilework. Open daily from 9 a.m. to 5:30 p.m. (7 p.m. in summer); admission is $3.

Taking stock at Solvang Theaterfest

The well-respected Pacific Conservatory of the Performing Arts stages a slate of plays and musicals at the 700-seat alfresco **Solvang Festival Theatre**, 420 Second St. (at Molle Way), from June through mid-October. Recent performances have included *Cabaret, Master Class, Taming of the Shrew,* and *Death Trap.* While this may not be Broadway, the performances are more often than not surprisingly good. Tickets run $18 to $20. You can get schedule info and tickets by calling ☎ 805-922-8313 or by going online to www.pcpa.org.

Exploring nearby Los Olivos

If you tire of the Danish kitsch, head down the road a bit to Los Olivos, a one-horse town that has blossomed with sophisticated art and craft galleries and wine-tasting rooms. Los Olivos is quiet, laid-back, and retains a bit of still-gentrifying authenticity — basically the antithesis of tourist-slick Solvang. A couple of hours are more than enough to see everything in town.

Shopping highlights on the main street, Grand Avenue (actually neither grand nor an avenue), include **Tatiana Maria Gallery** (☎ 805-688-9622), with an exquisite collection of Central and South American crafts, and **Oarlie's Antiques** (☎ 805-688-5027), for early-20th-century collectibles. If you're interested in sampling wines from the local Santa Ynez wine country, stop into **Richard Longoria Wines** (☎ 805-688-0305) or Los Olivos Vintners (☎ 800-824-8584 or 805-688-9665), both of which have charming tasting rooms right on Grand.

A few restaurants and gourmet sandwich shops will satisfy lunchtime visitors. Los Olivos is on Highway 154 just off U.S. 101; to reach it from Solvang, take Alamo Pintado Avenue or Highway 246 to 154.

Enjoying the great outdoors

This lovely reservoir at **Cachuma Lake Recreation Area** — created in 1953 by damming the Santa Ynez River — is the heart of a gorgeous county park rich with hiking, bird-watching, fishing, picnicking, and ballplaying opportunities. Wildlife-watching and eagle-spotting cruises are offered. This is a wonderful place to commune with nature. No swimming, though, as the lake serves as a prime water supply for the area. The park is open year-round from 8 a.m. to sunset. The day-use fee is $5. For more information, call ☎ **805-686-5054** or go online to www.sbparks.com.

Gathering More Information

Call the Solvang Conference and Visitors Bureau at ☎ **800-468-6765** or 805-688-6144, or point your Web browser to www.solvang.org. You'll also find useful information online at www.solvangca.com. After you arrive, stop at one of the two friendly staffed visitor centers: on Mission Drive and Fifth Street, and on Copenhagen Drive between First and Second streets.

Chapter 20

The Real Jewel of the Coast: Santa Barbara

● ●

In This Chapter

▶ Appreciating Southern California's prettiest beach town

▶ Choosing the best places to stay and dine

▶ Lounging on the beaches, seeing the sights, and taking in the local culture

● ●

*L*ooking for the perfect realization of the southern California dream? Stop reading now — you've found it. If Carmel is the gold standard of up-coast Golden State beauty (and it is), gorgeous Santa Barbara is the Southland version. Sunny California — the place of TV-inspired dreams and movie-made fantasies — simply doesn't get any better than this.

Santa Barbara has natural assets galore. This stretch of coast has a unique situation that makes all the difference: If you look at a map, you'll see that Santa Barbara lies at the foot of the Santa Ynez Mountains on a narrow strip of coastline that has the singular, jaunty confidence to run east-west rather than north-south. So even when it's cool, cloudy, rainy, or smoggy all over the rest of the region, this Spanish-Mediterranean beauty tends to sparkle in the sun like the rare jewel it is. Offshore islands and tide breaks even keep the Pacific waves calm and under control.

What's more, this picture-perfect beach hamlet remains unspoiled thanks to its distance from Los Angeles. Located about 100 miles to the northwest, it's a smidgen too far outside the beastly city's reach to be absorbed into the megalopolis, even by L.A.'s otherworldly commuting standards. Yay!

These idyllic, sun-drenched environs don't exactly inspire a bustling business world or low real estate prices — so don't quit your job to move here just yet. Santa Barbara is the self-proclaimed domain of the "almost wed and almost dead" — mainly college students (at UC Santa Barbara) and rich retirees who can afford to kick back and go with the mellow flow. So come join these well-rehearsed relaxees for a little downtime. You couldn't pick a better place to do it.

Timing Your Visit

Any time is a good time to visit Santa Barbara. The climate is mild and sunny year-round, with temperatures hovering between the low 60s and mid 70s most of the time. Santa Barbara has little in the way of an off-season, because the strolling and sightseeing are great no matter when you visit. Still, come before mid-October if you want guaranteed beach time and perpetual sunshine. Avoid weekends in summer and fall if you want to miss the capacity crowds.

Attention, moms and dads: Santa Barbara is family-friendly enough, but if you have very young ones in tow, you might prefer making even kid-friendlier Solvang your local base (see Chapter 19).

Plan on staying at least two or three nights so that you can enjoy Santa Barbara at the pace that it warrants — slow. Definitely give yourself the two days/three nights combo if you're planning to park yourself on the beach for an extended period or venture into the surrounding wine country.

Getting There

Santa Barbara is 134 miles southeast of Hearst Castle, 35 miles southeast of Solvang, and 102 miles northwest of Los Angeles U.S. 101 is the fastest and most direct route to Santa Barbara from points north or south. The highway runs right through town.

Attention, southbound travelers: For a scenic detour that will add no more than a few minutes to your drive, pick up the **San Marcos Pass (Highway 154)** near Los Olivos, about 35 miles northwest of Santa Barbara. Highway 154 offers a gorgeous peek at ranchlands and forest before depositing you back onto U.S. 101 just north of Santa Barbara. See "Getting There and Orienting Yourself" in Chapter 19.

Winging it

You can fly into Santa Barbara Municipal Airport (☎ **805-683-4011** or 805-967-7111; Internet: www.flysba.com), located 8 miles west of downtown in Goleta. Nonstop service is available from San Francisco, San Jose, and L.A. aboard American Airlines (☎ **800-433-7300**; Internet: www.aa.com) and United Airlines (☎ **800-241-6522**; Internet: www.ual.com). America West Express (☎ **800-235-9292**; Internet: www.americawest.com) serves Santa Barbara from Phoenix and Las Vegas only.

The car-rental companies with airport locations include Avis (☎ **800-331-1212**; Internet: www.avis.com); Budget (☎ **800-527-0700**; Internet:www.budgetrentacar.com); Enterprise (☎ **800-RENT-A-CAR**; Internet:www.erac.com); **Hertz** (☎ **800-654-3131**; Internet: www.hertz.com); and National (☎ **800-CAR-RENT**; Internet: www.nationalcar.com).

You can also catch a ride with Yellow Cab (☎ **805-965-5111**), Rose Cab (☎ **805-564-2600**), or Orange Cab (☎ **805-964-2800**), which usually have cabs lined up outside the terminal. Expect the fare into downtown Santa Barbara to cost $20 to $25, plus tip. If, for some reason, no cab is on hand, call Yellow Cab or Orange Cab and they'll send one right over. Rose Cab will schedule advance pickups with 24 hours' notice.

Before you pay for a taxi, check to see if your hotel offers complimentary shuttle service.

Riding the rails

Amtrak (☎ **800-USA-RAIL**; www.amtrak.com) offers daily service to Santa Barbara along its San Diegan and Coast Starlight routes. Trains arrive at the Amtrak station at 209 State St., just two blocks from the beach (☎ **805-963-1015**). Taxis are usually available, or you can pick up the electric shuttle; see the next section, "Orienting Yourself and Getting Around."

Orienting Yourself and Getting Around

Downtown Santa Barbara is laid out in a grid and is easily navigable. Restaurant- and boutique-lined State Street is the main drag. It runs perpendicular to the coastline, and serves as the east-west dividing line: Ortega Street, for example, is East Ortega to the east of State, West Ortega to the west. Cabrillo Boulevard runs along the ocean and separates the city's beaches from the rest of the town.

Even if you drive into town, you may want to leave your car parked for the duration of your stay, as parking can be tough to find downtown, and weekend traffic can be a nightmare.

Santa Barbara is a joy for strollers, and most attractions are easily reachable on foot. A popular method for exploring the coast is by bike or surrey; see "Hitting the Beaches" later in this chapter for rental info. Taxi companies like Yellow Cab, Rose Cab, or Orange Cab (see "Getting There" earlier in the chapter) can get you from your hotel to dinner and back again, or wherever else you'd like to go.

Another option is to hop aboard the *Downtown-Waterfront Shuttle*. These electric shuttles run along State Street every 10 minutes and Cabrillo Boulevard every half-hour daily from 10:15 a.m. to 6:00 p.m. The visitor-friendly shuttles are foolproof; you can pick them up at designated stops every block or two along each route. The fare is 25¢ (free for kids under 5); if you'd like to transfer to the other line at the junction of State and Cabrillo, ask the driver for a free transfer. For more info, call the Metropolitan Transit District (MTD) at ☎ **805-MTD-3702** or the visitor center at ☎ **805-965-3021,** or go online to www.sbmtd.gov.

Santa Barbara

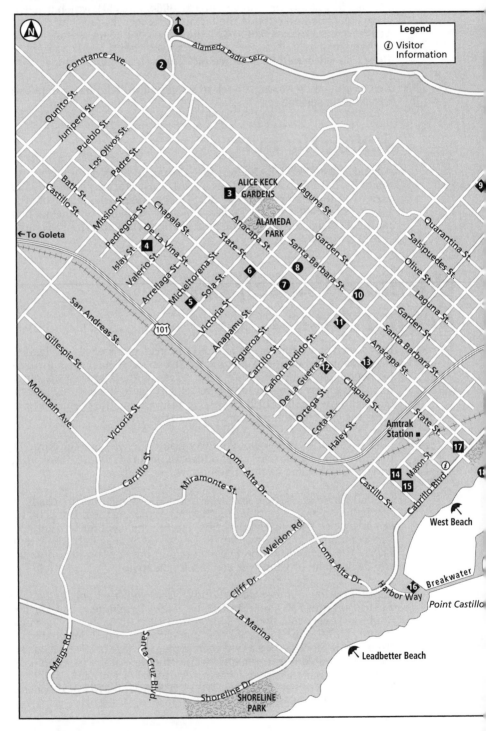

Legend

ⓘ Visitor Information

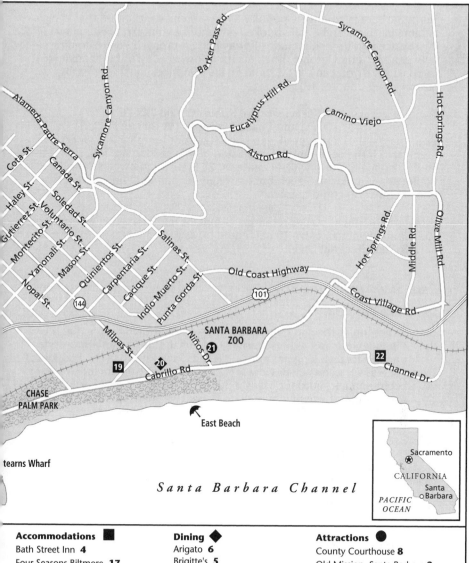

Accommodations ■

Bath Street Inn **4**
Four Seasons Biltmore **17**
Franciscan Inn **14**
Harbor View Inn **17**
Marina Beach Motel **15**
Motel 6 Santa Barbara #1 **19**
Simpson House Inn
   Bed & Breakfast **3**

Dining ◆

Arigato **6**
Brigitte's **5**
Brophy Bros. Clam Bar
   & Restaurant **16**
California Pizza Kitchen **12**
Citronelle **20**
Four Seasons Biltmore **22**
La Super-Rica **9**
The Palace Grill **13**
Wine Cask **11**

Attractions ●

County Courthouse **8**
Old Mission, Santa Barbara **2**
Santa Barbara Botanic Garden **1**
Santa Barbara Historical
   Society Museum **10**
Santa Barbara Museum
   of Art **7**
Santa Barbara Zoo **21**
Stearns Wharf **18**

Staying in Style

Santa Barbara is so hugely popular as a weekend destination that every lodging in town can be fully booked — so make your arrangements well in advance if your visit includes Friday and Saturday. If you're coming between May and October, book even a midweek stay as far in advance as possible. If you can't get a room on short notice, consider nearby Solvang (see Chapter 19).

Two free reservations services, **Hot Spots** (☎ 800-793-7666; www.hotspotsusa.com) and **Coastal Escapes** (☎ 800-292-2222; www.coastalescapes.com), can refer you to other reliable properties in the area if the accommodations listed in this section are full. Hot Spots also maintains a walk-in center at 36 State St., between Cabrillo Boulevard and Mason Street, but I strongly recommend having reservations before you come to town.

Be aware that most places require a two-night minimum stay on weekends. And expect an extra 10 percent in taxes to be tacked on to your hotel bill at checkout time.

Bath Street Inn

$$ Santa Barbara

Bath Street Inn is the top choice for value-minded B&B lovers. Each of the 12 immaculate and super-charming rooms in this Queen Anne–style Victorian has its own singular appeal, be it a clawfoot tub, a gas Franklin stove, or a sliver of an ocean view in the distance. The inn includes wonderful common and outdoor areas, and the lovely innkeeper serves elegant afternoon and evening munchies as well as breakfast. Frankly, she could charge more and this place would still be a stellar deal.

1720 Bath St. (just north of Valerio St.). ☎ *800-341-2284, 800-549-2284, or 805-682-9680. Fax: 805-569-1281. Internet:* www.bathstreetinn.com. *Parking: Free and easy street parking. Rack rates: $110–$170 double, $210 suite. Rates include generous breakfast, afternoon tea, and evening wine and cheese. Deals: Midweek rates 20 percent off Sept–June. Also ask about AAA, senior, and corporate discounts. AE, MC, V.*

Four Seasons Biltmore

$$$$$ Montecito

Built in 1927 and spread over 19 luxuriant acres, this Spanish-revival resort is the place to stay if you're looking to experience the "American Riviera" in its full, four-star glory. You won't want for anything here. The hotel includes 217 sumptuous rooms (including 12 cottages), amenities galore, and resort dining at its best. On the down side, the beach is not for swimming, and downtown is a 10-minute drive away. But at a resort as fab as this one, who wants to leave? Guests can enjoy the wonderful beachside pool at the Coral Casino Club, and a full-service salon with spa treatements provides nonstop pampering.

1260 Channel Dr. (use Olive Mill Rd. exit off of U.S. 101). ☎ 800-332-3442 or 805-969-2261. Fax: 805-565-8323. Internet: www.fourseasons.com. *Parking: Free self-parking, $16 to valet. Rack rates: $280–$555 double, $585–$2,100 suite. Deals: Ask about midweek rates and package deals, which may include tee times, American Express cardmember resort credits, and other perks. AE, DC, MC, V.*

Franciscan Inn

$-$$ Santa Barbara

Here's Santa Barbara's best motel bargain, bar none. Beautifully kept and smartly outfitted, it's way better than you'd expect for the money. All of the cute rooms have VCRs and free HBO. Suites are terrific for families, and most have fully equipped kitchenettes. The grounds have a nice heated pool and Jacuzzi, plus coin-op laundry. Movie rentals and morning newspapers are free. The staff is terrific, and West Beach is a block away. A real winner that will even please motel-o-phobes. Book well ahead.

109 Bath St. (at Mason St.). ☎ 805-963-8845. Fax: 805-564-3295. Internet: www.franciscaninn.com. *Parking: Free! Rack rates: $75–$134 double, $99–$250 suite. Rates include continental breakfast and afternoon cookies and drinks. AE, CB, DC, MC, V.*

Harbor View Inn

$$$-$$$$ Santa Barbara

It's pricey, but worth the splurge if you're looking for something special by the sea — and you couldn't dream up a better location. The hotel is built hacienda-style, like a mini Biltmore in the heart of town (and facing a better beach, no less). The gorgeous, contemporary-styled rooms are big enough to host a cocktail party; and all boast granite baths (some with oversize tubs) and patios or balconies. Ocean views are expensive, but you won't need one to be happy here. On-site is a restaurant, a gym, and a lovely pool. All of Santa Barbara is right out the front door.

28 W. Cabrillo Blvd. (at State St.). ☎ 800-755-0222 or 805-963-0780. Fax: 805-963-7967. Parking: Free! Rack rates: $180–$350 double, $350 suite. Deals: Inquire about 10 percent discounts for AAA or AARP members. AE, DC, MC, V.

Marina Beach Motel

$$ Santa Barbara

It's a mere 37 steps to the beach from this button-cute motel — just ask the friendly owners, who've turned the step-count into their biggest selling point. I like the Franciscan better, but this is also a very good bet. Rooms are spotless, and country/beachy touches save them from the budget doldrums. More than half have full-size kitchens at no extra charge, so ask for one when you book. Amenities include lovely tropical gardens, but no pool. Bicycles are on hand for your use.

21 Bath St. (at Mason St.). ☎ **877-627-4621** or 805-963-9311. Fax: 805-564-4102. Internet: www.marinabeachmotel.com. Parking: Free! Rack rates: $78–$160 double. Rates include continental breakfast. AE, CB, DC, DISC, MC, V.

Motel 6 — Santa Barbara #1

$ Santa Barbara

The first Motel 6 *ever* is the best super-cheap sleep in town — and it's less than a block from fab East Beach, no less. The rooms are what you'd expect, but they're well-kept, management is friendly, and there's a petite pool. Book as far ahead as possible, as this place fills up *way* in advance.

443 Corona del Mar (less than a block from Cabrillo Blvd.). ☎ **800-4-MOTEL-6** or 805-564-1392. Fax: 805-963-4687. Internet: www.motel6.com. Parking: Free! Rack rates: $61–$91 double. AE, CB, DC, DISC, MC, V.

Simpson House Inn Bed & Breakfast

$$$$ Santa Barbara

AAA's only five-diamond B&B (in all of North America!) is simply spectacular. Hidden behind towering hedges on dazzlingly manicured grounds, this Victorian oasis feels like a world unto itself. Rooms are decorated to perfection and overflowing with luxuries. The staff provides concierge-style service, and an evening hors d'oeuvres spread makes dinner redundant. Very expensive, but it's money well spent if you're celebrating. Some may find it too formal, though.

121 E. Arrellaga St. (between Santa Barbara and Anacapa sts.). ☎ **800-676-1280** or 805-963-7067. Fax: 805-564-4811. Internet: www.simpsonhouseinn.com. Parking: Free! Rack rates: $195–$500 double, suite, or cottage. Rates include full gourmet breakfast, evening hors d'oeuvres, and wine. AE, DISC, MC, V.

Dining Out

Reservations are *always* a good idea on weekends year-round and weeknights in summer.

If you're in town for the weekend, consider the all-you-can-eat Sunday brunch ($39.95 per person) at the **Four Seasons Biltmore** (see "Staying in Style," earlier in the chapter). This fabulous feast is the ultimate in elegant pig-outs — and trust me, you won't have to eat for the rest of the day.

Arigato

$$$ Santa Barbara   SUSHI

This chic sushi bar serves top-notch sushi to a hip crowd that appreciates the excellent quality and super-freshness of the fish, much of it flown in daily from Hawaii and Japan. The young servers are friendly and attentive, and the dimly lit room has a dash of romance about it.

In Victoria Court, 11 W. Victoria St. (just west of State St.). ☎ *805-965-6074. Reservations not taken. Sushi: 2-piece orders and rolls $4–$10; other dishes $9.50–$15. AE, MC, V. Open: Dinner daily.*

Brigitte's

$$ Santa Barbara   CAL-MEDITERRANEAN

This pretty, pretension-free bistro was the first Santa Barbara restaurant I ever dined in a dozen years ago, and it's just as wonderful as ever. The kitchen specializes in flavorful, unfussy cuisine that makes the most of such ingredients as fresh mozzarella, sun-dried tomatoes, roasted garlic, and mellow chiles. Look for wood-roasted meats, wood-fired pizzas, and Mediterranean-style fresh seafood preparations. The room is light, airy, and comfortable, and service is casual and friendly. A great value!

1325 State St. (at Sola St.). ☎ *805-966-9676. Reservations recommended. Main courses: $10–$16. AE, DC, DISC, MC, V. Open: Lunch Mon – Sat, dinner nightly.*

Brophy Bros. Clam Bar & Restaurant

$$ Santa Barbara   SEAFOOD

Serving fresh-off-the-boat seafood in a casual, boisterous maritime setting, Brophy Bros. is everything a good seafood house should be. Belly up to the bar for fresh-shucked clams, oysters on the half shell, or a bowl of killer chowder. Or take a table and choose from the day's catches, which can range from local thresher shark to flown-in Alaskan king salmon. Outdoor seating on two sides, but the bar also boasts great harbor views. The only down side? *Everybody* loves this place — locals and visitors alike — so the wait can be unbearable on weekend nights.

In the Santa Barbara Marina, 119 Harbor Way (at Cabrillo Blvd.), 2nd floor. ☎ *805-966-4418. Reservations not taken. Main courses: $8–$15. AE, MC, V. Open: Lunch and dinner daily.*

California Pizza Kitchen

$ Santa Barbara   PIZZA

The nation's premier single-serving pizza maker makes a great stop for a quick and affordable meal. You can't go wrong with the original BBQ chicken pizza, with red onions and smoked gouda; the Peking duck pizza, topped with crispy wontons and hoisin sauce, is a sweet-and-sour delight. Traditional-style pies, too, plus salads, pastas, and sandwiches.

In the Paseo Nuevo mall, on Chapala St. between Cañon Perdido and Ortega St. ☎ *805-962-4648. Reservations not taken. Pizzas and other main courses: $7–$10. AE, DISC, MC, V. Open: Lunch and dinner daily.*

Citronelle

$$$$ Santa Barbara CALIFORNIA

One of L.A.'s finest chefs, Michel Richard, maintains this Santa Barbara outpost, which serves up first-rate Cal-French cuisine and priceless panoramic ocean views from a second-floor perch. The vibe is a just-right blend of California casual and special occasion, and the food is always pleasing. A great local wine list is on hand, too. Book a window table for sunset and the world is yours — for the duration of your meal, at least.

At the Santa Barbara Inn, 901 Cabrillo Blvd. (at Milpas St.). ☎ 805-963-0111. Internet: www.santabarbarainn.com/citronelle.html. Reservations recommended. Main courses: $8–$13 at breakfast and lunch, $24–$32 at dinner. AE, DC, DISC, MC, V. Open: Breakfast, lunch, and dinner daily.

La Super-Rica Taqueria

$ Santa Barbara MEXICAN

This unassuming taco shack has earned a whopping 25 (out of a possible 30) rating from restaurant bible Zagat — no mean feat for a restaurant where nothing costs over $5.10. Portions are small, so order generously — but at these prices, you can afford to. The soft tacos are divine, and the weekend brings freshly made tamales. A few casual tables allow for instant satisfaction.

622 Milpas St. (just north of Cota St.). ☎ 805-963-4940. Reservations not taken. Main courses: $2–$5. No credit cards. Open: Lunch and dinner daily.

The Palace Grill

$$$ Santa Barbara CAJUN-CREOLE

This rollicking Creole-Cajun is a nice antidote to Santa Barbara's wealth of romance-inducing bistros. Come for big portions of bold and fiery N'awlins favorites like hearty gumbo, oysters Rockefeller, jambalaya, crawfish etoufee, house-smoked andouille sausage, and even bananas Foster for dessert. This fun place reaches maximum party potential with a jazz saxophonist and free appetizers for waiting diners on Saturday. Free valet parking is a nice plus.

8 E. Cota St. (between State and Anacapa sts.). ☎ 805-963-5000. Internet: www.palacegrill.com. Reservations accepted Sun – Thurs (Fri – Sat for 5:30 p.m. seating only). Main courses: $12–$21. AE, MC, V. Open: Lunch and dinner daily.

Wine Cask

$$$$ Santa Barbara CAL-ITALIAN

This utterly lovely restaurant is one of Santa Barbara's best. Choose between the gorgeous dining room (request a table by the fireplace for maximum romance) or the wonderful terra-cotta-tiled courtyard, complete with bubbling fountain. The menu features consistently terrific California fare with an Italian flair, and the award-winning wine list is an oenophile's dream come true. The Wine Cask is a true delight — and not overly pricey, considering the genuine special-occasion appeal.

In El Paseo, 813 Anacapa St. (between Cañon Perdido and de la Guerra St.). ☎ *805-966-9463. Internet:* www.winecask.com. *Reservations recommended. Main courses: $8–$15 at lunch, $18–$27 at dinner. AE, DC, DISC, MC, V. Open: Lunch Mon – Fri, brunch Sat – Sun, dinner nightly.*

Exploring Santa Barbara

For the best and most efficient overview, catch a ride on the **Santa Barbara Old Town Trolley** (☎ 805-965-0353). These motorized red trolleys offer narrated 90-minute tours of SB's main sightseeing areas, including State Street, the beachfront, and Santa Barbara's mission. It's a particularly good bet for those who are short on time and long on curiosity. The fee is $10 for adults, $7 for kids 12 and under. The trolley runs daily, and you can pick it up anywhere along the route. Call for the stop nearest you.

Hitting the beaches

Santa Barbara has a terrific collection of beaches. Most are flat and wide, boasting calm waters, gorgeous white sands, and lots of blanket space, even on busy summer days.

East Beach/West Beach

These sister beaches run as an unbroken strip along Cabrillo Boulevard for about two miles. **Stearns Wharf,** at the end of State Street, serves as the dividing line: The wide white sands to the east of the pier are **East Beach,** and those to the west are (you guessed it) **West Beach.** West Beach is fine, but East Beach is the real beaut. A grassy median and a marvelous palm-lined bike path separate it from the busy boulevard. On Sundays, a local artists' mart pops up along here. On the sand you'll find volleyball courts, a picnic area with barbecue grills, good facilities, and a landmark bathhouse from the 1920s. An excellent choice, and the best one for families.

Rent bikes, in-line skates, tandems for couples, and four-wheeled surreys to accommodate the whole family at *Beach Rentals,* just up from the beach at 22 State St. (☎ 805-966-2282). Rates are $6 to $32 for the first hour ($12 to $90 for 3 to 5 hours), depending on the kind of wheels you want. Beach toys are available, too.

Leadbetter Beach

On Cabrillo Boulevard just west of the harbor (turn left past La Playa School), this very pretty beach runs to Santa Barbara Point. Less protected than other local beaches, Leadbetter is popular with the local surfers when the waves kick up; fortunately, the waters generally stay calm for swimmers in summer. A great vantage point for watching boats cruise in and out of the harbor. The nice facilities include a sit-down cafe and limited free 90-minute parking. Otherwise, parking is $6 for the day.

You can rent kayaks, paddleboats, boogie boards, and other beach toys from **Kayak Rentals,** on the sand at Leadbetter Beach (☎ **805-266-2282**).

Shoreline Park

Long, grassy Shoreline Park sits atop the cliffs just past Leadbetter Beach. Spectacular panoramic ocean views make it a marvelous spot for a picnic. A lovely, bench-lined strolling path leads to neatly kept facilities and a small playground. Parking is free.

Arroyo Burro Beach County Park (Hendry's Beach)

Arroyo Burro Beach County Park is my favorite beach, and is well worth the 2-mile drive from downtown. This narrow but long crescent-shaped beach nestled below the cliffs feels secluded thanks to its dis-tance from the main road — and its status as a wetlands sanctuary for shorebirds adds an appealing natural element. The sands are dark but still lovely, and locals love 'em for sunbathing, shelling, and swimming. This beach makes a great choice for sunset strolling, too. The Brown Pelican restaurant is here, plus rest rooms, showers, and free parking. To get there, follow Cabrillo Boulevard west as it turns into Shoreline Drive. Turn right on Meigs Road, then left onto Cliff Drive; go 1.1 miles and turn left into the signed lot.

Seeing the county courthouse and other cultural highlights

The county courthouse serves as a great starting point for the **Red Tile Tour,** a self-guided walk covering a 12-square-block area of historic downtown. Pick up the map and brochure at the visitor center (see "Gathering More Information" at the end of this chapter). Allow 1½ to 3 hours to see everything along the route.

County Courthouse

In a city of stunning Spanish Colonial Revival architecture, the courthouse serves as the finest example of the vernacular. Completed in 1929 and taking up an entire downtown block, the building is utterly magnificent, and well worth a look. You can explore on your own. If the clock tower is open, you'll be rewarded for the climb to the observation deck with great views of the surrounding red-tile roofs and the ocean and mountains beyond. Don't miss the courtyard garden. Free guided tours are offered Monday, Tuesday, and Friday at 10:30 a.m. and Monday through Saturday at 2:00 p.m. — but times can vary, so call ahead.

1100 Anacapa St., between Anapamu and Figueroa sts. (enter mid-block from the Anacapa St. entrance to reach the information desk). ☎ *805-962-6464. Admission: Free! Open: Mon–Fri 8 a.m.–5 p.m., Sat–Sun 10 a.m.–5 p.m.*

Old Mission, Santa Barbara

Founded in 1786, this majestic hilltop complex is considered the "Queen" of the California mission chain. Even if you're not interested in the Spanish Colonial and/or Native American history of California, it's well worth a look. The mission set the architectural tone for the rest of Santa Barbara, and offers spectacular views all the way out to the Channel Islands. The self-guided tour includes a very cool cemetery.

2201 Laguna St. (at Los Olivos St., at the north end of town). ☎ *805-682-4149. Internet:* www.sbmission.org. *Admission: $4, free for kids under 12. Open: Daily 9 a.m.–5 p.m.*

Santa Barbara Botanic Garden

Situated in the foothills above town, this lovely garden is great for walkers, as 5½ miles of trails wind through indigenous California greenery. Guided tours are offered daily at 2:00 p.m., plus Thursday, Saturday, and Sunday at 10:30 a.m.

1212 Mission Canyon Rd. (1½ miles north of the mission). ☎ *805-682-4726. Internet:* www.sbbg.org. *To get there: From the mission, go north and turn right on Foothill Rd., then left on Mission Canyon; the garden is a half mile up on the left. Admission: $5 adults; $3 seniors, students, and teens; $1 kids 5–12. Open: Mar–Oct, Mon–Fri 9 a.m.–5 p.m., Sat–Sun 9 a.m.–6.p.m.; Nov–Feb, Mon–Fri 9 a.m.–4 p.m., Sat–Sun 9 a.m.–5 p.m.*

Santa Barbara Museum of Art

This little gem feels like a private gallery — one with works by Monet, Picasso, Braque, Chagall, Rodin, and other masters. It contains some good 20th-century Californian and Asian art, too, and is well worth an hour.

1130 State St. (at Anapamu St.). ☎ *805-963-4364. Internet:* www.sbmuseart.org. *Admission: $5 adults, $3 seniors, $2 students and kids 6–17. Open: Tues–Thurs and Sat 11 a.m.–5 p.m., Fri 11 a.m.–9 p.m., Sun noon–5 p.m.*

Santa Barbara Zoo

This charming, pint-size zoo is ideal for the little ones, and is easy to explore in less than an hour.

500 Niños Dr. (east of Milpas St., turn up Niños from Cabrillo Blvd.) ☎ *805-962-5339. Internet:* www.santabarbarazoo.com. *Admission: $7 adults, $5 seniors and kids 2–12. Open: Daily 10 a.m.–5 p.m. (arrive before 4 p.m.).*

Experiencing the harbor life

At the end of State Street is **Stearns Wharf,** a 19th-century vintage pier that offers great views but is otherwise pretty touristy. Head instead to **Santa Barbara Harbor** for a genuine look at local maritime life. To get there, follow Cabrillo Boulevard west, past Castillo Street, and turn left on Harbor Way. While you're there, **Brophy Bros. Clam Bar & Restaurant** makes a great place to soak in the atmosphere, not to mention some divine chowder and oysters on the half shell (see "Dining Out" earlier in this chapter).

If you want to hit the water, **Sea Landing** (☎ 805-963-3564) offers half- and full-day sportfishing trips. **The Santa Barbara Sailing Center** (☎ 800-350-9090 or 805-962-2826; www.sbsailctr.com) has a wide array of excursions, including dinner cruises, afternoon sailing, and whale-watching (February through May).

If you'd like to cruise over to **Channel Islands National Park,** check out the offerings from the fleet at **Truth Aquatics** (☎ 805-962-1127; www.truthaquatics.com), which offers hiking, camping, and natural history trips as well as fishing, diving, and whale watching.

Shopping 'til you drop

Boutiques abound along State Street and in the offshoot blocks, where you'll find such local treats as **Helena,** 130 E. Cañon Perdido, between Santa Barbara and Anacapa streets (☎ 805-963-0222), a stylish stop for fashionable women's separates and accessories.

Antiques hounds should seek out **Brinkerhoff Avenue**, a block-long passage 1½ blocks west of State between Cota and Haley streets that brims with vintage goodies. Most shops along Brinkerhoff are closed Monday, and close as early as 5 or 6 p.m. on weekdays.

Also worth seeking out is **El Paseo,** at 814 State St. (between Cañon Perdido and de la Guerra Street), a charming arcade lined with boutiques and galleries that's reminiscent of an old Spanish street. It also happens to be the oldest shopping street in southern California.

Touring the local wine country

In the past few years, Santa Barbara's wine country has really come into its own, with local labels achieving national prominence and wineries attracting visitors from the far reaches of the globe. If you'd like to explore the local tasting rooms — which include such familiar labels as Cambria, Firestone, Meridian, Au Bon Climat — stop into the local visitor center here or in nearby Solvang (see Chapter 19) and pick up the brochure and map called *Santa Barbara County Wineries.* You can also order a copy in advance by contacting the Santa Barbara County Vintners Association at ☎ 800-218-0881 or 805-688-0881. You can even download a version online at www.sbcountywines.com.

Gathering More Information

The Santa Barbara Conference and Visitors Bureau (☎ **800-549-5133** or 805-966-9222) has a wealth of information, much of it in easily printable form, at www.santabarbaraca.com. The Santa Barbara Tourist Information Center is just across from the beach at 1 Garden St., at Cabrillo Boulevard (☎ **805-965-3021**). This center offers good maps and other literature, and the friendly staff can answer specific questions. Open Monday through Saturday from 9 a.m. to 5 p.m. and Sunday from 10 a.m. to 5 p.m.

You may also want to pick up a copy of the *Independent*, a free weekly paper with comprehensive events listings. It's available from sidewalk racks and in shops and restaurants around town.

 American Express has two official travel offices in Santa Barbara: at the Santa Barbara Travel Bureau, in the heart of town at 3967 State St. (☎ **805-683-1666**), and in neighboring Montecito at 1127 Coast Village Rd. (☎ **805-969-7746**).

Part V
The Southland Cities and the Desert

The 5th Wave   By Rich Tennant

©RICHTENNANT

SID'S
TARANTULA, SCORPION,
AND RATTLESNAKE
PETTING ZOO

Welcome to
Death Valley

In this part . . .

This part focuses on **Southern California,** namely Los Angeles, San Diego, and Disneyland, along with California's real hot spots: the desert areas of Palm Springs, Joshua Tree National Park, and Death Valley National Park. Los Angeles, in addition to being rich in glitz and gloriously silly, is the state's finest museum town. Really. Disneyland is the original theme park, an unadulturated blast for kids of all ages. Disneyland sets the stage for San Diego, a significantly more easygoing city than L.A. — or even San Francisco, for that matter. This town has a wonderfully mellow vibe, golden beaches galore, and plenty of memory-making diversions.

Unlike the other destinations in this book — which are generally most popular in summer and largely pleasant to visit year-round — California is most fun to visit in any season *but* summer, when the scorching heat can be a bit much to bear. The Palm Springs area is the place to go for desert cool, and a day trip to unspoiled Joshua Tree National Park, with its mindbending shapes and otherworldly hues is a fascinating diversion. Both shockingly barren and stunningly beautiful, remote Death Valley National Park pumps up the otherworldliness to new heights, if you have the time and inclination to make the lengthy trek.

Chapter 21

Los Angeles

In This Chapter

▶ Knowing when to go and how to get there — and deciding how long to stay

▶ Getting to know the lay of La-La land

▶ Choosing your neighborhood and deciding on the best places to stay and eat

▶ Seeing the sights, shopping, and living it up after the sun goes down

Sunset Boulevard. Venice Beach. Rodeo Drive. Melrose Avenue. Hollywood and Vine. The names are so familiar that they roll off the tongue as if they were in your very own hometown.

Everyone knows Los Angeles, to some degree — such is the power of television. L.A. is sensational, glamorous, sunny, sprawling, smoggy, cynical. This is the city of the beautiful people. They all work in the entertainment biz and follow the latest fads and drive shiny new (or retro-cool) convertibles along cripplingly congested mega-freeways to get to their shrink's (or personal trainer's or holistic healer's or guru's) office. "Let's do lunch" is the social mantra, and movie premieres are the local equivalent of high culture.

Is all this true? To some degree, yes — gloriously, yes. Much of what we love to hate about L.A. are its greatest draws. Nowhere else can we better indulge our collective obsession with glamour, glitz, and fame than in this wild, wacky, brighter-than-bright, larger-than-life city. But, as with all stereotypes, the reality is so much more wonderfully complex.

For a much-photographed city, L.A. is not pretty. It contains *way* too many beige stucco strip malls for it to be called that. But it does have charisma, excitement, sexy allure, incredible diversity, and pockets of intense beauty — both natural and architectural. The city also wows with the pure power of scale.

What's more, L.A. is just plain fun. It's a blast to take movie studio tours, model your newest bikini on the beach, and rub shoulders with rock stars at chic bars. But set aside an afternoon or two for more high-minded pursuits, and you discover that L.A. also happens to be California's finest museum city (yes, even better than San Francisco). You can also explore a good bit of history, whether your interests lie with early Spanish colonialism or the Golden Age of Hollywood.

I would never suggest that you skip the silly stuff, by any means. But even those of you who can't tell Heather Locklear from Pamela Anderson Lee — and couldn't care less — will be surprised at how well you're able to connect with this town. The key to enjoying Los Angeles is just knowing where to look.

Timing Your Visit

Most people visit in summer, but Los Angeles is pleasant all year long. The daytime temperatures seldom drop below the mid-60s, and nighttime lows waffle between the 40s and 50s year-round (bring a jacket anytime you come).

Summer comes late to L.A. June is often on the cool side and plagued by "June gloom" — morning fog that doesn't burn off until early afternoon (and can actually last into August). On the up side, low humidity and ocean breezes keep things relatively dry and comfortable, even 20 miles inland, in the heat of summer (July and August). The valleys can get smoggy and miserable on the hottest days — which means you could end up broiling at Universal Studios — but otherwise you'll likely be comfortable.

My favorite months are September and October, when all the summer vacationers who have driven up hotel rates, booked up tables across town, and grabbed the best tickets for TV-show tapings have gone home, but beach weather still reigns. Rain is virtually nonexistent between May and November.

Winter provides a marvelous time for avoiding crowds and escaping the bitter cold back home. While the weather will likely be too cool for the beach, the occasional 80°F day will pop up, and hotel bargains are common (except at holiday time). Rain is rare, but the majority of the year's accumulation happens between February and April, and after the rain starts, it can sometimes continue for days.

L.A.'s attractions are spread out and traffic can be horrendous, which means one of two things:

✔ You need three full days to get a good overview of the city.

✔ If you're not a city person and you know that L.A. is going to get under your skin quickly (or you just don't have three full days to give), you should zero in on where your interests lie, see those attractions in a day or two, and skedaddle outta town.

For tips on how to plan your time, see "Suggested 1-, 2- and 3-Day Itineraries" later in this chapter.

Getting There

Los Angeles International Airport, commonly called LAX (☎ 310-646-5252; www.lawa.org), is the city's major gateway, and most likely where you'll fly in. LAX is on the ocean south of Marina del Rey at the intersection of the 405 and 105 freeways, 9½ miles from Santa Monica and 16 miles from Hollywood.

Burbank-Glendale-Pasadena Airport (☎ 800-U-FLY-BUR or 818-840-8840; www.burbankairport.com) is usually just referred to as "Burbank." You'll find it 8 miles northeast of Hollywood within a rough square bounded by the 5, 134, and 170 freeways. Burbank is far smaller and more manageable than LAX, and definitely the most convenient gateway if you're basing yourself in Hollywood. Most flights coming into Burbank arrive from other California cities or nearby cities like Phoenix and Vegas.

All of the major car-rental companies have branches at both airports. Each company provides shuttle service between the terminals and their off-site lot.

Getting to your hotel from LAX

If you're staying in Santa Monica, take Sepulveda Boulevard north and follow the signs to Lincoln Boulevard/Highway 1 (Pacific Coast Highway, or PCH) north. To reach West L.A., Beverly Hills, or Hollywood, take Century Boulevard to I-405 north; Santa Monica Boulevard east is the likeliest exit, but check with your hotel for exact directions.

If you won't be renting a car at the airport, SuperShuttle (☎ 800-554-3146 or 310-782-6600; www.supershuttle.com) offers door-to-door shuttle service. Expect to pay between $14 and $20 (plus tip) per person, depending on your drop-off point. Although you don't need reservations for your arrival, you must make them at least a day in advance for your return trip to the airport.

Taxis line up curbside at each terminal. Expect to pay between $31 and $40 (plus tip), depending on your destination. All LAX pickups include a $2.50 surcharge. Taxis can accommodate up to five riders.

Getting to your hotel from Burbank

Follow the signs to U.S. 101 south (the Hollywood Freeway), and exit at Vine Street for Hollywood hotels; continue south on the I-110 to the I-10 west if you're staying on the Westside or at the beach.

SuperShuttle (☎ 818-556-6600; www.supershuttle.com) offers door-to-door shuttle service from Burbank; expect to pay $15 plus tip to Hollywood. Reserve airport pickups and returns in advance. If you forget, taxis wait outside the terminal. Taxi fare will depend on your final destination, but expect to pay between $20 and $30 to Hollywood.

Arriving by car

If you're driving from Santa Barbara and coastal points north, follow U.S. 101 south to Interstate 405 (I-405):

- ✔ **For West L.A., Beverly Hills, or West Hollywood,** exit at Santa Monica Boulevard.

- ✔ **For Santa Monica,** pick up I-10 west, which will drop you right at the ocean.

- ✔ **If you're heading to Hollywood,** stay on 101 until it becomes the Hollywood Freeway (be sure to take the Hollywood Freeway/101 turnoff, or you'll end up in Pasadena before you know it). Exit the Hollywood Freeway at Vine or Gower streets.

If you're coming directly from San Francisco or Monterey and prefer to bypass the scenic coastal route for a much quicker route, follow Interstate 5 (I-5) through the middle of the state. Heading south on I-5, you'll pass a small town called Grapevine, which marks the start of the Grapevine Pass, a mountain pass that will lead you into the San Fernando Valley and L.A. Take I-405 south to Santa Monica, West L.A., Beverly Hills, and West Hollywood; for Hollywood, follow I-5 past the 405 to Highway 170 south to U.S. 101 south (this route is called the Hollywood Freeway the entire way).

From points east, either Palm Springs or Phoenix farther afield, take Interstate 10 (I-10) west, which dead-ends in Santa Monica. For Hollywood, take I-110 (the Harbor Freeway) to U.S. 101 (the Hollywood Freeway) north; for West L.A. and Beverly Hills, follow I-10 to I-405 north.

From Disneyland or San Diego, head north on I-5 (the Santa Ana Freeway). If you've been following along, you'll know to pick up I-405 north to Santa Monica, West Los Angeles, and Beverly Hills, and continue on to U.S. 101 for Hollywood.

Arriving by train

Amtrak (☎ 800-872-7245; www.amtrak.com) trains arrive at Union Station, 800 N. Alameda St. (☎ 213-624-0171), on the northern edge of downtown just north of U.S. 101. From here, you can take one of the taxis that line up outside.

Orienting Yourself and Getting Around

Los Angeles is sandwiched between mountains and ocean, on the flat-lands of a huge basin, with downtown L.A. as its midpoint 12 miles east of the Pacific. The huge, sprawling city includes dozens of neighborhoods and independent municipalities, so complex that even a city planner would need some serious time to sort it all out. The web of freeways knits it all together. The major freeways form a rough box around the area you'll concentrate your time in:

- ✔ **I-10 (the Santa Monica Freeway)** runs east-west from Palm Springs (actually from Georgia) all the way to the ocean in Santa Monica.

- ✔ **Highway 1 (the Pacific Coast Highway, or just "PCH")**, is a standard four-lane avenue called Lincoln Boulevard from just north of the airport to Santa Monica, where it turns into a surface highway and cuts west to hug the coast all the way to Malibu.

- ✔ **I-405 (the San Diego Freeway)** runs north-south through L.A.'s westside, roughly parallel to PCH and about 3½ miles inland from the coast.

- ✔ **U.S. 101** is the **Ventura Freeway** as it runs east-west through the San Fernando Valley (on the north side of L.A.), becoming the **Hollywood Freeway** after 101 takes a sharp turn right, running northwest-southeast to connect the Valley with downtown L.A. (The Ventura Freeway continues on directly east along Calif. 134.)

- ✔ **I-110 (the Harbor Freeway)** starts in Pasadena (as the Pasadena Freeway) and runs directly south. You'll likely use the section that runs along the western edge of downtown, connecting the Hollywood Freeway to I-10.

- ✔ **I-5 (the Golden State Freeway)** runs along the eastern edge of downtown on its way from San Francisco to San Diego.

An underlying grid of surface streets complements the freeways. The major east-west boulevards connecting downtown to the beaches are, from north to south, Sunset, Santa Monica, Wilshire, Olympic, Pico, and Venice boulevards.

Freeways are variously referred to both by their numbers and their names. You'll hear locals call I-10 both "the 10" and the Santa Monica Freeway.

A good city map is a must; even born-and-raised Angelenos carry one in their cars. AAA publishes the best maps of L.A., bar none. Members can stop in at one of the local offices (see "Quick Concierge" at the end of this chapter). If you're not a member, any good foldout map will do, as long as all streets and freeways are clearly marked and it has address number notations.

Los Angeles: The Neighborhoods in Brief

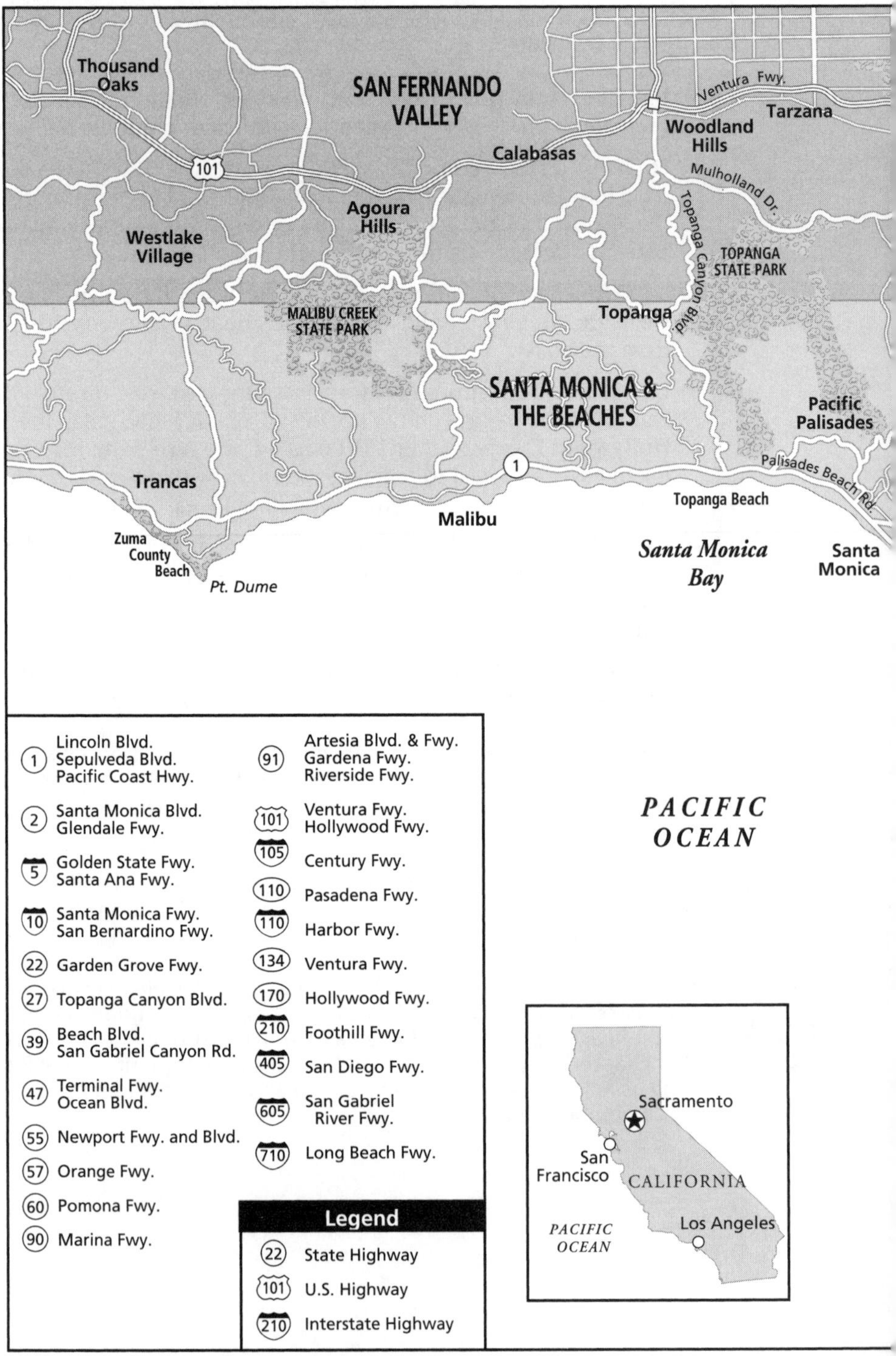
Thousand Oaks
SAN FERNANDO VALLEY
Ventura Fwy.
Tarzana
Woodland Hills
Calabasas
101
Mulholland Dr.
Agoura Hills
Westlake Village
Topanga Canyon Blvd.
TOPANGA STATE PARK
MALIBU CREEK STATE PARK
Topanga
SANTA MONICA & THE BEACHES
Pacific Palisades
1
Palisades Beach Rd.
Trancas
Topanga Beach
Malibu
Zuma County Beach
Pt. Dume
Santa Monica Bay
Santa Monica
PACIFIC OCEAN
1 Lincoln Blvd. Sepulveda Blvd. Pacific Coast Hwy.
2 Santa Monica Blvd. Glendale Fwy.
5 Golden State Fwy. Santa Ana Fwy.
10 Santa Monica Fwy. San Bernardino Fwy.
22 Garden Grove Fwy.
27 Topanga Canyon Blvd.
39 Beach Blvd. San Gabriel Canyon Rd.
47 Terminal Fwy. Ocean Blvd.
55 Newport Fwy. and Blvd.
57 Orange Fwy.
60 Pomona Fwy.
90 Marina Fwy.
91 Artesia Blvd. & Fwy. Gardena Fwy. Riverside Fwy.
101 Ventura Fwy. Hollywood Fwy.
105 Century Fwy.
110 Pasadena Fwy.
110 Harbor Fwy.
134 Ventura Fwy.
170 Hollywood Fwy.
210 Foothill Fwy.
405 San Diego Fwy.
605 San Gabriel River Fwy.
710 Long Beach Fwy.
Legend
22 State Highway
101 U.S. Highway
210 Interstate Highway
Sacramento
San Francisco
CALIFORNIA
PACIFIC OCEAN
Los Angeles

L.A.'s neighborhoods

I've separated the wheat from the chaff in a really big way, boiling down the city to the neighborhoods where most visitors (and most locals) head for sightseeing, entertainment, and general fun in the sun. Who really wants to go to Van Nuys, anyway?

Unlike in most cities, urban life in L.A. does not focus on downtown. You'll likely spend the bulk of your time in the beach communities, on the city's Westside, and in Hollywood.

Santa Monica

Santa Monica is L.A.'s premier beach community. It's fun, festive, and pretty, with a deserved left-of-center reputation. It extends for three miles along the coast, starting out artsy-funky around Ocean Park Boulevard and getting ritzier as you go north. Ocean Avenue runs blufftop along the coast, meeting Colorado Boulevard at the **Santa Monica Pier,** famous for its amusements. Dining and shopping north of Colorado centers on the **Third Street Promenade,** and along Main Street south of Colorado. I-10 drops you into the heart of the action.

Venice & Marina del Rey

South of Santa Monica is Venice, an early-20th-century planned community with its very own canals. But the real draw is wild, wacky, kinda skanky **Venice Beach,** which just may be the ultimate human carnival. Main Street will lead you into Venice from the north — you'll know you've arrived when it becomes Pacific Avenue — and Venice Boulevard and Washington Avenue serve as the main routes in from points east.

South of Washington is **Marina del Rey,** best known for its mammoth small-craft harbor. It's appreciably cleaner, more modern, more mall-ified, and more upscale than funky Venice.

Malibu

Malibu is the ultimate symbol of beachy super-celebrity. Its vast network of rugged canyons leads from Santa Monica north all the way to the northern border of L.A. County. Only the Pacific Coast Highway (and an almost-unbroken row of ocean-facing houses that are *much* larger — and pricier — than they look from PCH) separates Malibu's canyons from its gorgeous wide beaches. Malibu is extremely remote (one of its great appeals for the rich and famous) and without freeway access. Consequently, the drive to Malibu from just about anywhere else in the city takes around an hour.

West Los Angeles

West L.A. is basically an umbrella for the collection of middle- and upper-middle-class communities sandwiched between Santa Monica to the west and Beverly Hills to the east. Some of these communities lack exact labels beyond "West L.A." but they are perfectly nice nonetheless Among the most notable are:

✔ **Brentwood,** the upscale residential area north of Wilshire Boulevard and west of I-405 that O.J. Simpson made famous (to the chagrin of his former neighbors).

✔ **Westwood,** home to UCLA and a restaurant- and shop-laden village that caters largely to the college kids. It's the area between I-405 and Beverly Hills, bounded by Santa Monica and Sunset boulevards; the village is just north of Wilshire Boulevard.

✔ **Bel-Air** is the gated domain of the rich and famous north of UCLA above Sunset Boulevard.

✔ **Century City** is the pocket of high-rises just west of Beverly Hills, between Santa Monica and Pico boulevards. It offers the Westside its only real city skyline, but is otherwise quite sanitized and uninteresting.

Beverly Hills

You'd almost have to live under a rock not to know this one. The traditional bastion of L.A.'s ultra-rich and famous is a glitzy but easily enjoyable community. The area south of Wilshire Boulevard is largely upper-middle-class residential, and home to some surprisingly affordable hotels. North of Wilshire is the **Golden Triangle,** Beverly Hills' downtown, where you'll find the ritzy shops. North of Santa Monica Boulevard is the hilly, star-studded residential area.

West Hollywood

Ground zero for L.A.'s gay and rock 'n' roll communities, West Hollywood houses some of L.A.'s best (or liveliest, anyway) hotels, restaurants, bars, and clubs. It's long and narrow, shaped kind of like a house key, and feels either upscale or lowbrow, depending on where you are. The main drags are Santa Monica Boulevard and the stretch of Sunset Boulevard between Doheny Drive and Crescent Heights Boulevard known as the **Sunset Strip** — L.A.'s tattooed-and-pierced party central, packed with trendy bars and rocking clubs.

Hollywood

The original epicenter of Movie City glamour had degenerated into one of the seediest parts of town by the 1980s, but it's a whole different story of late. A major urban revitalization (much like the one that transformed New York's Times Square) was launched in the late '90s and continues apace. **Hollywood Boulevard** isn't ever going to be a bastion of high culture — in fact, L.A. hardly gets more touristy than this — but it's cleaner, safer, and more attractive than it has been in decades. The boulevard's **Walk of Fame** is the main attraction, but the neighborhood actually extends from Beverly Boulevard north into the Hollywood Hills, encompassing the famously funky alterna-shopping strip **Melrose Avenue.**

Mid-Wilshire District/Miracle Mile

This corridor flanks Wilshire Boulevard east from Beverly Hills to (roughly) Western Avenue. The highlight is the stretch of Wilshire between Fairfax and La Brea avenues, which serves as the city's impressive **Museum Row.**

L.A.'s Westside: Brentwood, et al

Stone Canyon Rd.

Benedict Canyon Rd.

Beverly Glen Blvd.

405

Bel Air

Holmby Hills

The Los Angeles Country Club

University of California Los Angeles

Kenter Ave.

Sunset Blvd.

Barrington Ave.

San Diego Freeway

Westwood

Veteran Ave.

Sepulveda Blvd.

Westwood Blvd.

2

San Vicente Blvd.

Brentwood Country Club

Brentwood

Montana Ave.

Wilshire Blvd.

Santa Monica Blvd.

Bundy Dr.

Sawtelle Ave.

405

Pico Blvd.

Attractions ●
Getty Center **2**
Museum of
    Television & Radio **10**
Museum of Tolerance **6**
Skirball Center **1**

Dining ◆
Chin Chin **3, 17**
Hard Rock Cafe **14**
Kate Mantilini **13**
Mimosa **15**

Nate 'n' Al's **9**
Spago Beverly Hills **16**
Swingers **17**
The Apple Pan **5**

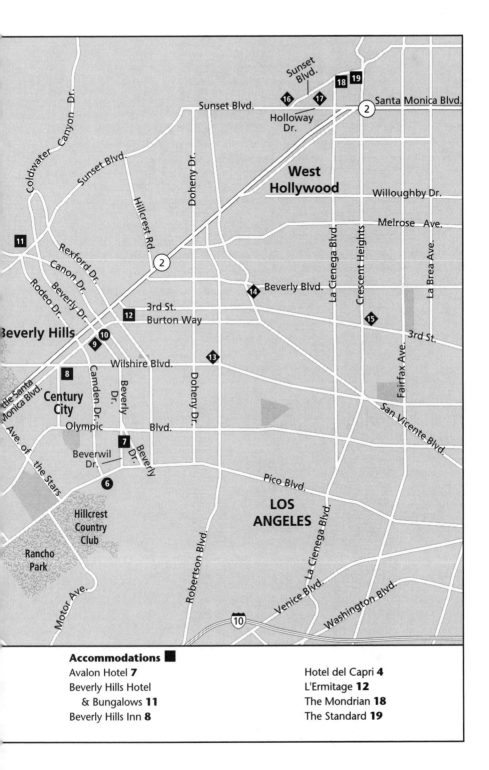

Accommodations ■

Avalon Hotel **7**

Beverly Hills Hotel
    & Bungalows **11**

Beverly Hills Inn **8**

Hotel del Capri **4**

L'Ermitage **12**

The Mondrian **18**

The Standard **19**

Hollywood

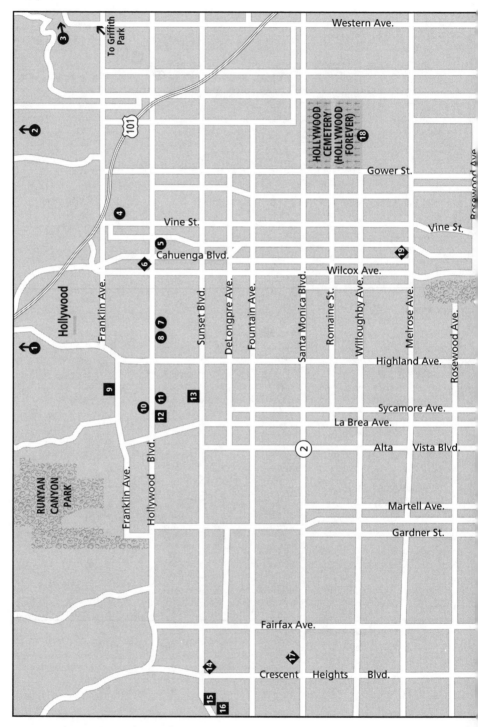

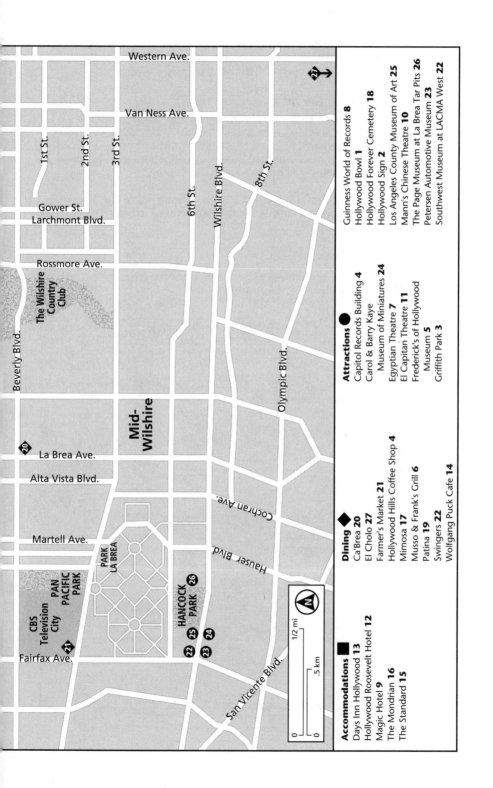

Western Ave.

Van Ness Ave.

1st St.

2nd St.

3rd St.

Gower St.
Larchmont Blvd.

Rossmore Ave.

The Wilshire
Country
Club

Beverly Blvd.

Wilshire Blvd.

6th St.

8th St.

Olympic Blvd.

Mid-
Wilshire

La Brea Ave.

Alta Vista Blvd.

Martell Ave.

Cochran Ave.

Hauser Blvd.

PARK
LA BREA

PAN
PACIFIC
PARK

HANCOCK
PARK

CBS
Television
City

Fairfax Ave.

San Vicente Blvd.

1/2 mi

.5 km

Accommodations ■
Days Inn Hollywood **13**
Hollywood Roosevelt Hotel **12**
Magic Hotel **9**
The Mondrian **16**
The Standard **15**

Dining ◆
Ca'Brea **20**
El Cholo **27**
Farmer's Market **21**
Hollywood Hills Coffee Shop **4**
Mimosa **17**
Musso & Frank's Grill **6**
Patina **19**
Swingers **22**
Wolfgang Puck Cafe **14**

Attractions ●
Capitol Records Building **4**
Carol & Barry Kaye
   Museum of Miniatures **24**
Egyptian Theatre **7**
El Capitan Theatre **11**
Frederick's of Hollywood
   Museum **5**
Griffith Park **3**

Guinness World of Records **8**
Hollywood Bowl **1**
Hollywood Forever Cemetery **18**
Hollywood Sign **2**
Los Angeles County Museum of Art **25**
Mann's Chinese Theatre **10**
The Page Museum at La Brea Tar Pits **26**
Petersen Automotive Museum **23**
Southwest Museum at LACMA West **22**

Los Feliz

This hip haven between Hollywood and downtown is most notable as a gateway to **Griffith Park,** the massive urban park that's home to the Griffith Observatory (remember *Rebel Without a Cause?*).

Universal City & Burbank

These San Fernando Valley communities are the joint capitals of TV Land, and all you need to know about the Valley. Universal City, west of Griffith Park between the Hollywood and Ventura freeways (U.S. 101 and Calif. 134), houses **Universal Studios Hollywood** and **Universal CityWalk,** the adjoining shopping-and-dining spread.

Just north of Universal City and the 134, Burbank hosts L.A.'s secondary airport and the **NBC** and **Warner Bros.** studios, open to the masses for TV tapings and tours.

Universal City & Burbank

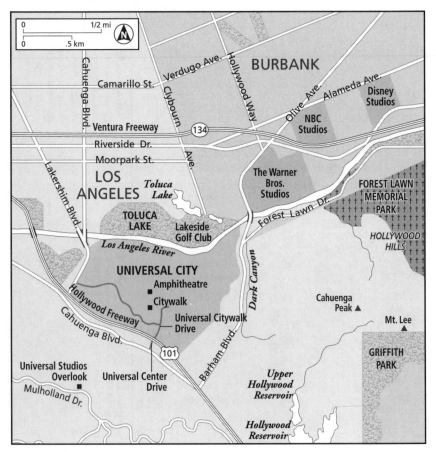

Downtown

Boxed in by the U.S. 101, I-110, I-10, and I-5 freeways, downtown is the entertainment-industry-free business center of the city. After a scruffy period, it has cleaned up quite nicely in recent years and has even drawn in some hip restaurants. But beyond the main visitor center and **El Pueblo de Los Angeles,** the original Mexican heart of the city, you won't find a whole lot of interest here, unless you hold tickets to an event at one of the spiffy performing arts venues.

Pasadena

Pasadena, blissfully free of Hollywood glam, is the premier draw of the San Gabriel Valley (the network of pretty, upscale bedroom communities east of the San Fernando Valley). The biggest day of the year here is January 1, when the **Tournament of Roses Parade** draws national attention to the attractive 'burb. You'll also find a few year-round attractions here, too, if you tire of the Tinseltown schlock.

Drive, she said — Getting around

Yes, driving around L.A. is a hassle. Yes, you pretty much have to do it. I've heard wild rumors about tourists who've gotten around using public transportation — but I've also heard wild rumors about the ghost of Montgomery Clift living at the Hollywood Roosevelt Hotel and three-headed monsters living in the sewer system, and I don't believe those, either.

The complex web of freeways and surface streets may seem intimidating at first. After you get the hang of it, however, it's not bad at all; driving in New York City, or even the daunting hills of San Francisco, is worlds more difficult. Just think of L.A. as one big, bad suburb and you'll do just fine.

Do yourself a favor and keep these tips in mind as you drive — and park — around the city:

- ✔ **Allow more time than you think it will actually take to get where you're going.** You need to make time for traffic and parking. Double your margin in weekday rush hours, from 7 to 9 a.m. and again from 3 to 7 p.m. I've often found the freeways to be much more crowded than I expect all day on Saturdays, too.

- ✔ **Plan your exact route before you set out.** Know where you'll need to exit the freeway and/or make turns — especially lefts — and merge in plenty of time. Otherwise, you're likely to find yourself waving to your freeway exit from an inside lane, or your turnoff from an outside one. Pulling over and whipping out your map if you screw up is never easy, and it's darn near impossible on the freeways.

- ✔ **Those kids you brought with you can come in handy.** Most freeways have a High Occupancy Vehicle (HOV) — a carpool — lane, which will let you speed past some of the congestion if you have three people in the car (sometimes two; read the signs). Don't flout the rules; if you do, expect to shell out close to 300 bucks for the ticket.

✔ **You can turn right on red as long as a posted sign doesn't tell you otherwise.** Come to a full stop first — no rolling.

✔ **Accept the fact that you will sometimes have to pay for parking.** Your hotel will cover your parking, either for free or a charge. Many other establishments (in some areas, most) don't have their own self-park lots, so free street parking is the holy grail. It's sometimes available, but not always. Side streets are often a good bet, but beware of residential neighborhoods, as an increasing number allow only permit parking — and you will be towed or ticketed. Metered street parking is much easier to find, but can still be tough to locate in the most popular areas of Santa Monica, Beverly Hills, and Hollywood.

Otherwise, expect to valet or garage it, and to pay between $3 and $10 for the privilege. Many restaurants, nightclubs, and even some shopping centers offer curbside valet parking.

✔ **Have plenty of quarters on hand.** Angelenos scrounge for parking-meter quarters like New Yorkers do for laundry quarters: They are the equivalent of pure gold. Save yourself some hassle and just buy a roll or two at your bank before you leave home.

✔ **Always read the street-parking signs, because they often limit your parking time.** You will be ticketed if you overstay your welcome. Read the meters as well as street signs. On the up side, meter fares are often waived in the evenings.

✔ **Don't lose your car in a parking garage.** Take it from a perfectly intelligent, well-educated person who's done it more than once — *it happens*. You know how you feel when you forget where you parked your car at the mall? Multiply that by 10 levels. Most garage levels and subsections are letter-, number-, and color-coded. Always make a mental note, or a physical one if need be.

If you must: By bus & metro

I don't recommend traveling by bus or metro. This city is too large to be covered by a good public transportation system, much less L.A.'s wildly inefficient one. Buses are really considered the domain of the marginalized here in Autoland — and who really thinks a subway system is such a good idea in earthquake-prone Los Angeles?

Still, if you just don't drive, are on an extra-tight budget, plan to park yourself in Santa Monica and not leave the immediate area, or you're a glutton for punishment, public transportation may be just the ticket. The Metropolitan Transit Authority (MTA) runs the bus network in addition to the limited three-line Metro Rail system, really conceived as a park-and-ride system for suburban commuters. For information, call ☎ **800-COMMUTE** (800-266-6883) or 213-626-4455, or go online to www.mta.net, where you'll find a custom online trip planner (have the exact addresses of your start and endpoint on hand).

By taxi

Taxis don't cruise the streets, so call well ahead for pickup. Keep in mind that distances are long, so the meter adds up quickly. If you need a cab, call L.A. Taxi (☎ **310-715-1968**) or Independent Taxi (☎ **323-666-0045**).

Staying in Style

In choosing Los Angeles's best hotels, I've concentrated on those neighborhoods that are the most visitor-friendly and offer the easiest access to L.A.'s main attractions. Still, consider what your major sight-seeing goals are before you decide where to stay. That beach hotel that's just right for some of you may be all wrong for others who are avid shoppers or club-hoppers.

Count on an extra 12 to 17 percent in taxes being tacked on to your hotel bill, depending on where you're staying. Ask what the local percentage is when you book.

Avalon Hotel

$$$ Beverly Hills

Housed in an apartment complex where Marilyn Monroe once lived, the Avalon is done in impeccable Atomic Age style, complete with kidney-shaped pool and Noguchi bubble lamps. But fashion doesn't forsake function — the rooms are comfy enough to please design dummies, too. They're gorgeous and restful, with VCRs, CD players, and fax machines. Ask about rooms 240 through 244, which include furnished terraces for no extra charge. Located in a lovely residential neighborhood, the Avalon is quieter and friendlier than other retro-chic hotels.

9400 W. Olympic Blvd. (at Canon Dr.), Beverly Hills. ☎ 800-535-4715 or 310-277-5221. Fax: 310-277-4928. Internet: www.srs-worldhotels.com/usa/beverly_hills. *To get there: I-405 to Olympic Blvd. east. Valet parking: $14. Rack rates: $185–$235 double, $300 suite. AE, DC, MC, V.*

Beverly Hills Hotel & Bungalows

$$$$$ Beverly Hills

If you really want to live Hollywood lore, pull out that platinum card and book a room at L.A.'s most famous temple to fabulousness. "The Pink Palace" has an Oscar-worthy legend at every turn, as well as a current

Hollywood following, thanks to a total overhaul in '95. You'll want for nothing in the hotel's ultra-luxurious rooms or on the lush, sprawling grounds. Don't miss the Dutch Apple pancakes in the iconic Polo Lounge.

9641 Sunset Blvd. (at Rodeo Dr.), Beverly Hills. ☎ *800-283-8885 or 310-276-2251. Fax: 310-281-2905. Internet:* www.thebeverlyhillshotel.com. *To get there: I-405 to Sunset Blvd. east. Valet parking: $21. Rack rates: $335–$390 double, from $600 suite. AE, DC, JCB, MC, V.*

Beverly Hills Inn

$$$ Beverly Hills

In terms of location, comfort, and overall quality, you can't beat this value-packed boutique hotel in the heart of ritzy Beverly Hills. It's attractively done in a contemporary style, and boasts extras that usually cost more, like fitness and business centers and a nice pool. A friendly staff and freebies galore — parking, breakfast, hors d'oeuvres — round out the excellent deal. A real find!

125 S. Spalding Dr. (south of Wilshire Blvd.), Beverly Hills. ☎ *800-463-4466 or 310-278-0303. Fax: 310-278-1728. Internet:* www.travelweb.com. *To get there: I-405 to Santa Monica Blvd. east; turn right on Wilshire. Parking: Free! Rack rates: $145–$160 double, $195 1-bedroom suite, $300 2-bedroom suite. Rates include full breakfast and evening hospitality hour. AE, CB, DC, MC, V.*

Cal Mar Hotel Suites

$$ Santa Monica

These well-tended and very spacious one-bedroom garden apartments are tucked away in a lovely residential neighborhood 2 ½ blocks from the ocean, and a block from Third Street Promenade dining and shopping. Not luxurious by any means — mix-and-match is the theme — but fully equipped kitchens, pullout sofas in the living rooms, and a heated pool make this a stellar bargain, especially for budget-minded families.

220 California Ave. (at 2nd St.), Santa Monica. ☎ *800-776-6007 or 310-395-5555. Fax: 310-451-1111. Internet:* www.calmarhotel.com. *To get there: Lincoln Blvd./Hwy. 1 to Santa Monica Blvd. west to 2nd St. north. Parking: Free! Rack rates: $119–$169 double. AE, MC, V.*

Days Inn Hollywood/Universal Studios

$–$$ Hollywood

Extras like free underground parking and breakfast make this newly renovated — and surprisingly nice — chain motel an especially good value. The location is east of the Sunset Strip action, but it's safe, freeway-convenient, and just minutes from Universal. For maximum bang for your buck, ask for a room overlooking the heated outdoor pool.

7023 Sunset Blvd. (between Highland and La Brea aves.), Hollywood. ☎ *800-346-7723 or 323-464-8344. Fax: 323-962-9748. Internet:* www.daysinn.com. *Parking: Free and secured! To get there: U.S. 101 to Sunset Blvd. west. Rack rates:*

$70–$160 double, $125–$200 Jacuzzi suite. Rates include continental breakfast. Deals: AARP and AAA discounts available, but even nonmembers can usually book a room for less than $100. AE, CB, DC, DISC, JCB, MC, V.

Hollywood Roosevelt Hotel

$$–$$$ Hollywood

This Tinseltown legend — host to the first Academy Awards, not to mention a few famous-name ghosts — also happens to be one of the best bargains in town. You'll get pedigree, comforts, and the kinds of services here that usually cost twice the price. Now under the Clarion banner, the hotel is as spiffy as ever, and the location is once again ideal, as this stretch of the Walk of Fame has cleaned up beautifully.

7000 Hollywood Blvd. (between La Brea and Highland aves.), Hollywood. ☎ 800-950-7667 or 323-466-7000. Fax: 323-469-7006. Internet: www.hollywoodroosevelt.com. To get there: U.S. 101 north to Gower St., U.S. 101 south to Vine St. Valet parking: $10. Rack rates: $159–$249 double, from $169 junior suite, from $299 suite. Deals: Almost no one pays rack here. Ask about AAA, senior, and other discounts, and check www.hotelchoice.com for special Internet rates (as low as $116 at press time). AE, CB, DC, DISC, EURO, MC, V.

Hotel California

$$–$$$ Santa Monica

Cute, clean, and friendly, this hacienda-style motel is the bargain of the beach. Only the suites have ocean views, but everybody has direct beach access down a courtyard path, plus loveseats, VCRs, minifridges, pretty florals, and freshly tiled baths. The location is A-1, just a stone's throw from the pier. Pay the extra $20 for a courtyard view, as the cheapest rooms face noisy Ocean Avenue and lack the polished wooden floors in the pricier units.

1670 Ocean Ave. (south of Colorado Ave.), Santa Monica. ☎ 800-537-8483 or 310-393-2363. Fax: 310-393-1063. Internet: www.hotelca.com. To get there: Lincoln Blvd./Hwy. 1 to Pico Blvd. west to Ocean Ave. north. Parking: $7. Rack rates: $125–$180 double, $175–$200 suite, $275–$350 suite with kitchen. Deals: Rooms sometimes go for as little as $99 midweek. AE, DISC, MC, V.

Hotel del Capri

$$ West Los Angeles

The spacious rooms at this older but still-pleasing motel complex are a good value, especially if you can score one of the many discounts on offer. Nothing is within walking distance of the ritzy high-rise neighborhood, but you'll have a hard time finding a more freeway-convenient or centrally located place to stay.

10587 Wilshire Blvd. (at Westholme Ave.), West Los Angeles. ☎ 800-44HOTEL (444-6835) or 310-474-3511. Fax: 310-470-9999. To get there: I-405 to Wilshire Blvd. east. Parking: Free! Rack rates: $110–$125 double, $135–$160 1-bedroom suite, $265

2-bedroom suite. Rates include continental breakfast. Deals: Discounts for AAA members and seniors, plus UCLA, airline, government, or corporate affiliations. AE, CB, DC, EURO, MC, V.

Hotel Oceana

$$$$$ Santa Monica

Considering how easily you can spend 300 bucks on an average room nowadays, these beachfront designer suites are a steal. Even the studios are huge and feature a full kitchen (better than home!), CD player, and SEGA Genesis game system; the one- and two-bedrooms also have a pull-out sofa. The primary colors and playful modern style suit the beachy location perfectly. Service is excellent, the hotel features a cute boomerang-shaped pool, and the neighborhood is one of L.A.'s loveliest.

849 Ocean Ave. (south of Montana Ave.), Santa Monica. ☎ *800-777-0758 or 310-393-0486. Fax: 310-458-1182. Internet:* www.hoteloceana.com. *To get there: Lincoln Blvd./Hwy. 1 to Pico Blvd. west to Ocean Ave. north. Valet parking: $18. Rack rates: $305–$325 studio suite, $345–$500 1-bedroom suite, $535–$700 2-bedroom suite. Rates include continental breakfast. Deals: Always ask for discounts; as low as $250 on summer weekends, even lower in the off-season, but they won't volunteer. AE, CB, DC, DISC, MC, V.*

L'Ermitage

$$$$$ Beverly Hills

If the Beverly Hills Hotel symbolizes Hollywood opulence as it was, L'Ermitage epitomizes what it is today. Each enormous, superbly decorated room is done in a contemporary Asian-influenced style that screams "understatement!" The real treat is the in-room technology, including 40-inch TVs, personal CD/DVD players, and "smart" bedside control panels that remember your lighting and climate preferences. Service is beyond impeccable. Millennial luxury doesn't get better.

9291 Burton Way (four blocks north of Rodeo Dr.), Beverly Hills. ☎ *800-800-2113 or 310-278-3344. Fax: 310-278-8247. Internet:* www.lermitagehotel.com. *To get there: I-405 to Santa Monica Blvd. east. Valet parking: $21. Rack rates: $325–$448 double, from $760 suite. AE, CB, DC, DISC, MC, V.*

Magic Hotel

$ Hollywood

This little hotel at the base of the Hollywood Hills is L.A.'s best budget deal. You won't see it in *Metropolitan Home* anytime soon, but everything is new and extremely well kept. Situated around a cute courtyard with a heated pool, each apartment-like unit has a big bath and a furnished patio; all but the smallest have a fully outfitted kitchen. A great location, free underground parking, and self-serve laundry clinch the deal. This place is an excellent value — book now!

7025 Franklin Ave. (between La Brea and Highland aves.), Hollywood. ☎ *800-741-4915 or 323-851-0800. Fax: 323-874-5246. Internet:* www.magichotel.com. *To get there: U.S. 101 to Franklin Ave. west. Parking: Free and secured! Rack rates: $55–$89 double or executive (studio) suite, $89–$119 1-bedroom suite, $109–$159 2-bedroom suite. Deals: Off-season and other discounts available. AE, DC, DISC, JCB, MC, V.*

The Mondrian

$$$$ West Hollywood

If you want creature comforts *and* a high hip factor, skip the Standard (below) and stay here. It's as pretentious as can be and not quite cozy enough for the price, but celeb-heavy Skybar is still L.A.'s hottest watering hole; book a room to guarantee admission. Early-to-bed types, beware — shutting out the din is difficult.

8440 Sunset Blvd., West Hollywood. ☎ *800-525-8029 or 323-650-8999. Fax: 323-650-9241. Internet:* www.mondrianhotel.com. *To get there: I-405 to Sunset Blvd. east. Valet parking: $20. Rack rates: $285–$375 double, $350–$565 suite. Deals: Ask about weekend discounts. AE, CB, DC, DISC, MC, V.*

Sea Shore Motel

$–$$ Santa Monica

This well-run motel is tucked away on Santa Monica's coolest shopping and dining strip. The accommodations are nothing special, of course, but they've been nicely renovated in the last few years and boast in-room fridges and dataports. Double-doubles do the job for budget-minded families who don't mind sharing; the suite is an even better deal.

2637 Main St. (just south of Ocean Park Blvd.), Santa Monica. ☎ *310-392-2787. Fax: 310/392-5167. Internet:* www.seashoremotel.com. *To get there: Lincoln Blvd./Hwy. 1 to Ocean Park Blvd. west to Main St. south. Parking: Free! Rack rates: $70–$95 double, $100–$120 suite. AE, DISC, MC, V.*

Shutters on the Beach

$$$$$ Santa Monica

Staying at Shutters is like staying at a really rich friend's L.A. beach house. Facing Santa Monica Beach in all of its gray-clapboarded glory, this oceanfront gem is a stunner. Rooms are airy and gorgeous, with such playful touches as rubber duckies in the whirlpool tubs and nighttime storybooks on the Frette-made beds. The food is great, and the casually elegant service is excellent.

1 Pico Blvd. (at the beach!), Santa Monica. ☎ *800-334-9000 or 310-458-0030. Fax: 310-458-4589. Internet:* www.shuttersonthebeach.com. *To get there: Lincoln Blvd./Hwy. 1 to Pico Blvd. west. Valet parking: $19. Rack rates: $335–$595 double, from $750 suite. Deals: Ask for weekend rates, honeymoon packages, and other special deals. AE, DC, DISC, MC, V.*

The Standard

$$–$$$ West Hollywood

If Austin Powers came to L.A., this is where he'd stay. This groovy neo-motel is a futuristic stunner for the under-35 "It" crowd whose expense accounts have limits (for now). It's a scene worthy of its Sunset Strip location, complete with a shag-carpeted lobby and DJ spinning ambient sounds nightly. Look beyond the silver bean-bag chairs, Warhol-patterned curtains, and Tang-orange bathrooms, and the rooms are little more than motel-standard — not worth it if you couldn't care less about the crowd. Beware: There are no nonsmoking rooms.

8300 Sunset Blvd. (east of La Cienega Blvd.), West Hollywood. ☎ *323-650-9090. Fax: 323-650-2820. To get there: I-405 to Sunset Blvd. east. Valet parking: $18. Rack rates: $95–$215 double, $650 suite. AE, DC, DISC, MC, V.*

Dining Out

To find L.A.'s original **Hard Rock Cafe** at the Beverly Center, 8600 Beverly Blvd., at San Vicente Boulevard (☎ **310-276-7605**), just look for the vintage Caddy sticking out of the roof. The newer — and better, in my estimation — **Hard Rock Hollywood** is at Universal CityWalk (☎ **818-622-ROCK**).

If you're planning on a special meal at any of the following restaurants, reserve a table before you leave home to avoid disappointment — especially on the weekend.

The Apple Pan

$ West Los Angeles   BURGERS

Pull up to the U-shaped counter, order a classic hickory burger (the tuna is also a tradition), and watch in awe as the behind-the-counter help (in paper hats, natch) prepares your meal with high-speed precision. Don't miss the fries, and finish up with home-baked apple or banana cream pie. A true legend — I can't imagine L.A. without it.

10801 W. Pico Blvd. (across from Westside Pavilion). ☎ *310-475-3585. To get there: I-10 to Overland Blvd. north; left on Pico. Main courses: $6 or less. No credit cards. Open: Lunch and dinner Tues–Sun.*

Border Grill

$$$ Santa Monica   MEXICAN

This modern cantina from Mary Sue Milliken and Susan Feniger, the Food Network's Too Hot Tamales (and the authors of *Mexican Cooking For Dummies*), is a brash, bold, colorful space serving up inspired South-of-the-Border cuisine. The ladies' creative cooking is firmly rooted in the traditional Mexican canon, so purists will be pleased as punch.

1445 4th St. (between Broadway and Santa Monica Blvd.), Santa Monica.
☎ *310-451-1655. Internet:* www.bordergrill.com. *Reservations recommended.*
To get there: I-10 to 4th St. Main courses: $8.50–$13 at lunch, $12.50–$22.50 at dinner.
AE, DC, DISC, MC, V. Open: Lunch Tues–Sun, dinner nightly.

Ca'Brea

$$$ Hollywood ITALIAN

Ca'Brea delivers flavorful, masterfully prepared northern Italian food in
a candlelit, white-tablecloth setting that feels far pricier. Expect excellently prepared house-made pastas, including Venetian spaghetti with
first-rate *frutti di mare*, and a braised veal shank that cuts like butter. This
is one of my L.A. faves — the best of the city's billions of trattorias, by far.

346 S. La Brea Ave. (north of Wilshire Blvd.), Los Angeles. ☎ *323-938-2863.*
Reservations recommended. To get there: I-10 to La Brea Ave. north. Main courses:
$11–$23 (most under $17). AE, DC, MC, V. Open: Lunch and dinner Mon–Sat.

Chin Chin

$ West Hollywood/Beverly Hills/Marina del Rey/West Los Angeles
CHINESE

This bright, cheery mini chain of modern Chinese cafes has made my
tummy happy for more than a decade now. This is Americanized Chinese,
but so what? The fresh, fluffy *bao* (buns) can stand up to any Chinatown
rivals, the dim sum and slow-roasted BBQ meats are always delightful,
and the shredded chicken salad is an L.A. classic.

In Sunset Plaza, 8618 Sunset Blvd. (west of La Cienega Blvd.), West Hollywood.
☎ *310-652-1818. Internet:* www.chinchin.com. *Reservations not taken. To get*
there: I-405 to Sunset Blvd. east; free parking in back. Main courses: $5–$9. AE, DC,
MC, V. Open: Lunch and dinner daily.

Also at: 206 S. Beverly Dr. (1 block north of Olympic Blvd.), Beverly Hills; ☎ *310-*
248-5252. 13455 Maxella Ave. (just east of Lincoln Blvd.), Marina del Rey;
☎ *310-823- 9999. 11740 San Vicente Blvd. (3 blocks east of Bundy Dr.), Brentwood;*
☎ *310- 826-2525.*

Ciudad

$$$ Downtown PAN-LATIN

TV's Too Hot Tamales (see the earlier entry for Border Grill) also run this
pan-Latin winner. Hearty, world-wise dishes like Argentine wild-
mushroom empanadas, short ribs glazed with South American BBQ
sauce, super-moist chicken bathed in sweet garlic, and traditional Cuban
pressed sandwiches are served in a sophisticated space that's a playful
blend of contemporary art and Austin Powers mod. Ciudad is perfect for
pre-theater dining — or as a special trip on its own.

445 S. Figueroa St. (at 5th St.), downtown. ☎ *213-486-5171. Internet:*
www.ciudad-la.com. *Reservations recommended. To get there: I-110 north to*
9th St.; left on Figueroa. Main courses: $9.50–$14 at lunch, $12.50–$22 at dinner.
AE, DISC, MC, V. Open: Lunch Mon–Fri, dinner nightly.

El Cholo

$$ Mid-Wilshire/Santa Monica MEXICAN

L.A.'s oldest Mexican restaurant — since 1927 — is as popular as ever, thanks to legendary frosty margaritas, marvelous green corn tamales, classic monster combo plates, and fresh, chunky guacamole that sets the standard. Nothing ground-breaking — but that's the whole, satisfying idea. For best results, bypass the newer beach location for the original pink hacienda on Hollywood's outskirts.

1121 Western Ave. (south of Olympic Blvd.). ☎ *323-734-2773. Reservations recommended for dinner. To get there: I-10 to Western Ave. north. Main courses: $8–$14. AE, DC, MC, V. Open: Lunch and dinner daily.*

Also at: 1025 Wilshire Blvd. (at 11th St.), Santa Monica. ☎ *310-899-1106.*

Farmer's Market

$ Hollywood GLOBAL

Can't agree on what to eat? No problem! Head to this L.A. landmark, the original food court. The 65-year-old indoor-outdoor bazaar is a global bonanza of good eats, from French crepes and Chinese combo plates to home-baked cakes and pies to gumbo and beignets and pizza and panini . . . you get the picture. You can choose from two sit-down diners (one trendy, one traditional), plus an oyster bar and a couple of beer-and-wine bars. The atmosphere is pleasingly festive, especially at weekend brunchtime, and the vendors are budget-friendly across the board.

6333 W. 3rd St. (at Fairfax Ave.), Hollywood. ☎ *323-933-9211. Internet:* www.farmersmarketla.com. *To get there: I-10 to Fairfax Ave. north. Main courses: Most meals less than $10. Open: Mon–Sat 9 a.m.–6:30 p.m., Sun 10 a.m.–5 p.m. (slightly later in summer).*

Hollywood Hills Coffee Shop

$ Hollywood AMERICAN

Famous for its cameo in the movie *Swingers* (this is where Vince Vaughn makes goo-goo eyes at the mom), this grade-A diner is much more than a stop on a silver-screen sightseeing map. The yummy eats are comfortingly familiar — burgers, turkey clubs, cowboy chili, meatloaf, breakfast all day — but ingredients are top-quality and the kitchen contains real talent. The friendly service is a pleasing blend of old-school charm and new-school hip. Great for star sightings, too: Celebs — who can afford to eat anywhere — are unfailingly loyal.

In the Best Western Hollywood Hills, 6145 Franklin Ave. (between Gower and Vine sts.), Hollywood. ☎ *323-467-7678. To get there: U.S. 101 north to Gower St., U.S. 101 south to Vine St. Main courses: $5–$10. AE, DISC, MC, V. Open: Breakfast, lunch, and dinner daily.*

Kate Mantilini

$$–$$$ Beverly Hills   ECLECTIC

This perennial favorite is still stylish and popular, especially among the late-night crowd. The mammoth menu offers something for everyone, including upscale takes on traditional American diner fare. The restaurant features a full bar, excellent meatloaf, and valet parking.

9101 Wilshire Blvd. (at Doheny Dr.), Beverly Hills. ☎ 310-278-3699. Reservations accepted for 6 or more. To get there: I-10 to La Cienega Blvd. north; left on Wilshire. Main courses: $7–$18. AE, DC, MC, V. Open: Breakfast, lunch, dinner, late dining daily.

The Lobster

$$$$ Santa Monica   SEAFOOD

Marvelous and ultra-modern, this new version of an old favorite is a deserved sensation. The Lobster presides over Santa Monica Pier, packing in a chic, party-hearty crowd drawn to the drop-dead-gorgeous indoor/outdoor setting, top-quality seafood menu, stellar cocktail scene, and the best ocean views in L.A., bar none. Book well ahead.

1602 Ocean Ave. (at Colorado Blvd.), Santa Monica. ☎ 310-458-9294. Internet: www.thelobster.com. Advance reservations highly recommended (2 weeks in advance for weekend dinner). Main courses: $9–$26 at lunch, $18–$39 (most under $30) at dinner. AE, DC, DISC, MC, V. Open: Lunch and dinner daily.

Mimosa

$$$ Los Angeles   FRENCH

Mimosa is a true slice of Provence — reinvented Hollywood style, of course. This traditional, tummy-pleasing country-French cooking deserves all the accolades it gets. Rustic standards like hearty cassoulet, steak frites, and Marseilles-style bouillabaise are served in the intimate butter-yellow dining room or out on the petite patio. And with a chic, Euro-trashy crowd at hand, the people-watching is almost as good as the eats.

8009 Beverly Blvd. (between Fairfax Ave. and La Cienega Blvd.). ☎ 323-655-8895. Internet: www.calendarlive.com/mimosa. Reservations recommended. Main courses: $9.50–$17.50 at lunch, $13–$25 at dinner. AE, DC, MC, V. Open: Lunch Mon–Fri, dinner Mon–Sat.

Nate 'n' Al's

$ Beverly Hills   DELI

L.A.'s best delicatessen is tucked away in the heart of 90210 territory. But don't expect any pretensions here — this is a true-blue Jewish deli through and through, from the white-aproned waitresses ("What'll ya have, hon?") to the homemade potato pancakes and kreplach. Comfort food hardly gets better.

414 N. Beverly Dr. (at Brighton Way), Beverly Hills. ☎ 310-274-0101. Main courses: $8–$13. AE, DISC, MC, V. To get there: I-405 to Santa Monica Blvd. east; turn right on Beverly Dr. Open: Breakfast, lunch, and dinner daily.

Patina

$$$$$ **Hollywood CALIFORNIA-FRENCH**

This supremely elegant Cal-French restaurant (more French than Cal, in my estimation) is one of L.A's finest places to eat, and a favorite place for locals to celebrate. Celeb chef Joachim Splichal keeps the kitchen in top form, and the dining room is as romantic as ever. Go to Spago if you're looking for gourmet glamour — but come here if you're looking for graceful understatement.

5955 Melrose Ave. (between Highland and Vine aves.). ☎ 323-467-1108. Internet: www.patinagroup.com. Reservations required. To get there: I-10 to La Brea Ave. north; follow Highland at split, turn right at Melrose. Main courses: $18–$32; tasting menu $79. AE, DC, DISC, JCB, MC, V. Open: Lunch Tues only, dinner nightly.

Pink's

$ **Hollywood HOT DOGS**

You can't miss the unpretentious take-out shack serving up L.A.'s favorite hot dog — just look for the clamoring crowds. To really experience the gourmet frank extraordinaire, order up a chili dog. Guaranteed to induce heartburn — the *good* kind.

709 N. La Brea Ave. (at Melrose Ave.). ☎ 323-931-4223. To get there: I-10 to La Brea Ave. north. Dogs: Less than $5. No credit cards. Open: Lunch, dinner, and late-night service daily.

Spago Beverly Hills

$$$$$ **Beverly Hills CALIFORNIA**

America's first celebrity chef, Wolfgang Puck, has created a fitting temple to California cuisine in his high-style signature restaurant. Expect accents from Puck's native Austria on the Cal-French menu, and a high glam factor in the crowd. Book a table on the twinkle-lit patio if the weather's nice — and if the elegant menu offers foie gras, don't pass it up. This place is excellent in every respect.

176 N. Canon Dr. (just north of Wilshire Blvd.), Beverly Hills. ☎ 310-385-0880. Internet: www.wolfgangpuck.com. Reservations a must. To get there: I-405 to Santa Monica Blvd. east; right on Wilshire Blvd. Main courses: $26–$35; tasting menu $85 ($125 with wine). AE, CB, DC, DISC, MC, V. Open: Lunch Mon–Sat, dinner nightly.

Swingers

$ Los Angeles AMERICAN

The best way to describe this place is classic-coffee-shop-meets-Kid-Rock, with a dash of *Love, American Style* retro-hip thrown in for good measure. The neo-diner grub is actually terrific, and nobody in town can beat the super-thick milkshakes. The restaurant is hugely popular with L.A.'s tattooed-and-pierced crowd — don't be surprised if you see a rock star roll in for breakfast (around 1 p.m., of course).

In the Beverly Laurel Motor Hotel, 8020 Beverly Blvd. (between Fairfax Ave. and La Cienega Blvd.). ☎ *323-653-5858. To get there: I-10 to La Cienega Blvd. north; right on Beverly. Main courses: $4.50–$11. AE, DISC, MC, V. Open: Breakfast, lunch, dinner, and late-night service daily.*

Valentino

$$$$$ Santa Monica ITALIAN

This supremely elegant Italian restaurant is a top choice for *amore* — but come anyway even if you don't have a lover in tow, because it's also one of the finest restaurants in the U.S. Just ask *Wine Spectator,* which named it one of the 10 best restaurants in 2000, singling out the wine cellar as peerless. The food is simple and stunning, the service at once impeccable and utterly soothing. For the ultimate seduction, ask owner Piero Selvaggio or one of his sophisticated minions to order for you.

3115 Pico Blvd. (west of Bundy Dr.), Santa Monica. ☎ *310-829-4313. Reservations required; jackets recommended for men. Main courses: $15–$30. AE, DC, MC, V. Open: Lunch Fri only, dinner Mon–Sat.*

Wolfgang Puck Cafe

$$ Universal City/Santa Monica/Hollywood CALIFORNIA

Turned off by the high prices — and pretensions — at Spago, but still interested in sampling cuisine from the man who brought gourmet pizzas to your grocer's freezer? These colorful, comfortable cafes serve up a more casual take on the quintessential California fare.

Universal CityWalk, 1000 Universal Center Dr., Universal City. ☎ *818-985-9653. Reservations accepted for 6 or more. To get there: U.S. 101 north to Universal Center Dr.; turn right. Main courses: $8–$18 (most under $15). AE, DC, MC, V. Open: Lunch and dinner daily.*

Also at: 1323 Montana Ave. (east of Ocean Ave.), Santa Monica; ☎ *310-393-0290. 8000 Sunset Blvd. (at Crescent Heights Blvd.), Hollywood;* ☎ *323-650-7300.*

Exploring L.A.'s Top Attractions

You can save a few bucks on admission fees to eight major attractions — including **Universal Studios, the Autry Museum of Western Heritage,** the **Petersen Automotive Museum, Hollywood's Egyptian Theatre,** the **Museum of Tolerance,** and the **Museum of Television & Radio** — by purchasing the pay-one-price *CityPass* for $49.75 ($38 for kids 3 to 11). You may not get to all the covered attractions, but because admission to Universal Studios alone is $41 ($31 for kids 3 to 11), you'll start saving with CityPass as long as you visit two additional attractions – not bad. You can purchase CityPass at any of the aforementioned attractions, or in advance from *Ticketweb* (☎ **310-641-TWEB;** www.ticketweb.com) or www.citypass.net.

Universal Studios Hollywood

Situated on the real Universal lot, the one-time studio tour has grown into a sizable theme park that will likely absorb an entire day.

The hour-long *Backlot Tram Tour* is still the heart of the matter. Tours take in such classic movie sites as the Bates Motel, plus a few silly-but-fun staged "disasters," including a not-so-secret one starring Jaws the shark. Silliness aside, this is an actual working studio, so you could see filming in action (though you're far more likely to see something happen on the Warner Bros. tour; see "Studio Tours," later in this chapter).

The rest of the fun is tied to more typical theme park—type rides and attractions, albeit with a movie slant. The big ones are impressively high-tech, especially the exciting new Terminator 2: 3D, a multisensory virtual adventure in Ah-nuld land, and the state-of-the-art, Spielberg-sanctioned Jurassic Park — The Ride. You may be sick of USA reruns, but don't skip Back to the Future — The Ride, a rollicking simulation-style ride that was the first of Universal's mega-budget thrill rides; it has stood the test of time well. You can rest your tootsies at one or two live-action shows; best are the WaterWorld stunt show (more fun than actually watching the Kevin Costner stinker) and Animal Actors, where fuzzy thespians get to strut their stuff.

You should come midweek if you can, preferably not in summer, to avoid long lines. Little ones will be plenty entertained, but the park really targets kids 7 and up. Adjoining the park is Universal's cartoony shopping-and-dining complex CityWalk (in case you haven't spent enough dough already), which boasts some very good after-park dinner options.

*100 Universal City Plaza, Universal City. ☎ **800-959-9688** or 818-662-3801. Internet: www.universalstudios.com. To get there: U.S. 101 to Universal Center Dr. or Lankershim Blvd. exit. Parking: $7. Admission: $41 adults, $36 seniors, $31 kids 3–11. Open: Daily 9 a.m.–7 p.m., 8 a.m.–10 p.m. mid-June–Labor Day; extended hours over spring breaks and holiday weekends.*

Hollywood Boulevard

Here is L.A. at its ticky-tacky worst. Still, if silver-screen history has drawn you to the city, you've got to see Hollywood Boulevard, because this is where it all began. The good news is that the boulevard is better than ever thanks to a massive (and still ongoing) makeover. Historic theaters have been restored, new museums have opened, and much of the grit and grime has been washed away. It'll be even shinier by the time you arrive, when the new **Hollywood & Highland** complex (www.hollywoodandhighland.com) between Highland and Orchid avenues, which was still a construction zone at this writing, will be going strong. The complex will include a state-of-the-art movie theater, the new **Renaissance Hollywood Hotel,** and at least a few retail shops.

Here are the boulevard's main tourist draws:

Hollywood Walk of Fame

Well more than 2,000 celebrities of stage, screen, and music have been honored along this literally star-studded sidewalk since Joanne Woodward received the first star on February 9, 1960.

You could spend hours browsing the stars; you're likely to tire of the activity before you exhaust the supply. Popular blocks include **Vine Street** just north of Hollywood Boulevard, where you'll find Judy Garland, haunted hero James Dean, Beatle John Lennon, and perennially misunderstood Marlon Brando.

Another good block is the south side of Hollywood Boulevard between **La Brea Avenue** and **Orange Drive,** where the chockablock sidewalk immortalizes Tom Hanks, Mary Tyler Moore, Walt Disney, Paul Newman, Sidney Poitier, and others. Elvis, fittingly, is on a little concrete island all by himself at 6777 Hollywood Blvd., at La Brea.

Call the Hollywood Chamber of Commerce at ☎ **323-463-8311** or check the official star directory at www.hollywoodcoc.org/walkoffame/frameset.html to find out where any specific star is located.

Want to see a celebrity earn his or her star? New stars are added to the legendary sidewalk as often as two or three times a month. You're invited to attend dedication ceremonies — an almost-guaranteed stargazing opportunity, because even the most famous honorees usually show up. Call the Hollywood Chamber of Commerce at ☎ **323-469-8311** for recorded info on who's being honored while you're in town.

Hollywood Blvd. between La Brea Ave. and Gower St.; also along Vine St. between Yucca St. (1 block north of Hollywood Blvd.) and Sunset Blvd. To get there: I-10 to La Brea Ave. north; or U.S. 101 north to Gower St., U.S. 101 south to Vine St. Parking: Various pay lots on and off Hollywood Blvd.

Mann's Chinese Theatre

Mann's Chinese is my favorite stop along the boulevard. I like the hand-
and footprint-filled forecourt of this legendary 1927 movie palace better
than the star-studded Walk of Fame, even though I feel like an Amazon
when I compare my shoe size to Elizabeth Taylor's — and even Sinatra's,
as a matter of fact. More recent impressions include Tom Cruise,
Mel Gibson, and Whoopi Goldberg.

*Between Orchid and Orange streets (☎ **323-464-6266** or 323-461-3331;* www.
manntheatres.com/chinese.html*). The forecourt is free and open to all;
first-run features are $9.*

Also of note along the boulevard are the following attractions:

The **El Capitan Theatre**, 6838 Hollywood Blvd., between Orange and
Highland avenues (☎ 323-468-8262), shows first-run films in the
gorgeously restored 1925 theater where Orson Welles premiered
Citizen Kane.

The **Egyptian Theatre,** at no. 6712, between Las Palmas and McCadden
(☎ 323-461-2020 or 323-466-3456; www.egyptiantheatre.com), is
another beautifully restored theater, this one from 1922. The Egyptian
screens American Cinematheque's hourlong *Forever Hollywood,* a
Tinseltown retrospective, plus rare and classic films.

The Guinness World of Records, at 6764 Hollywood Blvd. (☎ 323-
463-6433), is not really worth the $14.95 adults, $8.95 kids that you pay
to get into this place, though I should note that it's housed in
Hollywood's first movie house, which is now a registered landmark.

The **Frederick's of Hollywood Museum,** 6608 Hollywood Blvd. (☎ 323-
466-8506), is free and far more entertaining than most attractions
along the strip. Even if you don't need a new bra or panties or don't
plan to buy one for your sweetie, stop in to see the Celebrity Lingerie
Hall of Fame, which celebrates stars who made their names with the
aid of slinky underthings, from Milton Berle to Madonna.

Stop into **Musso & Frank's Grill,** 6667 Hollywood Blvd., at Cahuenga
(☎ 323-467-7788 or 323-467-5123), when you're ready for a break. Gone
are the days when Orson Welles held court, but little else has changed
at this legendary grill room: The waiters still wear kelly-green waist-
coats, the veggies come julienned, and the martinis remain the best in
town. Most people come for the marvelous old Hollywood vibe, as the
cooking is merely agreeable.

When you're done, head to Hollywood and Vine Street and turn north
to take a peek at the **Capitol Records Building,** one of Hollywood's
most recognizable landmarks, which really does look like a stack of
45s on a turntable (whether they meant it or not).

Lastly, look into the hills to see the **Hollywood Sign,** whose nine 50-
foot-high sheet-metal letters, which extend for 450 feet across, never
let anybody forget where they really are. For the best view, head south
to the corner of Sunset Boulevard and Bronson Avenue and look up.

Museum Row

Along Wilshire Boulevard in the Miracle Mile area lies L.A.'s greatest concentration of museums, including three standouts. To get there, take I-10 to Fairfax Ave. north.

Los Angeles County Museum of Art

The Getty Center (see the "More Surprisingly Terrific Museums" later in this chapter) is worth seeing for the house, but this museum complex (itself a wacko marriage of architectural styles) is the place to come if you want to see first-rate art collections. Most impressive is the Japanese Pavilion (the only building outside of Japan dedicated to Japanese art), which has shoji-like exterior walls that let in soft natural light, allowing you to see the magnificent collection as it was meant to be seen. The museum also excels at modern and contemporary works, and includes a mind-blowing Dada collection. You can also see a terrific costumes and textiles collection, excellent Southeast Asian and pre-Columbian galleries, and more. Because LACMA usually draws in the high-profile traveling collections (Van Gogh, Pharoahs of the Sun, and so forth), the special exhibitions are standouts more often than not.

LACMA can easily occupy you for an entire day, but I suggest not trying to see the whole place. Instead, pick up a map upon arrival, dedicate three hours to those areas that most interest you, and then move on to another museum along the Row for something completely different.

5905 Wilshire Blvd. (between Fairfax and La Brea aves.). ☎ *323-857-6000. Internet:* www.lacma.org. *Parking: Pay lots at Spaulding and Ogden drives. Admission: $7 adults, $5 seniors and students, $1 kids 6–17; free to all second Tues of the month. There may be an additional charge for special exhibits. Open: Mon–Tues and Thurs noon–8 p.m., Fri noon–9 p.m., Sat–Sun 11 a.m.–8 p.m.*

The Page Museum at La Brea Tar Pits

This bunker-like, semi-subterranean museum makes for a fascinating couple of hours. It sits right next to the source of its collections: A gooey, oily swamp that lured Ice Age critters with the promise of a drink and swallowed them up whole, preserving them for scientific posterity. Scientists have recovered thousands of mammals, birds, amphibians, and insects, including fantastical ones like saber-toothed cats, giant sloths, and woolly mammoths. Observation decks are erected over the pits, which include life-size replicas of some of the critters that were victims of the goo. Inside the museum, watch the short but fascinating film documenting the recoveries; you can also see scientists clean and repair recovered bones. Interactive exhibits bring home the scientific story to the kids.

5801 Wilshire Blvd. (just east of Fairfax Ave.). ☎ *323-934-7243 or 323-936-2230. Internet:* www.tarpits.org. *Parking: $5 with museum validation. Admission: $6 adults, $3.50 seniors and students, $2 kids 5–10. Open: Mon–Fri 9:30 a.m.–5 p.m., Sat–Sun 10 a.m.–5 p.m.*

Petersen Automotive Museum

The quintessential southern California museum is dedicated to — what else? — car culture. Four floors creatively display more than 200 sets of wheels, from the first Ford Model Ts to groovy hot rods, one-of-a-kind movie rides, and cars of the future. This terrific museum is a real blast — and so mythically, marvelously L.A. It is well worth a couple of hours; put it high on your sightseeing list.

6060 Wilshire Blvd. (at Fairfax Ave.). ☎ *323-930-2277. Internet:* www.petersen.org. *Parking: $4.50. Admission: $7 adults, $5 seniors and students, $3 kids 5–12. Open: Tues–Sun 10 a.m.–6 p.m.*

Also along Museum Row are a two special-interest museums of note: The **Carol & Barry Kaye Museum of Miniatures,** 5900 Wilshire Blvd., across from LACMA (☎ **323-937-6464;** www.museumofminiatures.com), the largest collection of miniature reproductions in the world; and the **Southwest Museum at LACMA West,** 6067 Wilshire Blvd., at Fairfax Ave (☎ **323-933-4510;** www.southwestmuseum.org), a satellite of downtown's Southwest Museum that focuses on Native American art and culture.

More surprisingly terrific museums

Autry Museum of Western Heritage

The Singing Cowboy himself, Gene Autry, founded one of California's finest museums. It chronicles the history of the American West from European-conquest-and-pioneer days (the good, the bad, and the ugly) through the Hollywoodization of the "Wild West." The first-rate collection is thoughtfully displayed from start to finish; even the lunch boxes have something to say about popular representations and the "merchandising" of the west. Lots of artifacts, film footage, and workshop-style fun for the kids (check the online calendar), plus notable special exhibits. Combine it with other Griffith Park sightseeing (see "Playing at Griffith Park," later in this chapter) for a solid half-day full of fun.

In Griffith Park, 4700 Western Heritage Way (across from the L.A. Zoo). ☎ *323-667-2000. Internet:* www.autry-museum.org. *To get there: I-5 north to Griffith Park or Zoo Dr. exit; or, from Los Feliz Blvd., go north on Riverside Dr. Parking: Free! Admission: $7.50 adults, $5 seniors and students, $3 kids 2–12. Open: Tues–Wed 10 a.m.–5 p.m., Thurs 10 a.m.–8 p.m., Fri–Sun 10 a.m.–5 p.m.*

Getty Center

If you're not the Universal Studios type, chances are good that you're coming to L.A. to see this high-profile arts center, which opened to great acclaim in late 1997 and houses 20th-century millionaire (sounds so quaint now, doesn't it?) J. Paul Getty's enormous collection of art. The collection includes not only the antiquities that were at the old Getty Museum, but also early Renaissance and Impressionist paintings (including van Gogh's *Irises*), French decorative arts, illuminated manuscripts, and contemporary photography and graphic arts.

The galleries are state of the art and the collections extensive, but, as a whole, not nearly as impressive as what you can see at LACMA (which also mounts the best traveling exhibitions) or, even better, the Norton Simon (detailed later in this section). Ultimately, Richard Meier's ultra-modern complex is the real draw. It presides over the landscape with appropriate grandeur, and the views are stunning. The alfresco spaces are as impressive as the interior ones, particularly the circular gardens.

The need for parking reservations is legend when it comes to the Getty. However, because the community hasn't embraced the new center like it did the old museum — and there's simply more available parking here — getting a reservation is much easier than it used to be. Still, book your reservation before you leave home, both to get your first-choice day and time and generally to avoid disappointment. Call as much as a month in advance for weekend and summer visits. (At press time, college students with valid ID did not need parking reservations, but it's a good idea to con-firm the continuance of this policy.) You may want to make dining reser-vations at the same time, but I found the restaurant to be disappointing and suggest skipping it. (The museum offers casual munchies, too.)

You'll park at the base and take a tram up the hill. Because the process is somewhat time-consuming, don't bother coming unless you have at least 3 or 4 hours to spare.

A great way to avoid the crowds is to visit later in the afternoon, espe-cially on Thursday or Friday, when the center remains open until 9 p.m. The sunset and after-dark panoramic views are marvelous, and the Westside and Santa Monica are convenient for a late dinner.

1200 Getty Center Dr., above Brentwood. ☎ *310-440-7300. Internet: www.getty.edu. To get there: I-405 to the Getty Center Dr. exit. Parking: $5; reser-vations required. Admission: Tues–Wed 11 a.m.–7 p.m., Thurs–Fri 11 a.m.–9 p.m., Sat–Sun 10 a.m.–6 p.m.*

You may want to pair your visit to the Getty Center with a stop at the new (and also strikingly modern) **Skirball Center**, 2701 N. Sepulveda Blvd., at Mulholland Drive (☎ **310-440-4500**; www.skirball.org), whose galleries focus on the marriage of Jewish life and the American Dream. It's quickly establishing a reputation for top-flight temporary exhibits, too. To get to the Skirball Center, take I-405 one exit north, to Skirball Center Drive, or just follow Sepulveda up the hill. Admission is $8 adults, $6 seniors and students, free for kids under 12. Open Tuesday through Saturday from noon to 5 p.m., Sunday from 11 a.m. to 5 p.m.

Museum of Television & Radio

This museum has a few galleries to see, but the real heart of the matter are the private consoles, which allow you to conjure up your favorite moments of broadcast history, from the Beatles' first appearance on Ed Sullivan to the crumbling of the Berlin Wall. Open screenings can range from "Laurence Olivier: Four Crowning Achievements" to "The World of Hanna-Barbera"; call or check the site for the current calendar. There's a 2-hour limit on the consoles — but if no one is waiting, getting a second library pass for a second 2 hours is easy.

465 N. Beverly Dr. (at Little Santa Monica Blvd.), Beverly Hills. ☎ *310-786-1000. Internet:* www.mtr.org. *To get there: I-405 to Santa Monica Blvd.; go 3 miles east, then right on Beverly Dr. Parking: $1 per hour; first 2 hours free. Admission: $6 adults, $4 seniors and students, $3 kids under 13. Open: Wed noon–5 p.m., Thurs noon–9 p.m., Fri–Sun noon–5 p.m.*

Norton Simon Museum of Art

Packaged-foods mogul Norton Simon gathered a mind-blowing art collection, now housed on the Rose Parade route (and under the direction of his widow, actress Jennifer Jones). It's a stunning — and undisputedly excellent — assemblage of European painting and sculpture spanning the 14th through 20th centuries, with the masters extremely well represented. The museum is well worth an afternoon excursion for serious art lovers.

411 W. Colorado Blvd. (at Orange Grove Blvd.), Pasadena. ☎ *626-449-6840. Internet:* www.nortonsimon.org. *To get there: I-110 north to Orange Grove exit and go north to Colorado. Parking: Free! Admission: $6, $3 seniors; at press time, free for students and kids. Open: Wed–Thurs noon–6 p.m., Fri noon–9 p.m., Sat–Sun noon–6 p.m.*

*If you're planning a trip to the Norton Simon, you may also want to budget time for the **Gamble House**, on Orange Grove Boulevard, just three blocks north of Colorado (☎ 626-793-3334;* www.gamblehouse.org*), one of the most spectacular examples of arts-and-crafts architecture in existence. One-hour tours are offered Thursday through Sunday every 20 minutes between noon and 3 p.m.; they often sell out, so come early and wear flat shoes (a requirement). Tickets are $5, $4 for seniors, $3 students.*

Hitting the beaches

The following sections describe L.A.'s best beaches as they run along PCH (Highway 1) from south to north.

Venice Beach and Ocean Front Walk

Starting at Venice Boulevard and running north to Rose Avenue is L.A.'s beach scene at its wackiest, wildest, and sleaziest. The sand is less the draw than the continuous carnival on the paved promenade known as **Ocean Front Walk** that runs along the beach, where vendors sell dirt-cheap merchandise from sunglasses to silly tchotchkes, and busking entertainers run the gamut from talking-parrot wranglers to chainsaw jugglers to Armageddon-obsessed evangelists. The constant crowd is the city's most eye-popping, and includes plenty of muscle-bound pretty boys, buxom beach bunnies on in-line skates, and tattooed biker types and their chicks.

Head elsewhere if you want to relax on the sand; come here for the color. Look in the blocks east of Pacific Avenue for a street parking space, or west of Pacific Avenue for a pay lot.

Santa Monica Beach and Pier

As you move north on Ocean Front Walk and cross into Santa Monica, the scene gets appreciably prettier and more subdued. The walk opens up for bikers and skaters, the beach is more suitable for playing and sunbathing, the bay waters are calm, and the food options and facilities improve.

The best beach access is along Bernard Way, which runs parallel to Ocean Avenue (called Neilson Way here) along the ocean from Marine Street (two blocks north of Rose Avenue) to Pico Boulevard. The scene is very relaxed; this is where locals come to kick back. The sands are wide, white, flat, and gorgeous, with grassy areas great for picnicking, good facilities, a playground, and lots of parking.

Those looking for a livelier scene and more facilities may prefer gathering midbeach on either side of the **Santa Monica Pier** (☎ 310-458-8900; www.santamonicapier.org), at the end of Colorado Avenue. After some years of neglect, the landmark wooden amusement pier is back in top form. It boasts a number of snack shacks and attractions, including a turn-of-the-century carousel (☎ 310-458-8867). **Pacific Park** (☎ 310-260-8744; www.pacpark.com) is a fun zone with a roller coaster, a dozen other rides, and old-fashioned midway games. You can also stop in **Playland Arcade** (☎ 310-451-5133) for high-tech arcade games. Below the carousel, at beach level, is the **UCLA Ocean Discovery Center**, 1600 Ocean Front Walk (☎ 310-393-6149; www.odc.ucla.edu), where you can learn a thing or two about the Santa Monica Bay marine environment (admission $3).

Weekends and summer daytimes are best for experiencing all the pier has to offer. If you're visiting at another time, call the specific attractions that catch your interest before you go to avoid disappointment. The pier is about a mile up Ocean Front Walk from Venice; it makes a great round-trip stroll.

North of the pier along Ocean Avenue is **Palisades Park,** a lovely, grassy blufftop park with benches. Anyplace along here is a good place to stop and take in the stunning ocean views; you'll find lots of metered parking (getting a spot is generally easier as you go north).

Rent bikes, in-line skates, boogie boards, baby joggers, beach chairs, and umbrellas from **Perry's Beach Cafe** (www.perryscafe.com), south of the pier at 2400 and 2600 Ocean Front Walk, at Ocean Park Boulevard (☎ 310-372-3138); and north of the pier at 930 and 1200 Pacific Coast Hwy. (☎ 310-458-3975 or 310-451-2021). Bike and skate rentals run $6 per hour or $18 per day ($4 and $12 for kids). Call for info on skate lessons if you're a newbie.

Santa Monica & Malibu Beaches

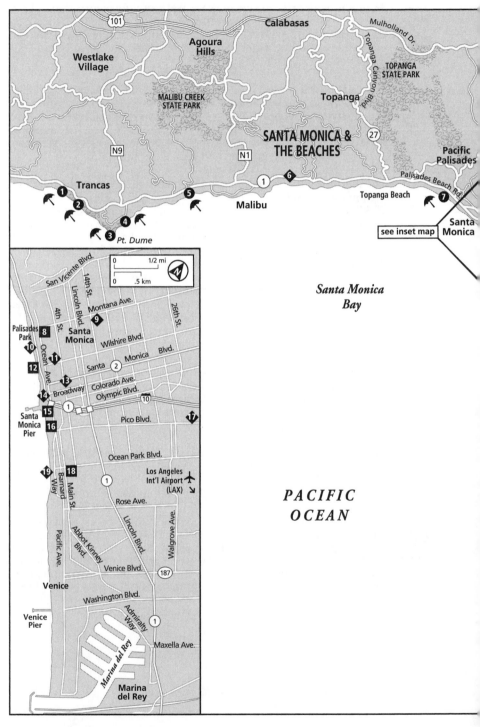

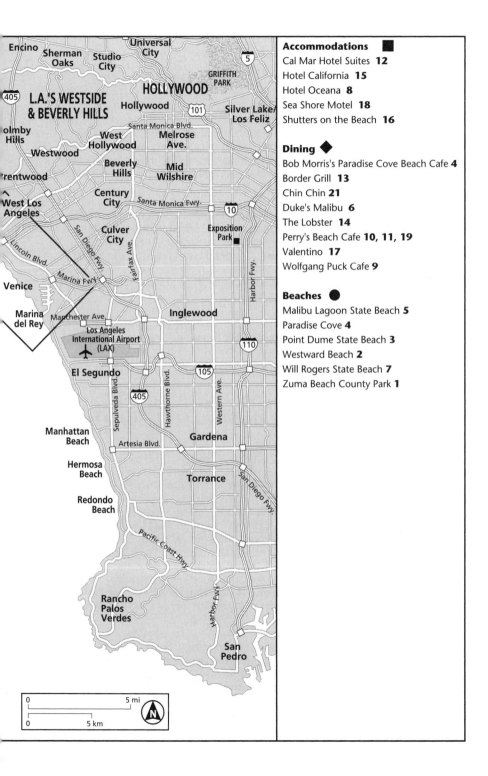

Accommodations ■
Cal Mar Hotel Suites **12**
Hotel California **15**
Hotel Oceana **8**
Sea Shore Motel **18**
Shutters on the Beach **16**

Dining ◆
Bob Morris's Paradise Cove Beach Cafe **4**
Border Grill **13**
Chin Chin **21**
Duke's Malibu **6**
The Lobster **14**
Perry's Beach Cafe **10, 11, 19**
Valentino **17**
Wolfgang Puck Cafe **9**

Beaches ●
Malibu Lagoon State Beach **5**
Paradise Cove **4**
Point Dume State Beach **3**
Westward Beach **2**
Will Rogers State Beach **7**
Zuma Beach County Park **1**

Encino
Sherman Oaks
Studio City
Universal City
GRIFFITH PARK
HOLLYWOOD
Hollywood
Silver Lake/Los Feliz
L.A.'S WESTSIDE & BEVERLY HILLS
Santa Monica Blvd.
olmby Hills
West Hollywood
Melrose Ave.
Westwood
Beverly Hills
Mid Wilshire
rentwood
Century City
Santa Monica Fwy.
West Los Angeles
Culver City
Exposition Park
Venice
Marina del Rey
Manchester Ave.
Inglewood
Los Angeles International Airport ✈ (LAX)
El Segundo
Manhattan Beach
Artesia Blvd.
Gardena
Hermosa Beach
Torrance
Redondo Beach
Pacific Coast Hwy.
Rancho Palos Verdes
San Pedro
San Diego Fwy.
Lincoln Blvd.
Marina Fwy.
Fairfax Ave.
Harbor Fwy.
Sepulveda Blvd.
Hawthorne Blvd.
Western Ave.
Harbor Fwy.

0   5 mi
0   5 km

The Malibu beaches

An alternative to coming up through Santa Monica to reach these beaches is to head west on Sunset Boulevard for a gorgeous, winding drive. Turn left on Temescal Canyon Road (follow the "to PCH" signs) to reach Will Rogers Beach; continue on Sunset all the way to PCH and turn right to reach the others.

Will Rogers State Beach, which runs from Temescal Canyon Road north to Sunset Boulevard, is where the Malibu vibe begins. The Temescal (south) section of the beach is especially nice — wide, flat, and pretty, with calm, swimmer-friendly surf, lifeguards, a snack bar, restrooms, beach-toy rentals, and easy parking ($2). Surfers hang out at the north end, near Sunset.

Malibu Lagoon State Beach, the curvaceous dark-sand beach and natural wetlands north of the Malibu Pier, is extremely popular with surfers. Swimming is allowed only in a small area near the pier, where the waters are protected by rocky shallows. Come instead to watch the locals hang-ten on the waves; weekends or after-work hours are best. The entrance is just south of Cross Creek Road. Parking is $2; do as the locals do and park along PCH to save the bucks.

If you want to rent a surfboard — smart only if you already know what you're doing — head to **Zuma Jay Surfboards,** about a ¼-mile south of Malibu Pier at 22775 PCH (☎ **310-456-8044;** www.zumajay.com). Surfboards are $20 for the day, wetsuits $8. You can also rent body-boards and kayaks.

Nearby is **Duke's Malibu,** 21150 PCH, at Las Flores Canyon (☎ **310-317-0777;** www.hulapie.com), for tropical-themed eats and drinks as well as stellar ocean views.

Paradise Cove is nestled well off the highway at the base of a cliff at 28128 PCH, a mile south of Kanan Dume Road. This lovely private cove beach is pricey to visit but well worth the dough if you're looking for a pretty place to spend the day. The beach is just a narrow curve, but a small parking lot keeps the crowds at bay. Come early (before noon on weekends); the $20 parking charge ($5 for walk-ins) keeps out the riff-raff, but plenty of families are more than happy to shell out for such a private haven. The waters are especially calm and well-protected, and therefore great for little ones. Claim your blanket space at the south end if you plan to spend the whole day, as the north end becomes shaded by mid-afternoon. On-site is **Bob Morris's Paradise Cove Beach Cafe,** plus picnic tables, rest rooms, and nice changing rooms with showers.

Zuma Beach County Park is L.A.'s largest beach playground. Zuma starts a mile north of Kanan Dume Road (watch for the turnoff on the right, which takes you under the highway). Beach-goers pack the more than 2 miles of sand on warm summer weekends. They're drawn by the wide sand beach and comprehensive facilities, including lifeguards, volleyball courts, swing sets, snack bars, and beach-toy rentals. Restrooms are strategically placed along the beach, so you're never far from a bathroom. The wide expanse of sand (and even wider parking lot) means that street noise isn't a big problem, especially when the revelers kick into high gear. Come midweek to have plenty of sand for yourself, on the weekend to catch the scene. Parking is $2; bring exact change in the off-season, as the fee is collected automatically.

You can separate yourself from the masses and the highway noise by heading to **Westward Beach,** hidden by sandstone cliffs at the south end of Zuma. To get there, turn left at Westward Beach Road (at the Malibu Country Inn), two minutes after the Heathercliff Road light (just before the right-hand turnoff for Zuma). At the end of Westward Beach Road is a $6 parking lot for **Point Dume State Beach,** another wonderful stretch of sand below the cliffs.

Being there: Attending TV show tapings

Attending the taping of your favorite (or any) TV show is a great way to see Hollywood at work — and maybe a famous face or two up close and in person.

Your best source is Audiences Unlimited (☎ **818-753-3470;** www. tvtickets.com), which distributes free tickets for most sitcoms (including *Friends, That 70s Show,* and *Everybody Loves Raymond*), plus *Whose Line Is It Anyway?,* a few talk and game shows, and pilots and specials. They're organized, informative, and fully sanctioned by production companies and networks. (In fact, they do such a good job that ABC doesn't even bother handling direct requests anymore.) The Web site is a great place to start. You can order tickets 60 days in advance over the phone, or 30 days in advance over the Web site.

You can also get tickets from some of the networks or shows directly. For *Politically Incorrect with Bill Maher,* call ☎ **323-575-4321** to make a first-come, first-served reservation, or order online at www.abc.com/pi.

The Price is Right tickets are generally available between a day and a week in advance; call ☎ **323-575-2458** or stop by the CBS ticket window at Beverly Boulevard and Fairfax Avenue (next to the Farmer's Market) during business hours.

For information on how to get tickets to shows taped at NBC Studios, 3000 W. Alameda Ave., Burbank, including *The Tonight Show with Jay Leno,* call ☎ **818-840-3537.** Or, after you're in town, stop by the ticket office in Burbank off California Street (take Highway 134 to Buena Vista exit and turn left; follow signs for "TV Tickets") for same-day tickets (the earlier the better, 8 a.m. if you have hopes for Leno tickets). NBC also operates a ticket booth at **Universal CityWalk** (see "Shopping 'til You Drop" later in this chapter), in the alley next to the Nature Company, which almost always has tickets available for something.

Paramount Pictures offers tickets to network sitcoms taped on its Melrose Avenue lot. Tickets become available up to five days in advance; call ☎ **323-956-5575,** or go online to www.paramountshowtickets.com.

Tickets are sometimes given away outside popular sites like Mann's Chinese on Hollywood Boulevard, as well as at visitor information centers (see "Gathering More Information" later in this chapter).

Pickings can be slim from April through July, when most series are on hiatus. Getting tickets to a big show like *Friends* or Leno is always harder than getting tickets to an as-yet-unaired new show or a five-days-a-week daytime gabfest, so start doing your homework well in advance if you have your heart set on seeing a ratings king. Allot four hours for a taping, and *always* bring a sweater (anybody who watches Letterman knows it's freezing in TV studios). If you have kids in tow, check age limits. If you'd like to be in the audience (or a contestant) on your favorite game show, your best bet is to watch the closing credits and contact the show directly.

Heading downtown for some history

The heart of historic L.A. is the **El Pueblo de Los Angeles Historic Monument,** across from Union Station, bounded by Alameda Street, U.S. 101, Spring Street, and Cesar E. Chavez Avenue (☎ **213-628-3562;** www.cityofla.org/elp). Despite some touristy schlock, this is a fun place to spend a couple of hours and get a taste of what Los Angeles may have been like before anyone ever even dreamed of motion pictures. Some of L.A.'s oldest buildings are in this colorful quarter, and the festive marketplace is rich with Latino flavor.

To get there, take U.S. 101 to the Broadway or Alameda exits. Parking is plentiful at pay lots; the most convenient are just north of the freeway on the west side of Main Street.

Start out at the Visitors Center, in the 1887 **Sepulveda House,** 622 N. Main St. (open Monday to Saturday from 10 a.m. to 3 p.m.), or at the information desk on the plaza at the end of Olvera Street, where you can pick up an orientation map. (Free guided tours leave from the desk Wednesday through Saturday at 10 a.m., 11 a.m., and noon.) Come on Saturday for the liveliest crowd as well as entertainment on the plaza; cruise past **Mission Nuestra Señora Reina de Los Angeles,** the prime structure on the west side of Main Street, and you're likely to see more than one Mexican-American wedding going on — quite a treat! The prime area to target is pedestrian-only **Olvera Street,** lined with ticky-tacky market stalls, food stands, and sit-down Mexican restaurants, the best of which is **La Golondrina,** a festive cafe at West-17 Olvera St. (☎ **213-628-4349;** www.lagolondrina.com) with bathtub-sized margaritas and generous combo platters. **Avila Adobe,** the city's oldest building (1818) at E-10 Olvera St., is worth a peek (open daily from 10 a.m. to 4 p.m.).

Playing at Griffith Park

Hilly, 4,000-acre **Griffith Park** (☎ 323-913-4688; www.cityofla.
org/RAP/grifmet/gp) is the nation's largest public park (five times as
large as New York's Central Park). It has a number of attractions worth
seeking out, and also makes a good place to unwind or let the kids run
off steam if you tire of the urban madness. The park is open daily from
6 a.m. to 10 p.m. To get there, take I-5 north to the Griffith Park or Zoo
Drive exit; or, from Los Feliz Boulevard, go north on Western Avenue,
Vermont Avenue, or Riverside Drive. For an overview, drive the loop
road that winds from the top of Western Avenue, past Griffith
Observatory, and down to Vermont Avenue.

In addition to the **Autry Museum of Western Heritage** (see "More
Surprisingly Terrific Museums" earlier in this chapter), the park's other
biggest attraction is the **Griffith Observatory,** 2800 E. Observatory Rd.,
at the end of Vermont Ave. (☎ **323-664-1191;** www.griffithobs.org).
The observatory houses a planetarium featuring narrated sky shows, a
Hall of Science with cosmic-minded exhibits, and some mind-boggling tel-
escopes through which you can view the cosmos after dark. Planetarium
admission is $4 adults, $3 seniors, $2 kids 5 to 12; all other exhibits are
free. Open Tuesday through Friday from 2 to 10 p.m., Saturday and
Sunday from 12:30 to 10 p.m. (from 12:30 p.m. daily in summer). But most
people don't even go inside; they just come to see the spectacular observatory itself, built in 1935 and made famous in *Rebel Without a Cause*. The
nighttime views from here are simply spectacular.

At the **Travel Town Transportation Museum,** 5200 Zoo Dr. (☎ **323-662-
5874**), where kids can climb aboard vintage trains. The adjacent **Los
Angeles Live Steamers** (☎ **323-664-9678**) can take you choo-chooing
on a scale-model steam train. Travel Town also rents bikes for two-
wheel exploring (☎ **323-662-6573**). Also in the park is the **Los Angeles
Zoo** (☎ **323-644-6400;** www.lazoo.org), not one of the city's best
attractions; I say skip it.

Seeing L.A. by guided tour

An introductory tour is a good bet for those of you with limited
time to explore the city. **Starline Tours** (☎ **800-959-3131;** www.
starlinetours.com) offers a dozen or so guided mini-van tours
through La La Land, with prices starting at $35 adults, $26 kids 3 to 11,
for the basic 2-hour **Movie Stars' Homes Tour,** which includes the
Playboy Mansion and Aaron Spelling's even bigger manse. This tour
leaves from Mann's Chinese Theatre every half-hour daily from 10 a.m.
to 6 p.m.; reserve longer tours a day in advance.

Euro-Pacific Tours (☎ **800-303-3005** or **310-574-0595;** www.
euro-pacific-tours.com) offers similar movie-stars-homes
and full-city tours, with prices starting at $30 adults, $22 kids.

Studio tours

The best of the studio tours, by far, is the **Warner Bros. VIP Studio Tour,** 4000 Warner Blvd., Burbank (☎ **818-972-8687;** www.studio-tour.com). The 2 ½-hour tour starts out with a short WB film retrospective and accelerates into a real-life golf-cart ride through the working lot, offering insight into the modern studio system as you go. The itinerary depends on what's happening on the lot at the time, but the guide makes a signifi-cant effort to show you something exciting. On my last (incognito) visit, we got to see a rehearsal of *Suddenly Susan* (complete with Brooke Shields) and spent a fascinating half-hour in the state-of-the-art sound-editing studio. Tours run weekdays between 9 a.m. and 4 p.m., and reser-vations are your best bet. Tickets are $30; kids under 10 are not admitted. To get there, take U.S. 101 north (the Hollywood Freeway) to Barham Boulevard exit and turn right; or Highway 134 to Pass Avenue, left on Riverside Drive, right on Hollywood Way.

The far side of fame

The former Hollywood Memorial Park, now **Hollywood Forever**, 6000 Santa Monica Blvd. (between Gower and Van Ness streets), Hollywood (☎ **323-469-1181**), is the resting place of many of early Hollywood's biggest names, from Rudolph Valentino and Cecil B. DeMille to Alfalfa from *The Little Rascals*. The new owners have spiffed up the place nicely and embrace its status as a bona-fide sightseeing attraction, so they're very friendly to sightseers. Stop in at the office to pick up a free map for a self-guided tour (open 8:30 a.m. to 5 p.m. on weekdays, 10 a.m. to 4 p.m. on weekends), or call for the current schedule of guided tours (offered most days).

Suggested 1-, 2-, and 3-Day Itineraries

Chances are good that, above all else, you came to L.A. to see **Universal Studios**, especially if you have kids in tow. So why not start **Day 1** there? Go early to make the most of the day, and start with a morning **Backlot Tram Tour** to get a feel for the place. Around noon, exit the park and head next door to CityWalk, where the lunch options are better. You'll find the **Wolfgang Puck Cafe** (see "Dining Out" earlier in this chapter), plus a half-dozen or so additional choices. After your tummies are full, head back into the park for the afternoon.

If you're not the Universal Studios type, spend your first day museum hopping. Spend the morning at the **Getty Center**, which requires advance parking reservations (see "More surprisingly terrific muse-ums" earlier in this chapter). After lunch, head over to Museum Row to catch some of the fine collections there — both the **Petersen Automotive Museum** and the **Page Museum at the La Brea Tar Pits** make for a nice change of pace.

If you haven't made a Getty Center reservation, start out on Museum Row, then head into **Griffith Park** to see the **Autry Museum of Western Heritage** after lunch. No matter which way you work it, the **Farmer's Market** (see "Dining Out") makes an ideal lunch stop.

Because you've had such a busy day, make dinner a low-key affair. If you have the kids, consider **Chin Chin** or **El Cholo**. If not, **Ca'Brea** is a nice, relaxing choice (see "Dining Out"). Follow up with a few laughs with improv meisters the **Groundlings** or catch some live music at **Largo** (see "Living It Up After Dark" later in this chapter).

Day 2

Dedicate **Day 2** to the real side of Hollywood (well, the more real side, anyway). Arrange in advance to take the insightful **Warner Bros. Studio Tour** in the morning. Start out with a hearty breakfast at one of the stars' favorite diners; the **Hollywood Hills Coffee Shop** (see "Dining Out") is a great choice, because it's right next to the on-ramp for the 101 freeway, which will whisk you right to the studio post-pancakes. If you haven't already arranged to attend a late-afternoon TV taping (see "Attending TV Show Tapings" earlier in this chapter), arrive in Burbank a bit early so that you can swing by the **NBC Studios** first to see if you can get any last-minute tickets for the day's tapings.

Spend the afternoon strolling **Hollywood Boulevard.** Or, if you've had enough of the silver-screen side of things, head to **Griffith Park** for some playtime with the kids, or go shopping. If Melrose or West 3rd Street is on the spending agenda, start out with lunch at **Sweet Lady Jane's,** on Melrose two blocks east of La Cienega (☎ **323-653-7145**), where the elegant salads and homemade soups are merely a prelude to the divine sweets.

If you're holding tickets to a TV taping, be sure to arrive early. Plan on dinner afterward, followed by some nightclubbing along the Sunset Strip if you're in a rock 'n' roll mood. Or, if a TV show isn't in the cards, plan on catching a play tonight.

Day 3

On **Day 3,** go to the beach. Head to Santa Monica in the morning and rent some bikes or in-line skates to cruise along Ocean Front Walk, or play on the pier, or just kick back on the sand for a couple of hours. Head over to Main Street for an easygoing lunch at an open-air cafe — the **Rose Cafe**, on the border between Santa Monica and Venice at Main Street and Rose Avenue (☎ **310-399-0711**), is one of my favorites — and maybe a little strolling and shopping.

In the afternoon, head to **Venice Beach** to catch the oddball human carnival. Or take a scenic drive to check out Malibu's fine beaches, stopping for an afternoon refreshment at **Duke's Malibu** or the cafe on the beach at **Paradise Cove** (see "Hitting the Beaches" earlier in this chapter). Stay in Santa Monica for dinner — you can't go wrong at **Border Grill** (see "Dining Out") for first-rate Mexican, followed by some after-dinner strolling along the lively **Third Street Promenade** (see "Shopping 'til You Drop" later in this chapter).

Or, if you're in the mood to splurge, head back to your hotel to clean up, then set out for elegant cocktails with a view at **Yamashiro,** or with a paper umbrella at **Trader Vic's** (see "Living it Up After Dark"). Follow with dinner at one of L.A.'s terrific special-occasion restaurants, such as **Patina** or **Spago Beverly Hills** (see " Dining Out"), to celebrate the success of your visit to L.A.

Shopping 'til You Drop

Ardent shoppers won't lack for diversions in Los Angeles. What follows are L.A.'s finest hunting grounds.

Santa Monica

If I had to pick one place to shop in L.A., it would be this charming, multifaceted beach town.

Third Street Promenade

This sunny pedestrian-only walk is a real crowd-pleaser, with something for everyone: record shops (both independents and chains), bookstores (**Borders Books & Music** and specialty shops), and familiar clothing chains and one-off boutiques. It's a browser's delight, and most stores stay open for after-dinner shopping. Take I-10 to 4th Street and park in a structure between 4th and 2nd streets.

Main Street

This hip, casual strip is the place to find the beach vibe in Santa Monica shopping. The nice mix of national favorites, one-of-a-kind boutiques, and sidewalk cafes between Rose Avenue and Strand (north of Ocean Park Boulevard) makes for a lovely stroll. Check out www.main-streetsm.com.

Bergamot Station

Bergamot Station is the city's top stop for contemporary art. Twenty beautifully browsable galleries run the gamut from Japanese paper to jewelry, painting, and sculpture. At 2525 Michigan Ave. (☎ 310-829-5854; www.bergamotstation.com); take I-405 to Cloverfield/26th Street, turn right on Cloverfield Boulevard, and right on Michigan; parking is free and plentiful.

Montana Avenue

This grown-up shopping strip at the upscale north end of town is wonderful for one-of-a-kind browsing. The best boutiquing is just east of 9th Street, where you'll find lots of casually elegant clothing boutiques for women. Visit www.montanaave.com for a rundown.

West L.A.

Skip the creatively challenged, teen-targeted shopping in **Westwood Village** and head to **Rhino Records,** 1720 Westwood Blvd., one block north of Santa Monica Boulevard (☎ **310-474-8685**). This record collector's dream of a new/used store spawned the wildly successful retro record label.

Beverly Hills's Golden Triangle

This world-famous corner of couture is more accessible than you may think. Anchoring the retail area north of Wilshire Boulevard between Santa Monica Boulevard and Rexford Drive are three high-fashion department stores, NYC's **Barneys New York** and **Saks Fifth Avenue,** plus Texas couturier **Neiman Marcus,** sitting like ducks in a row between 9500 and 9700 Wilshire.

Rodeo Drive is the most famous — and most exclusive — of the shopping streets, with two Euro-style, piazza-like couture malls (**2 Rodeo** and the **Rodeo Collection**), plus top designer boutiques from Tommy Hilfiger, Chanel, Van Cleef & Arpels, and many more. But you'll find plenty of reasonably priced booty throughout the easily walkable area, too. For a list, see www.bhvb.org/shop1.html. Expect to pay for a parking lot space unless you get lucky.

West 3rd Street

Right in the shadow of the famous **Beverly Center** mall — which sits like a prison at Beverly and La Cienega boulevards (☎ **310-854-0070**) — is one of the city's most appealing shopping streets. Running east from La Cienega, West 3rd's shops are whimsical, accessible, and just upscale enough, like **ga-ga,** 8362 W. 3rd St. (☎ **323-653-3388**), a magical spot for unique kids' gifts; **Traveler's Bookcase,** no. 8375 (☎ **323-655-0575**), and **The Cook's Library,** no. 8373 (☎ **323-655-3141**), two of the best specialty bookstores around; and **Freehand,** no. 8413 (☎ **323-655-2607**), a first-rate crafts gallery. You'll find easy meter parking.

West Hollywood

The **Sunset Strip** is most notable for its stargazing-while-you-shop opportunities. **Tower Records,** at no. 8801 (☎ **310-657-7300**) and the **Virgin Megastore,** no. 8000 (☎ **310-650-8666**) are often star-heavy, as is **Book Soup,** no. 8818 (☎ **310-659-3110**; www.booksoup.com) a browser's paradise just across from Tower (excellent magazine rack). Metered parking is your best bet.

Hollywood

If you want funky, this is your hood.

Melrose Avenue

L.A.'s wildest shopping strip starts out sophisticated at La Cienega Boulevard and gets progressively more rock-and-roll as you move east. This area is great for star sightings, especially obscure up-and-comers; I recently spotted Rose McGowan (Marilyn Manson's main squeeze) trying on tiny T-shirts at the super-trendy **Fred Segal** boutique mini-mall, at Crescent Heights (☎ **323-651-1800**). East of Fairfax is where the Angelina Jolie/Courtney Love skanky/cool style kicks in. **Retail Slut**, no. 7308 (☎ **323-934-1339;** www.retailslut.com), is one of many shops dealing in cutting-edge duds. You'll also find lots of faddish shoes and funky toys.

La Brea Avenue

The unsung stretch between Wilshire and Santa Monica boulevards is terrific for fashionable and retro-fascinated shoppers. Best is mammoth, eternally hip **American Rag, Cie.,** 150 S. La Brea, north of 2nd Street (☎ **323-935-3154),** for high-end vintage wearables and vintage-like new wear. Just south of Santa Monica is **Moletown,** 900 N. La Brea (☎ **323-851-0111;** www.moletown.com), your one-stop shop for official TV and movie merchandise.

Hollywood Boulevard

Come here if you're looking for dusty memorabilia shops full of vintage movie posters, autographed lobby cards, dog-eared scripts, and the like. You'll pay top dollar for top quality at **Hollywood Book & Poster,** 6562 Hollywood Blvd. (☎ **323-465-8764**).

Universal CityWalk

Adjacent to Universal Studios is this kid's dream of a mall (☎ **818-622-4455;** www.mca.com/citywalk). It's open-air and attention-grabbing, with neon-lit outsize storefronts like **Sparky's** (☎818-622-2925; www.reallyswellstuff.com) for new versions of retro toys like bobbing-head dolls and Pez dispensers; and **Glow** (☎ **818-761-3226**) for all things day-glo and black-lit. You can expect kid-friendly entertainment, such as face-painting or balloon-animal making, too. CityWalk also offers some good dining and nightlife options — but, at $7, the parking fee is inexcusable. Take U.S. 101 to Universal Center Drive or Lankershim Boulevard.

Living It Up After Dark

To see what's on, get the Sunday *Los Angeles Times* for its "Calendar" section, or the free *L.A. Weekly.* Also check "The Guide" at the back of the glossy monthly mag *Los Angeles.* Use the Web resources (see "Gathering More Information" later in this chapter) if you want to plan from home.

The major and the minor: Theater

One of the great surprises about L.A. is the high quality of its live theater scene. All those wannabes have to do something before they get their big break on the WB, right? Actually, movie and TV actors often feel the urge to conquer the stage after their celluloid successes — or to exercise their atrophied live-acting chops.

The Theatre League Alliance of Southern California, a.k.a. Theatre LA (☎ 213-614-0556), offers half-price same-day Web Tix. Here's how it works: Go online to www.theatrela.org (you can go to one of the Internet Centers in "Quick Concierge" at the end of this chapter if you don't tote a notebook and Web access isn't available at your hotel) before 6 p.m. Choose the show you want, enter your credit card number, and the tickets will be waiting for you at the box office. Full-price tickets for major stagings generally vary from $25 to $75, but smaller productions can be as cheap as $10; you'll pay half, plus a service charge between $2 and $5.

The major

The Performing Arts Center of Los Angeles, L.A.'s version of Lincoln Center, downtown at 135 N. Grand Ave. (between First and Temple streets), is home to the city's two top stages: the Ahmanson Theatre and the Mark Taper Forum, both the domain of the **Center Theater Group** (☎ 213-628-2772; www.taperahmanson.com). Productions at the **Ahmanson** tend toward familiar favorites and Broadway imports, while the more intimate **Mark Taper** focuses on new plays and creative restagings of contemporary works.

Another terrific stage is the **Geffen Playhouse,** 10886 Le Conte Ave., Westwood (☎ 310-208-6500 or 310-208-5454; www.geffenplayhouse.com), which tends to be more cutting-edge than the Taper.

The minor

This town contains so many small theaters that your best bet is to start with **Theatre LA** (☎ 213-614-0556; www.theatrela.org), which has all the current listings. Their Web site is particularly useful, but you can call if you don't have access. You can also find ads for plays in the *L.A. Weekly.* Companies worth seeking out include the **Colony Studio Theatre** (☎ 323-665-3011; www.colonytheatre.org), generally considered to be L.A.'s finest small company; the scrappy and irreverent **Actor's Gang Theater** (☎ 323-465-0566; www.actorsgang.com), which counts Tim Robbins among its founders; the **West Coast Ensemble Theater** (☎ 323-525-0022; www.wcensemble.org), known for smart stagings of familiar but well-chosen musicals and dramas; and **L.A. Theatre Works** (☎ 310-827-0889; www.latw.org), more often than not showcasing big-name actors in productions at the new Skirball Center.

A little night music

Hollywood Bowl

If you seek out one special venue before all others, it should be this legendary alfresco bandshell, set in the hills above Hollywood in a natural amphitheater. It's a magical place to see a show under the stars, whether it's the Los Angeles Philharmonic Orchestra (in residence all summer) performing Beethoven's Ninth or Rosemary Clooney and Michael Feinstein pairing up for classic pop songs. The season runs from June through September and always includes a jazz series, summer fireworks galas, and other events.

Box seats are usually sold to season subscription holders, so single-ticket buyers generally end up in the bleacher seats or on the lawn. The bleachers are packed tight for sold-out events, and the set-up is not overly comfortable. The magic of the evening more than compensates, but those of you who prefer more space should opt for the lawn instead. (That extra blanket in the closet of your hotel room will finally come in handy.)

One of the great Bowl traditions is picnicking, before or during the show. Most concertgoers bring their own gourmet spread and wine. If you'd rather not bother, order a portable feast (with or without wine) from the Bowl's Food Services Department, now under the ownership of Patina, one of L.A.'s best restaurants (see "Dining Out" earlier in this chapter). Pricing was not set at press time, but should be reasonable considering the quality of the grub. Order by phone ☎ **323-850-1885** at least a day prior.

2301 N. Highland Ave. (at Odin St.), Hollywood. ☎ 323-850-2000. Internet: www.hollywoodbowl.org. *To get there: U.S. 101 to Highland Ave. exit.*

Parking at the Bowl is extremely limited, so your best bet is to reserve a parking space in advance, or use one of the Bowl Park-and-Ride or shuttle services, for which you can purchase advance tickets. Call the Bowl at ☎ 323-850-2000, Ticketmaster at ☎ 213-480-3232, or go online to www.hollywoodbowl.org *and click on "Getting to the Bowl" for all the details.*

We're laughing with you!

Comedy Store

Pauly Shore's career may have fizzled, but his mom's is still going strong. Mitzi Shore owns this three-room standup showcase, which has launched the careers of too many big-time comics to name.

8433 Sunset Blvd. (1 block east of La Cienega Blvd.), West Hollywood. ☎ 323-650-6268. Internet: www.comedystore.com.

The Groundlings

This improvisational troupe has served as a major training ground for famous funnies, including Pee-Wee Herman, Lisa Kudrow, and the late, great Phil Hartman. The improv shows are gut-bustingly funny; the unpredictable comedy practically comes with a laugh-riot guarantee.

7307 Melrose Ave. (between Fairfax and La Brea aves.), Hollywood. ☎ *323-934-9700 or 323-934-4747. Internet:* www.groundlings.com.

The Improv

This venue is more clubby and intimate than the Comedy Store, but features equally impressive lineups. Now-famous faces like Drew Carey drop in on occasion.

8162 Melrose Ave. (between La Cienega Blvd. and Fairfax Ave.), West Hollywood. ☎ *323-651-2583. Internet:* www.improvclubs.com/hollywood.

Play it loud: Live music

B. B. King's Blues Club

This club is a genuine bastion of the blues tucked away in a veritable shopping-and-dining theme park. First-rate talent takes the stage; the man himself even drops by on occasion.

CityWalk, 1000 Universal Center Dr., Universal City. ☎ *818-622-5464 or 808-622-5406.*

Catalina Bar & Grill

This is the place for famous-name jazz talent and top-quality up-and-comers. Come here for great sound and good sightlines from all corners. Reserve ahead to ensure a spot.

1640 N. Cahuenga Blvd. (south of Hollywood Blvd.), Hollywood. ☎ *323-466-2210. Internet:* www.catalinajazzclub.com.

The Cinegrill

This landmark room showcases quality cabaret entertainment, including top-drawer talent such as Nell Carter and Eartha Kitt.

In the Hollywood Roosevelt Hotel, 7000 Hollywood Blvd. (between La Brea and Highland aves.), Hollywood. ☎ *323-466-7000.*

House of Blues

Despite the name (and the Beverly Hillbillies-meets-Chuck E. Cheese facade), this is a first-rate venue for famous-label rock 'n' roll. The Sunday gospel brunch is a thrill. The food is respectable, too; reserve ahead if you want to eat.

8430 Sunset Blvd. (at La Cienega Blvd.), West Hollywood. ☎ *323-848-5100. Internet:* www.hob.com.

Key Club

Hair-metal godfather Ben Gazzari would roll over in his grave if he saw what replaced his grungy club. This plush multimedia venue is so impressively high style that it's worth the cover for a look-see alone. Live music runs the gamut from local faves to Duran Duran. Word is that Dennis Rodman met Carmen Electra here.

9039 Sunset Blvd. (between Doheny Dr. and Hammond St.), West Hollywood. ☎ *310-274-5800.*

Largo

This intimate, easygoing sit-down club is the place to see acoustic and electric singer-songwriters, both familiar names and talented wannabes, working in the rock and pop idioms. If record producer Jon Brion (Fiona Apple, Aimee Mann) is still hosting his oft-star-studded Friday-night jams, don't miss it.

432 N. Fairfax Ave. (between Beverly Blvd. and Melrose Ave.), Los Angeles. ☎ *323-852-1073.*

Troubadour

Famous as a folk-rock launching pad in the '60s and a hair-metal one in the '80s (Linda Ronstadt, Elton John, and Guns 'n' Roses all got their first taste of fame here), the Troub is once again hip thanks to a savvy booker who brings in a terrific mix of established and up-and-coming alterna-acts.

9081 Santa Monica Blvd. (at Doheny Dr.), West Hollywood. ☎ *310-276-6168. Internet:* www.troubadour.com.

Viper Room

A quarter-century younger than the neighboring Whiskey but nearly as famous thanks to co-owner Johnny Depp, River Phoenix's unfortunate on-premises demise, and surprise late-night star turns from A-list acts. It's hot, sweaty, cramped, and crowded, but exciting as all get out.

8852 Sunset Blvd. (at Larrabee St.), West Hollywood. ☎ *310-358-1880. Internet:* www.viperroom.com.

Whisky A Go Go

This legendary Sunset Strip club has launched careers ranging from the Doors to Beck. It's still going strong, hosting full lineups of hopefuls who hope a little of the stardust will stick.

8901 Sunset Blvd. (at Clark St.), West Hollywood. ☎ *310-652-4202. Internet:* www.whiskyagogo.com.

Shake your groove thing

Century Club

The classy dance club for grown-ups who don't mind paying a high cover for a chic setting, a top-shelf bar, and clean bathrooms. A mainstream mix in the big room, R&B, hip-hop, funk, and jazz in the smaller ones.

101301 Constellation Blvd. (between Century Park East and Ave. of the Stars), Century City. ☎ *310-553-6000. Internet:* www.calendarlive.com/centuryclub.

The Conga Room

This is the place for live Latin music and dancing. Top-flight salsa orchestras dominate, but luminaries grace the stage on occasion. It's sexy, stylish, and hot, hot, hot.

5364 Wilshire Blvd. (west of La Brea Ave.), mid-Wilshire. ☎ *323-938-1696 or 323-549-9765. Internet:* www.congaroom.com.

The Derby

Ground zero of the neo-Swing movement, this place is still going strong. It offers class-A space, top-flight swing bands, and dance lessons for neophytes who come early.

4500 Los Feliz Blvd. (at Virgil Ave.), Los Feliz. ☎ *323-663-8979.* www.the-derby.com.

Come here often? Bars & lounges

Cat 'n' Fiddle

This indoor/outdoor pub is a longstanding local favorite, thanks to quality beers on tap, good pub grub, and an even better jukebox. The spacious and comfortable outdoor patio is the best alfresco drinking spot in the city. Completely unpretentious.

6530 Sunset Blvd. (between Highland Ave. and Cahuenga Blvd.), Hollywood. ☎ *323-468-3800.*

The Cat Club

Co-owned by Stray Cats drummer Slim Jim Phantom, this ultra-cool rock 'n' roll lounge is the ideal spot to launch a night of Sunset Strip club trawling. Don't be surprised if you spot a famous face or two.

8911 Sunset Blvd. (just west of San Vicente Blvd., next to the Whiskey A Go Go), West Hollywood. ☎ *310-657-0888.*

Father's Office

A beer connoisseur's dream come true, this pleasing pub deals strictly in top-flight microbrews. A warm, familial atmosphere and a well-worn board-game selection invite you to kick back and stay awhile.

1018 Montana Ave. (near 10th St.), Santa Monica. ☎ *310-451-9330.*

Lola's

This sweet, sexy spot has a cocktail menu to die for. Pricey but the size of bathtubs, the martinis will please purists and adventurous types alike (chocolate martini, anyone?). Expect a fashionista crowd, good New American food, and live jazz on Wednesdays.

945 N. Fairfax Ave. (1 ½ blocks south of Santa Monica Blvd.), West Hollywood. ☎ *213-736-5652.*

Trader Vic's

This place is the ultimate in Polynesian cool. Career bartenders serve up monster cocktails with names like the Honolulu and the Scorpion Bowl from a marvelously entertaining menu. It's hip and happening on weekends, but quietly romantic midweek (I spotted David Spade with a leggy model on a low-key Tuesday).

In the Beverly Hilton hotel, 9876 Wilshire Blvd. (at Santa Monica Blvd.), Beverly Hills. ☎ *310-274-7777.*

Yamashiro

Perched in the hills above Hollywood, this magical Japanese palace serves up stellar cocktails and jaw-dropping panoramic views. Skip the dining room in favor of the ultra-romantic bar, where you can also indulge in good-quality sushi and other Japanese nibbles. My favorite cocktail spot above all others.

1999 N. Sycamore Ave. (north of Franklin Ave.), Hollywood Hills. ☎ *323-466-5125. Internet:* www.yamashirola.com.

Quick Concierge

AAA
Multiple Tinseltown offices include 1900 S. Sepulveda Blvd., south of Santa Monica Boulevard in West L.A. (☎ 310-914-8500); 5550 Wilshire Blvd., between Fairfax and La Brea avenues, Hollywood (☎ 323-525-0018); and 2601 S. Figueroa St., at Adams Boulevard, downtown (☎ 213-741-3686).

American Express
You'll find L.A. offices at 8493 W. 3rd St., at La Cienega Blvd., across from the Beverly Center (☎ 310-659-1682); 327 N. Beverly Dr., between Brighton and Dayton ways, Beverly Hills (☎ 310-274-8277); and 1250 4th St., at Arizona St., Santa Monica (☎ 310-395-9588).

Baby-Sitters

Your hotel can usually recommend a reliable baby-sitter. If not, contact the Baby-Sitters Guild (☎ **323-658-8792** or 818-552-2229), L.A.'s only bonded baby-sitting agency and recently named best in the city by *Los Angeles* magazine. Book a Saturday-night sit no later than Thursday morning.

Emergencies

For police, fire, or other emergencies, press **911.**

Hospitals

Cedars Sinai Medical Center, 8700 Beverly Blvd., at San Vicente Blvd., a block west of La Cienega Blvd. (☎ 310-855-5000), has a 24-hour emergency room.

Internet Centers

Kinko's, 7630 Sunset Blvd., between Fairfax and La Brea avenues in Hollywood (☎ 323-845-4501), offers Internet access 24 hours a day for 20¢ per minute.

If you'd like a latte while you surf, head to Cyber Java, 7080 Hollywood Blvd., at La Brea (☎ 323-466-5600), where Web rates are $2.50 per 15 minutes, or $9 per hour.

Newspapers & Magazines

The daily is the *Los Angeles Times;* the "Calendar" section in the Sunday edition is the source for arts-and-entertainment listings. The *L.A. Weekly* is L.A.'s answer to New York's *Village Voice;* this free alterna paper is easily available around town. *Los Angeles* magazine is a glossy monthly with good coverage of L.A.'s dining and arts scenes.

Police

Dial **911** in an emergency. For non-emergency matters, call ☎ 877-ASK-LAPD or 213-485-2121.

In Beverly Hills, call ☎ **310-550-4951** for non-emergencies.

Post Office

Call ☎ 800-ASK-USPS to find the nearest post office.

Taxes

Sales tax is 8.25%. Hotel taxes range from 12% to 17%, depending on the municipality you're in.

Taxis

Call **L.A. Taxi** (☎ 310-715-1968) or **Independent Taxi** (☎ 323-666-0045).

Weather

Call ☎ 212-554-1212 for the daily forecast.

Gathering More Information

Contact the Los Angeles Convention & Visitors Bureau (☎ **800-366-6116** or 213-689-8822; www.lacvb.com) to request a free visitor's kit, learn about upcoming events, or ask specific questions.

After you're in town, you'll find an excellent walk-in Visitor Information Center downtown at 685 S. Figueroa St., between Wilshire Boulevard and Seventh Street; it's open Monday through Friday from 8 a.m. to 5 p.m. and Saturday from 8:30 a.m. to 5 p.m. You may also want to stop by the staffed Hollywood Visitor Information Center at 6541 Hollywood Blvd., just west of Cahuenga Boulevard, which is open Monday through Saturday from 9 a.m. to 5 p.m. You can find Hollywood info at www.hollywoodcoc.org.

In addition, many municipalities maintain their own visitor centers:

- ✔ The Beverly Hills Visitors Bureau is at 239 S. Beverly Dr., south of Wilshire Boulevard between Charleville and Gregory Way (☎ **800-345-2210** or 310-248-1015). Official Beverly Hills information is online at www.bhvb.org.

- ✔ The Santa Monica Convention & Visitors Bureau has a walk-up center in Palisades Park, 1400 Ocean Ave., near Santa Monica Boulevard (☎ **310-393-7593**). Santa Monica info is at www.santamonica.com.

- ✔ The West Hollywood Convention & Visitors Bureau is in the Pacific Design Center, 8687 Melrose Ave. (at San Vicente Blvd.), suite M25 (☎ **800-368-6020** or 310-289-2525; www.visitwesthollywood.com).

Your best source for the latest arts, entertainment, dining, nightlife, and event listings is the *Los Angeles Times's* www.calendarlive.com. Other good sources for the latest on what's happening in the city are the L.A. Weekly site at www.laweekly.com, and www.digitalcity.com/losangeles. The online version of *Los Angeles* magazine at www.lamag.com is another good source, especially if you're looking for more good restaurants to choose from.

Chapter 22

The Happiest Place on Earth: Disneyland!

In This Chapter

▶ Planning your visit

▶ Getting there

▶ Finding the perfect places to stay and eat

▶ Practicing proven tips for touring the legendary park

▶ Exploring Disneyland's newest attractions

*D*isneyland can't compete with Florida's Walt Disney World in size or breadth of attractions. Newer sister parks in Tokyo and France may be sleeker and more sophisticated. But Disneyland will always have what the others don't — the quixotic magic of true originality. The world's first family-oriented mega-theme park sprung directly from the fertile imagination of cartoonist and film pioneer Walt Disney. Despite changes and expansions over the years (the latest being California Adventure, set to open in mid-2001), Disneyland remains true to the vision of its creator.

Close enough for a day trip from Los Angeles or San Diego, Disneyland is also large enough for a dedicated stay. With that in mind, I include everything you need to know about planning a stay at or near the park, making the most of your vacation dollars, and filling every hour with pure Disney magic.

Choosing When to Visit

The best time to visit may be when you have vacation and the kids are off from school. If you're flexible with your schedule, though, a number of factors can influence your decision, because Disneyland has seasons of its very own.

✔ **Busiest times:** Disneyland is busiest in summer (between Memorial Day and Labor Day), but it can also be crowded on holidays (Thanksgiving week, Christmas week, President's Day weekend, Easter week, and Japan's "Golden Week" in early May) and weekends year-round. All other times make up the off-season.

During the busy summertime, Tuesday through Thursday is the best time to come; Friday and Saturday are the most crowded days.

✔ **Fireworks, shows, and parades:** If you want to see all the shows and parades, you'll have to come during the high season, because scheduling is sporadic on off-season weekdays. Disneyland's famed fireworks display only happens in summer.

✔ **Summer scorchers:** Consider the summer heat when deciding when to go. Scorching days in July, August, and September can make waiting to board a ride feel like a death march, with everyone crowding into available shady spots, and super-long lines to buy cold drinks. Visiting during these months can be fine; just plan to take advantage of the indoor attractions during the midday heat. Your reward later on will be a pleasantly balmy evening, when being outdoors becomes a delight.

✔ **Crowd-free days:** If you want to avoid crowds, visit on a weekday, preferably in November, December, or January (excluding Thanksgiving and Christmas weeks). You run the risk that some rides may be closed for maintenance (never more than three or four at a time), but visiting during this low, low season is the best way to maximize a single day.

✔ **First-quarter rains:** Southern California gets most of its precipitation between January and April, but only a sustained downpour should affect your Disney plans. If the forecast predicts rain, bring both a collapsible umbrella and waterproof rain poncho (or splurge on the cute Mickey Mouse ponchos that suddenly appear when the first raindrop falls). Even if you get wet, you'll enjoy the lightest crowds of the year!

Deciding How Long to Stay

You'll want to devote *at least* one (very) full day to the original park. If you're planning to visit during one of the peak periods, crowds and wait times will limit the attractions you're able to enjoy in a single day, so plan to spend the night and re-enter Disneyland fresh the following morning. After California Adventure opens in 2001, you should set aside two days to experience both parks.

Multi-day Flex passports (see "The Lowdown on Admission" later in this chapter) are a great deal for the money, and don't require you to visit on consecutive days (if you want to break up your Disney stay with a day at the beach, for example). Families with small children will especially want to consider the multi-day option, regardless of the season. While surviving a marathon Disney day is a badge of honor for older kids, you all know that naptime crankiness will eventually rear its ugly head.

All in all, I suggest allotting two or three full days for the Disney attractions, which gives you enough time to immerse yourself in the fantasy before moving on to the next leg of your California visit. (If you're staying elsewhere in Southern California but would like two days at the park, plan on spending the night at the park rather than driving back again the next day. Trust me, you'll be glad you did.)

Getting the Lowdown on Admission

At press time, admission to Disneyland — including unlimited rides and all festivities and entertainment — is $41 for adults and kids 10 and over, $39 for seniors, and $31 for kids 3 to 9 (kids under 3 enter free). These figures are given only as guidelines, since new prices will go into effect once California Adventure opens in February 2001.

Multi-day admission is available as well, and 2- and 3-day passports offer substantial savings. The days needn't be consecutive, but must be used within 7 days (for the 2-day) or 14 days (for the 3-day). Expect to pay a parking charge between $7 to $10, which may be included in some admission packages.

Your best multi-day deal, however, is the "Flex" passport, available for 3-, 4-, or 5-day admission, whose savings usually equal an entire free day. What's the catch? You must use the Flex passport within a shorter period of time (usually 5 or 7 days, respectively), and you cannot buy it at the main ticket booths. They're available for advance purchase on the Disneyland Web site, through travel agents and area hotels, and at Disney Stores nationwide.

It gets even better if you stay at one of the Disneyland Resort's three hotels. Disneyland Resort guests can purchase — separately, or as part of a lodging package — the *Ultimate Park-Hopper Ticket*. With it, you can "park-hop" between Disneyland and California Adventure as many times as you want each day, beginning with the day you check in and including the day you check out. This deal is exclusive to the Disney hotels; off-site overnighters should opt for a "Flex" passport, which allows for only one admission — to either park — each day.

As far as California Adventure goes, prices and policies had not yet been set at press time, but it is slated to have a separate admission charge. Combo ticket options will be available, of course.

Opening the starting gate

Disneyland is open every day of the year, but operating hours vary widely. Call for the information that applies to the time frame of your visit (☎ 714-781-4565). You can also find exact open hours, ride closures, and show schedules online at www.disneyland.com.

Generally speaking, the park is open from 9 or 10 a.m. to 6 or 7 p.m. on weekdays, fall to spring; and from 8 or 9 a.m. to midnight or 1 a.m. on weekends, holidays, and during summer vacation periods. If you'd like to receive a copy of the park's *Vacation Planner* brochure to orient yourself before you go, call the automated request line at ☎ **800-225-2057**.

If you plan on arriving during a busy time (when the gates open in the morning, or between 11 a.m. and 2 p.m.), purchasing your tickets in advance and getting a jump on the crowds at the ticket counters is your best bet. You can buy your tickets through the Web site, at Disney stores throughout the United States, or by calling the mail-order line (☎ **714-781-4043**).

Discovering the art of the (package) deal

If you intend to spend two or more nights in Disney territory, investigating the available package options can pay off. Start by contacting your hotel (even those in Los Angeles or San Diego) to see whether they offer Disneyland admission packages. Some of the airline vacation packagers include admission to Disneyland in their inclusive packages (see Chapter 6 for more information).

In addition, check with the official Disney agency, *Walt Disney Travel Co.* (☎ **800-225-2024** or 714-520-5050; www.disneyland.com), whose packages are value-packed time- and money-savers with lots of built-in flexibility. You can request a glossy catalog by mail or log onto the Web site and click on "Book Your Vacation" to peruse package details, take a virtual tour of participating hotel properties, and get online price quotes for customized, date-specific packages.

Hotel choices range from the official Disney hotels to one of 35 neighbor hotels in every price range. A wide range of available extras includes admission to other Southern California attractions and guided tours (such as **Universal Studios** or a Tijuana shopping trip) and behind-the-scenes Disneyland tours, all in limitless combinations. Rates are highly competitive, especially considering that each package includes multi-day admission, early park entry, and free parking (if you choose a Disney hotel), plus keepsake souvenirs and coupon books. If you want to add air transportation or car rental, the Disney Travel Co. can make those arrangements, too.

Getting to Disneyland

Disneyland is located in the heart of Anaheim in Orange County, about 30 miles south of Los Angeles, and 98 miles north of San Diego. To get there from either city, follow I-5 until you see signs for Disneyland; dedicated off-ramps from both directions lead directly to the park's parking lots and surrounding streets.

From the Palm Springs area, follow I-10 westbound to Highway 60 west. In Riverside, pick up Highway 91 west to Anaheim and then take

Highway 57 south. Exit at the Ball Road off ramp and turn right (west), proceeding 2½ miles to Disneyland. The drive totals 110 miles.

If you'd rather wing it, Los Angeles International Airport (LAX) serves as the region's major airport, about 30 miles away. You can rent a car at the airport and drive to Anaheim, or you can take advantage of the many public-transportation services at LAX; see Chapter 21 for details.

If you'd rather fly directly into Anaheim from another state or another California city, the nearest airport is John Wayne International Airport in Irvine, 15 miles from Disneyland at the intersection of I-405 and Highway 55 (☎ 949-252-5200; www.ocair.com). Most national airlines and major rental-car agencies serve the airport. To reach Anaheim from the airport, rent a car and take Hwy. 55 east, then I-5 north to the Disneyland exit.

You can also catch a ride with American Taxi (☎ 888-482-9466), whose cabs queue up at the Ground Transportation Center on the lower level; reservations are not necessary. Expect the fare to Disneyland to run about $26. If only two of you are making the trip, though, consider using Super Shuttle (☎ 800-BLUE-VAN; www.supershuttle.com), which charges $10 per person to the Disneyland area. Advance reservations are recommended.

Before you pay for a taxi or shuttle service, ask if your Anaheim hotel offers airport transportation when you make your reservation.

Deciding Where to Stay

I'll admit it right from the start — the official Disney hotels are my favorites, both for convenience and ambience. But lots of reasons exist to stay at one of the many other hotels and motels that line the surrounding blocks, not the least of which is that sometimes all 2,200-plus Disney guest rooms are full.

Staying in official Disney digs

Can't decide whether to stay "off-campus," or splurge on one of the official Disney hotels? The main advantages of going 100 percent Disney are:

- **The Disney monorail:** Circumnavigating the theme park, the monorail also stops at each official hotel (and soon at California Adventure as well). So when you get weary of hoofing it, simply hop aboard and zip straight to your room. Dedicated ticket booths and entry turnstiles at the monorail stations mean you can also avoid the main entrance crush.

- **Early admission:** All Disney hotel guests qualify for early admission. That's right — you get to enter the park 1½ hours early, which means you can enjoy the major rides before long lines form (be sure to wave to the patient folks roped off along Main Street).

This shouldn't be your deciding factor, though, because packages from other hotels may also include early admission.

✔ **Just plain fun:** The official properties are just plain fun to stay at. Each gets the patented Disney treatment, with fantasy settings and imagination-stimulating diversions. Rooms, too, bear the Disney touch: bath amenities, for example, are plastered with Disney characters — and simply scream "free souvenir"!

Disneyland Hotel

$$–$$$ Disneyland

The Holy Grail for committed Disney-goers has always been a stay at the "Official Hotel of the Magic Kingdom." This Disney-themed hotel is a wild attraction unto itself, and the best choice for families with little ones. The rooms aren't fancy, but they're comfortably and attractively furnished, like a good-quality business hotel, and all have balconies and good in-room amenities. More than 10 restaurants, snack bars, and cocktail lounges are on site, plus a fantasy swimming lagoon with a white-sand beach and a video game center.

1150 W. Cerritos Ave. (off West St.). ☎ *714-956-MICKEY or 714-956-6400 (central reservations); 714-778-6600. Fax: 714-956-6582. Internet:* www.disneyland.com. *Parking: $10 to self-park, $14 to valet. Rack rates: $185–$245 double, $425–$1,200 suite. Deals: See "The art of the (package) deal" earlier in this chapter. AE, MC, V.*

Paradise Pier Hotel

$$–$$$ Disneyland

Adjoining the Disneyland Hotel, the Paradise Pier Hotel (formerly the Pacific Hotel) offers a Disney version of Asian tranquility that adults and older kids looking for a more serene refuge will appreciate.

1150 W. Cerritos Ave. (off West St.). ☎ *714-956-MICKEY or 714-956-6400 (central reservations); 714-999-0990. Fax: 714-956-6582. Internet:* www.disneyland.com. *Parking: $10 to self-park, $14 to valet. Rack rates: $185–$245 double, $425–$1,200 suite. Deals: See "Discovering the art of the (package) deal" earlier in this chapter. AE, MC, V.*

Grand Californian Hotel

Cost undetermined at press time   Disneyland

Disney's newest hotel is scheduled to open in January 2001. Located inside California Adventure, the 750-room hotel will feature a complex of swimming pools, a wedding chapel, and a full-service spa.

For information on reservations, call ☎ *714-956-MICKEY or Disneyland Guest Relations at 714-781-4560. Although room rates hadn't been determined at press time, you can expect that the complete array of package deals and early admission privileges will also apply here.*

Bunking beyond the resort

You can usually find more economical rooms at the many hotels lining the streets surrounding the park. Naturally, they're not as lavish and entertaining as the Disney hotels; but if saving money is your prime concern, the off-campus hotels offer the following advantages:

- ✓ **Free shuttles:** Free shuttles run frequently from most nearby hotels (including all the ones listed below) to the park's main entrance, so you can enjoy similar in/out privileges as monorail riders, though with a bit more walking. By all means, take advantage of the shuttle. Driving to and parking at the park is an unnecessary extra step and cost if you're staying close by.

- ✓ **Free parking:** All of the non-Disney hotels I recommend have free parking, and access to your car (and the freeway on-ramps) is less complicated than if you stay at a Disney hotel.

- ✓ **Free breakfast:** The rates in a number of the non-Disney hotels I recommend include breakfast, a boon to budget-minded families. If not, you can start the day at one of several inexpensive coffee shops (like Denny's, Millie's, or Coco's) just outside the park, rather than spending more money at a Disney restaurant.

Anaheim Plaza Hotel & Suites

$$ Anaheim

Across from Disneyland's main gate sits this 1960s hotel, whose clever design shuts out the noisy world. The two-story garden buildings remind me more of Waikiki than busy Anaheim. On the down side, artificial turf surrounds the heated pool and whirlpool, and the plain motel furnishings are beginning to look a little tired. But nothing's changed about the light-filled lobby or the wallet-friendly rates. Amenities include room service from the casual on-site cafe, plus valet service and coin-op laundry.

1700 S. Harbor Blvd. ☎ 800-228-1357 or 714-772-5900. Fax: 714-772-8386. Parking: Free! Rack rates: $79–$150 double, $185–$200 family suite. Rates include continental breakfast. Deals: Low occupancy can bring rates as low as $49. AE, DC, DISC, MC, V.

Best Western Anaheim Stardust

$ Anaheim

Located on the back side of Disneyland, this modest hotel will appeal to budget-minded travelers who aren't willing to sacrifice everything just to save a buck. All rooms have a fridge and microwave, breakfast is served in a refurbished train dining car, and you can relax by the large heated pool and spa while using the laundry room. The extra-large family rooms accommodate virtually any brood.

1057 W. Ball Rd. ☎ 800- 222-3639 or 714-774-7600. Fax: 714-535-6953. Parking: Free! Rack rates: $64-$89 double, $105 family room. Rates include full, hot, sit-down breakfast. AE, DC, DISC, MC, V.

Candy Cane Inn

$$ Anaheim

This hotel is a gem near Disneyland's main gate for stylish bargain hunters: A standard U-shaped motel court that's been successfully spruced up with cobblestone drives and walkways, old-time street lamps, and flowering vines engulfing the balconies. The attractively painted rooms are decorated in bright florals with comfortable furnishings, while the courtyard boasts a heated pool, a spa, and a kiddie wading pool.

1747 S. Harbor Blvd. ☎ 800-345-7057 or 714-774-5284. Fax: 714-772-5462. Parking: Free! Rack rates: $84-$129 double. Rates include a surprisingly nice continental breakfast. Deals: AAA and AARP discounts knock a few bucks off. AE, DC, DISC, MC, V.

Howard Johnson Hotel by the Park

$$ Anaheim

Renovated in '99, this HoJo is situated directly opposite Disneyland, with a cute San Francisco–style trolley car running to and from the park. Rooms have fridges and balconies that face a garden with three heated pools (two for adults, one for kids). In summer, you can see the nightly fireworks from the upper park-side rooms. Try to avoid the back rooms, which get some freeway noise. Amenities include room service from the attached Coco's coffee shop, game room, coin-op laundry, and airport shuttle. Pretty classy for a HoJo's!

1380 S. Harbor Blvd. ☎ 800-422-4228 or 714-776-6120. Fax: 714-533-3578. Internet: www.hojoanaheim.com. Parking: Free! Rack rates: $83-$104 double. Deals: Ask about hotel/Disney packages, which can save you a few dollars. AE, CB, DC, DISC, JCB, MC, V.

Sheraton Anaheim Hotel

$$$ Anaheim

This nice chain hotel behind Disneyland Park rises to the theme-park occasion with its fanciful English Tudor architecture. The public areas are quiet and elegant, with intimate gardens, a plush lobby, and lounges — a pleasing change of pace after a frenetic day at the park. The rooms are modern and unusually spacious, but otherwise not distinctive. The grounds include a large pool surrounded by attractive landscaping.

1015 W. Ball Rd. (at I-5). ☎ 800-325-3535 or 714-778-1700. Fax: 714-535-3889. Internet: www.sheraton.com. Parking: Free! Rack rates: $170-$190 double, $290-$360 suite. Deals: Rooms commonly go for $100 to $130, even on busy summer weekends. Check the Web site, and call the hotel direct for park packages. AE, CB, DC, MC, V.

Dining Out

You'll go broke before you go hungry at the Disneyland Resort. You can find food everywhere: a dozen sit-down restaurants and cafeterias inside the park, and seven more full-service restaurants between the **Disneyland** and **Paradise Pier** hotels (with two more in the works at the **Grand Californian Hotel**), not counting snack carts, casual walk-up stands, and packaged food shops. And, as you would expect, you can find a number of good restaurants conveniently located outside the park and near your hotel.

Dining at the resort

Most dining facilities inside Disneyland are overrated, overcrowded, and overpriced, redeeming themselves only by convenience. Here are some noteworthy exceptions worth seeking out:

- ✔ Scattered throughout Disneyland — but thankfully plotted on the official park map — are **churro carts ($)**, which dispense these absolutely addictive cylindrical Mexican donuts (rolled in sugar) beginning at 11 a.m.

- ✔ Though the food itself is unremarkable, I never miss a chance to eat at New Orleans Square's **Blue Bayou Restaurant ($$-$$$)** the only restaurant in the park that requires reservations (stop by early in the day to make yours). It meticulously re-creates a classic New Orleans verandah, complete with lush, vine-wrapped ironwork, lazily chirping crickets, and (nonalcoholic) mint juleps. Its misty, sunless atmosphere comes from being literally inside the Pirates of the Caribbean ride, so boatloads of pirate-seeking parkgoers drift by during your meal!

- ✔ For healthy snack options, head to Adventureland for refreshments at the **Tiki Juice Bar ($)** and **Indy Fruit Cart ($)**, which offer tropical juices and unembellished fresh fruit for a natural sugar boost.

If you're visiting with kids, take them to one — or both — of the "character dining" choices at the hotels.

- ✔ At **Goofy's Kitchen ($$-$$$)** in the Disneyland Hotel, characters like Mickey, Donald Duck, and Goofy himself roam between tables, greeting you and your wide-eyed youngsters as you dine at an all-you-can-eat buffet (breakfast, lunch, and dinner) in cartoonish surroundings.

- ✔ At the Paradise Pier Hotel, **Breakfast with Minnie and Friends ($$-$$$)** entertains with a song- and dance-filled magic show featuring Minnie Mouse, Merlin the Magician, surprise character guests, and gleeful kid participation. Both Goofy and Minnie suggest reservations; call ☎ 714-956-6755.

The much-touted **Downtown Disney entertainment complex,** a non-gated feature bridging the two "sister" parks with the Disneyland hotels, is preparing to open a handful of promising eateries by mid-2001. Because a top-name foodie favorite manages each new venture, I predict Downtown Disney will quickly overshadow the old standbys. The following restaurants were in the works at press time; call ☎ **714-781-4565** or 714-781-4560 for the latest.

- ✔ **Ralph Brennan's Jazz Kitchen,** from the established New Orleans family restaurant group Brennan's, will combine a mix of traditional Cajun and Creole foods with hot jazz.

- ✔ The Los Angeles–based **Patina/Pinot** fine dining/bistro dynasty will serve Mediterranean-influenced fare at their casually elegant restaurant.

- ✔ **Rainforest Cafe** is adding to its chain of theme restaurants. Expect a lush and lively tropical setting with special effects, live animals, and "international" cuisine that doesn't challenge your palate.

- ✔ **ESPN Zone** will offer classic American food and lots of state-of-the-art sports programming to please armchair quarterbacks (and centers and shortstops and . . .).

- ✔ Hollywood–based **House of Blues** will revise its successful formula of marrying Delta-inspired down-home cuisine with a live-music nightclub featuring blues and jazz.

- ✔ **Naples Ristorante and Pizzeria,** a New York City import, will feature Southern Italian dishes prepared in an open kitchen with wood-burning pizza ovens.

- ✔ **La Brea Bakery,** which bakes L.A.'s best breads and pastries, will open a full-service bakery/cafe featuring oven-fresh breads and Mediterranean light fare.

Dining about town

Citrus City Grille

$$$ Orange CALIFORNIA

This sophisticated crowd-pleaser pays homage to the town's agricultural (citrus) legacy in a bold, industrial-chic setting. Globe-trotting main courses come from the Mediterranean (pastas and risottos), Mexico (carne asada with avocado-corn relish), the American South (Louisiana gumbo), and the American Mom's kitchen (meat loaf smothered in gravy and fried onions). The gleaming bar features an extensive martini menu, and outdoor tables are nicely sheltered from the street.

122 N. Glassell St. (½ block north of Chapman), Orange. ☎ *714-639-9600. Internet:* www.citruscitygrille.com. *Reservations recommended. To get there: Take Harbor Blvd. south to Chapman Ave.; go left 3½ miles to Glassell St. Main courses: $8-$13 lunch, $12-$24 dinner. AE, DC, MC, V. Open: Lunch and dinner Tues-Sat.*

Mrs. Knott's Chicken Dinner Restaurant

$ Buena Park AMERICAN

The down-home restaurant that launched the Knott's Berry Farm dynasty stands just outside that theme park's entrance, looking country cute, with window shutters and paisley aplenty. The featured attraction is the original fried chicken dinner, complete with soup, salad, buttermilk biscuits, mashed potatoes and gravy, and a slice of its famous pies. The restaurant also offers country-fried steak, pot roast, pork ribs, sandwiches, salads, and a terrific chicken pot pie. Boysenberries abound, from breakfast jam to traditional double-crust pies.

8039 Beach Blvd. (near La Palma), Buena Park. ☎ *714-220-5080. Reservations not taken. To get there: From I-5, take Hwy. 91 west to Beach Blvd. exit. Main courses: $5–$7; complete dinners $10.95. AE, DC, DISC, MC, V. Open: Breakfast, lunch, and dinner daily.*

Thee White House

$$$$ Anaheim ITALIAN

Once surrounded by nothing but orange groves, this stately 1909 Colonial-style mansion now sits on a wide industrial street just 5 minutes from Disneyland, carefully restored and exuding nostalgic gentility. Northern Italian cuisine is served in elegant white-on-white rooms. Dinners are whimsically named for big-name fashion designers (Versace whitefish, Prada rack of lamb), and sometimes arrive on oddly shaped platters that work better as artwork than dishware. But chef David Libby knows what he's doing.

887 Anaheim Blvd., Anaheim. ☎ *714-772-1381. Internet:* www.anaheimwhitehouse. com. *Reservations recommended at dinner. To get there: From Disneyland, take Ball Road east, turn left on Anaheim Blvd. Main courses: $10–$16 lunch; $18–$28 dinner. AE, MC, V. Open: Lunch Mon–Fri, dinner daily.*

Playing Your Best Bets for Touring the Park

Though many visitors tackle Disneyland systematically, beginning at the entrance and working their way clockwise around the park, the most effective method historically has been to arrive early and run to the most popular rides first — the **Indiana Jones Adventure, Star Tours, Space Mountain, Splash Mountain,** the **Haunted Mansion,** and **Pirates of the Caribbean** — where midday lines can last an hour or more.

This time-honored plan of attack may become obsolete, however, thanks to the newly implemented *FastPass* system. Here's how it works: Suppose that you want to ride Space Mountain, but the line is long, so long that the wait sign indicates a 75-minute standstill. When that happens, you can head to the automated FastPass ticket dispensers near the ride, swipe the magnetic strip of your Disneyland entrance ticket, and get a FastPass for later that day. Return at the appointed time (usually within a 90-minute time window), and you can bypass the stand-by line for a separate, streamlined FastPass entrance with a nominal wait of 5 to 15 minutes. With this convenience in place, you don't need to rush to ride FastPass rides first thing in the morning. But do plan to start getting your FastPasses early in the day, as you must use your current FastPass *before* obtaining one for a second attraction. At press time, rides equipped with FastPass were **Space Mountain, Splash Mountain,** the **Matterhorn Bobsleds, Indiana Jones Adventure,** the newly designed **Autopia,** seven rides at **California Adventure,** and **Roger Rabbit's Car Toon Spin.** The **It's A Small World** ride implements FastPass only during the Christmas season.

Tips from a pro

Avoid common pitfalls by learning from the mistakes of others:

- ✔ **Wear your most comfortable walking shoes,** whether they go with your outfit or not. You'll spend many hours walking, standing, and putting lots of strain on your legs and feet. Running or tennis shoes are the best. Open-toed shoes are fine, especially on hot days; just make sure they have impact-cushioning soles and will support your feet.

- ✔ **Expect a dramatic temperature drop after dark,** even in summer. Bring a sweatshirt or jacket, perhaps even long pants; you can store them in a locker, leave them in the car, or tote them in a backpack. Too many visitors have shown up in shorts and tank tops, only to discover by 10 p.m. that they're freezing their buns off!

- ✔ **Don't forget such bare necessities** as sunscreen (the park gets a lot of direct sun); camera film (more than you think you'll want) and spare batteries; extra baby supplies; bottled water or a sports bottle you can refill at drinking fountains; and snacks (if the kids get hungry in line, or you just balk at the concession prices). Although anything you may forget is available for purchase inside Disneyland, you'll cringe at the marked-up prices.

- ✔ **If you have only one day:** Get to the park early and start by riding the most popular rides (described in the following sections) first — or obtaining FastPasses early — so you don't waste precious time in line.

- ✔ **If you have two or more days:** You have the luxury of enjoying some Disney extras not essential enough to pack into a single day. Avoid the midday-rides crush by strolling along **Main Street U.S.A.,** shopping for Disney souvenirs, and ducking into **Great Moments with Mr. Lincoln,** the patriotic look at America's 16th president that was Walt Disney's first foray into audio-animatronics.

Rides for the little ones

Disneyland does have ride restrictions, based on age and height. For most attractions, you have to be 7 years or older to ride alone, for example. For the more active, high-speed rides, like **Space Mountain, Splash Mountain,** and **Big Thunder Mountain Railroad,** kids are required to be at least 40 inches high and 3 years old. Forty-inch-hand-stamps are issued at certain locations, to last throughout the day.

If you have small kids with you, concentrate on **Fantasyland** (behind Sleeping Beauty's Castle), a kids' paradise with fairy-tale-derived rides like **King Arthur Carousel, Dumbo the Flying Elephant, Mr. Toad's Wild Ride, Peter Pan's Flight, Alice in Wonderland, Pinocchio's Daring Journey,** and the Disney signature ride **It's A Small World.** Elsewhere in the park, little ones will enjoy clambering through **Tarzan's Treehouse,** singing along with the audio-animatronic **Country Bear Jamboree,** and doing space wheelies on **Rocket Rods,** which is tamer than the name implies (not worth a long wait for grown-ups). **Mickey's Toontown** is a wacky, gag-filled world inspired by the *Roger Rabbit* films, featuring endless amusement for young imaginations.

Adventures for thrill-seekers

If high-speed thrills are your style, then follow the **Indiana Jones Adventure** into the Temple of the Forbidden Eye, with hair-raising perils that include the familiar cinematic tumbling boulder — very realistic in the front seats!

Most of Disneyland's best action roller coasters are "mountain" themed. Perennial favorite **Space Mountain** is a pitch-black indoor roller coaster that assaults your ears and equilibrium. **Splash Mountain** is a water flume with a big, wet splash at the end (be prepared!). The **Matterhorn Bobsleds** offer a zippy coaster ride through faux-alpine caverns and fog banks, while runaway train cars careen through a deserted 1870s gold mine on **Big Thunder Mountain Railroad.**

Diverging from the mountain theme, stationary **Star Tours** encounters a space-load of misadventures on the way to the Moon of Endor. This *Star Wars*–inspired Tomorrowland virtual ride manages to achieve realistic queasiness with motion seats and video effects.

Longtime faves

Some of Disneyland's highlights are long-time favorites that have stood the test of time. Two all-time best bets are in New Orleans Square: The intriguingly spooky **Haunted Mansion** showcases the brilliance of Disney "imagineers" and boggles your mind with too many details to absorb in just one visit. **Pirates of the Caribbean** presents an enchanted world of swashbuckling and rum-running that you glide through via a realistic southern bayou.

I've been told by more than one parent that these two attractions have spooked their under-6 kids, so you may want to skip them if you have little ones.

Parade and show-going tips

The park's parades and shows draw huge crowds into relatively small areas. Parades usually run twice a day, in the late afternoon and mid-evening. If a parade doesn't interest you, make a point to steer clear of these areas during and immediately after the parade; use this time to take advantage of shorter ride lines in Frontierland (**Big Thunder Mountain Railroad**), Tomorrowland (**Space Mountain**), and New Orleans Square (**Haunted Mansion** and **Pirates of the Caribbean**).

Ditto for the nighttime fireworks spectacular above Sleeping Beauty's Castle. **Fantasmic!** is an after-dark pyrotechnic spectacular mixing music, live performers, and sensational special effects; Mickey Mouse even appears as the Sorcerer's Apprentice. New Orleans Square serves as the prime viewing ground, and ushers begin cordoning off the area about an hour before showtime. Get there early if you want to watch, or hightail it to the other side of the park (again, Tomorrowland and Fantasyland are good bets) to avoid the crowds.

Keep in mind that most folks leave right after the fireworks and/or Fantasmic!, so pedestrian and auto exit routes are most crowded then.

Doing Disney's Latest Addition: California Adventure

By the time you read this, Disney will be putting the finishing touches on **California Adventure,** a brand new "sister" theme park adjacent to Disneyland (built on space originally occupied by Disney's mammoth outdoor parking lot). At press time, the new park was to focus more on interactive and educational experiences than thrill rides, all tied together by the theme of celebrating California's unique climate, lifestyle, and diversity. Among the planned attractions:

- ✔ **Pacific Wharf,** celebrating California as the nation's bread basket. The highlight promises to be Robert Mondavi's wine country experience, featuring real vineyards and wine-tasting counters. Other participants include a fully operational Mission tortilla factory, and a Boudin sourdough bread bakery that uses a portion of the original "mother dough" dating back to the first loaf made in 1849.

- ✔ A **Hollywood-style studio district** with hands-on animation exhibits, plus a TV studio where you are both star and audience.

- ✔ **Muppet Vision 3-D,** an action- and illusion-packed show featuring Kermit, Miss Piggy, and other familiar Muppet faces, in a venue reminiscent of the original "Muppet Show" theater, complete with hecklers Statler and Waldorf in the balcony.

Additional plans call for an area that celebrates California outdoor adventures, where you'll explore forests, deserts, subterranean caverns, and other landscapes. The most daring among you can "soar" in hang gliders over the state's most picturesque locales, or take a whitewater "rafting" expedition. You'll also be able to take a nostalgic walk along a "seaside" boardwalk, complete with classic rides and games, sandy beach, and street artists.

Enjoying After-Dark Fun

Family-friendly Disneyland was hardly the place to be for after hours (that is, grown-up) fun. All that is changing, however, with the much-anticipated opening of **Downtown Disney,** an outdoor pedestrian esplanade (much like Universal Studios' CityWalk in L.A.) linking the park with the Disneyland Hotel. Downtown Disney already has some high-profile tenants on-board. In addition to several promising restaurants (see "Dining at the resort" earlier in this chapter) and a sister store to Florida's mega **World of Disney,** plans call for a 12-screen AMC Theatres megaplex and live entertainment at **House of Blues** and **Ralph Brennan's Jazz Kitchen.** If you have energy to spare after cavorting in the amusement park all day, Downtown Disney should provide an easy outlet.

Gathering More Information

For the latest **Disneyland** and **California Adventure** developments, call the park's information line at ☎ **714-781-4565,** or 714-781-4560 to talk to a real person. You can find online info at www.disneyland.com.

To get more information on the surrounding area, check with the Anaheim/Orange County Visitor and Convention Bureau, 800 W. Katella Ave. (☎ **714-765-8888;** www.anaheimoc.org). The bureau is located just inside the Convention Center (across the street from Disneyland), and welcomes visitors Monday through Friday from 8 a.m. to 5 p.m.

Chapter 22 written by Stephanie Avnet Yates

Chapter 23

San Diego

- -

In This Chapter

▶ Determining the perfect time to visit

▶ Getting there and orienting yourself, neighborhood by neighborhood

▶ Sleeping and dining in the city

▶ Exploring the city's sights, on your own or by guided tour

▶ Discovering San Diego's top shopping sites

▶ Enjoying a night on the town

▶ Taking a day trip to Tijuana

- -

*S*an Diego is California's grown-up beach town. Year-round sunshine, postcard-perfect beaches, vibrant Spanish-Mexican heritage, and three fantastic family-oriented attractions (four, if you count LEGOLAND in nearby Carlsbad) make an irresistible combination, especially for families — and anyone with a kid-like sensibility and a need to kick back.

Little more than an overgrown Navy base just a few decades ago, San Diego is really hitting its stride as a multidimensional city these days. An influx of new residents has forced San Diego to shed its image as "Iowa-by-the-Sea" (no offense intended, Iowans), and start keeping up with culinary styles and cultural trends. It's still not bright lights/big city — and it probably never will be, thankfully — but an astonishing growth rate does threaten to bring Los Angeles–style ills (traffic, noise, pollution) into the oasis best known for squeaky-clean fun. Still, the easygoing pace and sunny beach-town optimism you'll find here remains worlds apart from L.A.'s crippling congestion and practiced cynicism.

One or more of the city's animal-themed fun spots — the San Diego Zoo, SeaWorld, and the Wild Animal Park — will probably top your sightseeing agenda. But don't be surprised when the historic neighborhoods, picturesque beach communities, active-minded lifestyles, and mellow local attitudes draw you in. After the sand gets between your toes, you'll be hooked.

Deciding When to Visit — and How Long to Stay

San Diego has a reputation for reliably mild weather. Is it deserved? You bet. Average daytime highs range seasonally from 65° to 78°F, with nighttime lows between 46° and 66°F. The sun shines all year-round, except (believe it or not) in June and July, when ocean fog rolls in during the wee morning hours and burns off slowly, sometimes not until midafternoon. A puny 9½ inches of rain falls annually, primarily between mid-December and mid-April.

Summer — between Memorial Day and Labor Day — means crowds of people on the sand, in the restaurants, at the major attractions, and occupying hotel rooms reserved months before. The best time to visit is in the fall — September through early December — when the crowds have vanished, winter snowbirds are still months away, and the possibility of rain is nearly nil. You can still comfortably bare it all at the beach through October. No matter when you visit, though, pack a swimsuit because "freak" warm weather (often in November or January) is common.

The few weeks between Thanksgiving and mid-January constitute the city's only bona-fide low season, just in time for you lucky holiday travelers.

You'll likely want to spend 2 to 4 nights in town, depending on your sightseeing goals — mainly, how many animal parks you want to visit. You can get acquainted with the rest of the city in just a couple of days. For tips on how to plan your time, see "Suggested 1-, 2-, and 3-day sightseeing itineraries" later in this chapter.

Getting There

As a top destination, San Diego is accessible by plane and train as well as by automobile. So take your pick.

By plane

San Diego International Airport (☎ **619-231-7361;** www.portof sandiego.org), locally known as Lindbergh Field, is right on the water on Harbor Drive, just 3 miles from downtown. Most of the major domestic carriers fly here, and all the major car-rental agencies maintain offices at the airport.

Chances are very good you'll want to have a rental car (for more on this subject, see "Getting Around" later in the chapter). If not, taxis line up outside the airport and charge around $8 (plus tip) to take you downtown.

✔ **To reach downtown** from the airport, take Harbor Drive south to Broadway, the main east-west thoroughfare, and turn left.

✔ **To reach Hillcrest or Balboa Park,** exit the airport toward I-5, and follow the signs for Laurel Street.

✔ **To reach Mission Bay (home of SeaWorld),** take I-5 north to I-8 west.

✔ **To reach La Jolla,** take I-5 north to the Ardath Road exit, turning onto Torrey Pines Road.

If you're the plan-ahead type and would prefer to arrange for shuttle service, contact Cloud 9 (☎ **800-9-SHUTTLE** or 858-9-SHUTTLE; www. cloud9shuttle.com). Expect to pay $6 to $9 for downtown and Hillcrest, and$19 to La Jolla (quoted rates are for the first person; additional members of your party pay less).

San Diego hotels commonly offer airport shuttle service — usually free, sometimes for a nominal charge — so ask before you make other arrangements. Make sure the hotel knows when you're arriving, and get precise directions on where they'll pick you up.

By car

Interstate 5 (I-5) is the route from Los Angeles, Anaheim, and coastal points north. The drive is about 120 miles, or 2 hours flat, from L.A., and 97 miles from Disneyland.

Interstate 15 (I-15) leads from inland destinations and the deserts to the north. As you enter San Diego, take I-8 west to reach the main parts of the city. From Palm Springs, take I-10 west to Highway 60, then I-215 south to I-15 south. The distance is 141 miles, or about 2 ½ hours.

I-8 cuts across California from points east like Phoenix, crossing I-5 and ending at Mission Bay.

By train

Amtrak (☎ **800-872-7245;** www.amtrak.com) trains arrive at Santa Fe Station, 1850 Kettner Blvd. (at Broadway), within walking distance of many downtown hotels and 1½ blocks from the Embarcadero (waterfront). Taxis line up out front, the trolley station is across the street, and a dozen local bus routes stop on Broadway or Pacific Highway, a block away.

Orienting Yourself

Thinking of San Diego without envisioning the water is impossible. You'll probably never be more than five miles from the bay while in San Diego, and you may never even lose sight of the blue Pacific.

Introducing San Diego

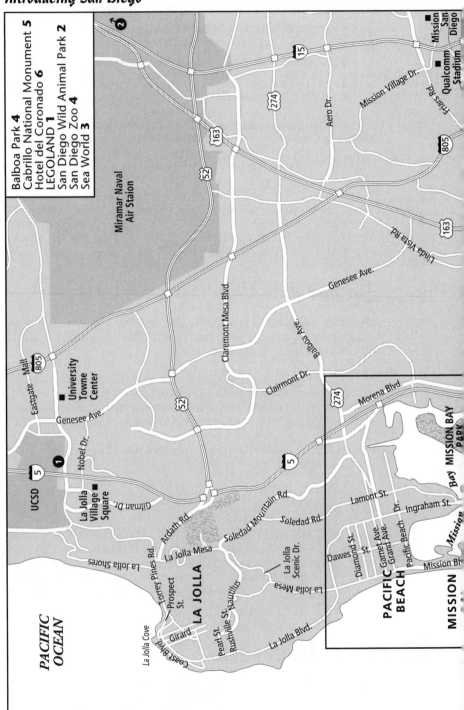

Balboa Park **4**
Cabrillo National Monument **5**
Hotel del Coronado **6**
LEGOLAND **1**
San Diego Wild Animal Park **2**
San Diego Zoo **4**
Sea World **3**

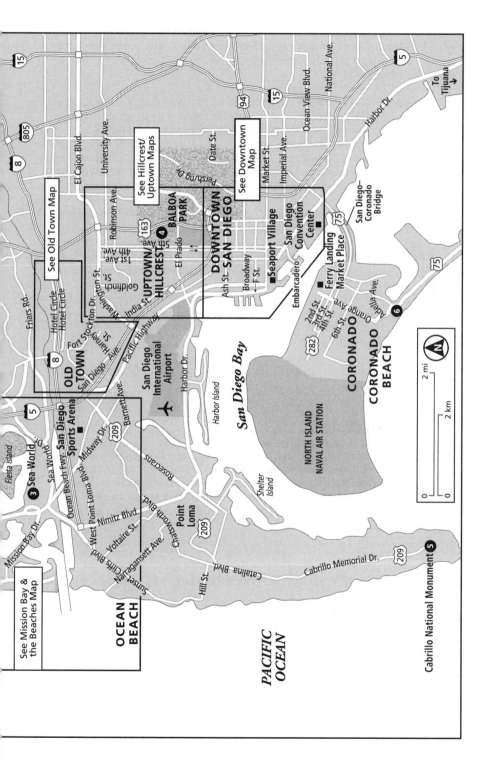

The bay is San Diego Bay — not to be confused with Mission Bay, which is a protected body of water, fed by the sea but isolated from it by thin strips of land. Mission Bay is directly north of San Diego Bay. The airport rests between the bays, merely a stone's throw from most city neighborhoods.

The neighborhoods are well-defined by the undulating geography of foothills, shallow canyons, and coastline: Downtown grew up on the waterfront, wrapping around San Diego's huge natural bay, which brought in crucial shipping commerce and, later, the influential U.S. Navy presence. Downtown, the historic Gaslamp Quarter sits several blocks inland from the bayfront Embarcadero, and the uptown neighborhood of Hillcrest has prime bay views from about a mile away.

Almost but not quite an island, Coronado lies smack-dab in the middle of San Diego Bay. The communities of Ocean Beach, Mission Beach, and Pacific Beach — as their names imply — sit directly on the water, upcoast from the city proper, with La Jolla (pronounced la-HOY-ya) occupying its own hilly peninsula at the northernmost edge.

You'll probably spend freeway drive time on I-5, which runs through San Diego north-south, jogging a bit around downtown before it leads straight to the border. East-west I-8 passes above Hillcrest and Old Town on its way to Mission Bay.

Here's a quick rundown of what you can expect in San Diego's main neighborhoods.

Downtown

The heart of San Diego still beats in its original downtown, especially the fun, commercial **Gaslamp Quarter.** Once known as a raunchy red-light district, the Quarter — loosely bounded by Broadway, Island Avenue, and 1st and 5th avenues — now boasts splendid late-19th- and early-20th-century buildings housing trendy restaurants, upscale nightspots, and art galleries.

Situated along Harbor Drive between Ash and Market streets, the **Embarcadero** is San Diego's waterfront, with hotels, attractions, and plenty of activity, from commercial fishing to a busy cruise-ship terminal.

North of the downtown core (between downtown and the airport), **Little Italy** is quickly gaining a reputation as an art and interior-design district. It stretches along India and Columbia streets and Kettner Boulevard between Cedar and Kalmia streets. And yes, it still boasts the best pizza and cannoli in town!

Downtown San Diego

Accommodations ■
La Pensione Hotel **3**
Holiday Inn on the Bay **4**
Gaslamp Plaza Suites **7**
Horton Grand **13**

Dining ◆
Croce's **9**
Filippi's Pizza Grotto **2**
Fio's **10**
Laurel **1**
The Fish Market/
   Top of the Market **5**

Shopping, Etc. ●
Horton Plaza **11**
Le Travel Store **12**
Many Hands **15**
Unicorn Antique Mall **14**
Seaport Village **15**

Nightlife ●
Croce's Nightclubs **9**
4th & B **6**
The Bitter End **10**
Martini Ranch **8**
Princess Pub & Grille **3**

Hillcrest

San Diego's early elite rode home in horse-drawn carriages to uptown neighborhoods with nicknames like "Banker's Hill" and "Pill Hill" (the doctors' 'hood). Preservation-minded residents, including a very active and fashionable gay community, have restored Hillcrest's charms after years of neglect. Think of Hillcrest as the local equivalent of L.A.'s West Hollywood or New York's SoHo. Loosely bounded by Washington and Hawthorn streets to the north and south, deep hilly ravines to the west, and 6th Avenue at the east, Hillcrest stretches along the edge of San Diego's green jewel, Balboa Park (see "The Best of the Rest: Balboa Park," later in the chapter).

Old Town

Its official name is **Old Town State Historic Park,** and this Williamsburg of the West is closed to vehicular traffic. Nestled into a wedge north of the airport where the I-5 and I-8 freeways intersect, the compact, Spanish-era core of San Diego is a genuine historic area that has been bastardized by commercialism. Nevertheless, I appreciate the opportunity to experience the vestige of history that remains. The interactive and educational aspects have been steadily improving (making it a great place to bring kids), and many of you will enjoy the history lesson and the notable 19th-century buildings. The shopping is generally avoidable unless you're prowling for souvenirs, but even locals come for the good restaurants.

Coronado

Located in the middle of San Diego Bay west of downtown, the "island" of Coronado is actually a peninsula, best known for the landmark **Hotel Del Coronado**, the Victorian grande dame most famous for its co-starring role — alongside Marilyn Monroe — in *Some Like It Hot.* Coronado is home to the U.S. Naval Air Station, a village of pretty cottages, charming shops along Orange Avenue, and a lovely duned beach. You can reach it from the "mainland" via the soaring Coronado Bay Bridge, a thrilling span to drive.

Mission Bay

This labyrinth of protected waterways may look artificial, but Mission Bay is really a natural saltwater bay that selective dredging has enhanced for use as an aquatic playground. Condos, cottages, and a few choice hotels line the shore, along with paved paths for joggers, in-line skaters, and bicyclists. **SeaWorld** is located on prime bayfront property.

The bay, bounded on the south and east by the San Diego River and I-5, is separated from the ocean by a narrow strip of land known as **Mission Beach,** a funky community of artists, free spirits, and surfers. This is a great place to base yourself if you want to be close to both the beach and downtown's attractions.

Hillcrest

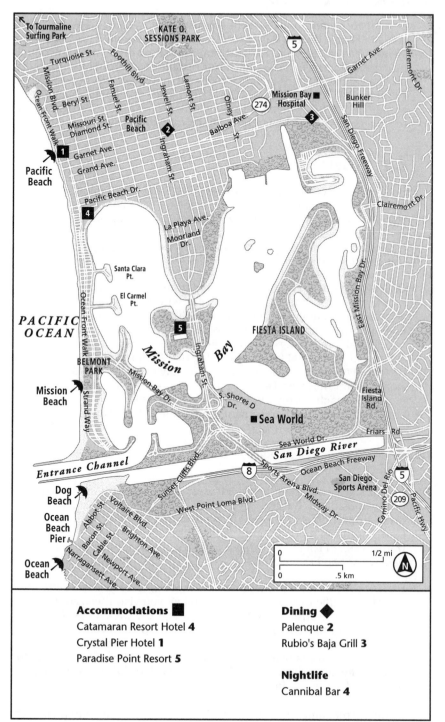

Accommodations ■

Catamaran Resort Hotel **4**
Crystal Pier Hotel **1**
Paradise Point Resort **5**

Dining ◆

Palenque **2**
Rubio's Baja Grill **3**

Nightlife

Cannibal Bar **4**

Pacific Beach

Looking for superlative dining or sophisticated culture? Then don't come to Pacific Beach. This water-hugging neighborhood north of Mission Bay is laid-back to the extreme, featuring acres of family-friendly beach and dozens of casual pub-style restaurants where the cuisine takes a back seat to the sunset view (and happy-hour discounts). **Ocean Front Walk** is a paved promenade featuring an eye-popping human parade akin to L.A.'s Venice Beach boardwalk. This is another great place to stay for easy access to both the beach and downtown.

La Jolla

Both chic and conservative, this wealthy Rodeo-Drive–meets-the-Mediterranean community is surrounded by beach and boasts out-standing restaurants and pricey shopping in "the village." The scenic spot that appears on most postcards is stunning **La Jolla Cove.** The cliffs above the cove hold grassy **Ellen Browning Scripps Park,** a per-fect spot for picnicking.

On the down side, La Jolla is insulated from most of San Diego, because it's at the northernmost edge of the city with no convenient freeway access. In rush hour, getting from the village to I-5 can take half an hour, plus a 10-minute drive to downtown. This makes La Jolla a poor base if you're planning to hop in the car every morning for far-flung sightseeing, but ideal for experiencing the "California Riviera" vibe that this jewel is known for. If you choose to stay elsewhere, La Jolla is worth an afternoon and evening for window-shopping and excellent dining. To reach Torrey Pines Road, La Jolla's main artery, take I-5 north to Ardath Road, or I-5 south to La Jolla Village Drive.

Getting Around

Chances are very good that you'll want to have a car. San Diego is pretty spread out, but the city is one of California's easiest cities to drive around. Streets are clearly marked, and traffic is relatively light except for brief morning and evening rush hours. Although the public transit system isn't as worthless as L.A.'s, it's certainly not as compre-hensive as San Francisco's.

Driving is a nuisance in certain areas, most notably the **Gaslamp Quarter,** Pacific Beach, and La Jolla. When you visit these spots, park your car on the street or in a parking garage and walk instead. If you stay in one of these neighborhoods and don't plan to venture much beyond it other than where public transportation can take you effi-ciently, you can easily make do without a car. But if you want to explore more of the city or visit the **Wild Animal Park** or **LEGOLAND,** mass transit will leave you in the lurch.

If you are planning to do without wheels, consult a map and pick your hotel carefully so you won't feel stranded.

Tips for driving and parking

Pay careful attention to freeway exits, because the names can differ from one direction to the other. For example, to reach La Jolla, you take Ardath Road from I-5 north, but La Jolla Village Drive from I-5 south.

Finding a place to stow a car is pretty easy in San Diego, but it may strain your supply of small change. Parking meters are plentiful in most areas: Posted signs indicate operating hours — generally between 8 a.m. and 6 p.m., even on weekends — and most meters accept only quarters.

In the **Gaslamp Quarter,** consider parking in Horton Plaza's garage (G Street and 4th Avenue), which is free to shoppers for the first 3 hours, $1 for every additional hour; it's also free daily after 5 p.m.

Spaces are elusive in downtown La Jolla, because street parking is free and public lots are scarce.

By bus and by trolley

The San Diego Metropolitan Transit System or MTS (☎ **619-685-4900** or 619-233-3004; www.sdcommute.com/sdmts) operates city buses and trolleys.

The terrific *San Diego Trolley* system runs bright-red trains south to the Mexican border (a 40-minute trip) and north to **Old Town** and **Mission Valley**, a sprawling slice of suburbia with mega shopping centers. Within the city, trolleys stop at many popular locations, and the fare is $1; the fare to the Mexican border is $2. Children under 5 ride free; seniors and riders with disabilities pay 75¢.

Trolleys operate on a self-service fare-collection system; purchase your ticket from machines in the station before boarding. Trains run every 15 minutes during the day, every half-hour at night. Trolleys generally operate daily from 5 a.m. to about 12:30 a.m., although the Blue Line, which goes to the border, runs around the clock on Saturday.

Unfortunately, the trolleys don't come close to covering the entire city. If they go where you're going, *hooray*. If not, take the bus.

Rectangular blue signs mark bus stops at every other block or so on local routes. Most fares range from $1.75 to $3, depending on the distance and type of service (local or express). Exact change is required ($1 bills are accepted). Get a transfer from the driver when boarding.

For recorded MTS information, call ☎ **619-685-4900.** To talk to a real person, call ☎ **619-233-3004** daily between 5:30 a.m. and 8:30 p.m. Because the MTS controls both the buses and trolleys, they do a pretty good job of providing you with info on using them in conjunction. The **Transit Store,** 102 Broadway, at 1st Avenue (☎ **619-234-1060**), is a complete information center, supplying passes, tokens, timetables, and maps. The store is open weekdays 8:30 a.m. to 5:30 p.m., Saturday and Sunday noon to 4 p.m.

The *Day Tripper pass* allows unlimited rides on the public transit system (buses and trolleys). Passes are good for 1, 2, 3, and 4 consecutive days, and cost $5, $8, $10, and $12, respectively. You can get Day Trippers from the Transit Store and all Trolley Station ticket vending machines.

Some hotels offer complimentary shuttles to popular shopping and/or dining areas around town. Check to see if yours does.

By taxi: Call ahead

Taxis don't cruise the streets, so call ahead for quick pickup. If you're at a hotel or restaurant, the front-desk attendant or maitre d' will call for you.

Among the local companies are Orange Cab (☎ 619-291-3333), San Diego Cab (☎ 619-226-TAXI), and Yellow Cab (☎ 619-234-6161). In La Jolla, use La Jolla Cab (☎ 858-453-4222).

Ferry on over to Coronado

The pedestrian-only **Coronado Ferry** (☎ 619-234-4111) is a charming way to get a quickie harbor cruise, and a boon if you're concerned about fighting street traffic on crowded summer weekends. It leaves from the Broadway Pier on the **Embarcadero** (at the foot of Broadway) every hour; the one-way fare is $2 per person.

After the 15-minute ride across San Diego Bay, the ferry docks at **Coronado's Ferry Landing Marketplace,** which is a stop along the Coronado Shuttle route (☎ 619-233-3004). Run by the MTS (and officially known as bus route no. 904), the Coronado Shuttle runs between Coronado's bay side and its ocean side primarily along Orange Avenue (Coronado's main drag) daily from 9:30 a.m. to 5:30 p.m. Stops include the **Hotel Del, Loews,** and the **visitor center.** The fare is $1.

Staying in Style

The San Diego lodging scene has multiple personalities. Downtown hotels cater to conventions, so they tend to have reduced weekend rates. Seaside hotels, on the other hand, sometimes offer deals mid-week, and always have lower prices after summer ends.

If you're planning to visit between Memorial Day and Labor Day, make your reservations several months in advance, especially if you want a hotel on the beach.

Some people worry about air conditioning in hotels, but San Diego's cooling ocean breezes make that a minor concern. Still, if you're visiting between July and September and are particularly sensitive, you should ask about A/C when booking.

Don't forget to count on an extra 10½ percent in taxes being tacked on your hotel bill.

Catamaran Resort Hotel

$$$ Pacific Beach

Lush palm groves and night-lit tiki torches amplify the Polynesian theme at this large, activity-oriented bay-front resort — imagine Gilligan's Island with in-room coffeemakers and poolside cocktails. Tower rooms offer the best views, while the low-rise rooms feel the most resortlike. After dark the Cannibal Bar pumps up the volume, and the Pacific Beach party scene is just a couple of blocks away.

3999 Mission Blvd., Pacific Beach. ☎ *800-422-8386 or 858-488-1081. Fax: 858-488-1387. Internet:* www.catamaranresort.com. *To get there: Take I-5 to Grand/Garnet exit; go west on Grand Ave., then 4 blocks south on Mission Blvd. Parking: $6 to self-park, $8 to valet. Rack rates: $195–$265 double. Deals: Rates often drop based on occupancy; packages are also available, like the B&B deal, which includes breakfast and room tax for as little as $140 per night. AE, DC, DISC, MC, V.*

Crystal Pier Hotel

$$–$$$$ Pacific Beach

Built on an ocean pier, these 26 wooden cottages (circa 1936, but recently renovated) are San Diego's most unusual lodgings. Like tiny vacation homes, they're as darling as can be, and book up *really* fast for summer. Each has a private patio, living room, bedroom, full kitchen, and breathtaking sunset views. Beach gear is available for rent, but BYO beach towels.

4500 Ocean Blvd., Pacific Beach. ☎ *800-748-5894 or 858-483-6983. Fax: 858-483-6811. To get there: Take I-5 to Grand/Garnet exit; follow Garnet Ave. to the pier. Parking: Free! Rack rates: Mid-June–mid-Sept, $135–$335 cottage; late Sept–early June, $105–$275 double. Deals: Rates are pretty much set, but most cottages sleep up to 4 people for the same price. DISC, MC, V.*

Gaslamp Plaza Suites

$$ Gaslamp Quarter

Once an office building and now a 64-room boutique hotel, this impeccably restored Victorian at the center of the vibrant Gaslamp Quarter boasts an elegance and drama that belie its bargain rates. Room appointments say "indulgence" rather than "economy," especially in the impressive bathrooms. Plenty of exquisite period detail — wood, marble, and etched glass — that must have cost a fortune in 1913. Beware the cheapest rooms — they're tiny — and the nighttime neighborhood revelry may disturb a light sleeper.

520 E. St. (at 5th Ave.), Gaslamp Quarter. ☎ *800-874-8770 or 619-232-9500. Fax: 619-238-9945. Valet parking: $11. Rack rates: $93–$139 double. Rates include a very basic continental breakfast. Deals: AAA members get a 10 percent discount. AE, CB, DC, DISC, MC, V.*

Hacienda Hotel

$$ Old Town

At this Best Western all-suite hotel perched above Old Town, walkways thread through attractive courtyards bearing a rustic Mexican Colonial ambience. This hotel is tops in its price range, with extensive in-room amenities, tons of on-site services, and plenty of fun 'n' food within easy walking distance.

4041 Harney St., Old Town. ☎ *800-888-1991 or 619-298-4707. Fax: 619-298-4771. Internet:* www.haciendahotel-oldtown.com. *To get there: Take I-5 to Old Town Ave. exit, turn left onto San Diego Ave. and right onto Harney St. Parking: Free! Rack rates: $135–155 double. Deals: Off-season rates available, plus AAA discounts. AE, CB, DC, DISC, MC, V.*

Heritage Park Bed & Breakfast Inn

$$–$$$ Old Town

Surrender to the romance of utterly charming bedrooms, polished and pampering service from a friendly staff, and attention to every conceivable detail in this exquisite 1889 Queen Anne mansion, set on a hillside a short walk from Old Town dining and shopping.

2470 Heritage Park Row (off Harney St.), Old Town. ☎ *800-995-2470 or 619-299-6832. Fax: 619-299-9465. Internet:* www.heritageparkinn.com. *To get there: I-5 to Old Town Ave. exit; turn left onto San Diego Ave., then right on Harney St. Parking: Free! Rack rates: $100–$235 double. Rates include an extravagant breakfast, abundant tea sandwiches, and in-room goodies. AE, DC, DISC, MC, V.*

Holiday Inn on the Bay

$$–$$$ Downtown

Sprawling along the Embarcadero, this predictable but appealing and well-maintained chain hotel offers 600 rooms in a variety of buildings; choose the tower for cool bay or city views. Airport-convenient, the hotel boasts a bevy of on-site dining options and swimming pools plus the restaurants and recreation of the bay boardwalk across the street, making families happy as clams.

1355 N. Harbor Dr. (at Ash St.). ☎ *800-HOLIDAY or 619-232-3861. Fax: 619-232-4924. Internet:* www.holiday-inn.com. *To get there: From the airport, follow Harbor Dr. south. Parking: $13 to self-park, $18 to valet. Rack rates: $189–$209 double. Deals: No one pays rack here; the zoo/breakfast package can be as low as $159, and AARP and AAA discounts are available year-round, bringing the rate as low as $110–$139. AE, DC, MC, V.*

Horton Grand

$$–$$$ Gaslamp Quarter

Two historic hotels (one a notorious brothel) were linked to form this full-service boutique hotel with the studied aura of yesteryear. Not pristine, but charming, frilly, and just steps from hot nightlife.

311 Island Ave. (at 4th Ave.), Gaslamp Quarter. ☎ *800-542-1886 or 619-544-1886. Fax: 619-544-0058. Internet:* www.hortongrand.com. *To get there: From the airport, take Harbor Dr. south to Market St. east; turn right on 4th Ave. Bus 1 or 4; Convention Center trolley stop. Valet parking: $10. Rack rates: $139–$169 double. Deals: Packages prices start at $165, including parking, tax, and tips, plus extras like breakfast and/or champagne. AE, DC, MC, V.*

Hotel del Coronado

$$$–$$$$$ Coronado

This grand old seaside Victorian is my favorite place to stay in San Diego. Opened in 1888, it's loaded with personality and storybook architecture. You can see the landmarked red turrets from miles away. Rooms range from compact to extravagant. Those in the original building overflow with antique charm and perfectly modern appointments, while Ocean Towers rooms sport a contemporary look. A pristine white-sand beach awaits, along with swimming pools, tennis, day-spa facilities, and a worthwhile guided tour. During Christmas, the hotel is festooned with thousands of tiny white lights that can be seen from miles around.

1500 Orange Ave., Coronado. ☎ *800-468-3533 or 935-435-8000. Fax: 935-522-8238. Internet:* www.hoteldel.com. *To get there: From Coronado Bridge, turn left onto Orange Ave. Parking: $12 to self-park, $16 to valet. Rack rates: $215–$340 double (garden or city view), $360–$640 double (ocean view). Deals: Sport, spa, and romance packages available. AE, CB, DC, DISC, MC, V.*

La Pensione Hotel

$ Little Italy

This remarkable value is conveniently located to Downtown attractions and draws folks who seek out economy without compromise (that is, no youth hostels). While not large, guest rooms make the most of their space and feature minimalist modern furniture that's durable without looking cheap. Extras include fridges and microwaves, plus Little Italy shopping and dining just outside. Ask for a city or bay view; the nearby train tracks may bother extra-light sleepers, but most guests never even notice the noise.

1700 India St. (at Date St.), Little Italy. ☎ *800-232-4683 or 619-236-8000. Fax: 619-236-8088. Internet:* www.lapensionehotel.com. *To get there: From the airport, follow Harbor Dr. south to A St. east; turn left on India. Bus 5. Parking: Free! Rack rates: $60–$80 double. AE, DC, DISC, MC, V.*

La Valencia Hotel

$$$$$ La Jolla

Within its bougainvillea-draped walls and wrought-iron garden gates, this cliff-top bastion of gentility has been La Jolla's crown jewel since it opened in 1926. Though the bathrooms can be smallish, every fabric and furnishing is of the finest quality, and the service is exceptional. The hotel overlooks La Jolla Cove and features the clubby Whaling Bar, heady with expensive Scotch. It's long been a hideaway for Hollywood celebs, and its colorful dome was used as a civil defense lookout during World War II.

1132 Prospect St. (at Herschel Ave.), La Jolla. ☎ *800-451-0772 or 858-454-0771. Fax: 858-456-3921. Internet:* www.lavalencia.com. *To get there: From Torrey Pines Rd., turn right on Prospect Place, which becomes Prospect St. Valet parking: $14. Rack rates: $275–$550 double. AE, DC, DISC, MC, V.*

Paradise Point Resort

$$$–$$$$$ Mission Bay

Situated on its own island in Mission Bay, this complex is as much a theme park as its closest neighbor, SeaWorld (a three-minute drive). You can have so much fun here that you may never want to leave. Single-story duplex bungalows dot 44 acres of tropical gardens and swim-friendly beaches. All have private patios (many facing duck-filled lagoons) and plenty of thoughtful conveniences. Recent renovations kept the low-tech '60s charm but lost the tacky holdovers; rooms now sport refreshingly colorful beach-cottage decor.

1404 W. Vacation Rd., Mission Bay. ☎ *800-344-2626 or 858-274-4630. Fax: 858-581-5977. Internet:* www.paradisepoint.com. *To get there: I-8 west to Mission Bay Dr. exit; take Ingraham St. north to Vacation Rd. Parking: Free! Rack rates: Memorial Day–Labor Day, $220–$350 double; mid-Sept–mid-May, $175–$325 double. Deals: Ask about packages and discounts, as you can always find a deal. AE, DC, DISC, MC, V.*

Sommerset Suites Hotel

$$–$$$ Hillcrest

This all-suite hotel on a busy street has an apartment-like ambience and unexpected amenities like huge closets, medicine cabinets, and fully equipped kitchens in all rooms; executive suites even have dishwashers. Other terrific touches include a basket of welcome snacks, a courtesy van to shopping and attractions, and an afternoon wine reception. Several blocks of chic Hillcrest lie within easy walking distance.

606 Washington St. (at 5th Ave.), Hillcrest. ☎ *800-962-9665 or 619-692-5200. Fax: 619-692-5299. Internet:* www.sommersetsuites.com. *To get there: I-5 to Washington St. exit. Parking: Free! Rack rates: $135–$195 double. Deals: Occasional discounts edge rates down to around $100, so be sure to ask. AE, DC, DISC, MC, V.*

Dining Out

No, San Diego will never compete with New York or San Francisco on the culinary playing field, but its growing sophistication has sparked a new spirit of experimentation and style.

Azzura Point

$$$$$ Coronado CALIFORNIA/MEDITERRANEAN

This stylishly contemporary dining room wins continual raves from deep-pocketed San Diego foodies willing to cross the bay for inventive and artistic Cal-Med creations from pedigreed chefs. The restaurant is the best in town for fine cuisine in a chic setting — plushly upholstered, gilded, and view-endowed.

In the Loews Coronado Bay Resort, 4000 Coronado Bay Rd., Coronado. ☎ 935-424-4000. Reservations recommended. To get there: From downtown Coronado, Orange Blvd. south, which becomes Silver Strand Blvd.; turn at Coronado Bay Rd. Main courses: $21–$35. AE, CB, DC, DISC, MC, V. Open: Dinner Tues–Sun.

Casa de Bandini

$$ Old Town MEXICAN

Margaritas and mariachis make this picturesque adobe hacienda a San Diego tradition. Old Town's best setting, particularly the vine-shaded patio next to the trickling tiled fountain, improves the predictable food. Locals and visitors alike keep the waiting lines long on weekends, while towering tostada salads also draw a devoted lunch crowd.

2754 Calhoun St. (opposite Old Town Plaza), Old Town. ☎ 619-297-8211. Reservations not accepted. To get there: Follow Juan St. to Mason St. for easy parking; the restaurant is just uphill. Main courses: $6–$15. AE, CB, DC, DISC, MC, V. Open: Lunch through dinner daily.

Croce's

$$$–$$$$ Gaslamp Quarter AMERICAN/ECLECTIC

The restaurant, founded by Ingrid Croce (widow of singer-songwriter Jim "If I Could Save Time in a Bottle" Croce), helped spark the Gaslamp Quarter's resurgence, and has grown to fill every corner of its 1890 building with dining rooms and hip nightspots. The menu's fusion of Southern soul food, Southwestern spice, and other whims succeeds fairly well. Without the distraction of jazz and R&B bands wafting in, diners may be more discerning; still, Croce's is always packed, and always happening.

802 5th Ave. (at F St.). ☎ 619-233-4355. Internet: www.croces.com. Call for same-day priority seating (before walk-ins). To get there: Bus lines 1, 3, 5, 15, or 16; 5th Ave. trolley stop. Main courses: $14–$23. AE, DC, DISC, MC, V. Open: Dinner nightly.

Extraordinary Desserts

$ Hillcrest PASTRIES/CAKES

Attention, dessert-lovers: Don't miss chef Karen Krasne's shrine to all things sweet, which serves only the favorite course (plus gourmet coffees and teas). Among the dozens of divine creations that blend Parisian style with exotic ingredients and homespun favorites are raspberry linzer torte layered with white-chocolate buttercream, and Grand Marnier chocolate cheesecake on a brownie crust and sealed with bittersweet ganache. Definitely extraordinary!

2929 5th Ave. (between Palm and Quince sts.), Hillcrest. ☎ 619-294-7001. Reservations not accepted. To get there: Bus 1, 3, or 25. Desserts: $2–$6. MC, V. Open: All day Mon–Fri, afternoon and evening Sat–Sun.

Filippi's Pizza Grotto

$–$$ Little Italy   ITALIAN

Several reasons explain why Filippi's has been a Little Italy anchor since 1950 —the food is molto bueno, the portions enormous, and the staff welcomes everyone like family. Just follow the intoxicating aroma of traditional Sicilian pizza, lasagne, spaghetti, and antipasto through the Italian grocery/deli to the back dining room, traditionally outfitted with Chianti bottles and red-checked tablecloths.

1747 India St. (between Fir and Date Sts.), Little Italy. ☎ 619-232-5095. Reservations not taken. To get there: Little Italy trolley stop or bus 5. Main courses: $4.75–$12.50. AE, DC, DISC, MC, V. Open: Lunch through dinner daily.

Fio's

$$$ Gaslamp Quarter   NORTHERN ITALIAN

The granddaddy of San Diego's trendy trattorias has a sophisticated ambience and a constant crowd. While the Northern Italian cuisine is no longer cutting edge, practice has made the kitchen consistently good at delivering delicately sauced pastas, crispy gourmet pizzas, and impressive meats like veal shank on saffron risotto. Come without a reservation and you can still get the full menu at the elegant bar.

801 5th Ave. (at F St.), Gaslamp Quarter. ☎ 619-234-3467. Internet: www. fioscucina.com. Reservations recommended. To get there: Bus 1, 3, 5, 15, or 16; 5th Ave. trolley stop. Main courses: $11–$25. Open: Dinner nightly.

The Fish Market/Top of the Market

$$$/$$$$ The Embarcadero   SEAFOOD

Ask any San Diegan where to go for the freshest fish, and they'll send you to the bustling Fish Market. Chalkboards announce the day's catches, available in a number of simple, classic preparations. Upstairs, Top of the Market offers similar fare at jacked-up prices; I recommend having a cocktail in the posh, clubby Top — which has stupendous bay views — then heading downstairs to the more cheery, casual restaurant for affordable eats, including treats from the sushi and oyster bars.

On the Embarcadero, 750 N. Harbor Dr. ☎ 619-232-3474 downstairs, 619-234-4867 upstairs. Internet: www.thefishmarket.com. Reservations not taken downstairs, recommended upstairs. To get there: Seaport Village trolley stop or bus 7/7B. Main courses: $9–$25 downstairs, $16–$32 upstairs. AE, CB, DC, DISC, MC, V. Open: Lunch and dinner daily.

George's at the Cove/George's Ocean Terrace

$$$$/$$–$$$ La Jolla CALIFORNIA

These sibling restaurants — a fancy downstairs dining room and a breezy upstairs cafe — share an *aah*-inspiring ocean view, attentive service, and tasty smoked chicken/broccoli/black bean soup. George's downstairs kitchen turns up the finesse factor for inventive and formal California cuisine, while the Ocean Terrace cafe offers crowd-pleasing versions. Both are great, so choose based on your mood and budget.

1250 Prospect St., La Jolla. ☎ *858-454-4244. Internet:* www.georgesatthe cove.com. *Reservations recommended at George's, not accepted at Ocean Terrace. To get there: From Torrey Pines Rd., right on Prospect Place, which becomes Prospect St. Main courses: George's, $10–$15 at lunch, $21–$31 at dinner; Ocean Terrace, $10–$15. AE, DC, DISC, MC, V. Open: Lunch and dinner daily.*

Laurel

$$$$ Downtown/Hillcrest FRENCH/MEDITERRANEAN

Here's a restaurant that takes itself seriously. It offers a swank room, formal service, and classic French cuisine tempered with some refreshingly rustic Mediterranean elements. This restaurant is pleasant evidence that the San Diego restaurant scene has gotten with it.

Laurel is the best choice for pre-theater dining, thanks to the shuttle service they offer to and from the Old Globe Theatre, which allows you to leave your car at the restaurant and not bother with Balboa Park parking. The ride is pleasant, efficient, and absolutely free (for the price of dinner, of course).

505 Laurel St. (at 5th Ave.), on the border between downtown and Hillcrest. ☎ *619-239-2222. Internet:* www.winesellar.com. *Reservations recommended. To get there: Bus 1, 3, or 25. Main courses: $15–$26. AE, CB, DC, DISC, JCB, MC, V. Open: Dinner nightly.*

Mixx

$$$ Hillcrest CALIFORNIA/ECLECTIC

Aptly named for its subtle global fusion fare, Mixx embodies everything good about Hillcrest dining: an attractive and relaxing room, a sophisticated crowd, thoughtfully composed meals, and polished, friendly service. Hip locals gravitate toward this comfy, jovial place to see what the inventive chef will think up next. Allow time to search for that elusive Hillcrest parking space!

3671 5th Ave. (at Pennsylvania Ave.) ☎ *619-299-6499. Reservations recommended, especially on weekends. To get there: Bus 1, 3, or 25. Main courses: $11–$19. AE, CB, DC, DISC, MC, V. Open: Dinner nightly.*

Palenque

$–$$ Pacific Beach MEXICAN

Palenque is hard to find, but oh-so-worth the search. The menu draws on culinary traditions from Mexico's central region. The earthy mole sauce is the best in San Diego, as are the freshly patted tortillas and homemade salsa. Everything tastes as if it was lovingly prepared by your very own Mexican grandma. Choose between patio and airy, casual inside dining.

1653 Garnet Ave. (at Jewell St.), Pacific Beach. ☎ *858-272-7816. Reservations not taken. To get there: Bus 27. Main courses: $4–8 at lunch, $9–$15 at dinner. AE, MC, V. Open: Lunch and dinner daily.*

Rubio's Baja Grill

$ Pacific Beach TACOS

Local-surfer-made-good Ralph Rubio brought home the simple recipe common to Mexican fishing villages — batter-dipped, deep-fried fish fillets folded in corn tortillas and garnished with shredded cabbage, salsa, and tangy *crema* sauce — and launched the you-can't-eat-just-one Baja fish tacos craze. Wash 'em down with an ice-cold something. All over San Diego, but the original is the most fun.

4504 Mission Bay Dr., Pacific Beach. ☎ *858-272-2801. Internet:* www.rubios.com. *Main courses: Most under $5. MC, V. Open: Lunch and dinner daily.*

Trattoria Acqua

$$$ La Jolla ITALIAN/MEDITERRANEAN

Enjoy the Italian Mediterranean ambience of this romantic restaurant, where diners are encouraged to relax and linger over rich pastas like veal-and-mortadella tortellini in fennel cream sauce. The menu always has plenty of *secondi* as well, and every pasta is available in an appetizer portion (how considerate!). The wine list is a perennial *Wine Spectator* award-winner.

1298 Prospect St. (on Coast Walk), La Jolla. ☎ *858-454-0709. Internet:* www.trattoriaacqua.com. *Reservations recommended for dinner. To get there: From Torrey Pines Rd., right on Prospect Pl., which becomes Prospect St. Main courses: $13–$25. AE, MC, V. Open: Lunch and dinner daily.*

The Vegetarian Zone

$ Hillcrest INTERNATIONAL VEGETARIAN

Even if you're wary of tofu and tempeh, you'll like this ethnically accented food, which is so mainstream — and good — you'll forget that it just happens to be vegetarian. Menu standouts include Greek spinach-and-feta pie, daily soups and stews, and homemade salad dressings that taste too good to be this healthy. San Diegans from all walks of life quickly fill the casual indoor/outdoor seating at mealtimes.

2949 5th Ave. (between Palm and Quince sts.), Hillcrest. ☎ *619-298-7302.*
Reservations not taken. To get there: Bus 1, 3, or 25. Main courses: $5–$10. AE, DC,
DISC, MC, V. Open: Lunch and dinner daily.

Exploring San Diego

What do San Diego and central Florida have in common? They both
feature big-name family attractions, the spend-all-day kinds of places
around which you're probably planning your stay. The following
section contains everything you need to know about them, plus
suggestions for filling any free time after you're done.

The "Big Four" — The animal and theme parks

Each of these parks deserves a full, dedicated day.

San Diego's three main family attractions have joined forces, offering
combo ticket deals that reward you with big savings for taking on what I
like to call the Vacation Endurance Challenge. Here's how it works: You
get to visit both the **San Diego Zoo** and **Wild Animal Park** (deluxe zoo
package, Wild Animal Park admission) for $38.35 adults and $23.15 for
kids 3 to 11. The two-park ticket includes one visit to each attraction,
which you must use within five days of purchase.

What's that? You say you want more? Add **SeaWorld** to your plans with
a three-park ticket (deluxe zoo package, Wild Animal Park admission,
SeaWorld admission) for $73.95 adults, $50.95 kids 3 to 11. With this
one, you get unlimited use at all three parks for five days from date of
purchase — wow!

SeaWorld

One of the best-promoted attractions in California, this 165-acre aquatic
playground is a showplace for marine life, made politically correct with
an only nominally "educational" atmosphere that I wish they took further. At its heart, it's a fun-filled family entertainment center with performing dolphins, otters, sea lions, walruses, and seals. Several
successive 4-ton black-and-white killer whales have functioned as the
park's mascot, Shamu.

The hands-on area called **Shamu's Happy Harbor** encourages kids to
play and get wet. The newest attraction is **Shipwreck Rapids,** a wet
adventure ride on raftlike inner tubes that float through caverns, waterfalls, and wild rivers. Shows for short attention spans run continuously
throughout the day, and you can rotate through the various theaters;
best is the silly, plot-driven sea lions-go-to-Gilligan's Island show. Other
draws include **Wild Arctic,** an extremely cool virtual-reality trip to the
frozen North, complete with polar bears, beluga whales, walruses, and

harbor seals, that's well worth making time for; and **Shamu Close Up,** where you can watch the whales in their off hours through underwater windows while keepers explain what you're seeing.

500 Sea World Dr., Mission Bay. ☎ *858-226-3901. Internet:* www.seaworld.com. *To get there: From I-5, take the Sea World Dr. exit; from I-8, take W. Mission Bay Dr. exit to Sea World Dr. Bus 9. Admission: $39 adults, $35 seniors, $30 kids 3–11. Open: Memorial Day–Labor Day, daily 9 a.m.–11 p.m. (sometimes midnight); Sept–May, daily 10 a.m.–5 p.m.*

San Diego Zoo

More than 4,000 animals reside at this world-famous zoo, founded in 1916. Even if other zoos have caught up to it in terms of animal awareness in the intervening century, this granddaddy is still highly respected in the field. Every new exhibit features an even more high-tech method for simulating the climate, flora, and other conditions of the residents' natural habitat, and the preservation of endangered species is a primary concern. It also happens to be a whole lot of fun.

The 1996 loan of two magnificent giant pandas from the People's Republic of China brought the zoo more attention than ever, and in 1999, Bai Yun and Shi Shi became the parents of Hua Mei, an adorable baby panda who's quite an achievement of reproductive research (pandas rarely conceive in captivity). The pandas are the big attention-getters — and deservedly so — but the zoo contains many other rare and exotic species: cuddly koalas from Australia, long-billed kiwis from New Zealand, wild Przewalski horses from Mongolia, lowland gorillas from Africa, and giant tortoises from the Galapagos. Zoo regulars — lions, elephants, giraffes, tigers, and bears — prowl around as well, all housed in moated enclosures that resemble their natural habitats.

The zoo offers two types of *bus tours,* a 35-minute guided tour, and an on/off bus ticket you can use throughout the day. Both provide a narrated overview and allow you to see 75 percent of the park. I strongly encourage first-timers, especially parents with young kids, to spend the extra few bucks on the bus, as the zoo covers a lot of acreage, much of it terraced and extremely hilly. You can then use your energy to revisit the creatures that you like best, and to see those not covered on the tour, like the pandas. Even by starting with the bus tour you'll have a hard time visiting everything in the course of a long day, so wear your most comfortable sneakers. Come extra-early or later in afternoon and plan on spending the evening in summer, as the animals tend to hibernate in the heat of day. And don't miss the hippos — if you get lucky, you'll see them frolicking, which is a sight to behold.

2920 Zoo Dr. (off Park Blvd.), Balboa Park. ☎ *619-234-3153. Internet:* www. sandiegozoo.org. *To get there: Bus 7/7B. Admission: $18 adults, $8 kids 3–11. Deluxe package (admission, guided bus tour, round-trip Skyfari aerial tram) $26 adults, $23.40 seniors 60 and over, $14 children. Open: Daily 9 a.m.–4 p.m. (grounds close at 5 p.m.); summer 9 a.m.–9 p.m. (grounds close at 10 p.m.).*

The Zoo versus the Wild Animal Park: How do we choose?

Do both if time allows. Both parks are so different that you won't regret it. If you can't, convenience may be enough of a deciding factor, because the zoo is in the heart of San Diego, while the Wild Animal Park is a hefty 45-minute drive from San Diego. Additionally, you might consider the following factors when making your choice:

✔ The safari-like **Wild Animal Park** gives you the chance to see greater numbers of bigger animals living in a vastly larger territory. The animals don't even know people are spying on them, which means that you have a much better opportunity to see them exhibit natural behavior. They're free (and have space enough) to display herd behavior, and are comfortable enough to do almost anything.

✔ The **San Diego Zoo,** on the other hand, is home to a much more diverse population of animals from around the globe, thanks to the zookeepers' intense effort to reproduce authentic habitats. What's more, shows and attractions lend the zoo more of a colorful amusement park atmosphere, which makes it a better choice if you have little ones in tow. And if you've got a passion for pandas, the zoo's for you, no question!

San Diego Wild Animal Park

Originally begun as a breeding facility for the **San Diego Zoo,** the **San Diego Wild Animal Park (WAP)** now holds around 3,200 animals — many endangered species — all roaming freely over the park's 1,800 acres. Approximately 650 baby animals are born every year in the park.

The real beauty of the park is that you, not the animals, are the caged ones. The park has recently added a network of paths (with catchy but meaningless names like "Kilimanjaro Safari Walk" and "Heart of Africa") that skirt many of the enclosures. The best way to see the animals, however, is by riding the monorail, which is included in the admission price; for the best views, sit on the right-hand side. During the 50-minute ride, you'll pass through vast landscapes resembling Africa and Asia. Trains leave every 20 minutes from the station in *Nairobi Village,* the commercial hub of the park, with souvenir stores and refreshment vendors. (The food is mediocre and overpriced, so think about smuggling in your own snacks.) Otherwise, Nairobi Village is not much more than a small, traditional zoo whose best feature is the nursery area, where you can watch irresistible young'uns frolicking, being bottle-fed, and sleeping — cute!

If you really want to experience the vast landscape and large animals that make the WAP so special, take a *photo caravan tour* ($65 to $95 per person, park admission included). The photo-taking is secondary — for me, anyway — to the enjoyment of crossing the fence to meet rhinos, ostriches, zebras, deer, and giraffes on their home turf. You can even feed the giraffes along the way — *an amazing experience.* Advance reservations are recommended.

15500 San Pasqual Valley Rd., Escondido (30 miles northeast of San Diego). ☎ 760-747-8702. Internet: www.sandiegozoo.org. *To get there: I-15 north to Via Rancho Pkwy.; follow signs for about 3 miles. Admission: $21.95 adults 12 and over, $17.95 seniors, $14.95 kids 3–11, free for kids under 3. Open: Daily 9 a.m.– 4 p.m. (grounds close at 5 p.m.); extended hours in summer and December.*

LEGOLAND

New in 1999, this theme park is the ultimate monument to the world's most famous plastic building blocks. Two other enormously successful LEGOLANDs exist in Denmark and Britain, but this is the only one in America.

LEGOLAND is very cool. Attractions include hands-on interactive displays; a life-size menagerie of tigers, giraffes, and other animals; scale models of international landmarks (the Eiffel Tower, Sydney Opera House, and so on) — all constructed out of real LEGO bricks. "MiniLand" is a 1-to-20 scale representation of good ol' American achievement, from a New England Pilgrim village to Mount Rushmore, with lots of mini-size activity and movable parts. You can even take a gravity coaster ride (don't worry — it is built of steel) through a LEGO castle and a boat ride (steel again) through an international LEGO land.

Although the official guidelines imply that the park is geared toward children of all ages, the average MTV- and Playstation-seasoned kid over 10 will find it kind of a snooze. Don't be afraid that your toddler is too young, though; LEGOLAND has plenty for the little ones to do, including a DUPLO building area. The sheer artistry of construction means that you'll likely enjoy it too, especially if you have nostalgic LEGO memories; Miniland alone kept me enthralled for a couple of hours.

1 Lego Dr., Carlsbad (30 miles north of San Diego). ☎ 877-534-6526 or 760-438-5346. Internet: www.legolandca.com. *To get there: I-5 north to Cannon Rd. exit east, following signs for Lego Dr. Admission: $32 adults, $25 seniors and kids 3–16. Open: Daily 10 a.m.–dusk; extended summer and holiday hours.*

The best of the rest: Balboa Park

Balboa Park is one of San Diego's must-see attractions. Not only does it house the world-famous **San Diego Zoo** (see the previous section), but this verdant wonderland — the second-largest city park in the country, after New York's Central Park — serves as the cultural and recreational heart of the city. Spanish-Moorish buildings originally built for the 1915 Panama-California Exposition house most of the city's museums, surrounded by a series of cultivated gardens, small forests, tropical oases, and shaded groves coaxed from a formerly scruffy brown canyon. Lest it all sound too refined for you, the park boasts plenty of places to play as well.

Balboa Park lies at the northern edge of downtown, bordered on the west by 6th Avenue. From downtown, 12th Avenue leads directly in, becoming Park Boulevard and passing the entrance to the zoo. From

6th Avenue, Laurel Street becomes El Prado, the park's main thorough-fare; many of the park's major museums, along with the Visitor Center, are lined up along this avenue. The park contains plenty of parking lots, though you may not have your first choice on busy days. That's all right, though, because walking from place to place is part of the fun. Distances are easily manageable, but if the hills start to dog you, hop aboard the free park *trams,* which run regularly through the park. (The one exception to the distance rule is the zoo. It sits far enough away that you'll want to use its own lot.)

Sure, San Diego has other museums in town, but because you have lim-ited time (not to mention limited patience), make sightseeing easy on everyone by choosing from among the park's 14-plus museums, which offer more museum fix than you'll need in the course of your visit. The best of the bunch are described in detail below; for a complete list of park attractions, go online to www.balboapark.org or, after you arrive, pick up a map at the well-staffed *Balboa Park Visitors Center,* 1549 El Prado (☎ **619-239-0512**). To get there, take either bus 7/7B, 16, or 25.

In the courtyard behind the center you'll find the brand-new **Prado** (☎ **619-557-9441**), an upscale *Nuevo Latino* restaurant set within the historic walls of the House of Hospitality. If you'd prefer something lower on the food chain price-wise, snack bars and casual cafes are scattered throughout the park.

All of the park's museums are *free* one Tuesday each month. The muse-ums participate on a rotating schedule so that three or more waive their entrance fees every Tuesday. If you plan to visit more than three of the park's museums, buy the *Passport to Balboa Park,* a coupon booklet that allows one entrance to each of 11 museums (the rest are always free) and is valid for one week. You can purchase the $21 pass-port at any participating museum or the visitor center.

Note that many park attractions are closed Monday.

San Diego Aerospace Museum

The number-two kid-pleaser in town (after the Fleet Science Center), this enormously popular museum provides an overview of national and local aviation history, from hot-air balloons to the space age, with plenty of biplanes and fighters in between. The Ford Motor Company built the stunning cylindrical hall, which houses an imaginative gift shop with goodies like freeze-dried astronaut ice cream, in 1935. Plan on spending 1 ½ to 2 ½ hours here.

2001 Pan American Plaza. ☎ *619-234-8291. Internet:* www.aerospacemuseum. org. *Admission: $8 adults, $3 kids 6–17. Free fourth Tues of the month. Open: Daily 10 a.m.–4:30 p.m. (open later in summer).*

Balboa Park

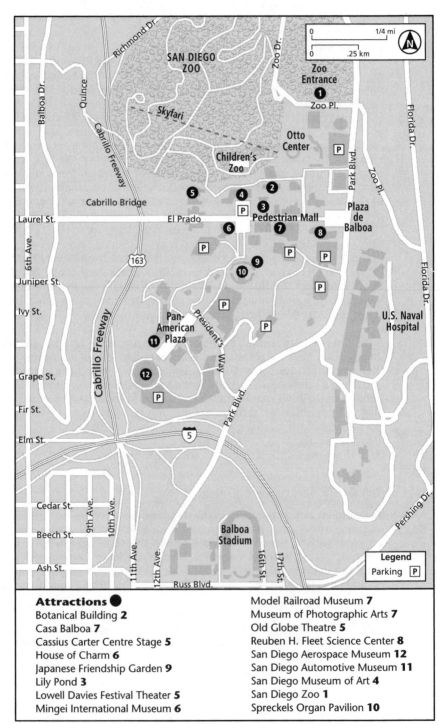

Attractions ●

Botanical Building **2**
Casa Balboa **7**
Cassius Carter Centre Stage **5**
House of Charm **6**
Japanese Friendship Garden **9**
Lily Pond **3**
Lowell Davies Festival Theater **5**
Mingei International Museum **6**

Model Railroad Museum **7**
Museum of Photographic Arts **7**
Old Globe Theatre **5**
Reuben H. Fleet Science Center **8**
San Diego Aerospace Museum **12**
San Diego Automotive Museum **11**
San Diego Museum of Art **4**
San Diego Zoo **1**
Spreckels Organ Pavilion **10**

Reuben H. Fleet Science Center

A must-see for kids of any age — yep, including grown-up kids. This tantalizing collection of hands-on exhibits is designed to provoke the imagination while teaching scientific principles. The newest feature is **SciTours**, a virtual-space simulator ride that resembles Disneyland's Star Tours ride. Although it doesn't seem to have any educational element, it's fun nonetheless. The Fleet also houses a 76-foot domed OMNIMAX theater, an excellent place to experience larger-than-life IMAX films. You'll need 1 ½ to 3 hours to explore all the exhibits, not counting IMAX movie time.

1875 El Prado. ☎ 619-238-1233; Internet: www.rhfleet.org. *Admission: (includes IMAX film, SciTours ride, and exhibit galleries) $11 adults, $9 seniors, $8 kids 3–12. Free first Tues of the month. Open: Mon–Tues 9:30 a.m.–6 p.m., Wed–Thurs 9:30 a.m.–9 p.m., Fri–Sat 9:30 a.m.–10 p.m., Sun 9:30 a.m.–9 p.m.*

San Diego Museum of Art

With one of the grandest entrances along El Prado, this museum also boasts outstanding collections of Italian Renaissance and Dutch and Spanish baroque art, along with an impressive collection of Toulouse-Lautrec's works. The museum often shows prestigious traveling exhibits, and the interactive computer image system allows you to locate highlights and custom-design a tour. Plan on spending 1 to 3 hours here.

1450 El Prado. ☎ 619-232-7931. Internet: www.sdmart.com. *Admission: $8 adults, $6 seniors and young adults 18–24, $3 kids 6–17. Free third Tues of the month. Open: Tues–Sun 10 a.m.–4:30 p.m.*

San Diego Automotive Museum

Even if you don't know a distributor from a dipstick, you'll ooh and aah over the classic, antique, and exotic cars here. Every one is in such pristine condition you'd swear it just rolled off the line, from the 1886 Benz to the 1981 DeLorean. You can easily see the collection in a little over an hour.

2080 Pan American Plaza. ☎ 619-231-2886. Internet: www.sdautomuseum.org. *Admission: $7 adults, $6 seniors, $3 kids 6–15. Free fourth Tues of the month. Open: Daily 10 a.m.–4:30 p.m. (later in summer).*

Museum of Photographic Arts

If names like Ansel Adams, Margaret Bourke-White, Imogen Cunningham, Edward Weston, and Henri Cartier-Bresson pique your interest, then don't miss this 3,600-plus image collection, one of few in the U.S. devoted exclusively to photography. Set aside 1 to 2 hours.

1649 El Prado. ☎ 619-238-7559; Internet: www.mopa.org. *Admission: $4 adults, free for kids under 13 (with adult). Free second Tues of the month. Open: Daily 10 a.m.–5 p.m.*

Model Railroad Museum

While not high culture as we know it, this museum is cool and cute, and well worth 30 to 60 minutes of your time, even if you don't consider yourself a train buff. Six permanent, scale-model railroads depict Southern California's transportation history and terrain with an astounding attention to detail. Kids will love the hands-on Lionel trains, and train buffs of all ages will appreciate the interactive multimedia element.

1649 El Prado. ☎ *619-696-0199. Internet:* www.sdmodelrailroadm.com. *Admission: $4 adults, free for kids under 15 (with adult). Free first Tues of the month. Open: Tues–Fri 11 a.m.–4 p.m., Sat–Sun 11 a.m.–5 p.m.*

Mingei International Museum

This museum offers changing exhibitions generally classifiable as folk art. Works by artists from around the globe run the gamut from textiles and costumes to jewelry and toys to pottery and sculpture. Thanks to the great natural light, the use of natural materials, and the artist's handiwork, it's easy to connect on a human level with the art on display. Anybody who's design-minded or who likes crafts will enjoy spending an hour more here.

1439 El Prado. ☎ *619-239-0003. Internet:* www.mingei.org. *Admission: $5 adults, $2 kids 6–17 and students with ID. Free third Tues of the month. Open: Tues–Sun 10 a.m.–4 p.m.*

Other Balboa Park highlights

Along El Prado, just beyond the Lily Pond, is the **Botanical Building,** a 250-foot-long wooden lath conservatory from the 1915 Exposition that looks like something out of a Victorian costume drama and houses about 1,200 tropical and flowering plants. Admission is free.

The largest outdoor pipe organ in the world is at **Spreckels Organ Pavilion,** south of El Prado (☎ 619-226-0819), an ornate, curved amphitheater offering free Sunday concerts at 2 p.m. year-round, and free evening concerts in July and August. The sound is stupendous, and the whole experience serves to amplify (pun intended) the old-fashioned Sunday-in-the-park quality of your visit.

The **Japanese Friendship Garden** (☎ 619-232-2721), adjacent to the organ pavilion, is a serene, meticulous oasis. From the elaborately carved gate, a crooked path (to confound evil spirits, who move only in a straight line) threads its way past nearly 100 carefully arranged plantings, a stream with colorful koi, and a traditional zen garden. Admission is $2, $1 for seniors and juniors, free to kids under 7.

The best of the rest: Old Town State Historic Park

Whether you're a history buff looking for an authentic slice of early California or a hungry theme-park refugee in search of a Mexican combo plate and a cheesy souvenir, chances are very good that you'll end up in **Old Town** — and you should.

The birthplace of San Diego — indeed, of California — Old Town was founded by Spanish friars in 1769, along with Mission San Diego. The town of San Diego grew up around the mission and its military presidio, which thrived here until the early 1870s. After San Diego's commercial core moved closer to the harbor (to "New Town," now the **Gaslamp Quarter**), Old Town was abandoned. In 1968, the park was established to preserve the structures that remained and rebuild several atop their original foundations. As the years have gone by, sensitivity to historical accuracy has improved greatly, making the park a combination of Disneyesque attractions and eerily authentic sites.

If you can get past the touristy veneer and into the true spirit of this pedestrians-only 6-block historic district, you'll step back to a time of one-room schoolhouses and village greens, when the people who lived, worked, and played here spoke Spanish. Depending on your interest level — whether you want only to cover the main points of interest, or see everything *and* have lunch — you can spend anywhere from 1 to 5 hours here.

Old Town is bounded by Congress, Juan, Wallace, and Twiggs Streets. To get there: Take I-5 to Old Town Ave. exit; parking is free in the many lots scattered around the park's perimeter, and the large lot for Old Town's trolley station (another option) holds more spaces, at the northwest end. Admission: Free, though donations are encouraged. Open: Daily 10 a.m. to 5 p.m.

Stop first at the **Seeley Stables Visitor Center,** on San Diego Ave. (☎ 619-220-5422), to get your bearings, join up with a walking tour (daily at 10:30 a.m. and 2 p.m.), or simply check out the old wagons, carriages, and stagecoaches. Other notable stops include:

- ✓ **La Casa de Estudillo,** the 1827 adobe home of a wealthy family, furnished with typical upper-class furniture of the period.
- ✓ **Robinson-Rose House,** built in 1853 and containing a scale model of Old Town the way it looked in 1872 before a fire destroyed much of the district.
- ✓ The **San Diego Union Building,** where a forerunner to today's *Union-Tribune* began publishing in 1868.
- ✓ The reproduction **McCoy House,** under construction at press time but slated to hold a fantastic new interpretive center by late summer 2001.

One of Old Town's top draws is its Mexican restaurants. See "Dining Out" for my top recommendation. See "The Top Shopping Areas" for the lowdown on Old Town shopping.

Old Town

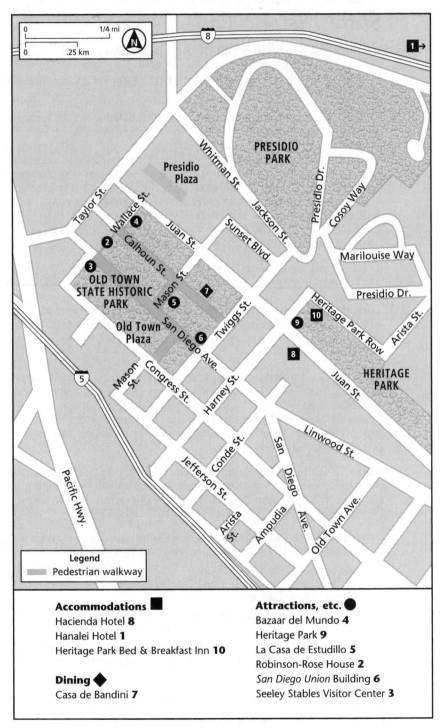

0 | 1/4 mi
0 | .25 km

N

PRESIDIO PARK

Presidio Plaza

Whitman St.

Jackson St.

Presidio Dr.

Cosoy Way

Taylor St.

Wallace St.

Juan St.

Sunset Blvd.

Marilouise Way

Presidio Dr.

Calhoun St.

OLD TOWN STATE HISTORIC PARK

Mason St.

Heritage Park Row

Arista St.

Old Town Plaza

San Diego Ave.

Twiggs St.

HERITAGE PARK

Mason St.

Congress St.

Harney St.

Juan St.

Pacific Hwy.

Conde St.

Jefferson St.

Linwood St.

San Diego Ave.

Old Town Ave.

Arista St.

Ampudia

Legend
Pedestrian walkway

Accommodations ■
Hacienda Hotel **8**
Hanalei Hotel **1**
Heritage Park Bed & Breakfast Inn **10**

Dining ◆
Casa de Bandini **7**

Attractions, etc. ●
Bazaar del Mundo **4**
Heritage Park **9**
La Casa de Estudillo **5**
Robinson-Rose House **2**
San Diego Union Building **6**
Seeley Stables Visitor Center **3**

Hitting the beaches

San Diego's justifiably famous beaches are its second-biggest visitor draw (after the animal parks). "Beach weather" lasts virtually all year. Any sunny day is perfect for a walk, a little inline skating, or a picnic.

Coronado Beach

If you're spending any time on Coronado, don't miss this wide, sparkling-sand paradise of a beach, framed by the fabulous Hotel Del Coronado and extending along Ocean Avenue up to grassy Sunset Park. It's a flat, benign beach perfect for sunbathing, strolling, and wading. Street parking (some metered) is plentiful even in summer, and the beach includes lifeguards, restrooms, and a picnic area with a few fire rings. The islands visible from here — "Los Coronados" — are 18 miles away and belong to Mexico.

Ocean Beach

This beach sits just across the channel from Mission Bay. To reach it, take West Point Loma Boulevard all the way to the end. The northern end of **Ocean Beach Park** is known as **Dog Beach** after the pooches who frolic on the sand. Surfers generally congregate around **Ocean Beach Pier,** mostly in the water but often at the snack shack on the end. Rip currents are strong here, so venturing in beyond waist depth is not a good idea. Facilities include restrooms, showers, picnic tables, and plenty of metered parking lots; the funky shops and food stands of Newport Avenue are a couple blocks away.

Mission Beach and Pacific Beach

These neighbors along Mission Boulevard share a popular boardwalk: **Ocean Front Walk,** a fun, free-for-all human parade. To the south, **Mission Beach** features several dozen blocks of narrow but popular sandy beach known for a youthful surf culture and beginner-friendly waves. Grassy **Belmont Park** sits at midpoint (at West Mission Bay Drive), offering rides and carnival-style entertainment.

Pacific Beach begins around Pacific Beach Drive, where the scene is only slightly more sophisticated, and the surfers a little more experienced. Waves break pretty far out, making this one of San Diego's best swimming beaches. One exception is **Tourmaline Surfing Park,** at the northernmost end of Pacific Beach, where the sport's old guard gathers to ride the waves. Swimming is prohibited, but come to watch the masters in action.

You can find metered lots spaced along Mission Boulevard's side streets, and maybe even a few curbside spaces, if you're lucky. Both beaches have lifeguards and well-spaced restroom facilities.

Mission Bay and the Beaches

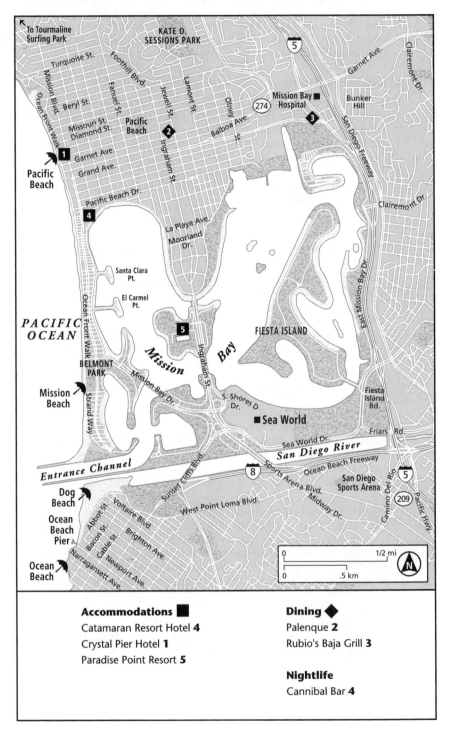

Accommodations ◼

Catamaran Resort Hotel **4**

Crystal Pier Hotel **1**

Paradise Point Resort **5**

Dining ◆

Palenque **2**

Rubio's Baja Grill **3**

Nightlife

Cannibal Bar **4**

Just east of Mission Beach is **Mission Bay,** whose labyrinth of calm
waters and pretty peninsulas are ideal for exploring. Check with
Seaforth Boat Rental, 1641 Quivera Rd. (☎ 888-834-2628 or
619-223-1681; www.seaforth-boat-rental.com/seaforth), which
offers half- and full-day rentals on powerboats, sailboats, personal
watercraft (PWCs), motorized skiffs, kayaks, or paddleboats. If you
don't want to get your feet wet, **Adventure Bike Tours,** also in the
Marriott (☎ 619-234-1500, ext. 6514), offers a guided "Bayside Glide"
for $22 per person; they also just rent bikes (about $8 an hour, $18 for a
half-day). For inline skates or traditional quads, **Hamel's Action Sports
Center,** 704 Ventura Pl., at Ocean Front Walk (☎ 858-488-8889), can set
you up with skates and all necessary safety gear.

La Jolla Cove

This scenic jewel appears regularly on La Jolla postcards, and is worth
the drive even if you're staying closer to downtown. Framed by grass-
carpeted bluffs and sheltering a snorkel-friendly marine preserve just
below the surface, the cove is also a terrific spot for swimmers of all
abilities. It's on the small side, so avoid peak summer weekends if you
can; the free parking spaces along Coast Boulevard tend to fill quickly
as well, but it's an easy walk from anywhere in the village.

Many visitors never know about the seals who hang out about four
blocks south of La Jolla Cove at **Children's Pool Beach,** a tiny cove
originally named for the toddlers who could safely frolic behind a man-
made seawall. These days, the sand is mostly off-limits to humans, who
congregate along the seawall railing or onshore to admire the protected seals who sun themselves on the beach or on semi-submerged
rocks. You can get surprisingly close — truly a mesmerizing sight.

Scanning the winter seas for whales

Whale-watching is a hugely popular pastime
between mid-December and mid-March.
California gray whales hug the shore on their
annual migration from Alaskan feeding grounds
to breeding lagoons in Mexico — and back
again, with calves in tow. If you've ever been
lucky enough to spot one of these gentle behe-
moths, you'll understand the thrill.

Grab binoculars and head to **Cabrillo National
Monument** (☎ 619-557-5450; www.nps.gov/
cabr), on Point Loma, where an elevated
glassed-in observatory offers a prime vantage
point. Take I-5 or I-8 to Highway 209/Rosecrans

Street and follow signs to the monument; admission is $5 per car.

On the UCSD campus in La Jolla, the outdoor
plaza at the **Birch Aquarium at Scripps
Institution of Oceanography** (☎ 858-534-3474;
www.aquarium.ucsd.edu) offers another
excellent whale-watching perch. Take I-5 to La
Jolla Village Drive, go west for a mile (past Torrey
Pines Road), and turn left at Expedition Way.

If you want to get a closer look, head out to sea
with **Classic Sailing Adventures** (☎ 800-
659-0141 or 619-224-0800).

Taking a Guided Tour by Trolley (and Other Means)

Not to be confused with the public transit trolley trains, the fully narrated **Old Town Trolley** (☎ 619-298-TOUR) is a constant favorite. You can get a comprehensive look at the city — or just the parts that interest you — aboard the old-fashioned motorized trolley car as it follows a 30-mile circular route. Hop off at any one of a dozen stops (ticket sales reps are on hand at each), explore at leisure, and reboard when you please (the motorized trolley runs every half-hour). Stops include the Embarcadero, Horton Plaza, Gaslamp Quarter, Coronado, San Diego Zoo, Balboa Park, and Heritage Park. The trolleys run daily from 9 a.m., with final pickup at each stop between 4 and 6 p.m. The tour costs $20 for adults and $8 for kids 6 to 12 (free for under 5) for one complete loop, no matter how many times you hop on and off; if you get on and stay on, the ride takes about 2 hours.

The old soft shoe (s)

Many parts of San Diego are quite walkable. The following are places that offer good walking tours:

✔ The **Gaslamp Quarter Historical Foundation** (☎ 619-233-4692; www.gqhf.com) offers 2-hour tours of San Diego's liveliest neighborhood. Tours depart Tuesday through Saturday from the **William Heath Davis House Museum,** 410 Island Ave., at 4th Avenue. A $5 donation is requested ($3 for seniors and students). Reservations are not required, but call for exact schedule.

✔ **La Jolla Walking Tours** (☎ 858-453-8219 or 619-291-2222; www.lajollawalkingtours.com) conducts 1 ½-hour tours of La Jolla. The tours depart from the **Grande Colonial Hotel,** 910 Prospect St. (between Fay and Gerard avenues), Friday and Saturday at 10 a.m. The cost is $9 per person, and reservations are strongly suggested (the guide won't come out if a minimum number of spots aren't booked).

✔ **Coronado Touring** (☎ 935-435-5993 or 935-435-5444) is a great way to learn a ton about charming Coronado. The 90-minute tour is upbeat and informative, including a delicious dose of local scandal and gossip. Tours leave at 11 a.m. on Tuesday, Thursday, and Saturday from the **Glorietta Bay Inn,** across the street from Hotel Del Coronado; the price is $7. Reservations are suggested, as walk-ins are subject to availability.

Bay cruises and gondola rides

When the weather's fine — which is most of the time — nothing says "San Diego" like a little waterborne sightseeing; the following companies do it well:

✔ **Hornblower Cruises** (☎ **800-ON-THE-BAY** or 619-686-8715; www.hornblower.com) is the local big cheese. In addition to one- and two-hour narrated tours of San Diego Bay, they offer evening dinner/dance cruises, Sunday brunch cruises, and whale-watching trips in winter. Prices start at $13 for harbor cruises, $36 for meal cruises; kids are half-price.

✔ **Gondola di Venezia** (☎ **858-221-2999**; www.gondoladivenezia.com) offers San Diego's most romantic cruise. Plying the calm waters of Mission Bay in Venetian gondolas — complete with singing gondoliers sporting straw hats, striped shirts, and perfect operatic pitch — while reclining with blankets, antipasto nibbles, and a chilled beverage (glasses provided; BYOB), is an unforgettable experience. An hour-long cruise for two is $72, and expanded packages are available. Hours of operation are noon to midnight daily, but evening is definitely *molto romantico*. Families are welcome, too. Advance reservations are required, although same-day bookings aren't out of the question, particularly midweek, during less-than-perfect weather, or off- season.

Suggested 1-, 2-, and 3-day sightseeing itineraries

On **Day 1,** plan to experience San Diego's prime attraction, **SeaWorld.** Get there when the gates open to maximize your time and enjoyment. Some families will want to spend the entire day, while certain grown-ups may have their fill by mid-afternoon. If you're ready for a change of pace, leave in time to enjoy a late afternoon stroll on the beach, stopping for a relaxing cappuccino or cocktail; the Green Flash is a scenic choice right on the boardwalk. Culture vultures may want to skip the beach and browse the shops and galleries of downtown's **Gaslamp Quarter,** which always promises a lively street scene.

If you opted for a full day at SeaWorld, head to your hotel to refresh (with a swim, weather obliging) before dinner. Either way, choose from one of the Gaslamp Quarter's abundant restaurants — **Fio's** is excellent, or neighborhood mainstay **Croce's** is just across the street — and stick around for some live music or nightclub dancing after dinner.

Substitute one of the other parks for SeaWorld if you think it will be too juvenile for you; this plan also works well with a 5- or 6-hour excursion to the **Wild Animal Park.**

Day 2

Day 2 is for enjoying the **San Diego Zoo** and the pleasures of surrounding **Balboa Park.** Once again, start your day early; not only will you catch the animals at their perky morning best (and avoid some human crowds), but you can allow time later for enjoying Balboa Park and peeking into a couple of its fantastic museums. The **Model Railroad Museum** and the **Museum of Photographic Arts** are two lighter choices that won't take a lot of time. Stop into the park's signature **Prado** restaurant, which serves lunch throughout the afternoon, segueing into a tantalizing *tapas* menu before dinner. If you're ready to leave Balboa Park, head for one of Hillcrest's stylish eateries, like **Mixx.** If you still have some evening energy, consider a theatrical performance at one of the **Old Globe** theaters.

An alternate plan for active types, if the weather is too perfect to believe, is to head for **Pacific Beach** for an energizing breakfast burrito at **Kono's Beach Cafe** (at the end of Garnet Avenue) before renting some recreational gear (bikes, skates, kayaks — they're all available). Spend several hours soaking up the sun along the shoreline, or exploring the perimeters of beautiful nearby **Mission Bay,** before returning to the hotel to refresh before a satisfying dinner in Hillcrest.

Day 3

Use **Day 3** for a trip into San Diego's past at **Old Town State Historic Park.** If you need a midmorning boost, stop into **Garden House Coffee & Tea** (set back from the street at 2480 San Diego Ave.) for a muffin and the city's best cafe mocha, then hoof it over to the park itself. Whether you opt for a guided tour (regularly scheduled tours depart from **Seeley Stables** daily at 10:30 a.m. and 2 p.m.) or explore at your own pace, you'll find plenty to keep you interested until lunchtime. Stick around for some Mexican chow at historic **Casa de Bandini,** then hop on the highway toward **La Jolla.** This shopper's paradise offers something for everyone; even doubters will find something to interest them at landmark **John Cole's Bookshop.** Start on Girard Avenue for a wide sampling of stores, and turn any corner that beckons. Meet up at **Children's Pool Beach** to say hello to the resident seals before checking in for dinner at La Jolla's best restaurant, **George's at the Cove.** If you're feeling grubby, or just plain casual, George's has a **Terrace Cafe** with many of the same dishes, including their signature smoked chicken/broccoli/black bean soup (don't miss it!).

Day 4

If your trip includes a **Day 4,** dedicate it either to taking the kids to **LEGOLAND** or heading south of the border on a day trip to Tijuana.

Shopping at the Top

If you're going to shop only once in San Diego, head to **Horton Plaza** in the **Gaslamp Quarter,** bounded by Broadway, 1st and 4th avenues and G Street (☎ **619-238-1596;** www.hortonplaza.com). This whimsical multilevel mall is the heart of the revitalized downtown, offering a superlative selection of stores in a lively outdoor setting.

The quarter is also known for its excellent art galleries, including **Many Hands,** 302 Island Ave. (☎ **619-557-8303**), a cooperative with 35 artists working in a variety of crafts. Le Travel Store, 745 4th Ave., between F and G streets (☎ **619-544-0005;** www.letravelstore.com), offers a good selection of luggage, travel books and maps, and groovy travel accessories.

Aunt Teek's guide to vintage treasures

Two enormous antique malls are guaranteed to leave the collectibles hounds among you with dusty hands and a lighter wallet: **Cracker Factory Antiques,** 448 W. Market St. (at Columbia Street), downtown (☎ **619-233-1669**), and **Unicorn Antique Mall,** 704 J St. (at 7th Ave.), just south of the Gaslamp Quarter (☎ **619-232-1696**). Merchandise ranges from kitschy collectibles to "real" antiques (you know, Louis the Whichever stuff).

Depending on your tastes, you may think the Embarcadero's **Seaport Village,** 849 W. Harbor Dr. (☎ **619-235-4014**), is quaintly appealing or completely contrived. This faux New England–style village is big for souvenir shopping and dining with a view. It's worth the trip, though, for a ride on the 1890 Looff carousel imported from Coney Island, New York.

Hillcrest

Compact Hillcrest is an ideal shopping destination. You can browse a unique and sometimes wacky mix of independent boutiques, vintage clothing stores, memorabilia shops, chain stores, bakeries, and cafes. Start at the neighborhood's hub — the intersection of University and 5th avenues — and prepare yourself to drop a few dollars on parking (either meters or lots).

Highlights include **Babette Schwartz,** 421 University Ave. (☎ **619-220-7048;** www.babette.com), a provocative pop-culture emporium named for a local drag queen. The **Village Hat Shop,** 3821 4th Ave. (☎ **619-683-5533;** www.villagehatshop.com), features head gear from straw hats to knit caps to classy fedoras, plus a mini-museum of vintage headwear.

If you love used and rare books, you'll want to poke around on 5th Avenue between University and Robinson. This block is also home to **Off the Record,** 3865 University Ave. (☎ **619-298-4755**), a new and used store with an alternative bent and the city's best vinyl selection. If vintage clothing is your passion, don't miss **Wear It Again Sam,** 3922 Park Blvd., at University Ave. (☎ **619-299-0185**), a classy step back in time.

Old Town

Yes, it's touristy (the local shopkeeper's motto is *"ka-ching!"*), but when you're looking for a classic souvenir of the cheesy variety — you know, San Diego-labeled T-shirts, baseball caps, snow domes, or those movable pens — this is ground zero. Milking the "old" even further, many of these shops boast a quasi-historic "general store" theme. Keep your eyes open for artist's workshops and bona-fide galleries tucked away amid the commercialism, where higher quality commands higher prices.

With mariachi music and Mexican archways setting the stage for import shops with wares from Central and South America, colorful **Bazaar del Mundo,** 2754 Calhoun St. (☎ 619-296-3161; www.bazaardelmundo. com), is worth seeking out. You won't find anything rare (or bargain-priced), but browsing can be fun.

La Jolla

Shopping is a major pastime here. Women's clothing boutiques tend to be conservative and costly, especially those lining Girard and Prospect streets. The many home-decor stores make for great window shopping, as do the ubiquitous jewelers — where Swiss watches, tennis bracelets, precious gems, and pearl necklaces sparkle in windows along every street.

No visit to La Jolla is complete without seeing **John Cole's Bookshop,** 780 Prospect St., at Eads Avenue (☎ 858-454-4766), a local legend housed in a turn-of-the-century wisteria-covered cottage. Look for cookbooks in the old kitchen, paperbacks in a former classroom, and CDs and harmonicas in the music corner. Sitting and reading in the patio garden is accepted, even encouraged.

Nightlife

For a rundown of the latest performances and evening events, check the "Night and Day" section of Thursday's *Union-Tribune* (www.union-trib.com). You can easily find copies of the free weekly *Reader* (www.sdreader.com) and *What's Playing?*, the San Diego Performing Arts League's bimonthly guide (www.sandiego-online.com/sdpal), around town.

You can save a bundle on theater and musical events at the half-price *Times Arts Tix* kiosk next to **Planet Hollywood** in Horton Plaza Park, at Broadway and 3rd Avenue. It's open Tuesday through Thursday from 11 a.m. to 6 p.m., Friday and Saturday 10 a.m. to 6 p.m.; tickets are available day-of-show only (except for Sunday and Monday shows, sold on Saturday). Cash only. Call ☎ 619-497-5000 for more information and the daily offerings, or go online to www.sandiegoperforms.com and click on "Arts Tix." *Parking tip:* The Horton Plaza garage is most convenient, and Arts Tix will validate.

The play's the thing

It's well worth making the effort to catch a show at the Shakespearean-style **Old Globe Theatre** or its adjacent theaters, the open-air Lowell Davies Festival Theater and the intimate in-the-round **Cassius Carter Centre Stage.** Not only do these venues occupy a magical setting within lovely **Balboa Park,** but they attract expertly casted classics along with thought-provoking regional and experimental offerings. The season runs from January through October, with two to four plays going at any one time. Ticket prices range from around $23 to $39, with discounts for students and seniors. Call ☎ **619-239-2255** or the 24-hour hotline at ☎ **619-23-GLOBE,** or go online to www.oldglobe.org.

The **La Jolla Playhouse,** on the UCSD campus at 2910 La Jolla Village Dr., at Torrey Pines Rd. (☎ **858-550-1010;** www.lajollaplayhouse.com), stages six productions each year, usually from April or May through November. Each one has something outstanding to recommend it, whether a nationally acclaimed director or a highly touted revival. Tickets range from $21 to $52.

Any unsold tickets are available for $10 in a "public rush" sale 10 minutes before the curtain goes up.

Play it loud: Live music

The Casbah

It may be a total dive, but this blaring downtown club has a well-earned rep for showcasing alternative and rock bands that either are, were, or will be famous. Consider buying advance tickets to avoid disappointment.

2501 Kettner Blvd., near the airport. ☎ *619-232-4355. Internet:* www.casbahmusic.com.

Croce's Nightclubs

This loud, crowded gathering place is the cornerstone of Gaslamp Quarter nightlife. Two separate clubs a couple doors apart offer traditional jazz (Croce's Jazz Bar) and rhythm and blues (Croce's Top Hat) nightly. The music blares onto the street, making it easy to decide whether to go in or not. The cover charge is waived if you eat at the restaurant (see "Dining Out" earlier in this chapter).

802 5th Ave. (at F St.). ☎ *619-233-4355. Internet:* www.croces.com.

4th & B

Haphazard seating (balcony theater seats, cabaret tables) and a handful of bar/lounge niches make this no-frills venue, housed in a former bank, comfortable. Their genre is no genre; everyone from B.B. King to Dokken to local-girl-made-good Jewel has performed here, in between regular bookings of the San Diego Chamber Orchestra.

345 B St. (at 4th Ave.). ☎ *619-231-4343. Internet:* www.4thandB.com.

Come here often? Bars & lounges

The Bitter End

With three floors, this self-important Gaslamp Quarter hot spot manages to be sophisticated martini bar, after-hours dance club, and relaxing cocktail lounge all in one. Weekends are subject to velvet rope/dress code nonsense.

770 5th Ave. (at F St.). ☎ ***619-338-9300.*** *Internet:* www.thebitterend.com.

Cannibal Bar

Attached to the lobby of the Polynesian-themed Catamaran hotel, this loud bar is the place to go for a mean Mai Tai. Party central at the beach for thundering DJ-driven music, the Cannibal also books some very admirable bands now and then.

3999 Mission Blvd., Pacific Beach. ☎ ***858-539-8650.***

Martini Ranch

The Gaslamp Quarter's newest crowd pleaser boasts a 30-martini menu that may stretch the definition of "martini" a bit, but nevertheless features an impressive selection of vodkas and gins. Downstairs resembles an upscale sports bar, while upstairs is dotted with love seats and conversation pits.

528 F St. (between 5th and 6th aves.). ☎ ***619-235-6100.***

Princess Pub & Grille

A local Anglophiles' haunt that's the place for a pint o' Bass, Fuller's, Watney's, or Guinness. This slice of Britain (in Little Italy, go figure) also serves up hearty pub grub.

1665 India St. (at Date St.). ☎ ***619-702-3021.*** *Internet:* www.princesspub.com.

Quick Concierge

AAA
Downtown at 815 Date St., between 8th and 9th avenues (☎ 619-233-1000; www aaa-calif.com).

American Express
A full-service office is downtown at 258 Broadway, at 3rd Avenue (☎ 619-234-4455).

Baby-Sitters
Marion's Childcare (☎ 619-582-5029) has bonded baby-sitters available to come to your hotel room.

Emergencies
For police, fire, highway patrol, or life-threatening medical emergencies, dial ☎ **911**. Hotel Docs (☎ 800-468-3537 or 619-275-2663)

is a 24-hour network of physicians, dentists, and chiropractors who claim they'll come to your hotel room within 35 minutes of your call.

Hospitals
The most conveniently located emergency room is at **UCSD Medical Center–Hillcrest,** 200 W. Arbor Dr. (☎ 619-543-6400); to get there, take 1st Avenue north, past Washington, and turn left on Arbor.

Internet Centers
In Hillcrest, the coffeehouse/study hall **Euphoria,** 1045 University Ave. (☎ 619-295-1769), has two Internet terminals. Open daily from 6 a.m. to 1 a.m.

Newspapers & Magazines
The city's daily is the *San Diego Union-Tribune,* available from newsstands and vending machines around town. The free alternative weekly **Reader** is available at shops, restaurants, and public hot spots.

Police
Dial **911** in an emergency. For non-emergencies, contact the downtown precinct, 1401 Broadway (☎ 619-531-2000).

Post Office
Post offices are located downtown, at 815 E St. (at 8th Avenue), and at 51 Horton Plaza (beside the Westin Hotel). Call ☎ 800-ASK-USPS or log onto www.usps.gov to find the branch nearest you.

Taxes
Sales tax in shops and restaurants is 7.75%. Hotel tax is 10.5%.

Taxis
Orange Cab (☎ 619-291-3333), **San Diego Cab** (☎ 619-226-TAXI), and **Yellow Cab** (☎ 619-234-6161). In La Jolla, use **La Jolla Cab** (☎ 858-453-4222).

Transit Info
☎ 619-685-4900 for 24-hour recorded info, ☎ 619-233-3004 daily from 5:30 a.m. to 8:30 p.m. to speak with a real live person.

Weather
For local weather and surf reports, call ☎ 619-289-1212.

Gathering More Information

The San Diego Convention and Visitors Bureau's International Visitor Information Center (☎ **619-236-1212**) is downtown on 1st Avenue at F Street, street level at Horton Plaza. They can provide you with the slick, glossy *San Diego Visitors Planning Guide,* as well as a money-saving coupon book. Open Monday through Saturday from 8:30 a.m. to 5 p.m., plus Sunday 11 a.m. to 5 p.m. June through August.

The Mission Bay Visitor Information Center (☎ **619-276-8200**) is on Mission Bay Drive at the end of Clairemont Drive. Near the San Diego Zoo is the Balboa Park Visitors Center (☎ **619-239-0512**), in the House of Hospitality on El Prado.

Information on La Jolla is distributed by the La Jolla Town Council, 7734 Herschel Ave., between Silverado and Kline streets (☎ **858-454-1444**). You'll find all you need to know about Coronado at the Coronado Visitors Bureau, 1047 B Ave., near Orange Avenue (☎ **800-622-8300** or 619-437-8788).

You can find San Diego's official Web site at www.sandiego.org. A guide to Gaslamp Quarter dining and shopping is at www.gaslamp.org. Official Coronado info is available at www.coronado.ca.us.

A great source for club and show listings is the *San Diego Reader* site at www.sdreader.com. *San Diego* magazine's www.sandiego-online.com features listings for dining and events. CitySearch's www.signon-sandiego.com, is run by the *Union-Tribune* and offers a mix of current news, entertainment listings, and visitor info. *Digital City San Diego,* at www.digitalcity.com/sandiego, targets locals, making it great for off-the-beaten-tourist-path recommendations.

Mexico? Muy Bueno! Side Tripping to Tijuana

Looking to add a shot of international flavor into your vacation? Then do as scores of San Diegans do, and head for the border.

Tijuana (tee-WAH-nah) is a mere half-hour from San Diego, yet Mexico's fourth-largest city offers a real window into traditional Mexican culture. Of course, most *Americanos* never get past the endless shopping opportunities, loading up on handcrafted pottery, woven blankets, embroidered dresses, beaded and silver jewelry, leather bags and sandals, blue-rimmed margarita glasses, and Cuban cigars. No matter. Whether your goal is cultural enlightenment or cheap souvenirs, a day spent in Tijuana is a whole lot of fun.

Going south of the border

Getting to Tijuana from San Diego is simple, quick, and inexpensive.

Driving yourself is a bad idea because: a1) U.S. insurance (and many rental-car agreements) is not valid across the border; b2) traffic is terrible in Tijuana; c3) getting through customs and back across the border can be more difficult if you're on your own; and d4) having an accident in Mexico, major or minor, is a *baaad* idea.

Just leave your car behind and hop aboard the **San Diego Trolley,** nicknamed the "Tijuana Trolley" for good reason. Get off at the last stop in San Ysidro. From there, just follow the signs to walk across the border. The one-way fare is $2, and the trolleys run constantly, with the last return from San Ysidro after midnight. On Saturdays, the trolley runs 24 hours. For more information on the trolley system, see "By Bus and Trolley," earlier in this chapter.

You can also leave your car at one of many border parking lots, which cost $8 to $10 for the day. Most lots are just a block or two away from the pedestrian walkway into Tijuana. While naysayers will grouse about perceived dangers in the lots, I've parked in them and felt very comfortable. After all, a constant stream of Americans coming and going fills the lots. Just take care after dark and don't be one of the last cars left.

Gray Line (☎ 800-331-5077 or 619-491-0011; www.grayline-sandiego.com) will take you to Tijuana for $28 ($38 with lunch). After a brief orientation tour, you'll be dropped off in the middle of town; you can spend a few hours or all day, catching any of the regularly scheduled buses back. **Contact Tours** (☎ 800-235-5393 or 619-477-8687; www.contactours.com) offers a similar tour for $26 round trip.

Getting around

After you're in Tijuana, getting around by walking or taxi is easy. Cabs line up around most of the visitor hot spots. Agreeing on a rate before stepping into the cabs is customary; one-way rides within the city cost $4 to $9. Tipping is optional.

A few helpful hints for your visit:

✔ Though a passport isn't required of U.S. citizens, carrying yours will speed up your return across the border. Be sure to at least have your driver's license handy. If your child does not have a passport or school photo ID, then a birth certificate will suffice.

✔ U.S. currency is legal tender nearly everywhere (small bills are preferred). Vendors often greet credit cards with a frown.

✔ To maneuver around someone on a crowded street or in a shop, say "*perdoneme*" (excuse me; pronounce all the syllables — per-*done*-eh-meh).

✔ Be alert to cheap rip-off goods when shopping, and remember that bargaining is expected everywhere except in the fanciest shops.

Seeing the sights

Tijuana's main event is bustling **Avenida Revolucion,** the city's original bawdy center for illicit fun. Changing times and civic improvement have toned it down a bit; shopping and drinking are now the main order of business.

Shoppers quickly discover that most of the curios spilling out onto the sidewalk look alike. Browse for comparison's sake, but duck into one of the many *pasajes,* or passageway arcades, for the best souvenir shopping. That's where you'll find items of a slightly better quality and merchants willing to bargain. Some of the most enjoyable *pasajes* are on the east side of the street between Calles 2 and 5.

If a marketplace atmosphere and spirited bargaining are what you're looking for, head to **Mercado de Artesanias (Crafts Market),** Calle 2 and Avenida Negrete, where vendors with pottery, clayware, clothing, and other crafts fill an entire city block.

For a taste of everyday Mexico away from the *Americano* crowds, visit **Mercado Hidalgo,** several blocks away at Avenida Sanchez Taboada and Avenida Independencia, a busy indoor-outdoor marketplace where vendors display fresh flowers and produce, sacks of dried beans and chiles by the kilo, and a few souvenir crafts, including some excellent piñatas. Morning is the best time to visit the market, and you'll be more comfortable paying with *pesos,* because most sellers are accustomed to a local crowd.

Anchoring the southern end of Revolucion is the landmark **Jai Alai Palace,** at Calle 7, a huge arena where jai alai (a fast-moving game that incorporates elements of tennis, hockey, and basketball, for those of you who haven't spent much time in places like south Florida) is played every day except Sunday. For more information, call ☎ 619-231-1910.

If you'd like to see a different side of Tijuana, start at the **Centro Cultural Tijuana (Tijuana Cultural Center)**, Paseo de los Heroes at Avenida Independencia (☎ 011-52-668-4-1111). You'll easily spot the ultramodern cultural center by its centerpiece dome housing an OMNI-MAX theater. The adjacent museum features Mexican artifacts from pre-Hispanic times through the modern political era. Open daily from 9 a.m. to 8:30 p.m. Admission to the permanent exhibits is free; you must pay a $2 charge for the visiting exhibit gallery, and tickets for OMNIMAX films are $4 for adults, $2.50 for kids.

Dining out

You can't spend five minutes on Avenida Revolucion without being beckoned into a cafe or bar by aggressive sidewalk barkers. Often your instinct and best judgment — not to mention your nose — will guide you to the good stuff. Most Tijuana restaurants are open all day, every day. Reservations are not necessary, although they may be helpful at **Cien Años** (see later in this section).

✔ One reliable choice in the heart of the action is **Cafe La Especial** ($–$$), Av. Revolucion 718, between calles 3 and 4 (☎ 011-52-668-5-6654), a bustling restaurant resembling an American-style coffee shop. It's tucked away in a downstairs shopping *pasaje* (turn in at the taco stand of the same name), and offers home-style Mexican cooking. The house specialty is *carne asada*, grilled marinated beef served with traditional accompaniments.

✔ If you prefer the culinary comforts of the good 'ol U.S.A., head for the Tijuana branch of **Hard Rock Cafe ($$)**, 520 Av. Revolucion, near Calle 1 (☎ 011-52-668-5-0206). Beware: prices are no bargain in competitive Tijuana.

A short cab ride from Avenida Revolucion will take you away from the tourist-pounded path to some more adventuresome choices:

✔ One of my favorites is **La Fonda de Roberto ($$)**, in La Sierra Motel, 2800 Blvd. Cuahutemoc Sue Oeste (a.k.a. Av. 16 de Septembre; ☎ 011-52-668-6-4687). This colorful dining room specializes in regional Mexican dishes so good that La Fonda regularly appears on San Diego "Best Of" lists.

✔ If you're interested in haute cuisine, the buzz around Tijuana is all about **Cien Años ($$$–$$$$)**, Jose Maria Velazco 1407 (☎ 011-52-663-4-3039 or 4-7262). This elegant *Zono Rio* (River Zone) eatery specializes in artfully blended Mexican flavors, using such disparate ingredients as tamarind, poblano chile, and mango, and stylishly presented dishes.

Gathering more information

Before you go, get information and maps from Baja California Tourism Information, 7860 Mission Center Court, no. 202, in Mission Valley (☎ **800-522-1516**, 800-225-2786, or 619-299-8518; www.travelfile. com/get/bajaca). Take I-8 east to Mission Center Road north (10 to 15 minutes from downtown); turn right at Mission Center Court. The San Diego Trolley stops 3 blocks away. You can also get a preview of events, restaurants, and more online at www.tijuana-net.com and www.tijuana.com.mx.

In Tijuana, you can pick up information at the Mexican Tourism Office, at Avenida Revolucion and Calle 1 (☎ **011-52-668-8-0555**), which is extremely helpful with maps and orientation, local events, and accommodations, should you want to stay overnight.

Chapter 24

The Palm Springs Resorts

In This Chapter

▶ Deciding when to go to the desert resorts — and how to get there

▶ Choosing the best places to stay and eat

▶ Exploring the top desert attractions

▶ Hitting the links in the heat — and living it up after the sun goes down

*M*y husband and I have a love/hate relationship with Palm Springs: I love it, he hates it.

He has an excuse: With four years of Phoenix living under his belt, he feels he's done his desert time — enough with the heat already. And he doesn't play golf.

I, however, can't get enough of Palm Springs. I love the perpetual sun, the unrepentant glamour, the high desert style. I love the frozen-in-the-'50s architecture and the martinis-and-bikinis vibe. This desert oasis dedicated to the easy life — swimming, sunning, spas — is A-OK with me. And I am not alone — anyone who's picked up a national shelter or lifestyle mag over the past year can testify to Palm Springs' newly minted ring-a-ding-ding hipness.

The other side of me — the nature-loving one — also loves Palm Springs. No matter how many times I return, I'm always wowed by the sheer beauty of the desert. At first, it may seem desolate — brown, dry, and baking under the relentless sun — especially if such extremes are new to you. But the majesty is undeniable: the soaring palms, the hearty flowering cacti; the surprising natural lushness and vivid hues of the landscape; the brilliant blue of the daytime sky, and the pink-purple glow that dusk ushers in; the jagged mountains that rise from the flat desert floor not too far in the distance. The scale alone is enough to impress.

So, unless you, too, have already had your fill of desert living, try to work the Palm Springs resort area into your trip agenda. It's a fabulous place to experience the kind of renewal that only comes from getting away from it all. Whether you draw inner peace from communing with spectacular nature or renewing your acquaintance with a gleaming set of nine-irons, Palm Springs has the answer for you. And bring the kids: Virtually all of the big resorts, and a few of the smaller ones, welcome them with open arms — and who's happier than a kid allowed to frolic the day away in the pool?

Timing Your Visit

Unlike most of the rest of California, Palm Springs' off-season is summer. From mid- or late May through September, daytime highs soar into the 100s. The strength of the sun and the heat that radiates off the street can really make you feel like you've jumped from the frying pan into the fire.

"In-season" is everything else: From October through April, average highs range between 69°F and 92°F. Keep in mind, however, that you can't always count on pool weather during these months; anyone who knows the desert will tell you that 70°F doesn't really feel like summer with virtually no humidity in the air and a sprinkling of clouds in the sky. The coolest months are usually December through February, when highs seldom get past the low 70s and nighttime temps dip into the 40s (perfect weather for you golfers, who probably don't relish the notion of a broiling midday sun). Fall and spring are best — that's when it feels like a regular summer, with highs generally in the 80s and nights in the 50s or 60s.

With the "season" comes the crowd, especially urban-escaping week-enders and "snowbirds" (annual refugees from colder climes, often retirees, who head back home — just like their feathered friends — 'round about April). Luckily, the area seldom feels overcrowded. Still, if you have your heart set on staying in a certain hotel, or you want prime tee times, you should plan ahead, especially if your visit falls over a weekend. Spring break — usually sometime around Easter — is worth avoiding if you can help it.

If you're not averse to packing an economy-size bottle of sunscreen and dealing with a little sizzling heat, off-season — summer — can be a bargain-hunter's bonanza. Call me crazy, but I like summer in the desert. Nothing is very crowded, and hotel rooms go for a song: You can get terrific accommodations for as little as $49, and luxury resorts sell $300-a-night rooms for less than $150. Of course, it's not a great time to take full-day hikes in the desert, but if your plan is to lie under the umbrella poolside, taking a cooling dip every once in a while, summer is just fine. Even you golfers can enjoy yourselves, as long as you book 6 or 7 a.m. tee times. After the sun goes down, summer evenings are lovely. Still, know what you're in for if you plan a July or August stay: The weather is going to be hot, hot, hot.

Coming to the desert is much like vacationing on an island — you need a couple of days just to unwind and settle into the laid-back vibe. I recommend three nights to work in enough do-nothing time, unless you're the type who gets antsy sitting around. Golfers will want to spend at the very least a day on the local courses.

If you want to work in a side trip to **Joshua Tree National Park** (see Chapter 25), you should set aside a full day for it.

Getting There

The Palm Springs resorts are about 108 miles east of Los Angeles and 141 miles north of San Diego.

✔ **From L. A.,** it's a straight shot east on Interstate 10; take the Highway 111 turnoff into Palm Springs, which will drop you directly onto North Palm Canyon Drive, the main thoroughfare. The drive takes about 2 hours.

If you're heading to Palm Desert, stay on I-10 past the Highway 111 junction. Exit at Monterey Avenue and turn right. The distance is 122 miles from L.A. to Palm Desert.

✔ **From San Diego,** take Interstate 15 north to I-215, then head east on Highway 60 until you connect to I-10 in Banning. From I-10, take the Highway 111 turnoff into Palm Springs, which will drop you directly onto North Palm Canyon Drive, the main thoroughfare. The 141-mile drive takes about 2 ½ hours.

If you're heading from San Diego to Palm Desert, the route changes a bit. Take I-15 north to Temecula, where you'll pick up Highway 79 to Highway 371 to Highway 74, which will lead you into Palm Desert from the south. This nice 122-mile drive takes about 2 ½ hours. If you'd rather stick to the interstate, follow the directions to Palm Springs and allow 3 hours.

Flying right in to Palm Springs is also easy. Pleasant Palm Springs International Airport is just a mile from the heart of downtown at 3400 E. Tahquitz Canyon Way, at El Cielo Road (☎ **760-318-3800;** www.ci.palm-springs.ca.us/Airport). These airlines fly in:

✔ Alaska Airlines: ☎ **800-426-0333;** www.alaskaair.com

✔ America West: ☎ **800-235-9292;** www.americawest.com

✔ American Airlines: ☎ **800-433-7300;** www.aa.com

✔ Continental: ☎ **800-525-0280;** www.continental.com

✔ Delta/Skywest: ☎ **800-453-9417;** www.delta-air.com

✔ United Express: ☎ **800-241-6522;** www.ual.com

✔ US Airways: ☎ **800-428-4322;** www.usairways.com

All of the national car-rental companies have airport locations. You can also set up a ride with one of the desert's many taxi companies, such as Airport Taxi (☎ **760-321-4470**) or Yellow Cab of the Desert (☎ **760-345-8398**). However, I strongly suggest renting a car, unless you plan on parking yourself at a destination resort or at one of the inns a walk away from Palm Springs' Palm Canyon Drive, and intend to do zero exploring.

Getting Your Bearings

The desert resorts are a breeze to navigate after you get a handle on what's where. They cover a roughly 25-mile-long stretch of desert running parallel to I-10, from Desert Hot Springs in the northwest to Indio in the southeast. With the exception of Desert Hot Springs (only worth a visit if you're visiting Two Bunch Palms; see "Ahh — the spa" later in the chapter), all of the big resort communities lie on the south side of the I-10, laid out in an angled grid pattern far enough away from the interstate that through traffic doesn't interfere.

Palm Springs, the oldest community, serves as the heart of the desert resort action. North Palm Canyon Drive is downtown Palm Springs' main drag, where many — but not all — of the restaurants and mall-and-boutique shopping are. Tahquitz Canyon Way meets North Palm Canyon at the town's primary intersection, tracking a straight line from the airport into the heart of town.

You find most of the luxury resorts and championship golf courses in newer communities to the east of Palm Springs, notably Rancho Mirage, Palm Desert, and La Quinta. The main connecting road between them is East Palm Canyon Drive, known as Highway 111 as soon as you leave Palm Springs. *Palm Desert* is the desert communities' other tourism-oriented commercial hub. Its central intersection is Highway 111 and Monterey Avenue, with El Paseo (often likened to Beverly Hills' Rodeo Drive), one block to the south, serving as the main dining-and-shopping drive.

Staying in Desert Style

If my favorites are full, you can book a room at one of the gazillion other places to stay in the area through the free reservation services offered by the Palm Springs Visitor Information Center (☎ 800-347-7746; www. palm-springs.org) and the Palm Springs Desert Resorts Convention & Visitors Bureau (☎ 800-41-RELAX [417-3529]; www.desert-resorts. com). The Palm Springs Visitor Information Center is particularly helpful if you're looking for gay-oriented accommodations.

An extra 10 to 11 percent in taxes will be tacked on to your hotel bill at checkout time.

Casa Cody

$$ Palm Springs

Founded by Buffalo Bill's cousin back in the '20s, Casa Cody is a charming, and surprisingly modern, place to stay. Two dozen lovely rooms, all decorated with Southwestern panache, are set hacienda style around two pools and a Jacuzzi. Studios and suites have equipped kitchens, and some have fireplaces and/or private patios. This is a terrific value — and a great location, too, with Palm Canyon shopping and dining a mere stone's throw away.

175 S. Cahuilla Rd. (between Tahquitz Canyon Way and Arenas Rd.), Palm Springs. ☎ *800-231-2639 or 760-320-9346. Fax: 760-325-8610. Internet:* www.palmsprings. com/hotels/casacody. *Parking: Free! Rack rates: $79–$139 double or studio, $149–$199 1-bedroom suite, $229–$359 2-bedroom suite or adobe house. Rates include expanded continental breakfast. Deals: Rates as low as $49 in summer; ask about midweek discounts. AE, CB, DC, DISC, MC, V.*

Estrella Inn

$$–$$$ Palm Springs

The standard rooms are charm-free, but even the most basic is 30 percent larger than other hotel rooms. Each has a minifridge, microwave, coffeemaker, and good-quality everything. If you want extra space or character, skip the hotel-standard suites in lieu of the historic bungalows (villas), which are excellently done with terra-cotta floors, full kitchens, and tons of charm — well worth the extra bucks. Lush grounds with three pools (including one for the kids) and two Jacuzzis, coin-op laundry, a central location, and an outstanding staff round out the appeal.

415 S. Belardo Rd. (between Ramon and Baristo rds.), Palm Springs. ☎ *800-237-3687 or 760-320-4117. Fax: 760-323-3303. Internet:* www.estrella.com. *Parking: Free! Rack rates: $125–$160 double, $185–$360 1- or 2-bedroom suite or villa. Rates include continental breakfast. Deals: AAA discounts available; ask about golf and other packages. AE, CB, DC, MC, V.*

Holiday Inn Palm Mountain Resort

$$ Palm Springs

Built around an excellent pool area with a Jacuzzi and poolside bar, this terrific property feels like a real resort. The nice rooms are done in an area-appropriate Southwest style; each has a microwave, minifridge, coffeemaker, and patio furniture. Go for a ground-floor poolside room, with only a sliding-glass door separating you from the drink. The location is A-1, a 2-minute walk from the heart of the Palm Canyon action. On site is a mid-priced Continental restaurant with a happy hour and early-bird specials. Nice!

155 S. Belardo Rd. (at Tahquitz Canyon Way), Palm Springs. ☎ *800-HOLIDAY or 760-325-1301. Fax: 760-323-8937. Internet:* www.palmmountainresort.com *or* www.holiday-inn.com. *Parking: Free! Rack rates: $89–$155 double. Deals: Ask for AAA and AARP discounts; check* www.holiday-inn.com *for special promotions. AE, CB, DC, DISC, JCB, MC, V.*

Ingleside Inn

$$–$$$ Palm Springs

For Rat Pack pizzazz, you can't beat this quirky but charming inn, the domain of Mel Haber, who's rubbed shoulders with celebs from Sinatra to Travolta for 25 years. Each unique unit has its own eccentricity (mine had a steam shower from the Eisenhower era), but all are comfortably outfitted. You have to cross the drive to reach the pool — odd — but the waistcoated servers will even bring your breakfast to you poolside. The well-regarded dining room, Melvyn's, and piano lounge still attract the crowd that dons sequins and dinner jackets for a night on the town.

200 W. Ramon Rd. (at Belardo Rd.), Palm Springs. ☎ *800-772-6655 or 760-325-0046. Fax: 760-325-0710. Internet:* www.inglesideinn.com. *Valet parking: Free! Rack rates: $95–$160 double, $145–$285 villa or minisuite, $355–$600 suite. Rates include continental breakfast. Deals: Check Web site or ask about specials. AE, DC, DISC, MC, V.*

La Quinta Resort & Club

$$$$$ La Quinta

If you want to hit the links or courts — or simply surrender to the lap of luxury — come to La Quinta. Destination resorts don't come any finer than this Spanish-style spread. Set in single-story casitas (freestanding houses) on lush, oasis-like grounds, each room has an air of intimacy and privacy. Championship golf and tennis, first-rate dining and spa facilities, kids' programs — the works. A bit far removed from the rest of the Palm Springs area, but who cares? You won't want to leave.

49499 Eisenhower Dr., La Quinta. ☎ *800-598-3828 or 760-564-4111. Fax: 760-564-5758. Internet:* www.laquintaresort.com. *Valet parking: Free! Rack rates: $275–$450 double, $475–$3,500 suite or villa. Deals: Rates from $165 double in summer. Always inquire about packages or other special deals. AE, DC, DISC, JCB, MC, V.*

Marriott Rancho Las Palmas Resort & Spa

$$$$ Rancho Mirage

This relaxing and attractive faux-hacienda-style resort is not quite as luxurious as La Quinta, but it's also far more down to earth. You'll find 27 terrific holes on a Ted Robinson–designed golf course, 25 tennis courts, a slate of restaurants to choose from, an excellent full-service spa, and a whopping 100-foot waterslide at the pool complex that the kids will just love. Guest rooms and public spaces are comfortable, attractive, and neatly suit the desert mood.

41000 Bob Hope Dr., Rancho Mirage. ☎ *800-I-LUV-SUN or 760-568-2727. Fax: 760-568-5845. Internet:* www.marriotthotels.com. *Valet parking: Free! Rack rates: $235–$370 double. Deals: Rates $150–$200 in summer. Great spa, golf, tennis, and romance packages almost always on offer, as are AAA and AARP discounts. AE, CB, DC, DISC, MC, V.*

Palm Desert Lodge

$$ Palm Desert

This family-run motel is a great bet for those who want to be near world-class golf or El Paseo shopping without paying resort prices. The rooms are clean, fresh, and attractive. Each has a minifridge, and most are double-doubles big enough to sleep four; some of the poolside units are even bigger and boast VCRs and/or fully equipped kitchens. A very nice pool and Jacuzzi area is simply but pleasingly landscaped.

74-527 Hwy. 111 (at Deep Canyon Rd.), Palm Desert. ☎ 760-346-3875. Fax: 760-773-0084. Internet: www.palmdesertlodge.com. *Parking: Free! Rack rates: $79–$179 double. Deals: Rates as low as $49 in summer; ask about autumn and senior discounts. AE, CB, DC, DISC, MC, V.*

Two Bunch Palms

$$$$ Desert Hot Springs

If you're coming to the desert to do the spa thing, here's your heaven. Push thoughts of bouffanted ladies in designer sweatsuits out of your mind — Two Bunch is intimate, easygoing, and understated, the kind of low-key oasis where multimillionaire movie execs and splurging suburban housewives are at one in their quest to de-stress. Spread over 56 lush acres, this eclectic low-rise complex has been here since the 1930s (Al Capone used it as a hideout). Accommodations range from simple but comfortable guestrooms to full-on villas. Frankly, they're nothing special; the real draw is the phenomenal menu of spa treatments, the oh-so-soothing natural mineral grotto, and the unparalleled service. More than divine — sublime.

67425 Two Bunch Palms Trail (off Palm Drive/Gene Autry Trail), Desert Hot Springs. ☎ 800-472-4334 or 760-329-8791. Fax: 760-329-1317. Internet: www.twobunchpalms.com. *Parking: Free! Rack rates: $175–$295 double, $325–$625 suite or villa. Rates include continental breakfast buffet. Deals: Money-saving spa packages are almost always on offer (at press time, as low as $275 with all meals, spa treatments, and other extras). Midweek and off-season discounts can be substantial. AE, MC, V.*

Villa Rosa Inn

$–$$ Palm Springs

This hidden gem is one of the finest bargains I've found in the entire state. Built hacienda style around a lovely courtyard pool, each homey unit features impeccable Southwestern decor and cool terra-cotta tile floors. The live-in owners keep this place in racing form; everything is top quality and fresh, fresh, fresh! Worth twice the price — really. A mere six units are available (four with full kitchens), so book as far in advance as possible.

1577 S. Indian Trail (off E. Palm Canyon Dr., between S. Palm Canyon and Sunrise Way), Palm Springs. ☎ 800-457-7605 or 760-327-5915. Fax: 760-416-9962. Internet: www.villarosainn.com. *Parking: Free and easy street parking. Rack rates: $49–$99 double, $99–$125 suite. 2-night minimum. Deals: 5 percent discount on stays of seven nights or more. AE, MC, V.*

The Willows

$$$$$ Palm Springs

Hideaways don't get more romantic than this glorious Mediterranean villa, which once played host to names like Gable, Lombard, and Einstein. Set against the mountains just a stone's throw from Palm Canyon Drive, it's both conveniently located and deliciously private at the same time. Eight luxurious rooms overflow with antiques, sumptuous textiles, and other impeccable appointments, plus modern comforts like TV. Gorgeous gardens and a fine pool complete the perfect picture. A stay here makes a worthy special-occasion splurge.

412 W. Tahquitz Canyon Way (just west of Palm Canyon Dr.), Palm Springs. ☎ *760-320-0771. Fax: 760-320-0780. Internet:* www.thewillowspalmsprings. com. *Parking: Free! Rack rates: $275–$525 double. Rates include three-course breakfast and afternoon hors d'oeuvres. Deals: Rates as low as $195 in summer. AE, DISC, MC, V.*

Dining Out

The Palm Springs area boasts lots of excellent restaurants, but don't expect much in the way of innovation. The trend is toward traditional styles of cuisine that I consider to be too formal or heavy for the desert. Desert dwellers really *love* classic French food served by tuxe-doed waiters on white linen and bone china. That said, diversity abounds — it's just a matter of knowing where to look.

Cuistot

$$$$ Palm Desert CAL-FRENCH

Here's the desert's best restaurant — no small claim in an area that invites so much disposable income. Expect dazzling French cuisine with enough innovation and lightness of touch to give it a distinct California flair; unpretentious, welcoming service; and the kind of perfectly cali-brated lighting that makes diamonds sparkle just that much more. Inside seating is preferable to the patio thanks to the winning ambience of the contemporary room. A real star — perfect for celebrating.

73-040 El Paseo (at Ocotillo Ave.), Palm Desert. ☎ *760-340-1000. Reservations highly recommended. Main courses: $21–$33. AE, MC, V. Open: Lunch and dinner Tues–Sat, dinner only Sun.*

Edgardo's Cafe Veracruz

$–$$ Palm Springs MEXICAN

Come to this marvelous, off-the-tourist-circuit Mexican cafe for authentic Mayan, Huasteco, and Aztec cuisine. Even if you don't know Mayan from Aztec, never fear — the menu will look plenty familiar. All the food is first rate; I dream of the fresh-made tortillas, the fresh fish tacos, and the tra-ditional beef tamales. The room is super-casual but attractive, and ser-vice is genuinely welcoming and attentive. Well worth seeking out.

494 N. Palm Canyon Dr. (btw. Baristo and Arenas rds.), Palm Springs.
☎ *760-360-3558. Reservations recommended for dinner. Main courses: $4.50–$15.*
DISC, MC, V. Open: Lunch and dinner Mon–Fri; breakfast, lunch, and dinner
Sat–Sun.

Europa

$$$$ Palm Springs   CALIFORNIA-CONTINENTAL

This longtime favorite is one of the desert's most romantic restaurants.
Housed in what was once ice skater and B-movie actress Sonja Henie's
house, the dining room sparkles with candlelight and old-world charm.
Expect lots of modern accents on the Continental menu; the succulent
rack of lamb is a standout. Everything is prepared with care and beautifully presented, including the divine desserts. The patio is pure magic on
a lovely desert evening.

At the Villa Royale, 1620 Indian Trail (off E. Palm Canyon Dr., between S. Palm
Canyon and Sunrise Way), Palm Springs. ☎ *800-245-2314 or 760-327-2314.*
Reservations recommended. Main courses: $17–$32. AE, DC, DISC, MC, V. Open:
Dinner Tues–Sun, Sun brunch.

La Provence

$$$ Palm Springs   FRENCH

This authentic slice of the south of France is a refreshing change from the
mostly classic, fairly snooty French restaurants that dot the desert. It's
charming, affordable, and unpretentious. You'll find Mediterranean
touches in the French comfort food, which is hearty without being heavy.
Highlights include phyllo-wrapped escargot on mushroom caps in
shallot-garlic butter — delicious! — and monster-size tiger prawns served
atop mushroom risotto in a not-too-rich red wine demi-glace. A winner!

254 N. Palm Canyon Dr. (between Andreas and Amado rds.), 2nd floor, Palm Springs.
☎ *760-416-4418. Reservations recommended. Main courses: $13–$29 (most less*
than $21). AE, DC, DISC, MC, V. Open: Dinner Tues–Sun.

Las Casuelas Terraza

$$ Palm Springs   MEXICAN

I like the food at Edgardo's better, but the Mexican here is terrific, too.
And hardly a better perch exists for Palm Canyon people-watching than
the sidewalk patio. Live music and an even livelier happy hour set the
tone for the festivities.

222 S. Palm Canyon Dr. (between Baristo and Arenas rds.), Palm Springs.
☎ *760-325-2794. Internet:* www.lascasuelas.com. *Reservations recom-*
mended for dinner. Main courses: $8–$17. AE, DISC, MC, V. Open: Lunch and dinner
daily.

Sammy's California Woodfired Pizza

$–$$ Palm Desert PIZZA

The menu at this bright and airy gourmet pizzeria also features entree-size salads, wraps, and pastas, but come for the pizza. Sammy's specializes in single-serving-size traditional pies as well as more innovative versions with toppings like smoked duck sausage and artichokes. The restaurant is friendly, well-priced, and satisfying.

At the Gardens of El Paseo (at Larkspur Dr.), 2nd floor, Palm Desert. ☎ *760-836-0500. Internet:* www.sammyspizza.com. *Main courses: $8–$17 (most less than $13). AE, DISC, MC, V. Open: Lunch and dinner daily.*

St. James at the Vineyard

$$$$$ Palm Springs ECLECTIC

A candlelit hacienda in the heart of the Palm Canyon action houses one of the desert's most thrilling restaurants. The kitchen excels at preparing innovative, globe-hopping cuisine, from coriander-steamed New Zealand mussels to rich curries with chutney and papadum to tequila-fired shrimp to homemade wild mushroom ravioli. The bold flavors, sophisticated ambience, gracious service, and top-flight wine list make for an exciting night on the town. The bar plays host to a lively weekend scene.

265 S. Palm Canyon Dr. (between Baristo and Arenas rds.), Palm Springs. ☎ *760-320-8041. Internet:* www.palmsprings.com/dine/stjames. *Reservations recommended. Main courses: $19–$36. AE, DISC, MC, V. Open: Dinner nightly.*

Tyler's

$ Palm Springs BURGERS

This cute and utterly casual indoor/outdoor burger shack serves up juicy burgers, crispy fries, and on-tap brew, plus hot dogs, turkey and egg-salad sandwiches, and yummy root-beer floats and malts. The burgers come piled high with traditional fixin's, and portions are generous. The Fridays-only clam chowder is a must for chowderheads.

149 S. Indian Canyon Dr. (at La Plaza), Palm Springs. ☎ *760-325-2990. Burgers and sandwiches: $2.50–$6. Cash only. Open: Lunch Mon–Sat.*

Exploring Palm Springs & the Resorts

You won't go begging for things to see and do in this pampering paradise.

Touring the top attractions

Palm Springs Aerial Tramway

Probably Palm Springs' best-known traditional sightseeing attraction is this cool funicular, which takes you on a 14-minute ascent 2½ miles to the top of Mt. San Jacinto, the second highest point in Southern California. It's quite a remarkable ride, straight up the side of the mountain through five different climate zones — somewhat akin to moving from Mexico to Alaska inside 15 minutes. The ride is perfectly stable, and sleek new Swiss funicular cars rotate to give everyone 360-degree views along the way. Still, it's not for anyone who's afraid of heights, as the car ascends at a very steep angle — that cable looks *mighty* small, even to bravehearts, after you're far enough off the ground to notice. Otherwise, the entire family will love it.

At the top is the 13,000-acre Mt. San Jacinto State Park & Wilderness Area, an alpine setting, complete with 54 miles of hiking trails, plus a '60s ski-lodge-style building housing a mini museum and the less-than-stellar cafeteria-style Alpine Restaurant (skip the Ride 'n' Dine package unless you're planning on spending the day). You can spend the whole day here, or just come up for the panoramic views and head back down on the next tram out. Temperatures are typically 40 degrees cooler than down on the desert floor, so bring a sweater in summer, a full-fledged coat in winter. Snow covers the ground in the cold months; locals bring the kids up for sledding and other snowy fun. An adventure center (☎ 760-325-1449) rents snow tubes, snowshoes, and cross-country skis. Guided mule rides are offered in spring, summer, and fall. The only down side of the whole adventure is the price, which is high. Bring your AAA card or check for an online coupon to soften the blow.

At the end of Tramway Rd. (turn toward the mountains off Hwy. 111/N. Palm Canyon Dr.), Palm Springs. ☎ 888-515-TRAM or 760-325-1391. Internet: www.pstramway. com. *Open: Cars depart every half-hour Mon–Fri 10 a.m.–8 p.m., Sat–Sun 8 a.m.–8 p.m. (daily to 9 p.m. Memorial Day–Labor Day). Admission: $19.65 adults, $17.65 seniors, $12.50 kids ages 3–12. Ride 'n' Dine combo (available after 2:30 p.m., dinner served after 4 p.m.) $23.65 adults, $15.50 kids; $19.65 seniors Tues–Thurs.*

Palm Springs Desert Museum

This small but well-endowed museum is Palm Springs' secret weapon in the culture wars, standing brave and tall against the schmaltz that tends to dominate the desert. Highlights include terrific Western and Native American art collections, as well as natural science and history exhibits focusing on the local Coachella Valley desert and its first people, the Cahuilla tribe. The well-curated special exhibits stick to similar themes.

The Palm Springs Desert Resorts

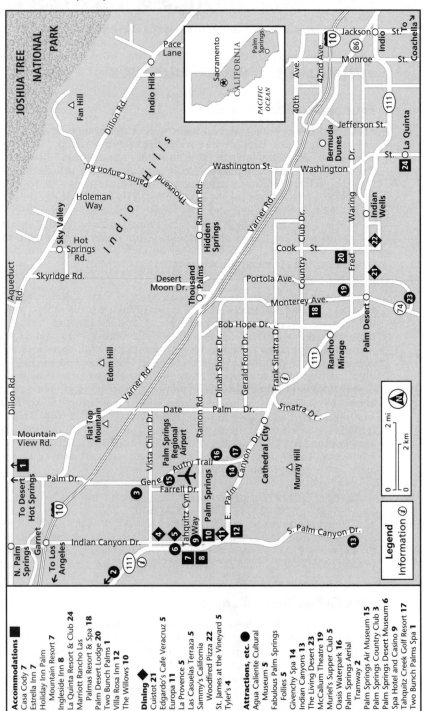

Accommodations ■
Casa Cody **7**
Estrella Inn **7**
Holiday Inn Palm
Mountain Resort **7**
Ingleside Inn **8**
La Quinta Resort & Club **24**
Marriott Rancho Las
Palmas Resort & Spa **18**
Palm Desert Lodge **20**
Two Bunch Palms **1**
Villa Rosa Inn **12**
The Willows **10**

Dining ◆
Cuistot **21**
Edgardo's Cafe Veracruz **5**
Europa **11**
La Provence **5**
Las Casuelas Terraza **5**
Sammy's California
Woodfired Pizza **22**
St. James at the Vineyard **5**
Tyler's **4**

Attractions, etc. ●
Agua Caliente Cultural
Museum **5**
Fabulous Palm Springs
Follies **5**
Givenchy Spa **14**
Indian Canyons **13**
The Living Desert **23**
McCallum Theatre **19**
Muriel's Supper Club **5**
Oasis Waterpark **16**
Palm Springs Aerial
Tramway **2**
Palm Springs Air Museum **15**
Palm Springs Country Club **3**
Palm Springs Desert Museum **6**
Spa Hotel and Casino **9**
Tahquitz Creek Golf Resort **17**
Two Bunch Palms Spa **1**

101 Museum Dr. (at Tahquitz Canyon Way, just west of N. Palm Canyon Dr.), Palm Springs. ☎ *760-325-7186. Internet:* www.psmuseum.org. *Open: Tues–Sat 10 a.m.–5 p.m., Sun noon–5 p.m. Admission: $7.50 adults, $6.50 seniors, $3.50 kids 6–17, free to all first Friday of the month.*

The Living Desert

Part museum, part zoo, and all learning center, this wildlife and botanical park is dedicated to introducing the wonders of the local ecosystem to those who consider the desert a flat, colorless, inhospitable wasteland. You can walk or take a tram ride through re-creations of several distinct desert zones, seeing and learning about the local geology, plants, insects, and wildlife as you go. Critters run the gamut from tarantulas to mountain lions, with bighorn sheep, roadrunners, and golden eagles in the mix. While you can't beat seeing the real desert with the help of an outfitter (see "Desert Excursions" later in the chapter), this is a great alternative for those not so inclined, or for families with little ones.

47-900 Portola Ave. (off Hwy. 111, between Monterey Ave. and Cook St.), Palm Desert. ☎ *760-346-5694. Internet:* www.livingdesert.org. *Open: Sept–mid-June, daily 9 a.m.–5 p.m. (last entrance 4 p.m.); mid-June–Aug, daily 8 a.m.–1 p.m. Admission: $8.50 adults, $7.50 seniors, $4.25 kids 3–12.*

Oasis Waterpark

Your kids will be in waterhog heaven at this 21-acre playground, which boasts 13 thrilling water slides (five dedicated to tots), the state's largest wave-action pool, an inner-tube ride, and lots more wet 'n' wild fun. Landlocked facilities include private beach cabanas, a video arcade, a 20,000-square-foot health club, and dressing rooms and lockers.

1500 S. Gene Autry Trail (between Ramon Rd. and E. Palm Canyon Dr.), Palm Springs. ☎ *760-327-0499. Internet:* www.oasiswaterresort.com. *Open: Mid-Mar–Labor Day, daily 11 a.m.–5 p.m.; Labor Day–Oct, Sat–Sun 11 a.m.–5 p.m. Admission: $19.95 adults, $12.95 kids 3–5 ft. tall.*

Palm Springs Air Museum

This museum holds one of the world's largest collections of WWII flyers. It's adjacent to the airport, so flying demonstrations are a regular part of the program. Many of the tour guides are veterans, so expect lots of good real-life stories, too.

745 N. Gene Autry Trail (between Ramon and Vista Chino rds.), Palm Springs. ☎ *760-778-6262. Internet:* www.air-museum.org. *Admission: $7.50 adults, $6 seniors and military, $3.50 kids 6–12. Open: Daily 10 a.m.–5 p.m.*

Hitting the links

If fairways and five-irons draw you to the desert, your best bet is to stay at one of the area golf resorts, such as **La Quinta** or **Marriott Rancho Las Palmas,** where you can play on some of the country's best championship golf courses without ever leaving the grounds (see

"Staying in Desert Style" earlier in the chapter). La Quinta, in particular, is home to some of the finest fairways around; in fact, three of the four are ranked in *Golf* magazine's "Top 100 Courses You Can Play."

Other resorts you may want to consider include **Hyatt Grand Champions** (☎ **800-633-7313** or 760-341-1000; www.hyatt.com) and **Westin Mission Hills** (☎ **888-625-5144** or 760-328-5955; www.westin.com). Westin's Resort Course is a stellar Pete Dye design that's more forgiving than most of his legendary greens. Expect greens fees to be between $135 and $175; twilight rates cut the fees nearly in half.

If you want to experience desert golf but you're not up to splurging on one of the big boys, consider **Tahquitz Creek,** 1885 Golf Club Dr., off East Palm Canyon Drive between Gene Autry Trail and Cathedral Canyon Drive, Palm Springs (☎ **800-743-2211** or 760-328-1005; www.palmergolf.com), whose two diverse courses run by the Arnold Palmer Group appeal to mid-handicappers. Greens fees range from $45 to $70, and discounted twilight rates are available.

Another good bet is **Palm Springs Country Club,** 2500 Whitewater Club Dr., off Vista Chino Road (☎ **760-323-2626**; www.palmsprings.com/golf/pscc.html), home to the oldest public course in Palm Springs, and especially popular with golfers on a budget. Greens fees are just $30 before 1 p.m., $20 after 1 p.m.

Tee times at many courses can't be booked more than a few days in advance (a problem for non-hotel guests who want to play at the big resorts), but several companies can make advance arrangements for you, the best of which is **Golf à la Carte** (☎ **760-324-5012**; www.palmspringsgolf.com). Go online to www.desertgolfguide.com and click on "Book Tee Times" for other visitor center–sanctioned agents, many of which can arrange a complete golf vacation for you.

And always ask about golf packages when you're making hotel reservations, because many area properties — even the most unassuming motels — offer packages that include tee times.

If you arrive in the desert without prebooked tee times, **Stand-By Golf** (☎ **760-321-2665**) specializes in same-day and next-day tee times. Ditto for **Next Day Golf** (☎ **760-345-8463**). **Palm Springs Tee Times** (☎ **760-324-5012**; www.palmspringsteetimes.com) may be able to book you in at a discount as much as 60 days in advance.

The visitors bureau is dedicated to making golfers happy, and can provide you with tons of additional golf information (see "Gathering More Information" later in this chapter). Their great *Desert Golf & Tennis Guide* is online at www.desertgolfguide.com, which also offers a complete list of the many tournaments held in the area (mainly from November to April), including celebrity pro-ams, if you're more the spectating type than a hands-on golfer. Other excellent sources include the online version of the free *Palm Springs Golfer* magazine (www.greatgolfing.com) and Golfer's Guide.com (www.golfersguide.com).

Ahhhh — The spa

The desert is the perfect place to indulge in some serious pampering. Without a doubt, my favorite place to relax is at **Two Bunch Palms** in Desert Hot Springs (☎ **800-472-4334** or 760-329-8791; www. twobunchpalms.com). You can enjoy this place even if you don't stay over. Book one of the little-advertised Day Spa packages, which include two 1-hour treatments, lunch or dinner, and full access to the grounds for 6 to 9 hours (ditto), plus taxes and gratuities for (at press time, at least) $235 to $275. You can even get a super-decadent 12-hour version that includes four treatments and two meals for $495 — plus the cost of a taxi back to your hotel when it's all over, because human Jell-O just can't drive. For further information, see "Staying in Desert Style" earlier in the chapter.

If you don't want to dedicate the majority of a day — or a few hundred bucks — to a spa, other resorts provide excellent full-service spas that offer more flexibility. If you're looking for chic, try the **Givenchy Spa** at Merv Griffin's Resort Hotel, 4200 E. Palm Canyon Dr., between Farrell Drive and Gene Autry Trail, Palm Springs (☎ **800-276-5000** or 760-770-5000; www.merv.com).

For something a little more down to earth, book a treatment or two at the **Spa Hotel and Casino,** 100 N. Indian Canyon Dr., Palm Springs (☎ **800-854-1279** or 760-325-1461; www.spa-hotel.com), run by the Aqua Caliente tribe on a square block of reservation land in the heart of town. The natural therapeutic hot-spring waters are the same that the local Indians have been taking for hundreds of years, but now they've built a sleekly modern, full-service spa around 'em.

Ol' Blue Eyes slept here

In the mood for some sanctioned gawking? Then hitch a ride on a nice air-conditioned bus on one of the **Palm Springs Celebrity Tours,** in the RimRock Plaza Center, at Gene Autry Trail and Highway 111 (☎ **760-770-2700**; www.celebritytour.qpg.com). Some actual history is thrown into the mix, but most of the tour is dedicated to seeing the stars' homes. The company also offers a streamlined 1-hour version for $15 adults, $13 seniors, and $7 kids 16 and under. But if you're gonna do it, go for the whole enchilada: The 2 ½-hour tour heads into Rancho Mirage and Palm Desert to take in the grandest estates of the biggest celebs — yep, including Sinatra — at a cost of $20 adults, $17 seniors, $9 kids. Make advance reservations.

Desert excursions

In addition to the following options, you may also consider a day trip to **Joshua Tree National Park** (see Chapter 25).

Taking a guided tour

To the untrained eye, the desert can look like a lot of nothing. Put yourself in the hands of a knowledgable and enthusiastic guide, however, and it's a whole different story — an entire, fascinating world you never knew existed will open up to you like a rare flower.

Hands down, the area's best tour operator is *Desert Adventures Jeep Eco-Tours* (☎ **888-440-JEEP** or 760-324-JEEP; www.red-jeep.com), whose off-road ecotours, offered in signature seven-seater red jeeps, are led by naturalist guides. The company is extremely reliable, and the experienced guides are great at communicating their vast knowledge of desert ecology, geology, history, and lore as well as earthquake science in a manner that's both smart and enjoyable. They're expert at giving meaning to what you see around you.

Still, the experience isn't for everyone. For one thing, the open jeep is very bouncy and dusty, and the weather can get really hot in summer. (Springtime, in particular, is a great time to go, as the weather is ideal and the wildflowers are in bloom.) Those of you with mobility issues should ask whether the tour can comfortably accommodate you. Kids, on the other hand, will love the rough-and-ready "on safari" feeling, although the tours do not accept children under six.

Offerings change periodically, so call or check the Web site to see what's on while you're in town. Most tours include a visit to the legendary **San Andreas Fault,** with detailed explanations of how tectonic forces work and a look at evidence of recent and ongoing fault activity. Those of you with cultural interests can choose to tour an authentically re-created ancient Cahuilla village to learn how Native Americans carved a life out of the barren land. Tours that include desert walks are also offered for hikers. Tours last 3 or 4 hours and vary in price from $79 to $129 ($5 off for seniors and kids under 12). Reservations are required; call at least a day in advance.

Hiking

The reservation land that comprises **Indian Canyons** (☎ **800-790-3398** or 760-325-5673; www.palmsprings.com/points/canyon), at the end of South Palm Canyon Drive (three miles south of the turnoff for East Palm Canyon/Highway 111), is terrific hiking territory. At press time, three stunning canyons were open to hikers of all levels; stop at the **Trading Post** for detailed trail maps.

Admission is $6 for adults, $3.50 for seniors and students, $1 kids 6 to 12. Open daily from 8 a.m. to 6 p.m.; tours are offered Monday through Thursday at 10 a.m. and 1 p.m., Friday through Sunday at 9 a.m., 11 a.m., 1 p.m., and 3 p.m. Call ahead in summer, because the canyons have been known to close from late June through Labor Day.

A visit to the **Agua Caliente Cultural Museum,** in the Village Green Heritage Center, 219 S. Palm Canyon Dr., at Arenas Road (☎ **760-778-1079** or 760-323-0151; www.prinet.com/accmuseum), pairs up well with a visit to Indian Canyons. Of particular note is the beautiful collection of basketry. Admission is free; call for hours.

Shopping

People looking to spend money will have no trouble in Palm Springs. Boutiques are abundant along Palm Canyon Drive and the side streets in the heart of Palm Springs. Antique and collectibles hunters — especially those with groovy midcentury-modern tastes — will enjoy the many '50s finds along North Palm Canyon, north of the downtown action.

Over in Palm Desert, you'll find Beverly Hills-style boutiquing along El Paseo, which curves south off Highway 111 between Fred Waring Drive and Cook Street and is lined with about 200 upper-end shops. For a complete directory of what's available, visit www.elpaseo.com.

The Gardens at El Paseo is a lovely open-air mall at El Paseo and Larkspur Drive (☎ **760-862-1990**), with offerings that run the gamut from Ann Taylor to terrific one-of-a-kind shops and galleries. One of my favorites is the **Tommy Bahama's Emporium** (☎ **760-836-0288**), a terrific source for island and desert resort wear.

Living It Up After Dark

For the latest bar and club happenings, pick up the free weekly *Desert Sun Weekend*, easily available around town. Also check out the *Desert Guide,* available at the visitor centers (see the next section).

Nightlife largely revolves around North Palm Canyon Drive, at the heart of downtown Palm Springs. Restaurants and bars spill out onto the street until late, so your best bet is to just wander down the street and pop into whichever establishment pleases you. Among the lively spots is **Muriel's Supper Club,** 210 S. Palm Canyon Dr., at Arenas Road (☎ **760-325-8839;** www.muriels.com), a chic dinner-and-dancing joint with an abundance of live music, from swing and mambo parties to concerts by funky New Orleans pianist Dr. John.

The rollicking street festival known as **VillageFest** takes over Palm Canyon Drive, between Amado and Baristo roads, on Thursdays from 7 to 10 p.m. (6 to 10 p.m. October through April). The all-ages fun offers art-and-crafts vendors, food booths, and street entertainers.

The **Fabulous Palm Springs Follies,** 128 S. Palm Canyon Dr. (☎ **760-327-0225;** www.palmspringsfollies.com), is a Vegas-style extravaganza filled with show tunes from the 1930s and '40s and lively production numbers complete with leggy showgirls. This silly show is so popular that it's celebrating its 10th anniversary; reserve in advance. Tickets run $33 to $65 for the 2 ½-hour show.

For more highbrow entertainment, see what's on at the **McCallum Theatre,** at the **Bob Hope Cultural Center,** 73000 Fred Waring Dr., Palm Desert (☎ **760-340-ARTS;** www.mccallum-theatre.org).

Gathering More Information

Palm Springs Desert Resorts Convention & Visitors Bureau (☎ **800-96-RESORTS** [967-3767] or 760-770-9000) can send you information and offer assistance with accommodations (call ☎ **800-41-RELAX** [417-3529] for accommodations info). It also operates a **24-hour activity hotline** (☎ **760-770-1992**) and an extensive Web site at www.desert-resorts.com.

You can get excellent assistance at the Palm Springs Visitors Information Center (☎ **800-34-SPRINGS** [347-7746] or 760-778-8418), which concentrates on Palm Springs proper and has a great site at www.palm-springs.org. The well-stocked and -staffed visitor center is at 2781 N. Palm Canyon Drive, just south of Tramway Road, an easy stop on your way into town.

If you're interested in Palm Desert, call the Palm Desert Visitors Information Center at ☎ **760-568-1441** or visit them online at www.palm-desert.com. The walk-in center is at Hwy. 111 and Monterey Avenue (pull into the Denny's parking lot).

Free publications with good maps are available at hotels, restaurants, shops, and visitor centers throughout the area. The best of the bunch is *Palm Springs Life* magazine's free monthly *Desert Guide.* Gay visitors will want to pick up the free *Palm Springs Gay Guide,* which is also easy to find. Other useful Web sites include www.palmsprings.com and www.inpalmsprings.com, the latter excellent for arts and entertainment coverage.

To check the local weather, dial ☎ **760-345-3711.**

American Express has an official travel office in Palm Springs at Andersen Travel Service, 700 E. Tahquitz Canyon Way (☎ **760-325 2001**).

Chapter 25

The Desert Parks: Joshua Tree and Death Valley

· ·

In This Chapter

▶ Getting to Joshua Tree National Park — and how long to stay

▶ Seeing the highlights — and deciding where to stay if you want to see more

▶ Considering the ins and outs of visiting far-flung Death Valley National Park

▶ Reaching Death Valley, seeing the sights, and deciding where to stay

· ·

*W*ant to experience the desert's rough-edged grandeur? Then visit one — or both — of these national parks dedicated to preserving the desert environment. They're refuges of rare beauty, otherworldly oases where living things thrive in a seemingly hostile world.

Joshua Tree National Park

Joshua Tree National Park is a great place to experience the wonders of the desert outside the carefully pruned environs of Palm Springs resort living. This seemingly barren, seemingly unkempt landscape thrives in ways that are not readily apparent to those of us who aren't from these parts, and easy to ignore when you're on a neatly manicured golf course or basking by the pool.

At first glance, you'll think you've landed on the moon, or at least in some inhospitable foreign land. The low, dry, scruffy terrain is vast and undeveloped, dotted with unwelcoming cactus and harsh, contorted mountains of rock. Rusted-out ruins of ranches and abandoned mines drive home the sense of a land that has stubbornly resisted civilization. Good, I say — it doesn't hurt us to realize that we're not always the winner in our attempts to conquer nature. That's when the respect comes — and the wows. You begin to notice the remarkable shapes and textures, the majestic scale, the vivid colors, and the true beauty in the sheer otherworldliness of it all.

The oddball tree that gives the park its name is actually a yucca, and a member of the lily family. At first glance, it seems like God's joke — or God's messenger, depending on your point of view. The early

19th-century explorer John C. Frémont summed up the common view when he called the Joshua tree "the most repulsive tree in the vegetable kingdom," while early Mormon settlers thought the stout trunk and bristly upraised limbs were nature's portrait of the prophet leading them to the Promised Land. The family resemblance is clearest in spring, when (if enough rain has fallen) the limbs sprout yellow lilylike blossoms.

The park actually encompasses two quite different desert environments: In the northwestern section — where you'll enter the park — is the **Mojave Desert,** the cragged, hilly land where rugged boulders set the tone and the Joshua tree lives. Head southeast through the park and the elevation drops and the landscape morphs into the **Colorado Desert,** which looks more like the desert you expect: hotter, drier, and dotted with cactus and creosote. Five groves of native fan palms dot the park; these oases point to natural water sources and serve as gathering spots for the park's wildlife — a range of critters, from roadrunners to golden eagles to bighorn sheep.

Making it a day trip

I highly recommend visiting the park as a day trip from Palm Springs. Unless you really want to become intimate with the desert environment, that's plenty. Do count on a very full day, though; leave early in the morning, and plan on a later dinner after you get back into town, with plenty of time built in to return and refresh. The park entrance is a good hour from the resorts, and the dry desert environment really takes it out of you. Trust me, you won't be up for a twilight round of golf when you get back.

If you'd like to stay close by to experience more of the park, the baby burb of Twentynine Palms, just outside the North Entrance, has a few basic options. See "Staying in nearby Twentynine Palms" later in this chapter.

Preparing for your visit to the park

If you've only been to well-developed parks like Yosemite or the Grand Canyon before, Joshua Tree will come as something of a surprise. This is true unspoiled wilderness, with no concessions at all within the park — no restaurants, no hotels, no gift shops with snow globes — and just a few rustic campgrounds. So prepare for your day trip with the following tips in mind:

- ✔ You'll need *water,* so load up the car with a few bottles before you enter the park. One gallon per person per day is the official recommendation, more if you're doing serious hiking.

- ✔ Make sure you fill the car with *gas,* too.

- ✔ You'll also need to bring in your own *food,* so pack a picnic lunch and snacks. If you don't do it in Palm Springs, Twentynine Palms has markets. If you enter at the West Entrance, you can buy box lunches at Park Center (see the next section).

✔ W*ear sturdy shoes,* preferably hiking boots. *Bring sunscreen, sunglasses, a hat, and a jacket or sweater,* as desert evenings can cool down quickly, and winter days can be chillier than you might expect. Even if the weather is hot in Palm Springs, it will be cooler at higher elevations; some of the northern portions of the park sit at 4,000 feet or more. You probably won't need another layer in summer, but throw it in the car anyway.

✔ After you're in the park, *stay out of abandoned mines and leftover structures.* Keep an eye on curious kids at all times.

Getting there

On the map, Joshua Tree National Park looks as if it's sitting just on the other side of the freeway from the desert resorts. Well, it does and it doesn't. None of the three access points is close to Palm Springs.

The South (Cottonwood Spring) Entrance is off I-10, 53 miles east of Palm Springs, but I don't suggest you use it. The **Cottonwood Visitor Center** is merely a ranger hut offering only basic information.

Instead, use either the West Entrance, at the village of Joshua Tree, or the North (Oasis of Mara) Entrance in Twentynine Palms. To reach both entrances from Palm Springs, take Gene Autry Trail to I-10 west; after six miles, take the turnoff for Highway 62 (the Twentynine Palms Highway), which curves around the west and north sides of the park. The distance is about 44 miles to the West Entrance, 55 miles to Twentynine Palms and the main gate.

At the West Entrance, in Joshua Tree village, is **Park Center,** 6554 Park Blvd. (☎ **760-366-3448;** www.parkcenter.net), open daily from 8:30 a.m. to 5 p.m. (turn right from Highway 62). This art gallery and gift shop-cum-visitor center is privately run but still very useful. The center includes a helpful information desk with maps and other park-relevant publications on hand, a convenience store, and a bakery and deli (open from 7 a.m. for early birds).

Farther down the highway, at the corner of National Park Drive and Utah Trail, a half mile south of Highway 62 in the funky desert town of Twentynine Palms, is the **Oasis Visitor Center,** the park's official main visitor center, open daily from 8 a.m. to 5 p.m. This is the place to pick up a detailed map, program and tour schedules, and ask any questions you have for the park rangers.

Admission to the park is $10 per car, good for seven days. Keep your stub to return.

Joshua Tree National Park

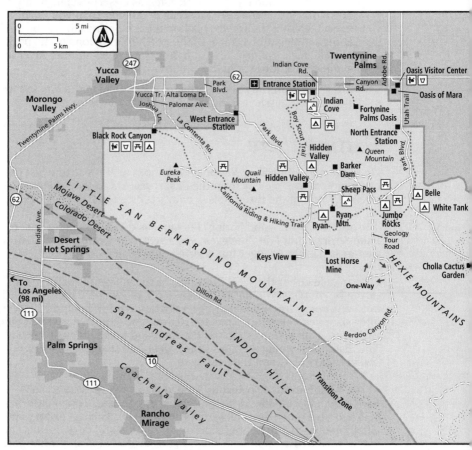

Exploring the park

The best bet for day-trippers looking for the full Joshua Tree experience is to enter the park at either the West or North entrance and explore the northern loop (Park Boulevard) first. Then follow the Pinto Basin Road to the southeast Cottonwood section of the park, where you can exit the park, go south to I-10, and be back in Palm Springs for dinner. This drive will take you past all the major highlights and through both desert climate zones. (The distance from the North Entrance to the Cottonwood gate is 41 miles.)

Entering the park via the West Entrance is most time-efficient because it doesn't require you to drive east and then backtrack west after you're in the park, like using the North Entrance does. But using the West Entrance also doesn't allow you to stop at the **Oasis Visitor Center** — which has geological, flora, and fauna interpretive displays that will help you to understand what you're seeing in the park — until after you've already driven the northern loop. The decision is up to you.

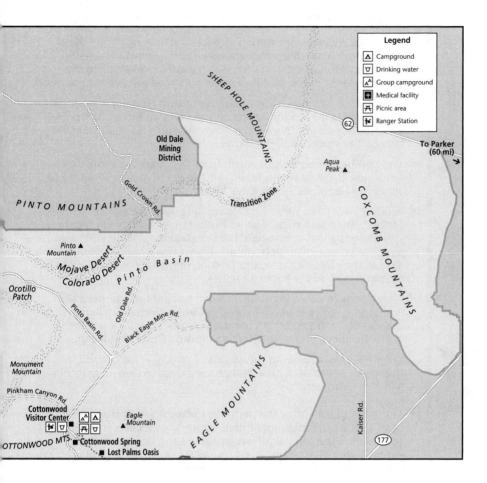

Legend

- △ Campground
- ▽ Drinking water
- ▲ Group campground
- ✚ Medical facility
- ⊼ Picnic area
- ▮ Ranger Station

SHEEP HOLE MOUNTAINS

62

Old Dale
Mining
District

Aqua
Peak ▲

To Parker
(60 mi)

Gold Crown Rd.

PINTO MOUNTAINS

Transition Zone

COXCOMB MOUNTAINS

Pinto ▲
Mountain

Mojave Desert

Colorado Desert

Pinto Basin

Ocotillo
Patch

Pinto Basin Rd.

Old Dale Rd.

Black Eagle Mine Rd.

Monument
Mountain

Pinkham Canyon Rd.

Cottonwood
Visitor Center

Eagle
▲ Mountain

EAGLE MOUNTAINS

Kaiser Rd.

177

OTTONWOOD MTS ▮ Cottonwood Spring

Lost Palms Oasis

If you want to be back in Palm Springs by early afternoon, stick with just the northern loop. Enter the park at the West Entrance, follow Park Boulevard past the main attractions, exit at the North Entrance, and follow Highway 62 back to I-10 and Palm Springs.

Seeing the highlights

To truly appreciate the park, you have to get out of your car and walk among the giant rocks and Joshua trees. Even if you're an experienced hiker, I recommend splitting your energy between a couple of easy trails in different areas rather than choosing one long or difficult hike, in order to get a broader experience of the park. The visitor center can supply you with an official park map so you can easily follow along, plus trail and topographical maps.

✔ **Jumbo Rocks** is one of the most striking — and fun — sections of the park. The rocks include an awe-inspiring collection of imaginatively shaped monster boulders (very Flintstones) and a Joshua tree forest that redefines the notion of "forest." The easy 1¾-mile **Skull Rock Nature Trail** takes you around one of the most personality-laden rock formations, and serves as a good introduction to the geology, plantlife, and wildlife. Expect your visit to take two hours.

✔ At Cap Rock Junction, where Park Boulevard (the northern loop) swings north, is the four-tenths mile paved **Cap Rock Nature Trail,** a super-easy alternative for those among you who don't want to take on the longer Skull Rock trail.

✔ The 2½-mile driving detour south from Cap Rock Junction, down Keys View Road, is worth taking for the grand desert views you'll enjoy from 5,185-foot-high **Keys View.**

✔ **Hidden Valley** is a former cattle rustlers' hideout and current rock-climbers fave tucked away behind more massive boulders. I love the easy, just-over-a-mile **Barker Dam** loop, which takes you past Native American petroglyphs (most easily visible along the base of the cliffs on the return portion of the loop) and to a small dammed lake. Allow about 1½ hours.

✔ After you turn down Pinto Basin Road toward the southern section of the park, the place to stop is **Cholla Cactus Gardens,** smack-dab in the middle of the park. A quarter-mile interpretive trail introduces you to the park's Colorado Desert landscape.

Keep your distance from the stands of cholla — nicknamed the "jumping cactus" — whose spines are drawn to skin and clothing like flies to honey.

✔ At the southern end of the park lies **Cottonwood Springs,** a lush oasis that's a favorite stop among visitors, especially in spring, when this is the top wildflower-viewing spot. Be sure to leave yourself enough daylight to enjoy it. An easy two-mile (round-trip) nature trail leaves from the campground.

Talking the talk: Ranger-led tours

Tours of **Keys Ranch** (also called Desert Queen Ranch) are most fascinating, and well worth planning your visit around. This early 20th-century homestead is tucked away in a remote rocky canyon (the Keys must've been hardy folks). You can only see it on a 1½-hour ranger-led half-mile walk, usually offered from October through May daily at 10 a.m., 1 p.m., and 3 p.m. Tickets are $5, $2.50 for kids 6 to 11. Reservations are recommended; you can book your spots up to five months in advance by calling ☎ 760-367-5555. If you don't make a reservation, ask at the Oasis Visitor Center if tickets are available for the day's tours and you may get lucky.

The rangers also offer lots of other guided walks and talks for various interests. The schedule is most active in spring and fall. Call ☎ 760-367-5500 or check the Web site at www.nps.gov/jotr.

Staying in nearby Twentynine Palms

The park offers no lodgings, but Twentynine Palms has a few basic options within five miles of the North Entrance:

✔ Near the visitor center, tucked in the palms of the Oasis of Mara, is the **29 Palms Inn ($-$$)**, 73950 Inn Ave. (☎ **760-367-3505;** www. 29palmsinn.com), a cluster of rustic frame cabins and adobe cottages from the 1920s attached to the best restaurant in town. You'll find lots of desert character here.

✔ The **Best Western Garden Inn & Suites ($$)**, 71487 Twentynine Palms Hwy. (☎ **760-367-9141;** www.bestwestern.com/ gardeninnsuites), is a comfortable and conveniently located motel with a pool and Jacuzzi.

✔ The **Roughley Manor ($$)**, 74744 Joe Davis Rd. (☎ **760-367-3238;** www.virtual29.com/themanor), is an immaculate B&B in a lovely restored homestead. Half of the rooms have private baths, and on-site facilities include a hot tub.

Gathering more information

Contact the Park Superintendent at ☎ **760-367-5500,** or point your Web browser to the official park site at www.nps.gov/jotr. The Joshua Tree National Park Association's site at www.joshuatree.org is even more useful. Also check www.desertgold.com, where you'll find a current schedule of ranger programs in addition to a wealth of other information.

For more information on the town of Twentynine Palms, contact the 29 Palms Chamber of Commerce (☎ **760-367-3445;** www.virtual29. com/chamber).

Death Valley National Park

I don't make a big deal out of **Death Valley National Park** because most of you won't have time to get there on your first trip to California. Or you may not want to go to the trouble: no easy way exists to get there, it's not close to anything, and services are minimal.

Still, plenty of people manage to work Death Valley in to their vacation plans, and I completely understand why. You can't deny the draw of such extremes: The hottest, the highest, the largest, the lowest, the driest — you want it, Death Valley's got it. The landscape is both savage and spectacular to the max. And heck, the name alone just begs for the defiance of a visit.

A living, breathing, singing desert

Even the most seemingly uninhabitable spots in Death Valley are often inhabited. At the desert bottom, the survival of tiny pupfish depends on whether or not the summer heat evaporates the Salt Creek pools the fish inhabit. Dunes dwellers include the kangeroo rat and the nocturnal sidewinder, a small rattlesnake that rarely comes out during the day. **Eureka Valley,** in the remote north end of the park, is famous for its rare plants, including the endangered Eureka Valley evening primrose, which only blooms at night. Look for desert tortoises and smoke trees — so named for their resemblance to puffs of smoke — in the **Owlshead Mountains,** in the extreme southern end of the park. Hardy bristlecone pines, believed to be the oldest living things on the planet, grow only on the park summits, in towering spots like **Telescope Peak;** if you're hardy, you might want to attempt the grueling hike to the top. Bighorn sheep can be seen in the folds of rugged canyon cliffs. Even the desert sand is alive. Visitors who climb to the top of Eureka Dunes, in the Eureka Valley, can actually hear the sand "singing" as the tiny grains shift and slide.

Getting there

Even though Death Valley is basically due east of the Central Coast, some pesky mountains and a couple of national forests conspire to make you go south — way south — to get there.

✔ **From Southern California:** Come via I-15 (which connects with I-10 midway between L.A. and Palm Springs) to Baker, where you connect with Highway 127 north to Highway 190 east. The drive is 300 miles or about 6½ hours.

Or you can take I-14 north from the L.A. area (it connects with I-5) to Highway 178 to Highway 190, which takes roughly the same amount of time.

✔ **From Yosemite:** In warm weather, you can also reach Death Valley from Yosemite National Park by traveling down the east side of the Sierras. (The Tioga Pass Road you'll need to take out of Yosemite is closed in winter.) Take Highway 120 east to I-395 south to Highway 136 to Highway 190, a 263-mile drive that also takes about 6½ hours. (See what I mean? Death Valley is not close to anything.)

✔ **From Nevada:** Take NV 374 from Beatty, located on U.S. 95.

Death Valley is a big, sprawling park, the largest national park in the lower 48 states. Because you need to set aside two days for driving alone, a visit to Death Valley requires a minimum of three days. Four is much smarter.

Death Valley

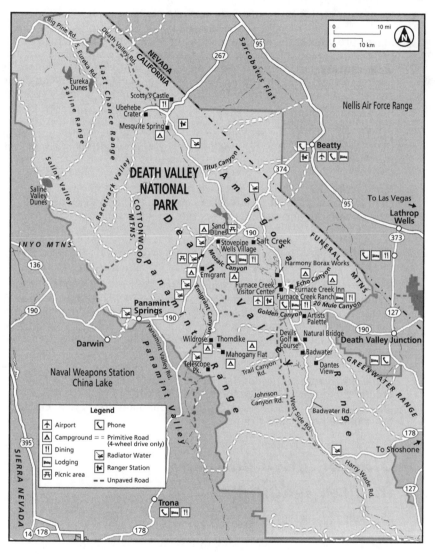

Surviving Death Valley: The basics

The place to start is Death Valley Visitor Center, in the middle of the park at **Furnace Creek,** 15 miles inside the eastern boundary at the junction of highways 190 and 178, open daily from 8 a.m. to 6 p.m. Admission to the park is $10 per car, and it's good for seven days; keep your stub.

Death Valley has been called a "windshield wilderness" because the best way to see the park is by car. Two-lane roads wind through a remote landscape devoid of telephone wires and commercial activity.

Note that you should only tackle many of the park's backcountry and primitive roads in a four-wheel-drive vehicle or a light truck; check at the visitor center for road conditions and maps.

Make sure your car is in good working order and fill it up with gas before setting out into Death Valley. Gasoline is only sold at a handful of far-ranging park outposts: **Furnace Creek, Scotty's Castle, Panamint Springs Resort,** and **Stovepipe Wells Village.** Packing a picnic lunch or snacks and plenty of water before the day's excursion is also a good idea. Restaurants and food concessions inside the park are remote and expensive, so packing a cooler full of drinks and snacks for the duration of your visit is smart. You can find a good range of food supplies in the towns of Baker, Beatty, Shoshone, Pahrump, and Ridgecrest and on the Furnace Creek Ranch.

Most people prefer to visit the park in the temperate months, from October through April. Heat-seekers come in the summer when the crowds thin out and daytime temperatures soar well past 100°F.

Exploring the park

If you're traveling out of the Furnace Creek Visitor Center, take the 24-mile drive through Furnace Creek Walsh badlands to **Dantes View,** a scenic overlook with a park basin panorama amid enveloping mountain ranges. Or take **Artists Drive,** which coils through colorful canyon terrain. **Devil's Golf Course,** a huge salt bed, can be found off a short spur road north of Badwater.

In the northwest section of the park is **Scotty's Castle,** a 1920s mansion built in the desert as a vacation retreat. It's got a pool fit for a desert — all 270 feet of it — and its own hydroelectric plant. Reserve ahead for tours of the house and grounds.

Staying alive and well in local lodgings

The valley holds four places to stay:

- ✔ The elegant **Furnace Creek Inn ($$$$)** is a beautifully restored 1930s desert oasis where you should reserve a room as far in advance as possible. It also has a formal dining room (☎ 760-786-2361).

- ✔ The **Furnace Creek Ranch ($$)** has moderately priced rustic cottages run by the same folks who run the inn. Among the food options here are a diner, a steak house, and a fully stocked grocery store (☎ 760-786-2345).

- ✔ **Stovepipe Wells Village ($)** offers budget-basic motel rooms, RV hookups, and a casual restaurant (☎ 760-786-2387).

- ✔ The **Panamint Springs Resort ($)** is a plain but perfectly appealing motel with a burgers-and-beer cafe (☎ 775-482-7680; www.deathvalley.com).

For *camping* info and reservations, call ☎ 800-365-CAMP (365-2267) or point your browser to reservations.nps.gov.

Gathering more information

For additional information, contact the Death Valley National Park Service at ☎ 760-786-2331, or go online to www.nps.gov/deva. Another quite useful source is www.deathvalley.com. For general information on preparing for your trip through the California desert, visit www.californiadesert.gov.

Part VI
The Part of Tens

In this part . . .

Every *For Dummies* book contains a Part of Tens. If Parts III through V are the main course of your meal, think of these fun chapters, each their own top-ten list, as dessert. If you feel like doing homework to get you in the proper California mood, check out Chapter 26. Or maybe you want to catch a whiff of genuine Left Coast zaniness while you're on the road? Read Chapter 27 to discover where you can get down and wacky like real Californians do.

Chapter 26

Ten Quintessentially California Movies to Watch Before You Leave Home

● ●

In This Chapter

▶ Seeing California through Hollywood's eyes

▶ Going on location through film

● ●

*T*he Golden State is synonymous with the silver screen, of course. So what better way to bone up for your vacation than to pop a few flicks into the VCR? Here are my picks, in no particular order, for the movies that best capture the spirit of the most dramatically diverse and phenomenally photogenic state in the Union.

What's Up, Doc? (1972)

This marvelous Peter Bogdanovich–directed, Buck Henry–scribed gem starring Barbra Streisand and Ryan O'Neal shows off the hilly streets of San Francisco — especially Chinatown — at their most colorful and romantic. *What's Up, Doc?* also happens to be one of my favorite screwball comedies of all time, with the incomparable Madeline Kahn stealing a very funny show.

Vertigo (1958)

Possibly the greatest movie director of all time, Alfred Hitchcock always used locations well — remember Mount Rushmore in *North by Northwest*? In *Vertigo,* the suspense master uses San Francisco to dizzying effect (pun intended).

You should watch for a few key locations. The Empire Hotel (where James Stewart eventually finds Kim Novak) is now the York Hotel, home to the sexy Plush Room cabaret showroom (see Chapter 9). Also, if you visit the Spanish mission, San Juan Bautista, featured in the film (it's a short drive from Monterey, near the junction of U.S. 101 and Highway 156), you'll find that it doesn't actually have a bell tower. Hitchcock's minions added the movie's bell tower with editing-room smoke and mirrors.

Monterey Pop (1969)

Monterey Pop, D.A. Pennebaker's first-rate rockumentary, chronicles the glorious three-day music festival that was actually a better realization of the Summer of Love dream than Woodstock ever hoped to be. The film wonderfully captures '60s' San Francisco's Haight-Ashbury vibe and the California sound, including groups such as the Mamas and the Papas (whose leader, John Phillips, was the brains behind the event), Jefferson Airplane, Janis Joplin with Big Brother and the Holding Company, Jimi Hendrix, Canned Heat, The Who, and others, plus a stunning performance by Otis Redding.

Star Trek IV: The Voyage Home (1986)

The Leonard Nimoy–directed movie — the fourth full-length feature in the *Star Trek* canon, and maybe the best — draws Kirk and crew to 20th-century San Francisco with the call of the humpback whale. The movie includes wonderful and hugely entertaining fish-out-of-water city scenes, marvelous footage shot at the Monterey Bay Aquarium and the Golden Gate Bridge, and a terrifically eco-minded Save the Whale storyline.

Star Trek V: The Final Frontier (1989) also features a noteworthy California location shoot, in which Kirk vacations (in anti-gravity boots, no less) at Yosemite National Park. The footage is brilliant, but the movie is not. Unless you're a diehard fan (in which case you've already seen it), just stick with the first 20 minutes and then move on to something else.

The Parent Trap (1961)

The Parent Trap is my absolute favorite family movie, in which groovier-than-thou dad Brian Keith presides over a picture-perfect California ranch, golfs at Pebble Beach, and takes his identical twins (Hayley Mills and Hayley Mills) camping on the Monterey Peninsula. I'm partial to the original (which plays regularly on the Disney Channel), but the 1998 remake, starring Dennis Quaid, Natasha Richardson, and Lindsay Lohan, also uses multiple California locations to their greatest Technicolor advantage, including the Napa Valley.

Play Misty for Me (1971)

Clint Eastwood made his directorial debut with *Play Misty for Me,* the winningly creepy thriller co-starring Jessica Walter (and Donna Mills, of quintessentially California *Knots Landing* fame). Young, studly Clint looks mighty fine, but the real star of the show is stunning Carmel, which Clint films with a genuine hometown love and a master's eye. (The multitalented superstar was elected mayor of Carmel-by-the-Sea in 1986, you may remember; he still owns the Mission Ranch, an elegant country inn, and resides in town.) Watch for the great footage of Big Sur's Bixby Bridge, too.

The Grapes of Wrath (1940)

The John Ford–directed, Academy Award–winning film of dispossessed "Okie" dustbowl farmers who migrate west to the promised land — California — wins a spot on this list not for its tremendous footage of the Golden State, but because it beautifully evokes California's agrarian story. An ideal moving-picture rendition of one of the many classic California novels written by Monterey's favorite son, John Steinbeck, *The Grapes of Wrath* also serves to curry excitement for a visit to the new National Steinbeck Center, a stone's throw from Monterey in Steinbeck's hometown of Salinas (often called the breadbasket of California).

Gidget (1965)

Perky Sally Field is the ultimate California beach girl in the ultimate California beach movie, *Gidget.* This innocent romp is really a joy to watch — far superior to the Frankie Avalon/Annette Funicello beach movies — with excellent footage of Malibu Beach and Pacific Coast Highway (cruisin' with the top down, of course). Dave Grusin is responsible for the super-groovy soundtrack.

Chinatown (1974)

Possibly the finest noir ever committed to film, *Chinatown* uses L.A. in the '70s to re-create L.A. in the '30s impeccably. Not only did director Roman Polanski (pre-exile) capture the City of Angels masterfully, but writer Robert Towne works in an essential slice of city history: the dirty dealing and power-grabbing of water rights that allowed — for better or worse — the infant desert city to blossom into the sprawling metropolis you'll find today. And, of course, this true classic features Jack Nicholson as the hard-boiled detective embroiled with femme fatale Faye Dunaway, plus legendary Hollywood heavyweight John Huston as the evil genius behind the Chandleresque web of intrigue.

The Player (1992)

Robert Altman's comeback film, *The Player* realistically captures the seedy underbelly and soul-selling seductive power of Hollywood influence and celebrity. Everybody who's anybody in the movie industry knows how scarily close to home Tim Robbins' portrayal of beleagured studio exec Griffin Mill hits. The film features great studio backlot shots and city footage throughout, plus some terrific scenes at my very favorite Palm Springs spa resort, Two Bunch Palms.

The restaurant where Griffin runs into Angelica Huston and John Cusack is the **Ivy,** still a hotter-than-hot power lunch spot at 133 N. Robertson Blvd. in West Hollywood (☎ **310-274-8303**).

Top Gun (1986)

San Diego serves as the setting for *Top Gun,* the Tom Cruise blockbuster about elite (and very studly) Navy flyboys. The movie is in top form whenever it's in the air, but the action really grinds to a halt on land, especially with the lack of chemistry between Cruise and Kelly McGillis. But so what? The sunny city looks great in the earthbound scenes, and the slick-as-can-be movie captures its star-spangled Navy-base heritage well.

Runners-up: The Ten Second-Best California Flicks

If you're not sated on my top ten, try these films for more California cool:

- ✔ *Some Like It Hot* (1959), stars Marilyn Monroe, Tony Curtis, Jack Lemmon, and San Diego's legendary **Hotel del Coronado.**

- ✔ In the original *Dirty Harry* (1971), gruff Clint Eastwood takes on the scum of the earth on the streets of San Francisco.

- ✔ *East of Eden* (1955), another classic John Steinbeck–scribed California story translated to film, features James Dean.

- ✔ In *Same Time, Next Year* (1978), Alan Alda and Ellen Burstyn rendezvous on the glorious Mendocino coast for 26 consecutive years.

- ✔ *The Lost Boys* (1987) may be a second-rate vampire flick, but it showcases a first-rate Santa Cruz backdrop.

- ✔ *Palm Springs Weekend* (1963), stars Troy Donahue, an apple-cheeked Connie Stevens, and America's coolest desert town in its full Atomic Age finery.

✔ Steve Martin's *L.A. Story* (1991) is the second-best movie, after *The Player,* about everything that's wonderfully silly about life in contemporary Tinseltown.

✔ *Valley Girl* (1983), starring a teenage Nicolas Cage, is an underdog in a teen genre that includes *Fast Times at Ridgemont High* and *Clueless,* but it comes out a winner because of its New-Wave-Boy-meets-mall-lovin'-Valley-Girl love story at the height of Valley Girl mania.

✔ *L.A. Confidential* (1997) is *Chinatown's* finest successor in the L.A.-as-noir-landscape category.

✔ *Pretty Woman* (1990) is appropriate for the Sunset Strip and Rodeo Drive locations.

Finally, check out any movie with "Beverly Hills" in the title (*Slums of Beverly Hills, Down and Out in Beverly Hills, Beverly Hills Cop . . .*).

Chapter 27

The Ten Wackiest Annual Events

● ●

In This Chapter

▶ Having a one-of-a-kind California experience

▶ Jumping frogs, racing worms, telling tales, and performing artistically

▶ Celebrating garlic, building sandcastles, showing weeds — all the doo-dah-day

● ●

*C*alifornia, in case you haven't heard, can be a kooky place. After all, strangeness is one of the Left Coast's most appealing qualities.

The yearly proceedings listed in this chapter — which hold their own on the annual statewide calendar next to such respected traditions as the Tournament of Roses Parade and cultured celebrations like the Monterey Jazz Festival — offer you the chance to throw your reserve to the wind and join in the nutty fun. Or you're welcome to just point and hoot from the sidelines, if you prefer.

Peg Leg Smith's Liars Contest

Where: Borrego Springs, San Diego County
When: Saturday nearest to April Fool's Day (natch)

This tall-tale-telling competition is the legacy of wooden-limbed yarn-spinner Thomas Long "Peg Leg" Smith, who, in 1829 or thereabouts (dates tended to be somewhat fluid in Peg Leg's world), found a few gold-specked rocks in the desert. Rather than actually bothering to look for more, Peg Leg spent the next 35 years weaving an increasingly Bunyanlike tale about his lost Borrego Springs gold mine into Old West legend.

Storytellers and listeners gather annually at the Peg Leg Monument in Anza Borrego Desert State Park to honor Peg Leg's chutzpah and have a little fun. You're welcome to gather around the campfire and just listen or do some spinning yourself, as long as your tale 1) has some-thing to do with gold mining in the Southwest, 2) doesn't last longer than five minutes, and 3) contains nothing that any reasonable listener might actually mistake for the truth. Call the Borrego Springs Chamber of Commerce at ☎ **800-559-5524** or 760-767-5555 for details.

Calaveras County Fair and Jumping Frog Jubilee

Where: Angels Camp, Gold Country
When: Third weekend in May

Inspired by Mark Twain's joyful short story "The Celebrated Jumping Frog of Calaveras County," this yearly competition is the Olympics of frog jumping. Really. Frog jockeys (yep, that's what they're called) arrive from all over the globe with their lean 'n' mean amphibians in tow, which compete for cash prizes as large as 5,000 smackeroos. The races are a hoot to watch, and the accompanying three days of festivities — which include the crowning of this year's Miss Calaveras (a human teenage beauty, not a frog) — are festive and fun. If you and your leaper dream of riches and glory, however, start training now: The current world frog-jumping record is 21 feet, 5¾ inches, set in 1986 by Rosie the Ribiter of Santa Clara, CA. Call the Calaveras County Fairgrounds at ☎ 209-736-2561 or visit www.frogtown.org.

World-Championship Great Arcata to Ferndale Cross-Country Kinetic Sculpture Race

Where: Humboldt County, Redwood Country
When: Memorial Day weekend

One of the country's coolest annual events is this ingenious race, in which wild and crazy people in wild and crazy people-powered sculptures race for three days and 38 miles across land, sand, and sea, from Arcata to the Victorian-cute town of Ferndale.

The mobile art must be entirely people powered, measure no more than 8 by 14 feet, and cannot be inherently dangerous to driver or spectator. Otherwise, anything goes and usually does; in the 30-plus-year history of the race, contraptions have ranged from giant watermelons to amphibious armadillos, and pilots have run the gamut from lone souls to teams of 12.

Just reading the rules is great fun; witness no. 201a, which includes the following provision: "Since mothers are discouraged from running alongside, racers must carry a comforting item of Psychological Luxury no smaller than a restaurant coffee cup at all times. An old security blanket (i.e., your 'binkie'), a soft teddy bear or sock doll will suffice. Teddy bears are highly recommended." Needless to say, it's about the race, not the winner. For more info on participating and spectating, call ☎ 707-786-9259 or visit www.humguide.com/kinetic.

International Worm Races

Where: Clearlake, Lake County (north of Napa Valley)
When: Independence Day

Launched in 1966 by a descendant of Mark Twain's, this hugely popular event wins first prize for sheer ridiculousness. The "race" track is a four-foot-square board with a two-foot target painted on it. Two to five worms — either night crawlers or reds — are placed on the bull's-eye, and the first to inch its way across the edge of the outer circle wins. The day's grand champion wins a $100 cash prize (which begs the question, what do worms do with money, anyway?).

The ultimate worm-on-worm challenge takes place at Clearlake's Redbud Park immediately following the annual Lions Club Fourth of July Parade. Entry is $2; sign up early, because the first 200 entrants receive official Worm Race Pins. Don't have your own red worm or night crawler to enter? No problem! You can rent fully trained worms from the worm "stable" (whatever that is) just prior to race time. Call ☎ **707-994-3600** for details and entry forms, or visit www.clearlake.ca.us.

Gilroy Garlic Festival

Where: Gilroy (east of Santa Cruz, south of San Jose)
When: Last full weekend in July

The Garlic Capital of the World celebrates its cash crop with this ultra-stinky food fest. This is one of the biggest, best, and most well-attended food festivals in the entire Golden State, ideal for garlic addicts (and you know who you are). In addition to garlicky eats from all over the culinary map — garlic ice cream, yum! — the festival features arts and crafts vendors, live bands, the Tour de Garlique bike ride, the Miss Gilroy Garlic pageant (a dubious honor if ever there was one), and a Listerine table (just kidding). Attention, cooks: Enter the Great Garlic Cook-off, and you could go home a thousand bucks richer. Call ☎ **408-842-1625** or visit www.gilroygarlicfestival.com for further details.

Pageant of the Masters

Where: Laguna Beach, Orange County
When: July–August

Ever think *The Last Supper* was too flat, the *Mona Lisa* too stiff, *The Blue Boy* a tad too, well, two-dimensional? Then this is the event for you. Watch master artworks spring to life in this truly bizarre yet awe-inspiring performance-art gala, first launched in artsy Laguna in 1932 and going strong ever since. This very serious affair features trained actors working on intricate artist-designed sets to create living, breathing tableaux that remain remarkably faithful to the original, with dramatic narration and full orchestral accompaniment in a lovely alfresco setting. This pageant is fantastic, in the truest sense of the word.

You can, and should, order your pageant tickets in advance by calling ☎ **800-487-3378** or 949-497-6582. Come early in the day so you can also enjoy the **Festival of the Arts,** an outdoor art show featuring first-rate artists working in all media. You can find additional details on the excellent Web site (www.foapom.com).

U.S. Open Sandcastle Competition

Where: Imperial Beach (just south of San Diego)
When: A three-day weekend in late July or August

What's more fun than sandcastles? Nothing — especially when they're astoundingly complex, larger-than-life sand sculptures of everything from Noah's Ark to lobsters (complete with melted butter- and lemon-shaped sand on the side) to scenes from the San Diego skyline. This world-class competition may be the best of California's many beach events — the huge crowds think so. The throng comes out in full force not only for the main competition but also for the pancake breakfasts, food and music vendors, parade, and kids' sandcastle-building competition. Even if you don't make it for the actual event, you may be able to view the leftovers in the weeks that follow — as long as rain doesn't wash 'em away, that is. Call ☎ **619-424-6663** or 629-424-3151, or point your Web browser to www.ci.imperial-beach.ca.us/sand-hm.htm.

Underwater Pumpkin-Carving Contest

Where: La Jolla
When: Weekend before Halloween

Underwater pumpkin carving seems even a couple of notches less practical than underwater basketweaving, yet plenty of sporting divers have turned out for this Halloween event each year since 1981. Nobody takes it real seriously — one year the panel of judges was the staff of a local dive shop, the next year five kids off the beach — but it's always a fun party, and the surfacing jack-o'-lanterns are mighty impressive. Even though the bulk of the action takes place below sea level, the event is still fun to watch. For details, call Ocean Enterprises at ☎ **858-565-6054.**

Weed Show

Where: Twentynine Palms (gateway to Joshua Tree National Park)
When: Usually the first weekend of November

No, this festival doesn't focus on *that* kind of weed. Still, you'll think the locals have been smokin' it, what with the mind-boggling sculptures they create in the name of art using found objects and, yes, weeds. Lest you think this desert event, sponsored by the Twentynine Palms

Historical Society, is small potatoes, think again: More than 250 entries are usually up for critique in multiple-judged categories during this weekend-long event. Call ☎ **760-367-3926** or 760-367-3445 for the exact date and additional details (including entry forms), or point your Web browser to www.twentynine.com.

Doo Dah Parade

Where: Pasadena
When: Thanksgiving weekend

This outrageous annual event — referred to in town as the "other" parade — was born way back in 1978 as a zany spoof of New Year's Day's annual Tournament of Roses promenade. Doo Dah has since grown into a left-of-center institution all its own, but age hasn't cost it an ounce of silliness.

Parading participants usually include the Synchronized Precision Briefcase Drill Team (whose twirling skills are unparalleled), drag queen cheerleaders (representing West Hollywood, of course), the BBQ and Hibachi Marching Grill Team, a kazoo-tooting marching band, and many more — plenty to make the Ministry of Silly Walks mighty proud. Radio personality Dr. Demento often serves as Master of Ceremonies.

New surprises pop up every year, so even if you've been before, joining the wild, weird party once again is worth the effort. Call ☎ 626-449- 3689 or the Pasadena Convention and Visitors Bureau at ☎ 626-795- 9311 for this year's date.

Appendix

Quick Concierge

American Automobile Association (AAA)
Call ☎ 800-564-6222 or visit www.aaa.com for national information. The **California State AAA** serves Northern California; call ☎ 800-922-8228 or visit www.csaa.com to locate the office nearest your current Northern California location (on the Web, click on "Member Services" for the office locator). The **Automobile Club of Southern California** is AAA's Southern California arm; call ☎ 800-222-8794 or point your web browser to www.aaa-calif.com for more information or to locate an office.

For *roadside assistance,* members can call AAA at ☎ 800-400-4AAA in California, ☎ 800-AAA-HELP anywhere else in the U.S.

American Express
San Francisco locations include 560 California St., between Montgomery and Kearny streets (☎ 415-536-2686), open Monday through Friday from 9 a.m. to 5 p.m.; and 455 Market St., at First Street (☎ 415-536-2600), open Monday through Friday from 8:30 a.m. to 5:30 p.m., Saturday from 9 a.m. to 2 p.m.

On the Central Coast, you'll find an official AmEx travel office in Cambria at **Traveltime,** 4210 Bridge St. (☎ 805-927-7799); and at two **Santa Barbara Travel Bureau** locations: 3967 State St., Santa Barbara (☎ 805-683-1666); and in neighboring Montecito at 1127 Coast Village Rd. (☎ 805-969-7746).

Los Angeles area locations include 8493 W. 3rd St., at La Cienega Blvd., across from the Beverly Center (☎ 310-659-1682); 327 N. Beverly Dr., between Brighton and Dayton ways, Beverly Hills (☎ 310-274-8277); and 1250 4th St., at Arizona St., Santa Monica (☎ 310-395-9588).

San Diego has a full-service office downtown at 258 Broadway, at Third Avenue (☎ 619-234-4455).

In Palm Springs, **Andersen Travel Service,** 700 E. Tahquitz Canyon Way (☎ 760-325 2001), serves as an official travel office.

To make inquiries or to locate other branch offices, call ☎ 800-AXP-TRIP or visit www.americanexpress.com.

ATMs
Unless you need dough in the backwoods of Big Sur, you'll have no trouble finding an ATM in California. Branches of the Golden State's most popular banks are everywhere, with virtually all connected to all the global ATM networks. Most supermarkets also contain ATMs.

One of California's most popular banks, with branches throughout the state, is **Wells Fargo Bank,** which is linked to all the major worldwide networks. To find the one nearest you, point your Web browser to www.wellsfargo.com/findus. You can also find ATMs on the **Cirrus** network by dialing ☎ 800-424-7787 or going online to www.mastercard.com; to find a **Plus** ATM, call ☎ 800-843-7587 or visit www.visa.com.

Emergencies
No matter where you are in California, dial ☎ **911** in any emergency, whether it requires police, the fire department, or an ambulance.

Highway Conditions
Call **CalTrans** at ☎ 800-427-ROAD (7623) or 916-445-1534, or point your Web browser to www.dot.ca.gov/hq/roadinfo for complete California highway information. Whether you call or go online, keep the highway numbers you're interested in handy at all times.

Information
The **California Division of Tourism** (☎ 800-862-2543) can send you a free vacation planner that serves as a good introduction to the Golden State. Their extensive Web site, at www.gocalif.com, is an equally useful source that can link you to local visitor bureaus throughout the state.

The state also runs convenient *welcome centers* in San Francisco at Fisherman's Wharf, Pier 39, at Beach and Embarcadero streets (☎ 415-956-3493); and in Los Angeles at 8500 Beverly Blvd. (☎ 310-289-5292).

See the "Gathering More Information" section of each chapter for the best local information sources for individual destinations.

Liquor Laws
The legal drinking age of 21 is strictly enforced throughout the state, so have your ID handy even if your college days were a decade or two ago. Liquor and grocery stores, as well as some drugstores, can legally sell packaged alcoholic beverages between 6 a.m. and 2 a.m. Restaurants and nightclubs are obligated to stop serving at 2 a.m.

Maps
Here's yet another reason to join AAA: They supply the best maps of California to members only, and they're absolutely free if you're a card-carrier. You can obtain a terrific freeway map covering the entire state, and pick and choose city and regional maps to suit your needs. For more information on becoming a member or locating the nearest office in California, see the American Automobile Association listing at the beginning of the Appendix, and check out "The AAA Advantage" in Chapter 4.

If you're not going the AAA way, or you just want other sources, a very good road guide is the comprehensive **Thomas Bros.** *California Road Atlas.* You can get this and other maps from major online booksellers and bookstores. I highly recommend acquiring a good state map before you come; you'll often get the best local maps after you arrive, especially in smaller towns.

Safety
For *general safety issues,* use your common sense, just like you would at home or anywhere else. Avoid deserted and poorly lit areas, especially at night. Always lock the doors of your rental car, and don't keep anything valuable inside; any thief worth his or her salt can get into your locked car quicker without a key than you can get in with one.

Be alert in hotels, and don't let strange folks into your hotel room unless they are clearly personnel that you expect or have summoned. Don't hesitate to call down to the front desk to verify an employee's identity; nothing's too silly where your safety's concerned. And be sure to store your valuables or cash in the in-room or behind-the-desk safe; don't just leave them laying around your hotel room.

If you have a *cellphone,* bring it with you, and make sure it's fully charged as you travel. You'll likely do a lot of driving, and having a cellphone with you can make all the difference in the world if your car breaks down.

In the unlikely event of an *earthquake,* keep these basics in mind: Don't run outside; instead, move away from windows and toward the building's center. Crouch under a desk or table or other sturdy piece of furniture, or stand in a doorway. If you must leave the building, use the stairs, *not* the elevator. If you're in the car, pull over to the side of the road and stay in your car — but don't pull over until you're away from bridges, overpasses, telephone poles, and power lines. If you're out walking, stay in the open, away from trees, power lines, and buildings.

Smoking
California has the best and worst smoking laws in the United States, depending on your point of view. Basically, the rule is this: If you're indoors, you're not allowed to light up.

Smoking is prohibited in virtually all indoor public spaces — yes, including restaurants (hence the proliferation of patio dining, where smoking is usually allowed). Many bars and clubs, however, openly defy the law.

A good number of hotels, especially smaller places, also prohibit in-room smoking, so be sure to ask, if it matters to you.

You must be 18 or older to buy cigarettes in California.

Taxes
California's statewide sales tax is 7.25 percent. Some cities tack on an additional percentage up to 1.25 percent. The base hotel tax is 10 percent, with some municipalities adding an additional surcharge (which is noted in the hotel section of each chapter).

Time Zone
California lies in the Pacific Time Zone, which is 8 hours behind Greenwich Mean Time, and 3 hours behind the East Coast. The entire state practices Daylight Saving Time from April to October.

Weather
To check the weather forecasts online, log onto www.weather.com or www.cnn.com/weather. Also note that many local visitor bureaus have weather links, so you may want to check each city or region's official site (listed in the "Gathering More Information" section of each chapter) to get a local link.

Useful Toll-Free Numbers & Web Sites

Airlines

Aer Lingus
☎ 800-474-7424 in the U.S.
☎ 01-886-8888 in Ireland
www.aerlingus.ie

Air Canada
☎ 800-776-3000
www.aircanada.ca

Air New Zealand
☎ 800-262-2468 in the U.S.
☎ 800-663-5494 in Canada
☎ 0800-737-767 in New Zealand

Alaska Airlines
☎ 800-426-0333
www.alaskaair.com

Aloha Airlines
☎ 800-367-5250 or 877-879-2564
www.alohaair.com

America West Airlines
☎ 800-235-9292
www.americawest.com

American Airlines/American Eagle
☎ 800-433-7300
www.americanair.com

American Trans Air
☎ 800-225-2995
www.ata.com

British Airways
☎ 800-247-9297
☎ 0345-222-111 in Britain
www.british-airways.com

Canadian Airlines International
☎ 800-426-7000
www.cdnair.ca

Continental Airlines
☎ 800-525-0280
www.continental.com

Delta Air Lines/Skywest
☎ 800-221-1212
www.delta-air.com

Hawaiian Airlines
☎ 800-367-5320
www.hawaiianair.com

Horizon Air
☎ 800-547-9308
www.horizonair.com

Northwest Airlines
☎ 800-225-2525
www.nwa.com

Qantas
☎ 800-474-7424 in the U.S.
☎ 612-9691-3636 in Australia
www.qantas.com

Southwest Airlines
☎ 800-435-9792
www.iflyswa.com

Trans World Airlines (TWA)
☎ 800-221-2000
www.twa.com

United Airlines
☎ 800-241-6522
www.ual.com

US Airways
☎ 800-428-4322
www.usairways.com

Virgin Atlantic Airways
☎ 800-862-8621 in Continental U.S.
☎ 0293-747-747 in Britain
www.fly.virgin.com

Car-Rental Agencies

Advantage
☎ 800-777-5500
www.arac.com

Alamo
☎ 800-327-9633
www.goalamo.com

Avis
☎ 800-331-1212 in Continental U.S.
☎ 800-TRY-AVIS in Canada
www.avis.com

Budget
☎ 800-527-0700
www.budgetrentacar.com

Dollar
☎ 800-800-4000
www.dollarcar.com

Enterprise
☎ 800-325-8007
www.pickenterprise.com

Hertz
☎ 800-654-3131
www.hertz.com

National
☎ 800-CAR-RENT

www.nationalcar.com

Payless
☎ 800-PAYLESS
www.paylesscar.com

Rent-A-Wreck
☎ 800-535-1391
rent-a-wreck.com

Thrifty
☎ 800-367-2277
www.thrifty.com

Major Hotel & Motel Chains

Best Western International
☎ 800-528-1234
www.bestwestern.com

Clarion Hotels
☎ 800-CLARION
www.hotelchoice.com

Comfort Inns & Suites
☎ 800-228-5150
www.hotelchoice.com

Courtyard by Marriott
☎ 800-321-2211
www.courtyard.com

Days Inn
☎ 800-325-2525
www.daysinn.com

Doubletree Hotels
☎ 800-222-TREE
www.doubletreehotels.com

Econo Lodges
☎ 800-55-ECONO
www.hotelchoice.com

Fairfield Inn by Marriott
☎ 800-228-2800
www.fairfieldinn.com

Four Seasons Hotels & Resorts
☎ 800-819-5053
www.fshr.com

Hampton Inn
☎ 800-HAMPTON
www.hampton-inn.com

Hilton Hotels
☎ 800-HILTONS
www.hilton.com

Holiday Inn
☎ 800-HOLIDAY
www.basshotels.com

Howard Johnson
☎ 800-654-2000
www.hojo.com

Hyatt Hotels & Resorts
☎ 800-228-9000
www.hyatt.com

La Quinta Motor Inns
☎ 800-531-5900
www.laquinta.com

Marriott Hotels & Resorts
800-228-9290
www.marriott.com

Motel 6
☎ 800-4-MOTEL6 (800-466-8536)
www.motel6.com

Quality Inns, Hotels & Suites
☎ 800-228-5151
www.hotelchoice.com

Premier Resorts
☎ 800-367-7052
www.premier-resorts.com

Radisson Hotels International
☎ 800-333-3333
www.radisson.com

Ramada Inns
☎ 800-2-RAMADA
www.ramada.com

Red Carpet Inns
☎ 800-251-1962
www.reservahost.com

Red Lion Hotels & Inns
☎ 800-547-8010
www.redlion.com

Red Roof Inns
☎ 800-843-7663
www.redroof.com

Renaissance Hotels & Resorts
☎ 800-932-2198
www.renaissancehotels.com

Residence Inn by Marriott
☎ 800-331-3131
www.residenceinn.com

Rodeway Inns
☎ 800-228-2000
www.hotelchoice.com

Sheraton Hotels & Resorts
☎ 800/325-3535
www.sheraton.com

Starwood's Luxury Collection
☎ 800-343-6320
www.luxurycollection.com

Super 8 Motels
☎ 800-800-8000
www.super8motels.com

Travelodge
☎ 800-255-3050
www.travelodge.com

Vagabond Inns
☎ 800-522-1555
www.vagabondinns.com

W Hotels
☎ 877-946-8357
www.whotels.com

Westin Hotels
☎ 888-625-5144
www.westin.com

Wyndham Hotels & Resorts
☎ 800-822-4200 in Continental U.S. and Canada
www.wyndham.com

Making Dollars and Sense of It

Expense	Amount
Airfare	
Car Rental	
Lodging	
Parking	
Breakfast	
Lunch	
Dinner	
Babysitting	
Attractions	
Transportation	
Souvenirs	
Tips	
Grand Total	

Notes

Fare Game: Choosing an Airline

Travel Agency: _____ Phone: _____

Agent's Name: _____ Quoted Fare: _____

Departure Schedule & Flight Information

Airline: _____ Airport: _____

Flight #: _____ Date: _____ Time: _____ a.m./p.m.

Arrives in: _____ Time: _____ a.m./p.m.

Connecting Flight (if any)

Amount of time between flights: _____ hours/mins

Airline: _____ Airport: _____

Flight #: _____ Date: _____ Time: _____ a.m./p.m.

Arrives in: _____ Time: _____ a.m./p.m.

Return Trip Schedule & Flight Information

Airline: _____ Airport: _____

Flight #: _____ Date: _____ Time: _____ a.m./p.m.

Arrives in: _____ Time: _____ a.m./p.m.

Connecting Flight (if any)

Amount of time between flights: _____ hours/mins

Airline: _____ Airport: _____

Flight #: _____ Date: _____ Time: _____ a.m./p.m.

Arrives in: _____ Time: _____ a.m./p.m.

Notes

Sweet Dreams: Choosing Your Hotel

Enter the hotels where you'd prefer to stay based on location and price. Then use the worksheet below to plan your itinerary.

Hotel	*Location*	*Price per night*

Menus & Venues

Enter the restaurants where you'd most like to dine. Then use the worksheet below to plan your itinerary.

Name	Address/Phone	Cuisine/Price

Places to Go, People to See, Things to Do

Enter the attractions you most would like to see. Then use the worksheet below to plan your itinerary.

Attractions	Amount of time you expect to spend there	Best day and time to go

Going "My" Way

Itinerary #1

- ☐ _____
- ☐ _____
- ☐ _____
- ☐ _____

Itinerary #2

- ☐ _____
- ☐ _____
- ☐ _____
- ☐ _____

Itinerary #3

- ☐ _____
- ☐ _____
- ☐ _____
- ☐ _____

Itinerary #4

- ☐ _____
- ☐ _____
- ☐ _____
- ☐ _____

Itinerary #5

- ☐ _____
- ☐ _____
- ☐ _____
- ☐ _____

Itinerary #6

- ☐ _____
- ☐ _____
- ☐ _____
- ☐ _____

Itinerary #7

- ☐ _____
- ☐ _____
- ☐ _____
- ☐ _____

Itinerary #8

- ☐ _____
- ☐ _____
- ☐ _____
- ☐ _____

Itinerary #9

- ☐ _____
- ☐ _____
- ☐ _____
- ☐ _____

Itinerary #10

- ☐ _____
- ☐ _____
- ☐ _____
- ☐ _____

Notes

Notes

Notes

Index

Accommodations Index

Restaurant Index

Notes

_____
_____
_____
_____
_____
_____
_____
_____
_____
_____
_____
_____
_____
_____
_____
_____
_____
_____
_____
_____

Notes

Notes

Notes

_____
_____
_____
_____
_____
_____
_____
_____
_____
_____
_____
_____
_____
_____
_____
_____
_____
_____
_____
_____

Notes

Notes

_____
_____
_____
_____
_____
_____
_____
_____
_____
_____
_____
_____
_____
_____
_____
_____
_____
_____
_____

Discover Dummies Online!

The Dummies Web Site is your fun and friendly online resource for the latest information about *For Dummies*® books and your favorite topics. The Web site is the place to communicate with us, exchange ideas with other *For Dummies* readers, chat with authors, and have fun!

Ten Fun and Useful Things You Can Do at www.dummies.com

1. Win free *For Dummies* books and more!
2. Register your book and be entered in a prize drawing.
3. Meet your favorite authors through the IDG Books Worldwide Author Chat Series.
4. Exchange helpful information with other *For Dummies* readers.
5. Discover other great *For Dummies* books you must have!
6. Purchase Dummieswear® exclusively from our Web site.
7. Buy *For Dummies* books online.
8. Talk to us. Make comments, ask questions, get answers!
9. Download free software.
10. Find additional useful resources from authors.

Link directly to these ten fun and useful things at
http://www.dummies.com/10useful

For other technology titles from IDG Books Worldwide, go to
www.idgbooks.com

Not on the Web yet? It's easy to get started with *Dummies 101*®: *The Internet For Windows*® *98* or *The Internet For Dummies*® at local retailers everywhere.

Find other *For Dummies* books on these topics:
Business • Career • Databases • Food & Beverage • Games • Gardening • Graphics • Hardware
Health & Fitness • Internet and the World Wide Web • Networking • Office Suites
Operating Systems • Personal Finance • Pets • Programming • Recreation • Sports
Spreadsheets • Teacher Resources • Test Prep • Word Processing

IDG BOOKS WORLDWIDE BOOK REGISTRATION

Register This Book and Win!

We want to hear from you!

Visit **http://my2cents.dummies.com** to register this book and tell us how you liked it!

- ✔ Get entered in our monthly prize giveaway.

- ✔ Give us feedback about this book — tell us what you like best, what you like least, or maybe what you'd like to ask the author and us to change!

- ✔ Let us know any other *For Dummies*® topics that interest you.

Your feedback helps us determine what books to publish, tells us what coverage to add as we revise our books, and lets us know whether we're meeting your needs as a *For Dummies* reader. You're our most valuable resource, and what you have to say is important to us!

Not on the Web yet? It's easy to get started with *Dummies 101*®: *The Internet For Windows*® *98* or *The Internet For Dummies*®3 at local retailers everywhere.

Or let us know what you think by sending us a letter at the following address:

For Dummies Book Registration
Dummies Press
10475 Crosspoint Blvd.
Indianapolis, IN 46256

BESTSELLING BOOK SERIES